THE CHEMISTRY DIMENSION

THE CHEMISTRY DIMENSION

A coursebook for GCSE

Bryan Slater

Senior Assistant Education Officer for Schools,
Devon County Council

Jeff Thompson

Professor of Education, University of Bath

MACMILLAN
EDUCATION

First published 1987

Published by
MACMILLAN EDUCATION LTD
Houndmills, Basingstoke, Hampshire RG21 2XS
and London
Companies and representatives
throughout the world

Designed by Linda Reed

Printed in Great Britain by Scotprint Limited, Musselburgh.

British Library Cataloguing in Publication Data
Slater, Bryan
The chemistry dimension: a coursebook for GCSE
1. Chemistry
I. Title   II. Thompson, Jeff
540   QD33
ISBN 0−333−37642−0

Contents

About this coursebook

The title of this book, *The Chemistry Dimension*, was chosen carefully. We wanted it to stand for the several 'faces' of chemistry which you will find inside.

The theme which links the contents of *The Chemistry Dimension* together is the chemical substances which make up the planets in our Solar System. You will learn about these different substances and how they behave. To help you understand these facts, you will meet atoms, molecules and ions, electrons, protons and neutrons – all tiny particles. So the study of chemistry takes us from objects the size of planets to objects the size of atoms – that is one part of the chemistry dimension.

You will see how chemistry affects your daily life through the objects and substances which chemistry has helped us to make, and how chemistry affects where people live and the quality of their surroundings. *The Chemistry Dimension* will also help you to see how chemistry helps in understanding issues in the modern world, and some of the ways you could use this understanding yourself after you have left school. All these are aspects or dimensions of the subject we call chemistry.

Sometimes your teacher will ask you to use *The Chemistry Dimension* for reading, sometimes for answering questions, sometimes for doing experiments and sometimes for carrying out research in writing or for setting up your own investigations. To help you, whenever a new word is used, it is explained and also put in capital letters. The index lists the page number where you will find each explanation. So use it when you find a word you have forgotten or don't understand. *The Chemistry Dimension* is divided into nine Sections, each divided into Units. At the end of each Unit there is a list of the new words found in it, and a summary of the main ideas and the facts which you should remember. You can use these summaries to look forward into new areas in the book, and to help you fix in your mind Units you have worked through. They are stepping stones through the different ideas you will find in *The Chemistry Dimension*.

BCS
JJT
1987

Acknowledgements

The authors and publishers wish to acknowledge the following photograph sources: Barnaby's Picture Library, p. 319; Beecham Research Laboratories. p. 212; BICC Research and Engineering Ltd, p. 258; British Gas Corporation, p. 87 (L); British Museum, p. 72; British Petroleum Co Ltd, p. 87 (R); British Steel Corporation, p. 254; Jim Brownbill, pp. 7 (L), 338, 367 (R), 368 (TL); Camera Press Ltd, pp. 1 (R), 62, 80 (T), 96 (L), 272, 300; J Allan Cash Ltd, pp. 105 (R), 107 (R), 144 (L), 184, 188, 252, 256, 361 (L); Central Electricity Generating Board, p. 30; CERN, p. 117; Cochranes of Oxford Ltd, p. 18; Dartington Glass Ltd, p. 264; De Beers Industrial Diamond Division (Pty) Ltd, p. 304; Ferranti Electronics Ltd, p. 80 (B); French Government Tourist Office, p. 91 (R); GEC Telecommunications Ltd, p. 368 (B); Geographical Museum, p. 20; Sally and Richard Greenhill, p. 107 (L); ICI Agriculture Division, pp. 279, 350 (L), 353; ICI Mond Division, p. 270; ICI Plastics Division, p. 162; Impalloy Ltd, p. 76 (TR); JBP Associates Ltd, p. 76 (BR); Rodney Jennings, pp. 36, 82, 110, 163, 183, 267, 282, 337 (R), 363; JET Joint Undertaking, p. 143; Kjell-Arne Larsson, p. 96 (R); Mansell Collection, pp. 19, 73 (T); NASA, pp. 193, 315, 346, 350 (R), 356; National Cavity Insulation Association, p. 85; National Coal Board, p. 86; New Zealand Government Tourist and Publicity Dept, p. 91 (L); Permutit, p. 320; Photo Source, pp. 93, 97, 101, 105 (L), 108, 118, 260, 331; Pilkington Brothers Ltd, p. 337 (L); Platinum Shop, p. 81; Popperfoto, p. 103; Richardson-Vicks Ltd, p. 361 (R); Rolls-Royce Ltd, p. 368 (TR); Royal Astronomical Society, pp. 144 (R), 324; RTZ Services Ltd, pp. 75, 76 (L); Science Photo Library, pp. 1 (L); 61; By kind permission of the Trustees of Science Museum (Crown copyright), p. 298 (R); Shell Photographic Service, p. 12; Sporting Images (Rod Organ), p. 187; John Topham Picture Library, p. 367 (L); Jim Turner, p. 305; Zefa Picture Library, p. 7 (R).

The authors and publisher thank Times Newspapers Ltd for the extract on p. 104 and the *Observer* for the extracts on pp. 106 and 150.

Illustrations by Taurus Graphics.

Background chemistry

UNIT 1.1 *What is chemistry?*

Chemistry is about substances. Everything that we can see, taste and feel is made up of substances. In chemistry, we study how these substances behave and we try to understand why it is that they do what they do. It does not matter whether you are at school learning about chemistry, or a research scientist – chemistry is always about these things.

In order to understand why chemical substances do what they do, we often need to find out what they are made of and how they are put together. So chemistry is really about taking substances apart to see how they are made up. Once we have found this out, and we understand how substances are put together, then we can use what we have discovered in order to help ourselves and our fellow men and women.

But how do we go about investigating the nature of chemical substances? One way of doing this would be to sit down and work out what seems reasonable from what we already know about the world. We could try to **think** our way to a better level of understanding. As long as what we decided did not conflict with what we already knew to be true, then we would probably be on the right lines. This way of doing things is all right – as far as it goes. The problem with it is – that it doesn't take us very far! The ancient Greek philosophers (thinkers) who lived hundreds of years before the birth of Christ tried to understand the world by this method. To be fair to them, some of the ideas which they **thought** must be true have now been **shown** by scientists to be correct – for instance that everything is made up of tiny particles called 'atoms'. The word 'atom' actually comes from an ancient Greek word, so it is not really a modern word at all! But the Greeks also thought that everything was made up of Earth, Air, Fire and Water put together in different ways – and this, as you will see yourself, is not true. You will see this because you will do something which the Greeks, in spite of their wisdom and learning, did not do. You will carry out EXPERIMENTS.

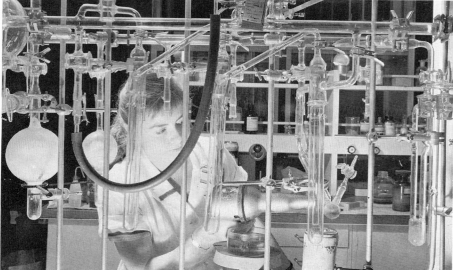

Fig. 1.1 *Chemistry is always about finding out why substances behave as they do*

Why do we do experiments, and why do they help us to understand the world better? The answer to this is that experiments give us more knowledge than we would otherwise have. We can use the knowledge gained from experiments to refine and improve our ideas. The Greeks could not get very far with their methods because they had only a fixed amount of information to go on (what they could see in the world about them) – and so, in the end, their level of understanding came to a halt, too.

When we carry out an experiment, it is to help us to answer a question which we have asked ourselves. Very often, this question takes the form 'What would happen if....?' From what we see, we can build up a better picture of how things are put together, and this then leads us on to ask another question.

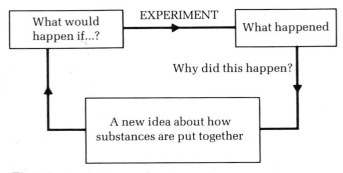

Fig. 1.2

Each time we ask a 'What would happen if ...?' question, it is a deeper question than the one that went before it. So this process, which is often called 'The Scientific Process', is more like a spiral, because each time we go round the loop, we improve our understanding.

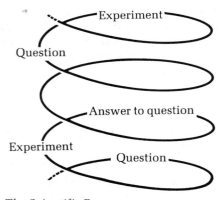

Fig. 1.3 *The Scientific Process*

We move up the 'spiral of understanding' by asking questions and by doing experiments. But what do we do with this understanding once we have it? In chemistry, we use our understanding of the way substances are put together to make new chemicals which will be useful to us, or to make chemicals that

we already know about in a way that is cheaper, or more efficient, or less polluting. In Britain alone, thousands of chemists are involved each day in increasing our understanding of the subject, and in finding ways to use this understanding. In the last 100 years, everyday life has been changed because of new chemicals made by scientists. Table 1.1 lists just a few of those substances.

drugs and anaesthetics for use by doctors
fertilisers, weedkillers and insecticides to increase food production
polythene, PVC, polystyrene (and others) for making all kinds of goods
petrol, paraffin and natural gas
silicon diodes for televisions, hi-fi sets, computers and calculators
steel and stainless steel for bridges, cars, ships, trains, buildings and many other uses

Table 1.1 *Substances made by chemists*

So chemistry is about understanding the way in which the substances in the world around us are put together, and then putting that understanding to use. But before we can take the first step in this investigation, it is important to make sure that we know what substances we are dealing with. It is particularly important to know whether the substance we are studying is a single chemical substance, or more than one chemical substance. If we know that we have a single pure substance, then the things that we find out when we do an experiment must be to do with that one substance and nothing else. But how do we get single substances, and how do we know if they are **pure**?

TOPIC 1.1.1

Pure substances

A substance is either a pure, single substance, or it is a mixture of more than one substance. We can divide all the things which go to make up the world into these two classes – pure substances and mixtures. Here are some examples of each type of substance:

Some pure substances	Some mixtures
water	earth
iron	air
polythene	wood
salt	paper
gold	glass
diamond	wool

Table 1.2

Do any of the substances in these lists surprise you? It seems odd to think that air is a mixture of more than one substance, because when you look at it (or, rather, through it) you can't see any evidence that there is more than one thing there. Why should air be a mixture, when water is a pure substance? If you take clean water, it looks perfectly clear, just like air – so how can we tell that it is a pure substance, but that air is not?

You may have already guessed the answer to this question – there is only one way to be sure. But before we decide finally what it is we would have to do, you can try the 'Greek' method for yourself.

PROJECT 1.1

Decide, just from what seems likely to you, whether each of the following substances is a pure substance or a mixture. Perhaps your teacher will discuss this with you.

Grass, steam, petrol, human beings (!), cotton, a cup of tea, washing-up liquid (apart from the colouring), a silver spoon, ink, an apple, leather and sugar.

Going by what seems likely can be misleading! The only sure way to decide whether something is a pure substance or not is to carry out an experiment. But what kind of experiment should this be? What test will tell us whether or not something is a pure substance?

To answer this question, we must first find out more about the differences between pure substances and mixtures.

▶ EXPERIMENT 1.1, page 4

So from Experiment 1.1 you have learned three things about mixtures:
1. The properties of a mixture are a mixture of the properties of the things in the mixture.
2. The properties of a mixture are not fixed, but vary depending on the amounts of the different things in the mixture.
3. The different things in a mixture can be separated from each other using a 'separation technique'.
Before Experiment 1.1 we asked ourselves what test would tell us whether or not something was a pure substance. We could put this another way and ask 'How can we tell a pure substance from a mixture?'.

You have seen some of the things that are true about all mixtures. If you have a substance and it is a mixture, then these things will be true about it also. If they are not true about it, then it cannot be a mixture. Anything which is not a mixture must be . . . a pure substance. So we can say that the following things are true about **pure** substances:

1. The properties of a pure substance are not a mixture of properties. They are the properties of that substance alone.
2. The properties of a pure substance are fixed, and they do not vary.
3. A pure substance cannot be separated into different things by using a 'separation technique'.

If we heat a solid, it will eventually turn into a liquid. The temperature at which it does this is called its MELTING POINT. If we heat a liquid it will eventually turn into a gas. The temperature at which it does this is called its BOILING POINT. You will learn more about melting and boiling in the next unit of this section.

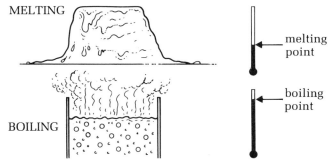

Fig. 1.4

A pure substance has an exact melting point, which does not change. A pure substance also has an exact boiling point, which does not change. For instance a particular pure substance could have an exact melting point of 23.1°C and an exact boiling point of 79.3°C.

A mixture does not have an exact melting point – it melts between a range of temperatures. For instance, it might melt between 17.5°C and 19.3°C. The melting point of a mixture (or really the **range** of temperature it melts over) also changes depending on the amounts of the different pure substances in it. For instance, we do not know the 'melting point' of a mixture of salt and sugar – it depends on how much of each of them we have in the particular mixture. The same is true for the 'boiling points' of mixtures – they are not exact, and they can change.

Question

Five substances were given to a scientist, and he had to decide whether they were pure substances or mixtures. So he did an experiment and found their melting points and boiling points. Here are his results:

Substance	Melting point/°C	Boiling point/°C
A	94 to 96.5	265
B	−117	78.5
C	79.9	218
D	−65	61.8 to 62.5
E	−34.5	114.9

⟶⟶ p. 5

EXPERIMENT 1.1
Looking at mixtures

You will need the following: powdered white blackboard chalk, powdered red blackboard chalk, 4 test-tubes, spatula, hand-lens, piece of white paper.

What to do

1   Use the spatula to measure out some powdered white chalk into three test-tubes. Put ten spatula-measures into the first tube, six into the second and three into the third. Leave a fourth tube empty.

2   Into the empty tube, measure ten spatulas of powdered red chalk.

3   Put seven spatulas of powdered red chalk into the tube which contains three spatulas of white chalk.

4   Put four spatulas of powdered red chalk into the tube which contains six spatulas of white chalk. Your four tubes will now look like this:

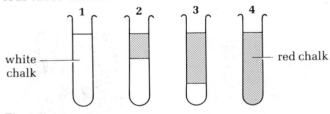

white chalk — — red chalk

Fig. 1.5

5   Now take each of the two tubes which contain a mixture. Put your thumb over the end, and shake until the powders are completely mixed.

6   How would you describe the colour of the mixture in each of the two tubes? Stand the tubes in a rack in order of the amount of white chalk which you put into them. What colours are in each?

7   **Discuss what you can see, and try to decide how these colours have come about.**

8   Write down what you have seen, and what you have decided.

What happened

You should have been able to see the following colours:

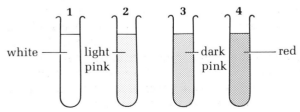

white — light pink — dark pink — red

Fig. 1.6

What we can decide

The two middle test-tubes appear to be pink – one darker pink (the one which had more red chalk to start with) and one lighter pink (the one which had more white chalk to start with). But you know that in each of the two middle tubes there is a **mixture of red chalk and white chalk**, not pink chalk. So the mixture looks pink, because red and white make pink. When we mix things together, the mixture looks like or behaves in a way that is a mixture of how the things that are in it look or behave. In science how something behaves is called a PROPERTY of that thing. The colour of a substance is one of its properties. We can always say about a mixture that its properties will be a mixture of the properties of the things which are in the mixture.

Property of things in the mixture	Property of mixture

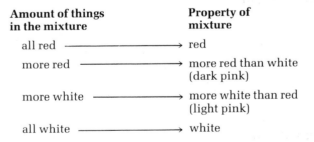

The two middle test tubes did not appear **identical**, however. The one which had more red chalk seemed redder, and the one which had more white chalk seemed whiter. So the colour of the mixture was not fixed, but it depended on how much of the different things in the mixture there were. In the same way, the properties of any mixture are not fixed. They vary, depending on the amounts of the different things in the mixture.

Amount of things in the mixture	Property of mixture
all red	red
more red	more red than white (dark pink)
more white	more white than red (light pink)
all white	white

If you pour some of one of the two mixtures onto a piece of paper, and look at it through a hand-lens, you will be able to see some white grains and some red grains. If you had a pair of tweezers and enough time, could you separate the white grains from the red ones? Try doing this just with the spatula. It's difficult, but with a bit of patience you will be able to separate a few grains from the rest. This shows you something else that is true of all mixtures – you can always separate out the things in the mixture using a 'separation technique'.

The scientist then turned to a table of melting points and boiling points for pure substances. Here is part of that table.

Substance	Melting point/°C	Boiling point/°C
ammonia	−77.7	−33.4
aluminium bromide	97.5	263.3
benzene	5.5	80.1
chloroform	−63.5	61.2
ethanol	−117	78.5
naphthalene	79.9	218
tin (IV) chloride	−33	114.1

(a) Which of the substances (A−E) was a pure substance?
(b) Which of the substances (A−E) was a mixture?
(c) For the pure substances, can you find the name of each substance?
(d) For the mixtures, can you decide what the main substance present is called?

TOPIC 1.1.2

How do we get pure substances from mixtures?

We have already said that we can use 'separation techniques' to get pure substances from mixtures. A separation technique is just a way of separating two substances. We can imagine the route to a pure substance as follows:

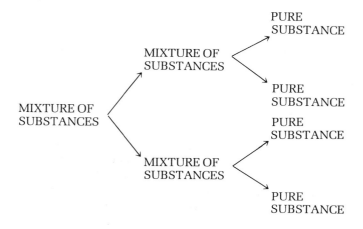

A good example of a separation technique is if you have a class of pupils made up of both boys and girls, and the teacher says 'Girls sit on the right-hand side of the class, and boys sit on the left-hand side'. The mixture of boys and girls would be separated into girls (on one side) and boys (on the other).

mixture of girls and boys

separation technique!

boys   girls

Fig. 1.7

But what different separation techniques are there in chemistry, and how do we carry them out? Remember how you would have been able to separate the red chalk from the white chalk in Experiment 1.1 – you would have used tweezers to pick out the different coloured grains. So, we could say that one separation technique is the 'tweezers method'! This is not as silly as it sounds – the 'tweezer method' was used to make one of the most important discoveries in modern chemistry. In 1848 the French chemist Louis Pasteur used a hand-lens and a pair of tweezers to separate two different types of crystals of the chemical sodium ammonium tartrate. Once he had done this, he made discoveries about the two types of crystal which led to a new branch of chemistry called 'stereochemistry' – which, incidentally, is nothing to do with music! (You have probably heard of Louis Pasteur before, but not because of this particular discovery. What is his most famous discovery?)

Now let us see what other separation techniques there are besides the 'tweezer method'.

▶ EXPERIMENT 1.2, page 6

EXPERIMENT 1.2
Separating sand from salt: 'filtration'

You will need the following: a mixture of salt and sand, a filter-funnel and filter-papers, a beaker (250 cm³), an evaporating basin, a glass rod, a hand-lens.

What to do

YOU MUST WEAR YOUR SAFETY SPECTACLES.

1   Take the salt and sand mixture, and put about ten spatula-measures of it into the beaker. Add **a little** tap water, and stir with the glass rod.

2   You will see that the salt starts to DISSOLVE, but that the sand does not. It will help later in the experiment if you can dissolve the salt in the smallest possible amount of water. To help you do this, you can take the beaker and warm it **gently** on top of a tripod and gauze. Keep stirring with the glass rod, and **do not let the water boil.**

3   If the salt has not all dissolved after a little gentle heating, add a little more tap water, and warm the beaker again. Carry on doing this until the salt has all dissolved.

4   You now have a clear liquid, mixed with sand. So you have to separate them. Your teacher will show you how to fold a piece of filter-paper so that it fits into a filter-funnel. Put **two** pieces of filter-paper, one on top of the other, into the filter-funnel. Now put the filter-funnel into a clamp (do not tighten too hard or you will break the glass). Alter the position of the funnel so that an evaporating basin will go underneath it, with a gap of about 2 cm.

5   Stir the mixture in the beaker, and use the glass rod to pour it through the filter-paper (your teacher will show you how). Do this a little at a time, and watch the evaporating basin to see that it does not overflow. Make sure that you scrape all the sand onto the filter-paper at the end. Keep the filter-paper and sand on one side.

6   Take the evaporating basin with the clear liquid in it, and put it on a tripod and gauze. Heat the basin gently.

7   You will see that the water starts to turn to steam. We say that the water is EVAPORATING. After a while, all the water will have evaporated, leaving behind a white solid.

8   Let the basin cool down, and then scrape out some of the white solid onto a piece of paper. Use the hand-lens to look at the solid more closely. Is there any sand mixed with it, or is it pure salt?

9   Now go back to the sand which is left in the filter-paper. Scrape some of it out onto a piece of paper, and look at it more closely with the hand-lens. Can you see any grains of salt? Are all the grains of sand the same? Do you think that sand is a single substance? How could you separate the different substances that go together to make up sand?

What happened

When you added the water to the mixture of sand and salt, the salt dissolved but the sand did not. This is because salt is SOLUBLE in water, but sand is INSOLUBLE

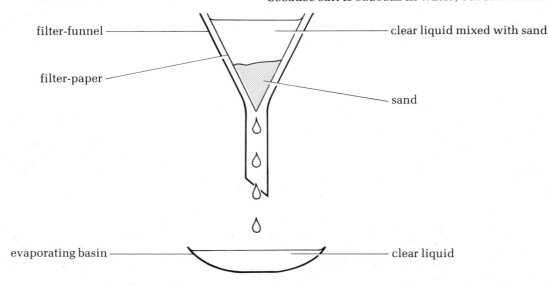

filter-funnel ———— clear liquid mixed with sand

filter-paper ————

———— sand

evaporating basin ———— clear liquid

Fig. 1.8

in water. A liquid in which other substances dissolve is called a SOLVENT. The substance which dissolves is called the SOLUTE. So in this case, water is the solvent and salt is the solute.

When all the salt had dissolved, you had a liquid (the SOLUTION of salt in the water) and a solid (the sand) in the beaker. A liquid will pass through a filter-paper, but a solid will not. So the salt solution ran through into the evaporating basin, and the sand was left behind on the filter-paper. In this way, the salt and the sand were separated. We call this way of separating substances FILTRATION.

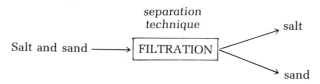

You should have been able to see that the salt in the evaporating basin was pure and that all the salt crystals looked very much like each other. The sand also contained no salt grains. So the separation

worked. But sand is made up of many different colours and shapes of particle.

What we can decide

1   Filtration is one separation technique. It will work when one of the substances in the mixture is a liquid and one is a solid. If both of the substances are solids, but one is soluble and the other is insoluble, then we can add a solvent to get one of them to dissolve. Then we can filter off the insoluble substance from the soluble one.

2   Sand is not a pure substance. It is a mixture of many different types of solid. We could separate the different solids in sand using the 'tweezer method'.

3   Salt is a pure substance. We could prove this by taking its melting point and comparing our result with tables.

4   Evaporation is another separation technique. It lets us separate a solvent from a solute.

Both filtration and evaporation are used every day by scientists in laboratories and on a large scale in industry to separate different substances. For instance, filtration is one of the ways that the water which we use for drinking is made pure. The water is made to pass through beds of finely divided rock and sand, and this filters out any solid substances which are in it (see Section 2, Topic 2.3.2). Evaporation is used in many cases in industry where a solvent has been used early in the process and has to be removed at the end. In very warm countries it is also used to get salt from sea-water (Fig. 1.10).

We use evaporation to remove the solvent from a

solute that we want to obtain. Sometimes, however, it is the solvent that is more valuable than the substance which is dissolved in it. When this is the case, we still use evaporation, but in such a way that we can 'keep' the solvent. The method we use is called DISTILLATION.

Distillation is really two processes in one. The first of these is evaporation of the solvent by boiling the solution. The second is catching the solvent by making it CONDENSE (turn back into a liquid). To make a vapour condense, we have to cool it. We do this by passing it through a tube which is surrounded by a flow of cold water in an outer jacket (called a Liebig condenser). The apparatus looks like Fig. 1.11.

Fig. 1.9 *Solid matter can be removed from water in filtration beds*

Fig.1.10 *The heat from the sun evaporates the sea water, leaving salt behind*

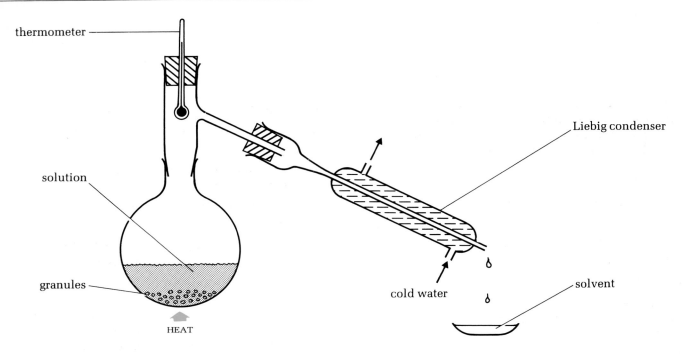

thermometer

solution

granules

HEAT

Liebig condenser

cold water

solvent

Fig. 1.11

An example of the use of distillation is again in the purification of water. Once solid impurities have been filtered out, the impurities which are left are those substances which are dissolved in the water. If we distil the water then the soluble impurities are left behind.

So far, we have seen how a solid which is soluble can be separated from a solid which is insoluble (filtration and evaporation), and how a dissolved solid and the solvent in which it is dissolved can be separated (evaporation or distillation). Suppose, however, that we had two **soluble** solids. How could they be separated? In order to separate two substances, we have to use something about them which makes one different from the other. If two solids are soluble, they are often soluble to different **extents**, and we can use this to separate them. The greater the difference between the solubilities of the two substances, the easier the separation is. We call the method we use FRACTIONAL CRYSTALLISATION.

▶ EXPERIMENT 1.3

We often use fractional crystallisation as a way of purifying a soluble substance which is contaminated with another soluble substance. We always use the minimum amount of water, so that we get a saturated solution of the substance we are purifying at the highest possible temperature. In this way, all the impurity is likely still to remain in solution, and to pass through the filter-paper as filtrate. Ideally, we should also carry out the cooling as slowly as possible, to avoid small amounts of the solution

(which would contain the impurity) being included in the forming crystals. We also have always to wash the crystals once they have formed, to remove drops of solution.

In the same way that we can use the difference in the solubility of two substances to separate them by fractional crystallisation, so we can also use the difference in the boiling point of two substances to separate them. We call this method of separation FRACTIONAL DISTILLATION. Your teacher may show you how this is done.

▶ EXPERIMENT 1.4, page 10

Fig. 1.12 *Carefully controlled copper stills used in making Scotch whisky*

EXPERIMENT 1.3

Separating potassium nitrate from copper(II) sulphate: fractional crystallisation

You will need the following: a mixture of potassium nitrate and copper(II) sulphate (ratio about 10:1 by volume), boiling-tube, filter-funnel, filter-paper, hand-lens, beaker (250 cm^3), glass rod.

What to do

YOU MUST WEAR YOUR SAFETY SPECTACLES.

1   Put some of the mixture on a piece of paper, and examine it closely with a hand-lens. How many types of crystal can you see?

2   Write down what you have seen.

3   Put about 10 spatula-measures of the mixture into a boiling-tube. Add about one third of a tube full of water.

4   Half-fill a beaker with water and place it on a tripod and gauze. Heat the water with a Bunsen burner. Place the boiling-tube in the beaker, and stir the contents with a glass rod.

5   Carry on stirring and heating until all the mixture dissolves. If this does not happen, add a **little** more water and continue heating and stirring, until it does.

6   Take the boiling-tube out of the beaker, and hold it under a running tap, until crystals begin to appear. Place the tube in a rack and leave it there until no more crystals form.

7   Filter off the crystals which have formed, and collect the solution which runs through the filter-paper in a beaker.

8   Take a very small volume of cold water and pour it over the crystals on the filter-paper. You will see that this 'washes' the crystals by taking away the drops of solution that were still there.

9   Take the filter-paper out of the funnel and carefully open it out. When the crystals are dry enough, look at them closely with the hand-lens.

10   Discuss what you have seen, and try to decide what has happened.

11   Write down what you have seen, and what you have decided.

What happened

You should have been able to see the following.

1   The mixture was made up of two types of crystal – white ones (potassium nitrate) and blue ones (copper(II) sulphate).

2   The crystals which you filtered off were white, once they had been washed.

3   The solution which passed through the filter-paper (we call this the FILTRATE) was blue.

What we can decide

When the mixture of crystals dissolved in the warm water, the solution which was formed was a mixture of potassium nitrate and copper(II) sulphate. When you cooled the solution crystals of potassium nitrate began to form, but there were no crystals of copper(II) sulphate. This is because the amount of potassium nitrate which will dissolve in a given amount of water gets much less as the temperature drops. At the point where the crystals of potassium nitrate began to form, the volume of water in the boiling-tube contained the maximum amount of potassium nitrate that it could hold at that temperature. We call such a solution a SATURATED solution. The more the temperature dropped, the more potassium nitrate was forced out of solution, and the more crystals formed.

The solubility of copper(II) sulphate also gets less as the temperature drops, but not to the same extent as for potassium nitrate. So when the solution became saturated with potassium nitrate, it was not yet saturated with copper(II) sulphate – so no crystals of it formed. Because only potassium nitrate crystals formed, you were able to filter these off, and therefore to separate them from the copper(II) sulphate. The filtrate was still a mixture of potassium nitrate and copper(II) sulphate in solution, but the potassium nitrate which you got was pure (once it had been washed).

EXPERIMENT 1.4
Separating ethanol from water: fractional distillation

> **Your teacher will show you this experiment**

The following will be needed: a mixture of ethanol (industrial methylated spirits) and water (1 part ethanol to 3 parts water), Liebig condenser, fractionating column and glass packing, thermometer (−10°C to 110°C), large round-bottomed flask, anti-bumping granules or broken porcelain, large watch-glass.

What to do

YOU MUST WEAR YOUR SAFETY SPECTACLES

1   Take a few drops of the mixture, and put them in a large watch-glass. Use a lighted spill to try to set fire to the mixture. Will it burn?

2   Put some anti-bumping granules (or broken porcelain) into a large round-bottomed flask, and then fill it about one-third full of the mixture of ethanol and water.

3   Clamp the flask above the bench so that it is resting on the gauze of a tripod.

4   Insert the fractionating column (which you have filled with glass rods or beads) into the neck of the flask, and clamp it into position. Put the thermometer into the top of the fractionating column. Attach the Liebig condenser, and clamp it in place.

Points to note about the apparatus:
1. The granules help the liquid to boil smoothly, without bumping.
2. The fractionating column is filled with small glass rods or beads to give a very large surface area. This means that the mixture condenses and boils many times. It gives a better separation.
3. The bulb of the thermometer must be opposite the entry to the Liebig condenser. This makes sure that the temperature that it shows is the temperature of the vapour which is being condensed and collected.
4. The Liebig condenser is a long glass tube surrounded with flowing cold water. We always set a Liebig condenser up so that the water from the tap enters the inlet at the bottom end of the condenser, and flows out of the outlet at the top of the condenser. This is for two reasons:
   (a) So that the condenser always has water in it. If there is an air-lock in the water coming from the tap, the condenser will not empty.
   (b) So that there is a gradual change in temperature along the length of the condenser. The hot vapour heats up the cold water in the jacket as it flows. So the water is coldest at the bottom and hottest at the top. If we put the water in at the top, then the hottest vapour would be in contact with the coldest water, and this might crack the glass of the condenser.

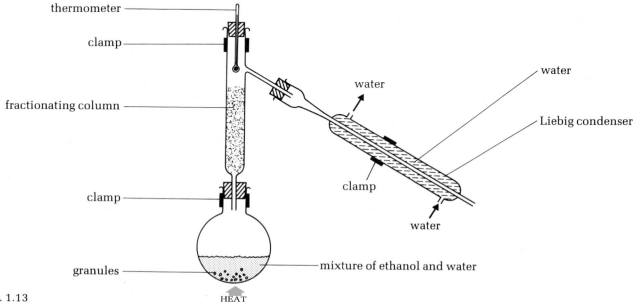

Fig. 1.13

5   Start the distillation. Watch the temperature shown by the thermometer as it rises. Use separate small beakers to collect the liquid coming out of the condenser (we call this liquid the CONDENSATE) as follows:

(a) Between 78°C and 82°C   Fraction 1
(b) Between 82°C and 86°C   Fraction 2
(c) Between 86°C and 90°C   Fraction 3
(d) Between 90°C and 94°C   Fraction 4
(e) Between 94°C and 98°C   Fraction 5

6   Try each liquid separately to see if it will burn, by putting it on a clean watch-glass and trying to ignite it with a lighted spill.

What happened

You should have been able to see the following.
1   The original mixture would not burn. It is made up of 25% ethanol and 75% water.

2   The early 'fractions' coming out of the condenser did burn, but the later ones did not. The make-up of the different fractions is roughly as follows:

Fraction 1   85% ethanol, 15% water
Fraction 2   75% ethanol, 25% water
Fraction 3   65% ethanol, 35% water
Fraction 4   55% ethanol, 45% water
Fraction 5   30% ethanol, 70% water

Can you say what has happened to the mixture as a result of the fractional distillation?

What we can decide

Fractional distillation changes the composition of a mixture of two liquids. The liquid which has the lower boiling point boils first, and then as the temperature of the liquid in the flask gets higher, more of the liquid with the higher boiling point boils. Eventually, only the liquid with the higher boiling point is left in the flask, and this then boils on its own. Suppose A (represented by ○) has the lower boiling point, and that B (represented by ●) has the higher boiling point (Fig. 1.14).

Theoretically, we can get pure A and pure B from a mixture of the two liquids using fractional distillation. Unfortunately, in reality this is only true for **some** mixtures. For many liquids mixed together (for instance, ethanol and water) we can never get a perfect separation by fractional distillation. The best we can hope to do in this particular case is to get a mixture of 96% ethanol and 4% water. Much effort has gone into perfecting this particular separation over the years, because ethanol is the substance which we usually call by the simple name 'alcohol'. Fractional distillation is used to increase the percentage of alcohol in the mixture which is produced by the brewing process. Whether the apparatus which is used is simple or complicated, the highest concentration of ethanol in the mixture is always the same.

The fractionating column is used to cause the mixture of vapours coming out of the flask to condense and boil many times before reaching the condenser. This helps the separation of the substances in the original mixture. At any one time, the top of the column is filled with a mixture which has a lower boiling point than the mixture at the bottom. Halfway down the column, the mixture will have a boiling point and a composition in between these two. So, to get the mixture we want, we could just set up a fractionating column.

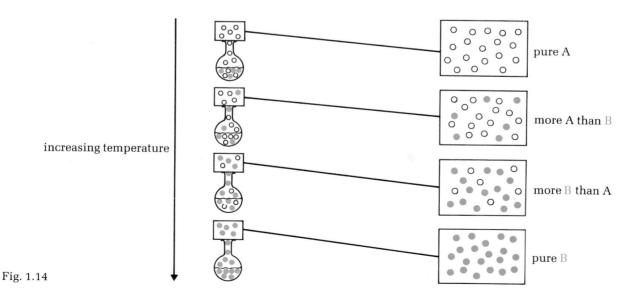

increasing temperature

pure A

more A than B

more B than A

pure B

Fig. 1.14

One of the most important uses of fractional distillation in industry is the separation of crude oil into different fractions. The fractionating column used is about 50 m high, and the different products are led off at different levels.

The products of the fractional distillation of crude oil are roughly as shown in Fig. 1.16.

Another way of separating two or more dissolved substances is called CHROMATOGRAPHY.

▶ EXPERIMENT 1.5

Fig. 1.15 *A fractionating column in an oil refinery*

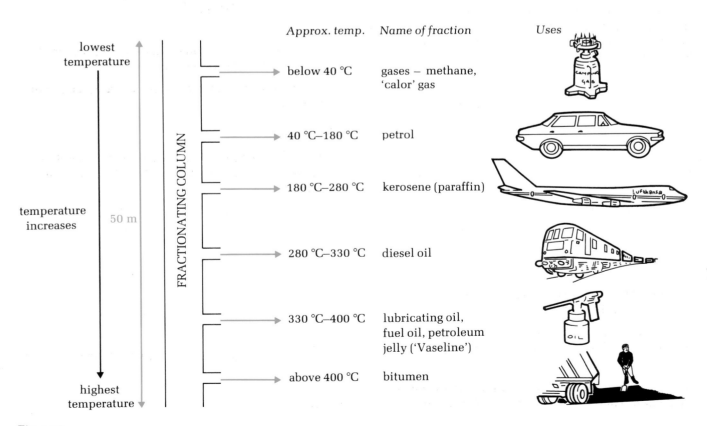

	Approx. temp.	Name of fraction	Uses
lowest temperature	below 40 °C	gases – methane, 'calor' gas	
	40 °C–180 °C	petrol	
	180 °C–280 °C	kerosene (paraffin)	
temperature increases 50 m	280 °C–330 °C	diesel oil	
	330 °C–400 °C	lubricating oil, fuel oil, petroleum jelly ('Vaseline')	
highest temperature	above 400 °C	bitumen	

FRACTIONATING COLUMN

Fig. 1.16

EXPERIMENT 1.5
Separating the dyes in different inks: chromatography

You will need the following: a solvent made up of butan-1-ol, ethanol and 2M ammonia solution (in the proportion 3:1:1), two boiling-tubes, capillary tubing, strips of filter-paper, a selection of different coloured inks, two drawing pins, corks (or bungs) for boiling-tubes.

What to do

1   Cut two strips of filter-paper, $1\frac{1}{2}$ cm wide, and 2 cm longer than a boiling-tube.

2   Take each strip and fold the end over so that it is wide enough to take a drawing pin. Pierce the flap with a drawing pin and use it to pin the strip of paper to the underside of a boiling-tube bung.

3   Put the bung into a boiling-tube, and look to see whether the paper reaches the bottom of it. Trim off any excess paper, so that the strip just touches the bottom when the bung is in the tube. Repeat this for the other strip of paper and boiling-tube.

4   Take each strip of paper, and use a pencil and ruler to draw a line, parallel to the bottom edge, but about 2 cm up from it.

5   Use a clean capillary tube to place a spot of the first ink on this line, just in from the edge. Do the same again on the other side of the paper with another ink. The paper will look like this:

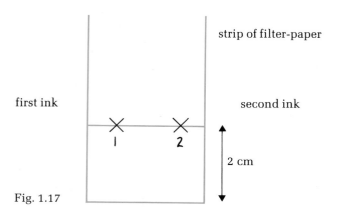

Fig. 1.17

6   Repeat this for the other tube, so that you have used four inks in all.

7   Let the spots of ink dry in the air, and mark the position of each in pencil with a number (as in the diagram).

8   To each boiling-tube add the solvent until it is 1 cm deep. Then lower the strip of filter-paper

carefully into the tube so that the bottom end of it is in the solvent. Check to see that none of the spots has gone below the level of the solvent. If this has happened, you will have to start again!

9   Leave the tubes to stand and observe what happens as the solvent soaks up the strips of filter-paper.

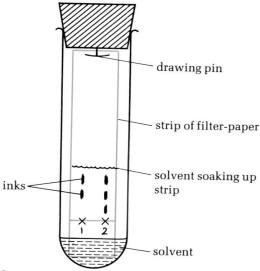

Fig. 1.18

10   Discuss what you can see happening, and try to decide why this is taking place.

11   **Write down what you have seen, and what you have decided.**

What happened

You should have seen that the inks were separated into two or more different dyes. A typical example would look like this:

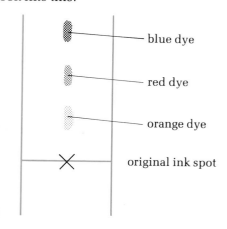

Fig. 1.19

Continued overleaf

What we can decide

Chromatography works because the different dyes cling to the paper with different strengths. So, as the solvent washes the dyes across the paper, different ones move at different speeds.

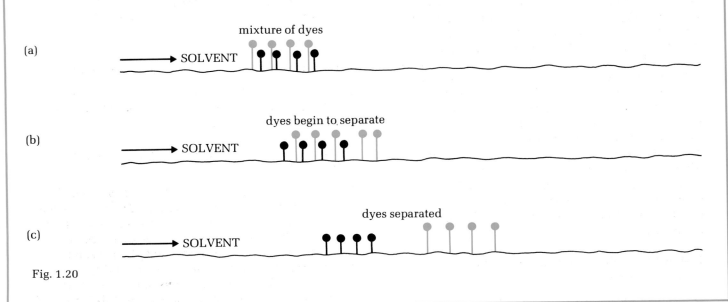

Fig. 1.20

Sometimes, chromatography is used to separate and collect dissolved substances (we do this by simply washing the dyes separately off the end of the paper and collecting them). However, it is used more often to identify substances. For a given solvent and a given type of paper, each substance will move a certain distance. So, we can tell what a substance is by how far it moves. If we use a substance that we know in the same chromatography experiment, and it moves the same distance as one of the 'unknown' spots, then we have identified the unknown (Fig. 1.21).

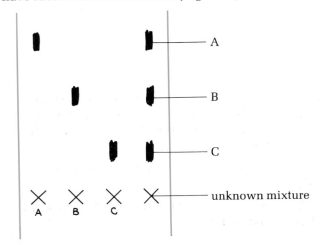

Fig. 1.21

It is this principle which forms the basis of one of the most sensitive detection methods known to modern science. GAS–LIQUID CHROMATOGRAPHY is basically the same process as the PAPER CHROMATOGRAPHY which was carried out in Experiment 1.5. The only difference is that the 'solvent' is a gas (usually nitrogen), and that instead of filter paper a liquid is used. The liquid is given a large surface area by coating it onto a powder. Tiny amounts of the unknown substance are introduced into the flow of nitrogen gas at one end of a long tube which contains the liquid-coated powder. The more soluble a substance is in this liquid, the longer it takes to pass through the tube.

The time taken for the different substances which were in the mixture to pass through the tube is measured very accurately. These times are compared with the times taken by known pure substances, and the composition of the unknown mixture is discovered. Because this method is so sensitive and accurate, it is now used in many places to spot small amounts of chemical substances. Police forensic laboratories are equipped with gas–liquid chromatography machines, and so are hospital laboratories, and the laboratories which check the accuracy of chemical processes. Gas–liquid chromatography machines are used in police laboratories to test drivers' breath for alcohol.

TOPIC 1.1.3

The difference between physical changes and chemical changes

So far in this section you have seen many different changes. You saw how red chalk and white chalk could go together to make something that seemed to be pink, and you also saw how it would be possible to change the mixture of chalks by separating out the red and white chalk again. You saw how sand could be separated from salt, and how salt crystals could be obtained from a solution of salt in water. You then saw how a mixture of soluble solids could be separated by fractional crystallisation, and how a mixture of miscible liquids could be separated by fractional distillation. You saw how useful chromatography can also be in separating and identifying substances.

Each of these changes had a number of things in common. To find out what these things are, you need to ask yourself some questions about the changes you have seen.

1. When the different substances were separated, did the change cause new substances to form?

For each of the changes you have seen the answer to this question is 'no'. Think back to the mixture of red chalk and white chalk. If you separated them, you would be left with two piles – one of white chalk and one of red. The change left us with the same substances that were there before – only they were no longer mixed together. The sand and salt that were separated by filtration were there at the beginning and at the end. The only difference caused by the change was that the substances which were mixed together at the beginning were separated at the end.

PROJECT 1.2

For each of the other changes which you have seen, decide what substances were there at the beginning, and what substances were there at the end.

The changes were: evaporation, fractional crystallisation, fractional distillation and chromatography.

2. Could the changes have been reversed easily?

For each change, the answer to this is 'yes'. You would simply have to mix together the substances which you had separated.

3. Was there a lot of heat given out or taken in by the change?

This question is a little more difficult to answer. For some of the changes, heat was used. So it may be that heat was taken in – for instance, during evaporation. However, this heat was used to change one of the parts of the mixture into a different physical state – for instance, to change water to steam during evaporation. The heat was not used for the actual separation itself. The easiest way to see this is to think of what would happen when you reversed the change – if, for instance, you mixed water with salt. If you did this there would be very little heat change indeed. It is easy to see that there is no heat change whatsoever when, for example, sand and salt are mixed together.

So the answer to this question is 'no', or 'very little'. Each of the changes you have seen so far was a PHYSICAL CHANGE. Now we can go on to look at a different sort of change – one that you will see much more of as you study chemistry.

▶ EXPERIMENT 1.6

EXPERIMENT 1.6

Chemical changes

You will need the following: magnesium ribbon, tongs, a small piece of clean copper foil, hydrated copper(II) sulphate crystals, boiling-tube.

What to do

YOU MUST WEAR YOUR SAFETY SPECTACLES.

A 1 Take a piece of clean magnesium ribbon, about 5 cm long, and hold one end in a pair of tongs. Hold the other end in a roaring Bunsen flame. When the magnesium starts to burn take it out of the flame. DO NOT LOOK DIRECTLY AT THE BURNING MAGNESIUM as this will hurt your eyes.

2 Collect together the substance that is left at the end.

3 **Discuss what you have seen, and try to describe what has happened.**

Continued overleaf

4   Write down what you have seen, and what the substance which is left at the end of the change looks like.

B 1   Take a small piece of clean copper foil, about 2 cm × 2 cm. Hold one end in the tongs, and heat it in the Bunsen flame. Do this for just a few seconds, and then take the copper out of the flame. After a few seconds, plunge the copper back into the flame for another short time.

2   Do this several times, until you can see a change.

3   Take the copper out of the flame, and let it cool down.

4   Scrape the surface of the copper with something sharp – what do you see?

5   Discuss what you have seen, and try to describe what happened.

6   Write down what you have seen, and what the substance which is left at the end of the change looks like.

C 1   Take a clean, dry boiling-tube. Put hydrated copper(II) sulphate crystals into the tube, so that there is a depth of about 3 cm of crystals.

2   Clamp the boiling-tube above the bench, at a slight angle. Now heat the crystals with a medium Bunsen flame.

3   Move the flame about, so that the heat does not crack the tube.

4   Keep heating until you see a change. If some liquid forms in the tube, try to get enough to collect a few drops by carefully pouring it into another tube.

5   Test any liquid which you can collect with anhydrous cobalt chloride paper.

6   Discuss what you have seen, and try to describe what happened.

7   Write down what you have seen, and what the substance which is left in the tube at the end of the change looks like.

8   Let the substance which is left in the tube cool down. Then take the tube, and hold it so that the base of the tube is in the palm of your hand. Now add a small amount of water *very carefully* – what happens?

9   Look at the contents of the tube – how have they changed?

10   Discuss what you have seen, and try to decide what happened.

11   Write down what you have seen, and what you have decided.

What happened

You should have been able to see the following.
A   The magnesium burned with a very bright light, and clouds of smoke were produced. The magnesium ribbon seemed to be turned into a grey/white powder.
B   The copper foil became coated in a black layer. This layer was very thin, and flaky.
C   The hydrated copper(II) sulphate crystals gave off steam, and slowly turned white. After the steam has condensed to form water, it will turn anhydrous cobalt chloride paper from blue to pink.

When water was added back to the white product of the change, a large amount of heat was given out, and the blue colour of the hydrated copper(II) sulphate returned.

What we can decide

When magnesium ribbon is heated, a change takes place which gives out a lot of heat and light. There is enough heat given out for the change to carry on, without the heat of the Bunsen burner. The substance left at the end of the change was not there beforehand. A new substance (the smoke and the powder are the same substance) is formed – we call this magnesium oxide. We would not find it easy to get magnesium ribbon from magnesium oxide powder. The change which has happened is a CHEMICAL CHANGE.

When copper foil is heated, a change happens which leaves a new substance which was not there beforehand. The new substance (the black layer on the surface of the copper foil) is called copper(II) oxide. We would not find it easy to get copper foil from copper(II) oxide. The change which has happened is a CHEMICAL CHANGE.

When we heat hydrated copper(II) sulphate crystals, a lot of heat is taken in. Two new chemicals, water and the white powder (which we call anhydrous copper(II) sulphate), are left at the end of this change. This change is another CHEMICAL CHANGE. It is one of the few chemical changes which we can make happen in the opposite direction by just adding the new chemicals together again. When we do this, we get hydrated copper(II) sulphate again, and the heat which the chemical change took in is given out again.

So, we can see that physical changes and chemical changes are different. The ways in which the two changes are different are set out in Table 1.3.

Physical changes	Chemical changes
No new substances formed	New substances always formed
Heat is often taken in or given out, but the amount is much less than for a chemical change.	Often, a large amount of heat is taken in or given out.
We can usually reverse a physical change very easily.	We cannot usually reverse a chemical change easily.

Table 1.3

We can imagine the situation in the following way:

A PHYSICAL CHANGE

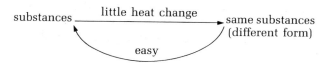

A CHEMICAL CHANGE

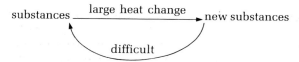

UNIT 1.1
Summary and learning

1 Chemistry is about the substances of which everything is made. We find out how they behave, and we try to understand why by finding out how they are made up. We use this knowledge to help ourselves and other people.

2 We refine and improve our ideas by carrying out experiments. We use experiments to try to find answers to questions which we have asked ourselves.

3 We can divide all substances into pure substances and mixtures.

4 We know the following about mixtures:
(a) The properties of a mixture are a mixture of the properties of the things in the mixture.
(b) The properties of a mixture are not fixed, but they vary depending on the amounts of the different things in the mixture.
(c) The different things in the mixture can be separated from each other using a 'separation technique'.

5 We know the following about pure substances:
(a) The properties of a pure substance are not a mixture of properties. They are the properties of that substance alone.
(b) The properties of a pure substance are fixed, and they do not vary.
(c) A pure substance cannot be separated into different things by using a 'separation technique'.

6 We can tell whether a substance is pure or a mixture by finding its melting point or boiling point. A pure substance has an exact melting and boiling point. A mixture has a melting point and boiling point which vary depending on its composition. Mixtures usually melt and boil over a range of temperatures, rather than at a specific temperature.

7 We can separate mixtures into pure substances using the following separation techniques.
   The 'tweezer method' – for solids that look different from each other.
   Filtration – to separate a liquid and a solid.
   Evaporation – To separate a solvent and a solute.
   Fractional crystallisation – to separate solids which have different solubilities.
   Fractional distillation – to separate liquids which have different boiling points.
   Chromatography – to separate many types of substance, but particularly coloured substances in solution.

8 There are a number of differences between physical changes and chemical changes (see Table 1.3). You should remember these differences.

9 You have learnt the meaning of these words:

experiments	distillation
property	condense
melting point	fractional crystallisation
boiling point	saturated
dissolve	fractional distillation
evaporating	condensate
soluble	chromatography
insoluble	gas-liquid chromatography
solvent	paper chromatography
solute	physical change
solution	chemical change
filtration	

UNIT 1.2   *What is matter made of?*

This may seem too simple a question. Matter is made, obviously, of matter! Why should it be of interest to us to probe this idea further?

We said in the last unit that chemistry is about understanding the way substances behave. To really understand this behaviour, we have to find out **why** substances do what they do. And to understand **why** chemical substances behave in certain ways, we have to find out how the substances themselves are put together. We have to discover what chemical substances are made of.

All chemists are involved in trying to unravel how chemicals are put together. For example, one of the most important discoveries ever made in biology was the way in which the molecule DNA (deoxyribonucleic acid) is put together. It was not until the structure of this chemical was worked out that scientists could understand how it is able to act as the chemical messenger of inheritance from one generation of living matter to the next. This discovery was made in 1953 by James Watson and Francis Crick, who were working at Cambridge University. Quite rightly, they were awarded the Nobel Prize for making this discovery.

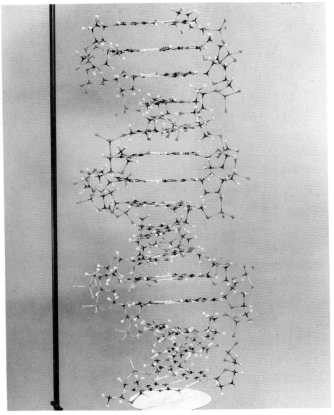

Fig. 1.22 *How the chemical DNA is put together*

DNA is a slightly more advanced example than you will have to think about now, but the process that went through the minds of Watson and Crick is the same as the one in which you are now going to be involved. How is matter put together?

TOPIC 1.2.1

Is matter made up of particles?

Let us start at the most basic level. Before we think about the different types of matter, and try to explain how they behave in terms of how they are put together, let's think about **all** matter. Is there something about the way all matter is put together that we ought to know before we go any further?

Perhaps there is. Suppose we ask ourselves the question 'What are the bits that make things up?'. Let's take as an example, say, a block of wood. What are the bits that make it up? Is it, perhaps, just made up of 'wood stuff', and nothing else? If it is, then there would not have to be any gaps between the bits of 'wood stuff' – it could just be one continuous lump. In the same way, metal might just be continuous 'metal stuff', water might be continuous 'water stuff', and air might just be continuous 'air stuff'.

But is there another possibility to consider? Well, an Ancient Greek called Democritus thought that there was. He thought that all matter, whether solid, liquid or gas, was made of tiny, invisible particles called ATOMS. His reasoning went this way. The streets of towns in the ancient world were paved with stones, and over a period of many years the wheels of carts passing over them wore grooves in the stone. Some of these can still be seen today in places like Pompeii, the Roman town that was buried by volcanic ash in AD 79. Since these grooves were worn by the passage of thousands of wheels over the same place, each individual wheel must have worn away something extremely tiny. So it must be that stone is made of very small objects which can be worn away one at a time.

Democritus' idea was that substances are made of millions of very tiny identical **particles**, rather than being one continuous lump of the substance. So when one layer of particles is worn away by the friction caused by a cart-wheel, the next layer of identical particles then becomes the surface – so the object still looks like it did before (stone).

So there are these two ideas – the 'one continuous lump' and the 'millions of identical tiny particles' theories. Which is right?

▶ EXPERIMENT 1.7

Fig. 1.23 *The grooves in the paving stones of the streets of Pompeii were made by thousands of wheels passing over the same spot*

EXPERIMENT 1.7
Do gases spread out?

Your teacher will show you this experiment

The following will be needed: bottle of concentrated ammonia solution, liquid bromine, gas-jar.

If your teacher takes the top off a bottle of concentrated ammonia solution, and puts it on the front bench, you will discover that the smell of ammonia gas soon reaches to all parts of the room. How can this be? What has carried the smell?
    Bromine is a dark red liquid, that is on the point of changing to a gas. If your teacher takes a small drop of bromine and puts it into a gas-jar full of air, you will soon see that the red colour spreads out until all the jar is the same shade of red. How is the colour spread?

What we can say

Both these experiments tell us that gases will 'spread out' into other gases if they are allowed to. The word we use for this is DIFFUSION. We say that gases DIFFUSE into one another. Diffusion is very good evidence that gases are made of particles.

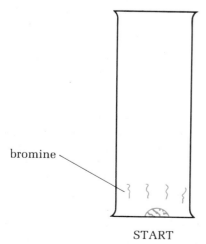
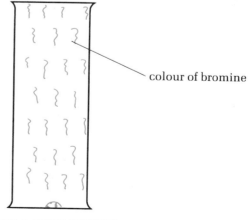

colour of bromine

bromine

START   AFTER A FEW MINUTES

Fig. 1.24

Think back to Experiment 1.1 when you mixed together different coloured chalks. Suppose you had taken, instead of chalk powder, a stick of red chalk and a stick of white chalk. If you put these sticks into a test-tube and shook them up, would they have mixed? No, of course they wouldn't. Continuous lumps cannot mix together. Only things which are divided into tiny particles can mix together.

So it seems that Democritus was right. Matter (solids, liquids and gases) is made up of millions of tiny particles. We say that matter is PARTICULATE.

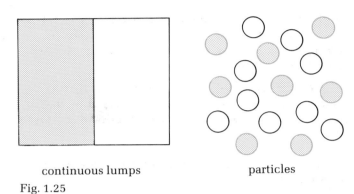

continuous lumps   particles

Fig. 1.25

▶ EXPERIMENT 1.8

So we can say that the particles which make up matter are extremely small. In fact, the experiment which you have just done gives us only a very rough answer. The actual diameter of a particle of the substance gold, for example, is about 3×10^{-7} mm (0.000 000 03 mm).

But how does the fact that we know that matter is made up of particles help us to explain how they behave? First of all, we can look at the nature of the different forms (or STATES) in which matter exists.

TOPIC 1.2.2
Solids, liquids and gases

There are in fact four states of matter altogether. These are the solid state, the liquid state, the gaseous state, and the state called 'plasma'. However, this last form is very rare indeed and is found only in extremely unusual surroundings such as inside the sun. So we can concentrate on the other three states of matter – those in which matter exists in everyday life.

Section 7 deals with the states of matter in some detail. For the moment, it will be enough to concentrate on the main properties of the three states, and our understanding of this behaviour in terms of the particles which make them up. We call this the KINETIC THEORY of matter, because it is based on the speed with which the particles move, and the kinetic energy which they have.

Solids

In a solid, the particles are held tightly together – so tightly in fact that they are not able to move away from each other. Each particle takes up its own position relative to the other particles, in a structure which we call a LATTICE.

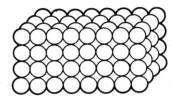

Fig. 1.26 *A solid lattice*

Although each particle has its own position, it does not stay completely still. Particles in the lattice will be moving all the time – vibrating about the position in which they are to be found most of the time. However, as long as the substance remains a solid, the particles do not actually break away. This means that a solid cannot flow, because the particles which make it up are not free to flow. Instead, a solid has a definite shape. For some solids, the particles in the lattice are arranged in a very regular pattern. When this happens, the shape which the solid takes up is also very regular – with straight edges and flat surfaces. We call such a solid a CRYSTAL.

Fig. 1.27 *Crystals of sulphur*

The speed with which the particles in the solid lattice vibrate depends upon the temperature of the surroundings. The higher the temperature, the faster the particles move, and the more kinetic energy they have. All the time, the particles in the solid lattice are straining against the forces of attraction between themselves which are holding them in place. For a given substance, this force of attraction will have a different value than for another substance. So for different substances, the temperature at which the particles have enough energy to overcome the forces holding the lattice together is different.

EXPERIMENT 1.8
How big are the particles?

You will need the following: test-tube and bung, beaker, measuring cylinder, crystal of potassium permanganate.

What to do

1 Take the measuring cylinder and put 10 cm³ of water into it.

2 Run this water into a test-tube, and mark the level it comes up to. Pour the water away.

3 This time, measure 100 cm³ water in the measuring cylinder, and run it into a beaker. Again, mark the level of the water in the beaker and pour the water away.

4 Take **one** small crystal of potassium permanganate, and put it on a piece of paper. Use a ruler to estimate its length in mm. Write down the length of the crystal.

5 Drop the crystal into the test-tube, and add a little water. Put the bung in the tube, and shake until the crystal is dissolved. Now fill the tube up to the mark which you made earlier. The solution of potassium permanganate which you have made contains all the particles that were in the crystal, but more spread out by about 100 times.

6 Pour the solution into the beaker. Fill the beaker up to the mark that you made earlier. The solution that was 10 cm³ in volume is now 100 cm³ in volume – so you have spread the particles out a further 10 times – or 1000 times in all.

7 Take the new solution, and fill the test-tube with it up to the mark. You have 'kept behind' 10 cm³ of the '1000 times spread out' solution. Pour away the rest of the solution in the beaker. Now put back the 10 cm³, and make the volume up to 100 cm³ by filling the beaker up to the mark with water. You have now spread the particles out a further 10 times, or 10 000 times in all.

8 Repeat the above, and record each time you spread the particles out a further 10 times. Keep doing this until you can only just see the very faintest colour of pink in the solution.

9 The very faint pink colour must be due to some potassium permanganate, and we will assume that it is caused by the very smallest amount possible – just one particle.

How to work out the size of a particle of potassium permanganate

Decide how many times you spread the particles out until there was just one particle. Suppose you made 10 dilutions in all. You must have spread the particles out 10 000 000 000 or 10^{10} times. You could have made this many solutions, each containing one particle, from the original crystal. So there must have been this many particles in the original crystal.

All these particles were packed into the crystal. From the length of the crystal in millimetres, you can work out the length of one of the particles in millimetres.

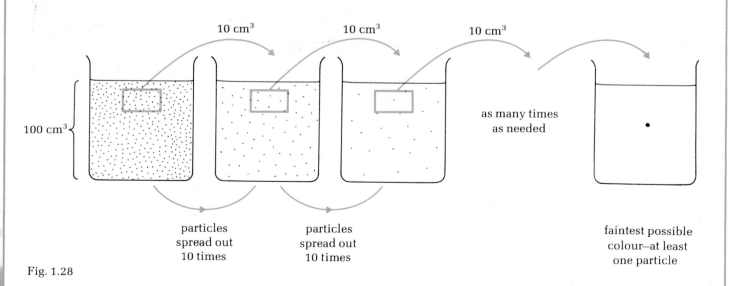

Fig. 1.28

When the particles are moving fast enough to break away from each other, the lattice starts to collapse, and liquid starts to form. The substance has started to melt. We call the temperature at which this starts to happen the MELTING POINT for that substance.

The temperature at which the particles have enough kinetic energy to equal the energy holding the particles together in the lattice is the temperature at which the solid will begin to melt. At that temperature, the particles will look as follows:

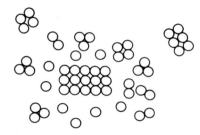

Fig. 1.29

Energy has to be supplied to the particles if they are to overcome the forces which are holding them back, and at the same time carry on moving away at the same speed. You can think of this energy as being similar to that which is supplied by the engines of a rocket which is being used to launch a space vehicle. Gravity pulls back on the rocket all the time, so it has to use up energy to keep itself moving away from the Earth. Eventually, if the rocket accelerates to a high enough speed, it will reach its ESCAPE VELOCITY, and no more energy is needed because it is effectively free. In the same way, only a certain amount of energy is needed to separate particles of a solid when they are melting – after it has been supplied, the particles are free. We call this energy the ENTHALPY OF FUSION and it is the amount of energy needed to convert a certain mass of the solid to the liquid, at the melting point. For instance, the amount of energy needed to convert one gram of ice to water at 0 °C is 334 joules. The stronger the forces of attraction are between the particles of a substance, the more energy will be needed to overcome them, and the higher the enthalpy of fusion will be.

Sometimes, the particles of a solid which have been freed from the lattice have enough energy to escape completely from each other. If they do this, they form a gas straight away without first becoming a liquid. When this happens, we say that the solid has SUBLIMED. The process is called SUBLIMATION. Such cases are, however, rare. For most substances, the state of matter which is formed from a solid is a liquid.

Liquids

In a liquid, the particles are free to move about. However, they are not totally free of each other's influence. The particles in a liquid are in constant movement, bouncing off each other, and sometimes forming small clusters which soon break up only to be replaced by clusters somewhere else.

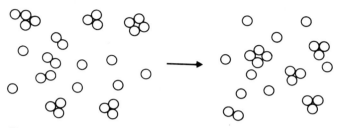

Fig. 1.30

Solids have a particular shape, and a particular volume. Liquids have no particular shape (they 'flow' and take up the shape of the bottom of whatever vessel they are in) but they do have a particular volume. This means that it is very difficult to compress a liquid into a smaller volume. Taken together with the fact that liquids flow, this means that liquids are particularly good at transmitting pressure from one point to another. If a pressure is put on part of a liquid, then the same pressure is immediately felt by all other points in the liquid. We use this property of liquids in the braking systems of cars and lorries, and in the moving parts of heavy machinery – we call the system HYDRAULICS.

Because the particles of a liquid are in constant motion, if we put a small particle of a solid (such as a very fine powder, or a pollen grain) onto the surface of a liquid, that speck of solid will be bombarded constantly by the particles in the liquid. If the speck is small enough, it will actually move about with a very rapid irregular, vibrating movement because of this bombardment. This fact was first spotted by a Scottish scientist Robert Brown, when he was looking at some pollen grains on the surface of a liquid through a microscope. We call this movement of small solid particles on the surface of a liquid BROWNIAN MOTION after the man who discovered it. Brownian motion is good evidence for the movement of the particles of a liquid – but remember that Brownian motion is not the word we use to describe the movement of the particles themselves – only the movement of something floating on the liquid.

Fig. 1.31 *Path of pollen grain on surface of water*

Although the vast majority of the particles in a liquid are held within the volume that the liquid takes up, some particles do occasionally escape from the surface of a liquid. The particles that can do this are those which are moving the fastest. Just as for particles of solid escaping into the liquid state, so also for particles escaping from the surface of a liquid into the gaseous state, there is a minimum 'escape velocity'. Just as for a solid, the higher the temperature, the faster the particles move, and so more have enough energy to escape from the surface of the liquid. The lower the temperature, the fewer the particles which are moving fast enough to escape. For different substances, the stronger the forces holding the particles together, the fewer particles can escape, at a particular temperature.

So, the number of particles which can escape from the surface of a liquid depends on two things – the kind of substance itself (since it is this that decides the strength of the forces between the particles), and the temperature.

When particles escape from the surface of a liquid, they start to form a vapour. We call this EVAPORATION. Because some particles escape from the surface of a liquid all the time, evaporation is always happening, whatever the temperature. Of course, the higher the temperature, the more evaporation there is. The vapour which is formed by evaporation has a pressure, which depends on the number of particles in the vapour. So, as the temperature increases, the VAPOUR PRESSURE above a liquid increases.

Suppose we have two substances, one with strong forces between the particles, and one which has weak forces. If we had each, first at a low temperature, and then at a high temperature, we would get the following values for the vapour pressure (Table 1.4).

We do not normally keep liquids in a vacuum. It is much more usual to have them in contact with another gas above the liquid surface. More often than not, this gas is just air. This would be the situation if we had, for instance, a beaker of water standing on a tripod in the laboratory. Imagine that we now start to heat this beaker. As the temperature of the water rises, the vapour pressure above the water will rise, because more particles can escape into the vapour. Eventually, as we go on, vapour pressure will be equal to the pressure of the air (which we usually call ATMOSPHERIC PRESSURE). At this point, **all** the particles of the water can theoretically escape and become vapour. We say that the water is boiling.

So, a liquid boils when its own vapour pressure is equal to the pressure of the surrounding gases. We call the temperature at which this happens the BOILING POINT. Remember that boiling and evaporation are different. Evaporation happens at any temperature. Boiling only happens at *one* temperature. The boiling point of a liquid depends on the nature of that liquid – it depends on the strength of the forces between the particles. If the forces are weak, the vapour pressure will equal the outside pressure at a low temperature. If they are strong, a higher temperature will have to be reached before this happens, and the boiling point will be high.

For water, the vapour pressure equals 1 atmosphere at 100°C. So this is its boiling point.

Question

The boiling point of two substances, A and B, was found when the pressure of the surrounding gases was
(a) 1 atmosphere   (b) 2 atmospheres.
Some of the results are in the following table, but some have been missed out. Copy out the table, and say what you can for the missing results:

	A	B
1 atmosphere	50°C	
2 atmospheres		90°C

	Low temperature	High temperature
Strong forces	low vapour pressure	medium vapour pressure
Weak forces	medium vapour pressure	high vapour pressure

Table 1.4

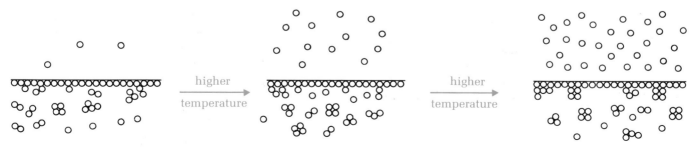

Fig. 1.32 *For a particular substance, the number of particles escaping from the surface increases as the temperature increases*

In the same way that melting uses energy, so also does boiling. We call this energy the ENTHALPY OF VAPORISATION. It is the amount of heat needed to convert a certain mass of the liquid to the vapour, at the boiling point. For instance, the amount of energy needed to convert one gram of water to steam at 100°C is 2255 joules. The stronger the forces of attraction between the particles in a substance, the higher the enthalpy of vaporisation will be.

So far, we have used the kinetic theory to describe solids and liquids. But what about the other state of matter? What does the kinetic theory tell us about gases?

Gases

As you will be able to tell from the description given above of the process of boiling, the particles in a gas are freer still of each other's influence than are the particles in a liquid. In fact, the particles in a gas are almost **completely** free to move wherever they wish.

We said earlier that solids have a particular shape and a particular volume, and that liquids have no particular shape but that they do have a certain volume. Gases have no particular shape, and no particular volume.

The kinetic theory says that gases are made up of particles moving at very great speeds. For a typical gas, the speed of the particles is about 1000 miles per hour! The particles collide with each other and with the walls of the vessel in which the gas is being kept. For a typical gas kept at room temperature and atmospheric pressure, each particle will make about 500 000 000 collisions **each second** with other particles! The particles bounce off each other and end up moving about totally at random. If we could 'freeze the action', the movement of particles in a gas would look something like this:

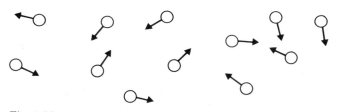

Fig. 1.33

At any instant, some of the particles will be moving **away** from the others. So they will carry on in this direction until they hit something. If they do not hit any other particles, they will eventually hit the wall of the vessel in which the gas is being kept. Many others will follow them, and so the whole of the space available will be taken up by the gas.

Gases always expand to fill the space available to them. You experienced this when your teacher showed you that gases spread out (Experiment 1.7). So gases do not have a shape of their own. Their shape is that of the space which contains them. They also have no fixed volume, because (given the chance) they will always spread out.

We have seen how the kinetic theory describes solids, liquids and gases. It tells us that the temperature at which a solid turns into a liquid (and the energy needed for this) depends on the strength of the forces holding the particles together. The same is also true for boiling. The stronger the forces holding the particles in a substance together are, the higher will be that substance's boiling point. So, substances which have weak forces holding the particles together will have low melting and boiling points. Substances which have strong forces will have high melting and boiling points.

If a substance is a gas under everyday conditions, its boiling point must be below room temperature. Substances which are liquids must have boiling points above room temperature, and melting points below room temperature. Substances which are solids must have melting points above room temperature.

We can summarise what we know about solids, liquids and gases in Table 1.5, below.

So, all matter is made of particles, and the strength of the forces of attraction between the particles in a substance decides whether it is a solid, a liquid or a gas at room temperature. But what causes there to be a difference for different substances in the strength of this force? We will go on to look at this in the next topic, when you will learn about the different **types** of particle which exist.

State of substance at room temperature	Melting point	Boiling point	Strength of forces between particles	Enthalpy of fusion	Enthalpy of vaporisation
solid	above room temperature	above room temperature	↑	↑	↑
liquid	below room temperature	above room temperature	increases	increases	increases
gas	below room temperature	below room temperature			

Table 1.5

UNIT 1.2
Summary and learning

1   All matter is made up of tiny, invisible particles. We say that matter is **particulate.**

2   We can estimate the size of these particles. The diameter of the particles which make up gold, for example, is about 0.000 000 03 mm.

3   The three most common forms or 'states' of matter are solids, liquids and gases.

4   We can understand the nature and the behaviour of these forms of matter in terms of the speeds with which the particles move. We call this way of looking at matter the 'kinetic theory'.

5   In solids, there are strong forces of attraction between the particles, and these are therefore held tightly together in a structure called a 'lattice'. As a result, solids have a fixed shape and size.

6   Substances which are liquids at room temperature have weaker forces of attraction between their particles. As a result the particles are able to move about, but do not escape completely from each other. Because of this, liquids can flow and have no fixed shape, but they do have a fixed volume.

7   If a substance is a gas at room temperature, it is because the forces of attraction between the particles are weak. The particles move about completely free from each other, apart from the collisions between them. For this reason, gases have no fixed shape and no fixed volume. A gas will expand to fill the space which is made available to it.

8   A solid begins to melt when the particles in the lattice have enough kinetic energy to overcome the forces holding them together. The amount of energy needed to convert a certain amount of solid (say 1 gram) to the liquid at the melting point is called the ENTHALPY OF FUSION. It has a different value for different substances.

9   A liquid begins to boil when the vapour pressure above its surface caused by evaporation is equal to the pressure of the surrounding gases (usually atmospheric pressure). The amount of energy needed to convert a certain amount of liquid (say 1 gram) to the gas at the boiling point is called the ENTHALPY OF VAPORISATION. It too is different for different substances.

10   You have learnt the meaning of these words:

atom	enthalpy of fusion
diffusion	sublimation
diffuse	hydraulics
particulate	Brownian motion
states (of matter)	evaporation
kinetic theory	vapour pressure
lattice	atmospheric pressure
crystal	enthalpy of vaporisation
escape velocity	

UNIT 1.3   *What are chemical elements and chemical compounds?*

So far, we have seen that all substances are either pure substances or mixtures of pure substances. We also know that all substances are made up of tiny particles, and that for different substances these particles might in some way be different to each other.

You have learnt how to separate mixtures into pure substances, and how to check on this purity. In chemistry we are interested in finding out how pure substances behave, and in explaining this behaviour in terms of the way the substances are put together.

So we now want to go on to look in more detail at pure substances, and the particles which make them up. The Ancient Greeks thought that all substances were made from Earth, Air, Fire and Water. They called these basic substances from which anything else could be made ELEMENTS. We now know that the Greeks were wrong, but only about which substances were elements, not about the fact that elements exist.

We have found out that the only way we can make new chemical substances is by carrying out a chemical change. Suppose we could find ways of making our chemical changes give us **simpler** chemicals each time we carried one out. Then eventually we would come to a halt because we would have reached a chemical which could not be made any simpler. Such a chemical would be an element. Elements are the building blocks for all chemicals.

So, all pure substances are either elements, or they are more complicated chemicals which have been made by combining two or more elements together using a chemical change.

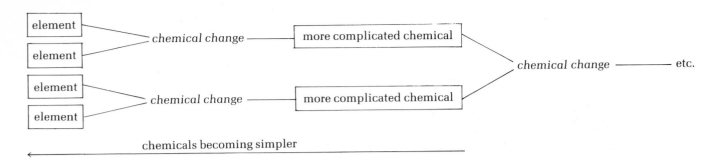

We can often tell that we have succeeded in splitting up a chemical because we end up with something which has a mass lower than the chemical we started with. For instance, we can break the substance water down using a chemical reaction, into two simpler chemicals, hydrogen and oxygen. The mass of hydrogen that we get is less than the mass of water which was used to form it. The difference between the two masses is the mass of oxygen which was formed at the same time as the hydrogen. If we now take the hydrogen and try to split it up into simpler chemicals we will fail, no matter how many different chemical changes we try. This is because hydrogen is an element. So is oxygen.

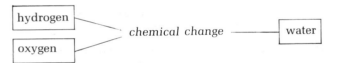

Water is one of those substances which is not an element itself, but which is made of different elements put together. These substances we get when we put elements together by a chemical change are called COMPOUNDS.

An element is a chemical which cannot be split into simpler chemicals using a chemical reaction.
A compound is a substance which is made of two or more elements which have been combined using a chemical change.

There are just over 100 elements and they go together to make the many millions of compounds which exist. Table 1.6 lists some everyday compounds and the elements they contain.

Compound	Elements
water	hydrogen, oxygen
sulphuric acid	sulphur, hydrogen, oxygen
ammonia	nitrogen, hydrogen
nitric acid	nitrogen, hydrogen, oxygen
polyvinyl chloride (PVC)	carbon, hydrogen, chlorine
carbon dioxide	carbon, oxygen

Table 1.6

Chemical elements

What makes an element an element? Why, for instance, is hydrogen hydrogen, and why is it different from oxygen?

This is a question to which science had no answer, even as recently as the year 1800. By that time, many elements had been discovered, and scientists were carrying out experiments on them to try to understand their properties. One of these scientists was an Englishman called John Dalton, who lived in Manchester.

Dalton was particularly interested in the **weights** of elements which combined together. Today in science we talk about mass, rather than about weight, because it is more precise in meaning. Dalton always talked about weight, but his experiments uncovered the fact that elements combine together in characteristic amounts. If, for instance, you take 1 g of the element hydrogen, and combine it with oxygen, then the mass of oxygen you will need is always 8 g, no matter how many times you do the experiment. The same held true in Dalton's time for all the elements – so each one seemed to have a fixed **weight** which was the amount of it that combined with the characteristic weight of other elements. Why should this be? What was it about the way elements were themselves made up which gave rise to this apparently strange behaviour?

Dalton knew of the particulate theory of matter, but he did not know for certain that it was true. In the time of the Ancient Greeks, and in the years before Dalton began his work, there had been strong disagreement about the ideas of particles which Democritus had first put forward. There were those who said that matter was made of small indivisible particles, which Democritus and others had called 'atoms' ('atoms' is the Greek word for 'indivisible'). There were others who said that this was not true, that matter could be divided indefinitely, and that atoms did not exist. We can imagine the two opposing groups, ranged in Dalton's mind.

FOR ATOMS   AGAINST ATOMS

Democritus (Greek)
b. 460 BC

Pierre Gassendi (French)
b. 1592

Aristotle (Greek)
b. 384 BC

Isaac Newton (English)
b. 1642

René Descartes (French)
b. 1596

Fig. 1.34

It was Gassendi, a French Catholic priest who became professor of mathematics at the Royal College of Paris, who 'rediscovered' the ideas of Democritus, which had been forgotten until his time. He disagreed with the brilliant and respected philosopher René Descartes, who lived at the same time as Gassendi and also in France, and who said that there was no limit to the divisibility of matter. The idea of atoms was then given a boost when the famous English scientist and mathematician Sir Isaac Newton wrote the following:

'It seems probable to me, that God in the beginning formed matter in solid, massy, hard, impenetrable, moveable particles, of such sizes and figures, and with such other properties, and in such proportion to space, as most conduced to the end for which He form'd them; and that these primitive particles being solids, are incomparably harder than any porous bodies compounded of them, even so very hard, as never to wear or break in pieces; no ordinary power being able to divide what God Himself made one in the first Creation.'

Newton, Opticks, 1704

Dalton decided that the only theory which could explain his findings was to say that **each element had its own type of atom.** The atoms of one element were all identical to each other, but different from the atoms of all other elements. One of the things which made the atoms of the different elements different was their mass. So hydrogen atoms all had the same mass as each other, but their mass was different to the mass of all oxygen atoms. These are Dalton's own words:

'Elementary principles which never can be metamorphosed one into another by any power we can control . . . That all atoms of the same kind . . . must necessarily be conceived to be alike in shape, weight, and every other particular.'

Dalton, New System of Chemical Philosophy, 1808 ('metamorphosed' means 'changed')

Dalton had hit upon a great truth, which can be said to be the starting point of modern chemistry. He not only proposed the idea that the different atoms each have their own mass, but he went on to work out from his own results what the masses of the atoms of the different elements were, relative to each other, and he devised a set of symbols for the elements.

Dalton's idea was that, when elements combine to form compounds, each individual atom of one type of element combines with a single atom of the other element, or two atoms of it, or three atoms of it (and so on). For a particular reaction, giving a particular compound, the ratio of the number of atoms of the different elements is always the same (that is, 1:1 or 1:2 etc). Since the ratio in which the atoms combine is fixed, and since the masses of the different atoms are fixed, then the actual number of grams of the two elements which combine must be fixed. Dalton thought that an atom of oxygen had a mass 8 times that of an atom of hydrogen, and that one of each of them combined to form a particle of water:

	oxygen	hydrogen	water
relative mass	1	8	9

So, whenever water is formed, the mass of oxygen involved is eight times the mass of hydrogen involved.

Dalton was not absolutely correct in the details of his theory, but his idea was a huge step forward in our understanding. It is for this reason that we give to him the honour of having discovered the idea of atoms and of having introduced it into science. We call Dalton's idea 'Dalton's Atomic Theory', and his name is still remembered in modern-day Manchester – a street is named after him, and one of the buildings at the University of Manchester.

Nowadays, we know the masses of the atoms of all the elements. We have discovered since Newton's time that the atoms of elements can be split up – but not into other atoms, only into the particles which go together to make up all atoms. However, as far as chemical reactions are concerned, what Newton said about atoms being indivisible is true, since the atoms of elements are never split up by the amount of energy involved in a chemical change. You will learn more about how matter is put together in Section 3. For the moment, you have seen that **the particles which make up elements are atoms.**

We can now go on to look at elements, and the way they behave, in more detail.

TOPIC 1.3.2

Different sorts of element

Which of the substances we see around us in everyday life are elements, and what do they look like? Can we divide elements up into different types?

The easiest way of answering these questions is to take some elements and see what they look like and how they behave.

▶ EXPERIMENT 1.9

EXPERIMENT 1.9

What do elements look like?

> **Your teacher will show you some elements. You may be allowed to examine magnesium, aluminium, iron, zinc, carbon, sulphur and iodine for yourself.**

The following will be needed: samples of the elements sodium, potassium, magnesium, aluminium, iron, zinc, mercury, carbon, sulphur, bromine and iodine; gas jars containing chlorine and oxygen; tile and knife; sandpaper.

What to do

DO NOT TOUCH IODINE WITH YOUR FINGERS — YOU MUST USE A SPATULA.

1   Your teacher will show you some elements, one at a time. For each one, write down the name of the element, and what it looks like.

2   For each element, write against its name whether it is a solid, a liquid or a gas. Also write down anything else you can say, such as the colour of the element.

3   For the elements sodium and potassium, your teacher will also show you what they look like when they have just been cut by a knife. Write down what you see.

4   Look at the elements which you have been given to investigate for yourself. Repeat the steps above for each one in turn, until you have described it. You will have some sandpaper available to clean the surface of some of the elements.

What you should have seen

One way of dividing elements up into different types is to separate the METALS and the NON-METALS. For each of the elements you have described, you will be told whether it is a metal or a non-metal. Now re-arrange your list of elements so that all the metals are together, and all the non-metals are together. You should end up with a table which looks like Table 1.7.

What we can decide

It would seem that there is a difference in the physical appearance of metals and non-metals. Apart from mercury, all the metals are solids. The non-metals are either solids, liquids or gases.

Several of the metals look alike, and they all have shiny surfaces when they are clean. The non-metals have various colours.

	Name of element	Solid, liquid or gas	What it looked like
Metals	sodium	solid	Kept under oil. Dull grey surface. Freshly cut surface is shiny silver, which soon goes grey.
	potassium	solid	Kept under oil. Dull grey surface. Freshly cut surface is shiny and silvery, but soon goes grey.
	magnesium	solid	Long strips (called 'magnesium ribbon'). Surface is dull grey but shiny and silvery after cleaning.
	aluminium	solid	Quite shiny, especially when it has been cleaned.
	iron	solid	Dull grey surface. Shiny after cleaning.
	zinc	solid	Rather dull, light grey colour.
	mercury	liquid	Very shiny, reflecting surface.
Non-metals	carbon	solid	Black powder or thin rods
	oxygen	gas	Colourless
	sulphur	solid	Yellow powder or lumps
	chlorine	gas	Pale yellow/green
	bromine	liquid/gas	Deep red/brown
	iodine	solid	Purple/black crystals

Table 1.7

Perhaps we can find other differences between metals and non-metals if we carry out some tests on them.

EXPERIMENT 1.10

Which elements pass electricity, and which pass heat?

You will need the following: power pack or battery (6 volts), bulb, connecting wires, crocodile clips, steel probes (several cm long), carbon rods, magnesium, iron, copper, aluminium, powdered sulphur, lumps of sulphur, a candle.

What to do

A 1 Set up a circuit with a battery a bulb and a gap for testing elements to see whether they will pass electricity. The ends of the gap should be two wires with crocodile clips which can be fastened to the element to test it. Test your circuit first, by touching the crocodile clips together.

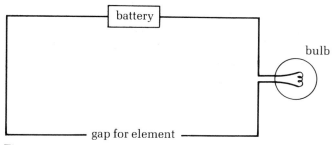

Fig. 1.35

2 Test each element in turn (use lumps of sulphur rather than the powder), and decide whether or not it will pass electricity.

3 **Discuss what you discover, and try to decide whether there is a difference between metals and non-metals.**

4 Write down what you have seen, and what you have decided.

B 1 Take a steel probe and a carbon rod of about the same length. Clamp them next to each other above the bench in a horizontal position. Light a candle, and drip the melted wax onto both, about 5 cm from one end, so that at least one blob of dried wax is left behind (make sure that you catch the falling drips on something suitable).

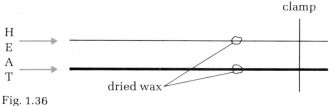

Fig. 1.36

Continued overleaf

2   You now have a way of comparing how well carbon and steel pass heat. Use a Bunsen burner to heat the ends of the two elements furthest away from the dried wax, so that both receive the same amount of heat. The more quickly the element passes heat, the sooner the heat of the burner will reach the wax and melt it.

3   Discuss what you see, and what it tells you about metals and non-metals.

4   Write down what you have seen, and what you have decided.

What happened

You should have seen the following:

1   All the elements except sulphur passed electricity.
2   The steel rods passed heat much more quickly than carbon.

What we can decide

Of the elements being tested, carbon and sulphur are non-metals, and all the others are metals. Carbon is one of very few non-metals which will pass electricity easily. The others are all poor at passing electricity. Metals, on the other hand, are all good at passing electricity. So we can say that, in general, metals pass electricity easily, but non-metals do not.

Fig. 1.37 *Metal wires are used to carry electricity from one place to another*

Carbon is like most other non-metals in being poor at passing heat. In contrast, metals are all good at carrying heat. This is another difference between metals and non-metals. Liquid sodium is used to carry the heat away from the core of nuclear reactors.

We have seen that there are differences in the properties of metals and non-metals. They look different, and they behave in different ways. But so far the properties which we have looked at have been only the **physical** properties of metals and non-metals. What about their **chemical** properties? To find out more about this, we would have to take some metals and some non-metals and make new chemicals from them by means of a chemical change.

▶   EXPERIMENT 1.11

A substance which causes universal indicator paper to go red is called an ACID. A substance which causes it to go blue is called an ALKALI. So we can say that the chemical produced when a metal burns dissolves in water to give an alkali, and that the chemical produced when a non-metal burns dissolves in water to give an acid. In fact, this is the best way we have of telling the difference between metals and non-metals:

A metal is an element which burns to give a chemical which forms an alkali when it dissolves in water. A non-metal is an element which burns to give a chemical which forms an acid when it dissolves in water.

So we have seen that there really are two types of element. They are different from each other in physical ways and in chemical ways. The chemical definition of metals and non-metals introduced the idea of acids and alkalis. What is an acid, and what is an alkali?

EXPERIMENT 1.11
What substances do we get when metals and non-metals burn?

You will need the following: length of magnesium ribbon (2–3 cm), small piece of calcium, powdered sulphur, test-tube full of carbon dioxide, tongs, emery paper, small beaker, broken porcelain, universal indicator paper.

What to do

YOU MUST WEAR YOUR SAFETY SPECTACLES. THE ROOM MUST BE WELL VENTILATED.

A *Magnesium*

1   Clean the piece of magnesium ribbon with the emery paper until it is shiny all over. Put a little water (about 1 cm depth) in a beaker. Have this beaker ready on the bench.

2   Put the magnesium on a piece of broken porcelain, and hold the porcelain carefully in a pair of tongs. Hold it in a roaring Bunsen burner flame until the magnesium begins to burn. DO NOT LOOK AT THE BURNING MAGNESIUM DIRECTLY.

3   When the magnesium has finished burning, use a spatula to scrape the ash into the beaker of water. Use the spatula to stir the water, and then test the solution with universal indicator paper. Record the colour of the paper.

B *Calcium*

1   Wash out the beaker and put 1 cm depth of clean water into it. Heat a small piece of cleaned calcium on a piece of broken porcelain in a strong Bunsen flame, for about 5 minutes.

2   At the end of this time, carefully put the calcium in the beaker and stir with a spatula. Test the solution with universal indicator paper. Write down the colour of the paper.

C *Powdered sulphur*

YOU MUST DO THIS PART OF THE EXPERIMENT IN A FUME-CUPBOARD OR NEAR AN OPEN WINDOW

1   Place a spatula measure of powdered sulphur on a piece of broken porcelain. Hold this in a pair of tongs and heat it in a roaring Bunsen burner flame. The gas which is given off is dangerous – DO NOT BREATHE IT IN.

2   Have some **damp** universal indicator paper ready. From time to time, take the broken porcelain out of the flame, and test the gas being given off from the heated

sulphur with this paper. Write down the colour of the paper.

D *Carbon dioxide*

1   Carbon dioxide is the chemical which is made when carbon burns. Take a piece of **damp** universal indicator paper, remove the bung from the test-tube containing carbon dioxide, and drop it in. Replace the bung straight away.

2   Write down the colour of the paper.

What happened

You should have been able to see the following.

A   The universal indicator paper went blue when it was placed in the solution formed by dissolving the chemical made when magnesium burns.

B   The chemical made when calcium burns dissolves in water to give a solution which turns universal indicator paper blue.

C   The chemical made when sulphur burns is a gas. This gas turns damp universal indicator paper red.

D   The chemical made when carbon burns is called carbon dioxide. Carbon dioxide turns damp universal indicator paper red.

What we can decide

We said that we wanted to see whether metals and non-metals have different chemical properties as well as different physical properties. So we have taken two metals (magnesium and calcium) and two non-metals (sulphur and carbon), and subjected them all to the same chemical change. We have burned each of them in air.

Immediately, we can see that the product of burning a metal in air is physically different from the product of burning a non-metal in air. When a metal burns the chemical which is made is a solid. When a non-metal burns the chemical which is made is a gas.

But the products of burning the two types of element are also different chemically. If we dissolve them in water, the products of burning metals turn universal indicator paper blue. When we do the same to the products of burning non-metals, the solution which we get turns universal indicator paper red.

TOPIC 1.3.3

Acids, bases, alkalis and the pH scale

When an element burns in air, the new chemical which is formed is called an OXIDE. An oxide is a compound which contains oxygen and one other element. The oxygen has been taken from the air.

When a metal burns in air, the compound formed is a metal oxide. We call metal oxides BASIC oxides. If a basic oxide is soluble, it gives an alkali when we dissolve it.

When a non-metal burns in air, the compound formed is a non-metal oxide. We call non-metal oxides ACIDIC oxides. If an acidic oxide is soluble, it gives an acid when we dissolve it.

Water is a compound which is made of the elements hydrogen and oxygen. So hydrogen is the only other element which it could add to the elements which are already there, for both basic and acidic oxides. So alkalis and acids must both contain hydrogen. However, we can **prove** that both alkalis and acids contain hydrogen, in the following way.

▶ EXPERIMENT 1.12

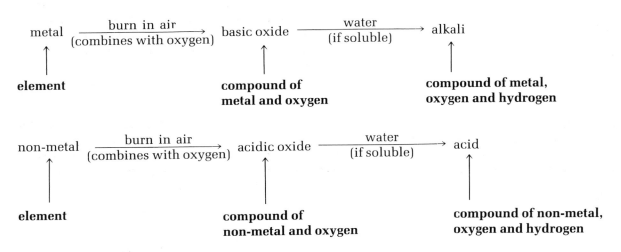

EXPERIMENT 1.12

Which other element do alkalis and acids contain?

You will need the following: granules of zinc, dilute hydrochloric acid, dilute sodium hydroxide solution.

What to do

YOU MUST WEAR YOUR SAFETY SPECTACLES.

A 1 Place a lump of 'granulated' zinc in the bottom of a test-tube. Now add about 2 cm depth of dilute hydrochloric acid, a little at a time. Light a Bunsen burner and have it ready on the bench.

2 Use your thumb to trap the gas which is being made by the chemical change. Hold the gas in until you can feel a strong pressure.

3 Now bring the tube up to the Bunsen burner, with your thumb still in place. Hold the tube close to the flame, but just below it, and take your thumb away.

4 Repeat this two or three times until you are sure of what you have seen. If hydrogen gas is in the tube, there will be a loud 'squeak' or 'pop'.

5 Discuss what you have seen, and try to decide where the hydrogen (if there was any) came from.

6 Write down what you have seen, and what you have decided.

B 1 Take a clean test-tube.

2 Repeat the steps above, but use dilute sodium hydroxide solution instead of dilute hydrochloric acid.

3 If no gas forms in the test-tube, warm it very gently.

4 Remember to keep the tube moving in the flame, and to hold it so that it is not pointing at yourself or anybody else.

5   Test to see if hydrogen gas forms in the test-tube.

6   **Discuss what you have seen, and try to decide where the hydrogen (if there was any) came from.**

7   Write down what you have seen, and what you have decided.

C 1   Take a clean test-tube and repeat the steps in (**B**), but use distilled water instead of sodium hydroxide solution.

2   Discuss your results, and try to decide if they help in telling where the hydrogen in (**A**) and (**B**) (if any) came from.

What happened

You should have been able to see that:

(a) zinc reacts with dilute hydrochloric acid, giving hydrogen;

(b) zinc reacts with dilute sodium hydroxide solution, giving hydrogen;

(c) zinc does not react with distilled water.

What we can decide

We know that zinc does not contain any hydrogen, because it is an element itself. So, the hydrogen must have come from one of the other chemicals which was there. A dilute acid and a dilute alkali both contain water. But you have seen that water itself does not react with zinc. So it must have been the acid in (**A**) and the alkali in (**B**) that reacted with zinc, giving hydrogen. This means that acids must contain hydrogen, and that alkalis must also contain hydrogen.

So, on the face of it, acids and alkalis seem to be similar. They both contain the elements oxygen and hydrogen. But they are not the same. While acids also contain a non-metal, alkalis also contain a metal.

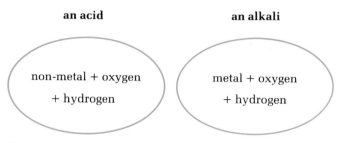

an acid   **an alkali**

non-metal + oxygen   metal + oxygen
+ hydrogen   + hydrogen

Fig. 1.38

Water contains two parts of hydrogen and one part of oxygen. We can think of it as being like this:

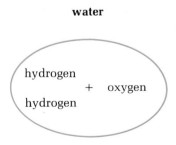

water

hydrogen
            +   oxygen
hydrogen

Fig. 1.39

For most of the time, the oxygen in water is 'between' the two hydrogens, not attached more to one than to the other. This forms a particle called a water MOLECULE.

But sometimes, just for a tiny instant, the oxygen is attached more closely to one of the hydrogens than to the other. This means that the water particle **splits up**

into two new particles. We call these particles IONS. So if we drew a picture of what water looks like, we would really need two diagrams. One for water most of the time (a molecule), and one for water a tiny fraction of the time (two ions).

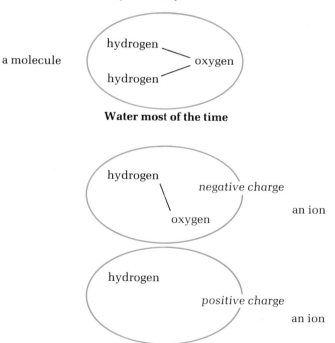

a molecule

hydrogen
            oxygen
hydrogen

Water most of the time

hydrogen
                negative charge
            oxygen   an ion

hydrogen
                positive charge
                                     an ion

Fig. 1.40   **Water a tiny fraction of the time**

The two ions soon go back together again to make a molecule. But in a beaker of water (for instance) there are millions and millions and millions of water molecules. So at any given moment there will be some that are split up into ions. So water **always** contains some ions, although only a very few compared to the number of molecules.

We write the water molecule as H_2O. The two ions are called the HYDROXIDE ION (which we write as OH^-), and the HYDROGEN ION (which we write as H^+). You will learn more about molecules and ions soon.

H_2O a water molecule OH^- a hydroxide ion
H^+ a hydrogen ion

When a water molecule splits up, it produces **one** OH^- ion and **one** H^+ ion. Therefore, if we have pure water, we have a balanced or neutral position. There are exactly equal numbers of hydroxide and hydrogen ions present all of the time. Water molecules constantly split up, and at the same time OH^- ions and H^+ ions constantly combine together again to make molecules.

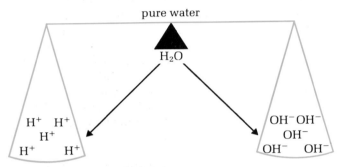

Fig. 1.41 *The water balance*

We say that pure water is 'neutral', because there are equal numbers of OH^- and H^+ ions all the time. Suppose, however, that we had something else dissolved in the water so that there were more of one of the ions than of the other. Then there would no longer be a balance, and the solution would not be 'neutral'.

We can now go back to look again at the make-up of an acid. As you will see shortly, non-metals tend to combine together chemically with other non-metals. The oxygen in an acid will combine with another non-metal, rather than with hydrogen, because oxygen itself is a non-metal.

an acid

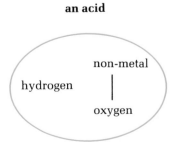

Fig. 1.42

So the hydrogen is left over, in the form of hydrogen ions (H^+). There are no OH^- ions produced at the same time to balance this out, so a solution of an acid in water has more H^+ ions than OH^- ions.

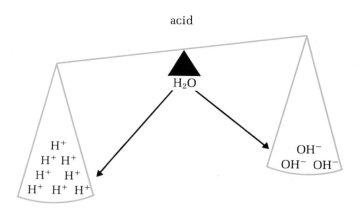

Fig. 1.43 *The acid balance*

In an alkali, the oxygen has no other non-metal with which to combine. So it combines with the hydrogen, and these elements go together to make OH^- ions.

an alkali

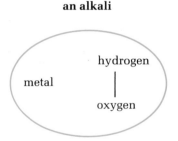

Fig. 1.44

There are no more H^+ ions made at the same time to balance the position again, so a solution of an alkali in water has more OH^- ions than H^+ ions.

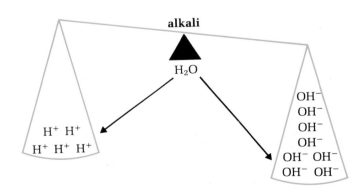

Fig. 1.45 *The alkali balance*

We can now define exactly what we mean by the words 'acid', 'base' and 'alkali'.

Acids

An acid contains very many H^+ ions. When it reacts with other chemicals, it is the H^+ ions that are involved. So we say that **an acid is a substance which is able to give H^+ ions to other chemicals during a chemical change**.

Since all acids have this in common, they all behave in similar ways. The following are the properties which all acids have in common.

(a) They react with metals above lead in the Reactivity Series to give hydrogen and a salt (see Unit 1.4).

(b) They react with carbonates to give carbon dioxide.

(c) They react with bases to give salts (see Unit 1.4).

Bases

A base is the chemical 'reverse' of an acid. So **a base is something which can take a H^+ ion from an acid during a chemical change**. The oxides of many metals are bases, and so are their hydroxides (which we get from the oxide of the metal by reacting it with water). If the basic hydroxide of a metal is soluble in water, we call it an alkali. An alkali is a special type of base.

Alkalis

An alkali is a basic hydroxide which is soluble in water. The most common alkalis are sodium hydroxide, potassium hydroxide, calcium hydroxide and ammonium hydroxide. Alkalis contain very many OH^- ions, and it is always this that is involved when they react with other chemicals. Because all alkalis are alike in this way, they have a number of properties which are common to them all.

(a) They react with non-metals to give a salt (see Unit 1.4).

(b) They react with ammonium salts to give ammonia gas.

(c) They react with acids to give salts (see Unit 1.4).

The pH scale, indicators, and the strength of acids and bases

It is often very important to us to know whether a particular solution is an acid, an alkali, or whether it is neutral. Fortunately there exist in the natural world a number of coloured substances which change their colour, depending on the acidity or alkalinity of their surroundings. Because we can use them to **indicate** the nature of a solution to us, we call these substances INDICATORS.

The coloured extracts from plants will often work as indicators – for instance the dyes from beetroot and red cabbage are good indicators. Each individual indicator is one colour in an acid, and another colour in an alkali. Table 1.8 gives a list of the indicators we use most often in chemistry.

Indicator	Colour in acid	Colour in alkali
phenolphthalein	colourless	pink
litmus	red	blue
methyl orange	red	yellow

Table 1.8

Often, however, it is not enough to know whether a substance is an acid or an alkali (that is, which side the balance is tipped to), but **how far** the balance is tipped to one side or the other. An acid, for example, could have a slight majority of H^+ ions over OH^- ions, or it could have a huge excess of H^+ ions. That is, an acid can be more acidic or less acidic. The same is true for alkalis, which can be more alkaline or less alkaline. So chemists have invented a scale to represent the extent of acidity or alkalinity in a solution. It is called the pH scale. A neutral solution, in which H^+ and OH^- ions are balanced, has a pH of 7. An acid has a pH of less than 7 and an alkaline solution has a pH of more than 7.

```
pH  0  1  2  3  4  5  6  7  8  9  10  11  12  13  14

        increasingly   N   increasingly
    ←──── acidic        E   alkaline ────→
                        U
                        T
                        R
                        A
                        L
```

We can imagine the pH scale as being like a scale attached to the acid or alkali balance. We could use the name 'pH balance' for all the balances we have thought of so far (look at Fig. 1.47 overleaf).

Universal indicator is a special combination of coloured substances which have been put together so that its colour gradually changes over the whole range of pH 0 to pH 14. So we can use it to gauge the pH of any solution (Fig. 1.46).

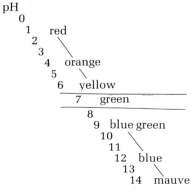

Fig. 1.46 *The colours of universal indicator*

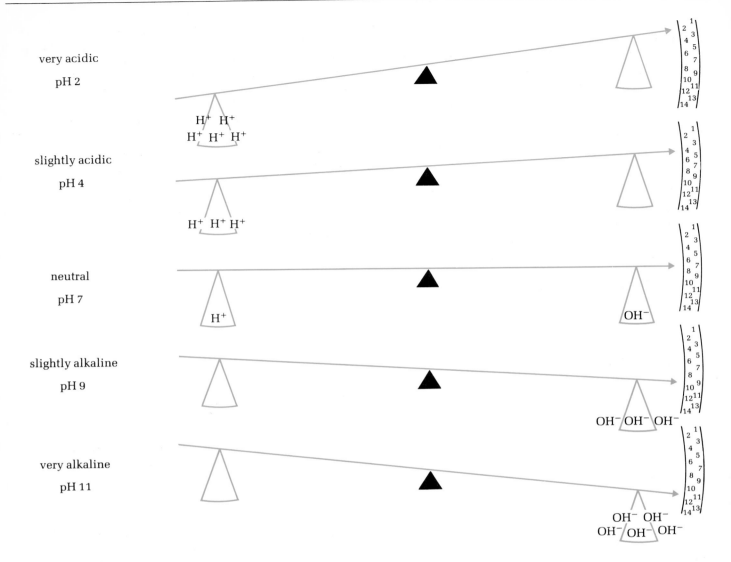

Fig. 1.47   *The pH balance*

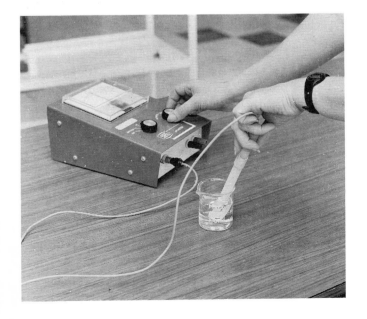

We can find the pH of a solution very precisely using a piece of apparatus called a 'pH meter'.

Fig. 1.48   *A pH meter being used to find the relative number of H^+ and OH^- ions in a solution*

The pH of a solution is a measure of the relative numbers of H^+ and OH^- ions which it contains. If the numbers are almost equal, then the pH will be close to 7 (on one side or the other). One way to make sure that this is the case is to have a solution which is almost all water. That is, if we have a very, very **dilute** solution of any chemical, the pH will be close to 7. Suppose, however that we have a concentrated solution, not a dilute one. What will decide the pH for such a solution?

If there is plenty of the actual chemical in a solution, then the extent to which H^+ ions are in the majority (if the substance is an acid), is decided by the extent to which the substance itself splits up to give H^+ ions in the first place. Some acids split up completely, and give as many H^+ ions as possible. Every particle of the acid splits up to give one H^+ ion. Such acids are called STRONG acids. If however, the acid is like water, it will only be split up to a small extent. So there will be fewer H^+ ions in the solution compared to a solution of a strong acid which has the same concentration. So the pH will be different. An acid which is not completely split up to give H^+ ions is called a WEAK acid.

Just as there are strong and weak acids, so there are strong and weak alkalis. A strong alkali is one in which all the particles are split up, producing OH^- ions. A weak alkali is one in which only some of the particles are split up into OH^- ions. So two things decide the pH of an acid or an alkali, and it is important not to mix them up:

(a) Whether it is **concentrated or dilute**
(b) Whether it is **strong or weak**

▶ EXPERIMENT 1.13

EXPERIMENT 1.13

The difference between 'strong' and 'concentrated' and the difference between 'weak' and 'dilute'

You will need the following: 12 test-tubes, solutions of hydrochloric acid, ethanoic acid, sodium hydroxide and ammonia (see below), universal indicator solution, test-tube racks.

What to do

1   There are six solutions of hydrochloric acid for you to test, with the following labels:

0.1M   0.01M   0.001M 10^{-4}M 10^{-5}M 10^{-6}M

Each solution is ten times more **dilute** than the previous one. Place about 3 cm depth of each solution in test-tubes which have been marked beforehand and put these in a test-tube rack.

To each test-tube, add 3 drops of universal indicator solution. Write down a description for each colour, and say roughly what the pH of each solution was. Keep the test-tube rack on one side.

2   Now repeat the above using the six solutions of ethanoic acid. Write down a description for each colour, and say roughly what the pH of each solution was.

3   Now compare the two test-tube racks by putting them side by side. **Discuss with the others in your group what you have seen, and try to decide the reasons for this**

4   If there is time, you can compare solutions of sodium hydroxide and ammonia by using the same method as above.

What happened

You should have been able to see that the colours of universal indicator in the solutions of ethanoic acid were different from those in the solutions of hydrochloric acid. The more concentrated solutions of ethanoic acid gave colours which were like the less concentrated solutions of hydrochloric acid.

What we can decide

Ethanoic acid is a 'weak' acid, but hydrochloric acid is a 'strong' acid. Although 0.01M hydrochloric acid and 0.01M ethanoic acid have the same **concentration**, there are more H^+ ions in a given volume of hydrochloric acid. Hydrochloric acid always splits up completely to give H^+ ions. Ethanoic acid never splits up completely to give H^+ ions.

If you repeated the experiment using solutions of sodium hydroxide and ammonia, you will have seen that ammonia is a 'weak' alkali, but sodium hydroxide is a 'strong' alkali. Sodium hydroxide always splits up completely into OH^- ions. Ammonia never splits up completely into OH^- ions.

From now on, you must be very careful which words you use to describe acids and alkalis. Remember, **'strong' does not mean the same as 'concentrated', and 'weak' does not mean the same as 'dilute'**.

Suppose we had a solution which was only slightly acidic, say pH 6. This could be because it is a weak acid or because it is a dilute solution of a strong acid.

If a solution is slightly alkaline, say pH 8, this could be because it is a weak alkali or because it is a dilute solution of a strong alkali.

Questions

1   Use your own words to describe the difference between a strong acid and a concentrated acid.

2   Use your own words to describe the difference between a weak alkali and a dilute alkali.

Here are the pH values of some everyday substances.

1 – battery acid
2 – lemon juice
3 – vinegar
4 – lemonade
5 – coffee
6
– milk
7 – water
– blood
8
9
10 – tooth paste
11 – milk of magnesia
12 – ammonia cleaner
13
14

All living things, both plants and animals, contain water. So the chemicals which they contain almost always exist as solutions. The pH of these solutions could, theoretically, vary. However, for the chemical reactions which happen inside living things to take place, the pH of the solution in which they exist must be very carefully controlled. For example, some plants will grow properly only in acidic soils, whereas others need alkaline conditions. So gardeners and farmers need to know the pH of their soil, or to add chemicals to it in order to get the right value.

In human beings too, the pH of the solutions inside our body must be of the right value. For example, the pH of blood is about 7.5.

Acids and alkalis are both compounds. This must be so, because they are not elements, and they are pure substances. You have seen that there are different types of elements – metals and non-metals. Are there also different types of compound?

TOPIC 1.3.4

Different sorts of chemical compound

Remember that we said that **a compound is a substance which is made of two or more elements which have been combined using a chemical change**. Because the change is a **chemical** one, we know that we cannot easily separate out the elements from a compound. The compound has its own properties, and not just a mixture of the properties of the elements which it contains.

So, to find out more about compounds, we have to carry out experiments on them, and we cannot simply rely on what we know about elements. To answer the question 'are there different types of compound', we will have to take some compounds and see how they behave.

One of the ways we used to find the different types of element was to see whether they would pass electricity. We can use the same test on compounds.

▶   EXPERIMENT 1.14

Electricity is charge. If something passes electricity it means that a charge has been passed. If a compound passes electricity, a charge must have passed between the carbon rods.

You know that all substances are made up of extremely small particles. You also know that these particles are not free to move about if the substance is a solid, but that they are if it is a liquid. When electricity passes through a compound which is in the liquid form, the charge is carried from one electrode to the other by the particles which make up the compound.

To be able to **carry** charge, the particles must be able to **move** from one place to another – so the substance must be in the liquid form. But the particles must also **have a charge themselves**.

The particles in any liquid are free to move – whether the substance is an ionic compound or a molecular compound. Both types of compound are alike as far as this is concerned. So the difference between them must be to do with whether their particles have a charge.

The particles which make up ionic compounds have a charge. The particles which make up molecular compounds do not have a charge.

Ionic compounds

There are two types of charge – positive charge and negative charge (in the same way that a battery has positive and negative sides). If a compound were made up of just one sort of charged particle, it would be either wholly positive or wholly negative.

EXPERIMENT 1.14
Which compounds pass electricity?

You will need the following: power pack or batteries (6 volts), bulb, connecting wires, crocodile clips, carbon rods, lead bromide, ethanol, potassium iodide, paraffin wax, 100 cm³ beaker, boiling-tube.

What to do

ETHANOL IS VERY FLAMMABLE. TEST IT FIRST, BEFORE ANYONE IN THE ROOM LIGHTS A BUNSEN BURNER.

1   Set up a circuit with a battery, a bulb and a gap for testing the compounds to see whether they will pass electricity. The ends of the gap should be two wires with crocodile clips which are fastened to carbon electrodes. Test your circuit, by touching the carbon electrodes together.

2   Put about 10 cm³ of ethanol in a 100 cm³ beaker. Use the circuit in Fig. 1.49 to see whether ethanol passes electricity. Ethanol is a liquid which is very flammable. The three other compounds which you are going to test are all solids, and you will be using a Bunsen burner to melt them. However, everyone in the room must use the ethanol first, before anyone lights a Bunsen. When you have finished with the ethanol, do not leave any of it on your bench. **Your teacher will tell you where to return the ethanol, and when it is safe for everybody to start the next part of the experiment.**

3   Take each of the three other compounds, in turn, and melt them in a small beaker or boiling-tube. When you have melted one of the compounds, take the

Bunsen burner away. You can then test the compound to see whether it will pass electricity when it is melted. Use just enough of each compound to make enough liquid to test.

4   Using a clean beaker or boiling-tube, melt and test another compound. Carry on until you have tested them all.

5   Decide which compounds conduct electricity, and which do not. Do you think that you can use your results to divide compounds up into two different types?

6   Write down what you have seen and what you have decided.

What happened

You should have seen the following:

1   Ethanol and melted paraffin wax did not pass electricity.

2   Melted lead bromide and melted potassium iodide did pass electricity.

What we can decide

All compounds can be divided up into those which pass electricity (when they are in the form of a liquid – some are solids which have to be melted), or those which do not. The compounds which do pass electricity are called IONIC compounds, and those which do not are called MOLECULAR compounds.

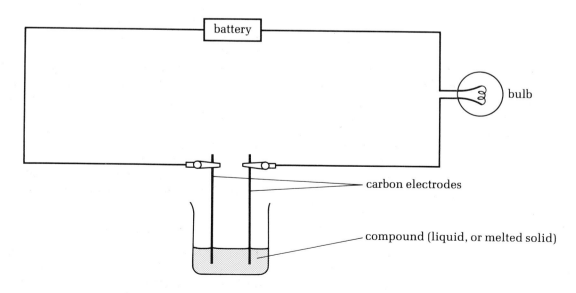

Fig. 1.49

Such a compound would be very strongly attracted by a magnet. But if we take an ionic compound like lead bromide and test it with a magnet, nothing happens. This is because, overall, ionic compounds are neutral. They all contain both positively and negatively charged particles, so that their total charges cancel out.

The charged particles which make up ionic compounds are called IONS. The ones which have a positive charge are called CATIONS. The ones which have a negative charge are called ANIONS.

A positive ion is called a cation
(CATIONS ARE PUSSITIVE).

A negative ion is called an anion.

When elements combine together to form compounds, there are these different possibilities.
1. A metal could combine with another metal.
2. A metal could combine with a non-metal.
3. A non-metal could combine with another non-metal.

Metals cannot combine with other metals to form compounds, and so only methods 2 and 3 work. Ionic compounds are made by method 2. **An ionic compound forms when a metal combines with a non-metal**.

When this happens, atoms of the metal form positively charged ions (cations). Atoms of the non-metal form negatively charged ions (anions).

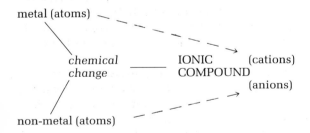

When an ionic compound is in the solid state, the ions are not free to move about, and so the compound does not pass electricity. When the ionic compound has been melted, the ions can move about and can carry the electricity from one place to another.

Molecular compounds

When a non-metal combines with another non-metal, the compound which forms is a molecular compound. The particles which make up molecular compounds are MOLECULES. For the moment, you can think of a molecule as being made up of the atoms of the different elements in the compound joined together. A molecule may look something like Fig. 1.50.

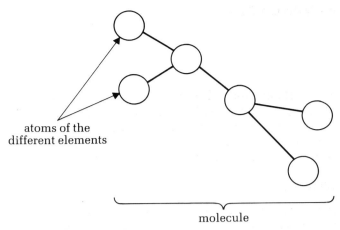

atoms of the
different elements

molecule

Fig. 1.50

A molecule contains at least one atom of each of the elements which make up the compound. The atoms in a molecule are held together very tightly, so the molecule is in fact a new, bigger particle. When a molecular compound is in liquid form, the molecules are free to move about, but they cannot carry electricity, because they do not have a charge.

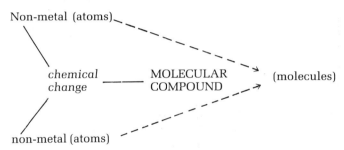

We have seen that there are two types of compound, and that one of the differences between them is that melted ionic compounds will pass electricity whereas molecular compounds in the liquid form will not. What other differences are there between ionic and molecular compounds, and how can we understand these differences from what we know about the particles which make them up?

In the last experiment, we turned ionic compounds into liquids by melting them. But there is another way of putting a solid into the liquid form. Instead of melting it, we could make a solution of it in some other liquid. Will solutions of ionic compounds pass electricity in the same way that the melted solids did?

▶ EXPERIMENT 1.15

You may have noticed that all the ionic compounds which you have come across are solids, whereas molecular compounds have been solids or liquids (and, in fact, many are gases). Perhaps there is a difference here between the two types of compound.

EXPERIMENT 1.15

Which compounds dissolve in water, and which solutions will pass electricity?

You will need the following: power pack or batteries (6 volts), bulb, connecting wires, crocodile clips, carbon rods, sodium chloride, potassium nitrate, ethanol, glucose, potassium iodide, paraffin wax, ethyl ethanoate, petroleum ether, distilled water.

What to do

ETHANOL, ETHYL ACETATE AND PETROLEUM ETHER ARE HIGHLY FLAMMABLE. KEEP THEM WELL AWAY FROM ANY FLAME. THE ROOM MUST BE WELL VENTILATED.

1 Set up a circuit with a battery, a bulb and a gap for testing the solutions which you are going to make to see if they will pass electricity. Test your circuit, by touching the carbon rods together.

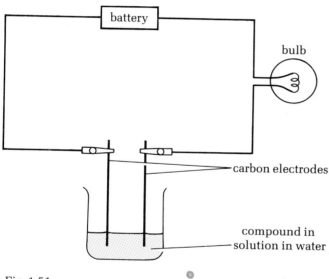

Fig. 1.51

2 Take each compound in turn, and place a little of it (half a spatula-measure if the compound is a solid) in a test-tube. Half-fill the test-tube with **distilled** water. Shake it to see if the compound dissolves.

3 For those compounds which are liquids, you should put a depth of about 1 cm in the test-tube, add the distilled water and shake. If the liquid is soluble, it will mix completely with the water. If it is not, you will be able to see two separate layers in the test-tube – one layer is water and the other is the compound.

4 If the compound you are testing is soluble in water, pour the solution into a beaker and use your circuit to see whether it will pass electricity.

5 Are all the compounds soluble? Do all the soluble ones pass electricity? **Discuss what you have found, and try to decide why you have obtained these findings**.

6 Draw up a table of soluble and insoluble compounds. Divide the soluble compounds into those whose solution passes electricity, and those whose solution does not pass electricity.

What happened

You should have been able to draw up a table like the one below:

Insoluble in water	Soluble in water	
	Pass electricity	Do not pass electricity
paraffin wax	sodium chloride	ethanol
ethyl ethanoate	potassium nitrate	glucose
petroleum ether	potassium iodide	

Table 1.9

What we can decide

Sodium chloride, potassium nitrate and potassium iodide are all ionic compounds. They are all solids at room temperature which are soluble in water. Their solutions will pass electricity. These three are typical ionic compounds. Most ionic compounds will have the same properties.

Paraffin wax, ethyl ethanoate, petroleum ether, ethanol and glucose are all molecular compounds. Most molecular compounds are not soluble in water, but a few like ethanol and glucose are. However, their solutions will not pass electricity, because they do not contain charged particles.

PROJECT 1.3
Differences in melting point and density

Here is some information about five typical molecular compounds and five typical ionic compounds.

Molecular compounds

Name	Melting point/°C	Density/g cm^{-3}
ammonia	−78	0.77×10^{-3}
carbon dioxide	−57	1.97×10^{-3}
ethanol	−117	0.79
methane	−183	0.72×10^{-3}
sulphur dioxide	−76	2.93×10^{-3}

Ionic compounds

Name	Melting point/°C	Density/g cm^{-3}
ammonium chloride	335	1.53
lead chloride	501	5.90
potassium nitrate	334	2.10
sodium chloride	804	2.16
magnesium oxide	2800	3.65

Draw a graph of melting point against density for these ten compounds. To help you, the axes you should use are shown in Fig. 1.52.

Use the graph which you have drawn to answer these questions:

1   Do ionic compounds tend to have high or low melting points?

2   Do ionic compounds tend to have high or low densities?

3   Do molecular compounds tend to have high or low melting points?

4   Do molecular compounds tend to have high or low densities?

5   Can you summarise the difference between ionic and molecular compounds in one sentence?

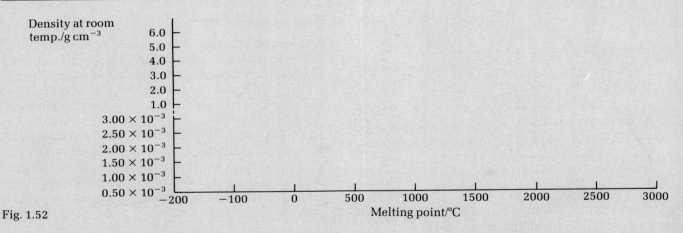

Fig. 1.52

As well as the difference in solubility between ionic and molecular compounds, and the difference between the ability of the liquid form of the two types of compound (either melted or dissolved in water) to pass electricity, there is also a difference in their simple physical properties. Ionic compounds are denser than molecular compounds, and have higher melting (and boiling) points. Another way of putting this is to say that while molecular compounds are often gases or liquids at room temperature (and only rarely solids), ionic compounds are **always** solids. We shall see why this is so shortly. First, however, there is one very important difference between ionic and molecular compounds which we have not yet discovered. This is to do with their **chemical** behaviour. When we describe a chemical change, we often use the phrase CHEMICAL REACTION – it means the same thing. You will now see an important difference between the chemical reactions of ionic compounds and the chemical reactions of molecular compounds.

▶   EXPERIMENT 1.16

EXPERIMENT 1.16
Differences in speeds of reaction

Your teacher will show you this experiment

The following will be needed:

A 'Quickfit' pear-shaped flask and reflux condenser, anti-bumping granules, dropping pipette, test-tube rack, concentrated sodium hydroxide solution, potassium permanganate crystals, benzyl alcohol (phenylmethanol), concentrated hydrochloric acid.

B Test-tube rack, solutions of sodium chloride, barium nitrate, lead nitrate, silver nitrate, sodium sulphate, potassium iodide, and potassium chromate.

What to do

YOU MUST WEAR YOUR SAFETY SPECTACLES.

A 1 Put 10 cm³ distilled water, 10 cm³ concentrated sodium hydroxide solution, and two spatula-measures of potassium permanganate crystals into the pear-shaped flask. Shake thoroughly, taking care not to splash any of the mixture. Add some anti-bumping granules.

2 Clamp the flask in a vertical position, and partly submerse it in a beaker of water which is itself on a tripod. Fix the reflux condenser into the top of the flask and maintain a steady flow of water through it. Add 1 cm³ of benzyl alcohol down the reflux condenser from a dropping pipette.

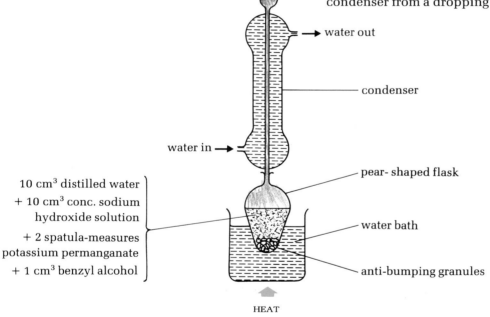

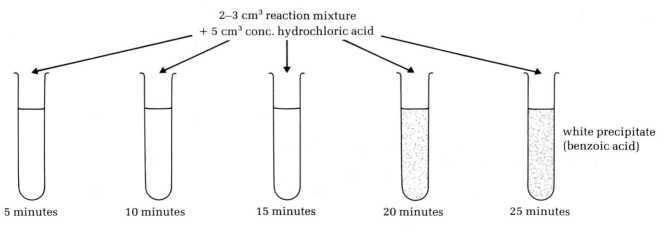

Fig. 1.53

Continued overleaf

3   Heat the water in the beaker until it boils. At intervals of five minutes, stop heating and let the apparatus cool down a little. Then remove 2–3 cm³ of the reaction mixture from the flask using a dropping pipette, by carefully disconnecting the reflux condenser. To the reaction mixture extract, add 5 cm³ of concentrated hydrochloric acid. Stand the test-tube containing the extract in a test-tube rack. Quickly replace the reflux condenser and continue heating.

4   If any benzoic acid has formed in the reaction mixture at the time when the extract is taken, it will form as a white precipitate as the mixture in the test-tube cools. The benzoic acid is formed by the reaction in the pear-shaped flask – adding hydrochloric acid simply allows us to see it.

While the reaction of benzyl alcohol above is taking place (benzyl alcohol is a typical molecular compound), the following reactions which involve typical ionic compounds can be demonstrated:

B   In each case, carry out the reactions below in a test-tube. You should note the speed with which the product of the reaction (a precipitate) forms.
1. Sodium chloride solution (3 cm³) + silver nitrate solution (5 drops).
2. Barium nitrate solution (3 cm³) + sodium sulphate solution (5 drops).
3. Lead nitrate solution (3 cm³) + potassium iodide solution (5 drops).
4. Barium nitrate solution (3 cm³) + potassium chromate solution (5 drops).

What happened

You should have been able to see the following.

1   The reaction of the molecular compound benzyl alcohol was very slow. It is normally about 20 minutes before any real quantity of the product of the reaction (benzoic acid) forms.

2   The reactions of the ionic compounds were very rapid. In each case, the precipitate, which is the product of the reaction, forms the instant that the chemicals mix together.

What we can decide

Since benzyl alcohol is a typical molecular compound, and since the chemicals in part (**B**) of the experiment are typical ionic compounds, we can decide that it will be true generally that the reactions of ionic compounds are very much quicker than those of molecular compounds.

You have seen that the fact that molten (melted) ionic compounds will pass electricity whereas molecular compounds (also in the liquid form) will not, can be understood from what we know about the particles which make them up. You saw that the particles which make up ionic compounds themselves have a charge, but that the particles which make up molecular compounds do not.

   You now know that there are other differences between ionic and molecular compounds. We can summarise all the differences we know about in Table 1.10.

Ionic	Molecular
Pass electricity when in the liquid form	Do not pass electricity when in the liquid form
Most will dissolve in water	Most will not dissolve in water
Solution in water will pass electricity	Solution in water will not pass electricity
Have high melting point, high boiling point and high density (most are solids at room temperature)	Have low melting point, low boiling point and low density (most are liquids or gases at room temperature)
Their reactions happen quickly	Their reactions happen slowly

Table 1.10

You will learn more about water and its properties in Section 7. For the moment we want only to explain why ionic compounds, and some molecular compounds, will dissolve in it. Whenever a liquid dissolves a solid, it is because the particles which make up the solid are able to attach themselves to the particles which make up the liquid. Water is made up of water molecules. Because of their special nature water molecules are strongly attracted to charged particles, and to particles which have sections which are like the water molecule. Obviously, then, water molecules will be strongly attracted to ions – both cations and anions. They are also strongly attracted to molecules which have oxygen and hydrogen (the atoms which are in a water molecule) grouped together. (There are one or two other groups of atoms which will cause the same thing to happen, but this is not important for the moment.) Ethanol and glucose are both molecular compounds which have oxygen and hydrogen grouped together in their molecules.

   When an ionic compound has dissolved in water, there are still charged particles present. So such a solution will still pass electricity. A solution of a molecular compound in water has no charged particles and will not pass electricity.

   In Topic 1.2.2 you learned about solids, liquids and gases. You should read through Topic 1.2.2 again.

Opposite charges attract each other very strongly. The particles in an ionic compound have either a positive or a negative charge. So each cation is strongly attracted to many anions, and each anion is strongly attracted to many cations. When all the cations and anions are put together, then, there are many strong forces of attraction between the particles. So ionic compounds are almost always solids at room temperature, and have high melting and boiling points. There are no such strong forces of attraction between molecules, and so molecular compounds are almost always liquids or gases at room temperature, with low melting and boiling points. Solids are very much more dense than liquids and gases, and so ionic compounds are very much more dense than molecular compounds.

When an ionic compound takes part in a chemical reaction, all that happens is that the ions of the different compounds present rearrange themselves. It is as if the different cations and anions 'change partners'. For instance, the change which happens when sodium chloride reacts with silver nitrate can be written out in the following way (we call this a WORD-EQUATION, because it represents in words what happens during the chemical change):

$$\text{sodium chloride} + \text{silver nitrate} \xrightarrow{\text{chemical change}} \text{silver chloride} + \text{sodium nitrate}$$

This is a simple change, and it can happen very quickly. However, when molecules of different molecular compounds come together to react, much more has to happen than a simple rearrangement. As you will learn in Section 3, the atoms which make up molecules are held together by CHEMICAL BONDS. These bonds have to be broken and new chemical bonds between different atoms have to be formed before a new chemical substance can be made. We have to pull the molecule apart, and put a new one together. This is a very slow process. For this reason, chemical changes which involve molecular compounds are usually slow.

There are millions and millions of molecular compounds. So many that they almost cannot be counted. Because of this, there are millions of ways of making the different molecular compounds which exist. The situation with ionic compounds is much simpler. Most ionic compounds are SALTS, and there is only a limited number of ways of making these. You will discover what salts are and what these different ways are in the next unit.

UNIT 1.3
Summary and learning

1   An element is a chemical which cannot be split into simpler chemicals using a chemical change.

2   A compound is a substance which is made of two or more elements which have been combined using a chemical change.

3   Each element has its own type of atom. All the atoms of the same element are identical, and different from the atoms of all other elements.

4   A metal is an element which burns to give a chemical which forms an alkali when it dissolves in water. Metals are usually solids, which have a shiny silvery surface when the surface is clean. Metals allow electricity and heat to pass through themselves very easily.

5   A non-metal is an element which burns to give a chemical which forms an acid when it dissolves in water. Non-metals may be solids, liquids or gases, and they have a variety of colours. In general, non-metals do not allow electricity or heat to pass through themselves easily.

6   An acid is a solution in water which has a pH of less than 7, an alkali is a solution in water which has a pH of more than 7. The pH of pure water is exactly 7.

7   An acid is a substance which is able to give hydrogen ions (H^+) to other chemicals during a chemical change. An acid will:
(a) react with metals above lead in the Reactivity Series (see Section 4) to give hydrogen;
(b) react with all carbonates to give carbon dioxide;
(c) react with bases to give salts.

8   A base is a substance which can take a hydrogen ion from an acid during a chemical change.

9   An alkali is a basic hydroxide which is soluble in water. An alkali will:
(a) react with non-metals to give a salt;
(b) react with ammonium salts to give ammonia gas;
(c) react with acids to give salts.

10   An indicator is a chemical whose colour changes depending on the pH of the surroundings.

11   When we talk about acids and alkalis, the word 'strong' means something different from the word 'concentrated', and the word 'weak' means something different from the word 'dilute'.

12   An ionic compound is formed when a metal and a non-metal combine together chemically. The particles which make up ionic compounds are called ions. Ionic compounds:
(a) pass electricity when they are in the liquid form;

(b) dissolve in water (usually), and their solutions pass electricity;

(c) have high melting points, high boiling points and high density;

(d) have chemical reactions which happen quickly.

13   A molecular compound is formed when two non-metals combine together chemically. The particles which make up molecular compounds are called molecules. Molecular compounds

(a) do not pass electricity when they are in the liquid form;

(b) do not dissolve in water (usually), but if they do their solutions do not pass electricity;

(c) have low melting points, low boiling points and low density;

(d) have chemical reactions which happen slowly.

14   You have learnt the meaning of these words:

element	hydrogen ion
compound	indicator
metal	strong (acid)
non-metal	weak (acid)
acid	ionic (compound)
alkali	molecular (compound)
basic oxide	cation
acidic oxide	anion
molecule	chemical reaction
ion	word-equation
hydroxide ion	chemical bonds

UNIT 1.4   *What are salts?*

You saw in the last part of this section that an acid is a compound which contains hydrogen, a non-metal and oxygen, and which is dissolved in water. You also saw that an acid contains hydrogen ions (which we write as H^+).

So the hydrogen in an acid makes the hydrogen cation, and the non-metal and oxygen together make the anion.

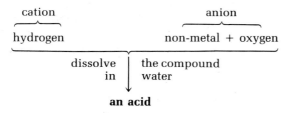

Fig. 1.54 *How most acids are made up*

For example, nitric acid is made up from hydrogen, the non-metal nitrogen and oxygen.

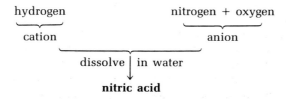

Fig. 1.55 *How nitric acid is made up*

This is not the whole story, because sometimes an acid is made when we take a compound which contains no oxygen and dissolve it in water. Instead, the compounds are made from hydrogen and a non-metal **only**. There are very few acids which we can make in this way, but one of them is an acid which we meet very frequently – hydrochloric acid. Hydrochloric acid forms when we make a compound between hydrogen and the non-metal chlorine, and dissolve it in water.

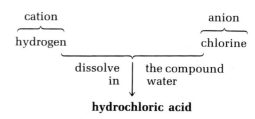

Fig. 1.56 *How hydrochloric acid is made up*

In hydrochloric acid, hydrogen makes the hydrogen cation and chlorine forms the anion. The anion which chlorine forms is called the CHLORIDE ion.

So, most acids contain an anion which is made up from a non-metal together with oxygen, but the anion in a few acids is made from a non-metal on its own.

But how does this help us with 'salts'? The clue comes when we realise that, in the same way that all acids contain an anion, all 'salts' also contain an anion. So what exactly is a 'salt'?

You know that an ionic compound is made when a metal and a non-metal combine together chemically. A SALT is a special type of ionic compound.

A salt is an ionic compound which is made up of a metal cation, together with an anion which could have come from an acid.

So, to get a salt from an acid, all we have to do is to replace the hydrogen cation by a metal cation.

$$\underbrace{\text{hydrogen cation + anion}}_{\textbf{an acid}} \longrightarrow \underbrace{\text{metal cation + anion}}_{\textbf{a salt}}$$

Question

Here are the chemical formulae of some acids, together with their names:

H_2SO_4 – sulphuric acid, H_3PO_4 – phosphoric acid, HBr – hydrobromic acid, H_2CO_3 – carbonic acid, H_2SO_3 – sulphurous acid, HI – hydroiodic acid

Use the chemical formulae to divide these acids into two groups – those which have oxygen in their anion, and those which do not have oxygen in their anion.

Many of the most useful chemicals (such as sodium carbonate, which you will learn about later) are salts, so we need to know how to make them. However, before we go on to look at the different ways which there are for making salts, we need first to learn how we give salts their names.

TOPIC 1.4.1
Giving names to salts

Since all salts contain an anion which can be found in an acid, we can give salts names based on the name of their 'parent' acid. The 'parent' acid is the one we might have used to get the anion to make the particular salt. Table 1.11 gives the rules for going from the name of the acid to the name of the salt.

Name of acid			Name of salt	
Start	end		Start	end
anything	**-ic**	→	stays almost the same	**-ate**
anything	**-ous**	→	stays almost the same	**-ite**
hydro-	**-ic**	→	drops 'hydro'	**-ide**

Table 1.11

Examples
Sulphur**ic** acid → a sulph**ate**
Sulphur**ous** acid → a sulph**ite**
Hydrochloric acid → a chlor**ide**

If you know these rules, you will be able to find the names of almost all the salts you will come across in chemistry.

TOPIC 1.4.2
Making salts

First of all, let us look at the different ways we might, in theory, make salts.

We know that to make a salt we must combine together a metal cation and either
(a) a non-metal anion, or
(b) an anion made from a non-metal and oxygen.
The easiest way to do the first of these is to react a metal and a non-metal **directly together.** So, for example, we can often make chlorides by reacting the metal directly with the non-metal chlorine.

To do the second, we have to find a way to put the anion from an acid together with a metal. So, we could start by reacting an acid itself with something – but what? We know that the following is true:

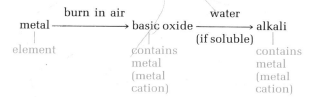

So, to make a salt, we could react an acid with:
1. a metal,
2. a basic oxide, and
3. an alkali
Each time we would get a salt – and what else? Obviously, if we are going to go to the trouble of making a salt, we will want to make sure that it is pure. This means that we have to find a way to separate the salt from any other chemicals which are made during the reaction. We can make things easier for ourselves if we find a way of making sure that there **are** no other chemicals made during the reaction(or at least, none that matter). For instance, if the other chemical which is made is water, we only need to find a way to dry the salt we have made. Then we will have it on its own. If, on the other hand, we could arrange for the other chemical to be a gas, then things would also be made easy. The gas would escape into the atmosphere, and would not have to be separated from the salt which we had made. (We would still have to dry the salt, of course, because of the water from the acid.) Fortunately, the other chemicals which are made along with the salt we are trying to get in the three methods above are either water or a gas:
1. when we react a metal with an acid – a gas (hydrogen);
2. when we react a basic oxide with an acid – water;
3. when we react an alkali with an acid – water.
So, each of these methods looks like being a good way

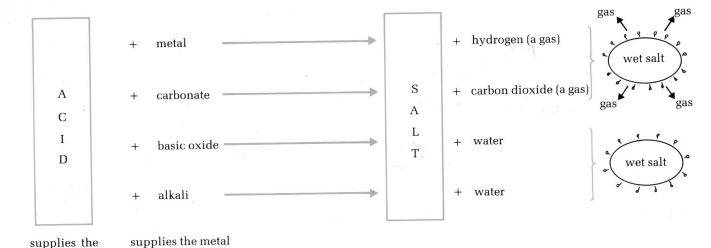

Fig. 1.57 *Some good ways for making salts*

of making salts. It so happens that there is another type of chemical which will react with acids to give a salt and 'harmless' by-products. (We use the word 'by-products' to describe the things which are made alongside the chemical we want. You may have heard this word used when people talk about the by-products of nuclear reactions. This subject is looked at in Section 3.) If we take a salt called a CARBONATE, and react it with an acid, we will get a salt, water and a gas (carbon dioxide). So this is another good way for making salts. (Fig. 1.57)

As well as making sure that we can separate the salt from other things which are made at the same time, we must also try to make it easy to get rid of any of the starting chemicals which are left over at the end. The easiest way to do this is to use solubility and insolubility.

Soluble and insoluble salts

	Soluble salts	Insoluble salts
nitrates	all of them	—
chlorides	all of them, *except:*	silver chloride and lead chloride
sulphates	all of them, *except:*	barium sulphate, lead sulphate and calcium sulphate
carbonates	sodium carbonate, potassium carbonate and ammonium carbonate	all other carbonates

Table 1.12

Questions

Use Table 1.12 to decide whether each of the following salts is soluble, or insoluble.

1. Sodium nitrate
2. Silver nitrate
3. Calcium chloride
4. Lead carbonate
5. Ammonium sulphate
6. Copper(II) chloride
7. Calcium sulphate
8. Magnesium carbonate
9. Zinc nitrate
10. Potassium carbonate

Making insoluble salts

The easiest way to make a salt which is itself insoluble, is to forget about starting from an acid and another chemical, but instead simply to react together two salts which are soluble. You can see from the table that all salts which are nitrates are soluble. Also, all salts of the metals sodium and potassium, as well as all ammonium salts, are soluble. We can use these facts to help us make insoluble salts. If we choose the right starting chemicals, we can make sure that we can react together two soluble salts, to give the insoluble salt we want, together with another salt which is soluble. All we have to do is to start with

(a) the nitrate salt of the metal which we want in the salt we are making – this must be soluble, because all nitrates are soluble;

(b) the sodium or potassium or ammonium salt of the anion which we want in the salt we are making – this must be soluble, because all sodium, potassium and ammonium salts are soluble.

When we mix these two soluble salts together, we will get

(i) the salt we are making – which is insoluble;

(ii) sodium or potassium or ammonium nitrate – which must be soluble.

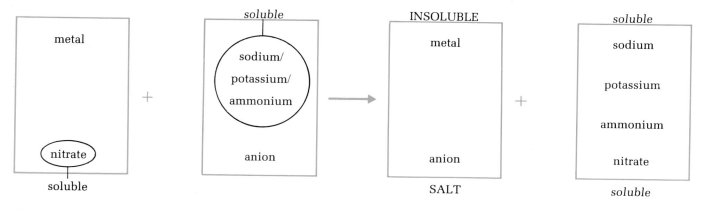

Fig. 1.58 *How to make insoluble salts*

This method will always work. The only insoluble chemical of all those which are there is the insoluble salt which we are trying to make. So we can filter it off. We use filtration as the separation technique.

For instance, to make barium sulphate we could mix together solutions of barium nitrate (soluble) and sodium sulphate (soluble). We would get barium sulphate (insoluble), and sodium sulphate (soluble). We could filter off the barium sulphate. You will see how it is possible to check that washing leaves us with the salt in the pure form, in the following preparation.

▶ PREPARATION 1.1

PREPARATION 1.1
Making barium sulphate

You will need the following: two 250 cm³ beakers, filter-funnel, filter-paper, plenty of distilled water, test-tubes and test-tube rack, two teat-pipettes, 0.2M barium nitrate solution (20 cm³), 0.2M sodium sulphate solution (20 cm³).

What to do

WARNING: BARIUM NITRATE IS VERY POISONOUS. MAKE SURE THAT YOU DO NOT TRANSFER ANY TO YOUR MOUTH FROM YOUR HANDS. WASH YOUR HANDS AT THE END OF THE LESSON.

1   Take the solutions of the two salts back to your bench. Put a little of each (a depth of 2 + 3 cm) in two separate test-tubes. Into each of these put a **clean** teat-pipette. Mark each solution, so that you know which is which.
2   Add together what is left of the two solutions in the beakers. You will see a solid forming from the solution. This is a PRECIPITATE of insoluble barium sulphate. We call what has happened PRECIPITATION.

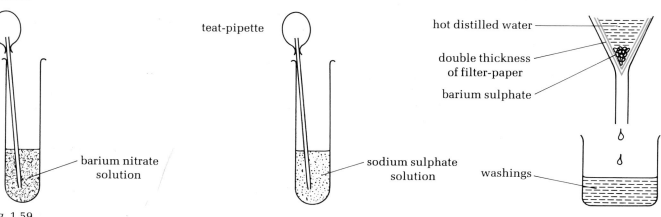

Fig. 1.59

Continued overleaf

3   Put a double thickness of filter-paper in a filter-funnel, and filter off the barium sulphate. You need a double thickness, because the grains of barium sulphate are very small. Many of them would pass through a single filter-paper.

4   The precipitate is contaminated with traces of each of the three soluble salts which are present (barium nitrate, sodium sulphate and sodium nitrate). Take some distilled water in a clean beaker and heat it until it is warm. Pour a small portion of the hot distilled water through the barium sulphate. Let it drain right through.

5   Pour another portion of distilled water through the precipitate, but this time collect a few drops of the WASHINGS as they come through, in each of two clean test-tubes.

6   To one of the samples of the washings, add two drops of barium nitrate solution using the teat-pipette. If a white precipitate forms, this means that there was some sodium sulphate in the washings, and the precipitate on the filter-paper cannot be clean. Return the teat-pipette to the correct tube.

7   To the other sample of the washings, add two drops of sodium sulphate solution using the teat-pipette. If there is a white precipitate, this shows that the washings contained some barium nitrate, and that the precipitate of barium sulphate cannot be clean. Return the teat-pipette to the correct tube.

8   Continue to add distilled water, collect some of the washings in two **clean** test-tubes and carry out the two tests until neither gives a white precipitate or cloudiness. Only at this point is the precipitate clean.

9   When the barium sulphate precipitate is clean, transfer it to a dry piece of filter-paper. Put another dry piece of filter-paper on top of the solid, and press it down with the back of a spatula. Carry on doing this until you can get no more moisture from the barium sulphate.

10   Let the barium sulphate dry completely in the air, by leaving it on the filter-paper, covered with another piece to protect it from dust. Examine the dry barium sulphate solid. You should be able to see that it is a pure white powder.

PROJECT 1.4

For each of the following insoluble salts, decide:
(a) which two soluble salts could be used to make them, and
(b) what tests you would need to carry out on the washings from the precipitate to show that it was pure.

1. Lead chloride
2. Magnesium carbonate
3. Calcium sulphate

So, making insoluble salts is fairly easy. What about making soluble salts?

Making soluble salts

You saw a little earlier (Fig. 1.57) that there are four good ways for making salts, starting from acids. We can use these methods, combined with what we know about solubility and insolubility, to help us make soluble salts.

If we make a soluble salt using one of these four methods, we will need to obtain the salt by crystallising at the end of the preparation (look again at Fig. 1.57). We will be left with a **solution** of the salt – remember it is **soluble** – in each case). We will want

to make sure that we have no other chemicals present before we crystallise. So, we will want to start with an **insoluble** chemical if possible, which we can react with the acid. **This will let us filter off the left-over chemical before we start to crystallise the salt**.

All alkalis are soluble. So we could not use this exact method for making soluble salts, starting from alkalis. We can use a different method for alkalis, which makes sure that none of the starting chemicals is left over. You will see what this method is when we look at a particular example. For the moment, let us return to the three other methods for making salts from acids.

As far as metals are concerned, they are all insoluble in water. The trouble is, that very reactive metals (like sodium) would react with water – so we could not use this method for making sodium salts for instance. Also, very unreactive metals will not react with acids. So this method will work only for metals which have 'medium' reactivity (such as magnesium, aluminium, zinc and iron). The idea of 'reactivity' and the reactivity of metals is explained in Section 4 of this book.

Only a few oxides of metals are insoluble – so this method will work only in a few cases. We usually use this reaction to make salts of lead and of copper, because their oxides are insoluble.

Many carbonates are insoluble (see Table 1.12 on page 48). So this is a good way for making many different types of soluble salt. Of course – it will not work for making sodium, potassium or ammonium salts (why not?). One metal for which this is a particularly good way of making salts is calcium, because each of the other methods has a disadvantage attached to it for calcium.

So we can now describe the four methods for making soluble salts from acids in a little more detail.

Method 1 React an acid with a metal (and use filtration).
Method 2 React an acid with an insoluble basic oxide (and use filtration).
Method 3 React an acid with an alkali (and use the special method below).
Method 4 React an acid with an insoluble carbonate (and use filtration).

We can think of the three methods which involve filtration (methods 1, 2 and 4) as working like Fig. 1.60.

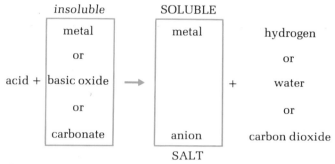

Fig. 1.60 *Some good ways for making soluble salts*

There is in fact one other way for making soluble salts – those whose anion contains no oxygen – by reacting a metal and a non-metal directly together. It is possible to make salts which are chlorides, bromides and iodides by this method, but we would normally use one of the other four methods whenever possible.

One salt which we have to make in this way is iron(III) chloride because we cannot make it by a method which involves water. If we heat some iron as we pass a stream of dry chlorine gas over it, then the two elements will combine together to make a salt. In this case, the salt forms a kind of 'smoke' as the iron 'burns' in the chlorine gas. So we have to have a special type of apparatus to make sure that we can collect and trap the iron(III) chloride (Fig. 1.61).

The particles of the iron(III) chloride 'smoke' collect on the inside of the large glass vessel. Iron(III) chloride would react with any water which could get to it – even water vapour in the air. So we have to dry the chlorine gas before we pass it into the apparatus, and we have to make sure that no moisture can get in from the other end. We can do this by making gases which pass into or out of the apparatus pass through a chemical which will absorb moisture (we call a chemical which will do this a DRYING AGENT). If we do all these things, we will make some dark brown iron(III) chloride, which we can scrape off the inside of the glass vessel and place in some dry surroundings to keep for later use.

Because the elements iron and chlorine combine together directly, we call this method of making salts DIRECT COMBINATION.

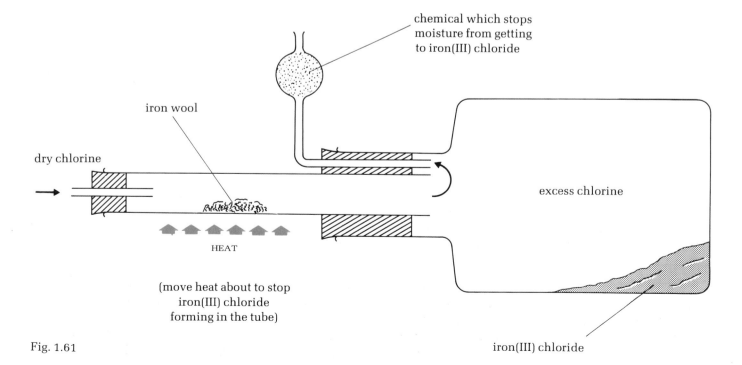

chemical which stops moisture from getting to iron(III) chloride

iron wool

dry chlorine

excess chlorine

HEAT

(move heat about to stop iron(III) chloride forming in the tube)

iron(III) chloride

Fig. 1.61

You can now see that, depending on the cation in the salt we want to make, we can decide which is likely to be the best of the four possible methods given above. If we include insoluble salts, and those whose anion contains no oxygen (chlorides, bromides and iodides) we can draw up a flow chart which we can use to decide which is the best method for making **any** particular salt.

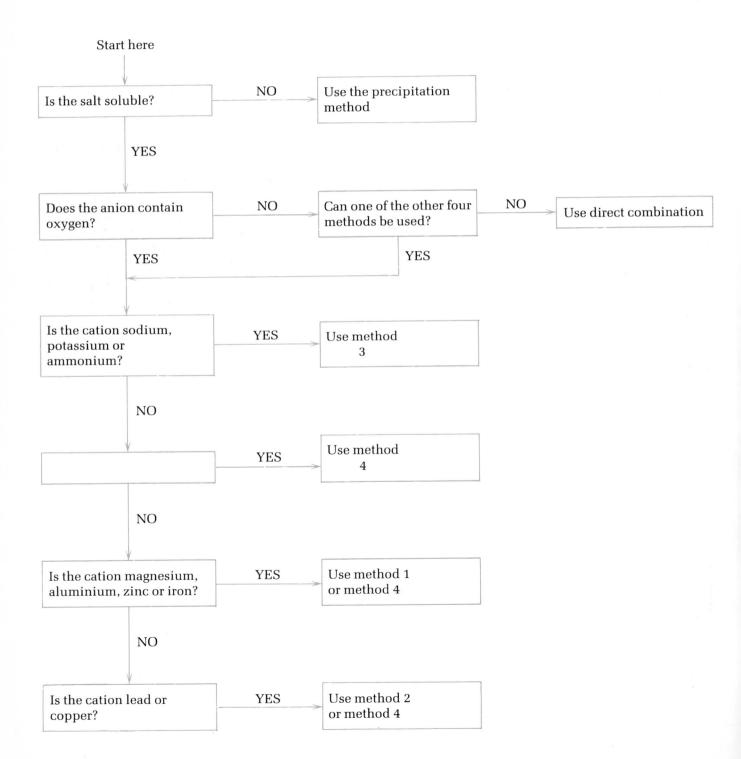

Questions

In each case, decide which would be the best method for making the given salt.

1. Magnesium chloride (it does not react with water)
2. Copper(II) sulphate
3. Sodium sulphate
4. Lead(II) chloride
5. Zinc nitrate
6. Calcium chloride (it does not react with water)
7. Ammonium sulphate
8. Lead sulphate
9. Aluminium nitrate
10. Calcium carbonate

Now you can go on to make some salts for yourself.

▶ PREPARATION 1.2

PREPARATION 1.2

Making magnesium chloride from magnesium metal

You will need the following: measuring cylinder, 250 cm^3 beaker, filter-funnel, evaporating basin, filter-paper, distilled water, magnesium ribbon (10 cm), hydrochloric acid (10 cm^3, approx. 0.5 M), sandpaper.

What to do

YOU MUST WEAR YOUR SAFETY SPECTACLES.

1 Use the measuring cylinder to put 10 cm^3 of the hydrochloric acid which has been provided into a 250 cm^3 beaker. Clean a piece of magnesium ribbon which is about 10 cm long, using sandpaper. Cut it into 1 cm lengths.

2 Add five of these pieces of magnesium to the hydrochloric acid and wait for them to dissolve. If this takes a long time, heat gently.

3 Now add more pieces of magnesium, one at a time, heating all the time.

4 DO NOT ALLOW THE SOLUTION IN THE BEAKER TO BOIL DRY. If this is going to happen, add some distilled water. (Keep the volume at about 10 cm^3 all the time.)

5 Continue until the last piece of magnesium which you have added does not dissolve. Filter the solution into a clean evaporating basin.

6 Heat the solution in the evaporating basin, until some solid starts to appear around the edge but take the heat away if it starts to 'spit'. Then place the evaporating basin on one side to cool. (At this stage, it is best to leave the solution for 2–3 days.)

7 Filter off the crystals which have formed, and dry them carefully on a piece of filter paper. These are pure crystals of magnesium chloride.

8 Examine the crystals, and try to describe them.

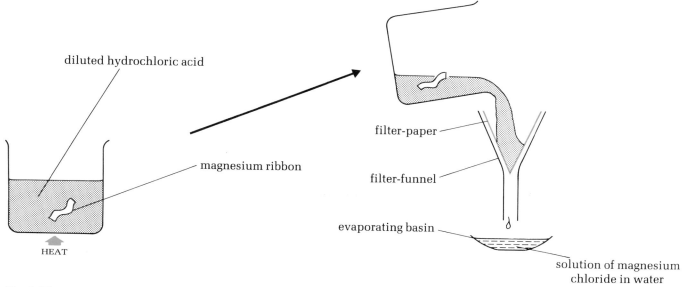

Fig. 1.62

When we use this method, we always make sure that there is some metal left unreacted at the end. This means that there must be no acid left in the solution for it to react with. So we know that all the acid has been used up, and that there will be none of it left to contaminate the salt which we are making. We can then filter off the metal.

PREPARATION 1.3

Making copper(II) sulphate from copper(II) oxide

You will need the following: 250 cm³ beaker, evaporating basin, glass rod, measuring cylinder, copper(II) oxide powder, dilute sulphuric acid, filter-funnel.

What to do

YOU MUST WEAR YOUR SAFETY SPECTACLES.

1   Place about 10 spatula-measures of copper(II) oxide powder in a beaker. Add 25 cm³ of dilute sulphuric acid and boil the mixture for 15 minutes. Throughout this time stir the mixture with a glass rod and make sure that there is always some solid in the beaker. If you need to, add some more copper(II) oxide powder. If it looks as though the beaker is going to boil dry, add some distilled water.

2   At the end of 15 minutes, add about 10 cm³ of distilled water. Filter off the unreacted copper(II) oxide and allow the solution of copper(II) sulphate which you have made to run into an evaporating basin.

3   Heat the solution in the evaporating basin, until some solid starts to appear around the edge, but take the heat away if it starts to 'spit'. Leave the solution to cool, and obtain crystals (as described in Preparation 1.2, notes 6 and 7).

4   Examine the crystals, and try to describe them.

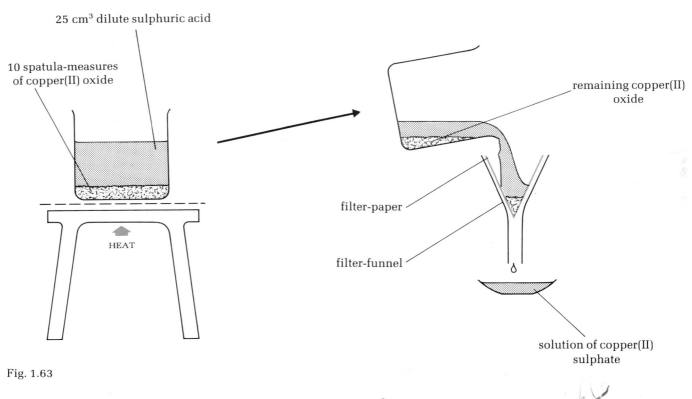

25 cm³ dilute sulphuric acid

10 spatula-measures of copper(II) oxide

HEAT

remaining copper(II) oxide

filter-paper

filter-funnel

solution of copper(II) sulphate

Fig. 1.63

Again, it is important that we always make sure that there is some basic oxide left unreacted at the end. This means that all the acid has been used up, and so none remains to contaminate the salt. Because the basic oxide is insoluble, we can filter it off.

PREPARATION 1.4

Making copper(II) sulphate from copper(II) carbonate

You will need the following: as for Preparation 1.3, but with copper(II) carbonate powder instead of copper(II) oxide powder.

What to do

YOU MUST WEAR YOUR SAFETY SPECTACLES.

1 Place 25 cm³ of dilute sulphuric acid in a beaker, and add 10 spatula-measures of copper(II) carbonate powder, one spatula-measure at a time. MAKE SURE THAT YOU ADD THE CARBONATE TO THE ACID, AND NOT THE ACID TO THE CARBONATE.

2 Boil the mixture for 15 minutes, making sure that there is some solid in the beaker all the time. If you need to, add some more copper(II) carbonate powder.

If it looks as though the beaker is going to boil dry, add some distilled water.

3 At the end of 15 minutes, add about 10 cm³ of distilled water. Filter off the unreacted copper(II) carbonate and allow the solution of copper(II) sulphate which you have made to run into an evaporating basin.

3 Heat the solution in the evaporating basin, until some solid starts to appear around the edge, but take the heat away if it starts to 'spit'. Leave the solution to cool, and obtain crystals as in the last two preparations.

4 Examine the crystals, and try to describe them.

Once more, we can make sure that all the acid has been used up by having some carbonate left at the end. Because the carbonate is insoluble, we can filter it off.

We now come to the method for making soluble salts which does not involve having to start from an insoluble chemical. You know that acids and alkalis react together (we say they 'neutralise' each other). When they do so, a salt is always produced. To obtain the salt free from any acid or alkali which might be left over, we have to react **exactly** the right amounts of acid and alkali together.

too much

acid + alkali → salt (+ left-over acid) + water

too much

acid +   alkali → salt (+ left-over alkali) + water

exactly the right amounts

acid + alkali → salt (pure) + water

So we cannot just add acid and alkali in any amounts. We must find what the exact amounts are, and **then** react them together. So, before we can make the salt, we have to do an experiment. Topic 1.3.3 explained how an indicator solution will tell us whether a solution is acidic or alkaline. So we can use an indicator to tell us when a solution **changes** from being acidic to being alkaline – or vice versa.

You know that acids and alkalis neutralise each other. So we can use an indicator to tell us when this happens. Suppose we take a certain amount of an alkali, and run acid into it. If there is an indicator in the alkali, it will show the colour for an alkali – up to the point where there has been just enough acid added to neutralise the alkali. One more drop – and the indicator will show the colour for an acid. We can measure the amount of acid which we have added, so we can find out the exact amount of acid which we need to react with the amount of alkali that we started with.

▶ EXPERIMENT 1.17, page 56, and PREPARATION 1.5, page 57

EXPERIMENT 1.17

Finding out how much dilute sulphuric acid reacts with a certain amount of dilute sodium hydroxide solution

You will need the following: 250 cm³ beaker, measuring cylinder, evaporating basin, burette, phenolphthalein solution, plenty of bench dilute sodium hydroxide solution and bench dilute sulphuric acid.

What to do

IF YOU HAVE NOT USED A BURETTE BEFORE, YOUR TEACHER WILL SHOW YOU HOW TO HANDLE THIS PIECE OF APPARATUS BEFORE YOU START THE EXPERIMENT. YOU MUST WEAR YOUR SAFETY SPECTACLES.

1   Put 25 cm³ of bench dilute sodium hydroxide solution (measured with a measuring cylinder) into a beaker. Add 2–3 drops of phenolphthalein solution. This will turn pink, because it is in an alkaline solution.

2   Place bench dilute sulphuric acid in the burette in the way you were shown by your teacher. Read the level of acid in the burette, and write down your reading.

3   Carefully run the sulphuric acid into the sodium hydroxide solution. Add about 1 cm³ of the acid, and then stop. Swirl the contents of the beaker to make sure that they mix. Then add another 1 cm³ of the acid, and so on.

4   Continue adding the acid until the indicator just becomes colourless. Now read the level of the acid in the burette again, and write down your readings.

5   The volume of acid which you have added is equal to the difference in the burette reading at the end of the experiment and at the beginning. Calculate the volume of acid which neutralised 25 cm³ of the sodium hydroxide solution.

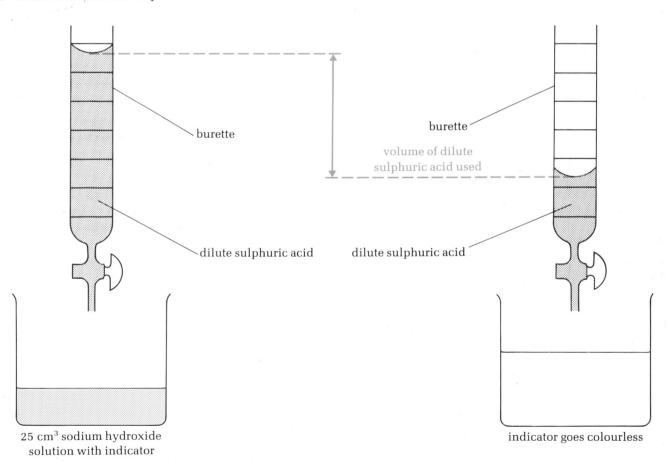

burette

volume of dilute sulphuric acid used

burette

dilute sulphuric acid

dilute sulphuric acid

25 cm³ sodium hydroxide solution with indicator

indicator goes colourless

Fig. 1.64

PREPARATION 1.5

Making sodium sulphate from sulphuric acid and sodium hydroxide solutions

You will need the following: as for Experiment 1.17, but this time you will not need any phenolphthalein indicator.

What to do

YOU MUST WEAR YOUR SAFETY SPECTACLES.

1 Repeat steps 1 and 2 of Experiment 1.17, but do not add any indicator to the alkali.

2 Work out what the final reading on the burette will be when you have added just enough acid to neutralise the alkali. Now you can run the acid into the beaker without stopping, until you have reached this mark on the burette.

3 You now have a pure solution of sodium sulphate. Pour it into a clean evaporating basin, and heat until some solid starts to form. Obtain crystals as in the last three preparations.

4 Examine the crystals, and try to describe them.

TOPIC 1.4.3

Testing for different salts

Sometimes, we may have a chemical, but not know exactly what it is. More often than not, we will want to carry out tests to find out what the chemical is. How can we do this?

You know enough about the properties of salts to be able to build up a series of tests which will let you identify almost any salt. You know that a salt is made up of a cation and an anion. To find out what an unknown salt is, then, all we have to do is to find out which cation it contains, and which anion it contains. We carry out tests for the two separately.

Tests for anions

(a) How to spot a sulphate

You know that barium sulphate is insoluble (see Table 1.12 on page 48). So if you take a soluble sulphate and add to it a soluble barium salt (barium chloride or barium nitrate) then there will be a precipitate of barium sulphate. The precise steps to carry out are set out below.

1. Take 2 spatula-measures of the unknown salt in a test-tube, and dissolve it in water. Use as little water as you can.
2. Add a little dilute hydrochloric acid, and then a little barium chloride solution.
3. If a white precipitate forms, add more dilute hydrochloric acid.
4. If the precipitate does not dissolve, then it is barium sulphate, and the unknown salt was itself a sulphate.

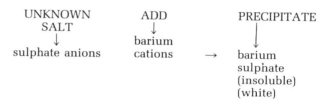

(b) How to spot a carbonate

You know that all carbonates will react with any acid to give off the gas carbon dioxide.

1. Take the unknown salt (either 2 spatula-measures of the solid, or a 2 cm depth of the solution if it is soluble) and put it in a test-tube.
2. Add a little dilute hydrochloric acid.
3. Test to see if any carbon dioxide is given off, by placing a test-tube which has a little lime-water in it in the position shown in the diagram.

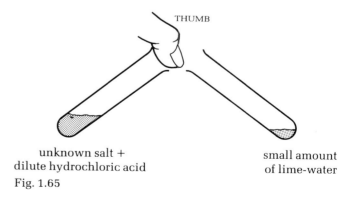

THUMB

unknown salt +
dilute hydrochloric acid

small amount
of lime-water

Fig. 1.65

4. If the unknown salt was a carbonate, and carbon dioxide is being given off, then the lime-water will turn 'milky' (a cloudy white precipitate of calcium carbonate forms).

```
                    GAS        ALLOW TO
UNKNOWN            GIVEN        REACT
SALT     ADD        OFF         WITH
  ↓       ↓          ↓           ↓
carbonate acid →  carbon      lime-water
anions            dioxide
```

```
                    ↓
              PRECIPITATE
                    ↓
     calcium carbonate (insoluble)
            ('milky' white)
```

(c) How to spot a chloride, a bromide or an iodide

You know that silver chloride is insoluble. So is silver bromide, and so is silver iodide. So, if you add a soluble silver salt to something which contains chloride, bromide or iodide ions, a precipitate will form. Fortunately, the precipitate is a different colour, depending on whether the anion present is chloride, bromide or iodide.

1. Take the unknown salt, and dissolve it in water.
2. Add a little dilute nitric acid, and then a little silver nitrate solution.
3. If a white precipitate forms, the unknown salt contained chloride anions. If the precipitate is pale cream, the anions were bromide ions, and if it is a rich cream/yellow colour, then the unknown salt contained iodide ions.

```
UNKNOWN         ADD          PRECIPITATE
SALT
  ↓              ↓                ↓
chloride anions  silver cations ──→ silver chloride
                                   (insoluble)
                                   (white)
bromide anions   silver cations ──→ silver bromide
                                   (insoluble)
                                   (cream)
iodide anions    silver cations ──→ silver bromide
                                   (insoluble)
                                   (cream/yellow)
```

(d) How to spot a nitrate

THIS TEST MUST BE CARRIED OUT IN A FUME-CUPBOARD, WITH **EXTREME CARE.** WEAR SAFETY SPECTACLES.

1. Take 2 spatula-measures of the unknown salt in a test-tube, and dissolve it in water. Use as little water as you can.
2. Take some iron(II) sulphate crystals, and dissolve them in water.
3. Add the solution of iron(II) sulphate to the solution of the unknown salt.
4. In a fume-cupboard, and with great care, carefully pour a small amount of concentrated sulphuric acid down the inside of the tube which contains the mixture you have prepared. Do this carefully and steadily, so that the sulphuric acid can form a separate layer below the mixture.
5. If the unknown salt contained a nitrate, then a brown ring will form in the test-tube, where the two layers meet. For this reason, this test is called the 'brown ring' test.
6. Unfortunately, bromides and iodides also give a brown ring with this test. So to be absolutely sure that the unknown salt was a nitrate, it is really necessary also to carry out the test for bromides and iodides (above), to make sure they are not present.

Tests for cations

Two simple tests form the basis of our means for spotting the different cations.

(a) The 'flame test'

Many cations will give a colour to a flame. The different cations give different colours. The steps to follow are set out below.

1. Take a nichrome or platinum wire, and dip it into some concentrated hydrochloric acid. Place the wire in a strong, non-luminous Bunsen flame.
2. Repeat the above, until there is no coloration given to the flame when the wire is put into it. This shows that the wire is clean.
3. Put the wire once more into concentrated hydrochloric acid, and this time dip the wire into the unknown salt (solid).
4. Now put the wire into the Bunsen flame, and note what colour is produced.

Cation	Flame colour
sodium	golden yellow, which cannot be seen through blue glass
potassium	lilac, which **can** be seen through blue glass
calcium	brick red
copper	green

Table 1.13

(b) Adding alkali to a solution of the cation

Cations which do not give a flame coloration can be spotted by the way they react with alkali.

You should always take about 1 cm depth of the solution in a test-tube.

WEAR YOUR SAFETY SPECTACLES FOR THIS TEST.

Cation in solution	Reaction with dilute sodium hydroxide solution
zinc	White precipitate forms. If more sodium hydroxide solution is added, this precipitate dissolves.
iron(II)	A green jelly-like precipitate forms.
iron(III)	A red/brown jelly-like precipitate forms.
lead	A white precipitate forms. If more sodium hydroxide solution is added, this precipitate dissolves.
ammonium	Add sodium hydroxide solution, and then boil the mixture very carefully in a small beaker. If the cation present in the unknown salt is ammonium, ammonia gas is given off. Ammonia gas will turn damp red litmus paper blue.

Table 1.14

You will see that zinc and lead give the same result when sodium hydroxide solution is added. We can decide which one of them we have by doing the following tests. (Table 1.15).

Test	Zinc	Lead
Take the white precipitate from the above test, and heat it strongly in a crucible	A solid forms which is yellow when it is hot, and white when it is cold	A solid forms which is yellow (hot and cold)
Make up a solution of the unknown salt, and add a little potassium iodide solution	No precipitate forms	A yellow precipitate forms

Table 1.15

▶ EXPERIMENT 1.18

EXPERIMENT 1.18
Identifying salts

You can use the tests set out above to identify unknown salts which your teacher will give you.

What to do

YOU MUST WEAR YOUR SAFETY SPECTACLES.

1   Take the unknown salts which you have been given one at a time.

2   Carry out **all** the anion tests **on one of the salts.** Set out your work like this:

Test	What happened	What this means

3   Carry out the two cation tests (the flame test and the reaction with sodium hydroxide solution) on this same salt. If you need to, carry out further tests to decide between zinc and lead. Set out your work like this:

Test	What happened	What this means

4   Now move on to the next salt.

UNIT 1.4
Summary and learning

1   A salt is an ionic compound which is made up of a metal cation together with an anion which could have come from an acid.

2   The anions which are found in acids are of two types. Some anions contain a non-metal and oxygen. The other type of anion consists of a non-metal on its own.

3   You should remember the rules for working out the names of salts from the names of their 'parent' acids, and you should remember which salts are soluble and which are insoluble.

4   We make insoluble salts by means of a precipitation. We react the sodium, potassium or ammonium salt of the anion with the nitrate of the cation. This ensures that the other product of the reaction, and both the salts we start with, are themselves soluble. This lets us filter off the insoluble salt which we have made, and purify it by washing.

5   We can make a salt which contains an anion which consists of a non-metal on its own by reacting a metal and a non-metal directly together. In most cases, however, we can use one of the other available methods as well, and these are usually easier.

6   There are four different ways which we can use to make soluble salts:
(a) an acid + a metal
(b) an acid + an insoluble base
(c) an acid + an alkali
(d) an acid + a carbonate
You should remember the details of the flow chart which helps us to decide which method to use for a particular salt. You should remember the practical details of the different ways which you have seen for making salts.

7   You should remember how to carry out tests to find
(a) the anion, and
(b) the cation
in an unknown salt.

8   You have learnt the meanings of these words:

chloride	precipitation
salt	washings
carbonate	drying agent
precipitate	direct combination

The chemical world – the chemical industry

UNIT 2.1 Where do chemicals come from?

You saw in the last section that chemicals are either elements, or compounds (if they are pure). But where do elements and compounds come from? Really, there are two ways to answer this question. We could look at where we find different elements and compounds in the world, and we can ask ourselves where they came from in the first place.

In this section we shall do both these things. The world's chemical industry is concerned with finding chemicals and turning them into the chemicals which we can use. The later parts of this section look at the chemical industry worldwide. But there would be no chemical industry if the chemicals did not exist already, and so first we shall look at the question of where matter came from, and how the Earth came to be made up of the chemicals which we find here.

TOPIC 2.1.1

The universe, galaxies, stars and elements

We use the word 'Universe' to mean all the physical matter which we know exists. The Universe is made up of millions of GALAXIES, which in turn are each made up of millions of stars.

If you stand outside on a clear night and stretch out your hand to arm's length, then the area covered by the tip of your finger would contain very many galaxies, together with a huge number of stars. The stars would all be members of our own galaxy, because stars exist only in a galaxy. Our galaxy is shaped like a spiral, like the one in Fig. 2.1. Our sun is one of about 100 million stars in the galaxy, and it is in one of the 'arms' of the spiral, a long way from the centre of the galaxy.

When we are talking about galaxies, the distances which are involved are so huge that we have to have a special unit of measurement. This is called a LIGHT

YEAR, and it is the **distance** which light will travel in one year (about 10 million million kilometres). It takes light about 8 minutes to reach the Earth from the Sun, and so the distance between the Sun and the Earth is about 8 light minutes. The moon is about 1 light second distant from the Earth.

Fig. 2.1 *This galaxy is like the one to which we belong*

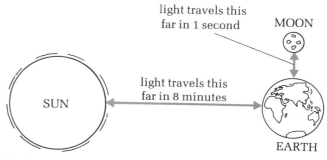

Fig. 2.2

You can get a picture of how big a galaxy is from the fact that it is about 30 000 light years from our sun to the centre of our galaxy. If we could stand out in space

looking back at the sun and its neighbours, we would
see the following sight (Fig. 2.3).

The nearest star to the sun is called Proxima
Centauri, about 4.3 light years away. So we always see
it as it was 4.3 years ago, because it has taken the light
that long to reach us.

Nobody has been able to count all the galaxies
which exist. Each time we build more powerful
telescopes, we are able to 'see' further into the
Universe and count more of them. However, the most
distant that we know of are several billion light years
away. Although we don't know how many galaxies
there are, we do know certain things about them.
Firstly, strange as it may seem, all galaxies appear to
be moving away from each other at a great speed. At
the same time, galaxies are not evenly distributed
throughout the vastness of the Universe. They are
grouped together in 'clusters', which are themselves
arranged like the beads on a necklace. This means that
there are whole areas of the Universe which contain
no galaxies, and therefore no stars and no planets. In
fact, galaxies occupy only about one hundred-
millionth of the volume of the Universe which we
know about. The Universe looks something like Fig.
2.4, with the shaded areas being those which contain
clusters of galaxies.

250 million light years

Fig. 2.4

There are about 30 galaxies in the group to which
our own galaxy belongs.

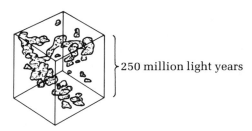

Fig. 2.5 *Our own galaxy is a member of a cluster similar to
this one*

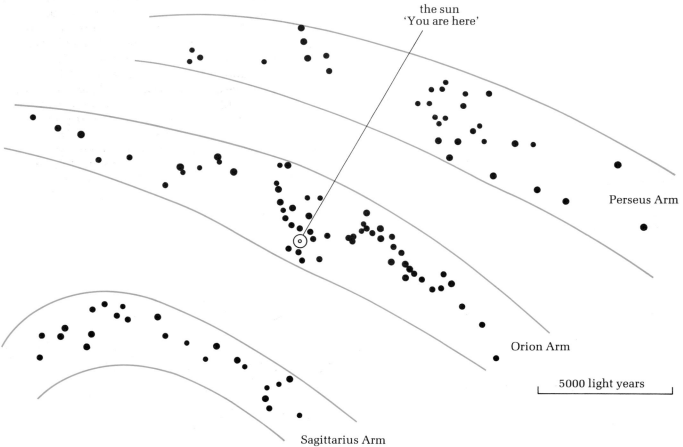

the sun
'You are here'

Perseus Arm

Orion Arm

5000 light years

Sagittarius Arm

Fig. 2.3

So our sun is just one star in the spiral arm of one of the millions of galaxies which exist. But where did the galaxies and stars come from, and what are they made of?

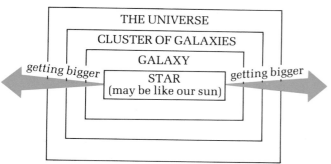

Fig. 2.6

There is another fact that we know about the universe that has led scientists to form a theory about how it began. Wherever we look in the universe, matter is not quite perfectly cold. 'Perfectly cold' means a temperature of 0 K (zero degrees Absolute, or ABSOLUTE ZERO). 0 K is the same as −273°C. Nothing can be colder than absolute zero, since it is the temperature at which all particles of matter stop moving. But instead of being at absolute zero, the 'background temperature' of the Universe is 3 K.

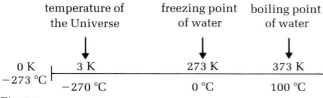

Fig. 2.7

Many scientists now believe that the Universe began in what they call a 'big bang' about 15 000 million years ago. The background temperature in the Universe of 3 K which we see today can be thought of as the fading afterglow of this fantastically hot explosion. In the 'big bang' space, time, matter and energy came into being – but of course nobody knows how or where from.

If there was a 'big bang', then the Universe as we know it today did not appear straight away. For instance, the nuclei of atoms (see Section 3) did not come into being until about 3 minutes had gone by, and atoms themselves did not form until the Universe was something like 100 000 years old. When atoms formed, light itself was also able to travel through space for the first time.

In the 'big bang', only hydrogen and helium (the two lightest elements) were formed. Gravity then drew these together into vast clouds, which collapsed further and further until, in those cases where there was enough matter there, a star formed. A star is a ball of hydrogen in which nuclear reactions are happening. These reactions produce heavier elements and huge quantities of energy. Nuclear reactions are explained in Section 3.

If the amount of hydrogen is too small to start a nuclear reaction, then what is left is something which can never become a star – it will forever be a relatively cold sphere of hydrogen. Such objects are called 'brown dwarfs', and an example is the planet Jupiter.

If the star has about the same mass as that of our own sun, then it will 'burn' steadily for millions of years, until the hydrogen is used up. At that point, the helium which has been made from the original hydrogen starts its own reaction, and this makes the element carbon. When this happens, the hydrogen which is left as outer layers of the original star is forced to expand, making the star seem suddenly much bigger (we call such a star a 'red giant'). At the same time, any planets which formed around the original star will be swallowed up. This is probably what will happen eventually to the Earth. The nucleus of the new star forms a very small, bright object, called a 'white dwarf'. Eventually, this runs out of energy and cools down. It leaves behind a massive lump of solid carbon, quite possibly in the form of a diamond, weighing billions and billions of tonnes! (Fig. 2.8)

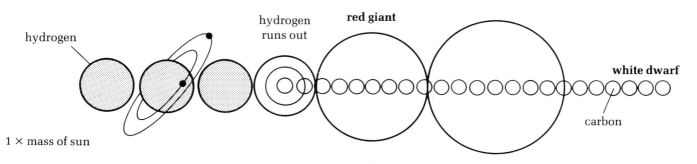

Fig. 2.8

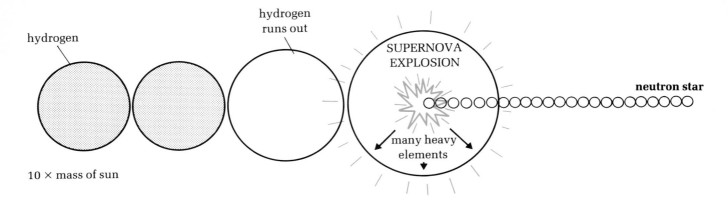

Fig. 2.9

If the original cloud of hydrogen had about ten times the mass of our own sun, then the 'death' of the star is different. Because there was more mass originally, the star will have been able to go beyond helium and carbon and make the heavier element, iron. When there is no more hydrogen left, the star suddenly runs out of energy, since iron cannot start a nuclear reaction in the same way as hydrogen and helium. So the nucleus of the star suddenly collapses under its own gravity. A superdense mass forms, which then rebounds outwards in a massive explosion (explained in more detail in Section 3), which results in heavier elements being formed. The core of the dead star becomes a 'neutron star' or 'pulsar'. (Fig. 2.9)

If there is about 30–50 times as much hydrogen in the original cloud as there is hydrogen in our own sun, then when the star which forms from it has burnt itself out, it simply collapses completely. The object which forms has so much mass that its gravitational pull is strong enough to stop anything – literally anything, including light – from escaping from it. Such an object is called a 'black hole'. Until recently, black holes were things which our theory predicted, but we did not know of any which actually existed. In 1983, one was discovered, and its mass was estimated to be about 100 million times that of our sun. (Fig. 2.10)

So, the elements hydrogen and helium were formed in the 'big bang', and other elements were made inside stars or in 'supernova' explosions.

But how did these elements come to form the chemicals which exist on the Earth?

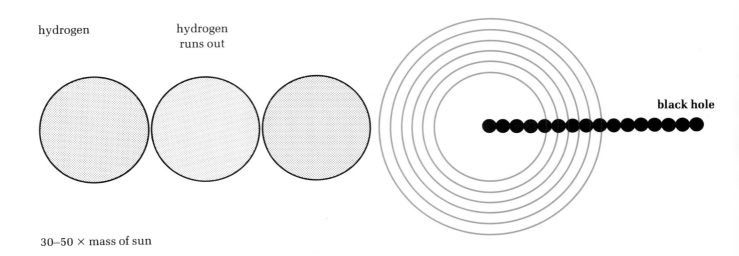

Fig. 2.10

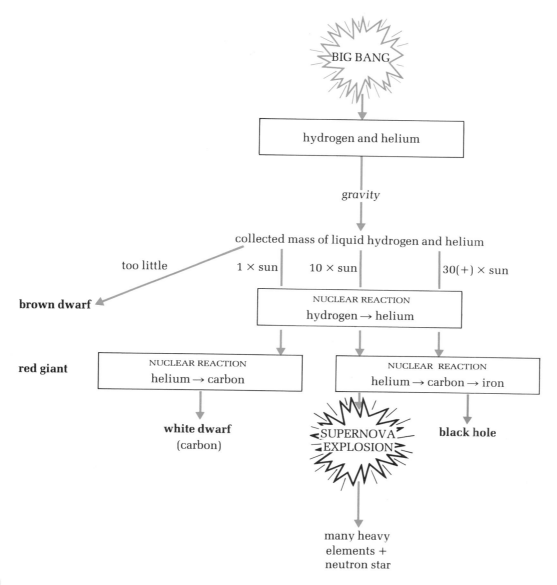

Fig. 2.11

How planets form

In the same way that we are not absolutely sure about how the Universe formed, we do not know for certain how the Earth and the other planets came into being. However, most astronomers believe that the planets formed at the same time as the sun, and out of the same material.

The elements which make up our solar system (the sun and the planets together) are probably a mixture of hydrogen and helium from the 'big bang', and heavier elements which were formed in a star, now long dead, which ended in a supernova explosion. As the sun formed at the centre of the mass of slowly swirling material, a disc of elements will have formed around it. Heavier elements will have collected towards the inside of the disc, and lighter elements towards the outside.

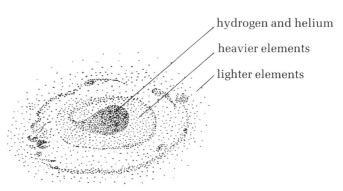

Fig. 2.12

Gravity will have caused these gases and dust to collect together first as rings and finally as planets. The planets nearer to the sun will be made of denser material, and those further away of less dense material (Fig. 2.13).

Whether or not this theory is true for the Universe as a whole (there must be planets around at least a proportion of other stars – and a cloud of dust around one of the stars nearest to us was discovered in 1983) we cannot be sure. However, the known facts about the planets in the solar system do fit with it, at least roughly. The solar system is made up of the sun, and nine planets – Mercury, Venus, Earth, Mars, Jupiter, Saturn, Uranus, Neptune and Pluto. By far the biggest object in the solar system is the sun itself.

The sun

The sun was formed about 4½ thousand million years ago from a cloud of gas which weighed about two million million million million million kilograms! The gas was made up of approximately 78% hydrogen, 20% helium and 2% of heavier elements (oxygen, carbon, nitrogen and iron). The radius of the sun is about 700 000 kilometres (so the Earth would fit more than 100 times across the sun's equator) and the temperature at its surface is about 5 500°C. The temperature at the centre of the sun is about 15 000 000°C! Each second, about 5 million tonnes of hydrogen are used up in the nuclear reaction inside the sun. The sun should burn for about another 4 thousand million years before it becomes a 'red giant'.

The density of the sun, on average, is about 1.4 times the density of water – which means that it has the same sort of 'runniness' as syrup!

The inner planets

Relatively near to the sun are four small planets which formed out of the heavier elements in the cloud of gas surrounding the early sun. These are Mercury, Venus, Earth and Mars. Each of them is almost certainly made up of a central core of the heavy elements iron and nickel, which is surrounded by a shell made up of lighter elements like silicon. Mercury probably has the largest heavy central core, and Mars the smallest. This is what we would expect, because we would expect the densest planet to be the one nearest to the sun (Fig. 2.14).

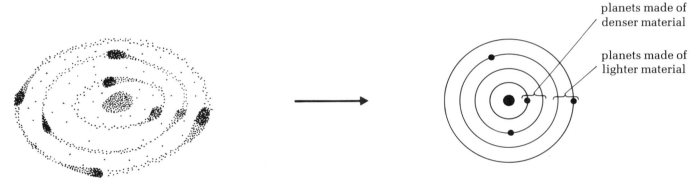

Fig. 2.13

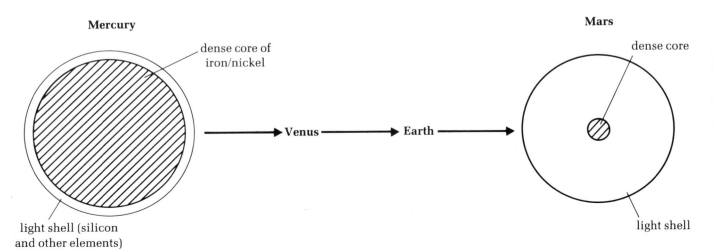

Fig. 2.14

Mercury is too small to have any real atmosphere (its gravity is too low – molecules of any gases just escape into space). The other inner planets all originally had atmospheres made up mainly of carbon dioxide and small amounts of nitrogen. Both Venus and Mars still have atmospheres made up in this way, although on Venus there are also clouds of sulphuric acid. The atmospheres of Venus, Earth and Mars are made up as follows (Table 2.1).

Planet	How its atmosphere is made up
Venus	97% carbon dioxide, 1–3% nitrogen. Clouds of sulphuric acid
Earth	78.09% nitrogen, 20.95% oxygen, 0.93% argon, 0.2% water vapour, 0.03% carbon dioxide
Mars	95% carbon dioxide, 2.7% nitrogen, traces of other gases

Table 2.1

You will see from the table that Venus and Mars still have atmospheres whose percentage make-ups are very similar. They are not the same, however, because Venus' atmosphere is about 100 times denser than our own: Mars' atmosphere is much thinner than the Earth's. Earth on the other hand, now has an entirely different type of atmosphere. The reasons for this will be explained in Section 9 of this book.

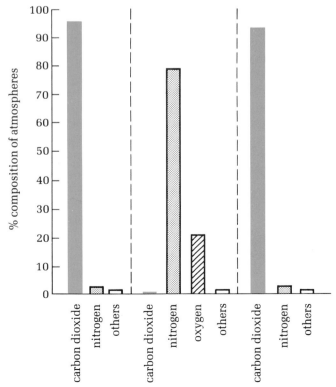

Fig. 2.15

The outer planets

Further away from the sun are five other planets. We do not know very much about the furthest planet, Pluto, but we do know that the four others are all very much larger than the four inner planets. They are also made out of material which is very much less dense.

Jupiter and Saturn are both **liquid** planets. They are made up of liquid hydrogen and helium, like the sun. They may have rock at their centre, but this is not known with any certainty.

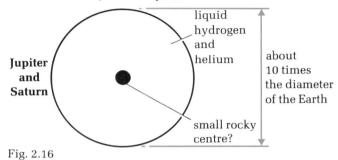

Fig. 2.16

After hydrogen and helium, the most common elements in the solar system as a whole are, in turn, oxygen, carbon and nitrogen.

1. Hydrogen
2. Helium
3. Oxygen
4. Carbon
5. Nitrogen

Table 2.2   *The solar system 'top 5' elements*

So far we have not really accounted for very much of any of these other elements. At the far edge of the solar system, very little heat arrives from the sun. As a result, temperatures are very low indeed. Because of these low temperatures, elements like oxygen, carbon and nitrogen will combine with hydrogen to form compounds. Oxygen forms water, carbon forms methane and nitrogen forms ammonia. (You will see in Section 3 why none of the elements combine with helium.) The next two planets, Uranus and Neptune, are made of a mixture of water, methane and ammonia. The surface of the planets is made of the frozen solids, and the inside is a mixture of the liquids.

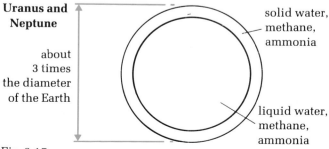

Fig. 2.17

The atmospheres of the four 'big' planets are all made up of a mixture of hydrogen, helium, methane and ammonia. Jupiter and Saturn also have nitrogen in their atmospheres.

We can compare the four inner planets with the four 'big' planets by looking at their size (radius), their density (compared to the density of water), and their distance from the sun. Use the graph in Fig. 2.18 to answer the questions which follow.

Questions

1. Which planet is most like the Earth in size?
2. Which planet is most like the Earth in density?
3. Which planet is the biggest?
4. Which planet has a density closest to that of the sun?
5. Which planet would 'float on water' (is less dense than water)?
6. Which planet has a density midway between that of the inner planets and that of the outer planets?
7. Which three planets are very similar in size and density?
8. Which two planets have sizes midway between that of the biggest and those of the inner planets?

So we have seen how the elements which were in the cloud out of which the sun and the planets formed came to give the sun and the planets their different natures.

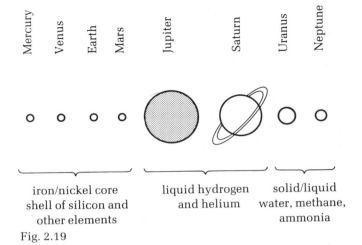

Fig. 2.19

The Earth is one of a group of similar planets towards the inside of the solar system. We can now go on to look in more detail at the chemical composition of the Earth.

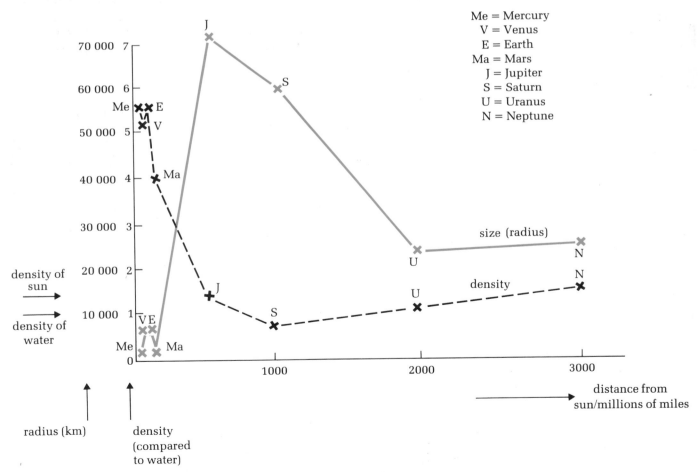

Me = Mercury
V = Venus
E = Earth
Ma = Mars
J = Jupiter
S = Saturn
U = Uranus
N = Neptune

Fig. 2.18

TOPIC 2.1.3

The chemicals which make up the Earth

If we could cut a slice through the centre of the Earth, we would see something which looked like Fig. 2.20.

At the very centre of the Earth is an INNER CORE which is solid, and which is probably made up of iron and nickel. Outside this, the OUTER CORE which is also made of iron and nickel, is a liquid. The whole of the core makes up about a third of the mass of our planet. Outside the core is lighter material, called the MANTLE. The mantle is what we could call 'molten rock'. It contains the elements oxygen, silicon, aluminium and iron. The surface layer of the Earth, or the Earth's CRUST, is solid, and made of material which is similar to the mantle.

But the surface of the Earth is not a dry solid, like the surface of planets such as Mars. Seventy per cent of the surface of the Earth is covered by water, and only thirty per cent by land. The importance of this covering of water cannot be over-estimated. Without it, there would certainly be no life here. It also helps to provide a stable environment without too great a variation in temperature. This is discussed in more detail in Section 7. The atmosphere also helps to protect us from radiations from space – again, this is discussed in Section 7.

You know that water always 'finds its own level' – it will flow downhill to fill up hollows and low-lying areas. The parts of the surface of the Earth which are covered by the seas and oceans are those areas which are low-lying. In fact, it is really the continents which are standing up above the level of the waters. The material of which the continents are made is slightly less dense than the rest of the 'crust'. So the continents 'float', not on the oceans, but on the denser crust.

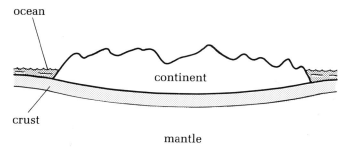

Fig. 2.21

Since there is only a certain amount of this lighter material which makes up the Earth's continents, the total amount of 'dry land' has always been about the same. In fact, we now know that 200 million years ago, all the continents which we know today were joined together into one giant land-mass, called

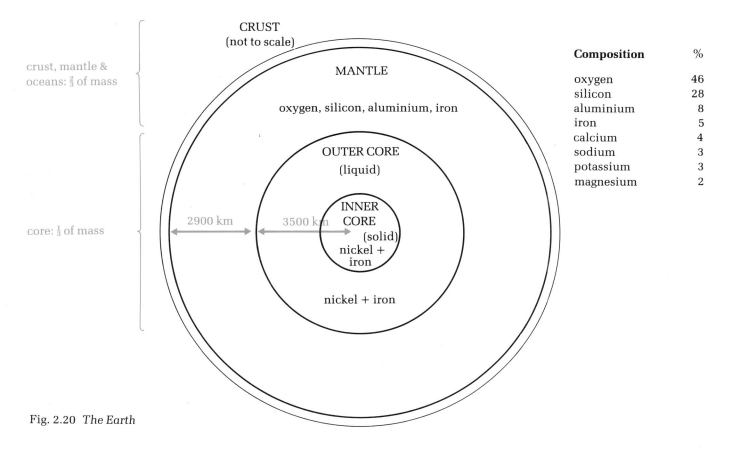

Composition	%
oxygen	46
silicon	28
aluminium	8
iron	5
calcium	4
sodium	3
potassium	3
magnesium	2

Fig. 2.20 *The Earth*

'Pangaea'. Over millions of years, the giant continent broke up and its pieces rearranged themselves. Even 50 million years ago, India was still not joined up with Asia, and Australia had not properly separated from Antarctica (which is a real continent covered with snow and ice: the Arctic, or North Pole ice-cap, is just that – a cap of ice floating on the ocean).

200 million years ago   50 million years ago

Fig. 2.22

We call this movement of continents CONTINENTAL DRIFT. It happens because the crust of the Earth is made up of at least twelve PLATES which are like pieces of a cracked egg-shell which is still in place around the egg (Fig. 2.23).

The boundaries of these 'plates' are the places on the Earth's surface where earthquakes and volcanoes happen. They are also the places where great mountain ranges are forced upwards by plates which are colliding with each other. Examples of this are the Himalayas, where India is colliding with Asia, and the Andes, where a plate is colliding with South America.

As well as being altered by continental drift, the land surface of the Earth has been changed since it was formed by the 'weathering' of rocks. This is another important role which is played by water, since it is very often a river that causes rocks to be broken down over a long period of time. Wind carrying rain and dust can also have the same effect. A good example of a place where rocks have been worn away by a river is the Grand Canyon in America.

Fig. 2.24 *Mud and sand settle in a river delta*

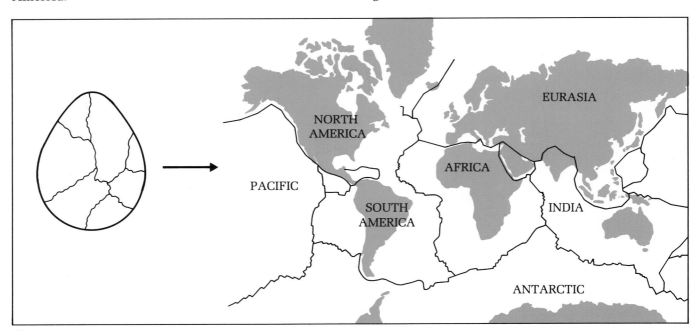

Fig. 2.23

The particles which wear away when rock is weathered are carried for great distances by rivers. Eventually, they settle when the river flows out into the sea. Over a period of millions of years, several layers of mud and sand form – and in time the pressure of the layers above will turn those below back into rock. We call this sort of rock SEDIMENTARY rock, so that we can think about it separately from the kind of rock that forms, for instance, when parts of the Earth's mantle rise to the surface. We see sedimentary rocks as layers of different thickness. The process of mountain-building may lift these layers high above the seas where they formed. So we find rocks of this type all over the Earth's surface (Figs. 2.25, 2.26).

In the same way that layers of mud and sand can form into rocks, so also the decayed remains of what were once forests can become buried over the years. There has been life on the Earth for a very long time, and for much of this time there have been plants and animals living in swampy areas. When the plants and animals die, their remains rot down to form a layer of material which is rich in compounds of the element carbon (since these are the compounds out of which plants and animals are made). If an area like this becomes buried under rocks, the massive pressure will make the material break down even futher. Coal, oil and natural gas all form in this way. It follows that the places where we find these fuels today need not be under the land. That is why it is possible to find oil in places like the North Sea, and coal in places like Antarctica, where no vegetation grows today.

So, the surface of the Earth has been changed since it formed. One important way in which this has happened is the rising up from inside the crust of mineral-rich rocks. In this way, substances like gold and diamond occur at particular places on the Earth's surface. (Fig. 2.27)

In the next topic, we will go on to look at the different types of chemical which are useful to man, where they appear on the surface of the Earth, and how they are used in the chemical industry.

Fig. 2.25 *These rocks were originally laid down in some ancient sea*

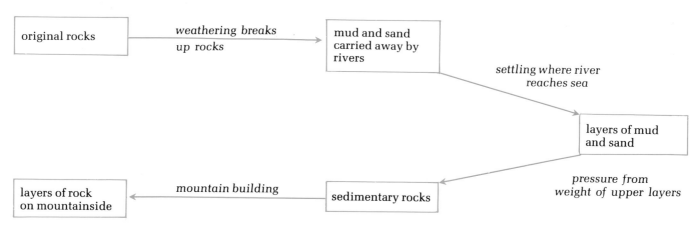

Fig. 2.26

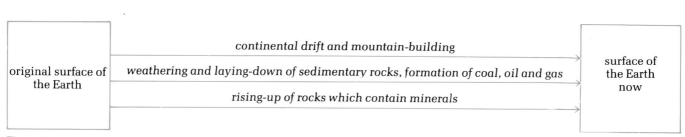

Fig. 2.27

UNIT 2.1
Summary and learning

1   You have learnt where galaxies and stars come from. You should remember the outline of this process. You should also remember how to convert temperature which is measured in degrees Absolute (K) to degrees Celsius (°C).

2   You should remember how the original elements in the Universe, hydrogen and helium, have been transformed into the range of elements which we see today.

3   You should remember how the sun and planets formed from the gases and dust left behind from a supernova explosion.

4   The inner planets are made up of similar chemicals, Jupiter and Saturn are similar and Uranus and Neptune are similar. You should be able to describe the chemical make-up of the three types of planet in outline, and of the Earth in detail.

5   You should remember the outline of how the surface of the Earth came to be in the form which we see today. You should be able to describe how sedimentary rocks and fuels such as coal, oil and natural gas have been formed.

6   You have learnt the meaning of these words:

galaxy	mantle
light year	crust
absolute zero	continental drift
inner core	plates (of the Earth)
outer core	sedimentary rocks

UNIT 2.2   *Raw materials for making things and for getting energy*

Ever since our ancestors discovered how to chip stones to make cutting edges and arrowheads, we have been using and adapting the things we find in the world around us to make them more useful. That is really what the chemical industry of the world does today – it takes the chemicals of which the world is made up, and turns them into things that people can use.

```
┌──────────────┐   the chemical   ┌──────────────────┐
│ chemical in  │ ───────────────→ │ something which   │
│ the ground   │     industry     │ we can use        │
└──────────────┘                  └──────────────────┘
```

The very early history of the human race is divided up into different periods by historians, according to the way in which people were using the natural things around them. For instance, the period when stones were carefully chipped to make sharp edges is called the Stone Age. This seems a very primitive form of technology to us today, but really this period was not all that long ago in terms of the age of the Earth. This is so much the case that some primitive tribes in remote parts of the world today are still in their own 'stone age', since they have never developed their technology any further. It would be a mistake, however, to think that these people are any less sophisticated or intelligent than so-called 'civilised' man. It is simply their **way of life** that has not developed. As far as we can tell, about 100 000 years ago (which is about the middle of the Stone Age) human beings lived in large numbers only in certain areas of the world – Europe, China and the south of Africa. So there are many remains of our Stone Age ancestors near where we live today. Stonehenge and the cave paintings of Lascaux in France belong to the Stone Age. Stonehenge may have been a religious site,

Fig. 2.28 *A flint axe-head . . . the beginning of technology*

or it may have been used to keep track of the sun, moon and planets – or both these things.

The first metals that people learnt how to use were probably copper, silver and gold. These exist on their own as elements in a few places on the Earth's surface. Other metals exist only in compounds. We call a compound which contains a metal (and which we can dig out of the ground) the ORE of that metal. To get a metal from its ore we have to carry out a chemical reaction. So it took our ancestors a little longer to find out how to do this.

metal ore	chemical reaction →	metal

Copper is also found in ores, and it was probably one of the earliest metals, along with others like tin and lead, that were obtained in this way. We say that the time when early people found out how to get hold of metals and use them is the beginning of the Bronze Age. This was about 5000 years ago.

Metals can be used to make tools and weapons which have a sharper and longer-lasting cutting edge than stone. Early people experimented with mixtures of different metals to try to improve this strength even further. A particularly successful mixture is that of copper and tin. We call this mixture 'bronze', and for thousands of years it was the most useful material for making things. We call a mixture of two or more metals an ALLOY. You will learn more about alloys in Section 5, when you look at the ways in which we try to improve the properties of alloys of another metal – iron.

In fact it was iron that eventually took over from bronze, about 2500 years ago. 'Iron Age' people lived all over Europe and the nearer parts of Asia. We could say that the ancient Greeks, the Romans, and the ancient Britons belonged to the Iron Age. However, iron was not the only metal used by these ancient civilisations. Many precious objects in gold and silver have survived from this period to the modern day.

Fig. 2.30 *The Iron Age was the Gold Age too!*

Fig. 2.29 *These fine paintings were made by Stone Age people*

Over the years we have found more and more ways to use the chemicals which we find on the Earth to make useful things. In the next few pages, the modern chemical industry, and the way in which it helps to give us our standard of living, will be described. But first, it is useful to look at the history of scientific discoveries and the dates of technological, chemical and medical advances – set against the history of the world.

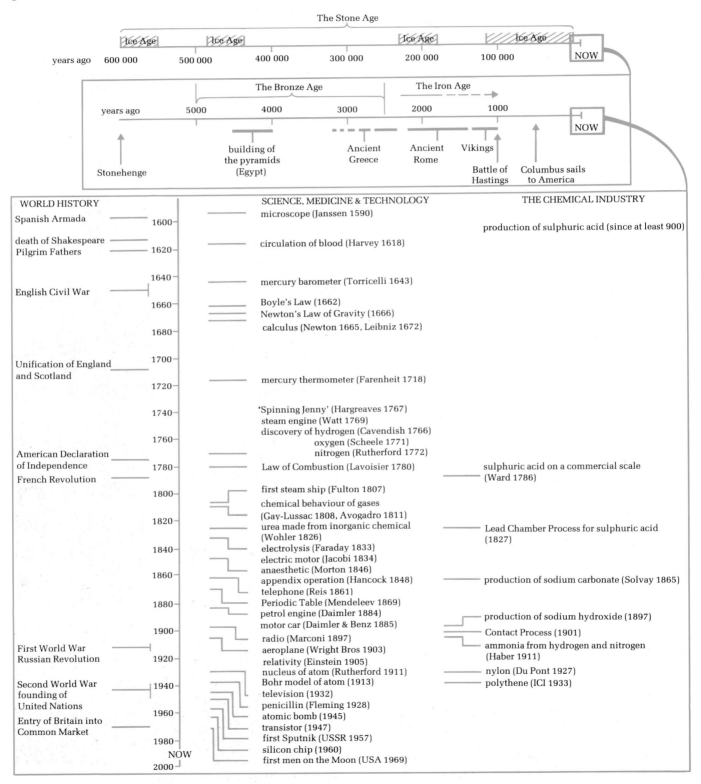

Fig. 2.31 *Chart of Scientific History*

PROJECT 2.1

Figure 2.29 contains a great deal of information. You should use it as the starting point in the work which you do in this Project.

Part 1: The first part of Fig. 2.29 shows that the Stone Age lasted for a very, very long time. Find out more about the type of existence which our ancestors had during the Stone Age. In particular, find out what the 'Ice Ages' were that happened during the Stone Age, and how human beings survived them. When is the next 'Ice Age' likely to happen? How would we be able to survive an 'Ice Age' if one happened now? Can you find out what it is that scientists think causes the 'Ice Ages' to happen? Some people think that some forms of pollution may 'trigger' the next 'Ice Age' before it is really due – try to find out why they say this.

Part 2: Pick one of the inventions or discoveries which have been made in the last 400 years (shown in the third part of Fig. 2.29). Find out what you can about the person (or people) who made the discovery and the difficulties which they had in making the discovery (and perhaps in getting others to accept it), and try to assess the change in our way of living that the invention or discovery has brought about. You should be able to find both good and bad effects of any invention!

Part 3: Pick a time in the last 400 years. If you went back to that time, what do you think the biggest differences that you would notice would be? You could write an essay to describe what you think you would feel.
OR
Suppose someone from Ancient Greece (or any of the other civilisations shown in the second part of Fig. 2.29) were transported to our modern world. Write an essay to describe the experiences which they would have because of all the changes which there have been between their time and our own.

TOPIC 2.2.1

Chemicals and the wealth of our world

You have just seen that the chemical industry has been part of the great scientific and technological changes which have taken place in the last 200 years. In fact, it can be said that it is the chemical industry which is to a large extent at the root of our modern way of life. Our 'standard of living' depends to a large degree on what the chemical industry does.

The chemical industry takes some naturally occurring resource (a chemical which can be dug out of the ground), and turns it into something useful. There are always a number of steps in this process, of course. First of all, the chemical must be mined, and separated from other chemicals. You learned several ways which we can use to separate different chemicals in the last section. Sometimes in the chemical industry, very special methods have to be used to separate the chemical which we want from the others. (We have to do this when the simpler methods do not work.) For instance, the ore of zinc has to be separated by floating it on oil droplets which are added to a SLURRY of the ore and the unwanted chemicals (a slurry is a mixture of water and very fine solid particles). So the first two stages in the use of zinc look like Fig. 2.32.

MINING

SEPARATION

Fig. 2.32 A. *Mining the ore of zinc*
B. *Zinc ore floats off on these bubbles*

If the chemical which we want is not the one which we dig out of the ground, but instead is only **contained in** the chemical which we have, then we have to carry out a chemical reaction. Very often we want to get a metal from a compound which contains it. We call this stage the EXTRACTION of the wanted chemical (Fig. 2.33).

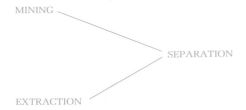

Fig. 2.33 *We heat zinc ore with coke in a furnace, and get zinc (the liquid at the bottom of the photograph)*

If the chemical is not in the form in which it will be used, then it has to be turned into the shape of object that we want. In the case of zinc, we usually manage to do this by pouring the molten metal into a mould of the right shape, and letting it set. This particular process is called DIE-CASTING, and the stage of processing of the chemical is called the FABRICATION stage (Fig. 2.34).

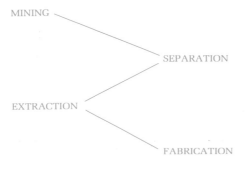

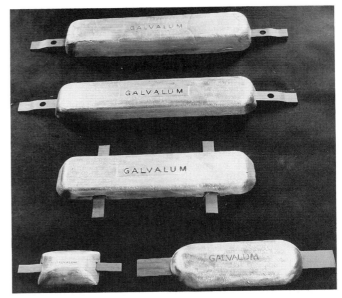

Fig. 2.34 *These zinc anodes were shaped in a die*

When we have the material we want in the form in which we will want to use it, then all that is left is to build the final product using what we have made. This step is called the ASSEMBLY stage. A typical use of die-cast zinc is shown in Fig. 2.35. Pieces of zinc attached to the hull of a ship will help to stop it rusting in sea-water.

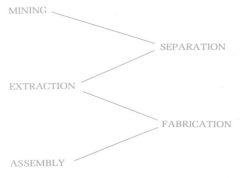

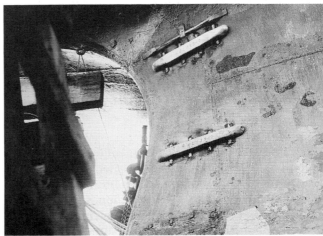

Fig. 2.35 *Zinc is put to the use for which it was mined*

These five stages will be used in turning any chemical resource into something which can be useful. Table 2.3 is a list of just some of the things which are made by the chemical industry.

chemical elements
nuclear fuels and radioactive elements
medicines and anaesthetics
cosmetics, hairdressings, shampoos, toothpastes, perfumes
paint, varnish, enamel, artists' colours
soap, soap powder, shaving cream, detergents
glass fibre, textile fibre, plastic, rubber, resins
dyes, pigments, food colouring
glues, wax, polish, explosives
weedkiller, fertilisers, disinfectants, ink, photographic film

Table 2.3 *Products of the chemical industry*

So, you have seen an outline of how the chemical industry goes about turning the chemicals of which the Earth is made into useful products, and you have found out how this works for particular examples. But how much does the chemical industry really contribute to the living standards of the world? This question is very difficult to answer accurately. In the first place, some of the figures are not always freely available, particularly from countries in eastern Europe and from places like China. Also, some countries count certain parts of industry as the chemical industry, while others may call the same thing, for instance, the textile industry. A third difficulty is that we do not get information until some years have gone by – by which time the situation may have changed considerably. However, we can certainly make a rough estimate of the value of the chemical industry to the world economy from the figures which we do have.

At the end of the 1970s, the activity of the world's 25 biggest chemical companies added up to **about 30 per cent of the total business carried out in the western world**. In one year, the world's chemical industry handles about £200 000 million worth of chemicals – a staggering amount! The contribution made by the chemical industry in different countries is as follows (Table 2.4).

	£ 000 million
USA	50
Japan	20
W. Germany	17
UK	10
France	10
Italy	7

Table 2.4 *Value of chemicals handled (1976 figures)*

So, for instance, the chemical industry in the USA handles about 25% of the world trade, and that in the UK about 5%. You will see from Table 2.3 that the products of the chemical industry are very largely the kinds of thing which make up our material wealth. So we can get a picture of the richness or poorness of different parts of the world from the amount of money which they can spend on these 'consumer' products. For the western world, the figures are as follows:

	% of western world spending	Amount per person per year
USA & Canada	34	£214
Western Europe	40	£150
Japan, Australia & N. Zealand	14	£170 (Japan) £140 (Aust. & NZ)
'third world'	12	£ 10

Table 2.5 *Amount of money spent on chemical products (1976 figures)*

Compare the amount of money which each person in the 'developed' world can spend with that for a person in a 'third world' country (the poorer countries in Africa, Asia and South America). Think of all the things which you use every day which are products of the chemical industry. Now think how your life would change if you had less than a tenth of these things.

PROJECT 2.2

Take **three** of the things in Table 2.3 and find out what chemicals they contain, where the chemicals come from and where and how the stages of separation, extraction, fabrication and assembly take place.

The chemical industry in the UK

The chemical industry is the third most important sector of the economy of the UK, and it makes up about 10 per cent of the national output (the first two are: (1) the food and drink industry, and (2) engineering). There are about 300 chemical firms, of which the largest, ICI, is the fourth largest company in the country.

The following are the types of chemicals which the chemical industry of this country handles (Table 2.6).

	%
pharmaceuticals (medical preparations)	15
organic chemicals (compounds of carbon – see Section 8)	14
inorganic chemicals	9
dyes and pigments	7
fertilisers	6
paints	5
cosmetics	4
soaps and detergents	3
all others	37

Table 2.6 *Sectors of the UK chemical industry*

The manufacture of medicines and other medical chemicals seems likely to become more and more important to the chemical industry in the UK since it does not need large quantities of natural resources.

There are, or have been, parts of the chemical industry in nearly every corner of the British Isles.

Fig. 2.36

In order to earn money, the chemical industry must sell its products to other countries. Chemicals make up one of the biggest exports from the country as a whole. The value of the exports of ICI to different parts of the world in 1982 are shown in this diagram.

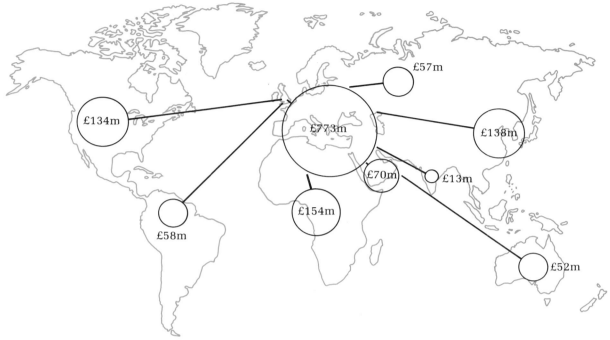

Fig. 2.37

Of the raw materials which the UK chemical industry needs, only a few can be mined here. The others have to be bought from other countries. The chemical industry is really a world-wide business, and so we should now look at the different types of chemical which exist in different parts of the Earth.

The Earth's store of chemicals

You will know that many people are worried today that the world's supply of many natural resources is 'running out'. You will certainly have heard of the so-called 'energy crisis', which is to do with the amount of coal, gas and oil which is left. This particular subject is dealt with in the next topic in this section.

But we also need to be concerned about the amounts of 'basic' raw materials like the metal copper which have not yet been used. For that reason, the next few pages will contain information about the rate at which the different chemicals are being used up, and the amounts of them which are left. This information is the best estimate which can be made at the present time in each case, and it is important to realise that it is only an estimate.

It costs money to search for new supplies of a chemical, and the rarer and more difficult to find the chemical is, the more it costs. So, it only makes sense to carry out the least expensive search possible – and to look for the most obvious new supply. Because this is the case, we cannot be sure that all the possible supplies of a chemical have been found. At the same time, it costs money to dig a chemical out of the ground once it has been found. Again, the harder it is to mine the chemical, the more it will cost. So there may be supplies of a chemical which we know about but which we do not count, because it would cost us so much to mine them that we would never get our money back. We say that it would be UNECONOMICAL to use such a resource. However, as time goes on, and supplies of a chemical become used up, we will be able to sell it for a higher and higher price. Eventually, a source of a chemical which has always been thought of as uneconomical may become worth mining – and so we can count it in with the amount of the chemical which is still left. So, we can never quite be sure how much of a particular chemical there is left at any one time. We can divide the chemical resources of the world into the following three groups:

1. Precious and rare metals
2. Metals used for making things
3. Fertilisers and other raw materials for industry

Petrochemicals, raw materials which are made from the chemicals in oil (and coal), are talked about in Section 8 (Unit 8.2).

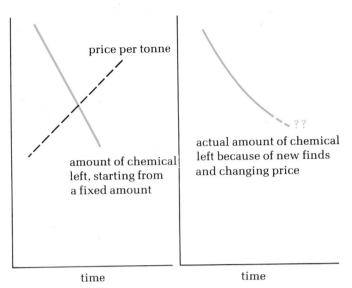

Fig. 2.38

Precious and rare metals: gold, silver, platinum and uranium

There are many different uses for each of these metals, but the main ones are shown in Table 2.7.

Metal	Uses
gold	jewellery, electronics, dentistry
silver	photography, electrical, electroplating
platinum	jewellery, special chemicals, 'catalyst', electrical
uranium	atomic energy

Table 2.7

Gold and silver have always been thought of as 'precious', not only because they are fairly uncommon, but particularly because they do not 'tarnish' like more reactive metals such as iron. So an object which is made out of gold or silver will last for a very long time indeed, staying relatively bright and shiny – almost as it was when it was made. Because they can be used in this way, gold and silver have always had a 'value'. It is not surprising, then, that when people thought of the idea of money (to stand as a **token** for something of value, rather than having to exchange the objects themselves) they decided to use the metals gold and silver to make coins. Nowadays, it has become too expensive to put gold and silver in our coins, and so we use cheaper substitutes. However, gold and silver are still the metals which are used as international currency. Gold has a certain value all over the world, and the wealth of a country can be

measured by the size of its 'gold reserves'. The gold reserves of many countries are kept at the Bank of England in London, and sometimes trolleys of gold bars are wheeled from one room to another when one country pays another for something!

Fig. 2.39 *The wealth of nations! An ounce of gold is worth about £250 – and each of these bars weighs 400 ounces. What is the value of what you can see?*

Sometimes, we move gold from one country to another, and sometimes it suffers an accident on the way. All over the world there are wrecks of ships containing gold which has been 'lost' when the ship was sunk.

But gold and silver are of value for other things than just being 'tokens'. Both are good at letting electricity pass through them, and so they are used for making electronic and electrical items.

Fig. 2.40 *This circuit contains many gold parts: all the wires are gold and the connection pins are gold plated*

In recent years, platinum has been used more and more for the same sort of purposes as gold and silver. Like them, it is shiny and does not easily become tarnished. It is white in colour, rather like silver, and so it will make jewellery. Platinum also has several very useful characteristics. One of these is that it will help chemical reactions to happen. Something which will do this is called a CATALYST. You will learn more about catalysts in Section 6. Platinum is particularly useful as a catalyst in the petroleum industry, where it helps us to split crude oil into the different chemicals which we get from it, such as petrol for cars.

Uranium is one of the elements which we can use to get nuclear power. You will learn more about this subject in the rest of this section, and in Section 3.

Originally, all four of these metals were brought to the surface of the Earth by hot rock rising up through the crust of the Earth. Over millions of years, the original deposits have been weathered, and the metals have become part of sedimentary rocks. However, they still tend to be in parts of the world where mountains have been formed, because it is here that rocks can rise up from within the Earth. We can now look at the places in the world where these precious and rare metals can be found (Fig. 2.42).

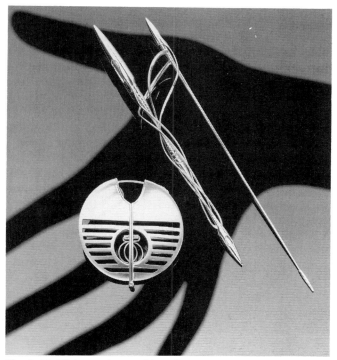

Fig. 2.41 *This earring and lapel pin are made from platinum (courtesy of The Platinum Shop, London)*

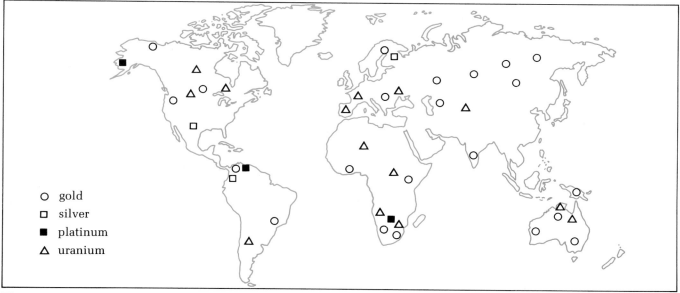

○ gold
□ silver
■ platinum
△ uranium

Fig. 2.42

Our best guess about the amounts of these metals which are left, is as follows (Table 2.8).

	Possible total world reserves/tonnes	Known total world reserves/tonnes	Western world %	Eastern bloc %	Third world %
gold	61 250	32 255	62	25	13
silver	770 000	255 000	51	24	25
platinum	60 000	20 000	91	9	—
uranium	2 720 000	1 729 000	46*	33*	21*

Table 2.8   *Figures for uranium are uncertain

Questions

1 Which parts of the world appear to have a high concentration of rare and precious metals?

2 Which parts of the world appear to have less than their fair share of these metals?

3 Table 2.8 shows how the reserves of precious metals that we know about are shared amongst the different parts of the world (as percentages). 'Eastern bloc' includes Russia, Eastern Europe and China. How does the amount of the different metals which are in the poorer parts of the world compare with the amount which the richer 'western' world has?

4 The following are the amounts of each of the metals which are mined all over the world each year:

World mine production each year	
gold	1 208 tonnes
silver	10 677 tonnes
platinum	46 tonnes
uranium	32 009 tonnes

For each metal, work out:
(a) when it will run out, based on present known reserves;
(b) when it will run out, based on possible total world reserves.

Metals used for making things: iron, copper, aluminium, zinc and lead

We use these metals for far more things than could be listed in this book. However, these are the main uses to which we put each of them (Table 2.9).

Metal	Uses
iron	All manner of metal goods, all forms of steel
copper	Electrical equipment, water pipes in houses, machinery
aluminium	Packaging (particularly food), building, ships and aeroplanes
zinc	Manufactured goods (die-casts), transport equipment, electrical equipment, machinery and chemicals
lead	Storage batteries, chemicals added to petrol, paints

Table 2.9

Clearly, these metals are all basic to our modern way of life. Each of them is used in some important way in the things which we use every day. For example, all of them are in use in Fig. 2.43. Can you decide where?

Fig. 2.43 *How are the different metals being used?*

You will learn more about each of these metals in Section 5. Copper, iron and lead are found where molten rocks have pushed their way to the surface, and also in sedimentary rocks. Zinc exists mostly as a result of the former of these processes, and aluminium deposits from which we can get the metal have come into being because of weathering. Figure 2.44 shows the places in the world where we can get these metals.

The amounts of these metals which we think are left are given in Table 2.10.

Questions

1 Which part of the world seems to be worst off for this kind of metal?
2 For which metals does the 'third world' have most of the known reserves?
3 Which part of the world has the best 'balance' of all the metals in the table?
4 The amounts of each metal which are mined in the world each year are:

World mine production each year	
iron	515 million tonnes
copper	8 million tonnes
aluminium	16 million tonnes
zinc	6 million tonnes
lead	3.5 million tonnes

For each metal, work out:
(a) when it will run out based on the present total known world reserves;
(b) when it will run out, based on possible total world reserves

Fertilisers, and other raw materials for industry: potash, phosphates, sulphur and nitrates

Potash is the oxide of the element potassium. The vast majority of the world's supply comes from Canada.

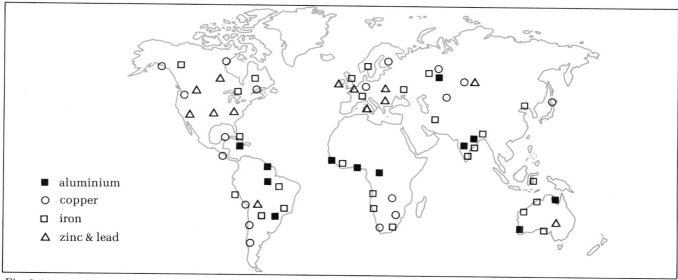

Fig. 2.44

	Possible total world reserves (million tonnes)	Known total world reserves (million tonnes)	Western world	Eastern bloc	Third world
iron	180 000	93 000	35%	34%	31%
copper	2317	493	32%	12%	56%
aluminium	8000	5100	30%	3%	67%
zinc	4400	162	62%	14%	24%
lead	288	127	63%	19%	18%

Table 2.10

Potassium, like nitrogen and phosphorus, is one of the elements which plants must have to grow successfully. It is for this reason that potash is in great demand as a fertiliser, as are phosphates (which supply phosphorus) and nitrates (which supply nitrogen) (see Section 9). Sulphur is involved in providing us with fertilisers, since it is used to make sulphuric acid – which in turn is used to make soluble fertilisers. Figure 2.45 shows the places in the world where these chemicals can be found.

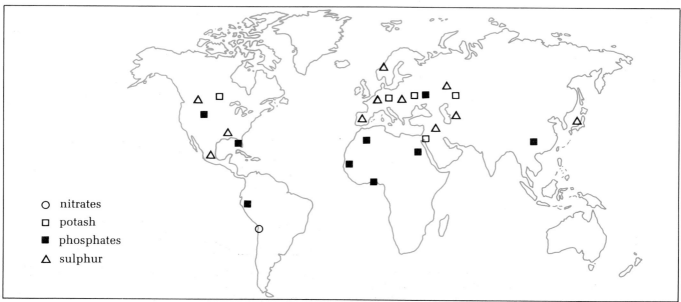

Fig. 2.45

The most densely populated parts of the world are India, China, Japan and Europe. You can see from the map that the places in the world which have most of the chemicals which we can use as fertilisers are Europe and America. Where are the parts of the world in which people are likely to have less to eat than the average? Try to find out the things which are being done to try to overcome this problem.

Fortunately, it seems that the world has very large supplies of fertiliser chemicals. For instance, there may be several thousand years' supply of potash, and many hundreds of years supply of phosphates. On the other hand, supplies of sulphur may run out much sooner – possibly within about 50 years. You will learn more about sulphur in Section 9.

Question

The following table shows the value of the different chemicals studied in this section which are mined each year. That is, it shows how much each of them adds to the world economy.

	Value per year (£000 million)
gold	12.0
silver	2.4
copper	10.5
iron	15.6
aluminium	18.3
zinc	3.6
lead	2.9
potash	2.3
sulphur	5.1
phosphates	4.0
nitrates	uncertain
uranium	2.1
platinum	0.7

Take the four largest money-earners, and look where they are found. Do you think that there is an even or an uneven spread of these valuable chemicals over the Earth as a whole? Explain how you have reached your decision.

TOPIC 2.2.3
Chemicals which give us energy

We need energy in the modern world for a wide variety of things. We need it to help us get raw materials out of the ground, and to turn them into useful products. We need it to help us make fertilisers, and therefore to grow food. We need energy for heating and lighting our homes and the places where we work, and we need it to provide motorised transport in cars and buses, and on ships, aeroplanes and trains. So the main areas for which we need energy are:

1. Manufacturing industry
2. Food production
3. Domestic and transport

The population of the world increases all the time. So we would expect that the total world need for energy would also increase all the time. Until recently, this was what happened, but in the most recent few years, the amount of energy used in the world has actually gone down. To understand the reasons for this, it is important first to find out who uses most of the world's energy. The map in Fig. 2.46 is a way of showing how much energy the different countries of the world use each year, relative to each other. The sizes of the blocks stand for amounts of energy.

Between them, the USA, Russia, Western Europe and Japan use up about 80% of the world's energy, although they contain only about 25% of the world's population. They are also the parts of the world where populations are **not** increasing.

So, these countries dominate what happens to the world's need for energy, and the increase in the number of people in other countries has almost no effect on the amount of energy used. Until 1973, the total amount of energy being used each year kept on increasing. Energy was relatively cheap, and industry needed more each year. But it was at that time that it was realised that the world's supply of energy-giving chemicals was running out – and the 'world energy crisis' was born. The amount of energy used suddenly dropped, but then after 1975 started increasing again. Since then great efforts have gone into cutting out energy waste both in industry and in people's homes. Energy has become much more expensive. The result of increased energy-saving has been a new fall in the total amount of energy being used, which started in 1979.

In 1981, the Department of Energy estimated that the total need for energy would drop to 80% of its present level in the next 20 years (Fig. 2.48).

We can divide the types of chemical which give us energy on a large scale into two separate groups:

1. fossil fuels, and
2. nuclear fuels.

There is also a range of alternatives to these ways of getting energy on a large scale, of which the most important is the use of the world's water resources to generate electricity. We call this type of energy HYDRO-ELECTRIC POWER. You will also learn about a third way of getting energy from chemicals, this time on a small scale, in Section 4.

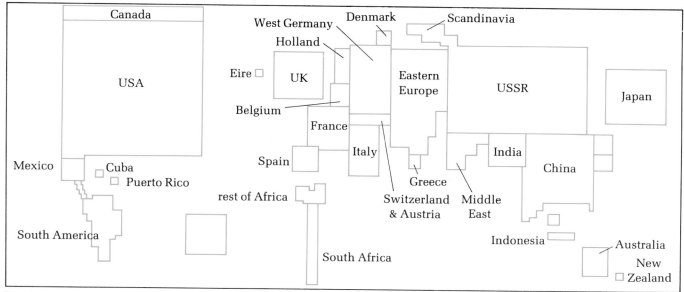

Fig. 2.46

Fig. 2.47 *This house is having insulation material pumped into the wall cavity – to cut down loss of heat*

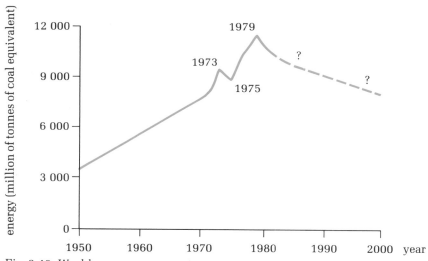

Fig. 2.48 *World energy consumption 1950–2000*

Fossil fuels

You saw how fossil fuels come about in Unit 2.1 and you will learn how the chemicals manage to store energy in themselves in Unit 4.1. There are three forms in which energy is stored as fossil chemicals – coal, oil and gas.

For many years, coal was the most important fossil fuel. Figure 2.36 (p. 78) shows that Britain has many coalfields. For many years coal kept the wheels of Britain's factories turning, and heated British homes. It also drove trains, ships and the occasional car or lorry!

In 1913, 20% of all the coal mined in the world was mined in Britain. In 1981, Britain exported about 4% of the amount of coal exported in 1913. The main reason for this change was the oil that became available from the Middle East in the 1950s. Oil is almost an ideal fuel – it is fairly cheap to produce, it burns efficiently, and it can be transported from one place to another. Coal, on the other hand, takes a lot of effort to dig out of the ground, is grimy to deal with, and contains less energy weight-for-weight than oil. So, much of the world switched to using oil. However, in spite of the slow-down in the use of energy, there is still only a very limited amount of oil left, and coal may come into its own again (see below).

Figure 2.49 shows how much coal the different parts of the Earth still have left, and how much they use each year. We can get an idea of how long the coal will last by dividing the amount which is left by the amount which is used each year.

Question

Work out the figure which should go in the last column:

	Amount of coal left/ thousand million tonnes	Amount used each year/ thousand million tonnes	How long the coal will last/ years
North America	187	0.57	328
South America	10	0.002	
Western Europe	82	0.393	
Eastern bloc	156	0.483	
China	99	0.439	
India	34	0.085	
South Africa	34	0.066	
Australia	27	0.06	

Where does it seem that the coal will last the longest?

The figure which you have just seen for the amount of coal which is left in the world tells us that it will last

for between 200 and 500 years in most places, and for about 300 years on average (if you add up the 'amount of coal left' column the total comes to 629 thousand million tonnes, and the total of the 'amount used each year' column is 2.2 thousand million tonnes). So there is plenty of coal left. In fact, there is probably vastly more than 629 thousand million tonnes of it – this is only the amount that we know about already, and that we can dig up with our present methods. Some people think that the total amount of coal still in the ground may be as much as 10 000 thousand million tonnes! If this is true, how long would the coal last?

Fig. 2.50 *In many parts of the world, the coal is near the surface and we can mine it with mechanical diggers. This open-cast mining is a very messy business!*

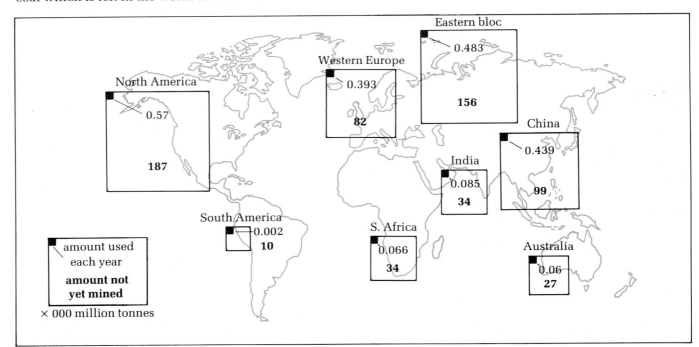

Fig. 2.49 *For many years, coal supplied many of our energy needs*

Most of the coal that we dig out of the ground is burned in power stations. The heat which this produces is used to turn water into steam, and the steam drives turbines which make electricity. Well over 80% of the electricity which we use every day comes from the energy which was stored in coal.

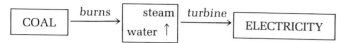

When coal burns, a mixture of smoke and different gases is produced. One of these gases is sulphur dioxide, which comes from the element sulphur which is an impurity in coal. Sulphur is a non-metal, and so sulphur dioxide forms an acid (sulphuric acid) when it dissolves in water. If a power-station releases large amounts of sulphur dioxide into the atmosphere, the result can be so-called 'acid rain'. Obviously, this is a major drawback to the use of coal (see Topic 2.3.1).

Another drawback to coal is the difficulty which there is in handling it, which was mentioned earlier. Since coal will probably last much longer than oil, scientists have been trying hard to find ways to turn it into a liquid or a gas so that there will be something which we can handle easily when the oil runs out. Making a liquid from a solid is called LIQUEFACTION, and making a gas from a solid is called GASIFICATION. Nobody has found a good way of making a liquid or a gas from coal on a large scale, although there are a number of trial plants in different parts of the world. In Britain, there is a trial coal gasification plant at Westfield in Scotland.

Fig. 2.51 *This plant makes coal into a gas*

We find oil and gas together under the ground, trapped in layers of 'spongy' rock which are between layers of hard rock. The hard rocks hold the oil and gas where they are. Also in the spongy layer will be large amounts of water. The oil and gas float on top of the water because they are both lighter than it.

Because the surface of the Earth has changed since the oil and gas were formed, the layers of rock have often become 'buckled'. Over many years, the oil and gas have collected at the highest points of the spongy rock (Fig. 2.52). The oil and gas have become compressed, and so they are at a high pressure (and often at temperatures as high as 95°C). This makes it easy for us to get them out of the ground, because all we have to do is to drill a hole through the rocks which keep them trapped, and the oil and gas will shoot out under their own pressure.

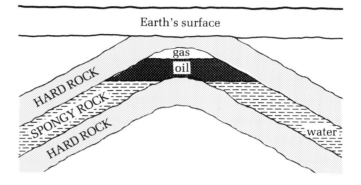

Fig. 2.52

Fig. 2.53 *This oil is rising from deep under the ground because of its own pressure ('gushers' like this rarely happen today, because the flow of oil is more carefully controlled)*

It is important that the hole is drilled through the very top of the underground 'peak', otherwise we will miss some of the oil (Fig. 2.54). So before the oil engineers start to drill, they must know exactly where the different rocks are under the ground. To find this out, they bounce shock-waves from an explosion on the surface off the different layers. From the pattern of the reflected waves, the engineers can find the top of the underground peak (Fig. 2.55).

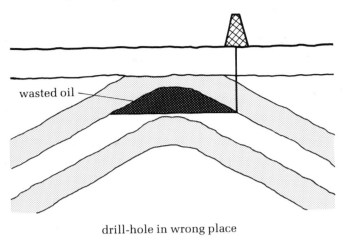

wasted oil

drill-hole in wrong place

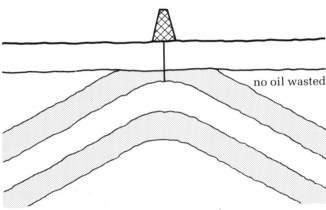

no oil wasted

drill-hole in right place

Fig. 2.54

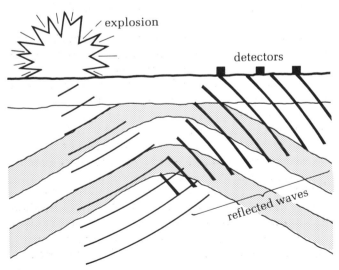

explosion

detectors

reflected waves

Fig. 2.55

In order to get all the oil out of a particular well, we sometimes have to make sure that the pressure under

the ground stays high. So we pump water or gas down another drill hole, as the oil comes out of the main well. If we did not do this, then the pressure might eventually drop and be too low to force the last of the oil out of the well (Fig. 2.56).

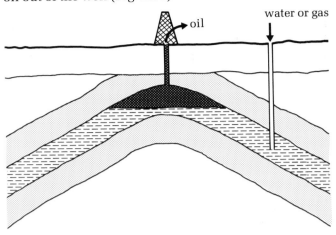

oil

water or gas

Fig. 2.56

As oil has become more precious, engineers have had to find ways of making sure that every last drop comes out of each well. Keeping up the pressure by forcing water or gas into a lower part of the reservoir is just one of the techniques which they use. We can see just why every last drop of oil is important if we look at how much oil we use each year, and how much there is left in the ground. Figure 2.57 shows how much oil there is left in the different parts of the world, and how much oil is used each year in them.

Question

Work out the figure which should go in the last column:

	Amount of oil left/ million tonnes	Amount used each year/million tonnes	How long the oil will last/years
North America	6134	490.8	12
South America	13 080	302.9	
Europe	3820	140.2	
Eastern bloc	14 186	737.7	
Middle East	61 548	618.7	
Asia/Pacific	3293	129.9	
Africa	9637	221.1	

Where does it seem the oil will last the longest?

The total amount of oil left in the world is 111 698 million tonnes, and the total amount which we use each year is 2644.4 million tonnes. This means that,

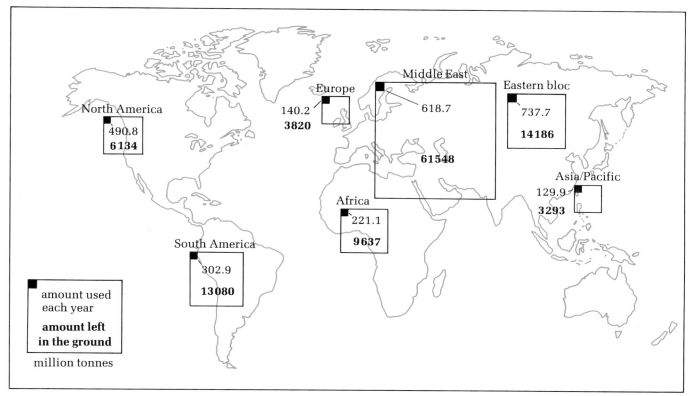

Fig. 2.57 *The world's oil*

overall, there should be enough oil to last another 42 years only. Some parts of the world will run out of oil much sooner than that. There is some hope that scientists will find new supplies of oil, but there is far less likelihood that the amount of oil left undiscovered is similar to the amount of coal which we do not yet know about. So the chances are that the world's oil will run out in the next 50 years. It is for this reason that scientists are now becoming more interested again in coal, with all its faults. At the beginning of the 1980s oil supplied about 40% of the total energy needs of the world. From now on, oil will have to be less and less important, and so many people fear that there will be an 'energy gap' because of the disappearing oil, by the end of the century.

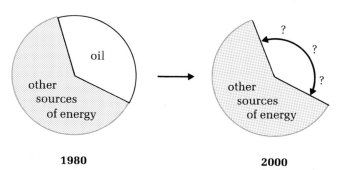

Fig. 2.58 *The coming energy gap*

Britain became self-sufficient in oil in 1981, thanks to the discovery of oil fields under the North Sea. In fact, there are many places in the world where oil is found under the sea rather than on dry land. This is because of the way the surface of the Earth has changed since the oil formed. Drilling for oil in the North Sea can be very difficult and dangerous. In some places the sea is hundreds of feet deep, and the weather in the area can be appalling, with many gales and waves which can be 15 metres high.

The amount of oil which we get from the North Sea will start to get smaller in the mid-1980s as the oil fields become used up. Depending on the rate at which new discoveries are made, and whether or not the amount of oil used each year increases or decreases, the country may still be able to produce all its own oil until the end of the century.

Natural gas is also a fossil fuel. It is mainly the compound methane, which you will learn more about in Section 8. Natural gas is a good way of providing heat at home and in industry, and almost all the gas used in Britain now comes from wells in the North Sea.

Like oil, natural gas will probably last for a much shorter time than coal. Table 2.11 shows the amount of natural gas left in the different parts of the world, and the amounts used each year.

	Amount of gas left/thousand million cubic feet	Amount used each year/thousand million cubic feet	How long the gas will last/years
North and South America	487 591	24 348	20
Europe	156 736	6142	26
Middle East	769 730	1799	428
Asia/Pacific	146 247	2176	67
Africa	189 423	1169	162
Eastern bloc	1 283 800	20 258	63
TOTAL	3 033 527	55 892	54

Table 2.11

You can see from the table that the Middle East is the part of the world where the supply of natural gas will last for the longest time. If other parts of the world did not then start to use the gas that was left there, it would last for over 400 years. However, the industrial world will need the gas in the Middle East, and so it too will soon be used up. If we compare the total amount of gas which we know exists in the world with the total amount used in the world each year, then it seems likely that the supply of natural gas will run out in about 50 years time, soon after the oil.

Nuclear fuels

The only way that the world will be able to supply itself with enough energy in the future will be if substitutes for oil and natural gas can be found.

OIL
&
GAS
will be replaced by →
NUCLEAR POWER
HYDRO-ELECTRIC POWER
SOLAR ENERGY
WIND POWER
TIDAL AND WAVE POWER
GEO-THERMAL ENERGY

Of these other possibilities, the only one which involves getting energy from chemicals is nuclear power. How this happens will be explained in Section 3 (Unit 3.2), where you will also learn about the dangers and advantages of using nuclear reactions to give us energy.

In 1977 there were 192 nuclear reactors in different countries in the world. The total amount of energy which they produced was over 90 thousand million watts – equivalent to the energy contained in 3.2 tonnes of coal **every second**, or the equivalent of 100 million tonnes of coal in a full year. More and more nuclear power plants are planned, and scientists expect that nuclear power will be one of the most important replacements for oil and gas (Fig. 2.59).

Alternative energy sources

Of the 'alternative' ways of getting energy, by far the most important is hydro-electric power. The energy from moving water is turned into electrical energy by turbines. The water can be moving under the influence of gravity or of some other force such as the tide at the edge of an ocean.

The Niagara Falls on the border of Canada and the USA is a good example of a place where water falls under the influence of gravity. If the water passes through turbines it turns them and makes electricity. Both the Canadians and the Americans have used the water at Niagara to make hydro-electric power.

In other cases, dams have been built across rivers to hold back huge amounts of water. When electricity is needed, the water can be allowed to carry on, but it has to pass through turbines as it goes. In France, a BARRAGE has been built across an estuary so that the sea water has to pass through the turbines it contains every time the tide changes (Figs. 2.60, 2.61).

All in all, about one quarter of all the world's electricity is made by tapping the power of moving water. In some countries, for instance Norway and Sweden, the majority of the electricity is made in hydro-electric plants.

At the moment, the energy which we get from all the other possible future sources added together is only a tiny fraction of the energy which we need. Trapping the energy which comes from the sun is an obvious candidate for the future, and many houses (and even some schools) have 'solar panels' which help to provide hot water. If we could trap **all** the energy from the sun which reaches the Earth, we would be able to solve all our energy problems – in just one day this is equivalent to the amount of energy which we could get by burning half a million million tonnes of coal. This would keep the entire world going for about 40 years!

Wind power and wave power may also help us in the future. Like the collection of the sun's energy, wind and wave energy will last for vast periods of time, and they do not cause pollution. Another possibility which scientists are looking at is the energy contained in the rocks beneath the ground. We call this energy GEO-THERMAL energy, and it might be possible to bring it to the surface by pumping cold water down one hole drilled into the hot rocks, which then comes up to the surface through another hole as

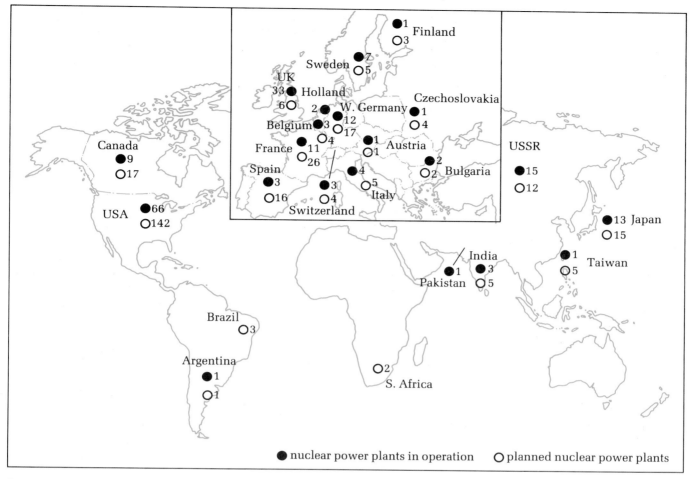

● nuclear power plants in operation   ○ planned nuclear power plants

Fig. 2.59

Fig. 2.60 *This dam and hydro-electric power station are in New Zealand*

Fig. 2.61 *This barrage at La Rance in France makes electricity from the tides*

hot water. Just such a system is undergoing trials near Stithians in Cornwall, England.

In spite of all these possibilities, it seems likely that the world will have to use more and more coal in the near future. This is going to cause many difficult problems, however, because burning coal, like other things which the chemical industry does, causes pollution.

UNIT 2.2
Summary and learning

1   The chemical industry takes a chemical which we find somewhere in the world around us, and turns it into something which we can use.

2   One of the most important chemical processes was started when people learnt how to make metal from metal ores.

3   The chemical industry has been part of the great scientific and technological changes which have happened in the last 200 years. Our standard of living depends to a very large extent on the chemical industry.

4   The different steps in a chemical process are:
   mining (digging up the raw chemical);
   separation (getting rid of unwanted chemicals);
   extraction (getting the chemical we want from the
      raw chemical);
   fabrication (shaping the chemical);
   assembly (making the finished produce).

5   In the UK, the chemical industry is widespread geographically, and is the third most important part of the economy. It depends very heavily on the import of raw chemicals.

6   You should remember why it is difficult to know accurately how much of any chemical there is left in the world.

7   You should remember the uses of, and the value of, each of the following types of chemical:
   precious and rare metals;
   metals which we use for making things;
   fertilisers and other raw materials.

8   You should remember where each of these types of chemical exist, and roughly how long they will last.

9   We need energy for:
   manufacturing industry;
   food production;
   heat, light and transport.

10   Together, the USA, the USSR, Western Europe and Japan use 80% of the world's energy, although they have only 25% of the world's population.

11   There is likely to be enough coal in the world to last for several hundred years. On the other hand, even though the amount of energy used in the world has dropped in recent years, it is still likely that the world's supply of oil will run out in about 40 years, and the natural gas in about 50 years.

12   You should remember how engineers go about getting all the oil from an oil well.

13   Along with nuclear fuels and other sources of energy, coal will need to be used more in the future to fill the gap left when the oil and gas run out. Coal is difficult to handle and to transport, and it causes pollution.

14   You have learnt the meaning of these words:

ore	uneconomical
alloy	catalyst
slurry	hydro-electric power
extraction	liquefaction
die-casting	gasification
fabrication	barrage
assembly	geo-thermal energy

UNIT 2.3 *The problem of pollution*

The word POLLUTION means adding things to our environment which are different from those that are there naturally. For the most part, we think of pollution as being harmful.

Pollution can come in many forms. For example, many people think that excessive noise is just as much pollution of the natural environment as is the oil spilled from a wrecked tanker.

Spilled oil is just one example of chemical pollution. You have seen that the chemical industry takes chemicals from the environment and makes them into something which is useful. In doing this, there are often other chemicals which we release into the environment – and so we cause pollution. The pollution which is caused by the chemical industry is a very real problem, and so in this unit you will see what the main causes of chemical pollution are, how they come about, and what can be done about them.

TOPIC 2.3.1

Pollution of air

In Unit 2.1 you learned that the air is made up of a mixture of different gases – mostly nitrogen together with oxygen. The air that we breathe today and the air that our Stone Age ancestors breathed was the same as

Fig. 2.62 *Sydney, Australia, at 8.30 in the morning. There are millions of people in there!*

far as these two gases go. However, the air that we breathe today is not the same as the Earth's 'natural' atmosphere, because it has been changed by man. It has been polluted.

As a percentage of the whole atmosphere, the amount of pollution is not very large. But even small amounts of 'unnatural' gases may be enough to cause illness, death and even widespread disaster which could affect millions of people.

In 1952 pollution of the air in London was so bad that a 'pea-soup' fog caused about 4000 people to die – poisoned by the gases they breathed in. Today in places like Sydney in Australia, pollution caused by industry and by cars and lorries causes a permanent haze of 'smog' to hang over the city (Fig. 2.62). The smog over Sydney contains all the different types of pollution of the air which exist. Some of this pollution causes what has become known as 'acid rain'.

Acid rain

You learnt about acids and the pH scale in Section 1. If you are not sure what an acid is or how the pH scale describes acidity, go back and read Topic 1.3.3 (p. 32).

Acid rain is what it says it is. It is rain which is acidic. Natural rain is **slightly** acidic, because the tiny amount of carbon dioxide which exists in the air dissolves in water to make it acidic. (How do you know? What kind of an element is carbon?) The pH of 'natural' rain is about 6. So when we talk about the acid rain which falls because of pollution, we mean rain which is more acidic than that – about as acidic as lemonade (pH 4). You know that the oxides of non-metals are likely to be gases, and that they will dissolve in water to form acids. So you might decide that the chemicals which cause acid rain because of pollution of the air are probably the oxides of non-metals.

If you think this, then you are right! Acid rain is caused by sulphur dioxide and by various oxides of nitrogen.

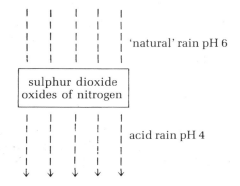

'natural' rain pH 6

sulphur dioxide
oxides of nitrogen

acid rain pH 4

All fossil fuels contain some sulphur. So when we burn them, as well as getting carbon dioxide and carbon monoxide (because they contain the element carbon) and water (because of the hydrogen in the compounds in a fossil fuel), we get sulphur dioxide.

FOSSIL FUEL

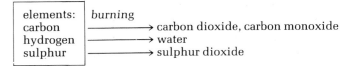

elements:
carbon
hydrogen
sulphur

burning

→ carbon dioxide, carbon monoxide
→ water
→ sulphur dioxide

The amount of sulphur dioxide which gets released into the air depends on the amount of sulphur in the fossil fuel, and the amount of fossil fuel which gets burned. (Several years ago, large amounts of sulphur dioxide used to get into the air when it escaped from chemical plants making sulphuric acid – see p. 364 – but this has now been almost completely stopped). You saw in Unit 2.2 of this section that the USA is the world's biggest user of energy, and therefore the world's biggest burner of fossil fuels. This means that the USA is also the world's biggest sulphur dioxide polluter.

Every year, about 100 million tonnes of sulphur dioxide are poured into the air throughout the world. A quarter of this total comes from the USA.

	million tonnes per year
USA	25
USSR	16
UK	5
Canada	5
W. Germany	4
E. Germany	4
France	4
Italy	4
Poland	4
Czechoslovakia	3
All others	26
World total	100

Table 2.12 *Sulphur dioxide pollution*

The total amount of sulphur dioxide poured into the air each year in Europe (including the USSR) is 60 million tonnes – 60% of the world total.

Part of the sulphur dioxide comes, of course, from the exhaust fumes of cars and lorries, because they burn a fossil fuel. In a car engine, petrol and air are mixed together and fed into the CYLINDERS of the engine. Each cylinder has a PISTON which can move up and down, and a SPARK PLUG. An electric current goes through the spark plug and causes a spark. This makes the mixture of petrol and air explode – and this pushes the piston upwards. This movement of the piston is turned into the power to drive the car forward (Fig. 2.63).

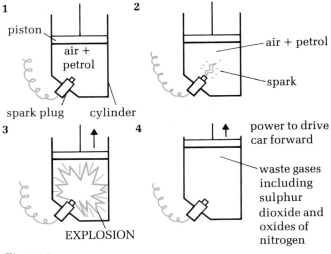

Fig. 2.63

The temperature of the spark is very high. It is high enough to make the oxygen and nitrogen in the air combine together chemically – to make various oxides of nitrogen. So cars and lorries are responsible for the oxides of nitrogen which help to make acid rain.

Acid rain often does not fall in the place that causes the pollution. Instead, the gases can be carried by air currents to other parts of the country, or even over great distances to other countries before they cause acid rain. For instance, scientists have measured the pH of the rain in Scotland at various places, and they have discovered that it gets more acidic towards the south and east (Fig. 2.64). To some extent, this is to do with where the pollution starts, but it is also to do with the way air currents bring polluted air from the industrial parts of Britain to south east Scotland.

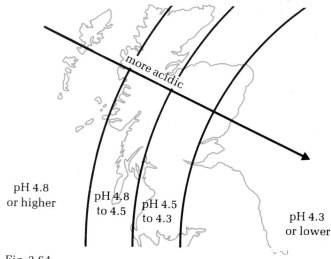

Fig. 2.64

In Sweden and Norway, the problem is even worse. These countries cause very little pollution of their own, and yet they suffer very badly from acid rain. This is because the direction of the air currents causes polluted air from all over Europe to pass over this part of northern Europe.

Norway
and
Sweden

Fig. 2.65

If we compare the amount of acid rain which falls in the different countries of Europe with the amount of sulphur dioxide that each produces, we can see which countries do the polluting, and which get polluted (Fig. 2.66). Because winds carry our sulphur dioxide pollution to other countries, the UK is one of the worst polluters in Europe.

Acid rain affects the **soil** on which it falls. Because it affects the soil, it affects the trees and plants which grow there. To grow properly, trees and plants need nitrogen, phosphorus, potassium and small amounts of some metals like calcium and magnesium. Normally, unpolluted soil can supply plants with all these things. However, acid rain can alter all that.

The first effect of acid rain is to actually **increase** the growth of plants. Because acid rain contains nitrogen, if it is only dilute and does not make the ground too acidic, the net effect is to help plants to grow (Fig. 2.67).

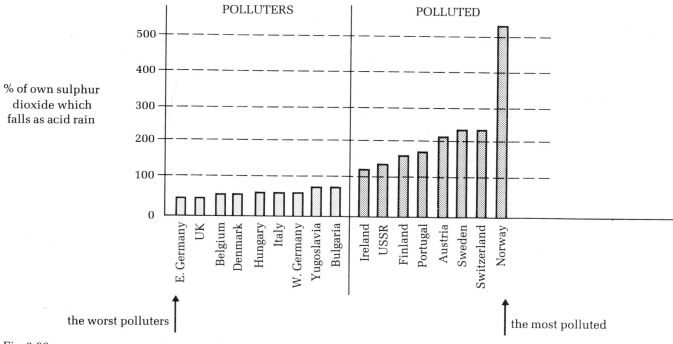

POLLUTERS   POLLUTED

% of own sulphur dioxide which falls as acid rain

the worst polluters ↑

the most polluted

Fig. 2.66

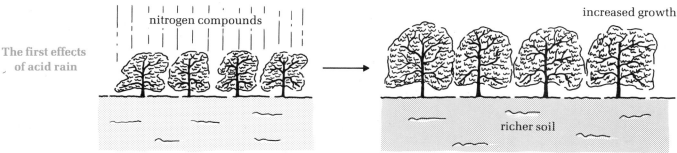

The first effects of acid rain

nitrogen compounds

increased growth

richer soil

Fig. 2.67

Soon, however, comes the second stage of acid rain pollution. The sulphur dioxide pollution forms sulphuric acid in the atmosphere, and so this is what falls as acid rain. As well as containing hydrogen ions, sulphuric acid contains **sulphate ions.** These wash through the soil, and carry with them the cations of metals which form soluble sulphates (like calcium and magnesium). So the sulphate ions flush out these essential plant nutrients from the soil. We say that they are LEACHED out of the soil (Fig. 2.68).

In the Harz Mountains in West Germany, thousands of hectares of forests are dying because the essential elements which they need to grow have been leached out of the soil by acid rain.

But there is worse to follow. Aluminium exists in soil in large quantities. It is harmful to plants and to animals, but fortunately it is locked away in insoluble compounds and causes no harm. That is, until acid rain alters the pH of the soil. When the pH reaches 4.2, aluminium ions become soluble and start to move. They are absorbed by the roots of trees, which become poisoned and diseased. The trees start to die, and because their roots are weakened, a strong wind will blow them over.

Even now the acid rain has not finished its destructive work. Once it has gone through the soil, it passes into rivers and streams, and may build up in lakes. If the pH of a lake drops to 5.5, fish will die or young fish will not develop properly. If aluminium ions get into the water, then all the fish will be killed, because aluminium interferes with their gills and they die of suffocation (Fig. 2.70).

The effects of acid rain are worst where the soil is thin, as it is in rocky or mountainous areas. This is because, to some extent, soil can resist the effects of acid rain. But if there is not much soil then it soon becomes exhausted. Norway and Sweden are mountainous countries which have many thousands of lakes. In southern Norway 2000 lakes have lost all their fish. In Sweden as many as 18 000 lakes have become acidified, and half of them are completely dead. There has been a tragedy on a massive scale.

Nearer home, the lakes of Scotland, South Wales and the Lake District are now suffering from the effects of acid rain. In North America, areas which have mountains and lakes are affected in the same way. As many as 48 000 lakes in central Canada may be in danger.

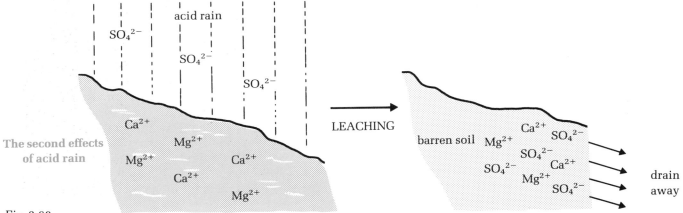

The second effects of acid rain

LEACHING

barren soil

drain away

Fig. 2.68

Fig. 2.69 *These trees were killed by the effects of acid rain*

Fig. 2.70 *There are no fish in this lake, because of acid rain*

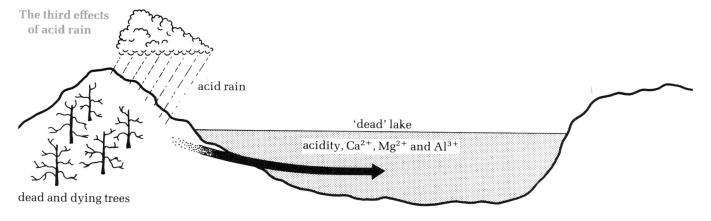

The third effects of acid rain

acid rain

'dead' lake

acidity, Ca^{2+}, Mg^{2+} and Al^{3+}

dead and dying trees

Fig. 2.71

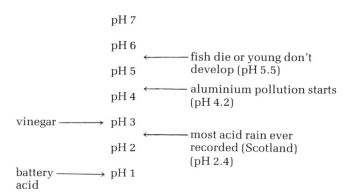

pH 7

pH 6

← fish die or young don't develop (pH 5.5)

pH 5

← aluminium pollution starts (pH 4.2)

pH 4

vinegar ⟶ pH 3

← most acid rain ever recorded (Scotland) (pH 2.4)

pH 2

battery ⟶ pH 1
acid

So what can be done? Science has caused the problem, but does science have the answers? In simple terms, the answer to this question is 'yes'. We **can** get rid of acid rain. The problem is that it would cost us about £150 to get rid of each tonne of sulphur dioxide. That may not seem like very much, but you can calculate for yourself what the 'clean up' bills would be.

Question

From the information in Table 2.12 on p. 94 work out the 'clean up' bill
(a) for the UK;   (b) for the whole world.

In the Ruhr, the industrial heart of West Germany, a modern coal-burning power station has been built at Bergkamen. Hardly any sulphur dioxide pollution comes out of this power-station's chimneys, because it is removed before it can get to the air. This is done by neutralising the chimney gases with a deluge of calcium hydroxide solution. We say that the gas is being SCRUBBED. In West Germany, people are so worried by the effects of acid rain caused by pollution from places like the Ruhr, that a decision has been taken to halve the amount of sulphur dioxide which gets into the air by 1990 – whatever the cost!

Fig. 2.72 *Air pollution in the Ruhr*

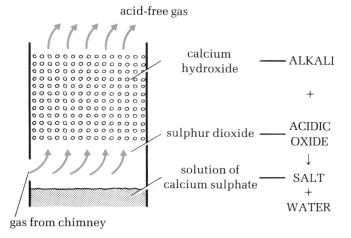

acid-free gas

calcium hydroxide —— ALKALI

+

sulphur dioxide —— ACIDIC OXIDE

↓

solution of calcium sulphate —— SALT

+

WATER

gas from chimney

Fig. 2.73 *Power station chimney gases can be 'scrubbed'*

Questions

Look back at Unit 2.2. Remember what was said there about the world's need for energy, and the amounts of the different fossil fuels that are left. Discuss the following issues with others in your group/class, and if you are asked to by your teacher, you can then put some thoughts down in writing.

1   Do you think that the problem of acid rain is likely to get worse or better in the coming years if nothing is done about it?

2   Is 'acid rain' an argument for more power to be made by nuclear reactors, do you think, rather than more coal being burned when the oil runs out? Or do you think that we should burn more coal, but stop sulphur dioxide getting into the air? Do you think there are other 'harmless' solutions to the world's coming energy gap?

3   'Acid rain' is an international problem. Do you think that the governments of different countries should get together to try to stop it, or do you think that it is a problem which the 'polluters' can forget about and leave to the 'polluted' to find an answer to?

The main gas that is produced when fossil fuels are burned is carbon dioxide. Many scientists now think that there may be as many dangers in pollution from carbon dioxide as there are in acid rain.

Carbon dioxide and the 'greenhouse effect'

The amount of carbon dioxide in the air today is different from the amount that there was in the Stone Age, and different even from the amount 100 years ago. Since fossil fuels started to be burned in large quantities last century, millions of tonnes of carbon dioxide each year have passed into the air. The rate is now about 18 000 million tonnes each year. Because of this, the amount of carbon dioxide in the air has increased, and it is still increasing. The exact amount of carbon dioxide in the air is 340 parts per million (0.034%). In the last century, it was only 265 parts per million (0.0265%). Some scientists think that by the middle of the next century, this level will have grown to about 600 parts per million, or nearly double what it is today.

You learned in Unit 2.1 that the amount of carbon dioxide in the Earth's atmosphere is tiny compared with the amounts in the atmospheres of Venus and Mars. The atmosphere of Mars is very thin – too thin to have much of an effect. But the atmosphere of Venus is not thin – in fact it is thicker than the Earth's. We can get some idea of what might happen if there were ever massive amounts of carbon dioxide in the Earth's atmosphere, by looking at Venus. The average temperature on the surface of the Earth is 15°C (although it is of course sometimes much higher and sometimes much lower). On Venus the average temperature is 400°C – four times as hot as boiling water!

The high temperature on Venus is not just because it is nearer to the sun than we are. It is because of the large amounts of carbon dioxide in its atmosphere. Of the energy from the sun which reaches the Earth's surface, about 10% escapes through the atmosphere back into space. On Venus, almost none of the energy escapes. This is because carbon dioxide lets light energy (the energy from the sun) pass through itself, but does not allow thermal energy (the heat caused by the sun's rays) to pass. So it 'traps' the sun's energy – in the same way that the glass in a greenhouse lets light in, but does not let heat out.

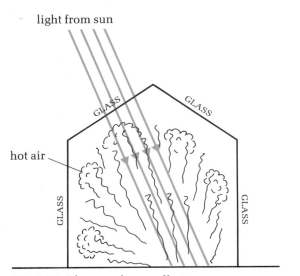

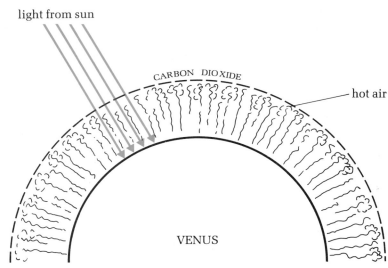

Fig. 2.74 *The greenhouse effect*

Now the questions we have to ask ourselves are:
1. will the temperature of the Earth rise because of carbon dioxide pollution, and
2. if it does, what will the effect be?

Scientists are divided on the first of these questions, some believing that doubling the amount of carbon dioxide in the atmosphere would mean an increase in temperature by as much as 10°C. Other scientists think that this figure is much too large, and that the effect of such a change might in fact be very small indeed. But there is not much dispute about what would happen if the temperature **did** rise. If it rose by as little as 2°C, then there would be a big change in the world's climate. Places like Britain would have warmer summers and colder winters, and the types of crop that could be grown would alter drastically. Much of the USA would become almost a desert, and the cereal growing area would move north to Canada.

If the temperature of the Earth rose by as much as 10°C, then the ice-caps at the North and South poles would begin to melt. This would mean that the level of the sea would rise by several metres – and much of the inhabited parts of the world would be flooded, including London!

To stop the amount of carbon dioxide in the air from rising, we could have huge plants to absorb it chemically from the air, but these would be extremely expensive. Or we could use nature. Trees and plants use up carbon dioxide when they make carbohydrates during photosynthesis. So we could plant very large tree plantations to take up the extra carbon dioxide, but the trouble is that they would each have to be as big as Europe to have any effect!

So, as far as carbon dioxide pollution and the greenhouse effect are concerned, we shall have to wait – and see!

PROJECT 2.3

Here is some background information.

A. Amount of carbon dioxide in the air above Hawaii/parts per million, 1958–1978

Year	Carbon dioxide/ppm	Year	Carbon dioxide/ppm
1958	315.5	1969	324
1959	316	1970	325
1960	316.5	1971	326
1961	317.5	1972	328
1962	318	1973	330
1963	319	1974	330.4
1964	319.5	1975	330.6
1965	320	1976	332
1966	321	1977	333
1967	321.5	1978	334.5
1968	322		

Table 2.13

B. Average annual temperature worldwide 1880–1980

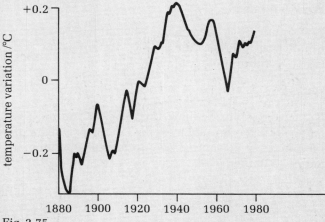

Fig. 2.75

1 Draw a graph of the amount of carbon dioxide in the air 1958–1978. Do you think that the rate of increase is getting greater? If so, why do you think this is?

2 Find out what you can about the rate at which the world's forests have been cut down. You should be able to find information on what is happening in the Amazon jungle, at least. What do you think the effect of this on the amount of carbon dioxide in the air has been, and what do you think the effect will be if the present rate of 'deforestation' continues?

3 Compare the shape of the graph you have drawn with the way the average temperature of the Earth has changed in the last 100 years. A direct comparison is not possible, but do you think that the two changes might appear to go hand-in-hand, at least? Or do you think we need more scientific evidence before we can be sure what is happening?

4 Find a topographical map (one that shows the height of the land above sea-level) of the British Isles. Draw the outline of the coast if the sea had risen by
(a) 20 metres,   (b) 50 metres.
Describe in your own words what you think the effects of these changes would be.

Other types of air pollution

Cars and lorries do not just give out sulphur dioxide, oxides of nitrogen and carbon dioxide. They also cause pollution by carbon monoxide and by lead. When a fossil fuel burns in plenty of oxygen, then carbon dioxide is one of the products. If there is not enough oxygen, then instead of getting carbon dioxide, we get carbon monoxide.

Carbon monoxide is poisonous. It can stop the haemoglobin in our blood from taking up oxygen properly, and so if there is enough of it in the air we breathe, we will die of lack of oxygen in our bodies.

Lead is added to petrol in the compound lead tetraethyl. We do this in order to help engines to run more smoothly, and so lead tetraethyl is called an ANTI-KNOCK. It allows us to use cheaper grades of petrol in our cars without doing any damage to the engine.

▶ EXPERIMENT 2.1

Lead is a poison which can build up in our bodies over a period of years, and so what seems to be important is the amount of it we are exposed to during our lifetime. Many scientists think that lead poisoning can affect the nervous system, and in particular that it can cause brain damage. Babies and young children are probably particularly sensitive to the effects of lead, and so many people are very worried about the effect which there might be on young people who live in areas where there is a lot of pollution from car exhausts (in cities). For this reason, the amount of lead in petrol is gradually being reduced, and in countries like the USA it is possible to buy lead-free petrol.

Another type of pollution in our air is tiny particles of solid matter. An obvious example of this is smoke. In smoke, tiny particles of soot (the element carbon) hang in the air. After the killing smogs in London, the Government passed the Clean Air Act (1956), which made it illegal to put smoke into the air in 'smokeless zones'. Even in very clean air, we probably breathe in about 40 000 particles of solid with every breath. It is not surprising therefore, that in air which is polluted by smoke all kinds of damage can be done to our lungs. In particular, smoke pollution can cause a disease called BRONCHITIS, from which many people in this country used to die each year.

Nowadays, other solid particles in the air give us cause to worry. For instance, people who work with the substance called ASBESTOS have to be very careful to wear masks and protective clothing. Tiny particles of asbestos can be carried in the air and they can cause a lung disease called ASBESTOSIS, from which many people have died.

It is possible that many solids carried on the air into our lungs can cause illness, and so we should always take steps to avoid breathing in any form of dust.

EXPERIMENT 2.1
Showing that petrol contains lead

You will need the following: filter-paper, small volume of petrol, dilute acetic acid (ethanoic acid), freshly prepared potassium iodide solution, ultraviolet lamp (if available).

What to do

IF AN ULTRAVIOLET LAMP IS USED, THIS MUST BE UNDER SAFE CONDITIONS. THERE MUST BE NO BUNSEN BURNERS ALIGHT IN THE LABORATORY AT ANY TIME.

1   Take a filter-paper and place it on top of an empty beaker, to support it.

2   Use a teat-pipette to drop petrol into the centre of the filter-paper, until the whole of it is saturated.

3   Now place the filter-paper in strong sunlight for several hours. If an ultraviolet lamp is available, use this AS SHOWN BY YOUR TEACHER for about ½ hour.

4   Now add dilute acetic acid to the filter-paper, followed by a few drops of freshly prepared potassium iodide solution.

What happened

You should have been able to see that within a few minutes of the potassium iodide solution being added, a yellow colour appeared.

What we can decide

If you saw a yellow colour, this was lead iodide. The lead iodide has formed from lead in the petrol and the iodide which you added. So this tells us that the petrol contained lead.

Fig. 2.76 *These workers are wearing masks to stop tiny particles of asbestos dust from getting into their lungs*

TOPIC 2.3.2

Pollution of water

Water is a pure compound, but it is rarely pure. You will see in Section 7 why water is a very good solvent for many different types of chemical. The fact that it is means that solids, liquids and gases will all dissolve in it. So it picks up impurities very easily.

But water is something which all living things must have. And that water must be fairly pure. In nature, water is purified by what happens to it during the WATER CYCLE.

Winds over the sea pick up moisture and clouds form, which are pure water vapour. When the clouds pass over high ground they rise higher into the atmosphere, where it is colder. So the water condenses and falls as rain. So creatures on dry land have a constant supply of fairly pure water (unless there is heavy pollution, of course!).

We can copy what nature does, by boiling water and condensing the steam. Distilled water is fairly pure water, and often science laboratories have water stills in order to make it.

Each of us uses about 150 litres of clean water every day, for drinking, washing, cooking, flushing the toilet and so on. It is very important that **all** of that water is pure enough to drink safely, and so a lot of money and effort goes into purifying our water supply – as we shall see shortly.

But we are not the only creatures that rely on water being pure. Ordinary freshwater streams and rivers contain about 10 parts per million of dissolved oxygen – if the water is pure. Fish need to have this amount of oxygen in the water in order to be able to survive by extracting it with their gills. Much water pollution results in the amount of dissolved oxygen being decreased, and therefore in the death of fish. We shall now look at the different ways in which we pollute our water supply.

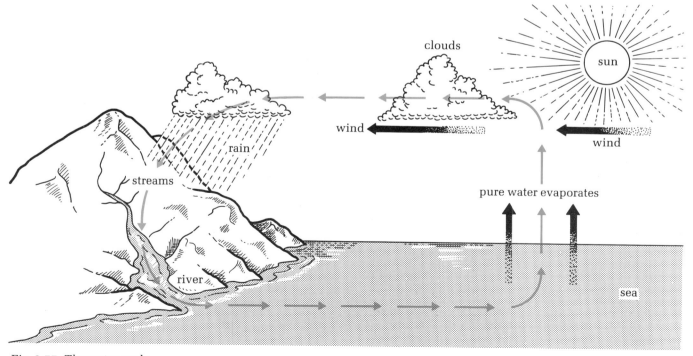

Fig. 2.77 *The water cycle*

Pollution by industrial waste

A typical example of this type of pollution of water is the tipping of waste from coal mines into the sea. Every year millions of tonnes of this and other sorts of waste from industry are dumped into the sea, because it is cheaper to do this than to go to the expense of getting rid of the waste on dry land in a way which is acceptable.

As well as the pollution of the sea, industrial waste causes pollution in our rivers. For many firms it used just to be simpler to pour waste from their factories into a passing river, than to dispose of it in any other way. The result was often the death of all living things in the river. The chemical nature of the pollution meant that it was oxidised by the dissolved oxygen in the water. This used up all the oxygen, and left none for the fish. One particular form of industrial waste, detergents, used to make this situation even worse. Detergents will poison fish in the first place, but they also used to stop oxygen getting into the water from the air. If the river passed over a weir or became agitated in some other way, then the detergent pollution would cause it to form a froth. This foam would then act like a blanket on the surface of the water, stopping any oxygen from dissolving. However, scientists have now found ways of making detergents which can be broken down by bacteria in the environment. We say that these modern detergents are BIO-DEGRADABLE. The secret lies in making the hydrocarbon part of the molecule from a chain which is straight and has no branches (see Section 8). Detergents now cause far fewer problems in our rivers.

Some forms of pollution, particularly metals like mercury, copper and lead, will build up in the bodies of fish. When the fish is caught and eaten, the level of metal which it contains may well make it poisonous to humans. The most well known example of this kind of thing happened some years ago in Japan. In that case, the pollution was mercury metal, and the result was the death of about 50 people. Very many more were paralysed because of the poison they had taken into their bodies.

Pollution by sewage

Sewage causes a problem only when it is 'untreated'. 'Raw' sewage, as it is called, contains nitrates and other nutrients in great abundance. This increases the rate at which micro-organisms in the water multiply and grow, and therefore the amount of oxygen which they take out of the water increases. Sometimes green algae will grow across the surface of a pond or a river – causing it to become stagnant.

Obviously, there is also a problem of disinfection with this type of pollution. Both these problems have to be dealt with in a sewage-works. The water that leaves a sewage-works has to be pure enough to return to a river.

The first stage of sewage treatment is to separate solids from liquids. This is done by simply letting the solids settle, and the stage is called CLARIFICATION. The sludge is taken away and used to make methane and fertilisers.

The water is purified in two stages, the first being FILTRATION. The water is made to trickle through gravel beds, where it picks up a lot of oxygen. This encourages micro-organisms to grow and to cleanse the water. The next stage is DISINFECTION. Chlorine is added to the water to remove the last remaining bacteria. A little too much chlorine is always added so that any bacteria which the water might pick up later before it is used by humans will also be killed.

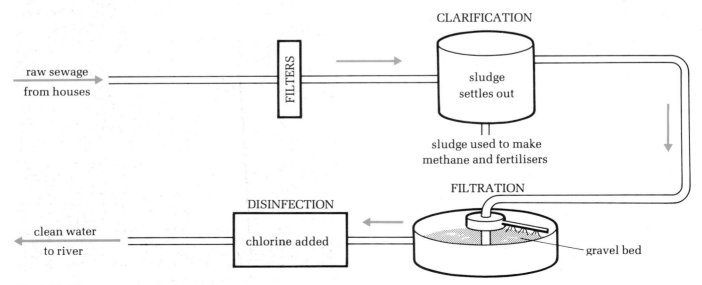

Fig. 2.78 *How a sewage plant works*

Pollution by fertilisers

Because farmers want to make sure that they grow the maximum amount of food on their land, they have added more and more artificial fertilisers. Fertilisers like nitrates and phosphates which are soluble wash off the land and eventually get into the water supply.

The effect of pollution by fertilisers is very similar to that caused by untreated sewage. Green algae will cover the surface of a pool and stop light getting to plants lower down in the water. So these plants die, and the water does not get the benefit of the oxygen which they released during photosynthesis. Fish and other creatures in the pond then die through lack of oxygen. This process is given the name EUTROPHICATION.

▶ PROJECT 2.4, p. 104

Pollution by heat

You already know that many chemical reactions produce heat. Because they do this, a way has to be found of getting rid of the heat, which is a nuisance like any other waste product.

One way of getting rid of heat is to pass cold water over the thing which has to be made cooler. As you will see in Section 7, water is good at absorbing heat.

So, chemical plants often take in cold water from a river or stream and put back hot water. So heat is a form of pollution. This means that the temperature of the river may be increased by several degrees. When this happens, the chemical reactions in the living things in the river speed up (we call these reactions the METABOLISM of the living thing). So a fish will burn up energy more quickly, and will need to have more oxygen. If the river has a low level of oxygen because of another form of pollution, the fish may soon run out of oxygen and die. If the temperature of the river gets too high, it will kill the fish on its own, even if the river is 'clean'.

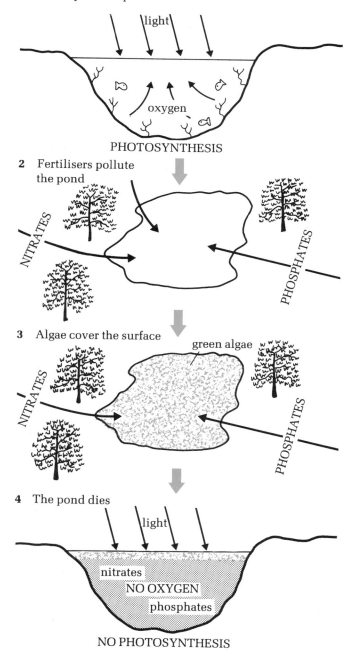

Fig. 2.79 *Eutrophication*

Fig. 2.80 *A combination of 'heat exhaustion' and other poisoning has killed these fish*

PROJECT 2.4

Many people are worried about the pollution of water which is caused by fertilisers. Read the newspaper extract below, and answer the questions which come after it.

Nitrate levels in drinking water breach safety limits, scientists report

By David Cross

Nitrate levels in drinking water have breached recommended safety limits, a group of scientists sponsored by the Royal Society said yesterday.

The problem is particularly acute in the South-east and Midlands where river water is drawn off during autumn and winter and stored.

"There the nitrate concentration may intermittently exceed the World Health Organization's European recommended limits", the scientists said in a 264-page report, *The Nitrogen Cycle of the United Kingdom.*

The study, under the chairmanship of Professor William Stewart, of Dundee University, took more than four years.

The report discloses that nitrate concentrations have risen between 50 and 400 per cent in 12 rivers where scientific data has been available for 20 years.

The Thames, which provided the main supply of drinking water for London, increased its mean annual nitrate concentrate from 2.5 milligrams per litre in 1928 to 8 mg in 1978. In 1981 and 1982, the nitrate concentration had risen above the recommended levels of 11.3mg several times.

In many areas, the report says, the nitrate levels will continue to rise as nitrates produced as fertilizers sink through the soil into underlying ground water. The average annual nitrate concentration in the Thames could reach 11.3 milligrams per litre in the mid 1990s, with maximum concentration well in excess.

Keeping concentrations below the 11.3 milligrams could cost between £200m and £1,600m at 1982 prices over the next 20 years.

Mr Hugh Fish, chief executive of Thames Water, said yesterday that if nitrate rose above acceptable levels it was reduced. Thames Water was also financing research into reducing nitrate levels biologically.

Nevertheless, the scientists say that there is "no good scientific reason" for the imposition of much stricter EEC regulations.

New Community rules state that the maximum acceptable concentration of nitrates in drinking water should be 11.3mg per litre, compared with up to 22.6mg laid down by the World Health Organization.

The Government has not decided whether to apply for an exemption to the limit which comes into effect next year.

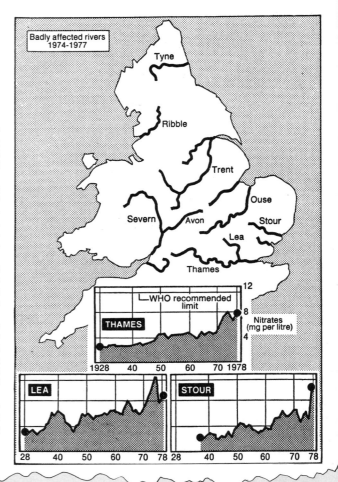

The Times, Wed. 25 January 1984

1   Which organisation has the stricter safety limit for the level of nitrates in water, the World Health Organisation or the European Economic Community (the EEC)?

2   Which is more serious, to exceed the EEC limit or to exceed the World Health Organisation limit?

3   In which parts of the country does the report say the safety limit set by the World Health Organisation has been exceeded?

4   Does the report seem to say that storing water from rivers during the autumn and winter means that higher levels of nitrate in the drinking water are produced? If so, why do you think this might happen?

5   If the limits set by the EEC are accepted, which rivers will have to be 'cleaned up'?

Pollution by oil

You know that the world uses up huge amounts of oil each year. The places where the oil is used are not always the same as the places where it is dug out of the ground. In particular, oil has to be moved from the Middle East to Western Europe. We do this in giant oil tankers, which each hold many thousands of tonnes of oil.

From time to time, one of these 'supertankers' is wrecked, and the oil escapes into the sea. The worst examples of this were the *Torrey Canyon* (off the west coast of England) and the *Amoco Cadiz* (off the coast of Brittany in France). Oil floats on the surface of the sea, and sea birds become covered in it. The oil clogs their feathers, and when they try to clean themselves, they swallow oil which kills them. When a major disaster happens, every effort is made to reduce the effects of the oil, using detergents and other chemicals, but these are sometimes more harmful than the oil itself.

Fig. 2.81 *Are tragedies like this unavoidable?*

Marine life has to suffer the effects of small amounts of oil pollution all the time, because many tankers 'wash out' holds which have been used to carry oil with sea water. This is illegal, of course, but it is very difficult to pin-point which ship has caused a particular oil-slick. More and more effort is going into ways of doing this, however.

TOPIC 2.3.3
Pollution of land

We pollute the land on which we live in many ways. One of these is the everyday problem of litter, caused by thoughtless people. Few forms of plastic, and no forms of tin can are bio-degradable. So they do not rot in hedgerows or rivers, they collect! So do old bicycles and bedsteads!

Factories and mines also cause solid waste – for instance, the slag heaps around coal mines are a pollution of the land. Careless disposal of dangerous

chemicals on the land is another form of pollution which could be avoided if more people took care, and if more people cared!

Fig. 2.82 *Does this have to happen?*

TOPIC 2.3.4
Industry against pollution

We have seen the many different forms of pollution of our environment which take place – some of them caused by the chemical industry itself. But the chemical industry is not just a **source** of pollution. Many thousands of chemists work every day to fight pollution.

Some of the steps taken against pollution have already been mentioned in Topics 2.3.1 – 2.3.3.

Question

Write down all the ways that were mentioned in Topics 2.3.1 – 2.3.3 for tackling different types of pollution.

▶ PROJECT 2.5, p. 106

PROJECT 2.5

Read the newspaper extract below, and answer the
questions which come after it.
'well briefed' means 'well informed'
'retort' means 'reply'
'her brief' means 'her information'
'a paper' means 'a report'

Britain blames cars for death of trees

NIGEL HAWKES on Mrs Thatcher's reply to acid rain claims

BRITAIN has prepared a new defence against charges that it is responsible for killing trees in Europe by 'exporting' acid rain.

It claims that trees dying in German forests are being killed, not by sulphur dioxide from British power stations, but by exhaust fumes from German cars. It does not deny that sulphur dioxide plays some role but claims that Britain's contribution to the sulphur falling on Europe has been greatly exaggerated.

Before last week's economic summit Mrs Thatcher made sure she was well briefed on the subject. She was fed up with repeated remonstrations from Chancellor Helmut Kohl of West Germany, who has raised the subject with her every time they have met in recent months. So she determined to deliver a crushing retort, given the opportunity.

Her brief for the summit included a quotation from a paper due to be presented by the German Government at an interna-

tional ministerial conference on the environment which opens in Munich next Sunday.

The German paper says that while acid precipitation was initially believed to be the main cause of die-back in forest trees, recently opinion has been changing. Now, it acknowledges, 'photochemical oxidants' derived from nitrogen oxides under the impact of sunlight and ozone also play a significant part.

The main source of nitrogen oxides is the exhaust from cars, and such pollution is not carried far. This means, according to British officials, that the primary pollutants causing German forest problems are car exhausts, local pollution, and sulphur dioxide from Eastern Europe.

Britain is not trying to fudge the issue, officials insist, but has been alarmed at demands from Europe, and particularly Scandinavia, to take action against sulphur dioxide emissions before it is even clear that they are the

principal causes of damage. Mrs Thatcher's brief last week said that Britain was in favour of 'swift, cost effective action, when the pollutant responsible is identified.'

It believes it would be pointless to spend hundreds of millions of pounds cleaning up power station emissions – the main source of sulphur dioxides – if the real villain was something else. And it claims that over most of Europe, Britain's share of the sulphur deposited is very small – 7 per cent in Germany and 9 per cent in Sweden, for example.

Only in Norway, where British sulphur represents 19 per cent of the deposition, are we a significant source. By contrast, 21 per cent of the sulphur which falls on Britain comes from the Continent, most of it from France.

The new emphasis on nitrogen oxides was also prominent in evidence given last week by the De-

partment of the Environment to a Commons select committee investigating acid rain. It pointed out that ozone levels in the Black Forest were similar to those in America, where ozone is known to cause forest damage.

Despite the combative attitude Mrs Thatcher took at the summit, and the British conviction that more research is needed before remedies for acid rain can be contemplated, Britain may feel obliged to make some concessions at the Munich conference.

Britain might, therefore, agree to fit sulphur-control equipment to some power stations, or even to join the '30 per cent club' – the group of nations which have pledged to cut sulphur polution by 30 per cent by 1995.

Alternatively, Britain might say that the car is the real villain of the piece, and back moves to cut exhaust pollution quickly.

The Observer, 17 June 1984

1   According to the British side of the story, what is the likely main source of the pollution that is killing German forests? Does the article say that we know the source with certainty?

2   If it is right that sulphur dioxide from power stations is still part of the problem, what information given in the newspaper article suggests that Britain is not the main culprit?

3   What does Britain say needs to be done before a lot of money is spent on solutions to acid rain?

4   If the main source of the pollution which is killing German forests is sulphur dioxide, what will need to be done?

5   If the main source of the pollution which is killing German forests is oxides of nitrogen, what will need to be done?

Getting rid of pollution from car exhausts

Much is already being done to cut down pollution from car exhausts. As you saw in the last topic, the pollution comes in the form of
(a) lead,   (b) carbon monoxide,   (c) carbon dioxide,
(d) sulphur dioxide, and   (e) oxides of nitrogen.
Lead pollution can be got rid of by taking the lead out of petrol. In the USA it is already possible to buy lead-free petrol quite widely, and many cars can run on it.

Fig. 2.83 *This car has been designed to run on petrol which contains no lead*

In Europe, it has been agreed that the amount of lead in petrol will be cut down in steps, and then eventually removed altogether. The other pollutants which can be got rid of are carbon monoxide, sulphur dioxide, and oxides of nitrogen. Carbon dioxide cannot be got rid of, as long as we use petrol to power cars. You will see why this is when you learn about the chemical reactions of the chemicals which make up petrol, in Section 8.

In Germany, steps are now being taken to fit all car exhausts with CATALYTIC CONVERTERS, which will get rid of carbon monoxide, sulphur dioxide, and oxides of nitrogen. These converters contain the metal platinum, which converts the harmful chemicals into harmless ones, or absorbs them. You will learn what a 'catalyst' is in Section 6. The trouble with catalytic converters is that they are fairly expensive, and they have to be replaced frequently. In Britain, another solution to car exhaust pollution is being looked into by scientists. This will consist of making car engines run on a much weaker mixture of petrol and air – so the amount of pollution will be much less. These engines are called 'lean burn' engines. Research engineers at the Ford research centre in Essex, England, have even gone to the length of making a special engine with hardened glass and quartz parts,

as part of the research. This engine will let them study the movement of air and petrol through the engine, using laser beams. The end result should be a design of car engine which will produce exhaust fumes which contain as little pollution as possible.

Getting rid of water pollution

You have seen how some forms of water pollution have already been tackled – for instance by sewage treatment, and by the use of detergents which are 'bio-degradable'.

Another form of water pollution is heat. This is really a problem for the individual chemical factory which has to use water to cool chemicals down. You will see how heat pollution is reduced when you look at specific manufacturing processes later in this book – for instance, the manufacture of sodium carbonate, in Section 5.

Pollution of the sea by crude oil from tankers has been combatted in the past by spraying detergents from ships onto the oil. The problem with this has been that the detergents have been almost as harmful to living things as the original oil. So scientists have had to find harmless 'dispersal agents' which make the oil sink to the sea-bed, where it is gradually broken up and made harmless itself by the action of the sea. Of course, it is much better if the oil does not get into the sea in the first place!

Fig. 2.84 *This ship is spraying an oil-slick with a special dispersal agent which is harmless to living things*

Getting rid of land pollution

There will, it seems, always be rubbish wherever there are humans. Science can help, though, by finding ways of using up some of what is thrown away. We call this RE-CYCLING of waste, because the object is turned from something of no use, to something useful again. So it has a 'second life'.

The main materials which can be re-cycled are glass, metals and paper. Of course, these have to be collected first. Glass is often collected at special points in supermarket car parks called 'bottle banks', scrap metal merchants collect old metal objects, and in some areas teams of workers collect old newspapers.

Fig. 2.85 *This bottle bank is the starting point in the recycling of glass*

PROJECT 2.6

Choose either the recycling of glass, of metals or of paper. Find out what happens to the material once it has been collected. What chemical reactions are used? What is the material changed into, and how is it used again? You should be able to find bottle banks, scrap metal dealers or paper collectors near to where you live!

Questions

1 Of all the different forms of pollution you have learned about, which do you think is the most dangerous? What do you think should be done to reduce it, or is enough being done already?

2 Which forms of pollution do you think science has been able to combat best? Do you think that we still need to do more?

3 Can you draw up a 'league table' of different forms of pollution – with those which scientists should do something about urgently at the top, and those which seem to be harmless or under control at the bottom?

UNIT 2.3
Summary and learning

1 We pollute the air we breathe, our water supply, and the land we live on.

2 You should remember what 'acid rain' is, what causes it, and the effects which it has. You should remember why acid rain is such a problem in places where the soil is thin.

3 You should be able to explain why it is that Norway and Sweden suffer particularly badly from acid rain.

4 You should remember which countries are the worst polluters in Europe, and which countries are the worst polluted.

5 You should be able to explain what 'leaching' means, and how acid rain turns aluminium in the soil from something harmless to something poisonous.

6 You should be able to describe ways in which we can prevent acid rain.

7 You should be able to say why it is that the level of carbon dioxide in the Earth's atmosphere has increased so much in the last 100 years. You should be able to describe how the 'greenhouse effect' is said to work.

8 You should remember what might happen to the world if the worst predictions of the effects of high levels of carbon dioxide in the air turn out to be correct.

9 You should remember what other forms of air pollution exist.

10 You should remember the different forms of pollution which affect water, and the problems which they cause.

11 You should be able to describe how eutrophication can be caused by fertilisers or by untreated sewage.

12 You should be able to describe how a sewage plant works.

13 You should remember the other forms of water pollution and their effects.

14 You should remember the ways in which the land becomes polluted.

15 You should remember the different ways in which scientists and engineers try to overcome pollution.

16   You have learnt the meaning of these words:

pollution	bronchitis	disinfection
cylinders	asbestos	eutrophication
piston	asbestosis	metabolism
spark plug	water cycle	catalytic converters
leaching	bio-degradable	re-cycling
scrubbing (a gas)	clarification	
anti-knock	filtration	

UNIT 2.4   *Inside the chemical industry – making decisions*

You have already learned a great deal about the chemical industry in this section. You have learned what the chemical industry does, the various stages in a typical chemical process, and the importance of the chemical industry to the economy of the world. In the last unit, you learned about the different forms of pollution which the chemical industry can cause.

But so far, one aspect has been missing – the human element. The chemical industry does not just 'happen', and it is not just a great machine that runs itself. At every stage people are involved – and those people have constantly to make decisions which will affect other people, and the chemical process which they are in charge of.

In any chemical company, there will be groups of people who have to look after different parts of the work. These different groups, and the work which they do, are shown in Fig. 2.86. If you were in the chemical industry, which part do you think you would fit into best?

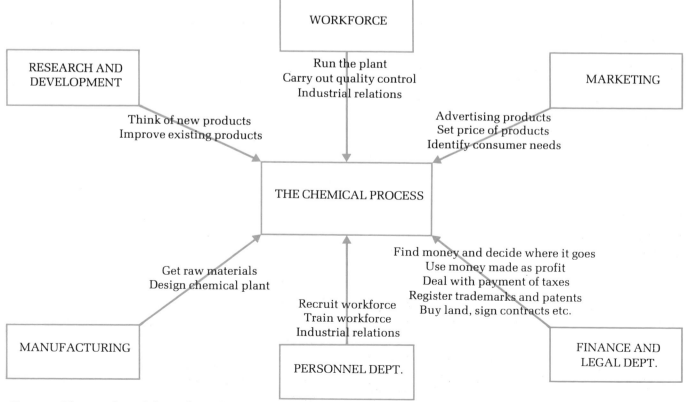

Fig. 2.86 *The people and their jobs in the chemical industry*

One of the jobs of the workforce is to carry out QUALITY CONTROL. This means checking regularly that the product which is being made is up to the necessary standard. In the chemical industry, this usually means checking that it is pure enough for the needs of the person who is buying the chemical. The workforce also regularly check that the plant is running under the right conditions (such as temperature and pressure) to give the best results. These conditions will have been decided upon beforehand by the people in charge of manufacturing (see below).

INDUSTRIAL RELATIONS are about the conditions which surround the workforce in their employment. Such things as wages, holidays and working hours have to be agreed between the employer and the employees. Usually a Union (or more than one Union) talks for the employees, and the Personnel Department of the company for the employer. In some places, this division between the employees and the employer is thought of as being old-fashioned, and instead everybody involved with the company is thought of as having an equal share in it. Industrial relations in the chemical industry are usually very good.

Every firm has to have somebody who tries to sell the product that is being made to a customer. If this does not happen, then there will be no money coming in to pay wages, or to buy fresh raw materials. The business will collapse, and everybody will lose their jobs. So the job done by the Marketing Department is vital. One of the things which a Marketing Department should always be doing is to find out if there are any products which the firm might be able to make which people want to buy. We call this MARKET RESEARCH, and the aim of it is to find out the needs of the people who might buy the thing which the company will make. We call people who buy the products the CONSUMERS. Each of us is a consumer – think of all the things which we use each day which are made in industry.

A TRADEMARK is a name or a symbol which is attached to a product which says that it belongs to the company. Other companies cannot copy the trademark. Familiar names like 'nylon' and 'polythene' were originally trademarks. A PATENT is a design or a formula which belongs to the person or company that invented it first. If the Research and Development Department of a company think of a new product, or a new way of making an old one, then the Legal Department will get a patent for what they have invented, so that others cannot use their idea.

Fig. 2.87 *The trademark on this product belongs to the firm*

We can now look at some of the decisions which people in the Chemical Industry have to make.

Investing in inventions

Every chemical company needs new ideas. So the Research and Development Department will be constantly coming up with possibilities which might make money. But there will always be a limited amount of money which can be used to turn bright ideas into something practical. So decisions have to be made about which idea to follow up. Somebody has to try to pick the winner.

If the wrong 'horse' is backed, then the waste can be enormous. It may amount to millions of pounds and thousands and thousands of hours of work.

An idea might fail for any one of the following reasons:
(a) it might not work in the first place;
(b) it might be too costly to make;
(c) it might turn out to be unsafe;
(d) nobody might want it when it has been made.

Question

The Managing Director of a chemical firm came into work one day and found a note on his desk from the Head of his Research And Development Department. The note read as follows:

_____ MEMO _____

I have just thought of a way to make a chemical which will stop grass from growing without killing it. People will rush to buy it to spray on their lawns and save them the time and effort of mowing.

I need £500 to make a small sample of the chemical. Can I have the money please? The rewards could be enormous!

Johnson

Grass wundachem

1. Send Johnson £500.

2. Give myself a pay-rise for spotting a winner.

3. Check with Marketing that people will buy "Grass wundachem."

4. Ask Johnson to make sure the thing works, that it's safe and cheap to make.

The Managing Director was very enthusiastic about the idea, and so he wrote on his note-pad a list of things to do, as shown above right.

Do you think that the order on the Managing Director's note-pad was the most sensible one? If not, can you suggest a better order?

More often than not, a manager will have not just one decision to make, but a choice between several possibilities. The purpose behind running a chemical firm is of course to make money. So if a manager has a certain amount of money which he can use to back possible new ideas (we would call this his INVESTMENT money), he will try to get the maximum amount of money back from his investment. The intention is to have research and development which at least covers its own costs.

Question

A Managing Director has £50 000 of investment money, and can choose from five different projects:

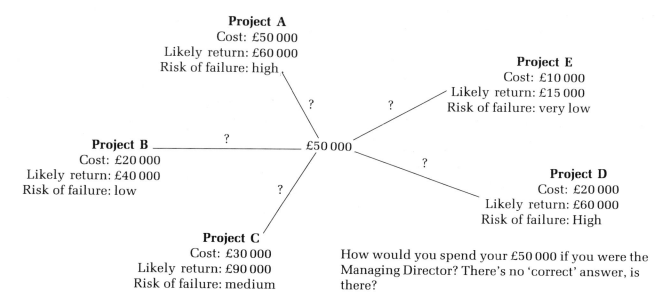

Project A
Cost: £50 000
Likely return: £60 000
Risk of failure: high

Project E
Cost: £10 000
Likely return: £15 000
Risk of failure: very low

Project B
Cost: £20 000
Likely return: £40 000
Risk of failure: low

£50 000

Project D
Cost: £20 000
Likely return: £60 000
Risk of failure: High

Project C
Cost: £30 000
Likely return: £90 000
Risk of failure: medium

How would you spend your £50 000 if you were the Managing Director? There's no 'correct' answer, is there?

TOPIC 2.4.2

How to get there

Often in chemistry there are several possible ways of getting the same chemical result. Only the route is different. This is exactly the same as the choice which motorists have when they get in their cars. There is (almost) always a choice of route from one place to another.

But the choice of which route to take is not always as obvious as it might seem. For instance, the motorway might be the **quickest** route between two places, but if you travel at 70 mph then you use up more petrol per mile than if you go at only 50 mph. So the motorway might not be the cheapest way to travel. It is often like that in the chemical industry – different routes to a chemical will have different advantages and drawbacks. For instance, one chemical route might need several separate stages (and so take a long time to complete) but it might be cheaper than a different reaction which causes the same overall change in one step (and which is quicker). So which chemical route do you choose? It all depends on which is more important – speed or cost.

Once we have decided which chemical route to take, we still have some important decisions to make. For instance, it is still possible to go along the same route at a different speed. You will learn in Section 6 that there are ways in which we can change the speed of a chemical reaction – but usually it costs us money to speed things up. So again, the choice is between speed and cost. (To go back to the picture of driving a car – once you have decided that the motorway is the best route, you can still decide whether to go at 70 mph or at 50 mph.)

SPEED ?

OR COST ?

Fig. 2.88

Another important decision which has to be made is how much chemical to make at a time. On what SCALE should a particular chemical be made? The more chemical we make at a time, the lower the cost of each tonne. There are a number of reasons why this is true.

(a) The cost of doubling the volume of a container is less than double (e.g. the amount of steel sheet which we need to make a container for 200 m³ of a liquid is less than twice the amount which we need for a container of the same shape which will take 100 m³. (Why is this? If you are not sure, you should ask your teacher.)

(b) There may be a minimum critical size for the reaction itself. If the scale is smaller, it becomes inefficient.

(c) The bigger the scale, the higher the proportion of each £ of cost which is turned into part of the production process (instead of being kept 'in reserve'). So you get more 'use' out of each £.

(d) In a big operation, workforce and managers can be more 'specialised' – they only have to look after a part of the plant. So they get to know their job more thoroughly and are better at it.

If we put all these factors together we get, in theory at least, a curve which looks like Fig. 2.89.

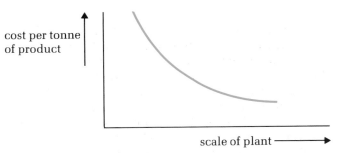

Fig. 2.89

For a particular chemical plant making a particular chemical, there is not always an increase of efficiency as the scale gets bigger and bigger. (For instance, the raw materials might be very expensive, and so the firm can only afford to buy them in fairly small quantities.) So there is usually an OPTIMUM SIZE for a particular type of chemical reaction. Somebody has to decide what this optimum size is, in each case.

For nearly all chemical reactions, there are two different ways in which the reaction can be carried out. It can be either a BATCH process, or a CONTINUOUS FLOW process. When you make a cup of tea in a teapot, you are carrying out a batch process. You make a certain amount at a time, with a certain amount of starting materials (the water and the tea-bags). The batch is the teapot-full, and if you want to make more you have to start a new batch. But suppose that you wanted so much tea that only a constant supply would give you enough. One way to get a constant supply would be to have a constant stream of boiling water passing through a teapot in which there were some tea-bags. You would need to replace the tea-bags with new ones from time to time, but you would have a constant supply of tea. This would be a continuous flow process.

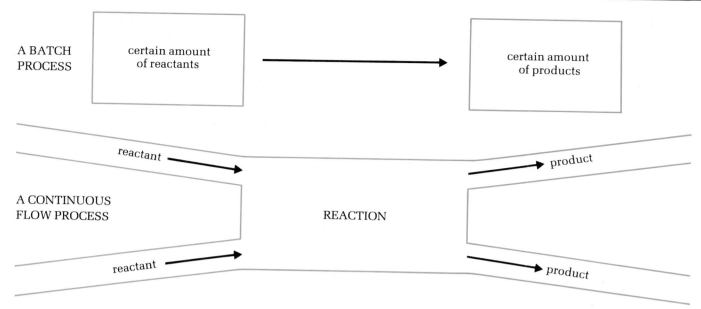

Fig. 2.90

In a chemical plant, the reactions often take place at a high temperature. But it takes a long time to heat up a large chemical plant to the right temperature. It may take several days in some cases, and this is valuable lost time. So, provided that a customer can be found for all the product that is made, it is more efficient for chemicals to be made by a continuous flow method. However, the decision as to whether to use a continuous flow or a batch method depends on the amount of product being made, the type of reaction being used, and what exactly the product is.

TOPIC 2.4.3
Where to put the chemical factory

Once a chemical process has been invested in and researched, and after it has been decided how to carry it out, with what kind of process and on what scale, there is still one crucial question to be answered. **Where** should the chemical plant be?

The simple answer to this question is – where all the requirements of the plant can best be met. Obviously, the needs will vary depending on the nature of the chemical process which is being carried out. You will learn more about the detailed requirements of different chemical processes later, but for now we can think in general terms about the kinds of thing which the person who decides where to build a chemical plant must have in mind.

A chemical plant must be able to make its product and deliver it to the customer as cheaply, quickly and safely as possible. So if possible the plant should be:

1. near to the source of the raw materials;
2. near to an adequate supply of fossil fuels, if these are needed;
3. near to a supply of water, if this is needed;
4. near to the customers;
5. near to good transport facilities (roads, railways, canals or navigable river) for getting the raw materials to the plant and for getting the product to the customer;
6. where the waste-products can be safely disposed of (if these are dangerous gases, then the plant cannot be near a centre of population);
7. where there is a nearby workforce;
8. where the land is cheap to buy.

It is never really possible to have the ideal position. So the best compromise has to be decided upon. You will learn in Section 5 about the way in which the chemical sodium carbonate is made in industry. The raw materials are sodium chloride and limestone (calcium carbonate), and there is a need for large amounts of cooling water. Some of the important customers who buy sodium carbonate are the glass manufacturing industry and the textile industry. Look at the map shown in Fig. 2.36 on p. 78. Where do you think a good place to make sodium carbonate would be?

There have been chemical plants making sodium carbonate in Cheshire for over 100 years. These are within a few miles of the salt deposits at Runcorn, and about 25 miles from a limestone quarry. The glass industry is nearby (in St. Helens) as is the textile industry of Lancashire. There is a navigable river, a canal system, and good road and rail links. The river provides cooling water. Now you can try some examples for yourself.

Questions

In each case, decide which of the possible sites is the best one for the type of chemical plant mentioned. You should explain your answer in a few short sentences.

1   Here are some facts about the steel industry:

Needs: iron ore
       coke (from coal)
       limestone
       workforce
Waste: slag and carbon dioxide
Customers: heavy industry (especially shipbuilding, car manufacture and the building industry)

Decide which of the possible sites would be the best one for a steelworks.

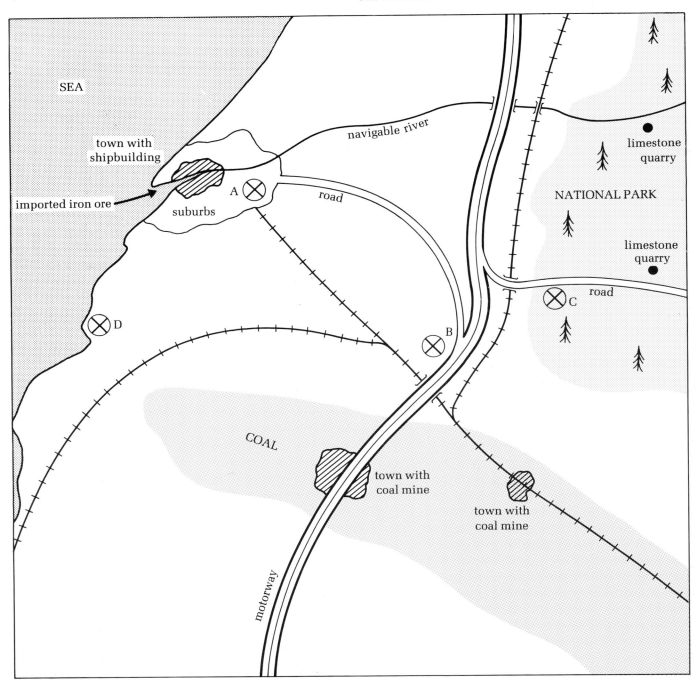

Fig. 2.91

2   Here are some facts about the manufacture of aluminium:

Needs: the ores bauxite and cryolite
          large amounts of electricity which is cheap
Waste: carbon dioxide
Customers: aircraft production, cooking utensils,
          aluminium paints

Decide which of the possible sites would be the best one for an aluminium plant.

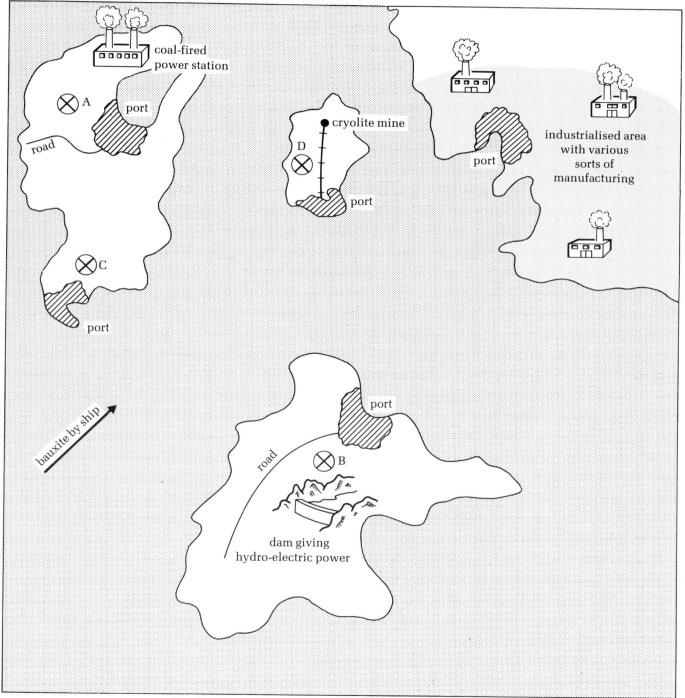

Fig. 2.92

UNIT 2.4
Summary and learning

1   The chemical industry is made up of many people who each have to make their own decisions which affect the whole process.

2   You should remember the roles which are played by the different people in the chemical industry.

3   One of the most important decisions which is made in the chemical industry is which ideas should be given financial backing.

4   For any chemical reaction which we decide to carry out on an industrial scale, we have to decide:
(a) which route to take;
(b) whether to go for speed or efficiency;
(c) what scale to carry out the process on;
(d) whether to use a batch process or a continuous flow process.

5   You should remember the different factors which have to be taken into account when someone decides where to put a chemical plant.

6   You have learnt the meaning of these words:

quality control
industrial relations
market research
consumers
trademark
patent

investment
scale
optimum size
batch process
continuous flow process

Elements and compounds

UNIT 3.1 Elements and the Periodic Table

TOPIC 3.1.1

How atoms are made up

Scientific discovery is a process which never ends. No matter how much we find out there is still more to be discovered. The spiral of 'the scientific process' (Section 1) has told us a great deal about the ways matter is put together, but we are still some way from finding a picture which is full and complete. Research is still going on to discover the secrets of the atom.

This research is so expensive and time-consuming that even individual countries cannot afford to do it on their own. In Europe, a huge complex has been built (called CERN – The European Centre for Nuclear Research) where scientists from many countries, including the UK, can carry out their work.

All research into the nature of the internal structure of atoms, as you will see shortly, has used the same technique. Particles moving at high speeds are fired at atoms, which are smashed to pieces. The idea is then to catch the pieces and work out what they are.

As we get deeper and deeper into the heart of atoms, we need more and more energy to make more progress. The particle which hits the atom has to be moving at greater and greater speeds. CERN is really a giant PARTICLE ACCELERATOR. It consists of a huge circle around which particles move, picking up speed all the time, until they are going fast enough to be useful. In the latest research, particles are being accelerated to speeds very close to the speed of light – as fast, as far as we know, as it is possible for anything to move.

CERN and research laboratories similar to it in the USA and the USSR are the latest step on a journey of understanding that began only relatively recently. Look at the Chart of Scientific History (Fig. 2.31, p. 74). You will see that all the important discoveries about the structure of the atom were made this century – that is, within the lifetime of many people living today.

Dalton made a great breakthrough in the early 1800s when he showed that the atoms of different elements are different. However, Dalton's picture of the atom

Fig. 3.1 The CERN complex is so big that part of it is in Switzerland and part of it in France

Fig. 3.2 This is a photograph of an atom being smashed by a high speed particle

was that it was a hard, unbreakable sphere. This idea of what atoms are like lasted for almost 100 years.

However, by the end of the 1800s it was becoming clear that there were other particles which existed besides atoms – electrons. Faraday (1833) , Helmholtz (1881) and J.J. Thomson (1890) had all shown that there was some relationship between chemicals and electricity (you have already seen some of what this relationship is for yourself). In 1908, Professor Soddy (who was later to work with Rutherford, himself on the point of a great breakthrough in 1908) gave a series of lectures in Glasgow. Of the electron, he said this:

> 'The electron is a new and somewhat startling conception to minds trained on the older lines, although traces of it date back to the discoveries of Faraday of the laws of electrolysis. The electron is an atom of electricity, divorced from matter. . . . Whatever the manner in which these electrons are produced, under whatever circumstances they result, they are always identical in their main characteristics.'

As well as the discovery of electrons, there were also some unsettling new ideas being formed about the nature of some of the elements themselves. Scientists working in France (the most important of these were a man called Becquerel and a woman called Marie Curie) had discovered that some chemical elements gave off 'rays' or 'radiations'. Obviously, this does not fit very well with the idea of atoms being unbreakable spheres, because the atoms must have been giving off a **part** of themselves. Electrons, too, must have been part of atoms. It was time for the idea of atoms being like hard spheres to change.

Rutherford, who was a New Zealander, had found out what the 'radiations' given off by one of these special 'radioactive' elements were. He called them α-particles, and he showed that they were fast-moving atoms of the element helium, which carried a positive charge. He soon hit on the idea of firing these small α-particles at other atoms, in order to see what would happen.

First of all, Rutherford fired a narrow beam of α-particles at a thin gold foil. He knew that in gold the atoms are closely packed together, with no spaces in between them. So he was very surprised to discover that the α-particles went straight through the foil – almost as if it were not there. It was obvious that the α-particles could not have passed **between** the gold atoms, so they must have passed **through** them. Atoms were not hard spheres at all. In fact, Rutherford worked out that the majority of the space taken up by atoms consisted of – nothing! In this early experiment, Rutherford noticed that a tiny proportion of the α-particles were deflected as they passed through the gold foil. So, in 1909, he set two students who were working with him, called Geiger and Marsden, the problem of finding out what was happening. They repeated Rutherford's experiment,

and found that not only were some α-particles deflected, some also bounced straight back off the foil! Rutherford was astounded at first, but he soon realised what was making this happen. He knew that α-particles carried a positive charge, and he also knew that opposite charges repel each other. He knew from his earlier experiments that if there was something 'hard' in an atom, it was extremely small. The object must also have a lot of mass compared to the α-particle, otherwise the α-particle would just have pushed it out of the way.

Rutherford had discovered the NUCLEUS. In the centre of each atom, there is a nucleus which:

(a) carries most of the mass of the atom, and a high positive charge;

(b) is very small indeed compared to the atom as a whole.

We now know that the nucleus is so small that 100 000 of them could stretch across the diameter of an atom. Put another way, it would take about 8 000 000 000 of them to fill up the space in an atom. To give you an idea of the scale, suppose we had a model of an atom which was as big as the average international cricket ground. Then the nucleus of the atom would be in the middle of the wicket – and could be represented by . . . a pin-head!

Fig. 3.3 *Can you see the pin-head at the centre of the wicket? Like looking for a needle in a . . .*

We now know that the nucleus is itself made up of two different types of particle – called PROTONS and NEUTRONS. (In fact, this is a vast simplification. The nucleus is really very complicated, and we still have not uncovered all its secrets even today. That is why experiments like those at CERN are being carried out. Fortunately for chemists, it is not the nucleus of an atom which we need to know about – but rather the rest of the atom, as we will shortly see.)

In order to study chemistry, we need only to think of an atom as being made up of three different particles:

1. the proton ⎫
2. the neutron ⎬ together, these make up the nucleus
3. electron – surrounding the nucleus, and taking up the rest of the space filled by the atom

But what do atoms look like? This is a very difficult question to answer. We can think of an atom as being like a 'cloud' of electrons surrounding the nucleus. We can think of a cloud, because the electrons are constantly moving at tremendous speeds. It's rather like the picture we would get if we photographed a swarm of bees around their hive, but left the camera shutter open for a few seconds. Compare this with the picture we get if we 'stop the action' (Fig. 3.4).

Fig. 3.4 A. The movement of the bees 'blurrs' the photograph

B. The usual photograph 'stops the action'

We cannot make a camera 'fast' enough to stop the action for the electrons in an atom. So a 'cloud' is the nearest we can get to what an atom looks like. This doesn't seem to get us very far, though, in our understanding of how atoms are put together. Fortunately, strange as it may seem from the picture of the atom which we have built up so far, the electrons in an atom have to obey certain rules as to where they can go and how they move. In particular, the velocity at which electrons rotate about the nucleus is limited to certain values. It is **as if** the electrons in an atom can only be in certain circular 'orbits' around the nucleus – those in which they are moving at the allowed velocity. Of course, the electrons in an atom do not all move around the nucleus in perfectly circular paths – but it is a great help to our understanding of atoms to think of them as if they do.

So we can picture an atom as being a nucleus surrounded by electrons arranged in spherical layers, or 'shells'.

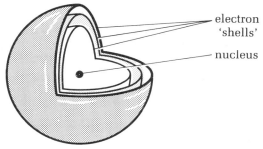

Fig. 3.5

We can simplify this picture still further in order to help our thinking. Suppose we cut a slice through the centre of an atom. Then we could represent the 'true' picture of shells with a drawing like Fig. 3.6.

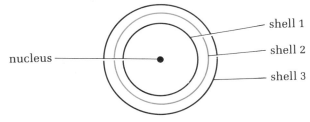

Fig. 3.6

This picture of an atom, with the electrons arranged in shells around the nucleus, was first put forward by the Danish scientist Niels Bohr, in 1913. Bohr was also one of Rutherford's students.

We also know some simple facts about the three particles which make up the atom. Electrons carry a charge, equal in value, but opposite in sign, to the positive charge carried by each proton. Neutrons are 'neutral' and have no charge. Protons and neutrons have almost the same mass as each other. Electrons have much less mass than the other two. It would need about 1840 electrons to have the same mass as a proton (or a neutron). We can summarise these facts in the following table. Together with the picture in Fig. 3.6 of the way in which electrons are arranged, they give us a good idea of the way atoms are put together.

	Charge (relative to each other)	Mass (relative to each other)
proton	+1	1
neutron	NIL	1
electron	−1	1/1840

Table 3.1

All the atoms of the different elements are put together by combinations of these three particles. But how many of each of them are there in the different atoms?

We know that the atoms of all elements are electrically neutral. That means that they must have **an equal number of positive and negative charges**. So an atom must always have an equal number of protons and electrons.

in an atom, number of protons = number of electrons

The atoms of **different** elements have **different** numbers of protons (they also have different numbers of electrons, therefore). **It is the number of protons in the atom of an element which decides which element it is.** We give this number a special name – the ATOMIC NUMBER. The symbol for it is Z.

atomic number = number of protons = number of electrons

The smallest number of protons we can have is, of course, 1. An atom of the element hydrogen is made up of a nucleus composed of one proton, which is circled by one electron. The atomic number of hydrogen is 1.

Fig. 3.7 *An atom of the element hydrogen*

You will see that there are no neutrons in the nucleus of a hydrogen atom. Hydrogen is the only element whose atom contains no neutrons. The next element which can exist is that which has an atomic number of 2. So the nucleus of the atom of this element must contain two protons, and outside it there must be two electrons. The nucleus in this atom also contains two neutrons. The element whose atomic number is 2 is helium. An atom of the element helium looks like Fig. 3.8.

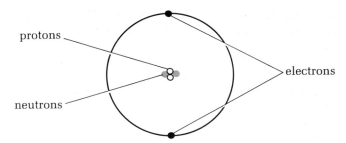

Fig. 3.8 *An atom of the element helium*

Since electrons have almost no mass, the mass of an atom depends on the number of protons plus the number of neutrons in the nucleus. We also give this number a special name – the MASS NUMBER. The symbol for mass number is A.

mass number = number of protons + number of neutrons

The mass number does not tell us what element we have – only the atomic number lets us identify the element. This is because the number of neutrons in the nucleus of an atom is not linked directly to the number of protons. So if we know the atomic number of an atom, we do not necessarily know its mass number. This means that it is possible for atoms of different elements (that is, atoms which have different numbers of protons from each other) to have the same mass number. This happens for some elements.

It is also possible for a given element to have more than one type of atom. The different types of atom of the same element are called ISOTOPES and they are different from each other in having different numbers of neutrons in their nuclei. They therefore have different mass numbers. But we shall come back to this subject later.

We have a shorthand way for representing a particular atom of a particular element. Suppose the symbol for the element is 'X'. Then we can write it down as:

$$^A_Z X$$

So the isotope of the element carbon (atomic number 6) which has a mass number of 12, can be represented by:

$$^{12}_6 C$$

But what are the symbols and names of the different elements? You learned in Section 1 that Dalton had some symbols for different elements. However, it was not long before so many elements had been discovered that no more symbols of the sort used by Dalton could be thought up. Nowadays we use letters to represent elements. The symbol for an element is either a single capital letter, or a capital letter followed by a small letter. A full chart showing the symbols and the names of all the elements is set out on p. 122. This chart is called the PERIODIC TABLE, and you will see shortly how it got its name. The elements are placed **in order of their atomic number** in the Periodic Table.

You will need to know the symbols for some of the elements by heart. The following table gives the names and symbols of the elements whose atomic numbers are 1–20.

Atomic number	Name	Symbol
1	hydrogen	H
2	helium	He
3	lithium	Li
4	beryllium	Be
5	boron	B
6	carbon	C
7	nitrogen	N
8	oxygen	O
9	fluorine	F
10	neon	Ne
11	sodium	Na
12	magnesium	Mg
13	aluminium	Al
14	silicon	Si
15	phosphorus	P
16	sulphur	S
17	chlorine	Cl
18	argon	Ar
19	potassium	K
20	calcium	Ca

Table 3.2

Some other elements and their symbols are:

Atomic number	Name	Symbol
26	iron	Fe
28	nickel	Ni
29	copper	Cu
30	zinc	Zn
35	bromine	Br
47	silver	Ag
53	iodine	I
56	barium	Ba
79	gold	Au
80	mercury	Hg
82	lead	Pb
92	uranium	U
94	plutonium	Pu

Table 3.3

You will see that some of the symbols correspond to the name for the element which they represent, but that others do not. This is because the names of some elements come from words in foreign languages. Table 3.4 below gives the origin of the names of some of the elements, together with the date the element was first discovered.

Name	Symbol	Origin	
hydrogen	H	means 'water maker' in Greek	(1766)
helium	He	'helios' is Greek for 'the sun'	(1868)
carbon	C	'carbo' is Latin for 'coal'	(prehistoric)
oxygen	O	means 'acid maker' in Greek	(1774)
neon	Ne	'neon' is Greek for 'new'	(1898)
sodium	Na	from the Arabic name for a salt of sodium (Natron)	(1807)
phosphorus	P	means 'light bringing' in Greek	(1669)
chlorine	Cl	'chloros' is Greek for 'light green'	(1774)
argon	Ar	'aergos' is Greek for 'does not work'	(1894)
potassium	K	from the word alkali, an Arabic word	(1807)
bromine	Br	'bromos' is Greek for 'stink'	(1826)
iodine	I	'iodos' is Greek for 'violet-coloured'	(1812)

Table 3.4

Question

Copy out the following table. Use what you know about atomic number, mass number, and the symbols for the elements to fill in the empty spaces.

Symbol	No. of protons	No. of neutrons	Mass no.	No. of electrons
S			32	
		10		9
	12	12		
Na		12		
			40	20
		14	28	
N			14	
		30		26
	10	10		
Li		4		

TOPIC 3.1.2

Atomic number and the Periodic Table

We have seen that we can think of the arrangement of the electrons in atoms as being like spherical 'shells' around the nucleus. We have also seen that each different element has a different number of electrons in its atoms. Perhaps the number of electrons in an atom has an effect on the way it behaves? To investigate this possibility, we first need to discover something more about the 'shells' in an atom. Remember that each shell represents a value for the velocity at which the electron moves around the nucleus. For any object to move in a circular path, there must be some sort of force pulling it towards the centre of the circle (otherwise it would fly off, moving in a straight line). This is the situation if you have a weight on a piece of string and spin it – it moves in a circle around your hand. The force which attracts electrons towards the nucleus of an atom is the attraction between opposite charges. An electron has a negative charge, and the nucleus has a positive charge.

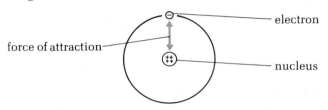

Fig. 3.9

The nearer an electron is to the nucleus, the stronger the force of attraction on it. Electrons further away will not be as strongly attracted.

So, the electrons in an atom can be thought of as being in shells – some closer to the nucleus (stronger

---

The Periodic Table of the Elements

1	2											3	4	5	6	7	0
1 H																	2 He
3 Li	4 Be											5 B	6 C	7 N	8 O	9 F	10 Ne
11 Na	12 Mg											13 Al	14 Si	15 P	16 S	17 Cl	18 Ar
19 K	20 Ca	21 Sc	22 Ti	23 V	24 Cr	25 Mn	26 Fe	27 Co	28 Ni	29 Cu	30 Zn	31 Ga	32 Ge	33 As	34 Se	35 Br	36 Kr
37 Rb	38 Sr	39 Y	40 Zr	41 Nb	42 Mo	43 Tc	44 Ru	45 Rh	46 Pd	47 Ag	48 Cd	49 In	50 Sn	51 Sb	52 Te	53 I	54 Xe
55 Cs	56 Ba	57 La	72 Hf	73 Ta	74 W	75 Re	76 Os	77 Ir	78 Pt	79 Au	80 Hg	81 Tl	82 Pb	83 Bi	84 Po	85 At	86 Rn
87 Fr	88 Ra	89 Ac	104 Rf*	105 Ha	106												

58 Ce	59 Pr	60 Nd	61 Pm	62 Sm	63 Eu	64 Gd	65 Tb	66 Dy	67 Ho	68 Er	69 Tm	70 Yb	71 Lu
90 Th	91 Pa	92 U	93 Np	94 Pu	95 Am	96 Cm	97 Bk	98 Cf	99 Es	100 Fm	101 Md	102 No	103 Lr

*Or Ku.

attraction), and some further away (weaker attraction). There are only a certain number of electrons allowed into each of these shells. Can we find out what this number is for each shell?

How many electrons are allowed in the different 'shells'?

You have seen that the different shells are at different distances from the nucleus in an atom. The closer the shell is to the nucleus, the stronger the force of attraction between the nucleus and an electron in that shell. We would expect, therefore, that the electrons in the innermost shell would be most strongly attracted to the nucleus, followed by the electrons in the second innermost shell, and so on.

We can measure the force of attraction between the electron in a particular shell and the nucleus, by measuring how much energy has to be used to pull the electron away from the nucleus. This energy is the energy we need to remove the electron from the atom altogether. When we take an electron from an atom, we make a cation – so the energy needed for this is the energy needed to make an ion, or the IONISATION ENERGY of the atom.

Suppose we think of an element like sodium. Its atom has 11 protons, 12 neutrons and 11 electrons. So, if we take an electron away, there will then be only 10 electrons, but still 11 protons. So overall, there is one more positive charge than negative charge – and the ION which we have formed has a positive charge. We represent an atom of the element sodium by the symbol Na, and an ion of sodium by Na^+ (to show that the overall charge which it has is +1). So we can represent the change which takes place when an atom of sodium is ionised in the following way:

$$Na \longrightarrow Na^+ + electron$$

the ionisation of an atom of sodium

Suppose we measured the ionisation energy of sodium, and then the ionisation energy of the next element, magnesium. If the electron which is lost when magnesium ionises was in the same shell as the electron which was lost from an atom of sodium, then we would expect the two ionisation energies to be similar. In fact, if we think about it a little harder, we would actually expect them to be similar, but slightly different. Magnesium has one more proton in its nucleus than sodium, and so the electron which is lost from magnesium has to overcome the attraction of one more positive charge. So if the electron in sodium is in the same shell as the electron in magnesium, we would expect magnesium to have a slightly **higher** ionisation energy than sodium.

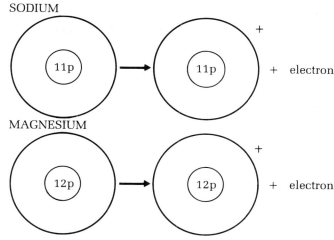

Fig. 3.10

Suppose you had 11 magnets on a table, each with their positive poles pointing towards the negative pole of another magnet, 5 cm away. If you held the magnet in your hand and tried to pull it away from the other 11, you would feel a resistance caused by the attraction between the opposite magnetic charges. Suppose that you then put another magnet with the first 11, with its positive pole also pointing towards the negative pole of the single magnet 5 cm away. If you tried to pull the single magnet away now, the resistance would be greater, because of the larger positive charge, 12 instead of 11, pulling back on the single magnet. This is similar to the difference between ionising sodium and ionising magnesium.

Suppose we now go to the next element, and then to the next, and so on. The same trend will appear **as long as the electron which is removed comes from the same shell.** There will be a gradual increase in ionisation energy as we go from one element to the next, because there is one more proton in the nucleus each time.

Suppose, however, that on going to the next element, we suddenly find a decrease in the ionisation energy compared to the element before it. This can only be because there is a much weaker force between the electron and the nucleus, even though the latter has one more proton. The electron must be much further away from the nucleus than was the electron in the previous element – we have found the point where a new shell starts.

Figure 3.11 (overleaf) shows the ionisation energy for the first 20 elements. You can see that the innermost shell is full when it contains 2 electrons. The electron which is lost from the element which has 3 electrons (lithium) obviously goes into the second shell. This in its own turn is full when we reach neon, which has 10 electrons in total – 2 in the innermost shell, and 8 in the second shell. The third shell is full

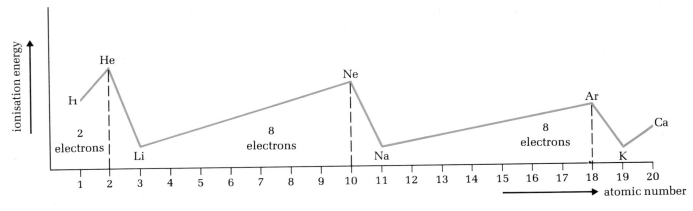

Fig. 3.11

when we reach argon, which has 18 electrons in total – 2 in the innermost shell, 8 in the next shell, and 8 in the third shell.

For each element, the electrons are always arranged as close to the nucleus as possible. We know that the maximum number of electrons in each shell, for the first 18 elements, is:

Shell number	1	2	3
maximum number of electrons	2	8	8

So we can work out the arrangement of the electrons in any atom of the first 18 elements.

Atomic number	Element	Arrangement of electrons Shell 1	2	3
1	hydrogen	1		
2	helium	2		
3	lithium	2	1	
4	beryllium	2	2	
5	boron	2	3	
6	carbon	2	4	
7	nitrogen	2	5	
8	oxygen	2	6	
9	fluorine	2	7	
10	neon	2	8	
11	sodium	2	8	1
12	magnesium	2	8	2
13	aluminium	2	8	3
14	silicon	2	8	4
15	phosphorus	2	8	5
16	sulphur	2	8	6
17	chlorine	2	8	7
18	argon	2	8	8

Table 3.5

To save time, we have a shorthand way of writing out the arrangement of electrons in an element. For instance, for sodium, we can simply write 2,8,1. For oxygen, we would write 2,6 and so on.

PROJECT 3.1

Use the shorthand method to write out the arrangement of electrons in the atoms of all those elements which have

(a) completely filled shells only;
(b) 1 electron in their outermost shell;
(c) 2 electrons in their outermost shell;
(d) 7 electrons in their outermost shell.

In each case, write the symbol for the element, and then the arrangement of its electrons. For example, if sodium comes in any of your lists, you will write   Na:2,8,1.

If you turn to the Periodic Table and look for the elements which have filled shells only, you will see that they are all together in a column at the extreme right. The other elements which are in this column – krypton (Kr), xenon (Xe) and radon (Rn) – also have all their shells filled. We call these vertical columns GROUPS of elements. There is a block of 30 elements in the Table called the TRANSITION elements. These elements do not really belong to groups, and we consider them separately, as you will see. But apart from the transition elements, all the elements in the Table belong to a group of elements. A group is a vertical column in the table.

The group of elements which have all their shells of electrons filled are called the 'Group 0' elements. Look at the table which gave you the origin of the names of some of the elements, and the date when they were discovered (Table 3.4). Find the elements which are in Group 0 in the Periodic Table.

What strikes you about these elements compared to the others? Look at the date when they were discovered. You will see that these elements were discovered much later than all the others. There are two reasons why this is the case. Firstly, the elements in Group 0 are rare on Earth. Most of them are present in the atmosphere to a tiny extent. By far the most plentiful is argon, and this makes up only 0.9% of the volume of the atmosphere. (Because they are so rare, an old name for this group of elements, which is not used much nowadays, is the 'rare earth' elements). The second reason that it took such a long time to spot these elements, is that they take part in no chemical reactions. (Well, this is not absolutely true. One or two of them have been forced by extreme measures into reacting – but even this did not happen until 1962.) Because they do not react, they form no compounds, and therefore exist as the element (they are all gases). A way to describe something which will not react is to call it 'inert'. The modern name for the Group 0 elements is the 'inert gases'. Because they are inert, it is very difficult to tell that they are there, and so for many years they went completely undetected.

But why are the Group 0 elements inert, and is it by chance that they are all in the same group in the Periodic Table? What is the link with the fact that they all have their shells of electrons filled?

The Periodic Table lists the elements in increasing order of their atomic number. So the group immediately before the inert gases all have one less electron than the inert gas which follows them. That means that their outermost shell is not filled, but it has space for one more electron in it.

We could work our way by this means back across the Table. All the elements in each group will have one less electron in their outermost shell. So the Group 6 elements all have room for 2 electrons in their outermost shell. By the time we get to Group 1, all the elements have only one electron in their outermost shell. So, in the Periodic Table, **elements in the same group have the same number of electrons in their outermost shell**.

But the people who worked out the Periodic Table knew nothing about atomic number, and they had no idea about electron shells or the number of electrons which atoms of the different elements had in them. So how did they discover how to draw up the Table?

Perhaps we can get a clue by looking more closely at the Table and the elements in it. You know that there are two basic types of element – metals and non-metals. Try to find the position of as many metals as you can in the Periodic Table. Now find the position of all the non-metals that you know.

So it seems that the nature of an element is related to its position in the Periodic Table – since we can see that all the metals are grouped together, and so are all the non-metals. We can investigate this link between chemical behaviour and position in the Table by looking more closely at the chemical properties of some of the elements.

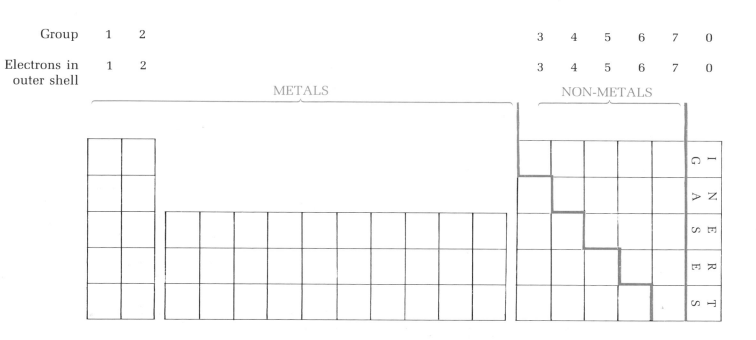

Finding the link between where an element is in the Periodic Table and how it behaves

The Group 1 elements (the 'alkali metals')

lithium (Li)
sodium (Na)
potassium (K)
rubidium (Rb)
caesium (Cs)

EXPERIMENT 3.1

The chemical properties of the 'alkali metals'

> **Your teacher will show you some of the reactions of these elements, and you will carry out another for yourself**

A   The following will be needed by your teacher: lithium, sodium and potassium, 3 gas-jars containing chlorine, 3 deflagrating spoons, 2 beakers containing small quantities of water, universal indicator paper, safety screen, small gauze or sheet of glass.

B   You will need the following: a small piece of lithium, tongs, beakers, universal indicator paper, small gauze or sheet of glass.

What to do

A   Your teacher will show you this part of the experiment.

A SAFETY SCREEN MUST BE USED, AND SAFETY SPECTACLES WORN.

1   Obtain a small piece of lithium by placing a large piece on a tile and cutting it with a knife.

2   Place the small piece of lithium on a deflagrating spoon, and ignite it in the air. While it is still burning, plunge it into one of the gas jars containing chlorine gas.

3   Repeat the above using first sodium and then potassium instead of lithium.

4   Take a small piece of sodium and add it to water in a beaker. Cover the beaker with a small gauze or a sheet of glass. Add a piece of universal indicator paper to the solution which forms as a result of the reaction between the sodium metal and the water.

5   Repeat this reaction with water, using a piece of potassium instead of sodium.

B   You may carry out this part of the experiment for yourself.

YOU MUST WEAR YOUR SAFETY SPECTACLES.

Your teacher will cut a small piece of lithium for you. Add it to a small amount of water in the bottom of a beaker. Cover the beaker with a gauze or a sheet of glass. Note what happens. When the reaction is over, add a piece of universal indicator paper to the solution.

What happened

You should have been able to see the following:

	Lithium	Sodium	Potassium
hardness	Hard to cut (about the same as cheese)	Fairly difficult to cut (about the same as cold butter)	Fairly easy to cut (about the same as soft butter)
reaction with air	Burns, after strong heating for a few minutes	Burns, after strong heating for about half a minute	Burns at once if heated strongly
reaction with chlorine	Burns. Produces clouds of smoke	Burns quite easily. Produces clouds of smoke	Burns very easily. Produces clouds of smoke
reaction with water	Moves about on the surface. Solution is alkaline	Moves about on the surface. Sometimes the gas produced catches fire. Solution is alkaline	Moves about on the surface. The gas produced always catches fire. Solution is alkaline

Table 3.6

What we can decide

You already know from Section 1 (Unit 3) that there is some similarity between these elements. First of all, they are all metals. you can now see why they are kept in oil – they react so violently with water that they have to be kept away from it. The easiest way to do this is to surround them with something with which they will not react, such as oil. Nevertheless, rubidium and caesium are so reactive that we do not normally keep them in schools. However, we may be able to find out what rubidium and caesium are like from what we have seen about the first three members of the group.

You can see from Table 3.6 that lithium, sodium and potassium are similar, but that they are not the same. As we go down the group, the elements become softer, and more reactive (with air, chlorine and water). Rubidium and caesium follow this trend – and so caesium is the most reactive of all the alkali metals. We can summarise this as follows:

		hardness	reactivity
down the group	lithium (Li) sodium (Na) potassium (K) rubidium (Rb) caesium (Cs)	becoming softer	becoming more reactive

We know that elements in one group in the Periodic Table (the inert gases) are similar to each other in the way they behave chemically. (The group 0 elements are similar to each other in **not** reacting chemically!) Now we have seen that the elements in another group (the alkali metals) are also similar to each other in the way they behave chemically. Perhaps it is true of the whole of the Periodic Table that the elements in the same group are similar to each other in their chemical properties. We can find out by looking at the behaviour of some of the elements in the remaining groups.

The Group 2 elements (the 'alkaline earth metals')

beryllium	(Be)
magnesium	(Mg)
calcium	(Ca)
strontium	(Sr)
barium	(Ba)

You also know quite a bit about the Group 2 elements already. You know that, like the Group 1 elements, they are all metals. So, for instance, they might be expected to react with acids making salts and the element hydrogen in the same way as Group 1 elements. The Group 1 elements react very violently with acids, but the Group 2 elements are in fact slightly less reactive. You have seen, for example how

one of the Group 2 elements, magnesium, reacts with an acid to form a salt and hydrogen. This reaction is fairly rapid, but it is gentle enough to be carried out safely in a school laboratory.

You also know that magnesium and calcium, when cleaned, will react with the air when heated to form a basic oxide. You carried out these reactions in Experiment 1.11. The other Group 2 elements are like magnesium and calcium in also having a dull protective layer on their surface. However, the metals get more and more reactive as we go down the group, and so this layer becomes less and less protective. Barium is so reactive, and its covering layer is so helpless to stop it reacting, that if we take some finely divided barium metal and place it in the air, it will burst into flames without being heated.

So, it seems that for the Group 2 elements, as for the

Group 1 elements, the behaviour of the members of the group is similar, but not identical. We can see whether this is true for the behaviour of these elements in general, by looking at another reaction – that with water.

From what you know so far, you might expect that the Group 2 elements will, like the alkali metals, react with water, but less violently. We can see whether or not this is true by seeing how two of the Group 2 elements, magnesium and calcium, react with water.

EXPERIMENT 3.2
The reaction of Group 2 elements with water

You will need the following: magnesium ribbon (about 5 cm), calcium turnings, sandpaper, beakers, test-tubes, filter-funnels, universal indicator paper.

What to do

YOU MUST WEAR YOUR SAFETY SPECTACLES.

1   Take a calcium turning, and a length of magnesium ribbon, and clean both of them carefully with a piece of sandpaper.

2   Take the piece of calcium and drop it into a beaker which is two-thirds full of water, in which you have previously placed an upturned test-tube which is itself full of water.

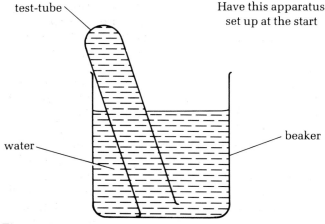

Have this apparatus set up at the start

Fig. 3.12

3   You will see that the calcium reacts straight away, and that a gas is given off. At the same time, the solution becomes cloudy. Now take a filter-funnel, and place it over the piece of calcium in the water. Move the test-tube in the beaker so that it is sitting over the narrow end of the filter-funnel, collecting the gas which is being given off by the reaction.

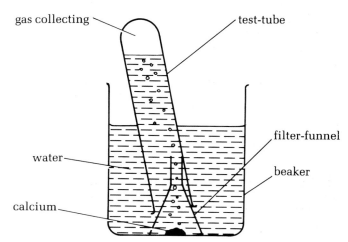

Fig. 3.13

4   When the test-tube is full of gas, test to see whether the gas is hydrogen. You learned how to test a gas to see if it is hydrogen in Section 1 (Experiment 1.12, p. 32). Test the solution which is left in the beaker with a piece of universal indicator paper.

5   Repeat the above, using a clean beaker and fresh water, with the length of magnesium ribbon in place of the calcium. You will see that if a reaction is happening, it is very slow. You will need to leave the apparatus for at least 1 week before any noticeable change takes place.

What happened

You should have been able to see that the calcium reacted with water to give hydrogen gas, and an alkaline solution. The magnesium reacted only very slowly with water, so slowly that there may not have been enough hydrogen formed at the end of 1 week to allow you to test it, and the solution may not have seemed appreciably alkaline.

What we can decide

The last reaction shows us that calcium, in general, reacts more rapidly than does magnesium. We can summarise what we know about the Group 2 elements in the following table.

	Reaction with air	Reaction with water
beryllium		—
magnesium	all have protective layer	reacts very slowly with cold water
calcium	all burn brightly when heated	reacts reasonably quickly with cold water
strontium		—
barium	ignites in air if finely divided	—

Table 3.7

Like the alkali metals, the Group 2 elements are similar to each other in the way they behave chemically, but not identical.

down the group

beryllium (Be)
magnesium (Mg)
calcium (Ca)
strontium (Sr)
barium (Ba)

becoming more reactive

The Group 7 elements (the 'halogens')

fluorine   (F)
chlorine   (Cl)
bromine   (Br)
iodine   (I)
astatine   (At)

The last two groups of elements were all metals. You saw that the elements in each group were similar to each other. Now we can switch to the other end of the Table to look at a group of elements which are non-metals. Does the same apply in this part of the Table? Are the elements similar to each other?

You saw what chlorine, bromine and iodine look like in Experiment 1.9. The appearance of all the 'halogens' is as follows:

fluorine – a faintly yellow gas
chlorine – a green/yellow gas
bromine – a red liquid/gas
iodine   – a black/purple solid

Like the alkali metals, the Group 7 elements are very reactive. Fluorine is so reactive that it even eats its way through glass apparatus! We need to have very special apparatus to handle fluorine, and for this reason we never keep it in school laboratories. However, as you will soon see, we can find out quite a bit about fluorine by looking at the other elements in its group. Astatine, at the other end of the group, is also an element which we have to do a lot of guessing about. It is one of those elements which, as you will learn in the next unit, have atoms which are very unstable. In fact, we cannot really get hold of enough astatine in one place at one time to find out much about it. But again, thanks to the Periodic Table, we can discover quite a lot about astatine too, without ever having seen it.

You know that chlorine will combine directly with metals like iron to form salts. Since the other Group 7 elements are also non-metals, they will behave in a similar way. Since they are so reactive, we almost always find the Group 7 elements combined with metals in this way. In contrast to fluorine and astatine, then, the other members of the group (chlorine, bromine and iodine) are very common in nature, and are an important part of the chemical world. Because they form salts so easily, the Group 7 elements have been given the name the 'halogens'. 'Halogen' is the Greek word which means 'salt-maker'.

▶ EXPERIMENTS 3.3 (p. 130) AND 3.4 (p. 131)

EXPERIMENT 3.3
Comparing the behaviour of chlorine and bromine

Your teacher will show you these reactions

The following will be needed: chlorine generator, bromine, iron wool, test-tube with hole at the end, 2 boiling-tubes, 1 test-tube and bung, universal indicator solution.

What to do

YOU WILL BE SHOWN THIS EXPERIMENT BY YOUR TEACHER. IT MUST BE CARRIED OUT IN A FUME-CUPBOARD.

1   Pass chlorine into some water in a boiling-tube. Add universal indicator solution.

2   Add a drop of bromine to a test-tube half filled with water. Insert the bung and shake vigorously. Add universal indicator solution.

3   Pass chlorine over heated iron wool as shown below, allowing pupils to observe whether a reaction has taken place (Fig. 3.14).

4   Pass bromine over heated iron wool in a test-tube, as shown, again allowing pupils to observe what happens. The Bunsen flame need not be applied directly to the bromine (Fig. 3.15).

What happened

Both chlorine and bromine dissolve in water. In each case, the solution which results has some of the colour of the halogen itself, and is slightly acidic.

Chlorine reacts easily with iron. The iron glows red hot because of the heat which is being given out by the reaction. Bromine also reacts with iron, but not as easily as chlorine. It is necessary to heat the iron wool all the time in the case of bromine, or the reaction will stop.

What we can decide

Chlorine and bromine are similar in the way they behave chemically, but not identical. Chlorine is the more reactive of the two elements, which suggests that iodine will be less reactive than bromine if there is a trend in reactivity which extends throughout the group (we already know that fluorine is extremely reactive).

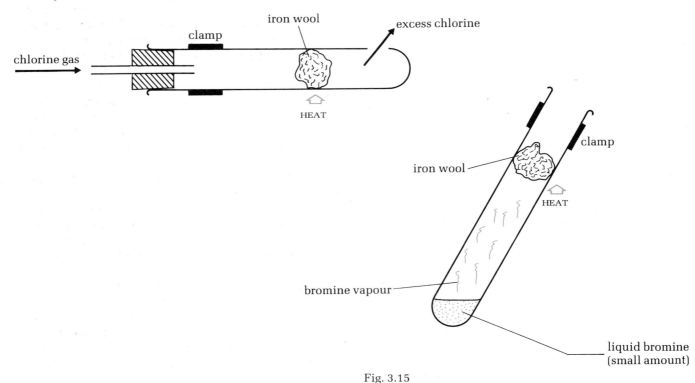

Fig. 3.15

EXPERIMENT 3.4
The behaviour of iodine

You will need the following: 2 crystals of iodine, iron wool, test-tube and bung, boiling-tube, universal indicator paper.

What to do

YOU MUST WEAR YOUR SAFETY SPECTACLES.

1 Place a small crystal of iodine in a test-tube. Add cold water, insert the bung and shake. Is the iodine soluble?

2 Remove the bung and heat the water carefully. Will the iodine crystal dissolve now? If it does, test the solution with universal indicator paper.

3 Pass iodine vapour over heated iron wool, using the same apparatus that your teacher used for the reaction between iron wool and bromine. **Use one crystal of iodine only**. You may need to heat the

iodine crystal **gently** to make it vaporise. Be careful not to heat so strongly that the purple vapour escapes from the tube. Does the iodine react with iron? How easily does it react?

What happened

You should have been able to see that iodine dissolves in water only with great difficulty. The solution which it forms is neutral. Iodine does react with heated iron wool, but less easily than bromine.

What we can decide

The reactivity of iodine fits in with the trend in reactivity within the halogen group of elements. It is less reactive than bromine, although its reactions are similar.

For both the groups of metals which we have looked at, the more reactive elements were those lower down in the group. For the halogens, the trend is in the opposite direction – the more reactive elements are at the top of the group:

		State	Reactivity
down the group	fluorine (F)	gas	
	chlorine (Cl)	gas	becoming
	bromine (Br)	liquid	*less*
	iodine (I)	solid	reactive

So if we now think of the Periodic Table as a whole, we can see that the general rule is that elements which are in the same group (and which therefore have the same number of electrons in their outermost shell) are similar to each other. This is true for both groups of metals and groups of non-metals.

For metals, the strength of reaction increases the further down the group the element is. For non-metals, it works the other way round – the higher up the group an element is, the more reactive it will be. Another way of putting this is to say that those elements which are the most strongly metallic are in the bottom left-hand corner of the Periodic Table. Those elements which are the most strongly non-metallic are in the top right-hand corner.

Suppose now that we consider the changes in chemical behaviour which there would be as we went **across** the Table instead of down it. The horizontal rows in the Periodic Table are called PERIODS. So the first period is Li → Ne, the second is the row Na → Ar,

and so on. We now come to the reason for the name of the Periodic Table as a whole. The elements are placed in the Table in order of their atomic number. When we do this we discover that similar elements appear at regular intervals. For instance, every eighth element is an alkali metal, or an alkaline earth metal, or a halogen. We say that the properties of the elements are **periodic** – hence the name Periodic Table.

So a period in the Table is the row of elements which take us from one type of element, through all the other types, until we get back to an element which is of the same type as the one where we started. If we go across a period in the Table, we see all the different types of element which there are.

If you look at Fig. 3.16, you can see why it is that the line which divides the metals from the non-metals is like a series of steps. Since the most strongly metallic elements are at the bottom left, and the most strongly non-metallic are at the top right, the two effects peter out along a line which runs diagonally down the table, from top left to bottom right. (Another consequence of this is that in the groups of elements in the centre of the Table, there must be both metallic and non-metallic elements. But we shall come to this later.) A good way to imagine the metallic and non-metallic nature of the elements in the Periodic Table is as being two hills, with a valley in between (Fig. 3.17).

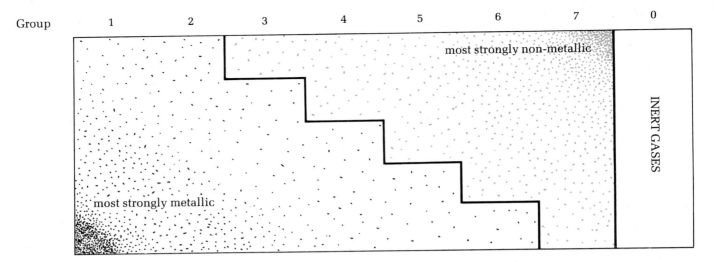

Fig. 3.16 *Simplified form of the Periodic Table (not showing transition elements), showing gradation of metallic and non-metallic behaviour*

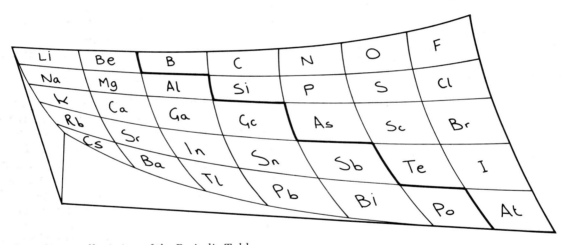

Fig. 3.17 *The 'silicon valley' view of the Periodic Table*

Suppose we decided to examine the second period – that from sodium to chlorine. We start with an element which is strongly metallic, move on to less strongly metallic elements progressively in magnesium and aluminium, come to a weakly non-metallic element (silicon), followed by increasingly strongly non-metallic elements in phosphorus and sulphur, before we come to a strongly non-metallic element (chlorine) at the end of the period. You could describe the nature of the path across **any** of the periods, using Fig. 3.16.

The second period Na, Mg, Al, Si, P, S, Cl

Since we know where each of the elements in the second period stands as far as being a metal or non-metal is concerned, we ought to a large extent to be able to predict their properties. Therefore we ought to be able to predict what changes in chemical behaviour there will be on going across the period from sodium to chlorine.

Before we do this, it will be useful to remind ourselves of what was said earlier about what acids, alkalis and water are made up of. You will find it helpful to go back now and read the paragraphs in Unit 1.3 which deal with this matter (pp. 32–35).

An acid is made up of H^+ cations, and anions containing a non-metal and oxygen (or in some cases, a non-metal only). We will use the symbol nM to stand for any non-metal in general. Then we can say that an acid is made up from:

H^+ cations
and $(nM{-}O)^-$ anions $\quad$ + water $\Big\}$ an acid

An alkali is made up of OH^- anions, and metal cations. If we use the symbol M to represent any metal in general, then we can write an alkali as:

M^+ cations
and $(O{-}H)^-$ anions $\quad$ + water $\Big\}$ an alkali

We know that water is mostly H_2O molecules, but that it is split up to a slight extent into:

H^+ cations
and $(O{-}H)^-$ anions $\Big\}$ water

When a metal reacts with another chemical, we know that the metal forms M^+ cations. So we can say that when hydrogen forms H^+ ions, it is behaving as if it were a metal. If we put two metals in competition to behave as metals, the one that is a stronger metal will win. It will form cations. So a metal could react with something which already contains H^+ ions **if it is a stronger metal than hydrogen**. The stronger metal wins the fight to behave as a metal, and makes the weaker metal (hydrogen) give up its place. The hydrogen is DISPLACED, as hydrogen gas. If a metal reacts with an acid,

metal
$\underbrace{H^+ \quad \text{and} \quad (nM{-}O)^-}_{\text{acid}} \longrightarrow \overbrace{M^+ \quad \text{and} \quad (nM{-}O)^-}^{\text{salt}}$
$\downarrow$
hydrogen (gas)
$\downarrow$

the products are a salt and hydrogen gas. If a metal reacts with water,

metal
$\underbrace{H^+ \quad \text{and} \quad (O{-}H)^-}_{\text{water}} \longrightarrow \overbrace{M^+ \quad \text{and} \quad (O{-}H)^-}^{\text{alkali}}$
$\downarrow$
hydrogen (gas)
$\downarrow$

the products are an alkali and hydrogen gas. You will learn which metals are stronger metals than hydrogen in Section 4 (Unit 4.1) A metal cannot replace the hydrogen in an alkali, because there the hydrogen is behaving as if it were a non-metal and not a metal. **So a metal does not react with an alkali as such**, although it can of course react with the water which is present with a solution of an alkali.

Similarly, **a non-metal will not react with an acid as such**, but only with the water that there is always present when we have an acid. But a non-metal will react with an alkali, or with water by replacing the hydrogen **in the hydroxide ion** (which is behaving as

if it were a non-metal). If we react a non-metal with an alkali,

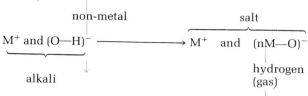

the products are a salt and hydrogen gas. If a non-metal reacts with water,

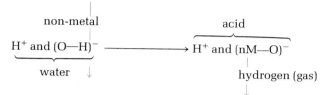

the products are an acid and hydrogen gas. We can summarise the above in the following word-equations:

metal + water $\longrightarrow$ alkali + hydrogen
metal + acid $\longrightarrow$ salt + hydrogen
metal + alkali $\longrightarrow$ NO REACTION (except with water present)

non-metal + water $\longrightarrow$ acid + hydrogen
non-metal + acid $\longrightarrow$ NO REACTION (except with water present)
non-metal + alkali $\longrightarrow$ salt + hydrogen

One further thing needs to be mentioned. You will notice that if a metal reacts with an alkali, it reacts with the water present – making more alkali. But there is plenty of alkali there in the solution at the beginning. It is a general rule in chemistry that if you already have one of the products of a reaction, it slows down the reaction that might have happened. In a similar way, any reaction between a non-metal and the water in a solution of an acid is slowed down by the presence of an acid. So metals react less violently with alkalis than they do with water on its own, and non-metals react less violently with acids than they do with water on its own.

It is also a general rule in chemistry that if one of the products of a reaction is taken away as soon as it is made, then it boosts the speed of the reaction. When a metal reacts with an acid, it can also react with the water present in the acid. The product of that reaction is an alkali – which is immediately taken away by reaction with the acid present. So the reaction with water is made quicker by the presence of the acid. We can therefore expect a metal to react more violently with an acid than it does with water on its own. The same applies to the reaction of a non-metal with an alkali – the reaction with the water present which is also going on at the same time is boosted by the alkali. So we can expect a non-metal to react more violently with an alkali than it would with water on its own.

▶ PROJECT 3.2 (p. 134)

PROJECT 3.2
Predicting the chemical properties of the elements in the period Na–Cl

You know that sodium, magnesium, and aluminium are metals and that silicon phosphorus, sulphur and chlorine are non-metals.

You know the way the strength of metallic and non-metallic behaviour of elements varies as we go across a period in the Table.

You know the general properties of metals and of non-metals, and you know the general properties of ionic and molecular compounds.

You know how metals and non-metals react with water, acids and alkalis.

Use this knowledge to answer the following questions for all the elements in the period Na–Cl:

1   How will they react with water, and what will the products of this reaction be?

2   How will they react with acids, and what will the products be?

3   How will they react with alkalis, and what will the products be?

4   With which other type of element (i.e. metals or non-metals, or both) will they form compounds?

5   Will the compounds formed with oxygen be ionic or molecular? For each element decide whether you expect its oxide to be a solid, a liquid or a gas, and whether it will be acidic or basic in nature.

6   Decide whether the chlorides of the elements will be ionic or molecular, and whether they will be solids, liquids or gases. Which of the chlorides do you expect to be soluble in water, and which do you expect to be soluble in ethanol? (Generally, molecular compounds are soluble in ethanol but ionic compounds are not.)

7   Decide whether the hydrides of the elements (compounds between the element and hydrogen) will be ionic or molecular, and whether they will be solids, liquids or gases. Ionic hydrides react with water to give an alkali and hydrogen gas. Molecular hydrides react with water to give acids. Decide which of the hydrides of the elements in the second period will react with water to give alkalis, and which will give acids.

For each of these properties, set out your answers in note form on a chart, of which the one below can be the start.

You now have a **theoretical** chart of the properties of the elements in the second period, and those of some of their compounds. Of the reactions in this chart, you have already seen several for yourself. For instance, you have seen the reactions of sodium and chlorine with water, the reaction between magnesium and dilute hydrochloric acid, the reactions of sodium, magnesium and sulphur with the oxygen of the air to form the oxide, and the nature of the oxides formed.

A   The elements

1   Reaction with water   Na   Mg   Al | Si   P   S   Cl

$\underrightarrow{\text{give alkali + hydrogen}}$ | $\underleftarrow{\text{give acid + hydrogen}}$
decreasing reactivity | decreasing reactivity

2   Reaction with acids

   etc.

B   Oxides of the elements

   etc.

C   Chlorides of the elements

   etc.

D   Hydrides of the elements

   etc.

EXPERIMENT 3.5
Further reactions of the elements in the period Na—Cl

If desired, the following reactions can now be carried out.

A   As demonstrations by the teacher

1   The reaction between magnesium and steam.
WEAR SAFETY SPECTACLES. USE A SAFETY SCREEN.

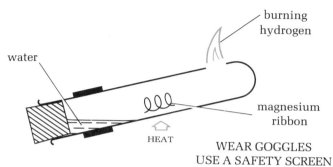

Fig. 3.18

2   The reaction between cleaned aluminium and dilute hydrochloric acid, and between cleaned aluminium and oxygen. The nature of the oxide.

Clean a small piece of aluminium foil with a piece of cotton wool soaked in mercury(II) chloride solution (A POISON). The reaction in air is spontaneous.

3   The reaction between red phosphorus and oxygen. The nature of the oxide.

B   As class experiments
YOU MUST WEAR YOUR SAFETY SPECTACLES

1   The reaction between magnesium and dilute sodium hydroxide solution, and between aluminium and dilute sodium hydroxide solution. Discover the nature of any gas which is given off.

You will see that some of the properties of the elements and their compounds do not fit into the theoretical pattern which you have worked out in Project 3.2. On page 136 is the chart of the actual properties of the elements in the period Na—Cl, and of those of their compounds.

Those properties which do not fit in with the theoretical pattern have been indicated by boxes. You will see that all these boxes lie along the dividing line between metals and non-metals.

The properties which do not fit are those which show aluminium to be not completely metallic (they are the properties which would be expected if it were a non-metal), and those which show silicon to be not completely non-metallic (they show that it has some metallic properties).

Aluminium

1. It reacts vigorously with alkalis giving a salt (called an ALUMINATE) and hydrogen.
2. The oxide of aluminium is both basic and acidic. It shows its basic nature by reacting with acids to give aluminium salts (containing the aluminium cation), and it shows its acidic nature by reacting with alkalis to give ALUMINATE salts (in which aluminium is combined with oxygen in an anion). An oxide which is both basic and acidic is called AMPHOTERIC.
3. The chloride of aluminium takes two forms. The hydrated (containing water) chloride is ionic, a solid and soluble in water. The anhydrous (containing no water) chloride is molecular.
4. The hydride of aluminium is molecular, a gas, and it reacts with water giving acids.

Silicon

1. Silicon does not form compounds by reacting with metals. It will form compounds only with non-metals.
2. The oxide of silicon is a solid (it is, however, molecular and not ionic).

These actual properties of some of the elements in the period Na—Cl show that we cannot simply say that all the elements up to and including aluminium are metals and that all the others are non-metals. The elements in the middle show some properties which are metallic and some which are non-metallic. Aluminium is metallic in most of its properties, but has a few which are non-metallic. Silicon is non-metallic in most of its properties, but has a few which are metallic.

However, we have seen that the properties of elements are periodic, and that the arrangement of the electrons in the outer shells of atoms is also periodic. So it seems that there is a direct link between the arrangement of the electrons in an atom, and the properties of an element. We shall investigate this link in the next unit.

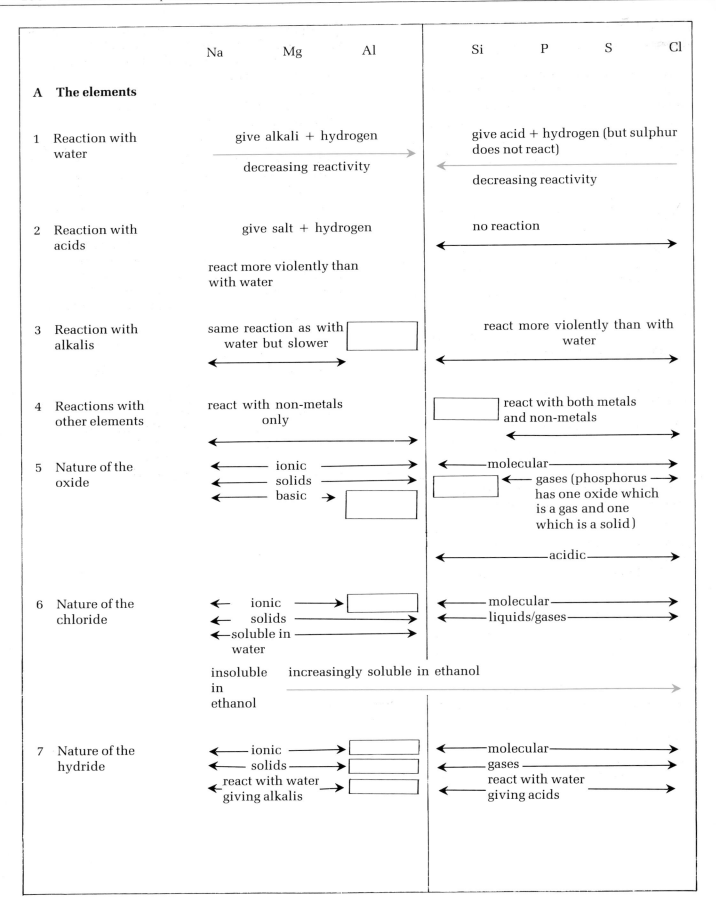

UNIT 3.1
Summary and learning

1   At the centre of an atom is the nucleus. The nucleus is tiny compared to the atom as a whole, but it contains nearly all the mass of the atom.

2   We can think of atoms as being made from three particles – the proton, the neutron and the electron. You should remember the mass and the charge of these particles relative to each other.

3   The nucleus in an atom is made up of neutrons and protons. The electrons in an atom surround the nucleus.

4   The atomic number of an element is the number of protons contained in its nucleus. It is also equal to the number of electrons which surround the nucleus. It is the atomic number which tells us which element we have.

5   The mass number of an atom is the sum of the number of neutrons and the number of protons in its nucleus.

6   We can symbolise any isotope of any element in the following way:

$${}^{A}_{Z}X$$ where A = the mass number
X = the symbol of the element
and Z = the atomic number

7   You should remember the names and the symbols for the first 20 elements, and those of the other elements which are listed on page 121.

8   The electrons in an atom can be thought of as being in spherical 'shells' around the nucleus. The maximum numbers of electrons which are allowed into the different shells are as follows:

Shell:	1	2	3
Maximum number of electrons:	2	8	8

9   You should be able to work out the arrangement of the electrons in the atom of any of the first 18 elements.

10   The Periodic Table lists the elements in order of their atomic numbers. The vertical columns are called groups of elements, and the horizontal rows are called periods of elements.

11   Elements in the same group in the Periodic Table have the same number of electrons in their outermost shell.

12   Elements in the same group in the Periodic Table have similar chemical properties. You should remember the general properties and the trends within the groups for:
   Group 1   the alkali metals
   Group 2   the alkaline earth elements
   Group 7   the halogens

13   You should remember why the Periodic Table is so called. A period in the Periodic Table takes us from one type of element through all the other types of element. You should remember the nature of the changes which we see when we go across the period Na–Cl.

14   The properties of an element are linked to the arrangement of the electrons in its atom, and particularly to the number of electrons in the outermost shell. This number repeats itself periodically if we list the elements in order of their atomic number.

15   You have learnt the meaning of these words:

particle accelerator	ionisation energy
nucleus	ion
proton	group
neutron	period
atomic number	transition element
mass number	displaced
isotope	aluminate
Periodic Table	amphoteric

UNIT 3.2 *The nucleus inside atoms*

In this unit, we will look at the nucleus of the atom more closely.

You already know that the nucleus of an atom is made up of protons and neutrons. The number of protons in a nucleus tells us which element we have. The number of neutrons tells us which isotope of the element we have.

Remember that different isotopes of the same element are only different because their nuclei contain a different number of neutrons. For example, there are two isotopes of the element chlorine. These are

$^{35}_{17}Cl$ and $^{37}_{17}Cl$

^{35}Cl has 17 protons and 18 neutrons in its nucleus. It has 17 electrons, arranged 2,8,7.
^{37}Cl has 17 protons and 20 neutrons in its nucleus. It has 17 electrons, arranged 2,8,7.

Because the arrangement of electrons is identical, the chemical properties of the two isotopes are identical. The only difference between them is their mass number. The chlorine we make in the laboratory has, roughly, 3 atoms of ^{35}Cl to every atom of ^{37}Cl.

Many other elements have more than one isotope. For instance, oxygen has the following:

Isotope	Relative amount
^{16}O	99.76%
^{17}O	0.04%
^{18}O	0.20%

Even hydrogen has three isotopes:

Isotope	Relative amount
^{1}H	99.985%
^{2}H ('deuterium')	0.015%
^{3}H ('tritium')	1 part in 10^{17}

So when we deal with a chemical element, we are usually dealing with a mixture of its different isotopes. While this makes no difference to the **chemical** properties which we see, it does make a difference to the physical properties, and particularly of course to the mass (or weight) of the element. The early chemists such as Dalton had no idea that isotopes might exist. So when they measured the weights of chemicals which reacted together, they did not realise that the weights which they calculated for elements were in fact average weights due to the existence of more than one type of atom of the same element.

Relative atomic masses, and early forms of the Periodic Table

Dalton carried out many experiments on the weights of elements which react together, as we have seen. From his results, he calculated the weights of the atoms of the elements relative to the weight of the atom of the lightest element, hydrogen. Nowadays we don't use the phrase 'atomic weights' to describe these values, as Dalton did. It is more correct to call them 'relative atomic masses'.

For many elements, the relative atomic mass which Dalton and the other chemists found was very close to a whole number. Even for an element such as oxygen, the percentage of atoms which are those of the second and third isotope is so small that the relative atomic mass would still be very close to a whole number. But for some elements, such as chlorine, the relative atomic mass was definitely **not** a whole number. The average mass of an atom of chlorine is the average weight of three atoms of ^{35}Cl and one of ^{37}Cl (four atoms in total):

$$\frac{(3 \times 35) + (1 \times 37)}{4} = \frac{105 + 37}{4} = \frac{142}{4} = 35.5$$

This was the value for the relative atomic mass of chlorine which the early chemists found by doing experiments.

You know that the Periodic Table gives the elements in order of their atomic number. But the early scientists only knew about relative atomic masses. As far as they knew, the relative atomic mass was the most basic property of an atom. As time went on, and more was discovered about the properties of more elements, it became clear that some elements were like others. At the same time, accurate values for relative atomic masses had been found by scientists such as Cannizzaro and Berzelius. Could atoms be sorted out into different types?

In 1863, an English chemist called John Newlands hit on the idea of writing down all the elements in order of their relative atomic mass. When he did this he discovered a pattern – periodicity. What he had hit upon was an early form of the Periodic Table – but one based on relative atomic masses, not on atomic numbers. Such a table is bound to be imperfect because, for instance, the order of relative atomic masses is not always the same as the order of atomic numbers. For example, tellurium (element number 82) has a relative atomic mass of 127.6 whereas iodine (element number 83) has a relative atomic mass of

126.9. According to relative atomic masses, iodine comes first. According to atomic numbers, tellurium comes first.

In 1871, a Russian chemist called Mendeleev drew up a full Periodic Table of the elements based on relative atomic masses, but he had the good sense to place tellurium and iodine in the order which made them fit in the table, and also to leave spaces where it seemed that there was a missing element. For instance, in 1871, element 32 (germanium) had not been discovered. So after gallium, the next known element was arsenic, followed by selenium and then bromine. If these are put down in order, there is a mis-match with elements above them.

Al   Si   P   S   Cl
Ga   As   Se   Br

Arsenic is similar to phosphorus (not silicon), selenium is like sulphur (not phosphorus) and bromine is like chlorine (not sulphur). Mendeleev realised that there must have been a missing element, and so he left a space for it. The other elements then fit into their proper groups:

Al	Si	P	S	Cl
Ga	↑ missing element	As	Se	Br

Mendeleev knew that elements in the same group had similar properties, so he could **predict** what the properties of the missing element should be. When the German scientist Winkler discovered a new element in 1886, he found that it had the properties which Mendeleev had predicted for the missing element, almost exactly. What is more, its relative atomic mass placed it between gallium and arsenic!!

Mendeleev's predictions about the missing element (made in 1871)	What Winkler found out about the new element (in 1886)
It will be a grey metal	It is a grey metal
It will have a high melting point	Its melting point is 958°C
It will have an amphoteric oxide	It has an amphoteric oxide
Its relative atomic mass will be 72	It relative atomic mass is 72.6

Table 3.8

Perhaps it was in order to show that not only Russian scientists were clever like 'I told you so' Mendeleev, that Winkler called the element he discovered after his own country – and gave it the name 'germanium'. If so, others had the same idea. Mendeleev in fact predicted several undiscovered elements, and two others were called after their native country by the

scientists who discovered them. Scandium (after Scandinavia) was discovered by a Swedish chemist, and gallium (after 'Gaul', the ancient name for France) was discovered by a French chemist.

Mendeleev's table was therefore the first accurate way of sorting out the chemical elements into their different types. However, it was still not perfect, because it was based on relative atomic masses, which meant that some elements had to be placed in reverse order to give the best fit (for example, tellurium and iodine). When the structure of the atom was worked out, scientists realised that atomic number was a more basic quality of an element than its relative atomic mass. The modern form of the Periodic Table was produced, when the elements were listed in order of their atomic number. The Periodic Table then became a perfect fit, as we have seen.

But this does not mean that relative atomic masses are an idea which can be thrown away, because they give us information about the actual masses of elements which we will meet in chemical reactions. Instead of using hydrogen as the standard mass we now use the mass of the most common isotope of carbon, ^{12}C. **The relative atomic mass of an element is its mass relative to 1/12 of the mass of an atom of ^{12}C.** It is **the average mass of the isotopes** in the mixture of isotopes which we find for that element.

TOPIC 3.2.2

Atoms which split up and atoms which do not

In the last topic, you saw that different isotopes of the same element have the same chemical properties. That is because chemical properties are due to the number of electrons in the outermost shell of an atom. Different isotopes of the same element have the same number of electrons, so they have the same number of electrons in their outermost shell, so they have the same chemical properties.

But different isotopes of the same element have different numbers of neutrons in their nuclei – so they have different mass numbers. So when the early chemists who were trying to sort the elements out into their different types used the relative atomic masses of elements, their results were sometimes confused because of isotopes. If an element had more than one isotope, the same chemical behaviour was coming from two (or more) atoms with different masses. So the relative atomic masses of elements and their properties do not always fit exactly with each other, as you have seen.

If different isotopes of the same element are identical **chemically**, how are they different? Well, since it is their nuclei that are different, we can expect that their nuclear behaviour will be different. But what do we mean by the 'nuclear' behaviour of an isotope?

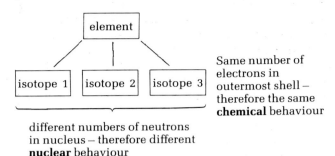

different numbers of neutrons in nucleus – therefore different **nuclear** behaviour

You know that some elements are 'radioactive' – that is, they give off 'radiations'. You have seen that one type of radiation which is given out by radioactive elements is called α–radiation ('alpha'–radiation). You also know that α–radiation is made up of particles.

There are two other main types of radiation: β-radiation ('beta'-radiation) and γ-radiation ('gamma'-radiation). (Alpha, beta and gamma are the first three letters in the Greek alphabet.) You will learn more about radiation shortly.

All three types of radiation are caused by the same thing – the breaking up of **the nucleus** of an atom. This happens whenever it is possible for a particular nucleus to make itself more stable by giving out one or more of the different types of radiation. If a particular nucleus is already 'stable', it does not need to split apart, and it is not radioactive.

stable nucleus   NOT RADIOACTIVE

unstable nucleus → another nucleus + α, β or γ radiation

We say that unstable nuclei DECAY to give more stable ones. When the radiation given out is α-radiation, we call the process α-DECAY. In the same way, we talk about β-DECAY and γ-DECAY.

In α- and β-decay, the new nucleus which is formed is that of a different element. In γ-decay, the nucleus just gets rid of excess energy, but does not change in any other way.

But what makes a particular nucleus stable or unstable? Well, it is to do with the balance between the number of protons and neutrons, and with the size of the nucleus. Very heavy nuclei (those with very many neutrons and protons) are always unstable. For smaller nuclei, it is the relative numbers of protons and neutrons which appears to matter most. So we can see that isotopes of the same element might be different from each other as far as their nuclear stability is concerned. They have a different ratio of protons to neutrons. So, for a particular element, some isotopes may have stable nuclei, while other isotopes have unstable nuclei. Of all the isotopes of all the

elements, those with **mass numbers** in the range 50 to 60 are the most stable.

Question

If isotopes of elements with mass numbers between 50 and 60 are the most stable, which elements are these likely to be? How many elements is this?

Why then, do not all other isotopes change into these most stable ones? Why do not only the few elements you have just seen exist? The reason is that there has to be a mechanism by which the more stable nuclei can be reached. That means that some physical process (like losing an α-particle) must exist which will cause the change to happen. Fortunately, there are about 269 isotopes of different elements for which no mechanism exists by which they can decay. So these isotopes can go on existing as if they were stable. This is just as well, because if only a few elements existed it is almost certain that life would not be possible, and none of us would exist either.

We can think of these 269 isotopes which cannot decay as being like hollows on the hillside on either side of a valley. Suppose we rolled some footballs down each slope – most would, naturally, reach the floor of the valley (the position of greatest stability). Others would get caught in the hollows, and would have to stay there because there was no way down.

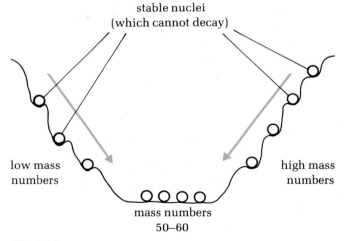

Fig. 3.19

Suppose there was a football at some point on either of the two slopes which was not one of the hollows. It would move to the nearest hollow, where it would stay. This is like the nucleus of an isotope which is radioactive. The nucleus is unstable relative to one of the 269 stable hollows. To move to the nearest hollow, the nucleus must give out radiation. Usually, this is β-radiation.

Once the nucleus has reached a certain size, no more stable hollows exist, and all heavier nuclei are unstable. All isotopes of all the elements heavier than bismuth (atomic number 83) are unstable, and break down by α-decay. If we plot a graph of the stable nuclei, it looks like Fig. 3.20. If an isotope is outside the stable area, it will be radioactive.

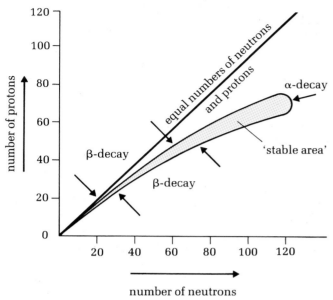

Fig. 3.20

Questions

1   Look at the graph in Fig. 3.20 and answer these questions.

(a) What can we say about the ratio of the number of neutrons to the number of protons in the 'stable area', compared to the ratio 1:1 which is shown by the straight line?

(b) How does this ratio for stable isotopes change as we go to heavier and heavier atoms?

2   Write down what you understand by the word 'isotope'. In your answer you should say what is similar about isotopes of the same element, and what is different about them. You should explain in your own words what we mean by stable isotopes and unstable isotopes.

TOPIC 3.2.3

Energy from nuclear reactions

Suppose we took one of the footballs in a stable hollow in Fig. 3.19 and gave it a kick to dislodge it. Then it would fall down to the next hollow, or if we had disturbed it enough, it might fall all the way down to the valley. When something becomes more stable, energy is given out (the difference between the higher energy, unstable starting point, and the lower energy, stable finishing point).

So we could take very small nuclei, and make them join together and energy would be given out. We would have to FUSE small nuclei together. This process is called NUCLEAR FUSION. On the other hand, we would also get energy out if we took heavy nuclei and split them up into nuclei the size of those in the 'valley' in Fig. 3.19. This process is called NUCLEAR FISSION.

Nuclear fission

Neutrons were discovered in 1932 by the English scientist James Chadwick. Almost straight away scientists started to use them to bombard atoms in order to find out more about their structure. They found that the neutrons were often 'captured' by the nuclei which they hit – swallowed up to form an unstable nucleus. This would then break apart to form much smaller nuclei, and at the same time other particles or radiation would be given out.

It was the German scientist, Hahn, who discovered that the nucleus of the uranium isotope $^{235}_{92}U$ would capture a neutron, and then split into two roughly equal parts. This particular example of nuclear fission is not really special, except for one thing – when the fission happens, more neutrons are formed (Fig. 3.21).

Every time fission happens, some energy is given out. But because neutrons are also produced, each fission can cause another one, two or three to happen. So a CHAIN REACTION is possible. Suppose we arrange matters so that just one of the neutrons is captured by another $^{235}_{92}U$ nucleus. We would simply get a steady

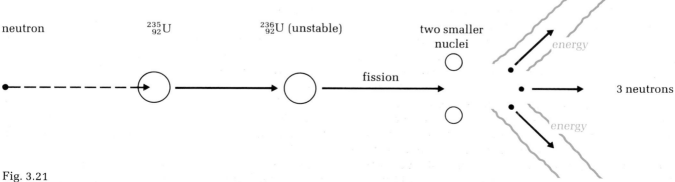

neutron $^{235}_{92}U$ $^{236}_{92}U$ (unstable)   two smaller nuclei   energy   3 neutrons   fission   energy

Fig. 3.21

flow of energy, until all the $^{235}_{92}$U was used up. This is what happens in a nuclear reactor. Two of the three neutrons produced by each fission are absorbed by some material like graphite, before they ever reach another $^{235}_{92}$U nucleus. Rods of graphite (called CONTROL RODS) can be pushed into the part of the reactor where fission is taking place (called the REACTOR CORE), to absorb neutrons and control the nuclear reaction. If necessary, the control rods can be used to absorb all the neutrons, and shut the reaction down completely.

Fig. 3.22 *Control rods in a reactor core*

Naturally occurring uranium is mostly the isotope ^{238}U, and contains only about 1% of ^{235}U.

Nevertheless, some nuclear reactors can use natural uranium, while others have to have as the fuel uranium in which the proportion of ^{235}U has been artificially increased. In a nuclear reactor, energy is given out in the form of heat from the uranium fuel, which is itself in the form of FUEL RODS. So the reactor core gets hot.

The heat from the core is taken away by a flow of carbon-dioxide gas (in the British design of reactor) or by a flow of water (in the design used in the USA). The hot gas or water is then used to generate steam, which in turn drives turbines, which make electricity. Figure 3.23 shows, in simplified form, the way a typical gas-cooled reactor works.

The early forms of nuclear reactor were all of this type – using ^{235}U as the fuel. There are other nuclei, however, which can be used in a similar way, the most important of which is an isotope of plutonium, ^{239}Pu. This isotope can be produced if ^{238}U (which is much more plentiful than ^{235}U) is bombarded with fast-moving neutrons. One source of fast-moving neutrons is ^{239}Pu. So if we use the fission reaction of ^{239}Pu to produce neutrons which then bombard ^{238}U, we can actually create more plutonium than we use! Nuclear reactors which do this have been made, and these are called FAST (because of the speed of the neutrons) -BREEDER (because they make their own fuel) reactors. A fast-breeder reactor makes so much heat that a very efficient conductor of heat, liquid sodium, is used to take it away. The core of a fast-breeder reactor looks like Fig. 3.24.

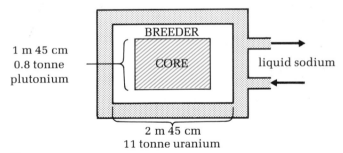

1 m 45 cm
0.8 tonne
plutonium

2 m 45 cm
11 tonne uranium

Fig. 3.24

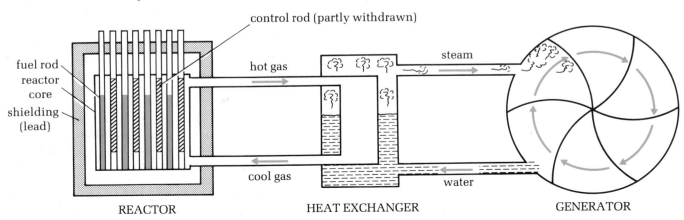

Fig. 3.23

Of course, a fast-breeder reactor does not have an infinite supply of fuel, because the plutonium of the core has to be replaced from time to time, as does the surrounding uranium. However, it can use up to 70% of the uranium atoms in naturally occurring uranium.

The place of nuclear power in fulfilling our energy needs in the coming years was discussed in Section 2, as were the problems and advantages of this way of making energy.

You will have heard about nuclear weapons, and may be wondering how 'the bomb' is related to nuclear reactors which are used for peaceful purposes. We have seen that when a ^{235}U atom splits up, three neutrons are produced. In a nuclear reactor, only one of these is allowed to cause a further nuclear reaction. But imagine for a moment what would happen if for every reaction which happened, three more were started. Very soon indeed, thousands, and then millions of reactions would be happening all at once. Huge amounts of energy would be released in a very short space of time – there would be a massive explosion.

A nuclear bomb is basically the same as a nuclear reactor, but without all the mechanisms for slowing the reaction down. In fact, to make a bomb, all that needs to happen is that more than a certain mass of ^{235}U is all together in one place. This is called the CRITICAL MASS.

Once the critical mass has been reached, an unstoppable chain reaction takes places extremely quickly. Below the critical mass, this simply will not happen, and it is for this reason that 'small' nuclear weapons are not possible. This is one of the factors that makes them so awesome and destructive.

Nuclear fusion

In nuclear fusion, the nuclei of elements with a very low atomic number are fused together to make heavier elements. The most abundant element in the Universe is hydrogen, and it is a nuclear fusion process involving hydrogen which powers stars like our sun.

In the sun, hydrogen nuclei are fusing together all the time to make helium nuclei. Scientists believe that the sun is about 4.5×10^9 years ($4\frac{1}{2}$ thousand million years) old, and that it has about as long again to go before it runs out of hydrogen.

In the same way that the energy from the process of nuclear fission can be harnessed to produce energy for peaceful purposes, so also can the process of nuclear fusion – at least in theory. (Unfortunately it can also be used to make atomic weapons – the 'H-bomb'.) The fusion of hydrogen nuclei will take place only at extremely high temperatures – the temperature of the surface of the sun is about 10^9K (about 1000 million K). Clearly, such a reaction cannot take place in an ordinary laboratory!

We can 'cheat' a little by starting from the isotopes of hydrogen, deuterium and tritium. Each of these is a bigger nucleus than the ^{1}H nucleus, and so we start 'part of the way there'.

$$^2D + {}^3T \rightarrow {}^4He + neutron$$

Even so, the temperature which we need is still about 10^8K (about 100 million K). At this temperature, normal matter cannot exist. This is because the electrons become separated from the nuclei of atoms at such a temperature, and we get what is called a PLASMA. A plasma is made up from nuclei and electrons swirling around independently in a kind of 'soup'. A plasma will of course instantly vaporise any matter it touches.

However, a plasma has one redeeming feature – it is magnetic. What this means is that a plasma can, in theory, be put into a magnetic 'bottle'. In fact, it has been discovered that the best way of controlling a plasma by a magnetic field, is to trap it in a doughnut-shaped ring. Such a ring is called a TORUS.

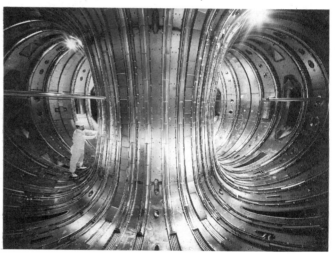

Fig. 3.25 *Inside the JET torus*

Research into the possibilities of fusion reactors is going on in America, Russia and Europe. The European team are working at the Culham Laboratories in Oxfordshire, and their project is called the JET Project – which stands for joint European torus. If all goes well, the JET team will succeed in obtaining power from a fusion reaction in the not too distant future.

Uranium and plutonium for use in fission reactors will eventually run out. Deuterium can be obtained from water, and tritium from the lithium which is found in china-clay (lithium is bombarded with neutrons, and tritium and helium are formed). In the more distant future, it may even be possible to send robot space vehicles to Jupiter or Saturn, where there are huge amounts of deuterium and tritium. The drawbacks of nuclear power from the fission process were mentioned in Section 2. These are that the radioactive by-products last for a long time, and that plutonium is extremely poisonous. Nuclear fusion is likely to suffer from such problems to a far lesser extent.

Fig. 3.26 *China-clay mine in Cornwall – fuel for the future?*

Look back at Fig. 3.19 (p. 140). Energy can be produced when large nuclei split up to form smaller ones, until atomic numbers around that of iron are produced. Alternatively, small nuclei can fuse together to make nuclei for which the atomic numbers are similar to that of iron.

The original element in the Universe was hydrogen, and stars are fuelled by the process of nuclear fusion. So how were elements with atomic numbers greater than that of iron made in the first place? They cannot have been made by the usual process of nuclear fusion, since to go beyond iron would need huge amounts of energy.

The answer is something called a SUPERNOVA. You learned about supernovae, in outline, in Section 2. You will remember that stars behave differently, depending on how big they were to start with. If a star is very big – about ten times the mass of our own sun – then when its core has been turned into iron, it dies. But its death is very spectacular. In less than a second, the core collapses under its own gravity into a superdense ball which rebounds outwards, saturating everything in its way with neutrons. There is a massive explosion – a supernova – which is brighter than a thousand million suns, and the star's outer layers become superheated. The intense flow of neutrons causes the nuclei of atoms to capture very many in one go, before they can disintegrate. In this way elements beyond iron are formed, with uranium and thorium being made in large quantities.

Since elements with larger atomic numbers than iron exist on Earth, it follows that the material which makes up our own solar system was itself the result of

a supernova explosion, which happened 4½ thousand million years ago.

Fig. 3.27 *The 'Crab' nebula is made up of material thrown out into space by a supernova explosion in* AD 1054

TOPIC 3.2.4

What is 'radiation'?

You know that there are three types of radiation, α, β and γ. You also know that when α and β radiation are produced by a nucleus, then a new element is always formed.

You are now going to learn more about the three different types of radiation. You have already seen that radiation can be dangerous, and that one of the problems associated with using nuclear reactions to obtain energy is that the by-products can exist for a long time. But which types of radiation are the most dangerous, and why? That is, exactly how does radiation harm us? What causes some radioactive elements to be longer-lived than others?

How long does it last?

Suppose we think of a collection of atoms of a radioactive element – let's call it element X. Suppose that when X decays, α-particles are given off, and a new element, Y, is produced. Suppose that Y is itself not radioactive. Then the quantity of radiation which we would detect in, say, a period of 10 seconds, depends on the number of atoms of X which decay into Y during those 10 seconds.

$$X \rightarrow Y + radiation$$

For each radioactive nucleus, a certain proportion of the atoms will split up during a given period. This proportion depends on the instability of the nucleus, and it is always the same for that nucleus.

Suppose, then, that we took a sample of a

radioactive element, and that we measured the radiation coming off it. How would the strength of that radiation change as time went on? We can detect and measure the radiation of a sample using a GEIGER–MÜLLER tube, and a counter. In effect, this counts the number of particles of radiation which are being given off.

Suppose that we started with 100 000 atoms of X, and that 1 in 10 of them split up every 10 seconds. Then the number which do so in successive 10 second periods, and therefore the level of radiation being produced, would change as shown in Table 3.9.

You can see that the level of radiation drops as time goes on. The rate at which it drops, however, is not constant. At the start, the rate is dropping quickly. As time goes on, the rate drops ever more slowly. If we were to carry on, we would eventually get to a point where the rate was dropping infinitesimally slowly, as the number of atoms of X becomes exhausted. If we draw a graph of the level of radiation against time, it would look like Fig. 3.28.

Such a curve is called an EXPONENTIAL curve. Theoretically, the point where there is no more of X left is reached only after an infinitely long time. We say that the 'radiation = zero' line is approached EXPONENTIALLY. We get the same type of curve for every radioactive nucleus. So the answer to the question 'how long does radiation last' is, theoretically, 'for

ever'. But in reality, infinitesimally low levels of radiation are always reached, sometimes very quickly. How can we compare different nuclei for their rate of decay? Clearly, we cannot compare the length of time taken for **all** the radiation to die away, since this would be meaningless. But we can compare the length of time take for the radiation to **halve**. We call this time the HALF-LIFE of the radioactive element. Different radioactive elements have different half-lives.

We can find the half-life for our imaginary element, X, from the graph which shows its decay. All we have to do is to find the time take for the radiation level to drop from (say) 10 000 counts per 10 seconds to 5000 counts per 10 seconds. (We could equally well find the time taken for the rate to drop from 8000 to 4000 per 10 seconds. The result would be the same.) You will see that this appears to be just less than 70 seconds.

So after 70 seconds, the level of radiation is half its original value. After 140 seconds, it is ¼ the original. After 210 seconds it has halved again, to ⅛ the original.

Your teacher will now show you an experiment to find the half-life for a real radioactive isotope. In this experiment, the radioactive isotope (an isotope of the element protactinium) first has to be separated from all the other chemicals found with it. The separation technique is called SOLVENT EXTRACTION. We do this

Number of 10 second period	Number of atoms of X at the start of this period	Number of atoms of X which decay during this period (= level of radiation)	Number of atoms of X left at the end of this period
1	100 000	10 000	90 000
2	90 000	9000	81 000
3	81 000	8100	72 900
4	72 900	7290	65 610
5	65 610	6561	59 049
6	59 049	5905	53 144
7	53 144	5314	47 830
8	47 830	4783	43 047
⋮	⋮	⋮	⋮

Table 3.9

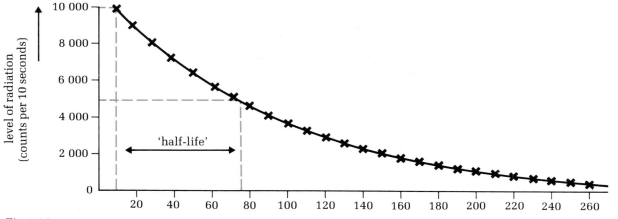

Fig. 3.28

because in the mixture of chemicals we start with, protactinium is being made as quickly as it decays, from other radioactive isotopes. After we have separated it, the protactinium is 'on its own', and we can see how quickly it decays.

EXPERIMENT 3.6
The half-life of ^{234}Pa

Your teacher will show you this experiment

The following will be needed: uranyl nitrate (1 g), 2-methylpentan-4-one (*iso*-butyl methyl ketone), concentrated hydrochloric acid, separating funnel (50 cm³), measuring cylinder, liquid G.M. counter (10 cm³), stopclock.

What to do

THE FOLLOWING SAFETY PRECAUTIONS MUST ALWAYS BE TAKEN WHEN HANDLING RADIOACTIVE MATERIALS:
1. Use only apparatus reserved for work with radioactive substances.
2. Wear disposable polythene gloves at all times.
3. Carry out the work in a large polythene tray which is lined with paper towels.
4. **Never** fill pipettes by mouth.
5. Make adequate provision for the proper disposal of waste which is radioactive.

1   Mix together 7 cm³ concentrated hydrochloric acid and 3 cm³ distilled water.

2   Dissolve the uranyl nitrate in this mixture.

3   Clamp the separating funnel and the G.M. tube in a retort stand.

4   Place about 10 cm³ of 2-methylpentan-4-one in the separating funnel, and add the uranyl nitrate solution. Start the stopclock.

5   Stopper the funnel, and shake for 30 seconds. Allow the phases to separate, and run the lower (aqueous) phase into a beaker.

6   Transfer 5 cm³ of the 2-methylpentan-4-one layer into the liquid counter, and start counting immediately.

7   Count for 10 second periods, with a 10 second wait to note the count and reset the counter. Follow the decay for about 10 minutes.

What happened

The following results are given to help in cases where schools may not possess the necessary apparatus to perform this experiment. They were obtained in an actual experiment.

Time elapsed/ min.s	Counts per 10 s period	Time elapsed/ min. s	Counts per 10 s period
1.35	1931	5.50	204
1.50	1604	6.10	164
2.10	1441	6.30	151
2.30	1227	6.50	127
2.50	974	7.10	115
3.10	854	7.30	99
3.30	718	7.50	66
3.50	553	8.10	55
4.10	474	8.30	63
4.30	387	8.50	43
4.50	343	9.10	53
5.10	294	9.30	52
5.30	258	9.50	35

You can use the results of your teacher's experiment, or those given above, to plot a graph similar to the one in Fig. 3.28. Use this graph to find the half-life of ^{234}Pa.

What we can decide

Your curve shows the decay of ^{234}Pa. This means that the separation of protactinium into the 2-methylpentan-4-one must have been successful. You should find that the half-life of ^{234}Pa is about 72 seconds.

The rate of decay of a radioactive isotope, and therefore its half-life, is related to the proportion of atoms of it that split up in a particular length of time. We can get an idea of the relative stability of different radioactive nuclei by calculating the proportion of atoms that split up in a given time from the value of the half-life (Table 3.10).

Nucleus	Half-life ($t_{1/2}$)	Proportion of atoms that split up in a given time
^{234}Pa	72 seconds	1 in 104 each second
^{234}Th	24 days	1 in 35 each day
^{238}U	4.5×10^9 years	1 in 6.5×10^9 each year
^{234}U	2.5×10^5 years	1 in 3.6×10^5 each year
^{14}C	5760 years	1 in 8309 each year
^{214}Pb	26.8 min	1 in 39 each minute
^{239}Pu	24 360 years	1 in 35 144 each year

Table 3.10

So it is the relative stability of a radioactive nucleus which decides how long-lived it is. We can show this by quoting either the half-life for the element, or the proportion of nuclei which split up in a certain length of time. But as well as the length of time for which a radioactive element lasts, it is the type of radiation which it gives off which decides how dangerous it is.

What are the different types of radiation like?

If we take some uranium, it gives off all three types of radiation. So we can use this to see what the difference between them is. If we take a narrow beam which is made up of α, β and γ radiation mixed together and make it pass through an electric field, we will see the following (Fig. 3.29).

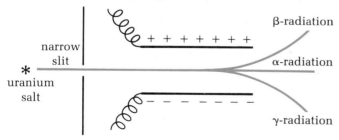

Fig. 3.29

The three forms of radiation behave differently, because they are made up of different things.

α-**particles** are nuclei of an atom of helium. They consist of two protons and two neutrons bound tightly together, with an overall charge of +2. So they are attracted towards the negative pole of an electric field. We represent an α-particle by the symbol $^4_2$He.

β-**particles** are electrons which are moving very

rapidly. Although they are electrons, they **do** come from the nucleus of a radioactive atom, and not from outside the nucleus. Because they are negatively charged, they are attracted to the positive pole.

γ-**rays** are not particles. They have no mass and carry no charge. So they are not attracted to either pole of an electric field. When γ-rays are lost by a nucleus, its mass number and atomic number do not change. So no new element is formed. γ-rays are electromagnetic radiation, like light or radio waves, but with very short wavelength (about 5×10^{-9} m).

What are the biological effects of radiation?

Because of their different natures, the different radiations can have a different effect on any living matter which they might meet. They do damage by interacting with the molecules of the chemicals in the living matter.

The amount of damage which a particular type of radiation can do is dependent on a combination of two factors:

(a) the extent to which the radiation causes ions to form in the chemicals which it passes through, and

(b) the amount of matter which it passes through before stopping.

α-particles produce a great amount of ionisation, but even the most rapidly moving α-particle is stopped by a layer of water just 0.13 mm thick. Even if α-particles strike naked skin, they will penetrate only to a tiny extent. However, other materials will easily stop α-particles, and so any radiation hazard from α-particles can be removed by wearing gloves and other garments. Nevertheless, if any radioactive chemical which gives off α-particles were to be taken **into** the body, it would be extremely dangerous.

β-particles cause less ionisation than α-particles, although they are slightly more penetrating. Even so, they are stopped by a few millimetres of lead. β-particles do not penetrate as far as the internal organs of the body, and the amount of damage which they can do from the outside of the body is therefore limited.

γ-rays cause very little ionisation, but are extremely penetrating. If a person is exposed to γ-rays, then these will penetrate right through the body, affecting internal organs and bones. Even shields of lead several centimetres thick do not stop γ-rays, and so it is clear that the dangers from external exposure to γ-rays are in general much greater than from α-particles or β-particles, although all are dangerous.

The most harmful effect of radiation is the damage which can be done to the DNA molecule in living cells. The structure of a DNA (which is short for 'deoxyribonucleic acid') molecule is shown on p. 18. It is made up of two spirals with cross-links between them. The DNA molecule is the carrier of the blueprint of information for making a whole living organism (such as a human being). If it is damaged, then the blueprint is wrong. Genetic damage of this sort can cause cancers to form. Radiation can cause

  (a) the double spiral to be broken;

  (b) the link between spirals to be broken;

  (c) the joining up of parts of the molecule which should not be joined.

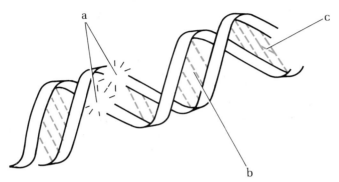

Fig. 3.30

The effect of one damaged DNA molecule can be multiplied millions of times over as the molecule copies itself.

Obviously, the most dangerous radiation is that which is extremely intense, or which affects people for a very long time. Victims of a nuclear bomb will have been exposed to very high levels of all the different forms of radiation mentioned above, together with others, such as neutrons and X-rays. Survivors of the nuclear bombs dropped on Japan at the end of the Second World War have now been discovered to be suffering from a variety of forms of cancer. Such a case, while it must not be forgotten, is different from the level of radiation to which most of us are exposed from day to day. How much radiation do we receive, where does it come from, and how dangerous is it?

▶ PROJECT 3.3

How can radioactivity be useful?

There are many ways in which radioactivity can be useful, in addition to the production of energy by the processes of nuclear fission and nuclear fusion. Briefly, these are as follows:

'Carbon 14 dating'

In the upper levels of the Earth's atmosphere, cosmic rays cause atoms to give up some of their neutrons, which in turn interact with nuclei of nitrogen atoms. The result is that small amounts of a radioactive isotope of carbon, ^{14}C, are formed:

$$^{14}_{7}N + ^{1}_{0}n \rightarrow ^{14}_{6}C + ^{1}_{1}p$$

This carbon enters the carbon dioxide in the atmosphere, is taken up by plants in photosynthesis, and is passed on to animals which eat the plants. So all living matter contains a certain proportion of its carbon as ^{14}C. As long as the plant or animal is alive, it constantly receives fresh supplies of ^{14}C through the normal life processes. But when the organism dies, the supply of ^{14}C stops, and it is as if an atomic clock starts to tick. The half-life of ^{14}C is 5760 years, which means that we can measure accurately the amount of it remaining in objects which died up to about 20 000 years ago. If we know how much ^{14}C the object contained when it died, and if we can measure the amount of ^{14}C left today, we can work out how long ago the plant or animal died, since we know the half-life of ^{14}C. There is a slight complication to this, however, since the amount of cosmic radiation which falls on the atmosphere is not constant. Therefore the amount of ^{14}C which is made is not constant. A way has been found to overcome this, by comparing the width of the rings from very old trees, called bristle-cone pines, in America. The trunk of a tree is a series of rings, each one corresponding to one year. The width of these rings varies, depending on the climate that year. So we can identify the same year in the rings from the trunks of different trees, by comparing the sequence of rings. If the life spans of two different trees overlap, we can go further and further back into history, counting one year for each ring. We know precisely (by counting!) which year each ring corresponds to. So if we find the amount of ^{14}C it contains, we can make up a calibration chart for all future datings using ^{14}C.

Because carbon dating covers the time for which humans have been active on the Earth, and since it can be used to find the age of any objects (such as wood, leather, paper, plant-dyes, bones and so on) which were once living, it is a very good way to fix an accurate date for archaeological finds. Some of the objects which have been dated by this method are:

1. the mammoth found buried in permafrost in Siberia – 12 000 years old;
2. the cave paintings at Lascaux in France – about 15 000 years old (see the photograph on page 73);
3. grain from a tomb of one of the Egyptian Pharaohs (which was still able to germinate!) – 4000 years old.

'Thermoluminescent' dating

This is like carbon dating, but it works for things like pottery, which are made from material which was never living. It uses the fact that radioactive ^{40}K in the soil causes atoms in the clay of a pot to become displaced. The original firing of the pot when it was made will have 'ironed out' all these displacements. So any which exist now are as a result of radiation which has fallen on the pot since it was made. All we have to do is to find the extent to which atoms in the clay which make up the pot are displaced, and the amount of radiation which the pot will have received each year in the spot where it has been lying, and then we can work out how long it has been there – that is, we can find its age.

This form of dating has been useful in conjunction with carbon dating of other remains in fixing the age of archaeological sites.

Dating of rocks

This is done by finding the ratio of ^{87}Rb to ^{87}Sr in the rock sample. It is by this method that the ages of the Earth and the solar system have been estimated.

Medical uses

Some forms of cancer can be treated by exposure to very high levels of γ-radiation for a very short period of time. Such irradiation is of course dangerous and has to be carried out with extreme caution in order that only the diseased tissue is destroyed. The source of γ-rays which is usually used is ^{60}Co. Isotopes of other elements have also been used successfully in treating other complaints – for example, radioactive iodine for treating disease of the thyroid gland.

Industrial uses

Many industrial uses of radioactivity have been found, and others are constantly being added. Examples are:
1. finding the depth of a liquid in a pressure vessel – put a β-emitter on one side of the vessel, and a detector on the other. Move both up and down until there is a sudden change in the amount of radiation received by the detector – this will be at the height of the surface of the liquid;
2. finding the thickness of metal sheet – by putting a β-emitter on one side and a detector on the other, which has been calibrated for known thicknesses;
3. finding cracks in pipes by detection of the escape of radioactive material – this has been used to check pipes carrying North Sea gas and oil ashore.

PROJECT 3.3

The following is information about the radiation to which we are all exposed.

1   Background radiation is radiation in the world around us which has always been there. In total, background radiation amounts to about $\frac{1}{5}$ of the level of radiation which it is safe for us to receive.

2   The different origins of background radiation, and their relative strength are given below.

From outside the body:

cosmic rays:	28%
terrestrial radiation (from rocks and radium in the air):	49%

From inside the body:

radioactive isotopes of common elements:	23%
	100%

3   As well as the radiation which comes from natural sources, we are all exposed to radiation which is man-made. The following figures are the approximate levels of radiation from different man-made sources, as a percentage of the natural background radiation:

'fallout' from explosion of nuclear bombs:	4%
escaping radiation from materials used in nuclear power plants:	0.3%

medical:

average diagnostic dose (e.g. dental X-ray):	30%
chest X-ray:	6% (man)
	15% (woman)
pelvic X-ray:	10 times background

You should try to write a few paragraphs to answer the following questions. You may have your own sources of information which you wish to draw on, but if you do say what they are. Try to base what you say on the scientific knowledge which we have about radiation, including that given above.

1   If it is 'safe' to receive up to 500% of the background level of radiation in any one year, which man-made sources will need to be most carefully monitored for most people? Does your dentist keep a record when you have had an X-ray? Do you think that people who work in hospitals with X-ray machines are more at risk than members of the general public? How can their safety be monitored? (You may have seen such people (and scientists working with nuclear power) wearing 'lapel-badges' which keep a check on the amount of radiation which each individual is receiving – try to find out how these work.)

Continued overleaf

Project 3.3 continued

2   The figure given above for the effect of nuclear 'fallout' is quite small. However, if there were ever to be a nuclear war, people fear that perhaps thousands of nuclear bombs would be used, and that any survivors would therefore be left in a world in which the radiation from 'fallout' would be extremely high. If bombs using ^{235}U or ^{239}Pu (plutonium) were used, the initial explosion would be accompanied by massive emissions of γ-rays. The products of the fission process are also radioactive, usually by β-decay, but some also involving further γ-ray emissions. The half-lives of these products range from less than a second (^{85}As, 0.43 s) to millions of years (^{129}I, 1.6×10^7 years). So β-particles and γ-rays would continue to be emitted by the 'fallout' from a nuclear war. The total energy of the nuclear explosion is shared out like this:

	%
original explosion (kinetic energy)	82.5
γ-rays from original explosion	3.5
β-particles from fission products	3.5
γ-rays from fission products	3.0
other	7.5

Should a nuclear war ever happen, what would be the effects of
(a) the initial radiation:
(b) the radiation from fallout, for any survivors?
Base your thoughts on what you know about the biological effects of the different sorts of radiation, and the levels and types of radiation involved. Would survivors of a nuclear war be able to eat any food they could find in safety?

3   The figure given above for the level of radiation which can be linked to the generation of power by nuclear reactions, is very low. This is, however, an average figure over the surface of the whole planet. Below is a recent newspaper article about a nuclear power-plant and reprocessing plant in England. When you have read it, and from what you know about the dangers of radiation, do you think:

(a) that we ought in general to be worried about radiation from nuclear power-plants?
(b) that people who live near to nuclear power-plants need have more concern than the majority of people?
c) that nuclear power plants could be made completely safe if it was made sure that there were adequate safety precautions, and enough money spent on keeping them up to date?
(d) that nuclear power is too unsafe to be used under any circumstances?

4   Find out what happened in 1986 following the Chernobyl disaster. How does it compare with what you have just read?

The Observer, Sun, 4 December 1983

Call for atom plant probe

by GEOFFREY LEAN, Environment Correspondent

DR DAVID OWEN, the SDP leader, is pressing for an urgent investigation into Windscale, the controversial Cumbrian nuclear complex, where there have been more than 300 accidents since 1950.

He has written to Mrs Thatcher urging her to set up in 'independent committee of inquiry' into the plant, which last week was the centre of renewed public concern when the Government warned people to keep off beaches in the area. Dr Owen's initiative follows an exclusive report in *The Observer* that the Government is cracking down heavily on Windscale's discharges of radioactive waste to the sea, and attempts by Greenpeace, punished last week by a £50,000 fine, to plug the waste pipe.

But while he wants the discharges to be reduced to 'near zero,' Dr Owen is also taking the issue farther by pressing for a scrutiny of the accident-prone plant itself.

That is particularly significant, since in the past Dr Owen has been a robust defender of the nuclear industry. He is not in favour of closing Windscale, now renamed Sellafield, but believes that public confidence must be restored urgently if it is to remain open.

In his letter to the Prime Minister he says he is 'very concerned' that a series of incidents at the plant over the past few years 'has greatly weakened public confidence and severely damaged the nuclear industry.'

An *Observer* investigation has established that there have been more than 300 accidents at Windscale since 1950. Since 1977 the plant has been responsible for nearly half the accidents in the whole of the British nuclear industry.

Disturbing

This disturbing record has attracted considerable pressure from the Nuclear Installations Inspectorate on British Nuclear Fuels Ltd, the nationalised firm that manages Windscale, to clean up the plant. About 400 buildings sprawl over the 485-acre site, which was once a munitions factory; Less than two years ago the inspectorate published a stinging report on the management of safety at Windscale.

Most of the recent incidents, it found, were caused by inadequate safety procedures, or by a failure to observe existing ones. Half the incidents resulted in the workers being exposed to, or contaminated by, radioactivity; a quarter by contamination above safety limits.

Several of them caused the inspectorate particular concern because they involved the failure or breach of a whole series of protective barriers and systems.

The report says: 'Our analysis revealed that such incidents might not have happened, or the consequences might have been mitigated, if in each case even one of the protective systems concerned had operated as intended.'

Thus silo 38 leaked radioactive caesium and strontium 90 (possibly for up to four years) before it was discovered in 1976; and two years later the same building was threatened by an explosion because of a build-up of hydrogen.

Both incidents were due to bad design, inadequate monitoring instruments, and inadequate arrangements for cooling and ventilation.

On Sunday, 4 February 1979 a fire started in a disused plant when oxy-acetylene equipment was being used to cut obsolete pipework. It was caused by failure to observe safety procedures.

When the fire started, the men found it hard to call the fire ser- vice because the fire alarm had been removed and the single telephone line to the fire station was engaged. And when the ser- vice finally arrived both their equipment and training were found to be defective.

The inspectorate's report showed that the maintenance of buildings at Windscale had been neglected and little money had been spent on repairs; that draw- ings were not kept up to date or were missing; that general housekeeping was poor; that the company had not kept up links with safety organisations; and that serious accidents were often partly caused by defective instru- ments, which had sometimes not been maintained or tested.

That was all at a time when the firm was improving safety standards, which had been allowed to deteriorate until the early 1970s.

Improvements continued throughout the decade, but by the end of it the inspectorate still found that industrial safety offic- ers did not carry out systematic inspections, that workers did not understand the effects that radiation might have on them, and that managers were uncer- tain about who was responsible for inspecting some pipelines and drains carrying radioactive substances.

Under the inspectorate's pressure the management at Windscale has continued to make improvements, and most of the deficiencies identified in the report have now been put right.

But there is still concern about the state of much of the repro- cessing and waste storage plant, which is old, initially designed at a time of laxer safety standards, and heavily labour intensive.

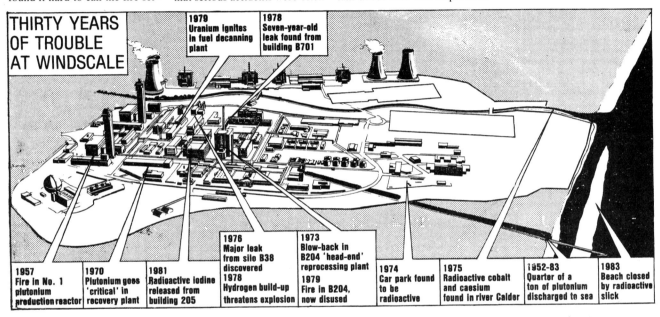

5   What do you think are the general dangers from radioactivity in the world around us? The following may help you.

(a) The danger from dying as a result of exposure to radiation in the general surroundings is about 1 in a million. The following represent equivalent risks from different causes:

Cause	Reason for death
smoking 1–3 cigarettes	cancer, heart-disease
living for two months in a stone building	cancer from radioactivity
working for 3 hours in a coal-mine	accident
working for 1½ weeks in a typical factory	accident
crossing the Atlantic by air	cancer from cosmic rays

(b) How dangerous is watching television? For every hour you spend watching a colour television, you receive about 0.02% of the background level of radiation. (It depends on how close you sit. At the surface of the screen, the level is 2% of the background every hour!) Work out roughly how much radiation **you** receive each year from watching television (assume about one-third this level for a black and white television).

UNIT 3.2
Summary and learning

1   The relative atomic mass of an element is the average mass of the isotopes of the element which are found in the normal isotopic mixture, relative to 1/12 of the mass of an atom of ^{12}C. You should remember why the existence of isotopes confused the early scientists as they tried to sort the elements into their different types, and how Mendeleev overcame the problem.

2   Radioactivity is caused by unstable nuclei splitting up. A given element may have some isotopes which are radioactive and others which are stable. Different isotopes of the same element have the same chemical properties, but different nuclear properties.

3   Of the stable nuclei, those which have atomic numbers in the region of iron in the Periodic Table are the most stable. In theory, even other stable nuclei should decay to give these most stable nuclei, but for 269 isotopes no mechanism for this change exists. These 269 isotopes are therefore not radioactive.

4   All other isotopes are radioactive, and give off α, β, or γ-radiation.
α-radiation is made up of helium nuclei.
β-radiation is made up of fast moving electrons.
γ-radiation is made up of electromagnetic radiation similar to light or radio waves.
You should remember how the three types of radiation behave in an electromagnetic field.

5   We can sometimes cause a stable nucleus to undergo nuclear fission by bombarding it with neutrons. When this process itself releases further neutrons, a chain reaction is possible, and self-sustaining reactions which release energy can be started. ^{235}U (uranium) and ^{239}Pu (plutonium) are nuclei for which this is possible. Both can result in uncontrolled reactions (nuclear explosions), or in the production of energy for peaceful purposes.

6   Energy can also be obtained from the process of fusing together very light elements. Again, this can be done either in a controlled or an uncontrolled way. The production of energy for peaceful purposes by fusion is unlikely to suffer all the drawbacks of nuclear fusion, although it is much harder to achieve.

7   The heaviest elements are made during supernova explosions. All the material of the solar system, including ourselves, was once part of a supernova explosion.

8   Each radioactive isotope decays at a rate which is measured by its half-life. The half-life of a radioactive isotope is the time taken for half the atoms to decay. From the value of the half-life, we can calculate the proportion of the atoms of the isotope which split up in a given length of time.

9   Of the three types of radiation, γ-rays are the most dangerous because of their ability to penetrate beyond the outer layers of the skin. However, if taken into the body, α-emitters and β-emitters are also extremely dangerous. You should remember the types of damage which radiation can cause to living things.

10   You should be aware of the relative dangers which result from exposure to radiation in everyday life (including that from man-made sources), from radiation associated with the production of energy in nuclear power-plants, and that which might result from the use of nuclear weapons.

11   You should remember the uses to which radioactivity can be put.

12   You have learnt the meanings of these words:

α-decay	fast-breeder reactor
β-decay	critical mass
γ-decay	plasma
nucleon	torus
nuclear fission	supernova
nuclear fusion	Geiger–Müller tube
chain reaction	exponential
control rod	half-life
reactor core	solvent extraction
fuel rods	

UNIT 3.3   *Chemical bonding between elements*

You know that the number of electrons in the outermost 'shell' in an atom has to do with the chemical behaviour of that element. You are able to work out from the atomic number of an element how many electrons its outermost shell will contain, and therefore which group in the Periodic Table it will belong to.

You know that elements with the same number of electrons in their outermost shell have similar chemical properties, and that as we go from the left-hand side of the Periodic Table to the right-hand side, there is a gradual change in the properties which the elements have, as the outermost shell becomes increasingly filled.

You know that the elements at the left-hand side of the Periodic Table are metals, and that metals will form only ionic compounds, in combination with non-metals. You know that the right-hand side of the Table contains the non-metals, and that non-metals can form two types of compound. They can form ionic compounds with metals, and molecular compounds with other non-metals.

Exactly how do these different types of compound come about, and why do metals and non-metals behave as they do? There is one further piece of knowledge which is the clue to finding an answer to this question. Some elements are basically unreactive – the Group 0 elements or 'inert gases'.

TOPIC 3.3.1

How ionic compounds are made up

The Group 0 elements all have one thing in common – their outermost shell of electrons is filled. They are also chemically inert (unreactive) – and the two things are related. The Group 0 elements form no compounds with other elements **because** they have filled outer shells. **All other elements do not have filled outer shells, and so they combine chemically with other elements in order to obtain a filled outer shell**.

Metals

Elements in Group 1 of the Periodic Table have one electron in their outermost shell. So, they can get a filled outer shell by gaining 7 electrons (which would be quite difficult) or by losing one electron (which is much easier). In the same way, elements in Group 2 can lose the two electrons which they have in their

outer shell, and elements in Group 3 can lose the three electrons which they have in theirs. So we can think of elements towards the left of the Periodic Table (metals) as **having too many electrons**, and needing to get rid of them to form something more stable (a filled outer shell).

When a metal atom loses an electron, a cation is formed. Elements in Group 1 in the Table all lose 1 electron, and so they form ions which have one more positive charge than negative charge. For instance, for sodium, the following happens (Fig. 3.31).

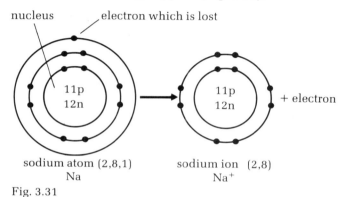

Fig. 3.31

In the same way, the following changes happen for the other Group 1 metals when they form an ion:

$$Li \rightarrow Li^+ \quad + \text{ electron}$$
$$K \rightarrow K^+ \quad + \text{ electron}$$
$$Rb \rightarrow Rb^+ \quad + \text{ electron}$$
$$Cs \rightarrow Cs^+ \quad + \text{ electron}$$

Elements in Group 2 all lose 2 electrons, and form ions which have an overall charge of $+2$, because the ion has two more protons in the nucleus than it has electrons:

$$Be \rightarrow Be^{2+} \quad + \text{ 2 electrons}$$
$$Mg \rightarrow Mg^{2+} \quad + \text{ 2 electrons}$$
$$Ca \rightarrow Ca^{2+} \quad + \text{ 2 electrons}$$
$$Sr \rightarrow Sr^{2+} \quad + \text{ 2 electrons}$$
$$Ba \rightarrow Ba^{2+} \quad + \text{ 2 electrons}$$

Elements in Group 3 lose 3 electrons, and so form ions which have an overall charge of $+3$. For example, aluminium forms Al^{3+} ions, because it loses 3 electrons. So metals always form cations when they react. The charge on the ion depends on which group in the table the metal is in.

Non-metals

Elements in Group 7 of the Table have 7 electrons in their outermost shell. So to get a filled outermost shell, they can lose 7 electrons (which would be difficult), or they can gain 1 electron (which is much easier). In the same way, elements in Group 6 can gain 2 electrons, and elements in Group 5 can gain 3 electrons. So we can think of elements towards the right of the Table (non-metals) as **having too few electrons**, and needing to gain the right number to make up a filled outer shell.

When a non-metal atom gains an electron, an anion is formed. For example, the following happens for chlorine (Fig. 3.32).

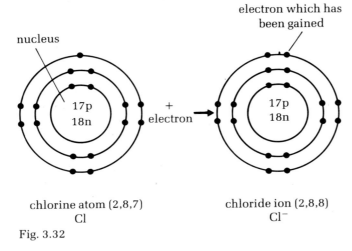

chlorine atom (2,8,7)   chloride ion (2,8,8)
Cl Cl^-

Fig. 3.32

In the same way, the following changes happen for the other Group 7 elements when they form an ion:

$$F + electron \rightarrow F^-$$
$$Br + electron \rightarrow Br^-$$
$$I + electron \rightarrow I^-$$

Elements in Group 6 all gain 2 electrons, and form ions which have an overall charge of -2 (because the ion has two more electrons than it has protons in the nucleus):

$$O + 2\,electrons \rightarrow O^{2-}$$
$$S + 2\,electrons \rightarrow S^{2-}$$

Elements in Group 5 gain 3 electrons, and so form ions which have an overall charge of -3. For example, nitrogen forms N^{3-} ions, because it gains 3 electrons. So non-metals always form anions when they react with metals. The charge on the ion depends on which group in the Table the non-metal is in.

The formulae of ionic compounds

For elements at the far left or far right of the Table, we can work out what the charge on its ion will be. However, there are other chemicals which form cations and anions. TRANSITION METALS (which you will study in detail in Section 5) can often form more than one type of cation, and the ammonium ion (NH_4^+) is not made up from just one element. The

most common cations are given in Table 3.11.

+1	+2	+3
NH^+ (ammonium)	Mg^{2+}	Al^{3+}
Li^+	Ca^{2+}	Fe^{3+} (iron(III))
Na^+	Ba^{2+}	
K^+	Fe^{2+} (iron (II))	
H^+	Cu^{2+} (copper(II))	
Ag^+	Zn^{2+}	
Cu^+ (copper(I))	Pb^{2+}	

Table 3.11

Similarly, there are other anions besides those formed by single non-metals. These are the anions which we find in acids. Table 3.12 gives the common anions.

-1	-2	-3
F^-	O^{2-} (oxide)	N^{3-} (nitride)
Cl^-	S^{2-} (sulphide)	PO_4^{3-} (phosphate)
Br^-	SO_4^{2-} (sulphate)	
I^-	CO_3^{2-} (carbonate)	
NO_3^- (nitrate)		
SO_3^- (sulphite)		

Table 3.12

All ionic compounds are electrically neutral. This means that the total numbers of positive and negative charges are equal. If a compound is formed between ions which have charges which are equal but opposite, then the ratio, of number of cations: number of anions, need only be 1:1. Some examples are given below:

NH_4Cl	MgO	$AlPO_4$
ammonium chloride	magnesium oxide	aluminium phosphate

You will see that when we write the formula of an ionic compound, we leave out the charges on the ions. Also, the 'formula' of an ionic compound does not represent anything which actually exists by itself. There is no particle which corresponds to MgO in magnesium oxide for example. Instead, what we write is the **ratio** in which the ions combine to form the compound. You already know that ionic compounds exist as huge lattices of oppositely charged ions, and you will learn more about them in Section 6.

But what about the formulae of ionic compounds in which the ions themselves do not have equal but opposite charges? The ions will combine together in a ratio such that the total number of positive charges is equal to the total number of negative charges, and we can represent this in the formula which we write.

Example 1   Magnesium chloride

Magnesium forms ions Mg^{2+} and chlorine forms ions Cl^-. So we need twice as many chloride ions as magnesium ions to have the same number of positive and negative charges. When we write a formula we show the relative number of ions by a number after the symbol (unless there is no number – that means '1'). So the formula of magnesium chloride is

MgCl$_2$

What this means is that when magnesium and chlorine react together, the ions which form combine together in the ratio of 1 Mg^{2+} cation to 2 Cl$^-$ anions.

Since magnesium chloride can be made by reacting the elements together directly, we can imagine in this case the actual transfer of electrons during the reaction. It is as if one magnesium atom gives one electron to each of two chlorine atoms, forming 1 Mg^{2+} ion and 2 Cl$^-$ ions (Fig. 3.33).

Example 2   Magnesium nitrate

We need twice as many nitrate ions as magnesium ions to have the same number of positive and negative charges. Whenever the number of anions which contain more than one element in the formula is greater than 1, we put a bracket round the whole of the anion, and then follow it with the number which we need. This is to show that the whole of the anion is included each time. So the formula of magnesium nitrate is:

Mg(NO$_3$)$_2$ (We say 'Mg, NO$_3$ twice')

Here are some more examples of formulae of ionic compounds:

ammonium chloride	NH$_4$Cl
ammonium sulphate	(NH$_4$)$_2$SO$_4$ ('NH$_4$ twice, SO$_4$')
iron(II) sulphate	FeSO$_4$
iron(III) sulphate	Fe$_2$(SO$_4$)$_3$
calcium phosphate	Ca$_3$(PO$_4$)$_2$
aluminium chloride	AlCl$_3$

Now you can try some formulae for yourself.

Questions

In each case, write the formula for the compound named:

1. Sodium chloride
2. Sodium carbonate
3. Calcium carbonate
4. Silver bromide
5. Zinc iodide
6. Aluminium nitrate
7. Copper(I) oxide
8. Copper(II) oxide
9. Lead sulphide
10. Iron(III) sulphate

How molecular compounds are made up

When an element needs to lose a small number of electrons to get a filled outer shell, there is only one thing it can do to reduce the number which it has – give some away. When an element needs to gain some electrons to get a filled outer shell, it can get more by obtaining some from another element. But there is also something else an element can do to 'get more' electrons.

Suppose we had two chlorine atoms – each of them needs to gain one electron to make up a filled outer shell. Clearly, this cannot be achieved for both atoms at the same time by the formation of a cation and an anion. There are just too few electrons to go round – the cation would be 2 electrons short of a filled shell. So how could the two atoms help each other to – effectively – have more electrons?

This is a bit like the type of problem which we call a 'brain teaser'. We might ask ourselves a question like 'Suppose you had nine buttons – how can you make two rows of five buttons?' The answer is like this:

One of the buttons belongs to two of the rows – but there are still two rows of five buttons! How does this help with the problem of the two chlorine atoms? Can you think of a way to make two shells of eight electrons starting with seven in each atom?

The answer is that atoms must **share** electrons. For our two chlorine atoms, we can imagine that the following happens:

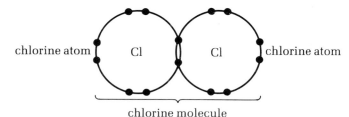

Fig. 3.34 *(only the outer electron shells are shown)*

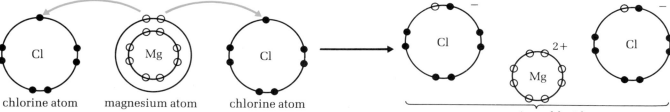

● electron originally belonging to Cl   ○ electron originally belonging to Mg

Fig. 3.33 *(only the outer electron shells are shown)*

It is as if the outer electron shells of the two atoms overlap. At the point where they do, there is a 'pool' of electrons which is held 'in common' between the two atoms. The common pool belongs equally to the two atoms, and so each can say that the electrons which it contains belong to its own outer shell. In this way, since each atom gives one electron to the common pool of two, the outer shell of each effectively contains one more electron – eight in all.

You can see that, unlike an ionic compound, there is an actual bond which links the two atoms together. The bond is the shared pair of electrons in the common pool. We call this bond a COVALENT bond, and this form of bonding COVALENT BONDING. Because the two atoms are physically joined together, **a new particle has been formed**. This particle is, of course, a molecule.

We have seen that two chlorine atoms can join together to make a chlorine molecule. When they do this, both effectively have filled outer shells of electrons. Surely, then, all chlorine atoms will want to do this? This is indeed the case... chlorine **exists as** chlorine molecules. The formula for a chlorine molecule is Cl_2, and we have a shorthand way of representing the shape of the molecule, showing the covalent bond:

Cl—Cl

One covalent bond is formed every time a pair of electrons is shared in the common pool between two atoms. As you will see shortly, it is possible for atoms to have two, and even three, covalent bonds between them. We know how many electrons elements in the different groups in the Periodic Table have in their outermost shells, and so how many each will need to gain by forming covalent bonds with other atoms, in order to get a filled shell:

Group: 4 5 6 7

Number of electrons needed: 4 3 2 1

So, elements in Group 7 will always want to form one covalent bond. (For this reason, all the halogens exist in the same form as chlorine, because they all form bonds with another atom of the same element. So all the halogens exist as DIATOMIC ('two-atom') molecules.) Elements in Group 6 will always want to form two covalent bonds, those in Group 5 will form three, and those in Group 4 will form four. Hydrogen has one electron in its outer shell, which would be filled if it contained one more. So hydrogen forms one covalent bond.

In order for two elements to form a covalent bond between them, **both** must need to gain electrons. **So molecular compounds can only be made when two (or more) non-metals react together.** Elements in Group 4 are non-metals, but do not have the choice of

forming anions in ionic compounds, since it is very difficult for ions having a charge of −4 to form. So the simple compounds of carbon and silicon are all molecular in nature (there can be more complicated chemicals which **contain** these elements and which are ionic, such as carbonates, of course). Table 3.13 gives the number of covalent bonds which some common elements will form:

Number of covalent bonds	4	3	2	1
Elements	carbon silicon	phosphorus nitrogen	oxygen sulphur	hydrogen halogens

Table 3.13

Question

Hydrogen exists in the form of diatomic molecules. Draw a diagram to show the arrangement of electrons in the hydrogen molecule, which will be of the same form as Fig. 3.34.

Both oxygen and nitrogen also exist as diatomic molecules. In oxygen, a double covalent bond forms between the atoms, and in nitrogen, there are three covalent bonds between the two atoms in the molecule. We can draw diagrams which represent what is happening in these two cases, as follows (Fig. 3.35).

For oxygen:

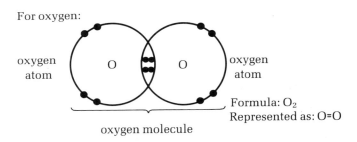

Formula: O_2
Represented as: O=O

oxygen molecule

For nitrogen:

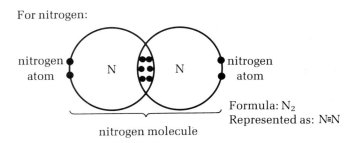

Formula: N_2
Represented as: N≡N

nitrogen molecule

Fig. 3.35 *(only the outer electron shells are shown)*

You will see that in these diagrams, electrons are always shown as being in pairs. This is because electrons actually do form pairs in this way. If the pair of electrons are in the common pool, we call them a BONDING pair of electrons. If the pair do not take part in the bonding, we call them a LONE pair of electrons. We will come back to bonding pairs and lone pairs shortly.

The formulae of molecular compounds

We can work out the formula of a molecular compound from what we know about the number of covalent bonds which each of the elements must form. **Each element must form the number of covalent bonds which it needs to get a filled outer shell**. So, often, the molecule will need to have more atoms of one element than of another. For instance, oxygen needs to form two bonds, but hydrogen can form only one. So, when oxygen and hydrogen combine to form a compound (water), two hydrogen atoms are needed in order that the oxygen atom can form two bonds.

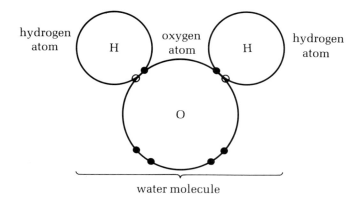

Formula: H₂O
Represented as H   H
            O

● electron originally belonging to oxygen
○ electron originally belonging to hydrogen

Fig. 3.36 *(only the outer electron shells are shown)*

In the case of a molecular compound, the formula does relate to something which exists – the molecule. The formula of a molecular compound tells us exactly how many atoms of each element there are in the molecule. The molecule is an individual particle of the molecular compound, in the same way that an atom is the smallest amount of an element which can exist on its own.

Suppose we take another example, the compound formed between nitrogen and hydrogen, ammonia. Again, we should think first of the element which needs to form the greater number of bonds. This is nitrogen, which needs to form three. As with water, hydrogen atoms can form only one bond each, and so in this case three are needed. The molecule will look like Fig. 3.37.

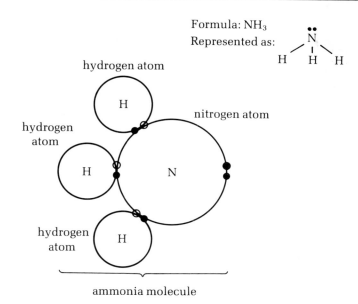

Formula: NH₃
Represented as:

ammonia molecule

● electron originally belonging to nitrogen
○ electron originally belonging to hydrogen

Fig. 3.37 *(only the outer electron shells are shown)*

What would be the formula of the compound between carbon and hydrogen? (In fact, as you will learn in Section 8, there are very many compounds between carbon and hydrogen. The simplest of these, however, is the one which has only one carbon atom.) If we start from the carbon atom, which needs to form four bonds, we can see that we will need four hydrogen atoms. The compound which we get as a result is called methane.

Formula: CH₄ Represented as:

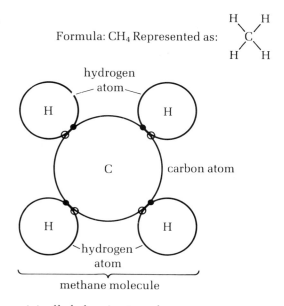

methane molecule

● electron originally belonging to carbon
○ electron originally belonging to hydrogen

Fig. 3.38 *(only the outer electron shells are shown)*

So far, we have only looked at examples where one of the atoms involved needs to form only one bond. Suppose we had a case where both elements needed to form more than one bond – can we use the same ideas to work out the formula of the molecular compound? A good example would be the compound between carbon and oxygen. Carbon needs to form four bonds, and oxygen needs to form two. So each carbon atom will need to form two bonds with each of two oxygen atoms. The compound which we get as a result is carbon dioxide.

Formula: CO_2

Represented as: O=C=O

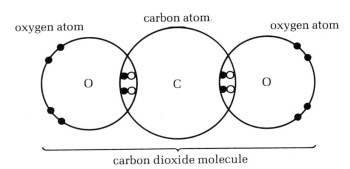

carbon dioxide molecule

○ electron originally belonging to carbon
● electron originally belonging to oxygen

Fig. 3.39 *(only the outer electron shells are shown)*

You can now try some examples for yourself.

Questions

In each case, work out the formula of the molecular compound which forms between the two non-metals which are named. Start from the element which will need to form the greater number of bonds. Draw a diagram to represent the arrangement of the electrons, give the formula, and show how the molecule would be represented.

1. Carbon, chlorine (the name of the compound is tetrachloromethane)
2. Phosphorus, hydrogen (phosphine)
3. Silicon, hydrogen (silane)
4. Hydrogen, chlorine (hydrogen chloride)
5. Hydrogen, sulphur (hydrogen sulphide)

The shapes of simple molecules

You will remember that the drawings which we have used to represent the electron shells in atoms are a simplification of what is really there. They are two-dimensional (flat) drawings of something which is really three-dimensional. We would be nearer the

truth if we thought of electron shells as being spheres.

All of the molecules for which we have worked out the formula have one thing in common. They all have a 'central' atom (the one which has to form the greater number of bonds), which ends up with four pairs of electrons in its outer shell. These electron pairs are either bonding pairs or lone pairs.

The pairs of electrons try to get as far away from each other as possible – because of the repulsion between the negative charges which they all have. But remember that they are really not round the edge of a circle, they are on the surface of a sphere. What shape do we get if we have four points on the surface of a sphere which are as far apart from each other as possible? We could get a picture in our minds by thinking about the Earth, and points on its surface. Suppose four people decided to get as far as possible away from each other. They could manage this, for instance, by one being at the South Pole, one in the Caribbean, another in Oman in the Persian Gulf, and the fourth in Hawaii. The shape which is produced if we join these points together is called a TETRAHEDRON. A tetrahedron is like a pyramid which has a triangle for a base rather than a square. It has four faces (hence its name: 'tetrahedron' comes from the Greek for 'four faces'). Its four points are all the same distance away from each other.

If we started at the point right in the centre of a tetrahedron, and drew four lines to the four corners, we would end up with a shape like that shown in Fig. 3.40. The angle between any two of the lines is 109°28′ (almost 109½°).

So, if we have four pairs of electrons in the outer shell of an atom, the basic shape which will always be produced is a tetrahedron. If all four of the pairs of electrons are bonding pairs, and each is in a bond to a single atom, the shape will be a perfect tetrahedron. This is the case for methane, CH_4. A methane molecule has the carbon atom at the centre of a tetrahedron, with a hydrogen atom at each of the four corners.

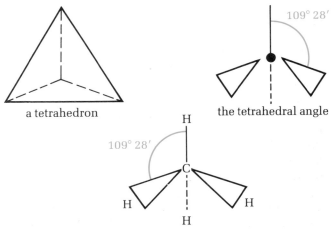

Fig. 3.40 *Methane – a perfect tetrahedron*

The angle between any two of the bonds (the H—C—H angle) is 109°28′.

If not all the electron pairs are bonding pairs, the tetrahedral shape becomes slightly distorted. Lone pairs of electrons cause a stronger repulsion than bonding pairs. So if we take a molecule like ammonia, the lone pair pushes each of the bonding pairs away more strongly than they push each other away, and the result is that the three hydrogen atoms get pushed closer to each other. This makes the angle between the bonds slightly less than in a pure tetrahedron – 107°.

Fig. 3.41 *Ammonia – a distorted tetrahedron*

In the water molecule, the central oxygen atom is surrounded by two lone pairs and two bonding pairs.

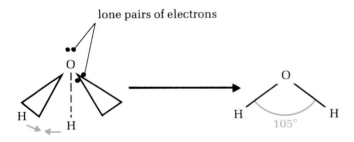

Fig. 3.42 *Water – a more distorted tetrahedron*

The strongest repulsion is between the two lone pairs, the next strongest is between the lone pairs and the bonding pairs, and the least strong is between the two bonding pairs. The result is that the hydrogen atoms in a water molecule are pushed even closer together than the hydrogen atoms in an ammonia molecule. The angle between the bonds is therefore less – 105°.

Obviously, molecules like O_2, N_2 and Cl_2 can only have one shape – because two points can only be joined by a straight line. In the same way, carbon dioxide is also a LINEAR molecule. Each oxygen atom forms two bonds to the central carbon atom. The four bonding pairs are not able to move away from each other – they are tied together in two pairs of two. These then move apart as far as possible – like the North and South Poles on the Earth's surface. The result is that the three atoms all lie in a straight line.

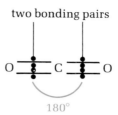

Fig. 3.43 *Carbon dioxide – a linear molecule*

Questions

Very roughly, what shape would you predict each of the following molecules would have?

1. Silane (SiH_4)
2. Carbon tetrachloride (CCl_4)
3. Phosphine (PH_3)

TOPIC 3.3.3

Other types of chemical bonding

Coordinate bonds

We have just seen one important effect of the lone pairs of electrons which sometimes exist in the outer electron shells of atoms. Another important effect of them is that they make the molecule able to 'attach' itself to some other atom. The lone pair of electrons can be 'given' to an atom which needs two to make up its outer shell. In fact, the bond which forms is exaxtly like all other covalent bonds – except in this case, both of the electrons come from one of the atoms only. We can see that ammonia and water are both in a position to form this special type of covalent bond, which is called a COORDINATE bond.

A hydrogen ion (H^+) has a nucleus (one proton and no neutrons) and no electrons in its outer shell. Hydrogen would have a filled shell if it had two electrons, and so a hydrogen ion can accept a pair of electrons into its outer shell. We can imagine what happens when a hydrogen ion meets an ammonia molecule:

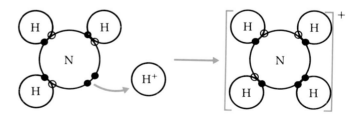

● electron originally belonging to nitrogen
○ electron originally belonging to hydrogen

Fig. 3.44

A shorthand way of representing this would be:

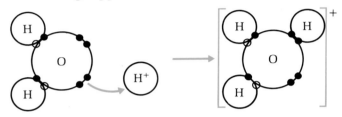

$H_3\ddot{N}\ \overset{\frown}{H}^+\ \longrightarrow\ [NH_4]^+$ Represented as: $\left[\begin{array}{c}H \qquad H \\ N \\ H \qquad H\end{array}\right]^+$

(Incidentally, what **shape** do you think an ammonium ion is? All four pairs of electrons are now bonding pairs.)

When a water molecule meets a hydrogen ion, a similar thing happens:

- ● electron originally belonging to oxygen
- ○ electron originally belonging to hydrogen

Fig. 3.45

or, in shorthand:

$H_2\ddot{O}\ \overset{\frown}{H}^+\ \longrightarrow\ H_3O^+$ Represented as: $\left[\begin{array}{c}H \qquad H \\ O \\ H\end{array}\right]^+$
hydroxonium ion

In fact, this will happen whenever a water molecule comes across a hydrogen ion, so that in any solution in water, 'free' hydrogen ions do not exist – they all have water molecules attached and exist as H_3O^+ ions. So an acid is really something which contains more hydroxonium ions (H_3O^+) than hydroxide ions (OH^-).

One group of metals, called the transition metals (these were mentioned earlier for another reason), can often accept pairs of electrons from molecules such as ammonia and water. The cation of the metal forms a coordinate bond with the molecule and forms a COMPLEX ION. We call the molecules which form complex ions with transition metal ions LIGANDS. So water and ammonia can both behave as ligands.

Ligands often have an interesting effect on transition metal ions – they cause them to have colour. You already know that hydrated copper(II) sulphate is blue, and that anhydrous copper(II) sulphate is white. In anhydrous copper(II) sulphate, the ligand (water) molecules have been removed. For most transition metal ions, when there are no ligands, they do not appear to have a colour. When they have ligand molecules attached, then we see a colour which depends on which transition metal we have, and which ligand molecules are attached to it.

So, for a particular transition metal ion, we can cause a change in the colour which we see by changing the ligand molecules. Your teacher may show you the following experiment.

▶ EXPERIMENT 3.7

Metallic bonds

You know that elements at the right of the Periodic Table (such as chlorine) exist as diatomic molecules. The same is true for non-metals like oxygen and nitrogen. Other non-metals such as sulphur and phosphorus exist as bigger molecules, while those in the middle of the Table (carbon and silicon) exist as 'giant' molecules – of which you will learn more in Section 7.

	Group 4	Group 5	Group 6	Group 7
METALS	giant molecules			small molecules

←——————————————
molecules getting bigger

Non-metals can form covalent bonds with each other, and so can form molecules. But you know that metals cannot do this, because they need to lose electrons, not to gain them. So how do atoms of a metal interact with each other? There must be some force which holds the atoms of metals together, otherwise they would fly apart and we would never see metals as 'lumps' of the element. And yet we know that metals do hold together – and very strongly indeed. Otherwise we would not be very wise in building bridges, buildings, cars and aeroplanes using metals!

We also know that metals will allow heat and electricity to pass easily through. Can we explain this ability?

Metals are very dense. Their atoms are packed closely together. We could imagine the atoms in a metal 'bumping up' against each other. But remember that atoms are not really hard spheres, and that our idea of 'electron shells' is only a picture which we use to help us. In reality, the outsides of atoms are 'fuzzy' and not 'hard'. Their outermost electrons can occupy a volume of space, and do not really move round an 'orbit'.

So when the atoms of metals get very close to each other, it is as if their outer 'shells' all mix together. Each outer electron can then move throughout the lattice of metal atoms, and does not have to stay with its own atom. So it is as if the metal atoms are all held together by a 'glue' of electrons.

EXPERIMENT 3.7
Changing the colour of a transition metal ion

> **Your teacher will show you this experiment**

The following will be needed: copper(II) sulphate crystals, dilute ammonia solution, boiling-tube.

What to do

1 Dissolve a little copper(II) sulphate in water in a boiling-tube.

2 Slowly add dilute ammonia solution.

3 Continue until there is no further change.

What happened

You should be able to see that when your teacher adds the ammonia solution to the copper(II) sulphate solution, the colour changes from blue to a very deep blue.

What we can decide

In aqueous copper(II) sulphate, the copper(II) ion has six water molecules which are attached to it by coordinate bonds. These six ligand molecules surround the copper(II) ion.

When ammonia molecules are present, they replace the water molecules as ligands (actually, only four of the six are replaced).

It is because molecules like water and ammonia can form coordinate bonds that they can behave as ligand molecules. As you saw the colour change happen when your teacher added ammonia, one type of coordinate bond was being replaced by another type of coordinate bond.

This structure is called a METALLIC BOND, and it is very strong indeed. It means that metals will not 'snap', and that they will therefore bear heavy loads.

does not happen easily

Fig. 3.46 *Metals do not snap*

At the same time, the 'glue' of electrons lets the rows of metal atoms in the lattice 'slip' over each other, but without coming apart. This means that metals can be pulled into very thin wires, again without snapping.

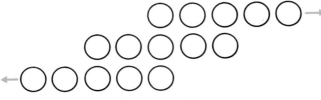

happens easily

Fig. 3.47 *Metals can be pulled into thin wires without snapping*

Because the electrons in a metal are free to move about over all the atoms, when we put another electron in at one end of a piece of wire, a different electron is pushed out at the other end. Since all electrons are identical, this does not alter the metal in any way. This is like what happens when a billiard ball hits a row of other billiard balls on a snooker table.

(a)   (b)

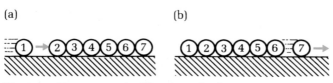

Fig. 3.48 *How to travel without moving!*

So a metal will be very good at letting an electric current (which is a flow of electrons) pass through it. It happens quickly, and with little loss of energy. Heat passes through a metal in a similar way.

Hydrogen bonds

We have seen that the forces of attraction between molecules are, generally speaking, very weak. However, there is one special arrangement of atoms which can cause there to be an extra force of attraction between some molecules. This force of attraction involves hydrogen, and is not really a bond. However it has become know as a HYDROGEN BOND.

There can be a hydrogen bond between two molecules if one of them has a hydrogen atom covalently bonded to a non-metal like oxygen, and the other molecule also contains a non-metal. Water is a good example of a chemical in which there are hydrogen bonds.

Although hydrogen bonds are really not very strong if we compare them to covalent bonds, they are much stronger than the ordinary forces of attraction between molecules. So those compounds which have hydrogen bonds between their molecules can have special properties. You will see the effect of hydrogen bonding on the properties of water in Section 7.

TOPIC 3.3.4

Finding formulae by doing experiments

So far, we have seen how we can use what we know about the structure of the atoms of the different elements in a compound to work out its formula. From knowing whether the elements are metals or non-metals we can work out whether the compound will be ionic or molecular. If it is ionic, we can find the charges which the cation and anion will have, by knowing the arrangement of the electrons in the atoms of the elements concerned. If we know the charges on the ions, we can work out the formula of the compound. If we know that a compound will be molecular, we can find the number of atoms of each element which there will be in the molecule, from knowing how many covalent bonds each atom needs to be involved in for it to get a filled outer shell of electrons. This, again, we get from what we know about the arrangement of the electrons in the atoms' outer shells.

nature of elements $\longrightarrow$ arrangement of electrons $\longrightarrow$ formula of compound

ionic compound $\longrightarrow$ charges on cation and anion $\longrightarrow$ ratio of no. of cations and no. of anions to make compound neutral

molecular compound $\longrightarrow$ no. of covalent bonds needed by each element $\longrightarrow$ no. of atoms of each element in the molecule

But suppose that we knew nothing about the arrangement of the electrons in the atoms of the elements which go to make up a particular compound. Is there any way in which we can still find the formula of the compound?

What else do we know about the atoms of the different elements? We know their mass, relative to each other (the relative atomic masses). Can we use this to help us find formulae?

Counting by weighing

A formula for a chemical compound is a relative **number** of atoms or ions. Can we get from weights to numbers? Well, this kind of thing is done every day in places like banks, where large numbers of coins have to be counted. In order to save having to count each coin, banks use the fact that we know exactly how much different coins weigh.

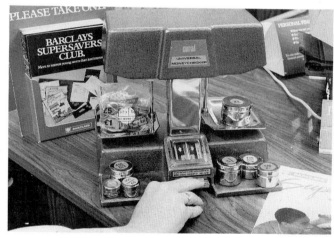

Fig. 3.49 *Weighing is quicker than counting*

Suppose the bag in the photograph is full of 10 p pieces. The bank clerk knows that a certain weight of 10 p coins will give the number which there are in £5. So there is no need to count them all – **the right weight will give the right number**.

We do the same thing, although not quite as precisely, for many everyday quantities. We weigh, rather than count, potatoes, peas, carrots, sweets, nails and many other items used in day-to-day living.

Comparing numbers by weighing

To count by weighing, you need to know the actual mass of one of the objects you are counting. That gives

the actual number of objects. But we do not know the **actual** masses of atoms – we know their masses **relative** to each other (on a scale in which the mass of the isotope ^{12}C is 12 units). Can this still help us in finding formulae?

Suppose our bank clerk has to compare the number of 5 p pieces in one bag with the number of 10 p pieces in another. Suppose also that a 10 p piece weighs exactly twice as much as a 5 p piece. Now, if the bank clerk discovers that the two bags weigh the same, what will the number of 5 p and 10 p pieces in the two bags be, relative to each other?

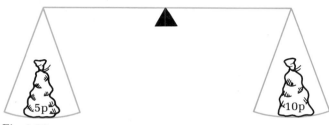

Fig. 3.50

	Relative mass of 'particles'	Relative total masses	Relative number of 'particles'
5 p coins	1	same	2
10 p coins	2	same	1

Table 3.14

For every 10 p coin in one bag, there must have been two 5 p coins in the other bag. So there were twice as many 5 p coins as 10 p coins. We do not know the **actual** number of 5 p and 10 p coins, of course, only the **relative** number of each.

Suppose that the two bags had not weighed the same. What if the bag containing the 10 p coins had weighed twice as much as the one containing the 5 p coins? What would the relative number of the two different types of coin have been then? What if the 5 p bag had weighed twice as much as the 10 p bag, what then? We can draw up a further table with these two examples.

		Relative mass of 'particles'	Relative total masses	Relative number of 'particles'
(a)	5 p coins	1	1	1
	10 p coins	2	2	1
(b)	5 p coins	1	2	4
	10 p coins	2	1	1

Table 3.15

In the first case it is easy to see that there must be equal numbers of the two types of coin. In the second example, there must be four times the number of 5 p coins as 10 p coins, since each one weighs half as much, and the total weight is double. You should be able to see that we could find the relative number of any two 'particles' as long as we know the relative mass of each, and the relative total masses. We could use this equation:

$$\frac{\text{relative number}}{\text{of particles}} = \frac{\text{relative total masses}}{\text{relative mass of particle}}$$

You should now go back and see how this relationship could be used to give the 'answers' to the three examples above.

We can use the relative atomic masses of elements to compare relative numbers of atoms. When we do this, we relate the number of atoms of each element to a 'standard' number. This is the number of atoms of carbon in 12 g of carbon. It is also the number of atoms of hydrogen in 1 g of hydrogen, and the number of atoms of oxygen in 16 g of oxygen, and the number of atoms of sodium in 23 g of sodium. We give this number the symbol 'N_A', and it is called Avogadro's Number. **The amount of an element which contains Avogadro's Number of atoms is called 1 MOLE of that element.** We can draw up the following table for elements:

Element	Relative atomic mass	Mass of element	Relative number of atoms
H	1	1 g	N_A
C	12	12 g	N_A
N	14	14 g	N_A
O	16	16 g	N_A
Na	23	23 g	N_A
Mg	24	24 g	N_A
Al	27	27 g	N_A
S	32	32 g	N_A
Cl	35.5	35.5 g	N_A
K	39	39 g	N_A
Ca	40	40 g	N_A
Cu	63.5	63.5 g	N_A
Fe	56	56 g	N_A
Zn	65	65 g	N_A

Table 3.16

So, from the mass of any element in grams, we can find out how many atoms are present, relative to the number of atoms in 12 g of carbon. So if we could find the relative masses of the different elements in a compound, we could find the relative number of particles (atoms or ions). This will give us directly the formula of an ionic compound, but as you will see

shortly, there is one further step needed to find the formula of a molecular compound.

However, we shall come back to this. First, you should practice using the idea of moles, by answering the following questions. Before you do, there is one more point to bear in mind. Hydrogen is a diatomic molecule, H_2. So the relative molecular mass of a hydrogen molecule is 2. So a mole of hydrogen **molecules** is 2 g of hydrogen, since it is this amount of the element which contains Avogadro's Number of molecules. In the same way, a mole of chlorine molecules is 71 g (2×35.5 g) of chlorine, and a mole of oxygen molecules is 32 g (2×16 g) of oxygen. In the same way that we can add up the relative atomic masses of the atoms in a diatomic molecule to find the relative molecular mass, so we can for a molecular compound. So the relative molecular mass of carbon dioxide is 44 ((1×12) + (2×16)), and a mole of carbon dioxide is 44 g of it. 44 g of carbon dioxide contains Avogadro's Number of molecules.

Questions

What are the following, in grams?

1. 2 moles of hydrogen atoms
2. 5 moles of carbon
3. ½ mole of magnesium
4. 1/10 mole of calcium
5. 1/5 mole of zinc

How many particles are there in the following?

6. 10 g of hydrogen molecules
7. 22 g of carbon dioxide
8. 32 g of oxygen atoms
9. 6.35 g of copper
10. 14 g of carbon monoxide (formula CO)

The formula of an ionic compound

▶ EXPERIMENT 3.8

The formula of a molecular compound

Suppose we had carried out an experiment like the one above to find the relative number of moles of the different elements in a molecular compound. We could use our results to find the relative number of atoms in the molecule. But would this give us the formula? The formula of a molecular compound is the actual number of atoms of the different elements in the molecule, not the relative number.

If we find the relative number of the different atoms in the molecule of a molecular compound, we have

⟶ p. 166

EXPERIMENT 3.8
Finding the formula of zinc iodide

You will need the following: zinc powder, iodine crystals, ethanol, test-tube to fit centrifuge, teat-pipette, access to centrifuge, access to top-pan balance (it will be useful to have several balances available), test-tube rack.

What to do

YOU MUST WEAR YOUR SAFETY SPECTACLES. REMEMBER THAT ETHANOL IS FLAMMABLE.

1   Take one of the special test-tubes which can be used in the centrifuge. Take it to the top-pan balance, and weigh it. Write down the weight of the tube.

2   On a piece of paper, weigh **approximately** 1 g of iodine. Put the iodine in the test-tube, and weigh it again. Write down the weight of the test-tube + iodine. Place the test-tube in the test-tube rack.

3   On a piece of paper, weigh **approximately** ½ g of zinc. Put the zinc in the test-tube, together with the iodine, and weigh again. Write down the weight of the test-tube + iodine + zinc.

4   The zinc and the iodine do not react unless they are dissolved in a suitable solvent. When they do, the weights of the two elements which are present will mean that all the iodine reacts, but that there will be some zinc left unreacted.

Use a teat-pipette to add ethanol (methylated spirits), drop by drop, to the two elements in the test-tube. Add only one or two drops of ethanol to start with and wait for a few moments. Keep adding ethanol in this way, a few drops at a time, until no further reaction happens (you will see the purple colour of dissolved iodine disappear when this point is reached). You should have added only a small amount of ethanol.

5   Centrifuge the test-tube **in a balanced centrifuge. If you have not used a centrifuge before, or you are not sure how to balance it, ask your teacher to help.** Centrifuge for about 30 seconds.

6   Use a teat pipette to remove the solution of zinc iodide which has formed. **Be careful not to take away any of the zinc at the bottom of the tube**.

7   Add a few drops of ethanol to the zinc which is left in the bottom of the tube. Shake, so that the zinc and liquid mix. Centrifuge again, and remove the liquid as before. Make sure that you take out as much ethanol as possible.

8   Lay the tube and wet solid on a gauze which you are warming with a very low Bunsen flame. REMEMBER THAT ETHANOL IS FLAMMABLE, SO BE CAREFUL. Keep heating until the zinc in the tube appears to be dry. Let the tube cool and weigh it again. Write down the weight of the test-tube + excess zinc.

Calculation

The following are typical of the results which might be obtained for this experiment:

Weight of test-tube	= 5.40 g
Weight of test-tube + iodine	= 6.33 g
Weight of test-tube + iodine + zinc	= 6.75 g
Weight of test-tube + unreacted zinc	= 5.58 g

To find the formula of zinc iodide, we need to find the weights of zinc and iodine which go together to make some of it. We can find these weights from the results above in the following way:

Weight of iodine	= 6.33 − 5.40 g = 0.93 g
Weight of zinc added	= 6.75 − 6.33 g = 0.42 g
Weight of unreacted zinc	= 5.58 − 5.40 g = 0.18 g
∴ Weight of zinc which reacted	= 0.42 − 0.18 g = 0.24 g

∴ **0.93 g of iodine react with 0.24 g of zinc to make zinc iodide**

You should use your own results to calculate the weights of iodine and zinc which reacted in your experiment.

The relative atomic masses of zinc and iodine are:
    $Zn = 65$, $I = 126$

Use your own results to calculate the number of moles of zinc and iodine which reacted together. Find out how many moles of iodine would react with one mole of zinc. There must be some experimental errors included in your results, so you can convert your answer into the nearest whole number. This will be the ratio of the number of ions of zinc and iodine which react together. We know that zinc iodide is an ionic compound, so this ratio will give us the formula of zinc iodide. From your results, what is the formula?

found what is called the EMPIRICAL FORMULA (provided we have expressed this ratio in its simplest form). To get to the MOLECULAR FORMULA (the actual number of atoms in the molecule), we need also to know the relative molecular mass of the compound. We can do different experiments to find relative molecular masses. The following examples will show you how this works.

Example 1

A compound of carbon and hydrogen was found by experiment to be made up of the following proportions of the elements by weight:

carbon: 92.3%   hydrogen: 7.7%

The relative molecular mass of the compound is 78. What is its molecular formula?

To find the molecular formula, we must first calculate the empirical formula. But the results above are in a slightly different form from those we have seen before. The percentage by weight of the compound which is each of the elements is another way of expressing the relative mass of each element. Carbon accounts for 92.3/100 parts of the weight, and hydrogen makes up 7.7/100 of the weight. So the relative masses of each element in the compound are 92.3:7.7. So we can find the relative number of particles (atoms) by dividing each by the relative atomic mass of the element concerned:

relative no. of atoms of carbon   = 92.3/12 = 7.7
relative no. of atoms of hydrogen = 7.7/1   = 7.7

So, the relative number of atoms is 7.7:7.7, or 1:1. Therefore, **the empirical formula is CH**.

The ratio of the number of atoms in the molecule must be the same ratio as that shown by the empirical formula. So, **the molecular formula must be a whole number multiple of the empirical formula**. We have to find whether this whole number is 1, 2, 3, 4, etc. If the number were 1, then the relative molecular mass of the compound would be 12 + 1 = 13. But we know that the relative molecular mass is 78. Now 78/13 = 6. So, the whole number by which we must multiply the empirical formula, in order to get the molecular formula, is 6.

Therefore, **the molecular formula is C_6H_6**.

A compound whose molecular formula is C_6H_6 is benzene. The molecule can be represented like this:

Example 2

Another compound of carbon and hydrogen was found by experiment to have exactly the same proportion by weight of the two elements as in the previous experiment. The relative molecular mass of the compound is 26. What is its molecular formula?

If the compound contains carbon and hydrogen in the same proportions by weight as in the previous experiment, then the empirical formula must be the same: CH.
The relative molecular mass is 26. And 26/13 = 2. So we must multiply the empirical formula by 2 to get the molecular formula.

Therefore, **the molecular formula is C_2H_2**.

A compound whose molecular formula is C_2H_2 is ethyne (acetylene). The molecule looks like this:

$$H - C \equiv C - H$$

These examples should show how to work out molecular formulae from empirical formulae, and how to work out empirical formulae from the percentage by weight of the different elements in the compound. They also show how two different molecular compounds can have the same empirical formula.

The following is a summary of the steps which you need to take in calculating the formulae of compounds from the results of experiments.

Calculating the formulae of compounds

Step 1: You will know either the actual weights of the different elements in the compound, or the relative weights. Divide each weight, or relative weight, by the relative atomic mass of the element concerned.

Step 2: The result of step 1 is the relative number of moles of the different elements which go to make up the compound. Decide whether the compound is molecular or ionic.

Step 3: If the compound is ionic, then the ratio of the number of moles which go to make it up (which will be the same as the ratio of the number of particles of the different elements), when put in its simplest form, gives the formula.

Step 4: If the compound is molecular, also put the ratio of the number of moles into its simplest form. Find what the relative molecular mass would be if the empirical formula were the same as the molecular formula.

Step 5: Divide the relative molecular mass by the figure obtained in step 4. The answer should be a whole number.

Step 6: Multiply the empirical formula by this number, to give the molecular formula.

You should now try some examples for yourself, **using the steps set out above**.

Questions

In each case, use the information which is given to find the formula of the compound.

1. Elements: nitrogen, hydrogen. Weights which react together: N, 0.84 g; H, 0.18 g, Relative molecular mass = 17.

2. Elements: calcium, carbon, oxygen. Percentage composition by weight: Ca, 40.0%; C, 12.0%; O, 48.0%.

3. Elements: phosphorus, chlorine. Percentage composition by weight: P, 22.5%; Cl, 77.5%. Relative molecular mass = 137.5.

4. Elements: sodium, sulphur, oxygen. Weights which react together: Na, 10.2 g; S, 14.2 g; O, 10.6 g.

UNIT 3.3
Summary and learning

1 Group 0 elements all have filled outer shells of electrons. All other elements do not have filled outer shells, and so they combine chemically with other elements in order to obtain filled outer shells.

2 Metals all need to lose electrons to obtain filled outer shells. When they form chemical compounds, they lose the electrons in their outer shells, and form a cation. The number of positive charges on the cation which a metal forms is equal to the number of electrons which have been lost.

3 Non-metals all need to gain electrons to obtain filled outer shells. They can gain the number of electrons which they need to make up a filled shell in one of two ways. They can gain electrons from a metal, and form an anion. The number of negative charges on the anion is equal to the number of electrons which have been gained. The other way a non-metal can gain electrons is by sharing with another non-metal. Each element puts one electron into a common pool which both share. This common pool is a covalent bond. A non-metal forms as many covalent bonds as the number of electrons which it needs to gain, because it effectively gains one electron for every covalent bond.

4 When an ionic compound forms, the total number of positive and negative charges is equal. The formula of an ionic compound is the ratio in which the cations and anions combine together.

5 The formula of a molecular compound is the actual number of atoms of the different elements which are in the molecule.

6 Many non-metals exist as diatomic molecules.

7 The repulsions between the pairs of electrons in the outer shells of atoms differ depending on whether they are lone pairs or bonding pairs. Two lone pairs repel each other more strongly than a lone pair and a bonding pair, and this repulsion is stronger than that between two bonding pairs. We can use this knowledge to work out what the shapes of simple molecules will be.

8 A coordinate bond is exactly the same as a covalent bond, with the exception that both of the electrons come originally from one of the atoms involved. Molecules in which the central atom has one or more lone pairs of electrons are able to form coordinate bonds.

9 You should be able to describe the type of bonding in metals, and to use this to explain the properties of metals.

10 You should know the circumstances in which a hydrogen bond may form between two molecules.

11 The amount of an element which contains the same number of atoms as there are in 12 g of the isotope ^{12}C, is called a mole. This number of atoms is called Avogadro's Number (N_A).

12 If we divide the weight (or the relative weight) of an element in a compound by its own relative atomic mass, we get the number (or relative number) of moles of the element which are present. From the relative number of moles of the different elements, we can find the relative number of particles, and hence the formula of the compound.

13 For a molecular compound, the simplest ratio of the number of atoms in the molecule is called the empirical formula. The molecular formula is a whole number multiple of the empirical formula.

14 You should remember the steps in calculating the formula of a compound.

15 You have learnt the meaning of these words:

transition metal	complex ion
covalent bond	ligand
diatomic molecule	metallic bond
bonding pair	hydrogen bond
lone pair	mole
tetrahedron	empirical formula
linear	molecular formula
coordinate bond	

Chemical changes – 1

UNIT 4.1   *What are chemical changes?*

A reaction is a change. A chemical reaction is a chemical change. It is a change from the chemicals we start with before the reaction to the chemicals we finish with after the reaction. The chemicals we start with are called the REACTANTS. The chemicals we finish with are called the PRODUCTS.

A chemical reaction is a bit like what you do when you turn water to steam by boiling a kettle. It is what you have to do to change something into something else.

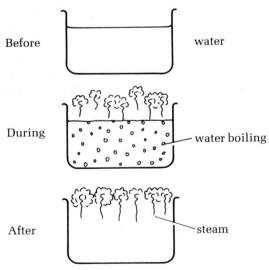

Fig. 4.1

You might boil a kettle because you wanted to get from water to steam. But water and steam are the same chemical. Boiling is a **physical** change. In chemistry you sometimes want to get from the chemicals you've got to some new chemicals. To do that, you have to do a chemical reaction.

Any change where new chemicals are produced from old ones is a chemical reaction. Chemical reactions are happening all the time in the world around us. Table 4.1 shows some examples.

Name	Chemical change
rusting	iron is changed into rust
breathing	oxygen is changed into carbon dioxide
cooking	raw food is changed into cooked food
gas fire burning	natural gas is changed into water and carbon dioxide
petrol engine running	petrol is changed into water, carbon dioxide and carbon monoxide.

Table 4.1

Can you think of any more? There are very many. But when you think that **everything** in the world is a chemical substance, chemical reactions are really very rare indeed. If all chemicals were constantly changing into other chemicals, it would be a strange world. Air is a mixture of chemicals, so is wood. Walls, floors, ceilings, windows, electric lights and decorations are all made of chemical substances. So are the pages of this book, and the ink that was used to print it. So are human beings!

Look at the laboratory you are in, or the room where you are reading this book. Write down any chemical reactions which are happening. (For instance, can you see a rusty window-catch or window frame? Is there something like a Bunsen burner or a gas fire alight in the room?)

Perhaps we should ask ourselves why some chemical changes happen, while for most of the time most chemicals do not react at all.

TOPIC 4.1.1

Why do chemical changes happen?

In the last section, you learnt about the halogen group

of elements. You did some reactions involving these
elements, and you saw some other reactions. You
compared the halogens chlorine, bromine and
iodine. You decided that chlorine was the most
'reactive'. You also decided that iodine was the least
'reactive'.

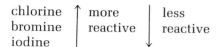

Look back at the work you did with the halogens in
the last section. Why did you say that chlorine was
the most reactive? Why did you say that iodine was
the least reactive?

Perhaps it is time to have another look at the idea of
reactivity. It may help us to understand why some
chemicals take part in chemical changes, while most
do not easily do so.

▶ EXPERIMENT 4.1 (p. 170)

If the products would be more reactive than the
reactants, no reaction happens (Figs. 4.2, 4.3).

Chemicals will move down the 'reactivity hill'
without any outside help. They will not move up the
reactivity hill without some help. As you will see
later, sometimes chemicals will move up the
reactivity hill with help from outside, but this is rare.

You know that when the halogens react they form a
halide, for instance, chlorine reacts to form a chloride
(a salt). All the halides have very low reactivity
compared to the halogens they are formed from. So we
could draw a reactivity hill for each halogen reacting
to form its halide. But we know that chlorine is more
reactive than bromine, which is more reactive than
iodine. So we know the heights of the three reactivity
hills compared to each other.

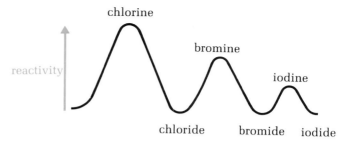

Fig. 4.4

Suppose you had some bromine, and that you could
react it with potassium chloride and with potassium
iodide. Would there be a reaction between bromine
and potassium iodide? The products would have to be
iodine and potassium bromide. Potassium takes no
real part in the reaction, so the reactants and products
are:

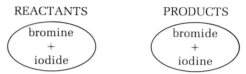

Look at Fig. 4.4. Are the reactants (taken together)
higher up or lower down the reactivity hills for the
halogens than the products (taken together)? So do
you think there would be a chemical change?

Now what about the possible chemical reaction
between bromine and potassium chloride. What
would the products of this reaction be, if it happened?
Again, potassium takes no real part in the reaction.
Are the reactants (together) more or less reactive than
the products (together)? So do you think this chemical
change would happen?

Now you can test your predictions.

▶ EXPERIMENT 4.2 (p. 171)

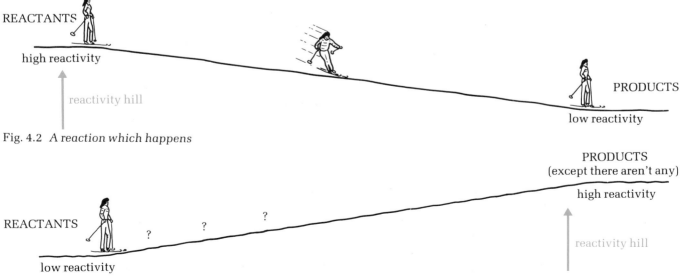

Fig. 4.2 *A reaction which happens*

Fig. 4.3 *A reaction which does not happen*

EXPERIMENT 4.1

Comparing the reactivity of chlorine with that of the other halogens

You will need the following: 3 test-tubes with bungs and a test-tube rack, chlorine water, solution of potassium iodide, solution of potassium bromide, solution of potassium chloride, trichloroethane.

What to do

YOU MUST WEAR YOUR SAFETY SPECTACLES.

1   Take some potassium iodide solution (about half a test-tube full) from the beaker provided by your teacher. Go to the fume-cupboard with this test-tube, and find the beaker which has the label 'chlorine water'. Use the teat-pipette which is there to put a few drops of the chlorine water into the test-tube with the potassium iodide solution.

2   Take this mixture back to your bench. Put a bung in the test-tube, and then shake it. Do you notice any change? If you do, write down what you see.

3   Go back to the fume-cupboard, and take your test-tube with you. Find the beaker which has the label 'trichloroethane'. Use the teat-pipette which is there to put a few drops of trichloroethane into the test-tube.

4   Take the test-tube back to your bench. Put a bung into the tube, and then shake it. Do you notice another change? If you do, write down what you see.

At this point, you should put your experiment to one side for a while. Sit down with the people who are working with you and try to decide between you what has happened in the test-tube. Before you start, read the following:
> Trichloroethane is not part of the chemical change. Instead it helps you to see what chemical change has happened. If there is any of the element iodine present, it will dissolve in the trichloroethane, and will make it go purple.

Was there any iodine in your test-tube? Where did it come from?
Write down what you have decided, and why you have decided it.

5   Repeat all the steps above (1–4), but use potassium bromide solution instead of potassium iodide solution. Any bromine present will dissolve in trichloroethane and make it go dark red. Remember this when you discuss your results.

6   Write down what you have decided and your reasons.

What happened

This table is a summary of what you should have seen:

	Chlorine only	Chlorine and trichloroethane
potassium iodide	solution goes brown/black	trichloroethane goes purple
potassium bromide	solution goes red	trichloroethane goes red

Table 4.2

When we put chlorine and potassium iodide together, a chemical reaction happens. A new chemical (iodine) forms. Chlorine also reacts with potassium bromide. This time the new chemical is bromine. So we can say:

chlorine + potassium iodide → iodine

and,   chlorine + potassium bromide → bromine

Questions

Now ask yourself these questions:
1   Is iodine more reactive, or less reactive than chlorine?

2   Is bromine more reactive, or less reactive than chlorine? Compare the answers you have just given to these questions, to what is written above. Which are the more reactive chemicals – reactant chemicals, or product chemicals?

What we can decide

The product chemicals are less reactive than the reactant chemicals. So it is the reactivity of the chemicals involved that decides whether or not a chemical change will happen. If the starting chemicals (the reactants) can react together to make chemicals (the products) which are less reactive than themselves, they do.

EXPERIMENT 4.2

Comparing the reactivity of bromine with that of other halogens

YOU MUST WEAR YOUR SAFETY SPECTACLES.

You will need the following: 3 test-tubes and a test-tube rack, bromine water, solution of potassium iodide, solution of potassium chloride, trichloroethane.

What to do

1   Repeat exactly steps 1–4 in Experiment 4.1, using potassium iodide solution and 'bromine water' from the fume cupboard.
Discuss your results, and try to decide what has happened.

2   Repeat these steps, using potassium chloride solution and 'bromine water' from the fume cupboard.
Discuss your results, and try to decide what has happened. (If the trichloroethane went **red**, then it is because **bromine** was present. Think carefully – does this mean that a reaction has happened?)
Write down what you have decided, and your reasons.

What happened

This table is a summary of what you should have seen:

	Bromine only	Bromine + trichloroethane
potassium iodide	solution goes brown/black	trichloroethane goes purple
potassium chloride	solution is red	trichloroethane goes red

Table 4.3

When bromine and potassium iodide are put together, a chemical reaction happens. A new chemical (iodine) forms:

bromine + potassium iodide
$\longrightarrow$ iodine (+ potassium bromide)

Look at Fig. 4.4. Iodide and bromide are both relatively unreactive. So the difference between the total reactivity of the reactants and the total reactivity of the products is the same as the difference between the reactivity of bromine and the reactivity of iodine. So we can draw the following diagram.

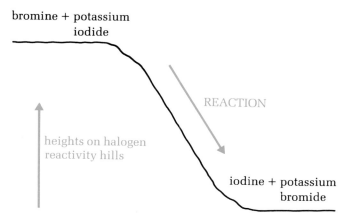

Fig. 4.5

When bromine and potassium chloride are put together, no reaction happens. The new chemical would have been . . . chlorine. Chlorine is higher up the reactivity hill than bromine, so the products would have been more reactive than the reactants and therefore no chemical change happens.

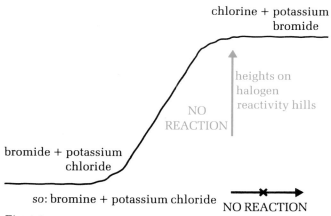

Fig. 4.6

What we can decide

If we know how reactive chemicals are relative to each other, we can predict whether or not chemical changes involving them will happen.

Question

Will a reaction happen if:
(a) iodine is put together with potassium bromide?
(b) iodine is put together with potassium chloride?
Explain each answer, and draw a diagram of the reactivity hill each time.

How to write down chemical changes in words

We have already written down many chemical changes in this book. If we write down the names of the reactant chemicals and the names of the product chemicals, with an arrow which shows the direction of the change, this is called a 'word-equation'. You met this idea first at the end of Unit 1.3. We put a '+' sign between the names of the reactant chemicals and between the names of the product chemicals.

Chlorine and potassium bromide react together to form bromine and potassium chloride. So the word equation is:

chlorine + potassium bromide
$\longrightarrow$ bromine + potassium chloride

Now try writing some word-equations for yourself:

	Reactants	Products
1	chlorine and potassium iodide	iodine and potassium chloride
2	bromine and potassium iodide	iodine and potassium bromide
3	hydrogen and oxygen	water (on its own)
4	carbon and oxygen	carbon dioxide (on its own)
5	sulphuric acid and sodium hydroxide	sodium sulphate and water

You know that all chemicals are either gases, liquids, solids or solutions. We can add this information (about the **state** of the chemicals) for every chemical in the word-equation. We do this by using a symbol:

(s) means 'solid'
(l) means 'liquid'
(g) means 'gas'
(aq) means 'solution in water' (short for 'aqueous', which means 'in water'. 'Aqua' is the Latin for 'water'.)

We use the symbol (l) for liquids which are pure substances (such as water). A solution is a liquid, but it is not a pure substance. A solution contains two chemicals – the substance which **has been** dissolved, and the liquid **in which** it dissolved. So we have to show the two types of liquids – pure liquids and solutions – differently. Think about salt dissolving in water. The word-equation would be:

salt(s) + water (l) $\rightarrow$ salt solution (aq)

Remember this example. It will help you to remember when to use '(l)' and when to use '(aq)' in word-equations.

Suppose we take as an example a particular reaction. This could be the reaction between hydrogen and oxygen, which produces water. Hydrogen is a gas, oxygen is a gas. Water is a liquid. The word-equation, with state-symbols, is:

hydrogen (g) + oxygen (g) $\rightarrow$ water (l)

If we turned the word-equation into a full sentence, the sentence would read as follows:

'Hydrogen gas reacts with oxygen gas and the product is the liquid called water'.

Questions

1   Write a sentence which explains what each of these word-equations means:

(a) sulphur (s) + oxygen (g) $\rightarrow$ sulphur dioxide (g)
(b) magnesium (s) + oxygen (g) $\rightarrow$ magnesium oxide (s)
(c) copper(II) oxide(s) + hydrogen (g)
$\longrightarrow$ copper(s) + water(l)

2   Write word-equations which match these sentences:

(a) Magnesium (a solid) reacts with lead oxide (a solid), and the products are magnesium oxide (a solid) and lead (a solid).
(b) Sodium (a solid) reacts with water (a liquid), and the products are hydrogen (a gas) and a solution in water of sodium hydroxide.

Understanding the reactivity of metals

We have used the idea of reactivity to explain why chemical changes happen. A reaction is a way of getting from more reactive chemicals to less reactive chemicals.

In Experiments 4.1 and 4.2 you saw why reactions which involve the halogen group of elements happen. **A reaction happened when one of the reactants was a more reactive halogen, and one of the products was a less reactive halogen.** We know the order of reactivity of the halogens, so we can say when a chemical reaction will happen and when it will not.

We can compare the reactivity of the halogens because they are similar to each other. Suppose we had some other elements which were also similar to each other. We would be able to compare their reactivity too. We could draw up an order of reactivity for these elements.

In Section 1, you learned about metals. Metals are elements and they are similar to each other. So we should be able to find an order of reactivity for metals.

(The fact that there is a 'reactivity series' for metals was mentioned in Section 1).

We know that a chemical change happens when we get a less reactive chemical at the end. Suppose we could try some chemical changes which involve metals. There would be a reaction **when a more reactive metal was one of the reactants, and a less reactive metal was one of the products.** This is exactly similar to what happened with the halogens.

For halogens:

$$\text{more reactive halogen} \xrightarrow{\text{REACTION}} \text{less reactive halogen}$$

$$\text{less reactive halogen} \xrightarrow[\times]{\substack{\text{NO} \\ \text{REACTION}}} \text{more reactive halogen}$$

For metals:

$$\text{more reactive metal} \xrightarrow{\text{REACTION}} \text{less reactive metal}$$

$$\text{less reactive metal} \xrightarrow[\times]{\substack{\text{NO} \\ \text{REACTION}}} \text{more reactive metal}$$

Metals will move down the 'reactivity hill' of metals of their own accord, but not up it.

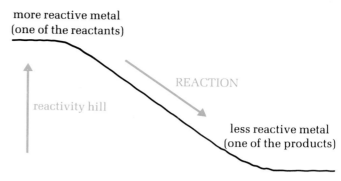

Fig. 4.7

If we start with a metal higher up as one of the reactants, there will be a reaction. We will get a metal lower down the reactivity hill as one of the products.

If we start with a metal lower down as one of the reactants, there will be no reaction. We will be left with the chemicals we started with.

So we can say that **the metal left at the end** (after there has been a reaction, or after there has been no reaction) **will be the one lower down the reactivity hill.** The metal left at the end will be the less reactive metal.

▶ EXPERIMENT 4.3

EXPERIMENT 4.3
Comparing zinc and copper for reactivity

You will need the following: test-tube, white tile, spatula, glass rod, zinc powder, copper(II) sulphate solution.

What to do

1 Take a test-tube, and half fill it with copper(II) sulphate solution. Take it back to your bench.

2 Get two spatula-measures of zinc powder on a piece of paper and take this back to your bench.

3 Make sure that everyone in the group sees the zinc powder, and remembers what colour it is. Later in the experiment you will have to compare the colour of zinc powder after it has reacted (with copper(II) sulphate solution) with the colour before it reacted. (If you want, you can keep a tiny amount of zinc powder separate from the zinc used in the reaction. Put a small pile of zinc in the corner of the white tile.)

4 Carefully pour the zinc into the copper(II) sulphate solution. (Use the paper as a funnel.) Stir several times with the glass rod.

5 Look to see if there are any changes happening in the test-tube. Is the colour of the solution changing? Hold the test-tube in your hand. Can you notice any other change?

6 When you can no longer see any changes, let the solution settle. Pour off most of the liquid. Use the spatula to scrape the wet powder out from the test-tube onto the white tile.

7 Now look at the wet powder. What colours can you see?

8 Ask yourself what colour copper metal is. **Now discuss what you have seen, and try to decide what has happened**.

9 Write down what you have seen and what you have decided.

Continued overleaf

Experiment 4.3 continued

What happened

You should have been able to see these changes.

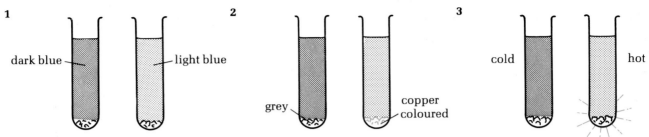

Fig. 4.8

1   The blue colour of the solution faded.

2   The grey colour of the zinc changed. It was coated in copper.

3   The test-tube got warmer.

Can you decide which metal is higher up the reactivity hill of metals: zinc or copper?

What we can decide

Zinc reacts with copper(II) sulphate solution. The products of the reaction are copper and zinc sulphate solution. The word-equation is:

zinc(s) + copper(II) sulphate (aq)
$\longrightarrow$ copper(s) + zinc sulphate (aq)

Zinc sulphate solution is colourless. So, as the reaction takes place, and copper(II) sulphate solution is replaced by zinc sulphate solution, the blue colour fades. At the same time, copper metal coats the zinc powder and so this seems to change colour.

The metal left at the end is copper. So copper is lower down the reactivity hill than zinc. **Zinc is more reactive than copper**.

In the reaction zinc changed into zinc cations, and copper changed from being copper cations. Both zinc cations and copper cations are much less reactive than the metals. So we can say that the reactivity hills for metals look like Fig. 4.9.

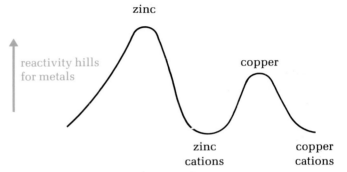

Fig. 4.9

We can also draw the following diagram for the chemical change which has happened.

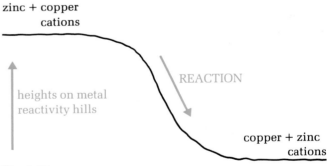

Fig. 4.10

The test-tube got warmer – but why was this? Where did the heat come from? We will ask ourselves this question in the next unit of this section. But at least it seems to be something to do with the reaction. Heat being given out is another clue that a reaction is taking place.

We can use the same method as that used for zinc and copper to find the order of reactivity for other metals.

▶ EXPERIMENT 4.4

EXPERIMENT 4.4
Putting more metals in their order of reactivity

You will need the following: microscope slides or white tiles, a glass rod or teat-pipette, the metals and solutions of metal compounds in the following list:

Metals	Compounds containing metals
magnesium ribbon	Solutions of:
lead foil	magnesium chloride
iron filings	lead nitrate
zinc foil	iron(II) sulphate
copper foil	zinc sulphate
	copper(II) sulphate
	silver nitrate

DO NOT LET THE SILVER NITRATE TOUCH YOUR SKIN. IF IT DOES, WASH IT OFF IMMEDIATELY.

What to do

1   Each reaction is between a metal and a compound containing a metal. You will carry them out on a microscope slide (or on a white tile) using only a drop of solution and a tiny piece of metal.

2   Take **one** of the solutions. Place a drop of it at each end of a microscope slide, using a glass rod or a teat-pipette. Repeat this with a second microscope slide. Take a third microscope slide, and put a drop of the solution in the middle of it. You will now have five drops of the solution in all. (If you are using a white tile, put a row of five drops of the solution down one side of it.)

3   Take a piece of magnesium ribbon, and put it in one of the drops of solution. Put a piece of each of the four remaining metals into the four remaining drops of solution. For iron, you will have to use 4 or 5 iron filings.

4   Look to see if a reaction is taking place in each drop of solution. If it is, you may see a different metal being produced, or the solution may change colour.

5   For each metal, write down what happens.

6   Repeat the experiment with a new solution, but make sure that your microscope slides are clean. If you have a white tile, separate the rows of drops and do not wash them off. Work systematically, putting the same metal in the same row each time. If you have time to do all the reactions, your tile will look like Fig. 4.11.

At the end of the experiment, you will be able to compare all the metals and all the solutions.

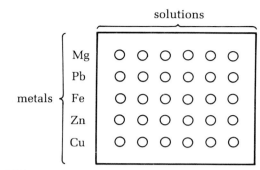

Fig. 4.11

What happened

For each solution, with each metal, decide whether a reaction took place or not. Put your results in a table like the one below. Show a reaction which took place with a tick (√), and one which did not with a cross (×).

	Mg	Pb	Fe	Zn	Cu
magnesium chloride	×	×	×	×	×
lead nitrate	√	×	√	√	×
iron(II) sulphate	√	×	×	√	×
zinc sulphate	√	×	×	×	×
copper(II) sulphate	√	√	√	√	×
silver nitrate	√	√	√	√	√

Table 4.4

What we can decide

When a chemical reaction takes place, the reactants are more reactive than the products. In a salt, the metal is present as a metal cation. So when, for instance, magnesium is put with copper(II) sulphate, it is the element magnesium and the copper(II) cation which have a chance of reacting.

In each of the reactions which took place, a metal was one of the products. At the same time, the reactant metal was used up. The metal which was a product of the reaction came from the metal cation in solution. This means that, **in all those cases where a reaction took place, the reactant metal was more reactive than the product metal**.

A general word-equation for all those reactions which took place is:

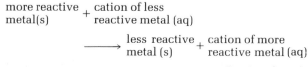

Continued overleaf

If no reaction took place, the reactant metal was less reactive than the metal contained in the salt.

$$\text{less reactive} \atop \text{metal(s)} \; + \; \text{cation of more} \atop \text{reactive metal(aq)} \xrightarrow[\times]{} \text{NO REACTION}$$

You can use these facts, together with your table of results, to find an order of reactivity for the metals. Suppose magnesium reacted with copper(II) sulphate. This would mean that magnesium is more reactive than copper. So we can write down:

increasing reactivity ↑   magnesium
                           copper

Now see if you can put any other metals above copper, from your results. For instance, is iron more reactive or less reactive than copper? If it is, it belongs above copper in the order of reactivity. But does it also belong above magnesium? To answer this question, you will have to decide whether magnesium is more reactive than iron, or whether iron is more reactive than magnesium.

Use your own results to try to work out a complete order of reactivity for the metals. How does your order compare with the theoretical order of reactivity for the metals?

The metal reactivity series

↑   sodium
                     calcium
                     magnesium   (This is the same
                     aluminium   order as the heights
                     zinc   of the metal reactivity
                     iron   hills if we drew them
increasing   lead   all.)
reactivity   copper
                     silver
                     gold

Remember that you carried out Experiments 4.1 and 4.2 to see if you could find a rule for predicting whether a particular reaction would take place. For reactions which involve metals, this rule is given by the position of the metal in the reactivity series of metals:

A metal higher in the series will react with a compound containing a metal lower in the series.

For example, suppose that you wanted to know whether magnesium will react with silver nitrate. What are the chemicals present?

magnesium metal   +   silver cation
        ↑   ↑
metal **higher** in the   cation of metal
reactivity series   **lower** in the
than silver   series than magnesium
            A CHEMICAL REACTION

The positions of magnesium and silver in the reactivity series tell us that a chemical reaction will take place.

As another example, would gold metal react with silver nitrate? What are the chemicals present?

gold metal   +   silver cation
        ↑   ↑
metal **lower** in the   cation of metal
reactivity series   **higher** in the reactivity
than silver   series than gold
            NO CHEMICAL REACTION

This time, there would be no reaction. Gold is lower in the reactivity series of metals than silver.

Now try some examples for yourself.

Questions

For each of the following questions, write down the chemicals present, and their positions relative to each other in the reactivity series. Do this as you were shown in the examples above. In each case, write down whether there would be a chemical reaction, or no chemical reaction.

1. Iron + zinc chloride
2. Lead + calcium nitrate
3. Aluminium + gold chloride
4. Potassium + aluminium sulphate
4. Copper + sodium chloride

We know that the less reactive metal is always a product of the reaction. We say that the more reactive metal DISPLACES the less reactive metal from the compound which contained it. 'Displace' means 'turn out'. (You met this word first in Section 3.) Suppose

we go back to the example of magnesium reacting with silver nitrate. We can describe it like this:

magnesium(s) + silver cation (aq)
        ⟶ silver(s) + magnesium cation (aq)

Magnesium displaces silver from silver nitrate

Question

Where you decided in the questions above that a chemical reaction would take place, write out a word-equation and description, as in the example just given.

The metal reactivity series can also be used to tell us about the reactivity of some other elements. These are elements which are not metals themselves, but which can behave sometimes as if they were metals. If an element does this, then it can be compared to other metals. One such element is the gas hydrogen. It takes part in displacement reactions exactly as if it were a metal. But what would these displacement reactions involving hydrogen look like? How could we do experiments to find a position for hydrogen in the metal reactivity series?

Some metals react with acids. When they do, they **displace** hydrogen (as a gas) from the acid. Some metals do **not** react with acids, and so they do not displace hydrogen from acids.

You saw in Unit 1.3 that all acids contain hydrogen. A metal which is very reactive is more reactive than hydrogen. So a very reactive metal will react with an acid, and will displace hydrogen from it. So it is as if hydrogen has a place on the reactivity series of metals.

But exactly where does hydrogen come in the reactivity series?

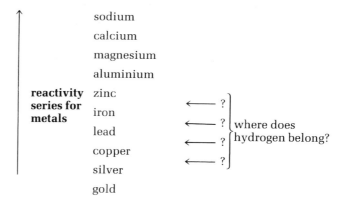

EXPERIMENT 4.5

EXPERIMENT 4.5
How reactive is hydrogen?

You will need the following: test-tube, dilute hydrochloric acid, a short piece of magnesium ribbon, zinc foil, a small piece of iron, copper foil, wood splints.

What to do

YOU MUST WEAR YOUR SAFETY SPECTACLES.

1   Take a test-tube, and half fill it with dilute hydrochloric acid.

2   Add a piece of magnesium ribbon to the acid. Does the reaction produce a gas? It it does, put your thumb over the end of the test-tube to trap some of it. When you can feel the pressure of the gas, quickly test it with a glowing splint. Hydrogen burns with a loud pop, and sometimes a squeak. Was the gas hydrogen?

3   **Discuss what you have seen, and try to decide what has happened.**

4   Write down what you have seen, and what you have decided.

5   Clean the test-tube. Repeat steps 1–4 for one of the other metals. If you cannot see a reaction taking place, warm the test-tube **very carefully**. DO NOT POINT THE TEST-TUBE TOWARDS YOURSELF OR TOWARDS ANYONE ELSE WHILE YOU ARE WARMING IT. Keep the tube moving all the time.

6   Carry on until you have tested the other three metals to see if they displace hydrogen from dilute hydrochloric acid.

What happened

You should have been able to see that the following happened:

magnesium ⎫
zinc   ⎬ react with dilute hydrochloric acid, giving
iron   ⎭ hydrogen gas
copper   does not react with dilute hydrochloric acid

What can you say about the reactivity of hydrogen? Where does it come in the metal reactivity series?

What we can decide

Magnesium, zinc and iron are all more reactive than hydrogen. Copper is less reactive than hydrogen. So hydrogen comes somewhere between iron and copper in the metal reactivity series.

The exact place for hydrogen is below lead and above copper:

The metal reactivity series
sodium
calcium
magnesium
aluminium
zinc
iron
lead
  ← hydrogen
copper
silver
gold

UNIT 4.1
Summary and learning

1   A chemical change is what happens when new chemicals are produced from old chemicals. We often call a chemical change a 'chemical reaction'.

2   When a chemical reaction happens, the product chemicals (taken together) are less reactive than the reactant chemicals.

3   We can represent chemical reactions by 'word-equations'. You should remember the list of 'state symbols', and this example:

  salt(s) + water(l) → salt solution (aq)

4   The metal reactivity series is the order of the heights of the reactivity hills for the metals. It lets us predict in advance whether a particular reaction which involves metals will happen or not. A metal higher in the series will react with a compound which contains cations of a metal which is lower down the series.

5   Hydrogen can behave like a metal, and so we can give it a position in the metal reactivity series. Hydrogen comes below lead and above copper.

6   You have learnt the meaning of these words:

reactants
products
displace

UNIT 4.2   *What else happens during a chemical change?*

We know that a chemical change is the change from the reactant chemicals to the product chemicals. We have looked at several chemical reactions to find out more about them, and to find a way of being able to tell if a chemical reaction will take place or not.

But is a change from the reactant chemicals to the product chemicals the **only** change that happens when there is a chemical reaction? Or can there be other changes as well?

If you think back through all the chemical reactions which you have seen, then you should be able to remember some 'other things' which happened. Can you remember a chemical reaction where there was a change in temperature? Can you remember one where light was given out? Can you remember a reaction which seemed to make a noise? Do you remember a chemical reaction where the chemicals change colour?

Question

Make a list of the changes which happen when there is a chemical reaction.

How is heat linked with chemical changes?

We can examine one of the other changes that goes with chemical changes in the following experiment.

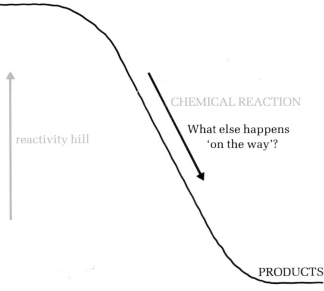

REACTANTS

reactivity hill

CHEMICAL REACTION

What else happens 'on the way'?

PRODUCTS

Fig. 4.12

▶   EXPERIMENT 4.6

EXPERIMENT 4.6
A closer look at hydrated copper(II) sulphate

You will need the following: 2 hard-glass test-tubes, 250 cm³ beaker, bung and bent glass tubing, retort stand and clamp, crystals of hydrated copper(II) sulphate.

What to do

YOU MUST WEAR YOUR SAFETY SPECTACLES.

1   Take one of the hard-glass tubes and fill it one-third full of crystals of hydrated copper(II) sulphate.

2   Put the stand and clamp together. Clamp the tube close to its neck, so that it is horizontal above the bench.

3   Put the bung and tubing in the neck of the tube holding the hydrated copper(II) sulphate. Alter the position of the tube so that it slopes **slightly** downwards, towards the bung.

4   Take the beaker and fill it half-full with water. Place the other tube in the beaker, so that it rests against its side.

5   Put the end of the tubing from the other tube into the tube in the beaker of water. Alter the position of the tube above the bench so that the end of the tubing is about half an inch above the bottom of the tube in the beaker.
The whole apparatus should look like this:

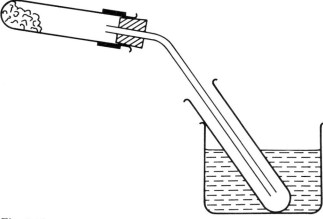

Fig. 4.13

6   Light a Bunsen burner and set the flame to a medium height.

7   Start to heat the hydrated copper(II) sulphate crystals gently. Keep the Bunsen flame moving all the time you are heating.

8   You will see that a vapour is given off. At the same time, a liquid will start to collect in the tube in the beaker of water. **Make sure that the end of the tubing stays above the level of the liquid.** If the liquid rises up the tube too far, alter the position of the tube which contains the hydrated copper(II) sulphate, so that the end of the tubing is lifted clear of the top of the liquid.

9   Keep heating until you can see no more vapour being given off. When you stop heating, **write down all the changes which you have seen. Discuss what you have seen so far.** What did the heat do to the hydrated copper(II) sulphate?

10   Let the test-tube cool for at least 10 minutes. When you are sure that it has cooled down, one of the group can take it out of the clamp.

11   Someone should hold the tube in the palm of their hand. By now, the tube will contain a white powder. Whoever is holding the tube should make sure that they hold it near the bottom, where the white powder is located.

12   Another member of the group can now take the other tube (the one in which the liquid collected) out of the beaker. They should add **a little bit** of this liquid to the tube which the other person is holding.

13   What happens when the liquid is added to the white powder? How many changes are there? **Write down all the changes which you have noticed. Discuss these changes, and the changes which you saw earlier. Try to decide what is happening.**

14   Each person should take turns to hold the tube while a little more liquid is added.

15   Write down what you have decided.

What happened

You should have been able to see the following.

1   When you heated the hydrated copper(II) sulphate, steam was produced. The steam condensed into water, and collected in the tube in the beaker. The hydrated copper(II) sulphate changed from being blue to being white.

2   When the water was added to the white solid left at the end of the heating, it turned blue again. At the same time, the test-tube got hot.

Can you say what the heat of the Bunsen burner caused to happen? Where do you think the heat of the

Continued overleaf

Experiment 4.6 continued

Bunsen burner **went** to?

Can you say what happened when the water was added to the white solid? Where did the heat come from?

What we can decide

When you heated the hydrated copper(II) sulphate crystals, **the heat made a chemical reaction happen**. The reactant chemical was hydrated copper(II) sulphate, and the product chemicals were the white powder and water. The water was given off in the form of steam, because the temperature was above 100°C. 'Hydrated' means 'with water'. The white powder is still copper(II) sulphate, but it is copper(II) sulphate 'without water'. The scientific word for this is 'anhydrous'. Now that we know the names of all the chemicals, we can write the word-equation for the reaction which the heat caused to happen.

$$\text{hydrated copper(II) sulphate(s)} \xrightarrow{\text{HEAT}} \text{anhydrous copper(II) sulphate(s)} + \text{water(g)}$$

The hydrated copper(II) sulphate did not react all by itself as soon as it was in the test-tube. It had to be heated first. So hydrated copper(II) sulphate is **unreactive**. It is at the **bottom** of the reactivity hill. The heat from the Bunsen burner gave the chemicals enough energy to climb the reactivity hill.

So we **can** make chemicals go from reactants of low reactivity to products of high reactivity. But to do this we have to supply the energy needed to climb the reactivity hill. This energy has to come from outside the chemical reaction. If we add heat energy from the outside, this will often make chemicals climb the reactivity hill.

Reactions which take in heat from the outside and use it to climb the reactivity hill are call ENDOTHERMIC reactions. 'Endo' means 'to the inside' and 'thermic' means 'heat'. So endothermic means 'heat to the inside', or 'heat goes in'. The product chemicals gain energy compared to the reactant chemicals, when a reaction is endothermic. They gain heat energy, which they take in from the outside.

We show that a reaction is endothermic by using a special symbol at the end of the word-equation. The symbol is $\triangle H$+ve. The way we say this is 'Delta H is positive'. Delta H is the change in energy, and +ve means that the change is an increase, rather than a decrease. The chemicals gain in energy as we go from the reactants to the products. For all endothermic reactions, $\triangle H$ is positive. This is because, if heat is taken in from the outside, the chemicals have more energy at the end of the reaction than at the beginning. The word-equation for the reaction which happened when you heated hydrated copper(II) sulphate in your experiment, is:

hydrated copper(II) sulphate (s)
$\longrightarrow$ anhydrous copper(II) sulphate(s) + water (l)
$\triangle H$ +ve

Anhydrous copper(II) sulphate and water are at the top of the reactivity hill. So why didn't they automatically react to make hydrated copper(II) sulphate? Think back to your experiment. The anhydrous copper(II) sulphate and the water could not react together, because one stayed behind in the test-tube and the other passed out of the test-tube as vapour. They could not get into contact with each other to react. It is as if a boy and his skis are at the top of the hill, but the boy is not wearing the skis. As soon as he puts on the skis, then they can both go down the hill together.

A reaction happens

Nothing happens

Fig. 4.14

This is exactly what happened as soon as you added the water back to the anhydrous copper(II) sulphate. They reacted together, and the product chemical was hydrated copper(II) sulphate. This time, **heat was given out** by the chemicals. A chemical reaction which gives out heat is called an EXOTHERMIC reaction. 'Exo' means 'to the outside'. So, exothermic means 'heat to the outside', or 'heat is given out'. The symbol for an exothermic reaction is $\triangle H$−ve.

The sign of $\triangle H$ is negative, because the chemicals lose energy. The chemicals move down the reactivity hill, and they have less energy at the end than at the beginning. The word-equation for the exothermic reaction which happened when you added water to anhydrous copper(II) sulphate in your experiment is:

anhydrous copper(II) sulphate(s) + water (l)
$\longrightarrow$ hydrated copper(II) sulphate(s)
$\triangle H$ −ve

We can imagine the changes which took place during your experiment as follows:

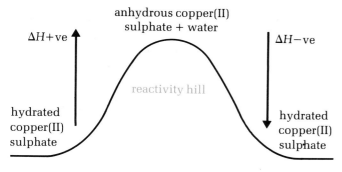

Fig. 4.15

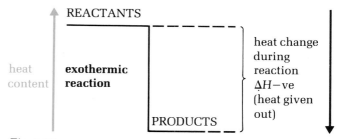

Fig. 4.17

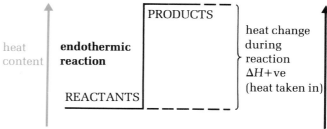

Fig. 4.18

Since we have managed to get back to where we started from (the chemical hydrated copper(II) sulphate), we can obviously carry out the same process again. We could do it as many times as we liked. The diagram to represent what happened would look like this:

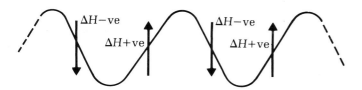

Fig. 4.16

If a reaction is exothermic, the surroundings get warmer. This is because the heat which the reaction gives out to the surroundings makes the temperature rise. So we normally spot an exothermic reaction by the fact that it makes the things around it get hotter. You noticed that this is what happened when you added water to anhydrous copper(II) sulphate.

When an endothermic reaction takes in heat from the surroundings, this makes the temperature fall. So we normally spot an endothermic reaction by the fact that it makes the things around it get cooler. You didn't notice this when hydrated copper(II) sulphate split up, because the Bunsen burner was making up for the heat taken in by the reaction. However, there are many chemical reactions which make their surroundings get cooler.

Table 4.5 is a summary of what you have just learned about endothermic and exothermic reactions:

Type of reaction	Heat is	Surroundings get	Sign of $\triangle H$
endothermic	taken in	cooler	+ ve
exothermic	given out	hotter	− ve

Table 4.5

We have a special way of representing the energy changes which take place during chemical reactions. These are called ENERGY LEVEL DIAGRAMS, and really they are a simplification of our idea of the reactivity hill.

For an exothermic reaction, the energy level diagram looks like this:

For an endothermic reaction, the energy level diagram looks like this:

Look back at the list that you made of changes which happen during chemical reactions. You know that heat is a form of energy. How many of the other changes are changes in energy? Do you think a change in energy is common during chemical changes? If so, perhaps we ought to find out why.

TOPIC 4.2.2

Where does the energy change during chemical reactions come from?

We know that, during a chemical reaction, new chemical compounds form and old ones are used up. If the reaction is between molecular compounds, this means that covalent bonds in reactant molecules have to break before any change can happen. Then, new covalent bonds have to form to make the product molecules. We can imagine what happens as being like this:

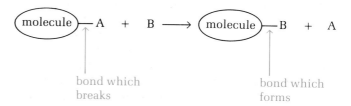

It takes energy to break the bond to element A in the reactant molecule. This is only like saying that it takes energy to snap a rubber band or a piece of string. **Forming** a bond gives out energy. So when a bond forms to element B, to make the product molecule, some energy is given out.

If the reaction is between ionic compounds, the forces involved (which have to be overcome to break up the reactants, and so on) are the forces of attraction between oppositely charged ions. Apart from this difference, the situation is the same as for molecular compounds. First, a force of attraction (the equivalent of a bond) has to be overcome, and this takes energy. Then a new force of attraction comes into being (like the new chemical bond when a product molecule forms), as the ions rearrange to form the product chemicals. As this new force comes into operation, energy is given out (in the same way that energy is given out when a new chemical bond is formed). We can imagine the situation for ionic compounds as being like this:

$$X^+ \text{---} Y^- + Z^+ \longrightarrow Z^+ \text{---} Y^- + X^+$$

    ↑   ↑

force of attraction   force of attraction
which has to be   which comes into
overcome   being

But if some energy is taken in (to break bonds) and some energy is given out (when bonds form), is energy taken in or given out, overall? For either type of chemical compound, the situation is the same. If the amount of energy which is needed to break up the reactants is greater than the amount of energy which is given out when the products form, then overall energy will be taken in. If the amount of energy needed to break up the reactants is less than the amount of energy which is given out when the products form, overall energy will be given out. So what matters is not what type of chemical compounds take part in the chemical reaction. What matters is the amount of energy needed to break up the reactant chemicals compared to the amount of energy which is released when the product chemicals form.

If the bond (or force of attraction) in a compound is strong, it will need a lot of energy to overcome it. In the same way, a lot of energy will be given out when a strong bond (or force of attraction) forms.

A weak bond (or force of attraction) needs little energy to overcome it, and it causes only a small amount of energy to be given out when it forms.

The overall energy change for a chemical reaction is the sum of all the energy taken in by bonds being broken, and the energy give out by bonds being formed. So if the bonds (or forces of attraction) which are being formed (those in the **product** chemicals) are stronger than the bonds (or forces of attraction) which are being broken (those in the **reactant** chemicals),

then the reaction overall will be exothermic.

If the bonds (or forces of attraction) in the products are weaker than those in the reactants, the reaction overall will be endothermic.

If the reactants have the stronger bonds, the reaction is endothermic.
If the products have the stronger bonds, the reaction is exothermic.

We can imagine what happens, in either case, in the following diagram.

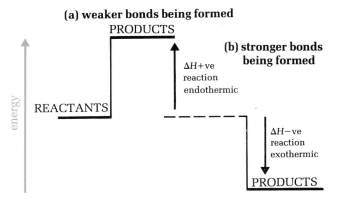

Fig. 4.19

Question

From the reactions which you have studied so far, choose one which is exothermic and one which is endothermic. Describe what happens to the bonds in both reactions, and how strong the different bonds must be relative to each other.

All chemical reactions, whether they are exothermic or endothermic, start with the breaking of chemical bonds. So **every** chemical reaction needs some energy to start with. To put it another way, we have to give all chemical reactions a 'push' to get them started. We call this push the ACTIVATION ENERGY of the reaction ('activation' means 'starting').

Think how many chemical reactions have to be heated before they will take place. This is because of the activation energy which they need. In a car engine, the chemical reaction which takes place is between petrol and the oxygen in the air. The reaction causes an explosion – it is **very** exothermic. But this reaction will not happen if petrol and air are simply mixed together. There has to be a spark or some other source of energy. So, all car engines have a mechanism for supplying a spark – which supplies the activation energy for the reaction (Fig. 4.22).

Suppose we now add the activation energy to the energy level diagrams which we drew in Topic 2.1. The complete picture for an exothermic reaction would be:

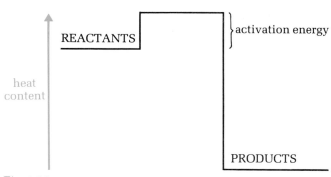

Fig. 4.20

In reality, the changes which happen during a chemical reaction are much smoother and more gradual than this shape suggests. So we should really draw a smooth curve, showing what happens during the course of the reaction:

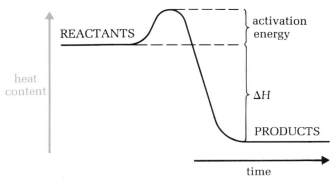

Fig. 4.21 *Potential energy diagram – exothermic reaction*

Such diagrams are called POTENTIAL ENERGY DIAGRAMS.

Questions

1 Draw a potential energy diagram, showing the activation energy and $\triangle H$, for an endothermic reaction.

2 Make a list of as many examples as you can (up to ten) of how the activation energy is supplied to everyday chemical reactions. For example, the activation energy for the chemical reaction when a match-head bursts into flames comes from the heat produced by friction when the match is being struck. Is cooking a chemical reaction?

TOPIC 4.2.3

Chemical changes which give us energy

You have just seen that chemical reactions can give out heat. Heat is energy, so chemical reactions can give us energy. You saw some of the reasons why we need energy in the modern world in Section 2 (Unit 2.2).

You also learned in Section 2 about the different types of fossil fuel and how they came about, and the problems of carbon dioxide pollution caused by burning fossil fuels. We might now ask ourselves two questions about fossil fuels.

1. How is energy stored in fossil fuels?
2. How is energy released when we burn a fossil fuel?

You know that fossil fuels come from decayed animal and vegetable matter, and that these are made up of

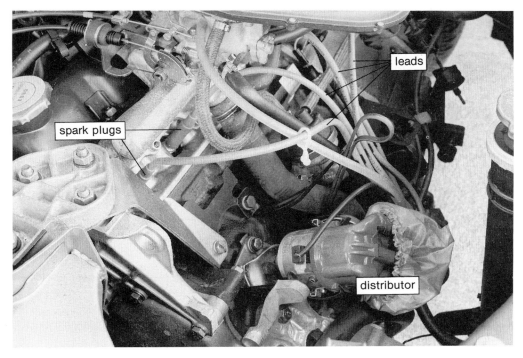

Fig. 4.22 *The distributor in a car engine provides a spark to each cylinder*

fairly complicated chemicals. But how did these complicated chemicals come into being in the first place?

Fig. 4.23 *Energy from the sun is being stored in chemical form in these sugar-beet*

Plants need to store energy so that they can use it later to grow. The energy that they store comes from the sun. It is 'trapped' in the form of chemicals. Plants use the energy of the sun to carry out an endothermic chemical reaction. The reactant chemicals are carbon dioxide and water, and the product chemicals are called SUGARS (oxygen is also produced). Plants that are able to do this are always green in colour because they have to contain a special green chemical called CHLOROPHYLL. You will probably have come across chlorophyll before. It is able to trap the energy in sunlight.

Green plants use the energy trapped by chlorophyll to build up complicated chemicals (sugars) from simple chemicals (carbon dioxide and water). The scientific word for 'building' is 'synthesis', and the

scientific word for 'light' is 'photo'. Put them together and you get 'photosynthesis', which means 'building-up with light'. So the scientific word for what green plants do when they make sugars using sunlight is PHOTOSYNTHESIS. The word-equation for photosynthesis is:

$$\text{carbon dioxide(g) + water(l)} \rightarrow \text{sugar(aq) + oxygen(g)}$$
$$\triangle H \text{ +ve}$$

So when a green plant makes sugars to trap the energy of the sun, oxygen is given out to the atmosphere. Before there were green plants, there was no oxygen to breathe! Over millions of years, trees and plants have made huge amounts of oxygen – so now there is plenty. Compare the amount of oxygen in the Earth's atmosphere with the amounts in the atmospheres of Venus and Mars (Unit 2.1, Fig. 2.15 and Table 2.1). Does it seem that there have ever been green plants making oxygen on Venus or Mars?

So green plants store energy from the sun in the form of chemicals called sugars. And they store sugars by turning them into a new chemical called STARCH. Plants take sugar molecules and join them up end-to-end to make very long molecules of starch. Often they store the starch in their roots. A potato is a store of starch for the potato plant (Fig. 4.24).

Starch is just a way of storing sugar molecules in a convenient form. The energy from the sun which was trapped by chlorophyll is stored in the sugar molecules themselves. But how exactly?

You saw in the last topic that if a chemical reaction is endothermic, then the bonds in the reactant chemicals are stronger than the bonds in the product chemicals. You know from Section 3 (Unit 3.3) that the covalent bonds in carbon dioxide are double bonds, and therefore very strong. Energy from the sun is used during photosynthesis to break these strong

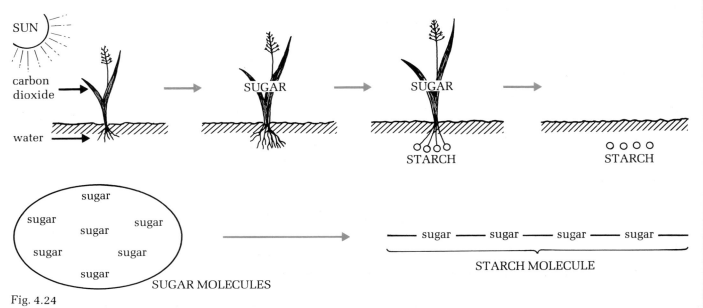

Fig. 4.24

bonds, which are replaced by weaker (single) bonds in the sugar molecules which are formed:

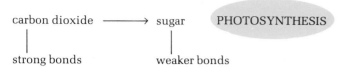

carbon dioxide ⟶ sugar   PHOTOSYNTHESIS

strong bonds   weaker bonds

Sugars and starch are both part of a group of chemicals called CARBOHYDRATES. Carbohydrates contain the elements carbon, oxygen and hydrogen. The chemicals in fossil fuels are called HYDROCARBONS.

Hydrocarbons are made up from the elements carbon and hydrogen. When the dead plant becomes fossilised (see Unit 2.1), the carbohydrates are turned into hydrocarbons. In hydrocarbons, the bonds are (for the most part) weaker single bonds like those in carbohydrates. So it is as if the hydrocarbons still contain the energy stored in the carbohydrates.

But how is the energy released from these chemicals? We need to take a closer look at what happens when something burns.

▶ EXPERIMENTS 4.7 AND 4.8

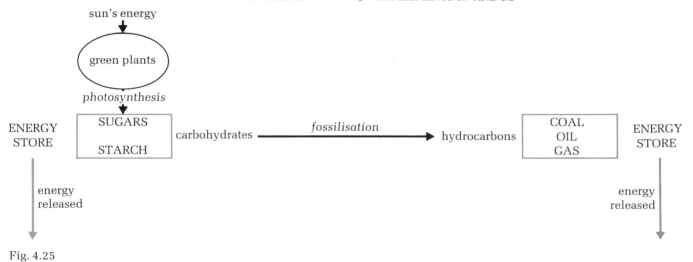

Fig. 4.25

EXPERIMENT 4.7
What happens when a candle burns?

You will need the following: candle (on a small clock-glass), a 250 cm³ beaker, a small piece of Plasticine, pieces of universal indicator paper, anhydrous cobalt chloride paper, white tile, lime-water.

What to do

1 Put the candle (on the clock-glass) on the white tile. Now light the candle, and place the beaker upside down over the burning candle. Seal the pouring-lip of the beaker with the piece of Plasticine.

2 Notice what happens to the flame. Write down what you have seen. Now take the beaker away, and allow a fresh supply of air into it.

3 Light the candle again, and put the beaker and the piece of Plasticine back into position. Notice what happens. Do this several times.

4 If some liquid forms on the inside of the beaker as a 'mist', test it with a piece of anhydrous cobalt chloride paper to see if it is water.

5 Light the candle again, and put it under the beaker. Put the Plasticine in place. When the flame has gone out, carefully pick up the beaker and the white tile together. Turn the beaker over, so that it is the 'right' way up, but do not let the white tile move.

6 Move the white tile to one side, so that there is a gap of about ½ inch at the top of the beaker. Pour **a little** lime-water through the gap, and slide the tile back into place. Now shake the beaker, carefully holding the white tile.

What happened

You should have been able to see the following.

1 The flame went out after a short time when it was under the beaker.

Continued overleaf

2   A liquid formed on the inside of the beaker. This liquid turned anhydrous cobalt chloride paper from blue to pink.

3   The gas which is left in the beaker after the candle has burned turns lime-water milky.

What we can decide

Every time the beaker was put over the flame of the candle, the flame eventually went out. When some more air was let into the beaker, the flame would burn again for a short time. So we can say that the candle **uses up** the air (or something in the air) when it burns. Eventually, the part of the air which is being used up is exhausted, and the candle goes out.

The part of the air which is used up when something burns is the oxygen. So oxygen is one of the reactant chemicals in the reaction which happens when something burns.

One of the product chemicals of burning a candle is water. We know this because the anhydrous cobalt chloride showed us that water had collected on the inside of the beaker. The water had come from the flame as water vapour, and condensed on the cold surface of the beaker. The lime-water test shows that carbon dioxide was left in the beaker after the reaction. So we know that another product of burning is carbon dioxide.

So, when something burns, there is a chemical reaction. The reactant chemicals are the thing which burns (in this case, the candle) and oxygen from the air. The product chemicals are water, carbon dioxide and sometimes soot. The reaction is exothermic. So we can write a word-equation for the reaction which happens when a candle burns:

$$candle\text{-}wax(s) + oxygen(g) \rightarrow water\,(l) + carbon\;dioxide(g)$$
$$\triangle H - ve$$

This equation should look a little familiar. We can go a step further if we take some sugar and burn it.

EXPERIMENT 4.8
Burning sugar

You will need the following: small amount of household sugar, crucible and crucible-holder (a 'pipe-clay triangle'), tripod.

What to do

1   Put the crucible-holder on the tripod (which should have had its gauze removed). Then put the crucible in the holder. Put 2–3 spatula-measures of sugar in the crucible.

2   Light the Bunsen burner. Adjust the flame so that it is about 5 cm high. Now open the air-hole.

3   Heat the sugar with the Bunsen burner flame, from above. Do this by holding the burner by its base, and direct the flame towards the sugar.

4   The sugar will melt and go black. Keep heating when this happens. After a short time, take the flame away to see if the sugar will burn on its own. Try to do this as many times as you can.

What happened

You should have been able to see the following.
1   After the sugar melted and went black, it started to burn. When the Bunsen was taken away, the sugar burned on its own for a short time.

2   The sugar could be re-lighted two or three times. In the end there was just a black solid left in the crucible, which glowed red when it was heated, but which would not burn.

What we can decide

Household sugar will burn. So it takes part in an exothermic reaction with the oxygen from the air. The word-equation is:

$$sugar(s) + oxygen(g) \rightarrow water(l) + carbon\;dioxide(g)$$
$$\triangle H - ve$$

You did not see the water because the heat from the Bunsen flame turned it to steam straight away.

You should be able to see that the word-equation for burning sugar is the reverse of the word-equation for photosynthesis. Burning and photosynthesis are the reverse of each other. When a sugar burns, something with stronger bonds (carbon dioxide) is one of the products. So we can write:

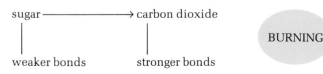

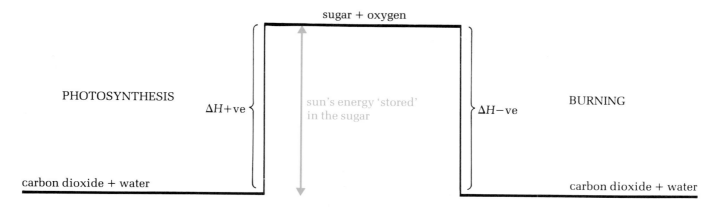

Fig. 4.26

Energy is stored in a sugar molecule because we can use it in a chemical reaction to get back to carbon dioxide. We can draw the energy diagram for photosynthesis and burning.

In Experiment 4.8 it was the heat from the Bunsen burner that supplied the activation energy for the reaction between sugar and oxygen. But you saw that the sugar would burn on its own, showing that the reaction was indeed exothermic. The energy being released was the energy taken in by the chemicals during photosynthesis, which came originally from the sun.

Suppose that, instead of being burned, the sugar had been eaten by an athlete who used the energy from it for running. What happens then? When you breathe in, you take in oxygen. When you breathe out you give out . . . what? Carbon dioxide and water! When a human being uses sugar for energy, the chemical reaction is exactly parallel to burning. The name for this process is RESPIRATION. The word-equation is the same as that above for burning a sugar.

Questions

1   Make a list of all the ways (at least three) in which burning and respiration are the same as each other.

2   Make a list of all the ways (at least three) in which burning and respiration are different from each other.

Fig. 4.27 *Respiration!*

When we burn a fossil fuel, the product chemicals are carbon dioxide and water and oxygen is used up. So the word-equation is:

fossil fuel + oxygen(g) → carbon dioxide (g) + water(l)
(s, l, or g) $\triangle H$ −ve

As with the burning of a sugar, the reaction is exothermic because the bonds in the product chemicals are stronger than the bonds in the reactant chemicals:

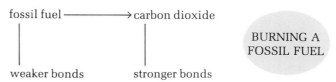

BURNING A
FOSSIL FUEL

Energy is stored in the fossil fuel because we can use it in a chemical reaction to get back to the carbon dioxide which originally came from the Earth's atmosphere. So we can say that there is an ENERGY CYCLE, which looks like Fig. 4.28.

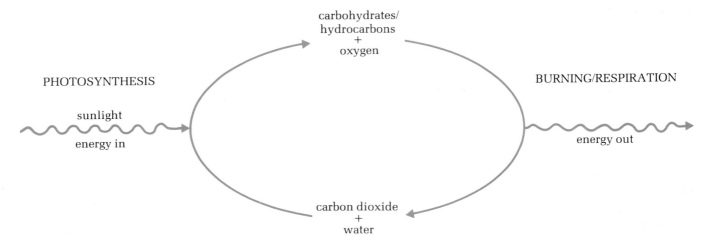

Fig. 4.28

PROJECT 4.1

Here is a photograph of a petrol pump . . . or is it? If you look carefully, you will see that the station is not selling pure petrol, but a mixture of petrol and alcohol. Alcohol is not a fossil fuel, but instead we get it by a chemical reaction from sugars made by photosynthesis.

You saw in Section 2 that the world's supply of oil (and therefore petrol) is running out. In some countries, alcohol has been added to petrol to stop oil being used up so quickly.

Find out how we get alcohol from sugars (Section 8 will help), and find out where Brazil is in the world. Why is it easier to make alcohol in vast amounts from sugars in Brazil than it would be in Britain?

Your teacher may take a drop of alcohol and show you that it burns, but you will not be allowed to handle any of the alcohol yourselves. When it is as concentrated as this, alcohol is extremely poisonous.

Fig. 4.29 *This photograph was taken in Brazil. Find out where Brazil is*

In Section 2 another way of getting energy from chemicals was mentioned. But this method is only good for using on a small scale, because the chemicals which are involved are fairly expensive. These are usually metals and their salts.

Simple chemicals which give us energy

In Experiment 4.3, you compared copper and zinc for reactivity. You found that zinc is higher up the reactivity hill than copper. You also found that when zinc metal reacts with copper(II) sulphate, heat is given out.

So, some metal displacement reactions are exothermic. That means that they might be useful ways of getting energy. The reaction which we would use would be between a reactive metal and the salt of a less reactive metal. Both of these are simple chemicals.

The experiment which you will do now will help you decide whether metal displacement reactions might be a good source of energy.

▶ EXPERIMENT 4.9

EXPERIMENT 4.9
Are metal displacement reactions good sources of energy?

You will need the following: magnesium powder, zinc powder, lead powder, M copper(II) sulphate solution, M zinc sulphate solution, stirring thermometer.

What to do

1   Take three test-tubes. Half-fill each of them with copper(II) sulphate solution. Take the temperature of the solution, and write down the result.

2   Add 2 spatula-measures of powdered magnesium to one of the test-tubes. Now stir with the thermometer. Keep stirring until the temperature stops rising. Write down the temperature when it stopped rising.

3   Add 2 spatula-measures of powdered zinc to one of the other test-tubes. Stir, and write down the highest temperature reached.

4   In the same way, add powdered lead to the last test-tube. Find the highest temperature reached.

5   **Discuss what you have seen, and try to decide whether these reactions would be a good source of energy.**

6   Write down what you have seen, and what you have decided.

7   Clean the test-tubes very carefully. Now half-fill each of them with zinc sulphate solution, and take the temperature of one of them.

8   Repeat what you did with copper(II) sulphate, using each of the three metals in the three different test-tubes.

9   **Discuss your results. Write down what you have seen, and what you have decided.**

What happened

You should have been able to see the following.

1   Some of the test-tubes contained reactions that gave out heat, and some did not.

2   Some of the mixtures in the test-tubes rose to higher temperatures than others.

Draw a table like the one below, and fill in the temperature reached in each test-tube. If the temperature in the test-tube did not change when you added the powdered metal, write 'no change' in the space.

	Temperature/°C		
	Magnesium	Zinc	Lead
copper(II) sulphate solution			
zinc sulphate solution			

What we can decide

Some of the test-tubes gave out no heat. This was because there was no reaction taking place in them. You should check this for yourself. Look at the positions of the metals involved in the reactivity series. You will see that those test-tubes which did not get warm contained a metal lower down the reactivity series than the metal in the salt. For instance, you would not have **expected** lead to displace zinc from zinc sulphate.

Most metal displacement reactions that do happen give out quite a lot of heat. So metal displacement reactions **are** good sources of energy.

You saw earlier in this section that a displacement reaction happens when a more reactive metal reacts with the salt of a less reactive metal. Another way of saying this is that the metal which is the more reactive is the one which forms the stronger bonds in the product chemicals:

more reactive metal(s) + cation of less reactive
          metal(aq)

              forms weaker 'bonds'

⟶ less reactive metal(s) + cation of more reactive
          metal(aq)

              forms stronger 'bonds'

But metal displacement reactions are not quite the same as the burning of a fuel to get energy. Your teacher will now show you that metal displacement reactions do not have to give out their energy in the form of heat. We can arrange things so that the chemicals do not get hot. Instead, the energy of the displacement reaction takes the form of electricity.

▶ EXPERIMENT 4.10 (p. 190)

EXPERIMENT 4.10
Getting electricity from a chemical reaction

Your teacher will show you this experiment

The following will be needed: U-tube, filter-papers soaked in saturated potassium nitrate solution, solutions of copper(II) sulphate and zinc sulphate, strips of copper and zinc, 2 V bulb and holder, voltmeter (0–5 V), electric motor (approx. 2 V).

What to do

1   Set up the apparatus shown in Fig. 4.30.

2   Connect the two metal strips together with a wire. The presence of a current in the wire can be demonstrated by putting a bulb in the circuit. The size of the voltage being created can be measured with a voltmeter.

What we can decide

Metal displacement reactions can be made to give up their energy as electricity.

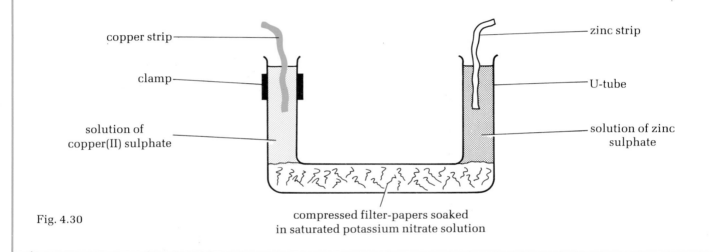

copper strip

clamp

solution of copper(II) sulphate

zinc strip

U-tube

solution of zinc sulphate

compressed filter-papers soaked in saturated potassium nitrate solution

Fig. 4.30

This is a more efficient way of getting electricity from a chemical reaction than by burning a fuel in a power-station. This is because all the middle steps are missed out. When we use a metal displacement reaction, we go straight to the electricity. In a power-station, there is some heat lost to the surroundings at each stage. This does not happen with a metal displacement reaction.

To get the energy from a metal displacement reaction as electricity, we always have to arrange the chemicals in the following way (Fig. 4.31).

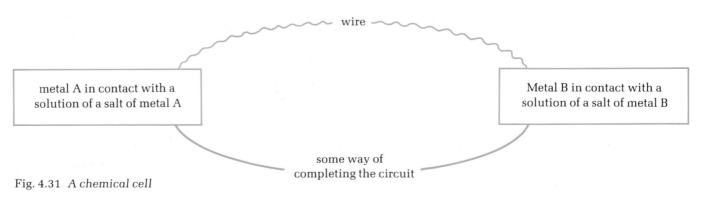

wire

metal A in contact with a solution of a salt of metal A

Metal B in contact with a solution of a salt of metal B

some way of completing the circuit

Fig. 4.31 *A chemical cell*

When we do this, the electricity flows through the wire **from the side with the metal higher in the reactivity series of metals to the side with the metal lower in the reactivity series. We call such an arrangement a CHEMICAL CELL.**

The net change which takes place in a chemical cell is that compounds with weaker forces of attraction holding them together are replaced by compounds with stronger forces of attraction. For instance, in Experiment 4.10 we can think of the chemical change as simply being compounds of a less reactive metal (copper) being replaced by compounds of a more reactive metal (zinc). So on the zinc side of the chemical cell, zinc passes into solution as zinc cations, and on the copper side of the cell, copper ions from the solution are left on the copper strip as copper atoms. Electrons flow through the wire from the zinc strip to the copper strip. So the zinc strip is the

negative terminal of the cell (because the electrons come from this side) and the copper strip is the positive terminal (Fig. 4.32).

The first man to notice that he could get electricity from a chemical reaction in this way was an Italian scientist called Volta. He did this in about the year 1800. He also discovered that a much higher voltage could be obtained if he connected many chemical cells together. When we have many identical things connected together, the word we use for this is a 'battery'. So we call the arrangement for getting electricity from metal displacement reactions a 'battery' too. The first battery ever made in the UK was composed of silver coins and zinc discs, but it worked!

Nowadays, we would use a chemical cell like the Daniell cell. The Daniell cell will give us a steady supply of about 1.1 volts for many hours (Fig. 4.33).

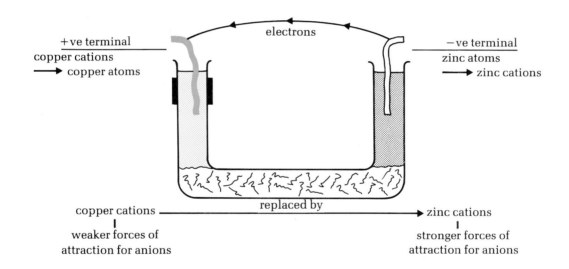

Fig. 4.32

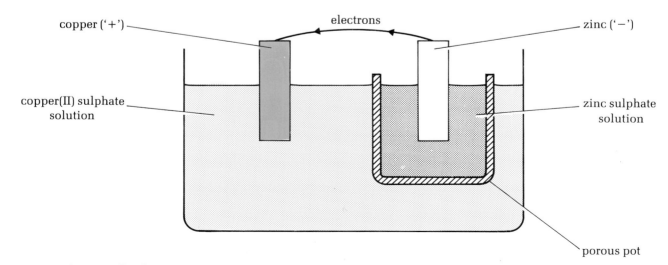

Fig. 4.33 *The Daniell cell*

In the Daniell cell, the two solutions are kept apart by a porous pot. The fact that there are liquids in the Daniell cell makes it heavy. Also, the liquids might spill out. These problems have been overcome by modern 'dry' batteries. The sort of batteries which we use in transistor radios, torches and calculators are dry batteries. The most common sort of dry battery looks like Fig. 4.34.

Another special type of chemical cell is called a FUEL CELL. A fuel cell does not use a metal displacement reaction. Instead, it uses a reaction which will give huge amounts of energy for a very low weight of chemicals. Your teacher will show you a simple form of fuel cell which uses the elements hydrogen and oxygen.

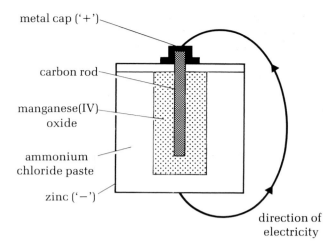

Fig. 4.34 *A 'dry' battery*

EXPERIMENT 4.11
A simple form of hydrogen/oxygen fuel cell

Your teacher will show you this experiment

The following will be needed: glass electrolysis cell (with carbon electrodes), M sodium hydroxide solution, high resistance voltmeter.

What to do

WEAR SAFETY SPECTACLES.

1   First, electrolyse the solution in order to obtain the gases for the reaction. Use a 6 volt d.c. supply.

2   When both test-tubes are full of gas, stop the electrolysis. Now connect a high resistance voltmeter across the two electrodes. A voltage is detected showing that the fuel cell is producing electrical power.

What we can decide

What your teacher has shown you proves that we can get electricity from the reaction between hydrogen and oxygen (giving water) if we arrange the chemicals in the right way.

Questions

1   Write down the word-equation for the reaction which took place in the fuel cell.

2   Draw a diagram of the reactivity hill for the reaction in the fuel cell.

3   Draw an energy level diagram for the reaction in the fuel cell.

4   What can you say about the strength of the chemical bonds in the different chemicals in the reaction which takes place in the fuel cell?

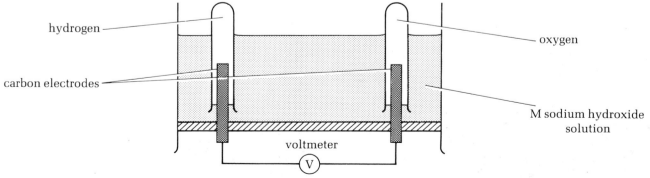

Fig. 4.35

The reaction between hydrogen and oxygen gives out huge amounts of energy. The mass of the chemicals is also very low. Can you think of ways in which this combination of plenty of energy and low mass would be useful? Imagine that a chemical reaction was being used to lift something vertically upwards. Now imagine that the chemical reaction is contained in the thing being lifted. The **mass** of the chemicals would be very important – because they have to lift **themselves**. The same thing can be true for human beings!

Fig. 4.36 *If they are just as strong as each other, the 10 stone boy can jump much higher than the 20 stone boy*

A space rocket has to lift itself into orbit. It carries its fuel with it. Energy is obtained from the fuel when it takes part in a chemical reaction. So, the more energy per gram of fuel, the better. For this reason, the rockets which carried men to the Moon for the first time were not powered by petrol or diesel, but by hydrogen and oxygen, which reacted together in the rocket's motors.

As well as needing a massive lift to put them into orbit, spaceships also have to have a source of electrical power. They carry huge amounts of electrical equipment – computers, life-support systems, communications equipment, and so on. All this has to be driven by electricity.

Fig. 4.37 *A Saturn 5B rocket, powered by a chemical reaction, lifts of the launch pad, carrying Apollo 13 to the Moon.*

The source of electrical power used in spacecraft has to produce plenty of electricity, and it also has to be very light. So – fuel cells are used. The reaction between hydrogen and oxygen puts rockets into orbit, and it provides them with electricity when they are there.

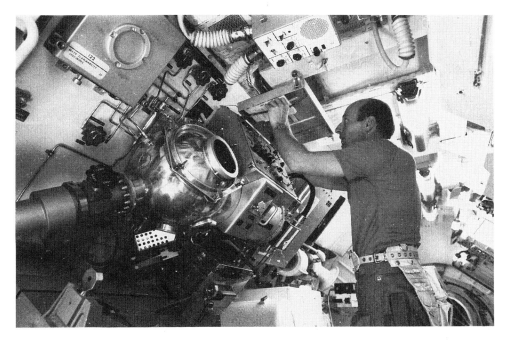

Fig. 4.38 *Some of the electrical equipment on board a spacecraft*

UNIT 4.2
Summary and learning

1   When chemicals react together to form new chemicals which are lower down the reactivity hill, heat energy is given out to the surroundings. This makes the surroundings get hotter. We say that such reactions are EXOTHERMIC. We represent an exothermic reaction by adding the symbol $\triangle H$ −ve at the end of the word-equation.

2   Sometimes, we can drive chemical reactions **up** the reactivity hill. We can do this by putting in heat from the surroundings. This makes the surroundings get cooler. We say that such reactions are ENDOTHERMIC. We represent an endothermic reaction by adding the symbol $\triangle H$ +ve at the end of the word-equation.

3   We represent the energy changes which happen during chemical changes in energy level diagrams. You should remember how to draw energy level diagrams to represent exothermic and endothermic reactions.

4   Every chemical reaction involves the breaking and formation of chemical bonds (or forces of attraction). If the bonds (or forces of attraction) are stronger in the products than in the reactants, the reaction will be exothermic. If the bonds (or forces of attraction) are stronger in the reactants than in the products, the reaction will be endothermic.

5   Because bonds have to be broken (or forces of attraction overcome), there is always an activation energy for a chemical reaction. If we include the activation energy in the energy level diagram, the result is a potential energy diagram. You should remember how to draw a potential energy diagram for an exothermic and for an endothermic reaction.

6   Green plants use energy from the sun to make chemicals which have weaker bonds (carbohydrates and oxygen) from chemicals which have stronger bonds (carbon dioxide and water). We call this process photosynthesis.

7   If a carbohydrate reacts with oxygen, energy is released because we go back to chemicals with stronger bonds (carbon dioxide and water). This is what happens when a sugar burns. Humans and animals get energy from food by the same method. We call this process respiration. You should remember how to draw energy level diagrams to represent photosynthesis and respiration/burning.

8   Fossilisation changes carbohydrates into hydrocarbons. However, we still get energy released when we burn a fossil fuel, because we still go back to chemicals with stronger bonds (carbon dioxide and water).

9   We can also get energy in the form of electricity on a small scale from metal displacement reactions. The chemicals have to be arranged in the form of a chemical cell so that the energy which is released by the reaction is produced in the form of a flow of electrons. You should remember the net chemical change which happens in a chemical cell, and how to work out which terminal will be '−ve' and which '+ve'. You should remember the arrangement of chemicals in a Daniell cell and in a 'dry' battery.

10   We can also use the reaction between hydrogen and oxygen (giving water) to give us electricity if we arrange the chemicals in the form of a fuel cell. This gives us a supply of electricity from chemicals which are very light.

11   You have learnt the meaning of these words:

endothermic	photosynthesis
exothermic	starch
energy level diagrams	hydrocarbon
activation energy	carbohydrate
potential energy diagrams	respiration
sugars	chemical cell
chlorophyll	fuel cell

UNIT 4.3 *How to write down chemical changes in symbols*

We know that we can write chemical substances in symbols. This is what we do when we write down their chemical formulae. But can we find a way to write down all of a chemical **reaction** in symbols?

Obviously, we can go from the word-equation for a reaction to a set of symbols just by writing in the chemical formula of each substance.

For example:

Word-equation

magnesium(s) + dilute hydrochloric acid(aq)
$\longrightarrow$ magnesium chloride (aq) + hydrogen(g)

Word-equation in symbols

$Mg(s) + HCl(aq) \rightarrow MgCl_2(aq) + H_2(g)$

But is this enough? Have we written a true representation of what happens during the chemical change?

We know that a chemical formula tells us the ratio of the number of atoms (or ions) in a chemical compound. We can use the chemical formula of a compound to work out **how much** (the relative masses) of the different elements there are in it.

Is what we have written for the chemical reaction between magnesium and dilute hydrochloric acid a true picture of **how much** (the relative masses) of the two chemicals react together? Perhaps it is not.

The formula of a compound represents the smallest amount of it that can exist. Each time we write the formula down, it represents 'one formula's worth', or one FORMULA-UNIT of the compound. A formula-unit of a molecular compound is a molecule, of course. We know that no actual **particle** exists for an ionic compound – just cations and anions in the ratio given in the formula.

To write down a true representation of a chemical reaction in symbols, we need to know how many 'formula's worth', or formula-units of one chemical react with how many formula-units of another, and how many formula-units of the different product chemicals we get.

So, suppose we had a reaction between chemical A and chemical B, making chemical C and chemical D. The question is,

$$A + B \rightarrow C + D$$

'What are the relative numbers of formula-units of the chemicals that are involved in the reaction?'

If we could say that 1 formula-unit of A reacts with 2 formula-units of B, to give 1 formula-unit of C and 2 formula-units of D, then we could write:

$$A + 2B \rightarrow C + 2D$$

This would be what we call a BALANCED EQUATION.

A balanced equation tells us the relative number of formula-units of the different chemicals which take part in the chemical reaction. So we would be able to use the balanced equation to tell us how much (the relative masses) of the different chemicals react, just as we can use the formula of a compound to tell us the relative masses of the different elements which are in it.

So perhaps we ought to try to discover some general facts about what happens to the amount of chemicals in chemical reactions. If we find some general rules, it will help us to work out how to write balanced equations.

TOPIC 4.3.1

What happens to mass during a chemical change?

The most obvious question we could ask ourselves about what happens to mass during a chemical reaction is: does mass increase or decrease? Or does it stay the same? Perhaps some matter is always lost during a chemical reaction – or perhaps the amount of matter is always greater at the end of a chemical reaction than at the beginning. Perhaps the total amount of matter remains constant, even though a reaction has taken place.

We can investigate these alternatives in a very simple way. If we measure the total mass of the reactants in a chemical reaction, allow the reaction to happen, and then measure the total mass of the products, we can decide whether matter has been created or destroyed during the reaction.

▶ EXPERIMENT 4.12 (p. 196)

The Law of Conservation of Mass is one important part of the knowledge you need to have before representing chemical reactions. It tells us that in our representation, whatever it finally looks like, we must make sure that **the total number of atoms (or ions) of each element on the reactants side of the representation is the same as the total number of atoms (or ions) of that element on the products side**. This will be true for all the elements involved. We know that this must be the case, because no matter is

$\longrightarrow$ p. 197

EXPERIMENT 4.12

Is matter created or destroyed during a chemical reaction?

You will need the following: access to top-pan balance, 250 cm³ conical flask with tight-fitting bung, small test-tube, barium nitrate solution, sodium sulphate solution, copper(II) sulphate solution, sodium hydroxide solution, lead(II) nitrate solution, sodium chloride solution.

What to do

BARIUM NITRATE SOLUTION IS POISONOUS. MAKE SURE THAT YOU DO NOT TRANSFER ANY TO YOUR MOUTH. WASH YOUR HANDS AT THE END OF THE EXPERIMENT.

1   There are three possible reactions for you to carry out. The word-equations are:

A barium nitrate(aq) + sodium sulphate(aq)
$\longrightarrow$ barium sulphate(s) + sodium nitrate(aq)
B copper(II) sulphate(aq) + sodium hydroxide(aq)
$\longrightarrow$ copper(II) hydroxide(s) + sodium sulphate(aq)
C lead(II) nitrate(aq) + sodium chloride(aq)
$\longrightarrow$ lead(II) chloride(s) + sodium nitrate(aq)

In each case both the reactants are solutions, and one of the products is a solid. So you will be able to see that a reaction has taken place.

2   You will carry out reaction A first. The arrangement of the apparatus is show in Fig. 4.39.

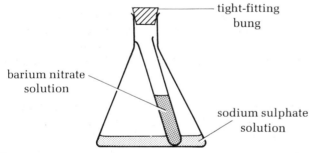

- tight-fitting bung

barium nitrate solution

sodium sulphate solution

Fig. 4.39

3   Be careful not to let the solutions mix. Put the sodium sulphate solution in the conical flask before introducing the test-tube which contains the barium nitrate solution. You may need to wipe the outside of the test-tube to remove any spilled barium nitrate solution, before you put it in the conical flask. If the test-tube will not stand up inside the conical flask, tie a piece of cotton around its neck, and trap the cotton between the bung and the side of the flask, so that the test-tube is supported.

4   Weigh the apparatus and the reactant chemicals by putting the conical flask on the top-pan balance. Write down the mass that is shown.

5   Make sure that the bung fits tightly, and then turn the apparatus upside down several times. You will see that a reaction happens.

6   Now weigh the apparatus and the product chemicals, using the top-pan balance.

7   Wash out the apparatus carefully, and repeat the experiment using copper(II) sulphate solution (in the test-tube) and sodium hydroxide solution (in the conical flask).

8   If you have time, you can look at the third reaction, between lead(II) nitrate solution (in the test-tube) and sodium chloride solution (in the conical flask).

What happened

For each reaction, you should compare the mass of the apparatus and the starting chemicals, with the mass of the apparatus and the product chemicals. We know that the mass of the apparatus will not have changed during the reaction. So any difference in mass must be due to a difference between the masses of the reactants and the products.

You should find that, in each case, the mass of the product chemicals is the same as that of the reactant chemicals.

What we can decide

What do your results tell you about what happens to mass during a chemical reaction? When a chemical reaction happens, new chemicals are formed by the breaking of chemical bonds in the reactants, and the formation of new chemical bonds to make the products. Remember that it is the breaking and formation of bonds that is the source of the energy changes that take place along with chemical reactions. The atoms (or ions) which make up the reactants are not destroyed. Neither are any new atoms or ions created. We could say that when a chemical reaction happens, the chemicals **rearrange** themselves to give the products. The amount of matter stays the same during a chemical reaction. Since this is true for **all** chemical reactions, we can put this in the form of a law, which is always true:

Matter is neither created nor destroyed during a chemical reaction.

We call this law the **Law of Conservation of Mass** (if something is 'conserved', it stays the same).

destroyed and none is created during a reaction. (And, of course, we know that elements do not change into other elements during chemical reactions.)

But there is one vital gap in our knowledge. When a reaction takes place between two chemicals, do the masses which react vary from day to day and from experiment to experiment, or are the relative amounts which are involved always the same? Suppose, for example, that we were reacting the chemicals A and B together to make two new chemicals (C and D). Our representation of this would be:

$$A + B \rightarrow C + D$$

Suppose also, that we started with 10 g of A and measured how much of B was needed to react with all the A present. If we repeat this several times, and always use 10 g of A, would the amount of B needed be the same each time? Perhaps there is no constant relationship between the amounts of chemicals which react together, and so perhaps the amount of B would always be different.

The only way we can find the answer to this question is to carry out an experiment. A reaction which we can look at is the one between magnesium metal and dilute hydrochloric acid. Each pupil, or group of pupils, can take the same amount of dilute hydrochloric acid, and see how much magnesium is needed to react with it. The word-equation is:

magnesium(s) + dilute hydrochloric acid (aq)
$\longrightarrow$ magnesium chloride (aq) + hydrogen(g)

The products of the reaction are a solution and a gas, so it is easy to see when all the magnesium is used up – no more solid material remains.

▶ EXPERIMENT 4.13 (p. 198)

Questions

In each case, write out the word-equation, but insert the missing mass of chemical. Explain your reasoning, as in the example below.

Example: Given that 32 g of sulphur will react with 32 g of oxygen to give sulphur dioxide only, what mass of sulphur dioxide is produced?
Solution: The word equation is:

sulphur + oxygen $\rightarrow$ sulphur dioxide
and we know that: 32 g + 32 g $\rightarrow$?
From the Law of Conservation of Mass, we know that the mass of sulphur dioxide must equal the sum of the mass of sulphur and the mass of oxygen = 32 g + 32 g
$$= 64 \text{ g.}$$
Answer: The mass of sulphur dioxide is 64 g.

sulphur + oxygen $\rightarrow$ sulphur dioxide
  32 g   32 g $\rightarrow$ 64 g

1   When 10 g of calcium carbonate is strongly heated, 5.6 g of calcium oxide is produced, together with a certain mass of carbon dioxide. There are no other reactants or products. What is the mass of carbon dioxide?

2   When sodium and chlorine react together, the only product is sodium chloride. When 46 g of sodium is used, 117 g of sodium chloride is produced.
(a) What mass of chlorine reacts with 46 g of sodium?
(b) What mass of chlorine reacts with 23 g of sodium?

3   When magnesium reacts with dilute hydrochloric acid, there are two products: magnesium chloride and hydrogen. It takes 24 g of magnesium and 73 g of hydrochloric acid to make 2 g of hydrogen.
(a) What mass of magnesium chloride is produced by this reaction when 2 g of hydrogen is formed?
(b) What mass of hydrochloric acid is needed to react with 12 g of magnesium?
(c) What mass of hydrogen is produced when 12 g of magnesium react with the necessary amount of hydrochloric acid?
(d) What mass of hydrogen would be produced from 46 g of magnesium?
(e) What mass of hydrogen would be produced from 120 g of magnesium?

4   Under the right conditions nitrogen gas and hydrogen gas will react together, making ammonia gas and no other products. 7 g of nitrogen will react with 1.5 g of hydrogen.
(a) What mass of ammonia is made when 7 g of nitrogen and 1.5 g of hydrogen react together?
(b) What mass of nitrogen, and what mass of hydrogen, are needed to make 17 g of ammonia by this method?

So now we know two important facts about chemical reactions which will help us build up a way of representing them. Firstly, we know that the number of atoms (or ions) of each element is the same on the reactants and the products sides of the reaction equation. Secondly, we know that chemicals react together in fixed amounts. From these two ideas, we can see that there must be a third rule which our representation of the amounts of chemicals in a chemical reaction must obey. Since the **amounts** of products are fixed and are related to the amounts of reactants (Law of Conservation of Mass), and since the **relative** amounts of reactants are fixed (Rule of Reacting Masses), so the **relative** amounts of products must be fixed. We could write this out in the following way.

If two chemicals C and D are formed by a chemical reaction, the ratio 'mass of C produced: mass of D produced' is always the same, no matter how many times the reaction is carried out.

EXPERIMENT 4.13
Do chemicals react together in fixed amounts?

You will need the following: measuring cylinder, 250 cm³ beaker, universal indicator paper, magnesium ribbon (approx. 10 cm), approximately 0.5 M hydrochloric acid (15 cm³)

What to do

YOU MUST WEAR YOUR SAFETY SPECTACLES.

1   Use a measuring cylinder to place **exactly** 10 cm³ of 0.5 M hydrochloric acid in a clean 250 cm³ beaker.

2   Take a piece of magnesium ribbon about 10 cm long, and clean its surface with sandpaper, until no dull surface layer is left.

3   Cut the ribbon into pieces which are exactly 1 cm long, using a ruler to measure with. Put any of the ribbon which is left over to one side.

4   Put one of the pieces of magnesium ribbon 1 cm long into the acid, and swirl the acid around in the bottom of the beaker. Be careful not to let any of the acid splash out. Keep swirling until all the magnesium has reacted.

5   If the first piece of magnesium dissolves completely, make a note of this, and then add a second piece. As before, swirl the acid around in the bottom of the beaker.

6   Each time that a piece of magnesium dissolves completely, make a note of this and then add another piece. Do not try to rush the experiment by adding two pieces together. This will spoil your results.

7   After a few pieces of magnesium ribbon have been added, the reaction becomes quite slow, but you can speed it up by heating. Take the beaker and place it on a tripod and gauze. Use a low Bunsen flame to heat gently. Try not to let the acid boil. If it does, take the heat away, but make sure that the temperature is kept fairly high.

8   From time to time, pick up the beaker carefully (it will be hot) and swirl its contents.

9   Do not let all the water boil away. If this looks like happening, add some distilled water, but only a little. (This does not ruin the experiment, because it does not alter the amount of acid in the beaker.)

10   Carry on, adding a piece of magnesium ribbon when necessary, until the reaction stops. You will be left with a piece of magnesium which has not reacted. Note down the number of pieces of magnesium which reacted **completely**.

11   Test the final solution with universal indicator paper to check that no acid remains.

What happened

How do the results of the different experiments carried out by the class compare? Was the same amount of magnesium needed to react with the same amount of acid? You should find that it was.

What we can decide

Can the results obtained above be used to say something about chemical reactions in general?

Whichever chemical reaction we take, the same thing happens. For a given amount of one reactant chemical, a given amount of another reactant chemical is always needed. If we double the amount of one reactant, we always double the amount of the other reactant needed. If we halve the amount of one, we halve the amount of the other.

We could put this rule in the following way:

If two chemicals A and B react together, the ratio 'mass of A reacting: mass of B reacting' is always the same, no matter how many times the reaction is carried out.

We could call this the **Rule of Reacting Masses**.

We could call this the **Rule of Product Masses.**

Using these rules, we will be able to write a representation showing the amounts of chemicals involved in chemical reactions. This representation will be the balanced equation. But first, it will be useful if we provide ourselves with a list of the different types of reaction which exist.

General word-equations

In Section 1, you learned ways of preparing salts. One way was to react a basic oxide with an acid. The products of the reaction were a salt and water. The same types of product are obtained no matter what the base and what the salt. So we can write a **general word-equation**, to cover the reaction between all bases and all acids. A general word-equation is a word-equation which describes, in terms of the **types** of chemicals involved, one of the several classes of chemical equation which exist.

General word-equation:

> **basic oxide + acid → salt + water**

Question

You also learned a number of other ways for preparing salts in Section 1. How many general word-equations can you find in that section?

Earlier in this section, we saw that some metals will displace other metals from solutions of their ions.

General word-equation:

> **metal   + salt of metal**
> **(higher in table)   (lower in table)**
>
> ⟶ **metal   + salt of metal**
> **(lower in table)   (higher in table)**

The following experiment will introduce some other types of reaction.

▶ EXPERIMENT 4.14 (p. 200)

We can now write out a list of general word-equations.

General word-equations

1. Basic oxide + acid → salt + water
2. Acid + alkali → salt + water
3. Acidic oxide + alkali → salt + water
4. Acid + carbonate → salt + carbon dioxide + water
5. Soluble salt + soluble salt
   → insoluble salt + soluble salt
6. Soluble salt + soluble hydroxide
   → insoluble hydroxide + soluble salt
7. Ammonium salt + alkali
   → salt + ammonia + water
8. Metal + non-metal → salt
9. Metal (above Pb) + acid → salt + hydrogen
10. Metal   + salt of metal → metal + salt of metal
    (higher)   (lower)   (lower)   (higher)

TOPIC 4.3.3

How to write balanced equations

Look back at Section 3, Topic 3.3.4. You learned there how to 'count by weighing'. You also learned that a mole of something is the mass of it which contains Avogadro's Number of particles. So a mole of hydrogen gas has a mass of 2 g, since it is made up of

H_2 molecules. A mole of hydrogen atoms has a mass of 1 g, since it also contains Avogadro's Number of particles (atoms).

When we write a chemical equation, we write down the relative number of particles of the different chemicals which react. So if in a chemical reaction

$$A + B \rightarrow C + D$$

one particle of A reacts with one particle of B, we may as well say that one million particles of A react with one million particles of B. Or, we might say that Avogadro's Number of particles of A react with Avogadro's Number of particles of B. That is, one **mole** of A reacts with one mole of B.

So when we have got our equation into the form where we are asking ourselves about the relative number of formula-units of the different chemicals which go into the balanced equation, we could instead talk about the relative number of **moles** of the different chemicals. It is just another way of talking about the relative number of particles.

These are really the same question {
What are the relative numbers of formula-units in the balanced equation?

$$A + B \longrightarrow C + D$$

What are the relative numbers of moles which react?
}

Suppose we take a chemical reaction like that between sodium hydroxide solution and dilute hydrochloric acid. To get to the balanced equation, we have to go through the following steps.

Step 1: Write the general word-equation
We know that sodium hydroxide solution is an alkali, and that dilute hydrochloric acid is an acid. So the general word-equation is:

> acid + alkali → salt + water

Step 2: Write the word-equation
From the general word-equation, we know that a salt is one of the products of the reaction. The salt will be made up from the metal part of the alkali (sodium) and the non-metal part of the acid (chloride). So its name is sodium chloride.

> acid   + alkali → salt   + water
>
> hydrochloric + sodium → sodium + water
> acid   hydroxide chloride

Step 3: Put in the chemical formulae of all the chemicals
From the rules given in Section 3, we can now give each substance its chemical formula:

> acid   + alkali → salt   + water
>
> hydrochloric + sodium → sodium + water
> acid   hydroxide chloride
>
> HCl   + NaOH → NaCl + H_2O

⟶ p. 201

EXPERIMENT 4.14
More general types of reaction

You will need the following: these solids; potassium nitrate, zinc nitrate, copper(II) sulphate, ammonium nitrate solution, sodium sulphite solution, dilute acidified hydrogen peroxide solution, universal indicator paper, Pyrex test-tubes, wooden splints.

What to do

YOU MUST WEAR YOUR SAFETY SPECTACLES. THE ROOM MUST BE WELL VENTILATED. BARIUM CHLORIDE IS POISONOUS. MAKE SURE THAT YOU DO NOT TRANSFER ANY TO YOUR MOUTH. WASH YOUR HANDS AT THE END OF THE EXPERIMENT.

1   Put a little potassium nitrate in a Pyrex test-tube and heat it strongly. Observe carefully what happens. Test the gas given off with a glowing splint.

2   In the same way, heat strongly a little zinc nitrate. Again, observe what happens, and test with a glowing splint.

3   Strongly heat a little copper(II) sulphate solid in a Pyrex test-tube. Note down what happens, and test the gas produced with damp universal indicator paper.

4   To a little ammonium nitrate solution in a test-tube, add some sodium hydroxide solution. Test any gas given off with damp universal indicator paper (it may be necessary to heat the reaction mixture gently).

5   Place some copper(II) sulphate solution in a test-tube and add some sodium hydroxide solution. Heat the product, and observe what happens.

6   To a little sodium sulphite solution in a test-tube, add an equal amount of acidified hydrogen peroxide solution. Then add 2–3 drops of barium(II) chloride solution.

What happened

In each case, a reaction took place. For each reaction, record carefully your observations, and try to write a word-equation. Do your results seem to fit into any of the general word-equations which you know so far?

What we can decide

For each of the three salts which were heated, the salt was broken down into different, simpler chemicals. But there was no general pattern to what happened. When one nitrate was heated, a colourless gas was given off. When the other was heated, two gases were produced – one colourless and the other brown. When copper(II) sulphate was heated, a different colourless gas to that produced by the nitrates was given off.

Each of these reactions is called a THERMAL DECOMPOSITION reaction. There is no general word-equation to cover all the different sorts of thermal decomposition. As you have just seen, the product chemicals of a thermal decomposition reaction depend on the exact nature of the starting chemicals. You will learn more about thermal decomposition later in this section.

When ammonium nitrate was heated with sodium hydroxide, ammonia gas was given off. This happens when any ammonium salt is heated with any alkali. So, in this case, we **can** write a general word-equation:

General word-equation:

ammonium salt + alkali → salt + ammonia + water

Copper(II) sulphate reacted with sodium hydroxide to give a blue gelatinous ('jelly-like') precipitate of copper(II) hydroxide. This is an example of another general reaction type. The general word-equation is:

General word-equation:

soluble salt + soluble hydroxide
⟶ **insoluble hydroxide + soluble salt**

When copper(II) hydroxide is heated, it decomposes and produces copper(II) oxide, which is black. This is another example of a thermal decomposition reaction.

Hydrogen peroxide is an example of a type of chemical called an OXIDISING AGENT. It **oxidises** sodium sulphite to sodium sulphate. (Look back at your results. How do you know that there was a sulphate present in the final reaction mixture?) Oxidising agents always react with chemicals called REDUCING AGENTS. There is no general word-equation to cover all reactions between oxidising agents and reducing agents. But we can always tell if a reaction is of the reducing-agent – oxidising-agent type. So we have a chemical 'nickname' for these reactions. We call them REDOX (red–ox) reactions. You will learn more about redox reactions later in this section.

Step 4: Is the Law of Conservation of Mass obeyed in what we have written?

We know that the formula HCl for hydrochloric acid represents one hydrogen ion combined with one chloride ion. NaOH for sodium chloride represents one ion of sodium combined with one hydroxide ion, and so on for the rest of the substances present. We can add up all the atoms or ions present on both sides of the equation. **For the Law of Conservation of Mass to be obeyed, the number of atoms or ions on the reactants side must be equal to the number of atoms or ions on the products side, for every element.**

We can make a table to compare the two sides of the equation:

	Reactants	Products
sodium	1	1
hydrogen	2	2
chlorine	1	1
oxygen	1	1

You can see that each element 'balances'. So the equation as a whole is also 'balanced'.

We can now add the state symbols:

Balanced equation:

$$HCl(aq) + NaOH(aq) \rightarrow NaCl(aq) + H_2O(l)$$

A more difficult example

We can use steps 1–4 above to find the balanced equation for any reaction. The equation for the reaction between hydrochloric acid and sodium hydroxide was balanced automatically once the formulae of the compounds were written in. Sometimes, however, when we write in all the formulae, the equation is **not** balanced. When this happens, we have to find a way to balance the equation ourselves.

Suppose we take as our example the reaction between potassium hydroxide and dilute sulphuric acid:

Step 1:

$$acid + alkali \rightarrow salt + water$$

Step 2:

dilute sulphuric acid + potassium hydroxide
$$\longrightarrow potassium\ sulphate + water$$

Step 3:

$$H_2SO_4 + KOH \rightarrow K_2SO_4 + H_2O$$

Step 4:

	Reactants	Products
hydrogen	3	2
sulphur	1	1
oxygen	5	5
potassium	1	2

In the table above, the figures were arrived at as follows:

Reactants
hydrogen: 2 from H_2SO_4 + 1 from KOH
sulphur: 1 from H_2SO_4
oxygen: 4 from H_2SO_4 + 1 from KOH
potassium: 1 from KOH

Products
hydrogen: 2 from H_2O
sulphur: 1 from K_2SO_4
oxygen: 4 from K_2SO_4 + 1 from H_2O
potassium: 2 from K_2SO_4

It is very important that you understand where these figures come from. If you do not, look back to Section 3, where you learned to write chemical formulae.

Step 4 shows us that, in this case, we have hit a problem. The equation written as step 3 is not balanced. The chemical formulae of all the compounds in the equation are correct, and cannot be changed. All that we can do is to **alter the number of formula-units (moles) of the chemicals present, until the equation becomes balanced. We can always get an equation that is balanced by doing this**.

The Rule of Reacting Masses tells us that there is a fixed relationship between the masses of reactant chemicals in a chemical reaction. But it does not tell us what this relationship is. The Rule of Reacting Masses does **not** say that one mole of one reactant must react with one mole of another reactant. It could be, for instance, that one mole reacts with two moles. Or it might be that two moles react with three moles. As long as we have **whole numbers** of moles, the rule will not be broken.

Look at the table in step 4. Which elements are out of balance? Here, it is hydrogen and potassium. We can change the number of moles of both these elements on the reactants side of the equation, by altering the number of moles of potassium hydroxide. Suppose we write **two** moles of potassium hydroxide instead of one. What will the effect of this be?

$$H_2SO_4 + 2KOH \rightarrow K_2SO_4 + H_2O$$

	Reactants	Products
hydrogen	4	2
sulphur	1	1
oxygen	6	5
potassium	2	2

The equation is still not balanced! There is too little hydrogen and too little oxygen on the products side. We can put this right by changing the number of moles of water.

$$H_2SO_4 + 2KOH \rightarrow K_2SO_4 + 2H_2O$$

	Reactants	Products
hydrogen	4	4
sulphur	1	1
oxygen	6	6
potassium	2	2

The equation is now balanced. All the chemical laws are obeyed. The balanced equation tells us that: 'One mole of dilute sulphuric acid reacts with two moles of potassium hydroxide, and when it does, the products are one mole of potassium sulphate, and two moles of water'. The final balanced equation, with state-symbols, is:

Balanced equation:

$H_2SO_4(aq) + 2KOH(aq) \rightarrow K_2SO_4(aq) + 2H_2O(l)$

If we did a careful experiment to find the actual amounts of the different chemicals which are involved in this reaction, our results would confirm that the balanced equation written above is correct. We can always find the balanced equation for any reaction by using the steps above. However, someone has always had to do an experiment to prove that the theoretical balanced equation is a true representation of what is happening in the test-tube. As with everything in science, the only way we can be certain about our facts is to carry out an experiment.

Questions

1–5 In each case, write a balanced equation for the reaction given. Write out each of the steps as in the examples above.
1. Dilute nitric acid reacting with potassium hydroxide solution
2. Dilute sulphuric acid reacting with copper(II) oxide
3. Magnesium metal reacting with copper(II) sulphate solution
4. Dilute hydrochloric acid reacting with calcium carbonate solid
5. Zinc metal reacting with dilute sulphuric acid

6–10 In each case, decide whether or not the equation which you are given is balanced. If it is not, find the correct balanced equation.

6. $CuSO_4(aq) + 2NaOH(aq)$
$$\longrightarrow Cu(OH)_2(s) + Na_2SO_4(aq)$$

7. $Mg(s) + HCl(aq) \rightarrow MgCl_2(aq) + H_2(g)$

8. $CaCO_3(s) \xrightarrow{heat} CaO(s) + CO_2(g)$

9. $SO_2(g) + 2H_2S(g) \rightarrow S(s) + 2H_2O(l)$

10. $NH_4NO_3(aq) + NaOH(aq)$
$$\longrightarrow NaNO_3(aq) + NH_3(g) + H_2O(l)$$

TOPIC 4.3.4

How to find balanced equations by doing experiments

So far, our understanding of balanced chemical equations is only really a **theory**. We have found a way of working out what the balanced equation for a particular reaction **should** be. We have not yet proved that our theory is correct.

▶ EXPERIMENT 4.15 (p. 204)

TOPIC 4.3.5

How to write balanced ionic equations

We can often simplify the equations which we write, if the chemicals involved are ionic. Suppose we take as our example the reaction between barium chloride solution and sodium sulphate solution. We know that both are ionic compounds.

A solution of barium chloride consists of Ba^{2+} ions and Cl^- ions. Sodium sulphate solution consists of Na^+ ions and SO_4^{2-} ions. In a solution in water, each individual cation and anion is attached to several water molecules. We say that each ion is AQUATED. So instead of writing $BaSO_4(aq)$ for a solution of barium chloride in water, we should write: $Ba^{2+}(aq) + 2Cl^-(aq)$. A solution of sodium sulphate in water should really be written: $2Na^+(aq) + SO_4^{2-}(aq)$, rather than $Na_2SO_4(aq)$.

The products of the reaction between barium chloride and sodium sulphate would be barium sulphate (which is insoluble), and sodium chloride (which is soluble). The solid barium sulphate forms as a precipitate if these two solutions are mixed. Since it is a solid, barium chloride does not consist of separately aquated cations and anions. It exists in the form of a giant lattice of ions, held in place by the charges on the ions. So we cannot write the ions separately. Also, the lattice overall is electrically neutral since the positive and negative charges cancel out. So we must always write an ionic solid as a unit, and without charges. For example, barium sulphate must simply be written as $BaSO_4(s)$. The sodium chloride also formed in the reaction will consist of separately aquated cations and anions, in other words $Na^+(aq) + Cl^-(aq)$.

So now we can rewrite the balanced equation for this reaction in 'ionic' form:

$BaCl_2(aq) + Na_2SO_4(aq) \rightarrow BaSO_4(s) + 2NaCl(aq)$

becomes:

$Ba^{2+}(aq) + 2Cl^-(aq) + 2Na^+ + SO_4^{2-}(aq)$
$\longrightarrow BaSO_4(s) + 2Na^+(aq) + 2Cl^-(aq)$

Examine the 'ionic equation' carefully. You will see that aquated chloride ions appear on both sides of the equation. In fact, they appear not to have been changed at all as a result of the chemical reaction. The same can be said for the aquated sodium ions. Both these ions actually play no part whatsoever in the chemical reaction. Since the balanced equation represents the change which happens during the chemical reaction, we ought really to leave out both sodium and chloride ions from the equation altogether. But there is one point we must be careful about when we do this. We must leave out **equal numbers** of each ion from both sides of the equation. That way, we can be sure that the equation which we end up with will still be balanced. The easiest way to do this is to write out the ionic equation in its full form, and then to cross out balanced numbers of the ions which do not take part in the reaction:

$Ba^{2+}(aq) + 2\cancel{Cl}^-(aq) + 2\cancel{Na}^+(aq) + SO_4^{2-}(aq) \rightarrow$
$\rightarrow BaSO_4(s) + 2\cancel{Na}^+(aq) + 2\cancel{Cl}^-(aq)$

So the balanced ionic equation is:

Balanced ionic equation:

$Ba^{2+}(aq) + SO_4^{2-}(aq) \rightarrow BaSO_4(s)$

The balanced ionic equation says that 'One mole of aquated barium ions reacts with one mole of aquated sulphate ions, and the product is one mole of barium sulphate solid'. In the balanced ionic equation, as well as the elements balancing, the total charge should also balance. In the example above, there are two negative and two positive charges on the reactants side, giving a total charge of zero. The charge on the reactants side of the equation is also zero.

Another example of an equation which can be written in ionic terms is the reaction between aluminium and lead nitrate:

Balanced equation:

$2Al(s) + 3Pb(NO_3)_2(aq) \rightarrow 3Pb(s) + 2Al(NO_3)_3 \ (aq)$

In ionic terms:

$2Al(s) + 3Pb^{2+}(aq) + 6NO_3^-(aq)$
$\longrightarrow 3Pb(s) + 2Al^{3+}(aq) + 6NO_3^-(aq)$

(NB: 3 moles of lead nitrate contain $3 \times 2 = 6$ moles of nitrate ion)

The nitrate ion takes no part in the reaction, so the balanced ionic equation is:

Balanced ionic equation:

$2Al(s) + 3Pb^{2+}(aq) \rightarrow 3Pb(s) + 2Al^{3+}(aq)$

The total charge on the reactants side is $3 \times 2+ = 6+$
The total charge on the products side is $2 \times 3+ = 6+$

If a molecular compound (like water) is present, it must of course be written in molecular and not ionic terms. For example, let us look at the reaction of dilute sulphuric acid with potassium hydroxide solution:

Balanced equation:

$H_2SO_4(aq) + 2KOH(aq) \rightarrow K_2SO_4(aq) + 2H_2O(l)$

Ionic equation:

$2H^+(aq) + SO_4^{2-}(aq) + 2K^+(aq) + 2OH^-(aq)$
$\longrightarrow 2K^+(aq) + SO_4^{2-}(aq) + 2H_2O(l)$

Balanced ionic equation:

$2H^+(aq) + 2OH^-(aq) \rightarrow 2H_2O(l)$

Since two moles of each substance are left in the equation, we can write a simpler version by dividing by 2:

Balanced ionic equation:

$H^+(aq) + OH^-(aq) \rightarrow H_2O(l)$

Potassium and sulphate ions are not involved in the final balanced ionic equation. So when dilute sulphuric acid reacts with potassium hydroxide, the only reaction which actually takes place is between one mole of hydrogen ions (from dilute sulphuric acid) and one mole of hydroxide ions (from potassium hydroxide), and the product is one mole of water molecules. **This is true for every acid reacting with every alkali**. If this seems unlikely, try writing some balanced ionic equations for reactions between different acids and different alkalis for yourself!

Questions

Write balanced equations for the following reactions. Remember that you must always write in non-ionic form all substances which are solids or which are molecular.

1. Magnesium + copper(II) sulphate solution
2. Hydrochloric acid + calcium carbonate solid
3. Zinc + dilute sulphuric acid
4. Carbon dioxide + sodium hydroxide solution
5. Copper(II) chloride solution + sodium hydroxide solution

EXPERIMENT 4.15
Finding the balanced equation for the reaction between lead nitrate and potassium iodide

You will need the following: M lead nitrate solution, M potassium iodide solution, (you will find both solutions in clearly labelled burettes around the laboratory), industrial methylated spirits, test-tubes to fit centrifuge (at least 3 for each working group), teat-pipette, access to centrifuge.

What to do

1   Take three of the special test-tubes which can be used in the centrifuge. Use one of the burettes around the laboratory to measure, as accurately as you can, 4 cm^3 of the solution which is marked 'M potassium iodide' into **each** tube

2   Use one of the other group of burettes to measure, again as accurately as you can, 1 cm^3 of the solution which is marked 'M lead nitrate' into **one** of the tubes which contain potassium iodide solution.

3   Into one of the other two tubes, measure exactly 2 cm^3 of lead nitrate solution, and into the third, measure exactly 3 cm^3 of lead nitrate solution.

4   Take a glass rod and make sure that it is clean and dry. Use it to stir the first solution and then wipe it dry. Stir the second solution, wipe the glass rod clean, and then use it to stir the third solution.
You must wipe the glass rod dry each time to stop solution being transferred from one test-tube to another.

5   Add two drops of industrial methylated spirits to each of the three test-tubes (this helps the precipitate to 'settle'), and then centrifuge **in a balanced centrifuge. If you have not used a centrifuge before, or if you are not sure how to balance it, ask your teacher to help**. Centrifuge all the tubes for the same length of time (30 seconds). The three test-tubes should now look like this:

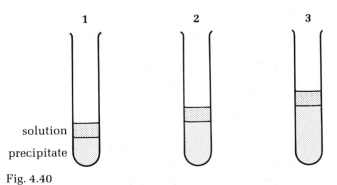

Fig. 4.40

1.   4 cm^3 M KI solution + 1 cm^3 M Pb(NO$_3$)$_2$ solution
2.   4 cm^3 M KI solution + 2 cm^3 M Pb(NO$_3$)$_2$ solution
3.   4 cm^3 M KI solution + 3 cm^3 M Pb(NO$_3$)$_2$ solution

5   Stand each test-tube upright. Measure the height of the precipitate in each tube, in centimetres, using a ruler.

What happened

The precipitate which forms in the test-tubes is lead iodide. The word-equation for the reaction is:

potassium iodide(aq) + lead nitrate(aq)
$\longrightarrow$ lead iodide(s) + potassium nitrate(aq)

The aim of the experiment was to find out how much lead nitrate reacts with how much potassium iodide. The solutions which you were given both had the same concentration. So the same volume of each solution contains the same amount of chemical. Therefore, to find the relative amounts of the two chemicals which react together, we only need to find the relative volumes of the two solutions which react.

We want to find, from the results of the experiment, the point where just enough M lead nitrate solution has been added to react with all the potassium iodide which there is in 4 cm^3 of M solution. We want to find out what amount of lead nitrate is EQUIVALENT to the amount of potassium iodide which was present in the test-tube.

We can find this out by looking at the amount of lead iodide precipitate which was formed. Suppose we imagine for a moment three different possible situations:
   A. There is too little lead nitrate added
   B. There is just enough lead nitrate added
   C. There is too much lead nitrate added
We can represent the amount of each chemical by the size of a box in which we write its formula. Where the amounts of the two chemicals do not balance exactly, one of the starting chemicals will be left over at the end. We say that this is the reactant chemical which is IN EXCESS. This will be potassium iodide in A, and lead nitrate in C.

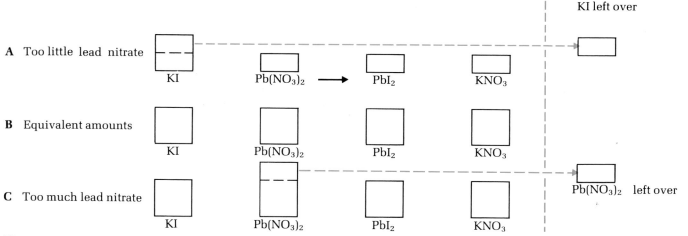

Fig. 4.41

We can see that the amount of lead iodide which is formed increases up to the point where there are equivalent amounts of the two reactant chemicals – and then **it stays constant**. So, to find the point where we have just added enough lead nitrate to make it equivalent to the amount of potassium iodide which is there, we need to find the point where the amount of lead iodide precipitate stopped increasing.

Can you use your own results to say what volume of M lead nitrate is equivalent to $4\,\text{cm}^3$ of M potassium iodide?

What we can decide

When we say that we have equivalent amounts of two chemicals, this does not mean that we have the **same** amounts. Equivalent amounts are really the ratio in which the number of moles of the two chemicals appear in the balanced equation. One mole of one

chemical may be equivalent to three moles of the other chemical, and so on.

Can you say, from the results of your experiment, what the equivalent volumes of the two chemicals were? Since the solutions had the same concentrations, this ratio will also be the ratio in which the number of moles of the two chemicals appear in the balanced equation. Can you write down the reactants side of the equation? Is it:

$$4KI + Pb(NO_3)_2$$
$$\text{or} \quad 2KI + Pb(NO_3)_2$$
$$\text{or} \quad KI + Pb(NO_3)_2 \quad ?$$

How does the result of your experiment compare with the theoretical balanced equation?

What would you need to do in order to use your experiment to find the **whole** of the balanced equation?

UNIT 4.3
Summary and learning

1   A balanced chemical equation represents the amounts of chemicals taking part in a chemical reaction.

2   Matter is neither created nor destroyed in a chemical reaction (the Law of Conservation of Mass).

3   If two chemicals A and B react together, the ratio of the mass of A reacting to the mass of B reacting is always the same, no matter how many times the reaction is carried out (the Rule of Reacting Masses).

4   If two product chemicals C and D are formed by a chemical reaction, the ratio of the mass of C produced

to the mass of D produced is always the same, no matter how many times the reaction is carried out (the Rule of Product Masses).

5   A general word-equation is a word-equation which describes, in terms of the **types** of chemical involved, one of the several classes of chemical reaction which exist. You should remember the 12 general word-equations.

6   The steps to be followed for finding the balanced equation for a chemical reaction are:
  (i) Write the general word-equation.
 (ii) Write the word-equation.
(iii) Put in the chemical formulae.
(iv) Check whether the equation is balanced for every
     element.

(v) If the equation is not balanced, use the Rule of Reacting Masses (and Product Masses) to obtain a balance by changing the number of moles of reactants or products (or both).

You should practice writing as many balanced equations as you can.

7   We can simplify the equations for reactions which involve ionic compounds by leaving out those ions which take no part in the reaction. When we write the equation in its ionic form, solids and molecular substances are always written in their non-ionic form. In a balanced ionic equation, the overall charge on the reactants side is equal to the overall charge on the products side.

8   You should remember that all chemical reactions first had their equations found by someone doing an experiment.

9   You have learnt the meaning of these words:

formula-unit	redox reaction
balanced equation	equivalent
thermal decomposition	in excess
oxidising agent	aquated
reducing agent	

UNIT 4.4   *How to use balanced equations*

We know that a balanced equation represents the amounts of chemicals which are involved in a particular chemical reaction. More accurately, it tells us what the relative number of **moles** of the different chemicals are.

Since 1 mole of a given chemical has a particular **mass**, we should be able to use balanced equations to tell us, very accurately, the masses of chemicals which react together. We should also be able to use the balanced equation to work out the masses of product chemicals for a known mass of reactant chemicals. If a reaction involves solutions of compounds rather than solids, we should be able to calculate their volumes and concentrations from the balanced equation.

In many reactions, the chemicals are gases at room temperature. Obviously, it is difficult to weigh a gas, but very much easier to measure its volume. So it is very much more useful to us to know the volume of a gas which is involved in a chemical reaction, than to know its mass. We shall go on, later in this unit, to see whether there is some way in which balanced equations can be used to give us information about the volumes, as well as about the masses, of chemicals which are gases.

We saw earlier that chemical reactions often have a heat, or enthalpy, change associated with them. We can measure the enthalpy change which happens when there is a reaction between the amounts of chemicals which are represented by the balanced equation. This lets us compare different reactions on an equal footing. It also lets us find out what the

enthalpy change would be for **any** quantity of chemicals. So, if we find the enthalpy change which goes with the balanced equation, we can put the balanced equation to yet another use.

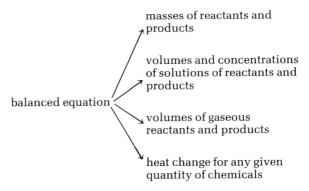

balanced equation
- masses of reactants and products
- volumes and concentrations of solutions of reactants and products
- volumes of gaseous reactants and products
- heat change for any given quantity of chemicals

TOPIC 4.4.1

The masses of chemicals which take part in chemical changes

Suppose that we take a balanced equation which has been obtained by the steps set out in the last unit. For instance,

$$CuCl_2(aq) + 2NaOH(aq) \rightarrow Cu(OH)_2(s) + 2NaCl(aq)$$

This tells us that 1 mole of copper(II) chloride reacts with 2 moles of sodium hydroxide, and that the products are 1 mole of copper(II) hydroxide and 2 moles of sodium chloride. So we can write under the balanced equation the masses of the different chemicals which are involved:

CuCl$_2$ + 2NaOH   → Cu(OH)$_2$ + 2NaCl
1 mole   2 moles   1 mole   2 moles
134.5 g   80 g   97.5 g   117 g

Suppose now that we wanted to make 10 g of copper(II) hydroxide, not 97.5 g. What masses of copper(II) chloride and sodium hydroxide should we start with?

We know that:

97.5 g Cu(OH)$_2$ are produced from 134.5 g CuCl$_2$

therefore,

1 g Cu(OH)$_2$ is produced from $\dfrac{134.5}{97.5}$ g CuCl$_2$

therefore,

10 g Cu(OH)$_2$ are produced from

$10 \times \dfrac{134.5}{97.5}$ g CuCl$_2$

= **13.8 g CuCl$_2$**

Also:

97.5 g Cu(OH)$_2$ are produced from 80 g NaOH

therefore,

1 g Cu(OH)$_2$ is produced from $\dfrac{80}{97.5}$ g NaOH

therefore,

10 g Cu(OH)$_2$ are produced from

$10 \times \dfrac{80}{97.5}$ g NaOH

= **8.2 g NaOH**

So we would need 13.8 g of CuCl$_2$ and 8.2 g of NaOH to produce 10 g of Cu(OH)$_2$.

We could do a calculation like this for the chemicals involved in any reaction, **as long as we know the balanced equation**. Suppose we take a different reaction now – such as the one between magnesium metal and dilute hydrochloric acid.

Mg(s) + 2HCl(aq) → MgCl$_2$(aq) + H$_2$(g)
1 mole   2 moles   1 mole   1 mole
24 g   73 g   95 g   2 g

Suppose we had plenty of dilute hydrochloric acid, and we were going to react 10 g of magnesium metal with it – what mass of hydrogen gas would we get? (In these circumstances, where there is enough dilute hydrochloric acid to react with all the magnesium, so that no magnesium was left at the end with the dilute hydrochloric acid left over, we say that the dilute hydrochloric acid is present IN EXCESS.)

We know that:

2 g H$_2$ are produced from 24 g Mg

therefore,

$\dfrac{2}{24}$ g H$_2$ is produced from 1 g Mg

therefore,

$10 \times \dfrac{2}{24}$ g H$_2$ are produced from 10 g Mg

$= \dfrac{5}{6}$ g H$_2$

= **0.83 g H$_2$**

So 0.83 g H$_2$ gas are produced when 10 g Mg reacts with excess dilute HCl.

In one of the above calculations, the number of grams of a product for a known number of grams of reactant was found. In the other, the number of grams of the product was known, and the number of grams of reactant were calculated. So we can do calculations like this going in either direction. In both cases, the steps which have to be followed are the same:

Calculations of reacting masses

Step 1: Obtain the balanced equation.
Step 2: Write down the number of moles of each chemical.
Step 3: Convert moles into grams for each chemical in the calculation.
Step 4: The question will tell you the known mass of one chemical (this may be a reactant or a product chemical). Scale down all the quantities, so that you have 1 g of this chemical.
Step 5: Scale up all the quantities, so that you have the mass of the known chemical which is given in the question.
Step 6: Write out the answer in the form of a sentence.

Now try some calculations for yourself, **using the steps given above**. Remember that the first step is to obtain the balanced equation.

Questions

1   Copper(II) oxide is a black powder. It dissolves in dilute sulphuric acid. What mass of copper(II) oxide would you need to react with excess dilute sulphuric acid, to get 100 g of copper(II) sulphate?

2   Zinc powder reacts with copper(II) sulphate solution. If 20 g of zinc powder is used with excess copper(II) sulphate solution, what mass of copper is produced?

3   If we heat potassium hydroxide and ammonium chloride together, one of the products is ammonia gas.
(a) If 112 g of potassium hydroxide are used with excess ammonium chloride, what mass of ammonia gas would be produced?
(b) What mass of ammonium chloride would react with 112 g of potassium hydroxide?
(c) If 120 g of ammonium chloride were used, what mass of it would be left over at the end?

4   Iron metal reacts with chlorine gas, and the product is iron(III) chloride. If you wanted to make 1 kg of iron(III) chloride, what mass of iron would you need to start with?

5   Carbon dioxide and calcium hydroxide react together to make calcium carbonate. If carbon dioxide was bubbled into a solution containing 7.4 g calcium hydroxide, until no more reaction took place, what mass of calcium carbonate was produced?

6   The calcium carbonate which was produced by the reaction in question 5 was carefully filtered off. It was reacted with excess dilute hydrochloric acid.
(a) What mass of carbon dioxide was produced?
(b) How does this compare with the mass of carbon dioxide which reacted originally with 7.4 g of calcium hydroxide?

7   Fill in the missing masses in the following diagram.

TOPIC 4.4.2
Calculations about solutions

Very often in chemistry, the substances which we use are solutions of chemicals in water. For any solution, we know that the mass of the dissolved chemical is related to the volume and concentration of the solution in the following way:

$$\text{mass(g)} = \text{volume(dm}^3) \times \text{concentration(g dm}^{-3})$$

So, instead of weighing solids, we can measure the volumes of solutions. Since the balanced equation for a reaction gives us the number of moles of the different chemicals involved, we usually think of the concentrations of solutions, not in g dm^{-3}, but in moles dm^{-3}. So we would use the fact that:

$$\text{no. of moles of dissolved chemical} = \text{volume(dm}^3) \times \text{molarity(moles dm}^{-3})$$

The MOLARITY of a solution is the number of moles of the dissolved chemical in 1 dm^3 of the solution. The symbol for molarity is M.
So if 5 moles of a chemical are dissolved in 1 dm^3 of solution, the solution produced is '5 molar' ('5 M'). A solution which is '0.1 M' contains 0.1 moles of chemical dissolved in 1 dm^3 of solution.
A solution which contains 1 mole of chemical dissolved in 1 dm^3 of solution is called a MOLAR SOLUTION. We could say that a molar solution is '1 M', but we usually just say that its molarity is 'M'.
If we know what the concentration of a solution is very accurately, we say that the solution is a STANDARD SOLUTION. (We may know the concentration in either g dm^{-3}, or in moles dm^{-3}, of course.)
We can use balanced equations to find either the volume of a solution whose molarity is known, or the molarity of a solution whose volume is known.

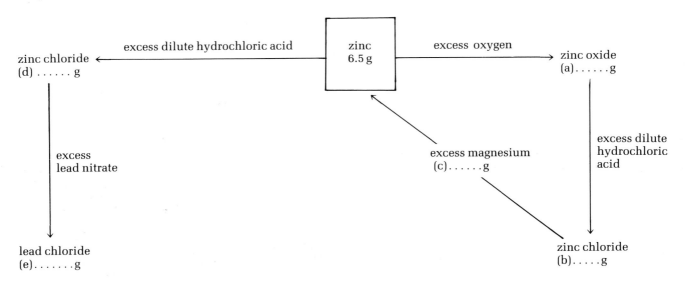

How to calculate an unknown volume

You should read very carefully through the example calculation which is set out below.

Example 1

What volume of 0.2 M sulphuric acid reacts with 25 cm³ of 0.2 M calcium hydroxide solution?

Balanced equation:

$$H_2SO_4(aq) + Ca(OH)_2(aq) \rightarrow CaSO_4(s) + 2H_2O(l)$$
$$\text{1 mole} \qquad \text{1 mole}$$

The balanced equation tells us that 1 mole of sulphuric acid reacts with 1 mole of calcium hydroxide. So the number of moles of sulphuric acid and the number of moles of calcium hydroxide are equal. We know the following:

For calcium hydroxide:

Volume: 25 cm³
Molarity: 0.2 M } We can call calcium hydroxide the 'known solution'

For sulphuric acid:

Volume: ?
Molarity: 0.2 M } We can call sulphuric acid the 'unknown solution'

We can calculate the number of moles of calcium hydroxide, because we know that

no. of moles = volume × molarity

KNOWN SOLUTION

No. of moles of $Ca(OH)_2$ in 25 cm³ of M solution
$$= \frac{25}{1000}$$
$$(1\,cm^3 = \frac{1}{1000}\,dm^3, \therefore 25\,cm^3 = \frac{25}{1000}dm^3)$$

$\therefore$ No. of moles of $Ca(OH)_2$ in 25 cm³ of 0.2 M solution
$$= \frac{25}{1000} \times 0.2$$

We can do the same calculation for the sulphuric acid, using x cm³ for the unknown volume:

UNKNOWN SOLUTION

No. of moles of H_2SO_4 in x cm³ of M solution $= \frac{x}{1000}$
$\therefore$ No. of moles of H_2SO_4 in x cm³ of 0.2 M solution
$$= \frac{x}{1000} \times 0.2$$

Since we know from the balanced equation that the number of moles of the two chemicals which react together are the same, we can write:

From volume and molarity of H_2SO_4	From volume and molarity of $Ca(OH)_2$

No. of moles of H_2SO_4 $= \frac{x}{1000} \times 0.2 = \frac{25}{1000} \times 0.2$

Therefore, **x = 25 cm³**

So 25 cm³ 0.2 M sulphuric acid react with 25 cm³ 0.2 M calcium hydroxide.

Is this the answer you would have expected? Both solutions had the same concentration, and the balanced equation tells us that equal numbers of moles of the two substances react together. Therefore the same volume of each solution will be needed. The answer for a more difficult example may not be so obvious, however.

Example 2

What volume of 0.5 M H_2SO_4 reacts with 25 cm³ of 0.5 M sodium hydroxide solution?

Balanced equation:

$$H_2SO_4(aq) + 2NaOH(aq) \rightarrow Na_2SO_4(aq) + 2H_2O(l)$$
$$\text{1 mole} \qquad \text{2 moles}$$

The balanced equation tells us that 1 mole of sulphuric acid reacts with 2 moles of sodium hydroxide. So the number of moles of sodium hydroxide is twice the number of moles of sulphuric acid. We know the following:

For sodium hydroxide:

Volume: 25 cm³
Molarity: 0.5 M } the 'known solution'

For sulphuric acid:

Volume: ?
Molarity: 0.5 M } the 'unknown solution'

KNOWN SOLUTION

No. of moles = volume(dm³) × molarity (moles dm⁻³)

No. of moles of NaOH in 25 cm³ of 0.5 M solution
$$= \frac{25}{1000} \times 0.5$$

No. of moles of H_2SO_4 required in reaction
$$= \frac{1}{2} \times \text{no. of moles NaOH}$$
$$= \frac{1}{2} \times \frac{25}{1000} \times 0.5$$

UNKNOWN SOLUTION

If x cm³ is the volume of 0.5 M H_2SO_4 which reacts, then

No. of moles of $H_2SO_4 = \frac{x}{1000} \times 0.5$

So we can say that:

From volume and molarity of H_2SO_4	From volume and molarity of NaOH, and balanced equation

No. of moles of H_2SO_4 $= \frac{x}{1000} \times 0.5 = \frac{1}{2} \times \frac{25}{1000} \times 0.5$

Therefore, $x = \frac{1}{2} \times 25 \, cm^3$

$x = 12.5 \, cm^3$

So 12.5 cm³ of 0.5 M sulphuric acid react with 25 cm³ 0.5 M sodium hydroxide.

A more complicated example still would be one where the two solutions have different molarities.

Example 3

What volume of 0.2 M H_2SO_4 reacts with 25 cm³ of 0.5 M sodium hydroxide solution?

Balanced equation:

$H_2SO_4(aq) + 2NaOH(aq) \rightarrow Na_2SO_4(aq) + 2H_2O(l)$
1 mole   2 moles

The balanced equation tells us that the number of moles of sodium hydroxide is twice the number of moles of sulphuric acid. We know the following:

For sodium hydroxide:

Volume: 25 cm³ } the 'known solution'
Molarity: 0.5 M

For sulphuric acid:

Volume: ? } the 'unknown solution'
Molarity: 0.2 M

KNOWN SOLUTION

No. of moles = volume(dm³) × molarity
(moles dm⁻³)

No. of moles of NaOH in 25 cm³ of 0.5 M solution

$= \frac{25}{1000} \times 0.5$

No. of moles of H_2SO_4 required in reaction

$= \frac{1}{2} \times$ no. of moles of NaOH

$= \frac{1}{2} \times \frac{25}{1000} \times 0.5$

UNKNOWN SOLUTION

If x cm³ is the volume of 0.2 M H_2SO_4 which reacts, then

No. of moles of $H_2SO_4 = \frac{x}{1000} \times 0.5$

So we can say that:

From volume and molarity of H_2SO_4	From volume and molarity of NaOH, and balanced equation
↓	↓

No. of moles of H_2SO_4 $= \frac{x}{1000} \times 0.2 = \frac{1}{2} \times \frac{25}{1000} \times 0.5$

Therefore, $x = \frac{5}{2} \times 25 \times 0.5$

$x = 31.25 \, cm^3$

So 31.25 cm³ of 0.2 M sulphuric acid reacts with 25 cm³ of 0.5 M sodium hydroxide.

You can see from these examples that, where we have standard solutions of both reactants, we can always find the volume of one if we know the volume of the other.

But what if we do not have standard solutions of the chemicals which are involved in the reaction? As long as we have a standard solution of **one** of the chemicals, and we know the volumes of the two solutions which react together, we can do a calculation to find the molarity of the other.

How to calculate an unknown molarity

Example 1

25 cm³ of hydrochloric acid react with 23.5 cm³ of 0.1 M sodium hydroxide. What is the molarity of the hydrochloric acid?

Balanced equation:

$HCl(aq) + NaOH(aq) \rightarrow NaCl(aq) + H_2O(l)$
1 mole   1 mole

The balanced equation tells us that 1 mole of hydrochloric acid reacts with 1 mole of sodium hydroxide. So the number of moles of the two chemicals are equal. We know the following:

For sodium hydroxide:

Volume: 23.5 cm³ } the 'known solution'
Molarity: 0.1 M

For hydrochloric acid:

Volume: 25 cm³ } the 'unknown solution'
Molarity: ?

KNOWN SOLUTION

No. of moles = volume(dm³) × molarity
(moles dm⁻³)

No. of moles of NaOH in 23.5 cm³ of 0.1 M solution

$= \frac{23.5}{1000} \times 0.1$

No. of moles of HCl required in reaction
= no. of moles of NaOH

$= \frac{23.5}{1000} \times 0.1$

UNKNOWN SOLUTION

If m is the molarity of the hydrochloric acid, then

No. of moles of HCl $= \frac{25}{1000} \times m$

So we can say that:

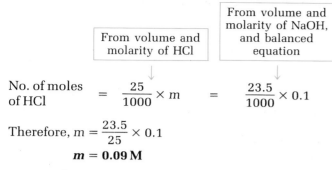

$$\text{No. of moles of HCl} = \frac{25}{1000} \times m = \frac{23.5}{1000} \times 0.1$$

Therefore, $m = \dfrac{23.5}{25} \times 0.1$

$$m = 0.09\,\text{M}$$

So 25 cm³ of 0.09 M hydrochloric acid react with 23.5 cm³ of 0.1 M sodium hydroxide.

Again, we should now try a more complicated example.

Example 2

25 cm³ of sulphuric acid react with 15.6 cm³ of 0.2 M potassium hydroxide. What is the molarity of the sulphuric acid?

Balanced equation:

$$H_2SO_4(aq) + 2KOH(aq) \rightarrow K_2SO_4(aq) + 2H_2O(l)$$
$$\text{1 mole} \qquad \text{2 moles}$$

The balanced equation tells us that 1 mole of sulphuric acid reacts with 2 moles of potassium hydroxide. So the number of moles of sulphuric acid is half the number of moles of potassium hydroxide. We know the following:

For potassium hydroxide:

Volume: 15.6 cm³ ⎫
Molarity: 0.2 M ⎬ the 'known solution'

For sulphuric acid:

Volume: 25 cm³ ⎫
Molarity: ? ⎬ the 'unknown solution'

KNOWN SOLUTION

No. of moles = volume(dm³) × molarity
(moles dm⁻³)

No. of moles of KOH in 15.6 cm³ of 0.2 M solution

$$= \frac{15.6}{1000} \times 0.2$$

No. of moles of sulphuric acid required in reaction

$$= \frac{1}{2} \times \text{no. of moles KOH}$$

$$= \frac{1}{2} \times \frac{15.6}{1000} \times 0.2$$

UNKNOWN SOLUTION

If m is the molarity of the sulphuric acid, then

No. of moles of $H_2SO_4 = \dfrac{25}{1000} \times m$

So we can say that:

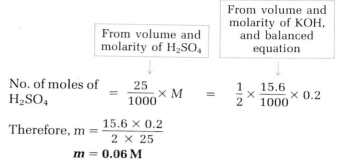

$$\text{No. of moles of } H_2SO_4 = \frac{25}{1000} \times M = \frac{1}{2} \times \frac{15.6}{1000} \times 0.2$$

Therefore, $m = \dfrac{15.6 \times 0.2}{2 \times 25}$

$$m = 0.06\,\text{M}$$

So 25 cm³ of 0.06 M sulphuric acid react with 15.6 cm³ of 0.02 M potassium hydroxide.

Whether you are asked to find the volume of a solution whose molarity is already known, or to find the molarity of a solution whose volume is already known, the steps are the same.

Calculations about solutions

Step 1: Obtain the balanced equation.
Step 2: Write down the number of moles of each chemical.
Step 3: Call the solution for which both the molarity and the volume reacting are known the 'known solution'.
Step 4: Calculate the number of moles of the 'known solution' which are present.
Step 5: Use the balanced equation to decide what the relationship is between the number of moles of the 'known solution' and the number of moles of the 'unknown solution'.
Step 6: Use the results of step 4 and step 5 to calculate the number of moles of the 'unknown solution'.
Step 7: Now calculate the number of moles of the 'unknown solution', using 'x cm³' for the volume (if this is not known), and 'm' for the molarity (if this is not known).
Step 8: You have now written down the number of moles of the 'unknown solution' in two ways. These must be equal to each other, so you can write an equation in which either 'x' or 'm' is the only unknown quantity. Calculate 'x' or 'm'.
Step 9: Write out the answer in a sentence.

Now try some calculations for yourself, using the steps given above. **Remember that you must obtain the balanced equation** before you start your calculation.

Questions

In questions 1–5, calculate the molarity of the solution given, in moles dm^{-3}.

1 2 g of sodium hydroxide dissolved in 500 cm^3 of solution.

2 112 g of potassium hydroxide dissolved in 2 dm^3 of solution.

3 10.6 g of sodium carbonate dissolved in 3 dm^3 of solution.

4 3.65 g of hydrogen chloride dissolved in 1 dm^3 of solution.

5 34.3 g of lead nitrate dissolved in 200 cm^3 of solution.

6 What volume of 0.1 M nitric acid reacts with 20 cm^3 0.1 M potassium hydroxide solution?

7 What volume of 0.2 M hydrochloric acid reacts with 100 cm^3 of 0.2 M sodium carbonate solution?

8 What volume of 2 M hydrochloric acid is needed to react with 6 g of magnesium ribbon? (Hint: calculate the number of moles of magnesium from its mass.)

9 What volume of 0.2 M potassium iodide reacts with 50 cm^3 of 0.1 M lead nitrate solution?

10 Calculate the mass of sodium carbonate present in the volume of 0.1 M solution which reacts with 25 cm^3 of 0.1 M nitric acid. (Hint: first find the volume of sodium carbonate solution. You can work out the mass of sodium carbonate which there would be in 1 dm^3 of 0.1 M solution. So you can calculate the mass in the volume of 0.1 M solution which reacts.)

11 12.5 cm^3 of a solution of calcium hydroxide react with 25 cm^3 of 0.2 M sulphuric acid. What is the molarity of the calcium hydroxide solution?

12 30 cm^3 of 2 M sodium sulphate react with 15 cm^3 of a solution of barium chloride. What is the molarity of the barium chloride solution?

13 50 cm^3 of 0.5 M sulphuric acid react with 50 cm^3 of sodium hydroxide solution. What is the molarity of the sodium hydroxide?

14 12 g of magnesium ribbon dissolve in 100 cm^3 of sulphuric acid. At the end of the reaction, the solution was exactly neutral. What was the molarity of the sulphuric acid? (Hint: a neutral solution means that all the acid reacted with all the magnesium ribbon.)

15 32 g of copper(II) oxide dissolve in 400 cm^3 of hydrochloric acid. At the end of the reaction, the solution was exactly neutral. What was the molarity of the hydrochloric acid? (Use Cu = 64 for this calculation. Hint: calculate the number of moles of copper(II) oxide from its mass.)

Volumetric analysis

Very frequently in chemistry, we need to find the concentration of a solution by carrying out an experiment. If we are finding out something about a chemical by doing an experiment, we can say that we are **analysing** the chemical. To find the concentration of a solution, we would need to find the volume of it which reacts with a known volume of a standard solution. Then we could carry out a calculation like those above, using the information which has been obtained during the experiment. Analysis of this sort, where we measure carefully the reacting volumes of chemicals, is called VOLUMETRIC ANALYSIS.

We can use volumetric analysis to find the concentration of any solution, provided we have a standard solution to react it with. Volumetric analysis is used by chemists whose job it is to discover the exact chemical composition of different substances. Such people are called analytical chemists, and the branch of chemistry in which they are experts is called analytical chemistry. Modern analytical chemistry uses many methods to find how things are composed, including very sensitive and accurate electronic devices. But volumetric analysis is still used very frequently in laboratories all over the world.

Fig. 4.42 *Analytical chemistry*

Examples of the work which analytical chemists do are listed in Table 4.6.

43

Analysis of rivers, the sea and the air for pollution.
Analysis of chemicals which have been dug out of the
ground for the presence of valuable minerals.
In forensic science (police) laboratories.
Analysis of the products of chemical processes in industry
(this is sometimes called 'quality control').
In chemical and biological research (finding out the exact
chemical nature of new substances which have not been
made before).

Table 4.6 *Some of the work done by analytical chemists.*

One of the commonest uses for volumetric analysis is
in finding out the concentrations of acids and alkalis.
This involves a special process which we call
TITRATION. In a titration, we react a standard solution
of an acid or an alkali with the solution whose
concentration we wish to find out. We discover the
exact amounts of acid and alkali which react together.

To do this we need:
1. A way of knowing when the amounts of acid and
   alkali which exactly react together have been
   mixed with each other.
2. A way of measuring accurately the volumes of the
   solutions involved.

We solve the problem of knowing when enough of the
reactants have been mixed together by using a
coloured chemical called an indicator. You met
indicators in Section 1. The indicator changes colour
at the point where exactly equivalent amounts of acid
and alkali have been added together. We call this
point the END-POINT of the titration. We overcome the
problem of measuring the volumes of the chemicals
very accurately by using very precise measuring
devices – a burette and a pipette.

▶ EXPERIMENT 4.16

EXPERIMENT 4.16

Volumetric analysis – finding the molarity of hydrochloric acid

You will need: burette, pipette (25 cm^3) with safety
filler, 3 conical flasks (250 cm^3), methyl orange
indicator, exactly 0.1 M sodium carbonate solution
(100 cm^3), approximately 0.2 M hydrochloric acid
(150 cm^3).

What to do

1   The standard solution used in this experiment is
0.1 M sodium carbonate solution. You will have to
measure it out exactly using a 25 cm^3 pipette. Your
teacher will show you how to use a pipette if you have
not done so before.

2   Wash out the pipette using water, and then using a
little of the 0.1 M sodium carbonate solution.

3   Wash out 3 conical flasks (250 cm^3), using distilled
water.

4   Use the pipette, in the way your teacher has shown
you, to run exactly 25 cm^3 of 0.1 M sodium carbonate
solution into each conical flask.

5   To each flask, add 2–3 drops of methyl orange
indicator solution. Methyl orange goes yellow in
alkaline solution.

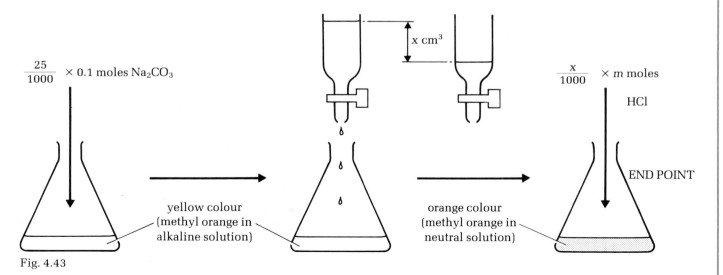

$$\frac{25}{1000} \times 0.1 \text{ moles Na}_2\text{CO}_3$$

x cm^3

$$\frac{x}{1000} \times m \text{ moles}$$

HCl

END POINT

yellow colour
(methyl orange in
alkaline solution)

orange colour
(methyl orange in
neutral solution)

Fig. 4.43

Continued overleaf

Experiment 4.16 continued

6   Wash out a burette, using first distilled water and then a little of the approximately 0.2 M hydrochloric acid. Fill the burette, using the filter funnel. Remove the filter funnel from the top of the burette. Now run some acid out through the tap, so that the tip of the burette is also filled with hydrochloric acid. Read the level of the acid in the burette.

7   Place one of the conical flasks underneath the burette on a white tile. Make sure that you can get the conical flask into position and remove it again without catching the tip of the burette, but that the burette is not too high above the neck of the flask.

8   Run 2 cm³ of the acid from the burette into the conical flask. Swirl the contents of the flask to mix them together. Add another 2 cm³ of the acid and swirl again. Keep on repeating this until you can see a definite pink colour in the solution when the acid is added to it before it has had chance to mix.

9   When this happens, add the acid only 0.5 cm³ at a time. Keep on doing this, swirling the contents of the flask each time, until the yellow colour returns very slowly.

10   Now you must add the acid as slowly as possible. If you can operate the burette carefully, you should be able to add only one drop at a time. Do this, and swirl the flask each time.

11   When the solution goes orange, **and stays orange after swirling**, you have reached the end-point of the titration. Read the level of the acid in the burette, and write down your result. If you add a further drop of acid, the solution should go pink because it is now acidic.

12   Use one of the remaining conical flasks containing sodium carbonate solution to repeat the above experiment. Before you start, make sure that there is enough acid in the burette to complete the reaction. If you have to add more acid to the burette to make sure there will be enough, do so with the conical flask well out of the way. Read the level of the acid in the burette before you start, and write down your result. If the volume of hydrochloric acid which is needed to neutralise the sodium carbonate in this second titration is different from the volume needed in the first titration by more than 0.1 cm³, carry out a third titration.

13   Carry on until you have two results which are within 0.1 cm³ of each other. Find the average of these two values for use in your calculation.

What happened

Set out your results in a table like the one below.

Titration	1	2	3	
Second burette reading				cm³
First burette reading				cm³
Volume of acid needed				cm³

Write down the calculation of the average of the two values which you will be using for your calculation.

Calculation

Calculate the molarity of the hydrochloric acid, from the balanced equation for the reaction, the number of moles in 25 cm³ of 0.1 M sodium carbonate, and the average value of the volume of hydrochloric acid used.

What we can decide

What was the molarity of the hydrochloric acid which you were given? Your teacher will probably collect together the results of all the groups in the class, to find the 'class average'. If there is any difference between your own value for the molarity of the hydrochloric acid and the class result, why do you think this might be? Where could the discrepancy come from?

TOPIC 4.4.3

Calculations about gases

Many chemical substances are gases. It was natural, therefore, for early scientists to study gases to see how they behaved during chemical reactions.

These scientists did not have modern laboratories, or modern scientific equipment. So they had to spend long hours painstakingly gathering information about gases, which would lead them – they knew not where. One of the researchers who studied the behaviour of gases during chemical reactions was a professor of chemistry in Paris, Joseph Gay-Lussac.

By the time he was 30 years old, in 1808, Joseph Gay-Lussac had discovered enough about gases to be able to say that there was something about the way they behaved which was common to them all. He put what he had discovered into the form of a chemical law, which all gases obey. Gay-Lussac's Law is about the **volumes** of gases which are involved in chemical reactions, and in many ways it is a simple law. Yet, in spite of this simplicity, what Gay-Lussac discovered led to scientists having to make basic changes to their ideas about chemistry.

1808 may seem a very long time ago. But if you compare it with the dates of other scientific breakthroughs, perhaps it isn't. Look at the Chart of Scientific History on p. 74. You will see that Gay-Lussac put forward his ideas only 25 years before the first electric motor was made, and only 50 years before telephones were invented.

▶ PROJECT 4.2 (p. 216)

Gay-Lussac's Law tells us that there is something special about gases which makes them different from liquids and solids. What is more, **all** gases behave in the same way. No matter how many gases are studied, no exceptions are found.

But why should this be so? Surely, there must be some explanation. It was three years before anyone came up with a theory to make sense of Gay-Lussac's Law. In 1811, an Italian scientist, Amadeo Avogadro, put forward the following suggestion (hypothesis).

Equal volumes of all gases (under the same conditions of temperature and pressure) contain equal numbers of particles.

'Avogadro's Hypothesis', as it is called, says that if a substance is a gas, the volume which it occupies depends upon the **number** of particles present. The **type** of particle does not matter.

We know today that the particles which make up gases are molecules – Avogadro did not know this in 1811. **So the volume of a gas depends on the number of molecules of it which are present. The same number of molecules of different gases will occupy the same volume.** If, for instance, we have a certain number of molecules of the gas methane (CH_4), and the same number of molecules of the gas ammonia (NH_3), the volumes occupied by the two gases will be the same (at the same temperature and pressure).

Suppose now that we think about a particular reaction, like the one in which ammonia gas is split up to make hydrogen gas and nitrogen gas. How does Avogadro's Hypothesis explain Gay-Lussac's Law? The balanced equation for the reaction is:

$$2NH_3(g) \rightarrow N_2(g) + 3H_2(g)$$
2 moles   1 mole   3 moles

You know that a mole of anything contains Avogadro's Number of particles (N_A). So, 1 mole of any gas contains N_A molecules, 2 moles of a gas contain $2N_A$ molecules, and so on. The number of molecules of the three gases represented by the equation is therefore:

ammonia	nitrogen	hydrogen
$2N_A$ molecules	N_A molecules	$3N_A$ molecules

Avogadro's Hypothesis links the number of molecules present to the volumes which the gases will occupy. The greater the number of molecules, the greater the volume. The ratio of the volumes of the gases will therefore be the same as the ratio of the number of molecules.

ammonia	nitrogen	hydrogen
2 volumes	1 volume	3 volumes

That is, **we expect volumes of gases which fit with Gay-Lussac's Law**. To recap:

	$2NH_3(g)$	$N_2(g)$		$3H_2(g)$
	2 moles	1 mole	+	3 moles
	$2N_A$ molecules	N_A molecules		$3N_A$ molecules
By Avogadro's Hypothesis (A.H.)	2 volumes	1 volume		3 volumes

results obtained experimentally, fitting Gay-Lussac's Law   (at same T & P)

PROJECT 4.2
Following in the footsteps of the famous

You will find it helpful to work in a group with one or two others during this project.

Joseph Gay-Lussac carried out many experiments before he put forward his law. Below are the results of some experiments which are similar to those performed by Gay-Lussac. Look at the volumes of the gases involved. Can you work out a description in words which will cover what is happening in each experiment? You should discuss your thinking with the other members of your group.

To help you, remember that Gay-Lussac would not have been able to write a balanced equation for any of the reactions. Even the idea of molecules did not exist in 1808! So you will not need to write a balanced equation yourself in order to follow Gay-Lussac's thinking.

Also remember that the results below were obtained from actual experiments, and that you might need to make allowances for small amounts of experimental error.

Experiment 1

Ammonia gas was passed over heated iron wool, giving the products hydrogen gas and nitrogen gas. The mixture of hydrogen and nitrogen was taken and passed over heated copper(II) oxide. This removed the hydrogen, leaving behind the nitrogen. From the volume of hydrogen and nitrogen together, and the volume of nitrogen on its own, the volume of hydrogen was calculated.

	ammonia	nitrogen	hydrogen
Volumes under experimental conditions	105 cm³	51 cm³	153 cm³
Volume corrected to room temperature and pressure	100 cm³	50.2 cm³	149.9 cm³

Experiment 2

Nitrogen monoxide gas was allowed to combine with oxygen gas, forming nitrogen dioxide gas only. The volumes of these were:-

	nitrogen monoxide	oxygen	nitrogen dioxide
Volume under experimental conditions (room temperature and pressure)	40 cm³	20 cm³	40.1 cm³

Experiment 3

Hydrogen gas and chlorine gas were allowed to mix together (in the presence of charcoal). The product was hydrogen chloride gas only.

	hydrogen	chlorine	hydrogen chloride
Volume under experimental conditions (room temperature and pressure)	30 cm³	30 cm³	59.9 cm³

Experiment 4

Hydrogen gas and oxygen gas were allowed to mix together. A spark was supplied to the mixture, which exploded. The temperature was above 100°C, so the product (water, in the form of steam) was also a gas.

	hydrogen	oxygen	steam
Volume under experimental conditions	40 cm³	20 cm³	42.3 cm³
Volume corrected to room temperature and pressure of 1 atmosphere	42.1 cm³	21.1 cm³	42.1 cm³

Take each experiment in turn and ask yourselves (talk about this in your group) if there is any sort of relationship between the volumes of the gases (once you have allowed for a small experimental error). Does there seem to be a pattern covering all the experiments which you can put into words? If you think you have arrived at a statement which will be a copy of Gay-Lussac's Law, discuss your finding with your teacher.

To help your thinking, your teacher may show you Experiments 1 and 2 in the laboratory. These can be carried out fairly simply with pieces of apparatus called 'gas syringes'. You may also be allowed to pass electricity through some acidified water in such a way that the volumes of hydrogen and oxygen which are produced can be compared.

At the end of your project, your teacher will put Gay-Lussac's Law into a form which all the groups in the class can accept.

A hypothesis is not the same as a law. A law has been proved, a hypothesis has not. It is not really possible to prove Avogadro's Hypothesis directly. However, so many experiments have now been carried out which support it, that it is often called 'Avogadro's Law'.

But how can we use Avogadro's Hypothesis to help us calculate the volumes of gases involved in chemical reactions? As you will see below, there are three types of calculation which we can do.

Calculations of relative volumes of different gases in the same reaction

Avogadro's Hypothesis tells us that the volumes of different gases involved in the same reaction are in the same ratio as their number of moles. Suppose that we again take the example of the reaction in which ammonia breaks down into nitrogen and hydrogen. Suppose that we start with a certain volume of ammonia (say 20 cm³). Can we calculate the volume of nitrogen and the volume of hydrogen which are formed?

$$2NH_3(g) \rightarrow H_2(g) + 3H_2(g)$$
2 moles	1 mole	3 moles
By A.H. 2 volumes	1 volume	3 volumes (at same T & P)

So for every 2 volumes of ammonia, 1 volume of nitrogen and 3 volumes of hydrogen are formed.

volume NH_3: volume N_2 = 2:1
        volume of NH_3 = 20 cm³
Therefore, the volume of nitrogen = 10 cm³
($\frac{1}{2} \times 20$ cm³ = 10 cm³) and,
volume NH_3: volume H_2 = 2:3
        volume of NH_3 = 20 cm³
therefore, the volume of hydrogen = 30 cm³
($3/2 \times 20$ cm³ = 30 cm³)

$$2NH_3(g) \rightarrow N_2(g) + 3H_2(g)$$
2 moles	1 mole	3 moles
By A.H. 2 volumes	1 volume	3 volumes (at same T & P)
20 cm³	10 cm³	30 cm² (at same T & P)

We can also work backwards from the volumes of products to the volumes of reactants. Suppose we found that 50 cm³ of sulphur trioxide was obtained in the reaction between sulphur dioxide and oxygen. We could work out the volumes of sulphur dioxide and oxygen which had reacted (at the same T & P).

$$2SO_2(g) + O_2(g) \rightarrow 2SO_3(g)$$
2 moles	1 mole	2 moles
By A.H. 2 volumes	1 volume	2 volumes (at same T & P)
50 cm³	25 cm³	50 cm³ (at same T & P)

(volume of SO_2: volume of SO_3 = 2:2 = 1:1
volume of SO_2 = 1 × 50 cm³   = 50 cm³
volume of O_2: volume of SO_3 = 1:2
volume of $O_2 = \frac{1}{2} \times 50$ cm³   = 25 cm³)

Now try the following calculations for yourself.

Questions

1   30 cm³ of hydrogen gas was reacted with 50 cm³ of chlorine gas. What volume of chlorine was left unreacted, and what volume of hydrogen chloride gas was formed? (All volumes measured at the same temperature and pressure.)

2   What volume of oxygen is needed to convert 100 cm³ of nitrogen monoxide into nitrogen dioxide? What volume of nitrogen dioxide is formed? (All volumes measured at the same temperature and pressure.)

Calculations involving one gas in a reaction

The same number of molecules of different gases occupy the same volume. The number of molecules in one mole of any gas is Avogadro's Number. So one mole of any gas must occupy the same volume as one mole of any other gas.

If we measure the volume taken up by 1 mole of a gas at 0°C and 1 atmosphere pressure, it is always 22.4 dm³. 0°C and 1 atmosphere are called STANDARD TEMPERATURE AND PRESSURE (s.t.p.). The volume occupied by a mole of gas is called the MOLAR VOLUME. At s.t.p. this volume is 22.4 dm³.

We sometimes use the fact that the molar volume at room temperature and pressure is approximately 24 dm³.

We know what volume a given number of moles of any gas will occupy (at s.t.p.). So, if we know what mass of a gas we have, we can work out the volume it will occupy from the number of moles which are present.

Example 1

6 g of magnesium was reacted with excess dilute hydrochloric acid. What volume of hydrogen (measured at s.t.p.) was formed?

$$Mg(s) + 2HCl(aq) \rightarrow MgCl_2(aq) + H_2(g)$$
1 mole	$\longrightarrow$	1 mole
1 mole	$\longrightarrow$	22.4 dm³ (at s.t.p.)
∴ 24 g	$\longrightarrow$	22.4 dm³ (at s.t.p.)
∴ 1 g	$\longrightarrow$	$\frac{22.4}{24}$ dm³ (at s.t.p.)
∴ 6 g	$\longrightarrow$	$6 \times \frac{22.4}{24}$ dm³ (at s.t.p.)

= 1/4 × 22.4 dm³ (at s.t.p.)
= 5.6 dm³ (at s.t.p.)

Therefore 6 g of magnesium, when reacted with excess dilute hydrochloric acid, will produce 5.6 dm³ of hydrogen (at s.t.p.).

We can also use a known volume of a gas to work out the mass of a reactant or product chemical.

Example 2

250 cm³ of sulphur dioxide (measured at s.t.p.) was reacted with excess hydrogen sulphide gas, giving sulphur and water. What mass of sulphur was formed?

$$2H_2S(g) + SO_2(g) \rightarrow 3S(s) + 2H_2O(l)$$
$$ 1 \text{ mole} \rightarrow 3 \text{ moles}$$

The mass of 3 moles of sulphur is $3 \times 32\,g = 96\,g$. Therefore 1 mole of sulphur dioxide gives rise to 96 g of sulphur.

$$22.4\,dm^3\ SO_2\ (\text{at s.t.p.}) \rightarrow 96\,g\ S$$
$$1\,dm^3\ SO_2\ (\text{at s.t.p.}) \rightarrow \frac{96}{22.4}\,g\ S$$
$$\therefore\ 250\,cm^3\ SO_2\ (\text{at s.t.p.}) \rightarrow \frac{250}{1000} \times \frac{96}{22.4}\,g\ S$$
$$= \frac{1}{4} \times \frac{96}{22.4}\,g\ S$$
$$= \frac{24}{22.4}\,g\ S$$
$$= \textbf{1.07 g of S}$$

Therefore, 250 cm³ of sulphur dioxide (measured at s.t.p.), when reacted with excess hydrogen sulphide, give rise to 1.07 g of sulphur.

Now try the following calculations for yourself.

Questions

1   When calcium carbonate is heated strongly, it undergoes thermal decomposition. It breaks up to form calcium oxide (a solid) and carbon dioxide gas. What volume of carbon dioxide (at s.t.p.) is produced from 10 g of calcium carbonate?

2   When sulphur is burned in oxygen, the gas sulphur dioxide is formed. If 2.8 dm³ of sulphur dioxide (at s.t.p.) is produced, what mass of sulphur was burned?

Calculations involving conditions other than s.t.p.

More often than not, the temperature and pressure at which chemical reactions are carried out are different from s.t.p. So we often find that we have made a measurement of the volume of a gas which we wish to convert to the value it would have at s.t.p., in order to find out about the number of moles involved. But how can we carry out this conversion?

Gases obey very precisely some simple laws, which link together pressure, volume and temperature. These laws, which were discovered by scientists doing large numbers of experiments on gases, are called, not surprisingly, the Gas Laws.

Boyle's Law links together the pressure and volume of a gas: 'The volume of a given mass of a gas is inversely proportional to the pressure, if all measurements are carried out at the same, constant, temperature.'

'Inversely proportional' means that the higher the pressure is, the smaller the volume is. The lower the pressure, the greater the volume. Another way of putting this is to say that **the volume and the pressure of a gas compensate for each other**. An increase in pressure is compensated for by a decrease in volume. A decrease in pressure is compensated for by an increase in volume.

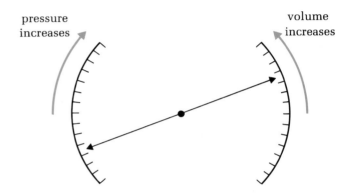

Fig. 4.44

To put this mathematically, the volume of a gas multiplied by its pressure always gives a constant value. If we halve the pressure, we double the volume, and so on. So, as long as we have a fixed **amount** (mass) of a gas, and as long as its temperature is kept constant, the value we get by multiplying the volume and the pressure together will always be the same. We say that,

$$P \times V = \text{constant} \quad \text{(at constant temperature)}$$

Suppose that the volume of a certain amount of gas is 2 dm³ at 1 atmosphere and 15 °C, and that we then decrease the pressure to $\frac{1}{2}$ atmosphere, at the same temperature. What would the new volume be? We know that $P \times V$ gives the same value, so:

If P_1 = original pressure (1 atmos.),
     V_1 = original volume (2 dm³)

and P_2 = new pressure ($\frac{1}{2}$ atmos.),
      V_2 = new volume (?)

We can write

$$P_1 \times V_1 = \text{certain value} = P_2 \times V_2$$
$$\text{or,} \quad \boldsymbol{P_1 V_1 = P_2 V_2}$$
$$\therefore \quad 1 \times 2 = \tfrac{1}{2} \times V_2$$
$$\therefore \quad \boldsymbol{V_2 = 4\,dm^3}$$

So, the new volume would be 4 dm³. We can always use Boyle's Law (in the form of $P_1V_1 = P_2V_2$) to do this sort of conversion. But what if the temperature does not stay constant?

Charles' Law links together the volume and the temperature of a gas: 'The volume of a given mass of gas is directly proportional to its temperature measured in degrees absolute (K), if all measurements are carried out at the same, constant, pressure.' 'Directly proportional' means that the higher the temperature, the higher the volume is. The lower the temperature, the lower the volume. Another way of saying this is that **the volume and the temperature of a gas parallel each other**. An increase in temperature is matched by an increase in volume. A decrease in temperature is matched by a decrease in volume.

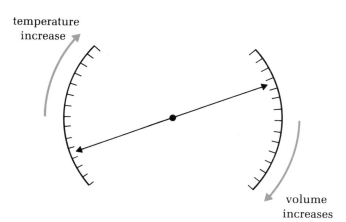

temperature increase

volume increases

Fig. 4.45

To put this mathematically, the volume of a gas divided by its absolute temperature always gives a constant value. If we double the absolute temperature, we double the volume, and so on.
We say that:

$$\frac{P}{T} = \text{constant} \qquad \text{(at constant pressure)}$$

Suppose that we again take our 2 dm³ of a certain amount of a gas, at 1 atmosphere and 15°C. If we increased the temperature to 60°C, what would the new volume be?

If V_1 = original volume (2 dm³)
     T_1 = original temperature (15°C)

and V_2 = new volume (?)
     T_2 = new temperature (60°C)

We can write

$$\frac{V_1}{T_1} = \text{a certain value} = \frac{V_2}{T_2}$$

or, $\dfrac{V_1}{T_1} = \dfrac{V_2}{T_2}$

Now remembering that we must add 273 to the

temperature in °C (Celsius) to get the temperature in K (Absolute),

$$\frac{2}{(15 + 273)} = \frac{V_2}{(60 + 273)}$$

$$\therefore \frac{2}{288} = \frac{V_2}{333}$$

$$\therefore V_2 = \frac{333 \times 2}{288} \text{ dm}^3$$

$$\therefore V_2 = 2.3 \text{ dm}^3$$

So the new volume would be 2.3 dm³.

From Boyle's Law we get

$$P_1V_1 = P_2V_2 \qquad \text{(at constant temperature)}$$

and from Charle's Law we get

$$\frac{V_1}{T_1} = \frac{V_2}{T_2} \qquad \text{(at constant pressure)}$$

We are allowed mathematically to combine these two relationships together to get a single formula which covers all possible changes of temperature and pressure:

$$\frac{P_1V_1}{T_1} = \frac{P_2V_2}{T_2} \qquad \textbf{The Ideal Gas Equation}$$

The Ideal Gas Equation allows us to convert from one set of conditions (temperature and pressure) to a new set of conditions, for any gas. The following example will show you how this can be used in a calculation about a chemical reaction.

Example

Iron(II) sulphate decomposes when it is heated, and the products are iron(III) oxide, sulphur dioxide and sulphur trioxide. Calculate the volume of sulphur trioxide, measured at 200°C and 800 mm pressure, which is obtained when 19 g of iron(II) sulphate are heated.

$$2FeSO_4 \rightarrow Fe_2O_3 + SO_2 + SO_3$$
$$\text{2 moles} \qquad\qquad\qquad\quad \text{1 mole}$$

1 mole of $FeSO_4$ weighs 152 g. So 2 moles weigh 304 g.

$$\therefore 304 \text{ g } FeSO_4 \rightarrow 1 \text{ mole } SO_3$$

$$\therefore 304 \text{ g } FeSO_4 \rightarrow 22.4 \text{ dm}^3 SO_3 \text{ (at s.t.p.)}$$

$$\therefore \quad 1 \text{ g } FeSO_4 \rightarrow \frac{22.4}{304} \text{ dm}^3 SO_3 \text{ (at s.t.p.)}$$

$$\therefore \quad 19 \text{ g } FeSO_4 \rightarrow \frac{19 \times 22.4}{304} \text{ dm}^3 SO_3 \text{ (at s.t.p.)}$$

$$= \frac{22.4}{16} \text{ dm}^3 SO_3 \text{ (at s.t.p.)}$$

$$= 1.4 \text{ dm}^3 SO_3 \text{ at s.t.p.}$$

'A pressure of 800 mm' means a pressure equal to that needed to support a column of mercury 800 mm high.

Atmospheric pressure is equivalent to 760 mm of mercury. So, we can write down

$P_1 = 760 \text{ mm}$ $P_2 = 800 \text{ mm}$
$V_1 = 1.4 \text{ dm}^3$ $V_2 = ?$
$T_1 = (0 + 273)\text{K}$ $T_2 = (200 + 273)\text{K}$

The Ideal Gas Equation

$$\frac{P_1V_1}{T_1} = \frac{P_2V_2}{T_2}$$

$$\therefore \frac{760 \times 1.4}{273} = \frac{800 \times V_2}{473}$$

$$\therefore V_2 = \frac{473 \times 760 \times 1.4}{273 \times 800} \text{ dm}^3$$

$$\therefore V_2 = 2.3 \text{ dm}^3$$

The volume of SO_3, measured at 200°C and 800 mm pressure, is 2.3 dm³.

Now try a calculation of this sort for yourself.

Question

20 g of calcium carbonate was reacted with excess dilute hydrochloric acid. What volume of carbon dioxide, measured at 15°C and 750 mm, was produced?

We can now summarise the steps involved in calculations about gases.

Calculations which involve gases

Step 1: Obtain the balanced equation.
Step 2: Write down the number of moles of the chemicals which are involved in the calculation.
Step 3: If the calculation is about the volumes of more than one gas, use Avogadro's Hypothesis to find the relative volumes from the relative number of moles.
Step 4: If the calculation is of the volume of a gas from the number of moles of a reactant or a product chemical, find the number of moles of the gas.
Step 5: From the number of moles of the gas, and the molar volume at s.t.p. (22.4 dm³), find the volume of the gas at s.t.p.
Step 6: If the calculation requires you to find the volume of the gas under conditions other than s.t.p., use the Ideal Gas Equation to find the volume under the conditions given. Remember that you must use absolute temperatures, and that 1 atmosphere = 760 mm.

TOPIC 4.4.4

The heat changes that happen with chemical changes

We have seen that many chemical changes are exothermic, and that many are endothermic. We have also seen that different reactions are likely to have different heat changes associated with them. But how do we relate the heat change in a chemical reaction to the balanced equation? The easiest way to see how this is done is to see how we can find the enthalpy change for a reaction that goes with its balanced equation.

▶ EXPERIMENT 4.17

The theoretical value for the energy change per mole for the reaction in Experiment 4.17 is $\triangle H - 217$ kJ mol^{-1}. We call this figure the ENTHALPY OF REACTION.

If we know the enthalpy of reaction for a particular chemical change, we can use it to find the heat change which there would be for any quantity of the chemicals in the reaction. Suppose, for instance, that we had 10 g of zinc, and that we reacted it with excess copper(II) sulphate solution. What would the heat change be?

We can write:

$Zn(s) + CuSO_4(aq) \rightarrow Cu(s) + ZnSO_4(aq)$ $\triangle H - 217$ kJ
1 mole $\longrightarrow$ $\triangle H - 217$ kJ
$\therefore$ 65 g $\longrightarrow$ $\triangle H - 217$ kJ
$\therefore$ 1 g $\longrightarrow$ $\triangle H - \dfrac{1}{65} \times 217$ kJ
$\therefore$ 10 g $\longrightarrow$ $\triangle H - \dfrac{10}{65} \times 217$ kJ
$\therefore$ 10 g $\longrightarrow$ $\triangle H - 33.4$ kJ

So, if we react 10 g of zinc with excess copper(II) sulphate, 33.4 kJ of energy will be given out.

EXPERIMENT 4.17
Finding the enthalpy change for a chemical reaction

You will need the following: polystyrene beaker (about $100\,cm^3$), stirring thermometer, 0.2 M copper(II) sulphate solution, $100\,cm^3$ measuring cylinder, zinc powder.

What to do

1   Use the measuring cylinder to measure out $20\,cm^3$ of the copper(II) sulphate solution.

2   Put this in the polystyrene beaker and measure its temperature. Leave the thermometer in the solution for at least 5 minutes before recording its temperature.

3   Weigh out about 0.4 g of powdered zinc onto a piece of paper. You do not have to record the exact weight of the powdered zinc, but make sure that you have between 0.3 and 0.5 g.

4   Add the powdered zinc to the copper(II) sulphate solution, and stir with the thermometer. Record the highest temperature which is reached.

What happened

Write down the initial temperature of the solution, and the final temperature.

Calculation

You have reacted a certain number of moles of copper(II) sulphate with an excess of zinc powder. The heat given out by this displacement reaction was absorbed by the solution itself, and so its temperature rose. You carried out the reaction in a polystyrene beaker, in order to minimise the heat lost to the surroundings. For the purposes of your calculation, you can assume:

1. that all the heat given out by the chemicals was absorbed by the solution, and that none was lost to the surroundings;
2. that the heat absorbed by the polystyrene beaker and the remaining zinc powder is insignificant compared with the heat absorbed by the solution. These two assumptions will allow us to carry out a calculation as if the temperature rise of the solution is a perfect measure of the heat given out by the chemicals during the reaction. To a large extent, this is true.

So,

energy given out by reaction
= energy absorbed by solution
= mass $\times$ specific heat capacity $\times$ temperature rise

One cm^3 of solution weighs 1 g, so $20\,cm^3$ of solution weigh 20 g.

$$mass = mass\ of\ 20\,cm^3 = 20\,g = \frac{20}{1000}\,kg$$

specific heat capacity = specific heat capacity of water
    $= 4.2$ kilojoules kilogram^{-1}°C^{-1}

temperature rise = final temperature
    $-$ original temperature

$\therefore$ Energy given out by reaction =
$\frac{20}{1000} \times 4.2 \times$ temperature rise (kilojoules)

This calculation would give us the amount of heat given out by the amount of chemicals which we had in the polystyrene beaker. The only way we could use this result to compare this reaction with others is to convert it into the amount of heat given out **per mole of reactant chemical**. To calculate this, we must first decide what fraction of a mole we had in the beaker in this experiment.

We had $20\,cm^3$ of 0.2 M copper(II) sulphate solution. If we had had $1\,dm^3$ of 0.2 M solution we would have had 0.2 mole.
$\therefore$ In $20\,cm^3$ of 0.2 M solution there must be
$\frac{20}{1000} \times 0.2$ mole.

So, to use the results of this experiment to find the amount of heat given out per mole, we must multiply the amount of heat given out by the chemicals which reacted in the beaker by

$$\frac{1000}{20 \times 0.2} = \frac{1000}{4} = 250$$

$\therefore$ Energy given out per mole of reactant

$= 250 \times \frac{20}{1000} \times 4.2 \times$ temperature rise (kilojoule mole^{-1})

$= 5 \times 4.2 \times$ temperature rise (kJ mole^{-1})

$= \mathbf{21 \times}$ **temperature rise** (kJ mole^{-1})

From the results of your experiment, calculate the amount of heat given out per mole of copper(II) sulphate used up.

What we can decide

The balanced equation for the reaction is:

$Zn(s) + CuSO_4(aq) \rightarrow Cu(s) + ZnSO_4(aq)$
$\triangle H - ?\ kJ\ mol^{-1}$

Write out the complete balanced equation, including the value of the enthalpy change.

We know that there are many types of chemical reaction which give out heat. Of course, we can measure the heat of reaction for all the different types. One obvious example is burning, or COMBUSTION. If we measure the amount of energy given out when one mole of a chemical burns, we call this the ENTHALPY OF COMBUSTION for that chemical.

EXPERIMENT 4.18

Finding the enthalpy of combustion of ethanol

You will need the following: small alcohol burner, tin can or copper calorimeter (big enough to hold at least 100 cm^3 water), stirring thermometer, access to top-pan balance.

What to do

REMEMBER THAT ALCOHOL IS FLAMMABLE.
YOU MUST WEAR SAFETY SPECTACLES.

1   Weigh the can or copper calorimeter. Place approximately 100 g of water in it, and weigh it again. Write down your results.

2   Your alcohol burner should be about half-full before you start the experiment. If it is not, ask your teacher to put some more alcohol into it for you. Then weigh the burner. Write down the weight of the burner.

3   Use the thermometer to find the temperature of the water in the can or calorimeter.

4   Use a clamp with wide jaws to hold the can or calorimeter above the burner. Light the burner, and make sure that the flame touches the bottom of the can or calorimeter (you may have to move the can up or down slightly until it is at the best height).

5   If there are draughts in the laboratory which make the flame move around too much, you should ask your teacher how to arrange a screen. It is important that as much heat as possible from the flame goes into heating the water.

6   From time to time, stir the water with the thermometer. When the temperature has increased by about 20°C, turn out the flame or blow it out if the wick does not work mechanically. Keep stirring, and keep a close watch on the thermometer. When the temperature does not rise any further, stop stirring. Write down the highest temperature which the water reaches.

7   Now weigh the alcohol burner again. Write down its weight.

What happened

You will have the following results from your experiment:

Mass of can or calorimeter
Mass of can/calorimeter + water
Temperature of water before heating
Temperature of water after heating
Mass of burner + alcohol before heating
Mass of burner + alcohol after heating

From these values find the following:

Mass of water in can/calorimeter
Temperature rise of water
Mass of alcohol used up during burning

Calculation

You have burned a certain amount of the alcohol 'ethanol'. You know the mass of ethanol which burned, because this is the amount of ethanol which was used up during the experiment.

The heat given out by the burning of this quantity of ethanol was 'trapped' by the water in the can/calorimeter. You can calculate the amount of heat which the water absorbed, from the mass of water, the temperature rise, and the specific heat capacity of water.

So you can find out how much heat was given out when a certain mass of ethanol burned. You can use this to work out how much heat would have been given out if 1 mole of ethanol had been burned. 1 mole of ethanol weighs 46 g.

What we can decide

The balanced equation for the reaction which took place is:

$$C_2H_5OH(l) + 3O_2(g) \rightarrow 2CO_2(g) + 3H_2O(g)$$
$$\triangle H - ? \, kJmol^{-1}$$

Write out the complete balanced equation, including the value of the enthalpy change.

The theoretical value for the heat of combustion of ethanol is $1240\,kJ\,mol^{-1}$. We can use this value to calculate the amount of heat which would be given out by the combustion of any mass of ethanol. Suppose we burned 20 g of ethanol. What would be the amount of heat given out?

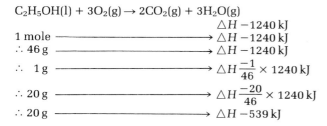

$$C_2H_5OH(l) + 3O_2(g) \rightarrow 2CO_2(g) + 3H_2O(g)$$

So, if we burn 20 g of ethanol, 539 kJ of energy will be given out.

Another type of reaction which gives out heat is the reaction of an acid with an alkali. This is a particular example of a group of reactions called NEUTRALISATION reactions. If we measure the amount of energy given out when one mole of an acid is neutralised by an alkali, we call this the ENTHALPY OF NEUTRALISATION of that acid.

▶ EXPERIMENT 4.19 (p. 224)

The theoretical value for the energy change per mole for this reaction is $\triangle H\ -57\,kJ\,mol^{-1}$. In Topic 4.3.5, you learnt that the ionic equation for the reaction of **any** acid with **any** alkali is the same. One mole of aquated hydrogen ions reacts with one mole of aquated hydroxyl ions, to give one mole of water molecules. It is this reaction for which the energy change is $\triangle H\ -57\,kJ\,mol^{-1}$. So, the heat of neutralisation of any acid with any alkali is $\triangle H\ -57\,kJ\,mol^{-1}$. ($mol^{-1}$ means per mole of $H^+(aq)$ ions). So we can write:

$$H^+(aq) + OH^-(aq) \rightarrow H_2O(l) \qquad \triangle H\ -57\,kJ\,mol^{-1}$$

We can use this balanced equation to work out the amount of heat which would be given out by the neutralisation of any quantity of an acid with the equivalent amount of alkali. For instance, suppose we had $50\,cm^3$ of a 0.2 M solution of hydrochloric acid, and that we neutralised it with excess alkali. How much heat would be given out?

$$H^+(aq) + OH^-(aq) \rightarrow H_2O(l) \qquad \triangle H\ -57\,kJ\,mol^{-1}$$
1 mole $\xrightarrow{\hspace{3cm}} \triangle H\ -57\,kJ$

$50\,cm^3$ of M solution would contain $\dfrac{50}{1000}$ mole

$\therefore 50\,cm^3$ of 0.2 M solution contains $\dfrac{50}{1000} \times 0.2$ mole
$= 0.01$ mole

0.01 mole $\xrightarrow{\hspace{3cm}} \triangle H\ 0.01 \times -57\,kJ$
$= -0.57\,kJ = -570\,J$

So, the amount of heat given out by the neutralisation of $50\,cm^3$ of 0.2 M hydrochloric acid with excess alkali is 570 J.

We can now summarise the steps involved in calculations about the heat changes associated with reactions:

Calculations which involve heat changes

Step 1: Obtain the balanced equation, showing $\triangle H$ per mole.

Step 2: Write down the number of moles of the relevant chemical and the corresponding value of $\triangle H$.

Step 3: If the calculation is about the mass of one of the chemicals in the reaction, convert the number of moles of it which react into a number of grams. Find what $\triangle H$ would be for 1 g of this chemical. Then find what $\triangle H$ would be for the number of grams of the chemical which are given in the question.

Step 4: If the calculation is about the volume of a solution of known concentration of one of the chemicals in the reaction, work out the number of moles of the chemical which will be present. From the value of $\triangle H$ for 1 mole, find the value of $\triangle H$ for this number of moles.

Now try some calculations for yourself, **using the steps given above.** Remember that the first step is to obtain the balanced equation.

Questions

1 The enthalpy of reaction of silver nitrate with sodium chloride is $\triangle H\ -65.5\,kJ\,mol^{-1}$. $10\,cm^3$ of 0.05 M silver nitrate was reacted with excess sodium chloride solution. How much heat was produced?

2 Below are the balanced equations for the combustion of ethanol and of liquid propane:

Ethanol $\quad C_2H_5OH(l) + 3O_2(g) \rightarrow 2CO_2(g) + 3H_2O(g)$
$\triangle H\ -1240\,kJ$

Liquid $\quad C_3H_8(l) + 5O_2(g) \rightarrow 3CO_2(g) + 4H_2O(g)$
propane $\qquad\qquad\qquad\qquad\qquad\qquad \triangle H\ -2036\,kJ$

Work out the amount of heat given out when 20 g of ethanol (relative molecular mass = 46) and when 20 g of liquid propane (relative molecular mass = 44) are burned.

Which of the two chemicals would be the better fuel for use in cars (from the amount of energy stored per gram point of view)? Explain your answer in a sentence.

3 Calculate the amount of heat which is given out when $25\,cm^3$ of M sodium hydroxide solution reacts with excess dilute sulphuric acid.

EXPERIMENT 4.19

Finding the enthalpy of neutralisation of hydrochloric acid with sodium hydroxide solution

You will need the following: polystyrene beaker, 25 cm³ pipette with safety filler, stirring thermometer, 2 M hydrochloric acid, 2 M sodium hydroxide solution.

What to do

1   Use a beaker to take about 50 cm³ of the 2 M hydrochloric acid which has been prepared for you back to your bench.

2   Use a pipette-filler to fill the pipette with 2 M hydrochloric acid. Run the acid into the polystyrene beaker.

3   Use the thermometer to measure the temperature of the acid.

4   Use another beaker to take back to your bench about 50 cm³ of the 2 M sodium hydroxide solution.

5   Wash the pipette with water. Use the pipette-filler to run a little sodium hydroxide solution into the pipette. Swill the solution around the pipette, so that all its inner surface has been washed. Run the sodium hydroxide away, and wash it down the sink with tap-water.

6   Use the pipette-filler to fill the pipette with sodium hydroxide solution. Run the alkali into the acid in the polystyrene beaker. Immediately stir the mixture with the thermometer, and record the highest temperature which is reached.

What happened

Write down the initial temperature of the solution in the polystyrene beaker, and the final temperature.

Calculation

You have reacted a certain amount of hydrochloric acid with **an equivalent amount** of sodium hydroxide solution. So the acid will have been neutralised by the alkali.

You used a polystyrene beaker in order to prevent heat given out by the reaction being lost to the surroundings. In your calculation, you will have to assume that there was no loss of heat, and that all the heat given out by the reaction was absorbed by the solution. So the rise in temperature of the solution is a measure of the heat given out by the reaction.

Energy given out by reaction
= energy absorbed by solution
= mass × specific heat capacity × temperature rise

$$\text{mass} \quad = \text{mass of 50 cm}^3 = 50\,\text{g} = \frac{50}{1000}\,\text{kg}$$

specific heat capacity = specific heat = $4.2\,\text{kJkg}^{-1}{}^{\circ}\text{C}^{-1}$ capacity of water

temperature rise = final temperature − original temperature

∴ Energy given out by reaction
$$= \frac{50}{1000} \times 4.2 \times \text{temp. rise (kJ)}$$

This is the amount of heat given out by the amounts of the chemicals which were in the polystyrene beaker. But these were not one mole of acid and one mole of alkali. So we will have to convert the value which the calculation above gives to the value for one mole of each reactant chemical.

We had 25 cm³ of 2 M solution.
If we had had 1 dm³ of 2 M solution, we would have had 2 moles.

∴ In 25 cm³ of 2 M solution there must be $\frac{25}{1000} \times 2$ moles.

So, we must multiply by $\frac{1000}{25 \times 2}$ to get the amount of heat given out by one mole.

∴ Amount of heat given out by one mole
$$= \frac{1000}{50} \times \frac{50}{1000} \times 4.2 \times \text{temp. rise (kJ)}$$
$$= \textbf{4.2} \times \textbf{temp. rise (kJ)}$$

From the results of your experiment, calculate the amount of heat given out per mole of reaction.

What we can decide

The balanced equation for the reaction which took place is:

$$\text{HCl(aq)} + \text{NaOH(aq)} \rightarrow \text{NaCl(aq)} + \text{H}_2\text{O(l)}$$
$$\triangle H - ?\,\text{kJmol}^{-1}$$

Write out the complete balanced equation, including the value of the enthalpy change.

UNIT 4.4
Summary and learning

1   We can use the balanced equation for a chemical reaction to calculate the masses of reactant and product chemicals which take part. You should remember the steps for carrying out such calculations.

2   The balanced equation also lets us carry out calculations about the volumes and concentrations of solutions of chemicals involved in a reaction. The molarity of a solution is the number of moles of the dissolved chemical in 1 dm³ of the solution. We use the symbol 'M' for the molarity of a solution. A molar solution is one which contains 1 mole of chemical dissolved in 1 dm³ of solution.

You should remember the steps for carrying out such calculations.

3   A standard solution is one whose concentration is known very accurately. We can use standard solutions to find the molarity of others, by volumetric analysis. You should remember what the terms 'indicator', 'end-point', and 'titration' mean.

4   Gay-Lussac's Law tells us that 'The volumes of different gases involved in the same chemical reaction (if measured at the same temperature and pressure) are simple multiples of each other'.

Avogadro's Hypothesis, which was put forward to explain Gay-Lussac's discovery, was 'Equal volumes of all gases (under the same conditions of temperature and pressure) contain equal numbers of particles'.

Avogadro's Hypothesis helps us to calculate the relative volumes of different gases which will be involved in the same chemical reaction, from the balanced equation.

We call 0°C and 1 atmosphere pressure (760 mm of mercury) standard temperature and pressure. We know that the volume occupied by 1 mole of any gas at s.t.p. (the molar volume) is 22.4 dm³. We can use this fact to calculate the volume of any gas involved in a chemical reaction, if we know the number of moles of it from the balanced equation.

The Ideal Gas Equation,

$$\frac{P_1 V_1}{T_1} = \frac{P_2 V_2}{T_2},$$

allows us to convert from one set of conditions of temperature and pressure to a new set of conditions, for any gas. So we can find the volume of a gas involved in a chemical reaction under any conditions of temperature and pressure.

You should remember the steps involved in calculations to do with gases.

5   We can carry out experiments to find the value of the heat change involved with particular chemical reactions. This heat change is given in kJ mol⁻¹ of one of the reactant chemicals. We can use the balanced equation for a reaction to find the heat change which would be involved for any quantity of reactant chemicals.

You should remember the steps involved in such calculations.

6   You have learnt the meaning of these words:

molarity	molar volume
molar solution	enthalpy of reaction
standard solution	combustion
volumetric analysis	enthalpy of combustion
titration	neutralisation
end-point	enthalpy of neutralisation
standard temperature and	
pressure	

UNIT 4.5   *More types of chemical change*

In Experiment 4.14 (Topic 4.3.2) you saw two further types of reaction to those which you had come across before – thermal decomposition and redox reactions. In this unit, you will learn more about each of these types of reaction, and you will study the chemical changes which an electric current can cause.

TOPIC 4.5.1

Reduction–oxidation (redox) reactions

'Redox' reactions are very common in chemistry. Many of the chemical changes which you have already come across under another name could also have been called redox reactions. For instance, metal/metal ion displacement reactions and halogen/halide ion displacement reactions are particular types of redox reaction. A redox reaction is the chemical change which happens when an oxidising chemical and a reducing chemical react together to form new chemicals.

When a redox reaction happens, the chemical which is an oxidising chemical (or OXIDISING AGENT) **oxidises** the other chemical. The other chemical, the reducing chemical (or REDUCING AGENT) **reduces** the

oxidising agent. We will look more closely at what we mean exactly by the words 'oxidise' and 'reduce' in a short while. But for the moment you should remember that 'oxidation' and 'reduction' are chemical necessities of each other.

For oxidation to happen, reduction must also happen at the same time. For reduction to happen, there must also be an oxidation happening. The two go together and cannot be separated. So in this type of reaction, two changes happen at the same time, as the reaction takes place. One is a reduction and the other is an oxidation.

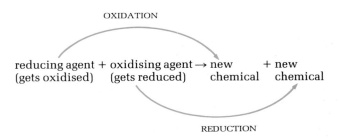

OXIDATION

reducing agent + oxidising agent → new   + new
(gets oxidised)   (gets reduced)   chemical   chemical

REDUCTION

Your teacher will now show you a number of different types of reaction, each of which is a redox reaction.

▶   EXPERIMENT 4.20

EXPERIMENT 4.20

Different types of redox reaction

Your teacher will show you these reactions

The following will be needed: gas-jars full of oxygen, carbon dioxide and hydrogen sulphide, apparatus for the laboratory preparation of chlorine (see below), magnesium ribbon, yellow or white phosphorus, tongs, deflagrating spoon, litmus solution.

What to do

CHLORINE MUST BE PREPARED IN A FUME-CUPBOARD. PUPILS MUST WEAR THEIR SAFETY SPECTACLES.

1   In a fume-cupboard (preferably where pupils can observe the reaction) set up the apparatus for the production of chlorine, as shown in Fig. 4.47.

NB: Double check that you are using conc. hydrochloric acid and not conc. sulphuric acid (conc. sulphuric acid is much denser and does not fume in air).

Allow the reaction to take place, and collect at least one gas-jar full of chlorine gas. The reaction between potassium permanganate and concentrated hydrochloric acid is itself a redox reaction.

2   Take a gas-jar full of chlorine, and place over it a gas-jar containing hydrogen sulphide, but with the cover-slips still in place. Now remove the cover-slips, and allow the gases to mix. A reaction takes place, and sulphur soon coats the inside of both gas-jars. This reaction is a redox reaction (Fig. 4.46).

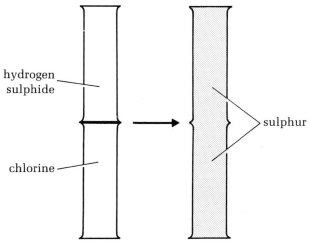

Fig. 4.46

3   Take a gas-jar full of carbon dioxide, and place it on the front bench where pupils can see it. Clean a piece of magnesium ribbon about 5 cm long, using sandpaper. Hold the magnesium in a pair of tongs, and ignite it in air. Immediately plunge the burning magnesium into the gas-jar. **Pupils must be warned not to look directly at the burning magnesium**. A redox reaction takes place between magnesium and

carbon dioxide, which results in the formation of white clouds of magnesium oxide and a black deposit of carbon.

4   Take a gas-jar full of oxygen and put a small amount of litmus solution into it. Place the gas-jar in a prominent position in the fume-cupboard. Also in the fume-cupboard, under the surface of water in a mortar cut a small pellet of white phosphorus from the body of the solid. **Great care is essential, as white phosphorus gives off very poisonous fumes, is poisonous itself, and can easily burst into flames in moist air, especially when being cut, due to friction.** Light a Bunsen burner in the fume-cupboard, and use it to warm the pellet of white phosphorus on a deflagrating spoon. When the phosphorus begins to burn, plunge it into the gas-jar. The phosphorus will burn with a very bright flame, and white clouds of oxides of phosphorus will be produced. At the end of the reaction, show the gas-jar to the class, in order that they can see the colour of the litmus solution. This will have turned red as a result of the reaction between the oxides of phosphorus and the water in the litmus solution, producing phosphorous and phosphoric acids. The reaction between phosphorus and oxygen is a redox reaction.

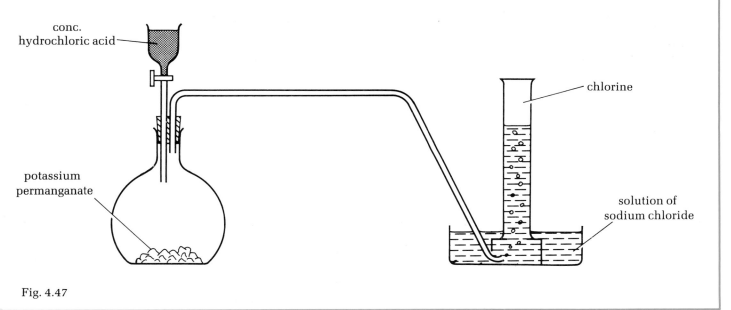

Fig. 4.47

You should be able to see from the experiments which your teacher has shown you that redox reactions can take place between a wide variety of types of chemical. Those which you have seen are:
1. An acid (conc. hydrochloric acid) reacting with a salt (potassium permanganate).
2. A halogen (chlorine) reacting with hydrogen sulphide (which we can think of as being an acid).

3. A metal (magnesium) reacting with the oxide of a non-metal (carbon dioxide).
4. A non-metal (phosphorus) reacting with oxygen.
What have these reactions all got in common, which lets us call them 'redox' reactions? To answer this question, we will need to look in more detail at what we mean by oxidation, and what we mean by reduction.

Oxidation/reduction in terms of oxygen and hydrogen

Originally, the word OXIDATION was used to describe what happens when an element reacts with oxygen. Later, it was also used for reactions of oxygen with compounds, and then for any reaction in which oxygen is added to another chemical. **So, oxidation is the addition of oxygen.** The oxygen may come from oxygen itself, or from a compound which contains oxygen.

CHEMICAL + oxygen → (CHEMICAL – oxygen)

OXIDATION

If oxidation is the addition of oxygen, then **reduction must be the removal of oxygen.** The chemical which gives up the oxygen is 'reduced'.

(CHEMICAL – oxygen) → CHEMICAL + oxygen

REDUCTION

You will see how these ideas work, if you consider the reaction between magnesium and carbon dioxide. The balanced equation is:

$$2Mg(s) + CO_2(g) \rightarrow 2MgO(s) + C(s)$$

Magnesium gains oxygen, and magnesium oxide forms. So magnesium is OXIDISED to magnesium oxide.

Carbon dioxide loses oxygen, and carbon forms. So carbon dioxide is REDUCED to carbon. We can write:

oxidation

$$2Mg(s) + CO_2(g) \rightarrow 2MgO(s) + C(s)$$

reduction

The chemical which is responsible for the oxidation is carbon dioxide. So carbon dioxide is the oxidising agent. The chemical which is responsible for the reduction is magnesium. So magnesium is the reducing agent. We can summarise what happens in the reaction in the following way.

Magnesium: Is the reducing agent. It reduces carbon dioxide to carbon.
Gets oxidised. It is oxidised to magnesium oxide.

Carbon dioxide: Is the oxidising agent. It oxidises the magnesium to magnesium oxide.
Gets reduced. It is reduced to carbon.

Can we use the same ideas to describe another of the reactions which you saw in Experiment 4.20? Suppose we take the reaction between phosphorus and oxygen. The balanced equation is:

$$P_4(s) + 5O_2(g) \rightarrow P_4O_{10}(s)$$

Phosphorus gains oxygen, and phosphorus pentoxide

forms. So phosphorus is oxidised to phosphorus pentoxide.

Oxygen loses oxygen (part of the oxygen molecule is given up each time there is a reaction with an atom of phosphorus), and phosphorus pentoxide forms. So oxygen is reduced to phosphorus pentoxide. We can write:

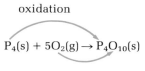

oxidation

$$P_4(s) + 5O_2(g) \rightarrow P_4O_{10}(s)$$

reduction

The chemical which is responsible for the oxidation is the oxygen. So oxygen is the oxidising agent. The chemical which is responsible for the reduction is the phosphorus. So phosphorus is the reducing agent. We can summarise what happens in the following way:

Phosphorus: Is the reducing agent. It reduces oxygen to phosphorus pentoxide.
Gets oxidised. It is oxidised to phosphorus pentoxide.

Oxygen: Is the oxidising agent. It oxidises the phosphorus to phosphorus pentoxide.
Gets reduced. It is reduced to phosphorus pentoxide.

If we tried to use these ideas to describe what happens when chlorine reacts with hydrogen sulphide, we would have a problem. There is no oxygen involved in this reaction, and so we could not use the definition of oxidation and reduction which worked in the last two examples. It was to overcome problems of this sort that another definition of oxidation and reduction was added to the one above, which is based on the loss or gain of oxygen. As you will see, this second definition allows us to include many more chemical reactions under the heading of redox reactions.

In the world of chemistry, one of the most common substances is water. Water is made up of oxygen and hydrogen, and it is common because these two elements combine together very easily. Wherever they are present in the same reaction and they are able to, they will react together to make water. So oxygen and hydrogen are a bit like the **chemical opposites** of each other. Therefore, **if oxidation is the addition of oxygen it is also the removal of hydrogen.** In the same way, **if reduction is the removal of oxygen it is also the addition of hydrogen.**

	Oxidation	Reduction
oxygen:	addition	removal
hydrogen:	removal	addition

Let's see if this new definition of oxidation and reduction will help us to describe the reaction between chlorine and hydrogen sulphide. The balanced equation is:

$$H_2S(g) + Cl_2(g) \rightarrow S(s) + 2HCl(g)$$

Hydrogen sulphide loses hydrogen, and sulphur forms. So hydrogen sulphide is oxidised to sulphur.

Chlorine gains hydrogen, and hydrogen chloride forms. So chlorine is reduced to hydrogen chloride. We can write:

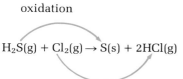

The chemical which is responsible for the oxidation is chlorine. So chlorine is the oxidising agent. The chemical which is responsible for the reduction is hydrogen sulphide. So hydrogen sulphide is the reducing agent. We can summarise the redox reaction which has taken place in the following way:

Hydrogen sulphide: Is the reducing agent. It reduces chlorine to hydrogen chloride. Gets oxidised. It is oxidised to sulphur.

Chlorine: Is the oxidising agent. It oxidises hydrogen sulphide to sulphur. Gets reduced. It is reduced to hydrogen chloride.

Sometimes, we can describe a redox reaction best using both the definitions above, in combination. For instance, the only reaction which you saw in Experiment 4.20 which we have not yet described is the reaction between conc. hydrochloric acid and potassium permanganate. The word-equation for this reaction is:

$$\text{potassium permanganate} + \text{conc. hydrochloric acid}$$
$$\longrightarrow \text{potassium chloride} + \text{manganese(II) chloride} + \text{chlorine} + \text{water}$$

Hydrochloric acid is oxidised to chlorine (it loses hydrogen). Potassium permanganate is reduced to manganese(II) chloride (it loses oxygen). So the oxidising agent is potassium permanganate, and the reducing agent is conc. hydrochloric acid.

You can now try some examples for yourself.

Questions

In each of the following questions, use the balanced equation to decide which chemical is the oxidising agent, and which the reducing agent. State which chemical is oxidised (and why). State which chemical is reduced (and why).

1 Hydrogen peroxide reacts with a solution of sodium sulphite. The products are sodium sulphate and water. The balanced equation is:

$$Na_2SO_3(aq) + H_2O_2(aq) \rightarrow Na_2SO_4(aq) + H_2O(l)$$

2 Sulphur (solid) reacts with oxygen (gas). The only product is sulphur dioxide (gas).

3 Carbon (solid) reacts with oxygen (gas). The only product is carbon dioxide (gas).

4 Iron (solid) reacts with oxygen (gas). The only product is tri-iron tetroxide (solid, formula Fe_3O_4).

5 Manganese dioxide reacts with concentrated hydrochloric acid. The products are manganese(II) chloride, water and chlorine. The balanced equation is:

$$MnO_2(s) + 4HCl(aq) \rightarrow MnCl_2(aq) + 2H_2O(l) + Cl_2(g)$$

6 Chlorine reacts with a solution of sulphur dioxide in water. The products are sulphuric acid and hydrochloric acid. The balanced equation is:

$$2H_2O(l) + SO_2(g) + Cl_2(g) \rightarrow H_2SO_4(aq) + 2HCl(aq)$$

7 Zinc oxide (solid) reacts with carbon (solid). The products are zinc (solid) and carbon dioxide (gas).

8 Copper(II) oxide reacts with carbon monoxide (gas). The products are copper (solid) and carbon dioxide (gas).

9 Sulphur dioxide reacts with potassium dichromate acidified with hydrochloric acid. The products are chromium(III) chloride, potassium chloride, sulphuric acid and water. The balanced equation is:

$$8HCl(aq) + K_2Cr_2O_7(aq) + 3H_2SO_3(aq)$$
$$\longrightarrow 2CrCl_3(aq) + 3H_2SO_4 + 4H_2O + 2KCl(aq)$$

NB: Sulphur dioxide reacts with the water present to give sulphurous acid (H_2SO_3).

10 Copper(II) oxide (solid) reacts with hydrogen (gas). The products are copper (solid) and water (liquid).

It is important to realise that chemicals are either oxidising or reducing agents **relative to other chemicals**. A given chemical will have a certain strength as an oxidising or reducing agent. You will see shortly how this relative strength of oxidising or reducing power can be worked out very precisely, at least as far as metals are concerned. Because oxidising/reducing power is relative to the other chemical in the reaction, one or two chemicals will behave as an oxidising agent with one chemical, and as a reducing agent with another chemical. For instance, water will oxidise carbon, and yet it will also reduce fluorine.

Water as an oxidising agent

$$\text{oxidation}$$
$$C(s) + H_2O(g) \rightarrow CO(g) + H_2(g)$$
$$\text{reduction}$$

Carbon is oxidised to carbon monoxide by steam (it gains oxygen).
Steam is reduced to hydrogen by carbon (it loses oxygen).
Water is the oxidising agent, carbon is the reducing agent.

Water as a reducing agent

$$\text{oxidation}$$
$$2H_2O(l) + 2F_2(g) \rightarrow O_2(g) + 4HF(aq)$$
$$\text{reduction}$$

Fluorine is reduced to hydrogen fluoride by water (it gains hydrogen).
Water is oxidised to oxygen by fluorine (it loses hydrogen).
Water is the reducing agent, fluorine is the oxidising agent.

However, for most chemicals, we can say that they will usually be either an oxidising agent or a reducing agent. Table 4.7 lists some common oxidising agents and common reducing agents:

Oxidising agents	Reducing agents
oxygen(g)	hydrogen(g)
hydrogen peroxide(aq)	hydrogen sulphide(g)
chlorine(g)	carbon(s)
manganese dioxide(s)	carbon monoxide(g)
potassium permanganate(aq)	sulphur dioxide(g)
potassium dichromate(aq)	potassium iodide(aq)
nitric acid(aq) (dilute & conc.)	metal(s)
sulphuric acid(aq) (conc. only)	

Table 4.7

▶ EXPERIMENT 4.21 (p. 232)

If you tried to explain the redox reactions which took place in steps 2 and 3 of Experiment 4.21 in terms of oxygen and hydrogen, you would not be able to. For both these reactions, and for many other redox reactions, a different definition of oxidation and of reduction has to be used.

Oxidation/reduction in terms of the transfer of electrons

Suppose we consider first the reaction between potassium iodide and hydrogen peroxide. The balanced equation is:

$$H_2O_2(aq) + 2KI(aq) + H_2SO_4(aq)$$
$$\longrightarrow 2H_2O(l) + I_2(aq) + K_2SO_4(aq)$$

In fact, we could have used any iodide, and any acid, to carry out this reaction. So we could write the equation above in its ionic form, and it would be just as valid. At the same time, we can show which chemical is oxidised and which is reduced:

$$\text{oxidation}$$
$$H_2O_2(aq) + 2I^-(aq) + 2H^+(aq) \rightarrow 2H_2O(l) + I_2(aq)$$
$$\text{reduction}$$

It is easy to see that hydrogen peroxide is reduced, because it loses oxygen. However, what is happening to the iodide? The only way in which we can answer this question is to write down what is called the HALF-REACTION for iodide:

$$2I^-(aq) \rightarrow I_2(aq) + 2 \text{ electrons}$$

The iodide ions lose electrons, and the iodine molecule forms. We know that the iodide is oxidised, so we can say that **oxidation is the loss of electrons**. If oxidation is the loss of electrons, then **reduction is the gain of electrons**.

This definition of oxidation and reduction is the most modern one which chemists have produced, and it allows us to understand all other reactions which can be called redox reactions. Suppose we look at the reaction between iron(II) sulphate and hydrogen peroxide. Will this new definition help us? The balanced equation is:

$$2FeSO_4(aq) + H_2O_2(aq) + H_2SO_4(aq)$$
$$\longrightarrow Fe_2(SO_4)_3(aq) + 2H_2O(l)$$

If we write the equation in its ionic form, and show where the reduction and oxidation are happening, we will get:

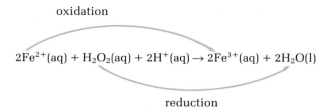

oxidation

$$2Fe^{2+}(aq) + H_2O_2(aq) + 2H^+(aq) \rightarrow 2Fe^{3+}(aq) + 2H_2O(l)$$

reduction

Again, it is easy to see that the hydrogen peroxide is reduced, because it loses oxygen. But what about the iron(II) ion? If we write the half-equation for what happens to the iron, this will only balance if electrons are lost:

$$Fe^{2+}(aq) \rightarrow Fe^{3+}(aq) + electron$$

The iron(III) ion forms when the iron(II) ion loses an electron. So we can say that the iron(II) ion is oxidised to the iron(III) ion.

Earlier in this section you learned about metal/metal ion displacement reactions. We can use this new definition of oxidation and reduction to include such reactions as redox reactions. Suppose we take a reaction like the one between magnesium ribbon and copper(II) sulphate. The products are magnesium sulphate and copper. If we write the equation in its ionic form, we can begin to see the redox process:

$$Mg(s) + Cu^{2+}(aq) \rightarrow Mg^{2+}(aq) + Cu(s)$$

The half-equations are:

for magnesium $Mg(s) \rightarrow Mg^{2+}(aq) + 2$ electrons
for copper $Cu^{2+}(aq) + 2$ electrons $\rightarrow Cu(s)$

So the magnesium loses electrons, and it is oxidised to Mg^{2+}. The copper(II) ion gains electrons, and it is reduced to copper. Magnesium is the reducing agent, and the copper(II) ion is the oxidising agent.

We know that the higher up the reactivity series a metal is, the more reactive it is. It will react with the ion of a metal lower down the series than itself. We now know that this reaction is a redox reaction, in which the metal is the reducing agent, and the metal ion is the oxidising agent. So we can say that the higher a metal is in the reactivity series, the stronger a reducing agent it will be. Metals high in the series are very reactive because they are easily oxidised (they easily lose an electron/electrons to form a cation).

	reactivity increases	strength as a reducing agent increases
sodium		
calcium		
magnesium		
aluminium		
zinc		
iron		
lead		
copper		
silver		
gold		

A metal higher in the reactivity series will reduce the cation of a metal lower in the series.

Another type of displacement reaction which you have met before is the reaction of a halogen with a halide. You know that a halogen higher in the halogen group in the Periodic Table will react with a halide lower in the group. For instance, chlorine will react with a bromide. The ionic equation is as follows:

$$Cl_2(aq) + 2Br^-(aq) \rightarrow Br_2(aq) + 2Cl^-(aq)$$

The half-equations are:

for chlorine $Cl_2(aq) + 2$ electrons $\rightarrow 2Cl^-(aq)$
for bromine $2Br^-(aq) \rightarrow Br_2(aq) + 2$ electrons

So chlorine gains electrons, and is therefore reduced (to chloride ions). The bromide ions lose electrons, and are therefore oxidised (to bromine). Chlorine is the oxidising agent and bromide ions are the reducing agent. So, the higher up the halogen group we go, the stronger the halogens become as oxidising agents.

	reactivity increases	strength as an oxidising agent increases
fluorine		
chlorine		
bromine		
iodine		

Now try some examples for yourself.

Questions

In each of the following questions, use the balanced equation (in ionic form) to decide which chemical is the oxidising agent, and which is the reducing agent. State which chemical is oxidised (and why). State which chemical is reduced (and why).

1   Zinc metal displaces silver from a solution of silver nitrate. The products are silver and a solution of zinc nitrate.

2   When chlorine gas is bubbled through a solution of iron(II) chloride, the iron(II) is converted to iron(III). The other product is chloride ions.

3   If chlorine gas is passed over heated copper, the only product is copper(II) chloride (solid).

4   Chlorine reacts with a solution of potassium iodide. The products are iodine and potassium chloride.

5   Magnesium metal displaces gold from a solution of gold(I) nitrate. The other product is magnesium nitrate.

It is very useful sometimes to be able to tell whether an unknown chemical is an oxidising agent, and whether it is a reducing agent. So we have worked out ways of testing with the kinds of chemical which are available in chemistry laboratories. These tests

→ p. 233

EXPERIMENT 4.21
Some more redox reactions

You will need the following: lead(II) oxide (litharge), charcoal block, metal blowpipe, metal container for hot charcoal blocks, hydrogen peroxide solution ('20 volume'), solution of potassium iodide (acidified with dilute sulphuric acid), iron(II) sulphate crystals, starch solution (freshly prepared), solution of sodium hydroxide, dilute sulphuric acid.

What to do

THE ROOM MUST BE WELL VENTILATED.
MAKE SURE THAT YOU WEAR YOUR SAFETY SPECTACLES THROUGHOUT THIS PART OF THE EXPERIMENT.

1   Take a charcoal block, and put a small amount of water in the hole on one side of it. (Use just enough to wet the surface. If there is no hole, your teacher will show you how to make one with a coin.) Now add two spatula-measures of lead(II) oxide to the hole. Your teacher will show you how to use the blowpipe to heat a small area of the charcoal. Heat the area around the lead(II) oxide very strongly indeed. Do not blow too hard, or you will blow out the lead(II) oxide (the moisture will help to hold it in place). Notice carefully what happens, and record any changes which you see.
WHEN YOU HAVE FINISHED WITH THE CHARCOAL BLOCK, PUT IT IN THE METAL CONTAINER WHICH IS PROVIDED (remember that the block will still be very hot).

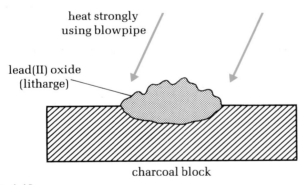

heat strongly
using blowpipe

lead(II) oxide
(litharge)

charcoal block

Fig. 4.48

BE CAREFUL NOT TO GET ANY HYDROGEN PEROXIDE ON YOUR SKIN. IF YOU DO, WASH IT OFF AT ONCE, AND TELL YOUR TEACHER.

2   Take a clean test-tube, and put into it 2–3 cm³ of the solution of acidified potassium iodide which has been prepared for you. Now add a few drops of the solution of hydrogen peroxide. Note what happens.
  Now add a few drops of starch solution. Again, note carefully what happens.

3   Take a spatula-measure of iron(II) sulphate crystals, and put these into a clean test-tube. Add about $\frac{1}{3}$ test-tube full of dilute sulphuric acid. Stir with a glass rod until all the crystals have dissolved.
  Take a small part of the solution and put it into a separate test-tube. Add sodium hydroxide solution until you can see a definite change. Write down what you see.
  Now take the original solution, and add to it several drops of the solution of hydrogen peroxide. (BE CAREFUL WITH THE HYDROGEN PEROXIDE, AS IN 2 ABOVE.) Now add sodium hydroxide solution, again until you can see no further change. Write down what you see.

What happened

For each part of the experiment, you should have recorded carefully any changes which could be seen. Can you interpret any of your results in terms of redox equations?

What we can decide

1   Carbon reduces lead(II) oxide to lead. You should have been able to see the formation of beads of lead during the experiment. The other product of the reaction is carbon dioxide. The balanced equation is:

oxidation

$$2PbO(s) + C(s) \rightarrow 2Pb(s) + CO_2(g)$$

reduction

Can you say which chemical is the oxidising agent, and which the reducing agent?

2   Hydrogen peroxide oxidises the potassium iodide to iodine. The presence of iodine is shown by the black/blue coloration which is produced when starch solution is added.

3   Hydrogen peroxide oxidises the iron(II) sulphate to iron(III) sulphate. Iron(II) sulphate gives a green jelly-like precipitate (iron(II) hydroxide) when sodium hydroxide is added. Iron(III) sulphate reacts with sodium hydroxide to give a brown jelly-like precipitate of iron(III) hydroxide. You should have been able to see from the production of these two precipitates that iron(II) sulphate was converted into iron(III) sulphate by the hydrogen peroxide.

involve reactions which you have come across in this topic, and each one gives a change which can easily be seen, if it takes place.

Tests for oxidising agents

If a chemical is an oxidising agent, it will react with a reducing agent. For instance, an oxidising agent will oxidise potassium iodide (in acidic solution) to iodine. If starch is then added, a very deep blue colour forms. Starch/iodide paper contains both iodide and starch, so it can detect an oxidising agent by itself. An oxidising agent turns starch/iodide paper deep blue.

An oxidising agent will also oxidise acidified sodium sulphite to sodium sulphate. We can tell when a sulphite has been oxidised to a sulphate, because a sulphate will react with a solution of barium chloride whereas a sulphite will not. When a sulphate reacts with barium chloride the product is a white precipitate of barium sulphate. So if we take the chemical we want to test, and react it with sodium sulphite and then add barium chloride solution, we will know if the chemical was an oxidising agent or not. If the chemical was an oxidising agent, a white precipitate will form. The original sodium sulphite must be acidified with a dilute acid which is not an oxidising agent (why?), and which does not contain sulphate ions (why?). So we use dilute hydrochloric acid. (Table 4.8)

Tests for reducing agents

A reducing agent will reduce an oxidising agent. For instance, a reducing agent will reduce acidified potassium permanganate solution to manganese(II) ions. Potassium permanganate is purple, and manganese(II) ions in solution are colourless. So, a reducing agent will appear to remove the colour of potassium permanganate which is in an acidic solution. We sometimes say that a reducing agent DECOLORISES acidified potassium permanganate solution.

A reducing agent will also reduce acidified potassium dichromate to chromium(III) ions. The colour of the solution changes from orange to green when this happens. (Table 4.9)

Chemical changes which are caused by heat

You met 'thermal decomposition' reactions in Experiment 4.14. The name of this type of reaction comes from the fact that they consist of chemicals being split up into simpler chemicals (decomposed) by heat (thermally). The chemicals which you heated in Experiment 4.14, and the results which you obtained, were as follows:

sodium nitrate – a gas (oxygen) came off.
zinc nitrate – two gases came off. One of the gases was oxygen.
copper(II) sulphate – a gas came off which was an acid when it dissolved in water (the gas is sulphur dioxide).
copper(II) hydroxide – one product was copper(II) oxide.

Can we fit these results into any pattern? Perhaps it is possible to find some rules about the way different salts will split up when they are heated.

There are two nitrates and two copper(II) salts in the list above. We could start by comparing how the two nitrates split up. In each case, oxygen comes off when the nitrate is heated. Perhaps oxygen is one of the products when **any** nitrate is heated – but what else can we say? When zinc nitrate is heated, another gas comes off as well as oxygen – so whatever is left behind when the nitrate has split up (giving oxygen) breaks up further.

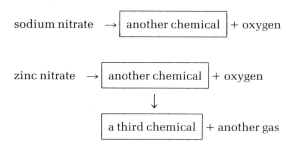

Chemical	Change caused by oxidising agent	Change revealed by	Change seen
acidified KI(aq)	$2I^-(aq) \rightarrow I_2(aq)$	starch solution	goes blue
sodium sulphite solution +, dil. HCl	$SO_3^{2-}(aq) \rightarrow SO_4^{2-}(aq)$	barium chloride solution	white precipitate forms

Table 4.8

Chemical	Change caused by reducing agent	Change seen
acidified potassium permanganate(aq)	permanganate(aq) $\rightarrow$ manganese(II)(aq)	purple $\rightarrow$ colourless
acidified potassium dichromate(aq)	dichromate(aq) $\rightarrow$ chromium(III)(aq)	orange $\rightarrow$ green

Table 4.9

One way we could describe this is to say that zinc nitrate **breaks down further** than sodium nitrate when we heat them both. That is, the zinc nitrate is split up into more things than is the sodium nitrate. The actual word-equations are:

sodium nitrate → sodium nitrate + oxygen
zinc nitrate → zinc oxide + dinitrogen tetroxide
+ oxygen

Zinc is lower down the reactivity series of metals than is sodium. So perhaps the further down the reactivity series the metal is, the more the nitrate splits up when it is heated. We can only decide if this is true by looking at what happens when another nitrate is heated. If we took some crystals of silver nitrate, and heated them gently, this is the thermal decomposition reaction which could happen:

silver nitrate → silver + dinitrogen tetroxide + oxygen

So the nitrate in this case splits down as far as it is possible to do – until only silver metal is left. Our idea looks as though it is correct. In fact, if we took the nitrates of many metals and heated them, we would see that most of them behave in the same way as zinc nitrate – they split up into the oxide of the metal, dinitrogen tetroxide and oxygen. But in no case would our rule be broken. So we can say that the further down the reactivity series the metal is, the more a nitrate splits up when it is heated.

But does this rule also hold for other salts? So far, we have only heated two different salts of copper, so we cannot say. In order to be able to answer this question, we will need to carry out some more experiments. We need to heat different salts of different metals and to decide what the product chemicals are, if a thermal decomposition reaction happens.

▶ EXPERIMENT 4.22

EXPERIMENT 4.22
Some more thermal decomposition reactions

You will need the following: these solids; sodium sulphate, calcium sulphate, sodium carbonate, calcium carbonate, sodium hydroxide, acidified potassium dichromate paper, freshly prepared lime-water, universal indicator paper, wooden splints, Pyrex test-tubes.

What to do

THE ROOM MUST BE WELL VENTILATED.
YOU MUST WEAR YOUR SAFETY SPECTACLES THROUGHOUT THIS EXPERIMENT.

1   Your teacher will tell you whether you will heat all the salts in the list above, or whether there will only be time for some groups to heat some salts, while other groups heat others. If time is short, your teacher will tell you which salts to heat. **If sodium hydroxide is in the list of salts which you will be heating, you must be careful not to let it touch your skin – so always use a spatula to touch it with**. If you accidentally touch some sodium hydroxide, wash your skin immediately with plenty of water.

2   Take one of the salts, and place a little of it in a Pyrex test-tube. Heat strongly. For each salt, you should test whether any of the following gases comes off:
oxygen – test with a glowing splint
sulphur dioxide – test with acidified potassium dichromate paper. What will happen if any sulphur dioxide is present? Look back at the section about redox reactions. Potassium dichromate is orange, chromium(III) chloride is green.
carbon dioxide – test with a small amount of lime-water in a test-tube.
Also test to see whether an acidic gas comes off, in each case.

3   Take each salt in turn, heat strongly, and carry out the tests above.

What happened

For each salt you heat, write down the result of each test which you carry out. It is as important to record that a particular gas is **not** given off, as to record that it is. Can you find any general pattern from what you have found out? Do your results (when added to what you already know for copper(II) sulphate and copper(II) hydroxide) seem to show a similar trend to that which exists in the case of nitrates? It will help you if you consider the different types of salt (sulphates, carbonates and hydroxides) separately.

What we can decide

You should be able to see from the results which you obtained that the other salts follow the same rule as do nitrates.

Sodium sulphate does not decompose at all when it is heated, whereas calcium sulphate gives calcium oxide, sulphur dioxide, and oxygen. Copper(II) sulphate is broken down as fully as is calcium sulphate, but in this case less heat is needed, and this means that sulphur trioxide comes off instead of sulphur dioxide and oxygen. (In the case of calcium sulphate, sulphur trioxide is formed at first, but the intense heat makes this split up into sulphur dioxide and oxygen.)

Sodium carbonate does not decompose at all when it is heated, whereas calcium carbonate gives calcium oxide and carbon dioxide.

Sodium hydroxide does not decompose when it is heated, whereas copper(II) hydroxide give copper(II) oxide and water.

So we can summarise what we know about the effect of heating salts in the following way:

The metal reactivity series

↑

The higher up the reactivity series, the less completely the salt is decomposed by heat, and the higher the temperature which is needed.
Salts get **harder** to decompose by heating.

TOPIC 4.5.3

Chemical changes which are caused by an electric current

Earlier in this (Topic 2.3), you saw that chemicals could be arranged so that the energy given out by a chemical reaction was produced as electricity. To put it another way, a chemical reaction can cause an electric current to flow.

You learnt in Section 1 that ionic compounds will conduct electricity when they are molten or when they are in a solution in water. When they do this, the compounds themselves become changed chemically. In other words, when chemicals conduct electricity, a chemical reaction takes place. We call this type of chemical reaction an ELECTROLYSIS reaction.

The difference between a battery and an electrolysis reaction is that a battery produces an electric current from a chemical reaction, whereas in electrolysis an electric current causes a chemical change to happen.

reactant chemicals $\xrightarrow{\text{REACTION}}$ product chemicals + electric current

A battery

reactant chemicals + electric current $\xrightarrow{\text{REACTION}}$ product chemicals

An electrolysis reaction

There are two questions which we ought to ask ourselves about electrolysis reactions. Firstly, how do chemicals manage to pass an electric current? Secondly, how do the chemical changes which take place during electrolysis come about? To find out what happens during electrolysis, we will need to carry out some electrolysis reactions.

▶ EXPERIMENT 4.23 (p. 236)

EXPERIMENT 4.23
Looking at electrolysis

You will need the following: lead iodide, small crucible, tripod and gauze, holder for electrodes and two graphite electrodes, connecting wires, crocodile clips, power pack or batteries (12 volts), stand and clamp.

What to do

MAKE SURE YOU WEAR YOUR SAFETY SPECTACLES.
THE ROOM SHOULD BE WELL VENTILATED.

1   Put some lead iodide crystals into a small crucible, so that they are 2 – 3 cm deep.

2   Place the crucible on a tripod, and arrange the electrical circuit so that you will be able to pass an electric current through the lead iodide. You will need to clamp the holder for the electrodes above the crucible. Remember that the area around the crucible will get very hot. You should make sure that the connecting wires are held well away from the heat.

3   Heat the lead iodide until it melts. Then lower the graphite electrodes into the liquid. Make sure that both the electrodes are below the surface of the lead iodide.

4   Now start to pass the electric current. Look to see if you can see any changes happening to the lead iodide. If you can see something happening, try to decide exactly **where** it is happening. You can describe one electrode by saying that it is connected to the negative terminal on the battery, and the other by saying that it is connected to the positive terminal.

5   After 5 – 10 minutes, turn off the electric current, and take away the heat. Leave the electrodes in the liquid.

6   Let the lead iodide cool down until it becomes solid again, and until it is cool enough to handle.

7   Use a spatula to break open the solid lead iodide. You should look to see if there is any more evidence of a chemical change having happened. In particular, can you find anything in the area around the electrodes?

What happened

For each electrode, decide whether there was a chemical change because of the passage of the electric current. If there was a change, can you say what it was?

What we can decide

When an electric current passes through a chemical, a chemical change takes place at each electrode. You should have been able to see that iodine vapour was given off at one electrode (the one connected to the positive terminal of the battery) when you passed an electric current through molten lead iodide. At the other electrode (the one connected to the negative terminal of the battery) a small bead of a soft, silvery solid was formed. This was a bead of the metal lead.

We call the chemical which is being electrolysed the ELECTROLYTE.

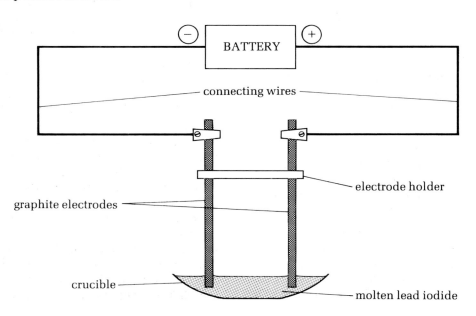

Fig. 4.49

So, passing an electric current through a chemical causes there to be a chemical change at each electrode. In the case of molten lead iodide, iodine forms at one electrode, and lead metal at the other. But this does not tell us what is happening to the rest of the lead iodide, and how the electricity is transported through it. The following simple experiment will help to throw some light on these questions.

EXPERIMENT 4.24
How do ionic compounds transport electricity through themselves?

You will need the following: crystals of potassium permanganate and copper(II) sulphate, microscope slide, strips of filter-paper to fit microscope slide, connecting wires, crocodile clips, power pack or batteries (20 volts).

NB: THE POWER PACK (IF USED) SHOULD BE CAPABLE OF PROVIDING NO MORE THAN 25 VOLTS.

What to do

1 Take a strip of filter-paper and wet it with water. The paper should be thoroughly moistened, but there should be no excess water.

2 Clip the wet filter-paper to a microscope slide, with crocodile clips (one at each end) which are attached to the connecting wires. Place the microscope slide flat on the bench.

3 Connect the wires to the source of electricity.

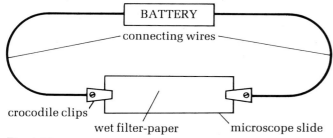

Fig. 4.50

4 Take a small crystal of potassium permanganate, and drop it on the microscope slide, about in the middle of the wet filter-paper.

5 Let the electric current pass for several minutes, and as it does so, look to see if there is any change taking place. You can describe one end of the filter-paper by saying that it is connected to the negative terminal of the battery, and the other by saying that it is connected to the positive terminal.

6 Take a clean piece of filter-paper and wet it. Place it on the microscope slide as before, and connect to the battery. This time, drop a small crystal of copper(II) sulphate on the middle of the filter-paper. Again, look to see if there is any change happening as the electric current flows. Describe what you see in terms of the terminal of the battery to which the two ends of the filter-paper are connected.

What happened

For both chemicals, potassium permanganate and copper(II) sulphate, decide whether there was any change caused by the passage of the electric current. If there was a change, try to explain what you think was happening.

What we can decide

In the case of potassium permanganate, you should have been able to see that, as the electric current was being passed, the purple colour moved towards the end of the filter-paper which was attached to the positive terminal of the battery. In potassium permanganate, it is the permanganate anion which is purple. The potassium cation is colourless. So the fact that the purple colour moved towards the positive end of the filter-paper means that it is the permanganate anion which is moving in this direction.

When you place a crystal of copper(II) sulphate on the filter-paper, you should have been able to see that the blue colour moved. The direction of this movement will have been towards the end of the filter-paper which was attached to the negative terminal of the battery. In copper(II) sulphate, it is the copper cation which is blue. The sulphate anion is colourless. So the blue copper(II) cations moved towards the negative end of the filter-paper.

The results of this experiment should tell us two things. In the first place, we can see that when an electric current is passed through a chemical, **the ions in the solution move towards the electrodes**. We can also see that the anions in the solution (which carry a negative charge) move towards the end which is connected to the positive terminal of the battery. The cations (which have a positive charge) move towards the end which is connected to the negative terminal of the battery. So, **the ions move towards the electrode which has the opposite charge to their own**.

Perhaps we can use the results of Experiment 4.24, and the results of Experiment 4.23, to work out a general picture of what happens when an electrolysis reaction takes place.

We know that a chemical reaction happens at each electrode. We know that the ions in the solution move towards the oppositely charged electrode. We know that an electric current passes. We also know that, in the electrolysis of molten lead iodide, lead was produced at one electrode, and that iodine was produced at the other.

First of all, we must look a little more closely at the electrodes which we use to carry out an electrolysis reaction. There are two types of electrode – one is called a 'reactive' electrode, and the other is called an 'unreactive' (or 'inert') electrode. A reactive electrode is one that takes part in the chemical change involved in the electrolysis. The most common types of reactive electrode are copper and silver metals – we will study them a little later on. An unreactive (inert) electrode is one which does not become involved in the chemical changes which take place. It simply allows the electric current to pass. The most common types of inert electrode are graphite (carbon) and platinum metal. Whether electrodes are reactive or inert, we call the electrode to which the cations move the CATHODE. We call the electrode to which the anions move the ANODE. So the cathode is negative, and the anode is positive. We can draw a diagram which will describe any electrolysis 'cell':

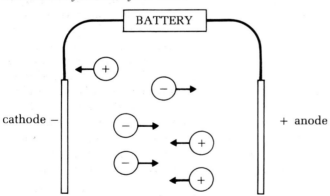

electrolyte (ions move to oppositely charged electrode)

Fig. 4.51 *An electrolysis cell*

For the moment, we will concentrate on electrolysis reactions in which the electrodes are inert.

Electrolysis of molten salts

If we take a molten salt, then the only ions which are present are those which come from the salt itself. The ions in a salt in the solid state are all held in position in the crystal lattice. So they are not able to move. If we melt the salt, the ions can then move. In order for a salt to conduct electricity, the ions must be able to move. It is for this reason that salts will not conduct electricity if they are in the solid state.

Let us consider the example of molten lead iodide. The ions which are present are lead(II) ions and bromide ions. When we start to pass an electric current through molten lead iodide, the lead(II) ions move to the negative electrode (the cathode) and the iodide ions move to the positive electrode (the anode).

When the lead(II) ions get to the cathode, they meet electrons from the battery. These electrons react with the lead ions. They cause the ions to lose their charge and become lead atoms. We say that the lead(II) cations have been DISCHARGED. We can write an equation for this discharge, called the ELECTRODE–EQUATION. In the electrode-equation, we need as many electrons to produce one atom of lead as there are charges on the lead ion:

$$Pb^{2+}(l) + 2e^- \rightarrow Pb(s) \qquad \text{cathode reaction}$$

We could say that one mole of lead(II) ions reacts with two moles of electrons, to give one mole of lead atoms. This equation fits with the results of Experiment 4.23, because you saw that lead metal was produced at the cathode of the electrolysis cell.

Now let us think about the iodide ions. They move to the anode which, instead of supplying electrons like the cathode, is itself short of electrons. Therefore, the iodide ions lose their negative charge in order to supply the anode with electrons. For every iodide ion which does this, the anode gets one electron. You know that iodide atoms will always combine to form iodine molecules, so the electrode-equation in this case is:

$$2I^-(l) \rightarrow I_2(g) + 2e^- \qquad \text{anode reaction}$$

Two electrons are used up at the cathode, while two electrons are produced at the anode. So the electrolysis cell 'balances'. This must always be so, because we could not have a build-up of electrons at any one point – there must always be a steady flow of electrons round the circuit. We can imagine that, at the same instant that a lead(II) cation is discharged at the cathode, two iodide ions lose their charge at the anode (Fig. 4.52).

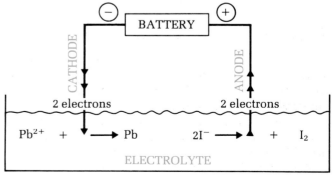

Fig. 4.52

So, when an electric current is passed through molten lead iodide, lead is produced at the cathode, and iodine is produced at the anode. At the same time, electrons are used up at the cathode, and are released at the anode. So it is as if the electrolyte has passed an electric current through itself. In fact the electricity is transported from one side of the electrolysis cell to the other by the movement of the ions and their discharge.

We can use what we have discovered about lead iodide to decide what will happen when other molten salts are electrolysed.

Example 1   The electrolysis of molten sodium chloride, using graphite electrodes

At the cathode	At the anode
Ion present: $Na^+(l)$	$Cl^-(l)$
Electrode-equation:	
$Na^+(l) + e^- \rightarrow Na(l)$	$2Cl^-(l) \rightarrow Cl_2(g) + 2e^-$
Balanced electrode-equations:	
$2Na^+(l) + 2e^- \rightarrow 2Na(l)$	$2Cl^-(l) \rightarrow Cl_2(g) + 2e^-$

Sodium metal is produced at the cathode, and chlorine gas is produced at the anode.

Example 2   The electrolysis of molten potassium iodide, using graphite electrodes

At the cathode	At the anode
Ion present: $K^+(l)$	$I^-(l)$
Electrode-equation:	
$K^+(l) + e^- \rightarrow K(l)$	$2I^-(l) \rightarrow I_2(g) + 2e^-$
Balanced electrode-equations:	
$2K^+(l) + 2e^- \rightarrow 2K(l)$	$2I^-(l) \rightarrow I_2(g) + 2e^-$

Potassium metal is produced at the cathode, and iodine gas is produced at the anode.

Now try the following example for yourself.

Question

Describe what happens when an electric current is passed through molten silver bromide, using graphite electrodes. Find the balanced electrode-equations, and describe in words the changes that take place.

Electrolysis of salt solutions

You know that as well as conducting electricity when in the molten state, salts will also conduct when they are in solution. This is because the ions are also free to move when a salt has been dissolved in water.

In a solution of a salt in water, the ions from the salt itself are not the only ions which are there. Water also provides a very small fraction of ions, because the water molecule can split up to give ions, as you learned in Section 1. You should remember that these ions are always present in water, to a very tiny extent.

$$H_2O \rightleftharpoons \underset{\substack{\text{hydrogen}\\\text{ion}}}{H^+} + \underset{\substack{\text{hydroxide}\\\text{ion}}}{OH^-}$$

(The sign $\rightleftharpoons$ means that the chemical change is going in both directions at the same time, at the same rate. You will learn more about this in Section 6.)

Very approximately, one water molecule in 50 million splits up in this way, at room temperature. If, however, the ions produced by the splitting up of this one molecule are removed, another water molecule will immediately split up to replace the hydrogen and hydroxide ions which have gone. This happens automatically, and is nothing to do with the electric current. However, this means that in practice there is an unlimited **supply** of ions in water, even though the actual number of them which are there at any one time is very small indeed.

Does this mean that water will itself become involved in the chemical changes which take place during electrolysis?

▶ EXPERIMENT 4.25 (p. 240)

Suppose we look at the first reaction carried out in Experiment 4.25 – the electrolysis of dilute hydrochloric acid.

The cation present in the solution is the hydrogen ion. This comes from both the dilute hydrochloric acid and from water. So hydrogen ions are discharged, and the gas hydrogen forms. At the anode, two ions will arrive, attracted by the positive charge. There will be chloride ions from the hydrochloric acid, and hydroxide ions from the water. So there is a choice as to which anion is discharged. The rule is that **whenever hydroxide ions are present, these are discharged in preference to any other ion, except concentrated chloride ions**. In this case, the chloride is dilute, and so hydroxide ions are discharged. When this happens, oxygen gas forms. We can summarise what happens in the electrolysis of dilute hydrochloric acid as follows:

	At the cathode	At the anode
Ions present:	$H^+(aq)$	$OH^-(aq)$, dilute $Cl^-(aq)$
		$OH^-(aq)$ preferred
Electrode-equation:	$2H^+(aq) + 2e^- \rightarrow H_2(g)$	$4OH^-(aq) \rightarrow O_2(g) + 2H_2O(l) + 4e^-$
Balanced electrode-equations:	$4H^+(aq) + 4e^- \rightarrow 2H_2(g)$	$4OH^-(aq) \rightarrow O_2(g) + 2H_2O(l) + 4e^-$

Hydrogen gas is produced at the cathode, and oxygen gas is produced at the anode. $H^+(aq)$ and $OH^-(aq)$ ions are removed from the solution. More water molecules split up to replace them, and the solution becomes more concentrated. Eventually, $Cl^-(aq)$ ions would be discharged at the anode.

EXPERIMENT 4.25
Can water influence the products of an electrolysis reaction?

You will need the following: solutions of potassium iodide and copper(II) sulphate, dilute hydrochloric acid, electrolysis cell to allow the collection of gases, power pack or batteries (12 volts).

What to do

1   Half-fill the electrolysis cell with dilute hydrochloric acid. Place filled test-tubes over the electrodes so that any gases produced can be collected.

2   Pass an electric current, and look to see if you can see any changes taking place. If any gases form, carry on until the test-tubes are nearly full. Disconnect the electricity supply, and carefully remove the test-tubes which contain gas. Test each gas with a glowing splint (to see whether it is oxygen) and with a lighted splint (to see whether it is hydrogen).

3   Empty the electrolysis cell. Wash it with water, and replace the dilute hydrochloric acid with a solution of potassium iodide. Carry out the electrolysis as before, and test any gases which are formed.

4   Again, wash the electrolysis cell, and this time, half-fill it with copper(II) sulphate solution. Carry out the electrolysis, collecting and testing any gases. If no gas forms, look to see whether there is any other change happening.

What happened

For each solution, try to decide from what you have seen, what happened at each electrode. You should have been able to see the following:

	Cathode	Anode
dilute hydrochloric acid	hydrogen gas forms	oxygen gas forms
potassium iodide solution	hydrogen gas forms	oxygen gas forms
copper(II) sulphate solution	copper metal forms	oxygen gas forms

Table 4.10

What we can decide

You should be able to see that the products of the electrolysis reactions above are, in each case, different from those which would have been obtained if a molten compound had been electrolysed. So water affects the chemical changes which happen. But why does this happen, and can we find a way of working out what the products of a particular electrolysis which involves water will be?

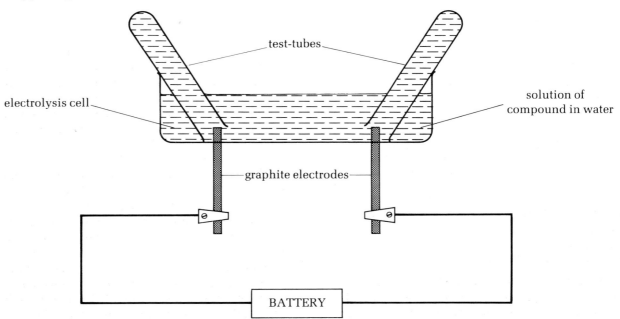

Fig. 4.53 *Electrolysis cell for solutions of compounds in water*

In the case of the electrolysis of potassium iodide solution, there is a choice of ion at each electrode. At the anode, the choice is between hydroxide ions (from water) and iodide ions (from potassium iodide). In line with the rule given above, the ion which is discharged is the hydroxide ion. The electrode-equation is as above.

At the cathode, there are hydrogen ions (from water) and potassium ions (from potassium iodide). The rule at the cathode is that **the element which is lower in the reactivity series of metals is the one which is discharged**. If you look back to the early part of this section (Experiment 4.5, p.177) you will see that hydrogen is lower in the reactivity series than any othe metal, except copper, silver and gold. So, if these ions are not present in solution, hydrogen ions are always discharged at the cathode when a solution is electrolysed. We can now summarise what happens when a solution of potassium iodide is electrolysed:

	At the cathode	**At the anode**
Ions present:	$H^+(aq)$, $K^+(aq)$ $H^+(aq)$ preferred	$OH^-(aq)$, $I^-(aq)$ $OH^-(aq)$ preferred
Electrode-equation:	$2H^+(aq) + 2e^-$ $\rightarrow H_2(g)$	$4OH^-(aq)$ $\rightarrow O_2(g) + 2H_2O(l) + 4e^-$
Balanced electrode-equations:	$4H^+(aq) + 4e^-$ $\rightarrow 2H_2(g)$	$4OH^-(aq)$ $\rightarrow O_2(g) + 2H_2O(l) + 4e^-$

Hydrogen gas is produced at the cathode, and oxygen gas at the anode. $H^+(aq)$ and $OH^-(aq)$ ions are removed from the solution. More water molecules split up to replace them, and the solution becomes more concentrated.

When copper(II) sulphate solution is electrolysed, there is also a choice of ion at each electrode. At the anode, it is again the hydroxide ion which wins. At the cathode, the choice is between hydrogen ions (from water) and copper(II) ions (from copper(II) sulphate). In this case, it is copper which is the lower in the reactivity series, and so the copper wins:

	At the cathode	**At the anode**
Ions present:	$H^+(aq)$, $Cu^{2+}(aq)$ $Cu^{2+}(aq)$ preferred	$OH^-(aq)$, $SO_4^{2-}(aq)$ $OH^-(aq)$ preferred
Electrode-equation	$Cu^{2+}(aq) + 2e^-$ $\rightarrow Cu(s)$	$4OH^-(aq)$ $\rightarrow O_2(g) + 2H_2O(l) + 4e^-$
Balanced electrode-equations:	$2Cu^{2+}(aq) + 4e^-$ $\rightarrow 2Cu(s)$	$4OH^-(aq)$ $\rightarrow O_2(g) + 2H_2O(l) + 4e^-$

Copper metal forms as a coat on the surface of the cathode, and oxygen gas is produced at the anode. $Cu^{2+}(aq)$ and $OH^-(aq)$ ions are removed from the solution. The ions which are left behind are $H^+(aq)$ and $SO_4^{2-}(aq)$. After a long time, therefore, the solution becomes dilute sulphuric acid.

Now that you know the rules for what happens at the cathode and at the anode when there is a choice of more than one ion, you can try some examples for yourself.

Questions

In each case, describe the chemical changes which take place when an electrolysis is carried out, using the electrodes which are given. Find the balanced electrode-equations, and describe in words the changes that take place.

1. A solution of silver nitrate, using graphite electrodes.
2. A solution of zinc sulphate, using platinum electrodes (these are inert, remember).
3. A solution of sodium sulphate, using graphite electrodes.
4. Dilute nitric acid, using platinum electrodes.
5. Concentrated aluminium chloride solution, using graphite electrodes.

Reactive electrodes

Reactive electrodes only affect what happens at the anode. If the anode is made of either copper or silver, then instead of an anion being discharged, the metal of the anode gives up electrons and forms metal ions. These metal ions then pass into solution. The electrode-equations are as follows:

REACTIVE ELECTRODES	copper	$Cu(s) \rightarrow Cu^{2+}(aq) + 2e^-$
	silver	$Ag(s) \rightarrow Ag^+(aq) + e^-$

▶ EXPERIMENT 4.26 (p. 242)

In both the electrolysis reactions in Experiment 4.26, what happens at the anode is the reverse of what happens at the cathode. So metal is transferred from the anode (which therefore decreases in mass) to the cathode (which increases in mass). The amount by which the anode gets lighter is the amount by which the cathode gets heavier.

The electrode-equations for an electrolysis reaction are linked together, because the number of electrons used up at the cathode must equal the number of electrons which are produced at the anode. So, when we write the **balanced** electrode-equations, we are writing down the amount of the reactions which take place at the two electrodes. The balanced electrode-equations for the electrolysis of copper(II) sulphate solution using copper electrodes tells us that whenever one mole of copper(II) ions are discharged at the cathode, one mole of copper metal passes into solution as copper(II) ions at the anode. So the mass lost by the anode is equal to the mass gained by the cathode.

EXPERIMENT 4.26

If there is time, your teacher may let you carry out the electrolysis of copper(II) sulphate solution using copper electrodes, or the electrolysis of silver nitrate solution, using silver electrodes.

Since we know what happens at each electrode, we should be able to work out the overall changes which occur for these two electrolysis reactions.

1 The electrolysis of copper(II) sulphate solution, using copper electrodes

	At the cathode	At the anode (copper)
Ions present:	$H^+(aq)$, $Cu^{2+}(aq)$ $Cu^{2+}(aq)$ preferred	$OH^-(aq)$, $SO_4^{2-}(aq)$ reactive anode
Electrode-equation: (balanced)	$Cu^{2+}(aq) + 2e^-$ $\rightarrow Cu(s)$	$Cu(s)$ $\rightarrow Cu^{2+}(aq) + 2e^-$

Copper metal forms as a coat on the surface of the cathode, and the copper of the anode passes into solution as copper(II) ions. The solution remains unchanged.

2 The electrolysis of silver nitrate solution, using silver electrodes

	At the cathode	At the anode (silver)
Ions present:	$H^+(aq)$, $Ag^+(aq)$ $Ag^+(aq)$ preferred	$OH^-(aq)$, $SO_4^{2-}(aq)$ reactive anode
Electrode equation: (balanced)	$Ag^+(aq) + e^- \rightarrow Ag(s)$	$Ag(s) \rightarrow Ag^+(aq) + e^-$

Silver metal forms as a coat on the surface of the cathode, and the silver of the anode passes into solution as silver ions. The solution remains unchanged.

Question

Explain, using your own words, why the mass of silver gained by the cathode is equal to the mass of silver lost by the anode, when silver nitrate solution is electrolysed with silver electrodes.

Electrolysis reactions with reactive electrodes are very useful in chemistry. The metal that forms as a layer on the surface of the cathode is **pure**. This is because it is made up of the atoms formed when ions from the solution have been discharged – and nothing else. So we can use electrolysis for purifying metals. If we make the anode a lump of impure copper, and the cathode out of pure copper, at the end of the electrolysis reaction there will be a lot more pure copper on the cathode than there was at the start. So some of the impure copper which started as the anode will end up as pure copper on the cathode – it will have been purified (Fig. 4.54).

You will see how this fact is used in industry to get pure metals such as copper from the chemical compounds which contain them, in Section 5.

As well as being pure, the layer of metal which forms on the cathode is very thin. To cover the surface of the cathode completely, the layer of metal only has to be one atom thick. So an object can be completely coated with a very thin layer of a metal such as silver, and it will look as though it was made of solid silver. For instance, suppose we took a knife or a fork made of a cheap metal, and used them as the cathode for the electrolysis of silver nitrate solution, with an anode

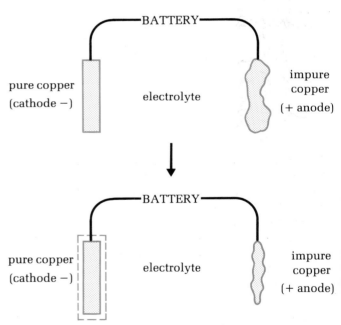

Fig. 4.54

made of silver. A thin layer of silver would form on the surface of the piece of cutlery – and it would look as if it was made of solid silver. It would, however, have been much cheaper to make than the real thing.

When we coat something with a layer of a metal in an electrolysis reaction, the layer is called a PLATE. So we call this process ELECTROPLATING.

If you look very carefully at pieces of cutlery that seem to be made of silver, you will often find the letters 'E.P.N.S.' somewhere on the handle. This stands for 'electroplated nickel-silver', and tells you that the object is not all that it seems to be!

Calculations about electrolysis reactions

Suppose we carried out the electrolysis of copper(II) sulphate solution using copper electrodes. The electrode-equation at the cathode would be:

$$Cu^{2+}(aq) + 2e^- \rightarrow Cu(s)$$
$$\text{1 mole} \quad \text{2 moles} \quad \text{1 mole}$$

This tells us that one mole of copper(II) ions reacts with two moles of electrons, and the product is one mole of copper metal.

A mole of electrons is called a FARADAY. (Michael Faraday was an English scientist who lived from 1791 to 1867, and who carried out many experiments to investigate the nature of electricity and magnetism. In 1833 he discovered the rules which describe how to find the quantities of chemicals which are involved in electrolysis reactions.) So we can say that we need two faradays of electricity to form 1 mole of copper as a deposit on the surface of a cathode in an electrolysis reaction.

Suppose the particular reaction is the electrolysis of copper(II) sulphate solution using **carbon** electrodes. The balanced electrode-equations are:

At the cathode
$$2Cu^{2+}(aq) + 4e^- \rightarrow 2Cu(s)$$

At the anode (graphite)
$$4OH^-(aq) \rightarrow O_2(g) + 2H_2O(l) + 4e^-$$

Because 4 faradays flow through the anode, 4 faradays must also flow through the cathode. So, for instance, 2 moles of copper are deposited at the cathode every time 1 mole of oxygen is formed at the anode. So, if we know the balanced electrode-equations, we can always find out the relative amounts of the chemicals which are involved at the two electrodes. This lets us carry out many different sorts of calculation about electrolysis reactions.

Example 1

When dilute sulphuric acid was electrolysed using platinum electrodes, 100 cm³ of hydrogen was formed at the cathode. What was the volume of oxygen which formed at the same time at the anode?

	At the cathode	At the anode (platinum)
Balanced electrode-equations	$4H^+(aq) + 4e^-$ $\rightarrow 2H_2(g)$ 2 moles $\longrightarrow$	$4OH^-$ $\rightarrow O_2(g) + 2H_2O(l) + 4e^-$ 1 mole
By Avogadro's Hypothesis:	2 volumes $\longrightarrow$ 100 cm³ $\longrightarrow$	1 volume (at same T and P) 50 cm³ (at same T and P)

(volume of O_2: volume of $H_2 = 1:2$
volume of $O_2 = \frac{1}{2} \times 100$ cm³ $= 50$ cm³)

The volume of oxygen produced at the anode was 50 cm³

Example 2

Molten lead chloride was electrolysed using graphite electrodes. If the mass of lead which was deposited at the cathode was 20.7 g, what volume of chlorine gas was formed at the anode (measured at s.t.p.)?

	At the cathode	At the anode (graphite)
Balanced electrode-equations:	$Pb^{2+}(l) + 2e^- \rightarrow Pb(s)$ 1 mole 207 g $\rightarrow$ 20.7 g $\rightarrow$	$2Cl^-(l) \rightarrow Cl_2(g) + 2e^-$ 1 mole 22.4 dm³ (at s.t.p.) 1/10 × 22.4 dm³ = 2.24 dm³ (at s.t.p.)

The volume of chlorine produced at the anode was 2.24 dm³ (at s.t.p.)

Example 3

Silver nitrate solution was electrolysed with silver electrodes. It was discovered that at the end of the electrolysis, the mass of the cathode had increased by 10.8 g. Another electrolysis cell was put in series with this cell before the electrolysis started. The second cell contained copper(II) sulphate solution, and copper electrodes. By how much did the cathode in the second cell increase in mass? (Fig. 4.55)

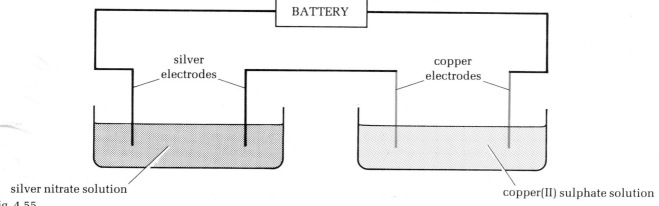

silver nitrate solution

copper(II) sulphate solution

Fig. 4.55

Balanced electrode-equations:

	At the cathode	**At the anode** (silver/copper)
Cell 1	$Ag^+(aq) + e^- \rightarrow Ag(s)$	$Ag(s) \rightarrow Ag^+(aq) + e^-$
Cell 2	$Cu^{2+}(aq) + 2e^- \rightarrow Cu(s)$	$Cu(s) \rightarrow Cu^{2+}(aq) + 2e^-$

Since the cells are connected in series, the same amount of electricity must flow through them both. So, the number of faradays in the equations for the two cells must be the same. So we can write for the two cathode reactions:

Cell 1 $2Ag^+(aq) + 2e^- \rightarrow 2Ag(s)$
Cell 2 $Cu^{2+}(aq) + 2e^- \rightarrow Cu(s)$

Every time one mole of copper is deposited, two moles of silver are deposited.
The mass of silver deposited = 10.8 g = 1/10 mole
$$\text{mass of copper deposited} = \tfrac{1}{2} \times \text{no. of moles of silver}$$
$$= 1/20 \text{ mole}$$
$$= 1/20 \times 64 \text{ g}$$
$$= 3.2 \text{ g}$$

The mass of copper deposited was 3.2 g

In a moment, you can do some examples for yourself, but first there is one more type of calculation which you must learn about.

A faraday is a certain amount of electricity. So it is equivalent to a certain current flowing for a certain time. If a current of 1 amp flows for 1 second, we say that a COULOMB of electricity has passed (Coulomb was a French scientist). So a faraday must be equal to a certain number of coulombs. In fact, 1 faraday = 96 500 coulombs. This may seem like a large number, but remember that a faraday is a mole of electrons, and you know what a large number a mole is.

If we know the current (amps) which flows through an electrolysis cell, and if we know the length of time for which it flows (seconds), we can calculate the number of coulombs. If we know the number of

coulombs, we know the number of faradays. If we know this, we can work out how much of each chemical forms at the two electrodes.

Example 4

A steady current of 5 amps was passed through a solution of copper(II) sulphate for 25 minutes. What weight of copper was lost by the anode?

At the anode (copper)
Electrode-equation $Cu(s) \rightarrow Cu^{2+}(aq) + 2e^-$
                                  1 mole   2 moles

1 mole of copper is deposited when 2 faradays of electricity pass.

$$\text{Actual no. of faradays} = \frac{\text{no. of coulombs}}{96\,500}$$
$$\text{no. of coulombs} = \text{amps} \times \text{seconds}$$
$$= 5 \times 25 \times 60$$
$$= 7500$$
$$\text{no. of faradays} = \frac{7500}{96\,500} = 0.08$$

2 faradays deposit 1 mole of copper
1 faraday deposits $\tfrac{1}{2}$ mole of copper
0.08 faradays deposit $\tfrac{1}{2} \times 0.08$ moles copper
$$= \tfrac{1}{2} \times 0.08 \times 64 \text{ g copper}$$
$$= 2.56 \text{ g copper}$$

The mass of copper deposited = 2.56 g

We can now write a summary of the steps involved in calculations about electrolysis, starting with the steps for getting the correct balanced electrode-equations.

Calculations about electrolysis

Step 1: Decide what change takes place at each electrode. You can use the following flow-charts:

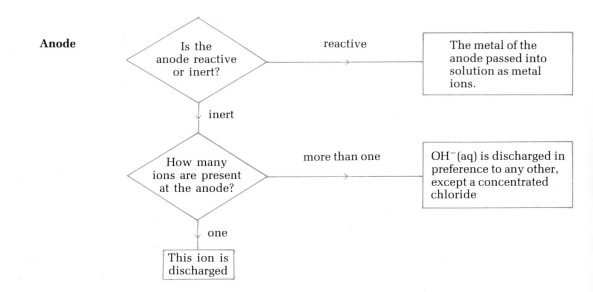

Cathode

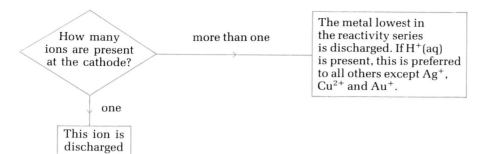

Step 2: Write the balanced electrode-equations.

Step 3: Write down the number of moles of the chemicals which are involved in the calculation, and the number of faradays of electricity if necessary.

Step 4: Scale up or down from the mass or volume of the known chemical to get the mass or volume of the unknown chemical.

Step 5: If you are given the value of the current, and the time for which it passes, find the number of coulombs by multiplying the current (amps) by the length of time (seconds). 1 faraday = 96 500 coulombs.

Now try some questions for yourself. Remember that the first step is to decide what happens at each electrode.

Questions

1 **Concentrated** sodium chloride solution was electrolysed using platinum electrodes. Write the balanced electrode-equations. What volume of each gas was produced, measured at s.t.p., if the current of 10 amps flowed for 10 minutes?

2 Dilute sodium hydroxide solution was electrolysed with platinum electrodes. Write the balanced electrode-equations. If the volume of gas collected at the cathode was 200 cm^3, what volume of gas (under the same conditions) was collected at the anode?

3 Write the electrode-equations for the electrolysis of a solution of silver nitrate, using
  (a) silver electrodes;
  (b) graphite electrodes.
Describe how the solutions left at the end of these two electrolysis reactions would be different from each other.

4 How long would a current of 20 amps have to flow in order for 32 g of copper to be deposited on the cathode of an electrolysis cell composed of copper electrodes and an electrolyte of copper(II) sulphate solution?

5 Do you think that an electrolysis reaction can be thought of as a 'redox' reaction as well? If so, where does oxidation take place in electrolysis, and where does the reduction happen?

UNIT 4.5
Summary and learning

1 A 'redox' reaction is a chemical change which takes place between an oxidising agent and a reducing agent. Reduction and oxidation must always happen together.
  Oxidation is the addition of oxygen, or the removal of hydrogen. It is the removal of electrons.
  Reduction is the removal of oxygen, or the addition of hydrogen. It is the addition of electrons.
The oxidising agent is the chemical which causes the oxidation to take place, and the reducing agent is the chemical which causes the reduction to take place.
  You should remember which chemicals usually behave as oxidising agents, and which chemicals usually behave as reducing agents.
  You should remember the tests for oxidising agents and the tests for reducing agents.

2 A thermal decomposition reaction is one in which a chemical is broken down into simpler chemicals by heat.
  The salts of metals higher in the reactivity series need to be heated to a higher temperature before they decompose (some do not decompose at all). When they do decompose, they do so less completely than the salts of metals lower in the reactivity series.

3 An electrolysis reaction is one in which a chemical reaction is caused by the passage of an electric current.
  You should remember the evidence which you have seen for the movement of ions during an electrolysis reaction.
  You should remember the rules for deciding what happens at each electrode, and you should remember the names of the electrodes.
  You should remember the steps for carrying out calculations about electrolysis reactions.

4   You have learnt the meaning of these words:

oxidising agent   anode
reducing agent   discharge
oxidation   electrode-equation
oxidise   reactive electrodes
reduce   plate
half-reaction   electroplating
decolorise   faraday
electrolysis   coulomb
cathode   electrolyte

The chemical world – metals and metal compounds

UNIT 5.1 Transition metals

You have already learned many things about metals. You know that they are one of the two basic types of element. You learned about the way they behave physically in Section 3 (Topic 3.3.3).

The way metals behave chemically has been explored in Section 1 (Topic 1.1.3), in Section 3 (Topic 3.1.3, where you learned how the structure of the atom of an element and its chemical behaviour are linked) and in Section 4 (Topic 4.1.3 where you learned about the reactivity of metals). In summary, we can say that the following things are true about all metals (Table 5.1).

Chemical behaviour	Physical behaviour
They form oxides which dissolve in water to form alkalis, or which are insoluble bases.	They have very shiny surfaces
They only form compounds with non-metals.	Generally, metals cannot easily be bent – they are physically strong.
Each metal has a particular reactivity, so we can draw up a reactivity series for the metals.	Although they are strong, metals can be pulled into wires.
	Metals pass an electric current very easily.
When metals react, they lose electrons and form cations.	Metals pass heat very easily.

Table 5.1 *Properties of metals*

In Section 3 (Topic 3.1.2) you also learned that there were 30 metals which do not belong to groups of elements in the same way as the alkali metals. These metals are called 'transition metals'. As well as having all of the properties listed above, transition metals also have some special properties of their own.

Question

Find the word 'transition' in a dictionary. Why do you think the word is used to describe the block of 30 elements in the middle of the Periodic Table?

TOPIC 5.1.1

What are 'transition metals', and how do they behave?

Turn to the Periodic Table on p. 122. You will remember that the 'transition metals' are a block of 30 elements in the middle of the table:

the transition metals

Ca	Sc	Ti	V	Cr	Mn	Fe	Co	Ni	Cu	Zn	Ga
Sr	Y	Zr	Nb	Mo	Tc	Ru	Rh	Pd	Ag	Cd	In
Ba	La	Hf	Ta	W	Re	Os	Ir	Pt	Au	Hg	Tl

Table 5.2

You will also recall that the properties of the other elements in the Periodic Table vary gradually across the periods **as if the transition metals were not there**. Element 31 (gallium) follows on after element 20 (calcium), element 49 (indium) after element 38 (strontium), and so on. It is as if the transition metals form a 'bridge' across the middle of the table. But what do we know about the transition metals? Well, to start with, have another look at the metal reactivity series. Here it is again, with the transition metals highlighted.

The metal reactivity series

sodium

calcium

magnesium

aluminium

zinc

iron

lead

copper

silver

What can we say about transition metals? Are they generally reactive, or unreactive? It is pretty clear that transition metals are less reactive than metals in Group 1 and Group 2, for instance.

What else do we know? In Section 2 (Topic 2.2.2), a number of metals which are important in the modern world were investigated. These were:

gold (Au)
silver (Ag)   } precious and
platinum (Pt) } rare metals
uranium (U)

AND

iron (Fe)
copper (Cu)
aluminium
(Al)   } metals for
zinc (Zn)   } making things
lead (Pb)

You should remember that an important reason for a metal being thought of as 'precious' is that it does not corrode or tarnish. Obviously, reactive metals will tarnish much more quickly than unreactive ones. Gold, silver and platinum are all transition metals, and so this is more evidence that transition metals are generally fairly unreactive. What about the metals which we use for making things? Use Table 5.2 to find those which are transition metals.

As well as being fairly unreactive (how long, for instance, would a bridge that was made out of sodium last?), metals which we use for making things must also be **strong**. So it would seem that, generally speaking, transition metals are amongst the strongest of the metals.

In Section 3 (Topic 3.3.3), you saw that some molecules (such as water and ammonia) can form coordinate bonds to metal cations (such as Cu^{2+}). You learned that such ligand molecules can be associated with giving something which appears coloured. Copper is a transition metal. So we can ask ourselves whether it is true for the transition metals generally that their ions have a colour.

▶ EXPERIMENT 5.1

EXPERIMENT 5.1

Do ions which contain a transition metal usually have a colour?

You will need the following: the solids – sodium carbonate, copper(II) sulphate, potassium permanganate, potassium chloride, potassium dichromate and iron(II) sulphate; microscope slide, strips of filter-paper to fit microscope slide, connecting wires, crocodile clips, power pack or batteries (20 volts).
NB: IF A POWER PACK IS USED, IT SHOULD BE CAPABLE OF PRODUCING NO MORE THAN 25 VOLTS.

What to do

1   Take each of the six solids in turn. Describe the colour (if any) of each of them.

2   Make a solution in water of each of the solids. Again, describe the colour of each solution.

3   For each substance, write down the colour which you see in the solid form, and when it is dissolved in water.

4   **Stop working, and discuss with the others in your group what you think you can decide from your findings.** The anion in potassium permanganate is MnO_4^- and that in potassium dichromate is $Cr_2O_7^{2-}$. **Write down what you have decided, and why you have decided it.**

5   It might be helpful to know which ion – the cation or the anion – in those salts which have a colour is the one which causes the colour. You already know the answer to this question for potassium permanganate and for copper(II) sulphate (from Experiment 4.24). But you can now repeat what you did there for the other salts which have a colour.

6   Take a strip of filter-paper and moisten it with water. Clip it to a microscope slide, using crocodile clips attached to connecting wires. Place the microscope slide flat on the bench, and connect the wires to the source of electricity. (Look at Fig. 4.50 on page 237.)

7   Drop a small crystal of the substance which you are testing onto the microscope slide, near the middle. Let the electric current pass for several minutes. Does any colour move towards the end

of the filter-paper which is attached to the positive terminal of the battery, or towards the one attached to the negative terminal?

8 Discuss what you think you can decide from your findings. Write down what you have decided and why you have decided it.

What happened

The chemicals which had a colour were: copper(II) sulphate, potassium dichromate, potassium permanganate and iron(II) sulphate. All have much the same colour in solution as does the solid.

When you tested iron(II) sulphate, you should have seen the colour move towards the negative terminal. For potassium dichromate the colour will have moved towards the positive terminal.

What we can decide

Each of the four salts which has a colour contains a transition metal. For two salts (copper(II) sulphate and iron(II) sulphate), the transition metal forms the cation. For potassium permanganate and potassium dichromate, the transition metal is in the anion. In each case, it is the transition metal which causes the substance to have a colour.

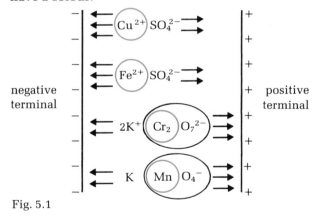

Fig. 5.1

We can say that many transition metals cause ions which contain them to have a colour. But what else can we find out about them?

In Section 3 (Topic 3.3.1) you learned that transition metals can form more than one type of cation. For instance, copper forms Cu^+ ('copper(I)') and Cu^{2+} ('copper(II)'), and iron forms Fe^{2+} ('iron(II)') and Fe^{3+} ('iron(III)'). We can now look at this ability to form different cations more closely.

▶ EXPERIMENT 5.2

EXPERIMENT 5.2
Different ions which contain vanadium

> **Your teacher will show you this experiment**

The following will be needed: ammonium metavanadate (vanadate(V)), powdered zinc, 2M sodium hydroxide solution, M sulphuric acid, large measuring cylinder.

What to do

1 Dissolve approximately 3 g of ammonium metavanadate (vanadate(V)) in 40 cm³ of 2M sodium hydroxide. Add 80 cm³ of M sulphuric acid.

2 Place a little powdered zinc at the bottom of a large measuring cylinder and just cover it with dilute sulphuric acid.

3 Now add the solution of ammonium metavanadate, carefully, in order not to disturb the layer of zinc.

4 Let the measuring cylinder stand for about a week.

What happened

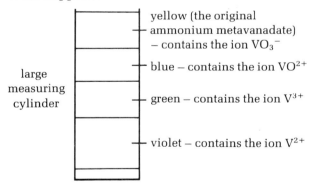

Fig. 5.2

You should have been able to see a series of coloured bands which move up the measuring cylinder, as shown in Fig. 5.2.

What we can decide

Each of the different coloured bands is caused by a different ion which contains vanadium. The ions which are responsible for the different colours are shown in Fig. 5.2. You will see that one of these is an anion, and the others are cations.

So we can say that the different ions which contain the same transition metal, whether they are cations or anions, will have a different colour. We can often use these colours to find out which ion we have, as you saw in Section 1 (Topic 1.4.3). Before you start the next experiment, go back to Section 1 and remind yourself of how we can spot iron(II) and iron(III) ions.

EXPERIMENT 5.3

Different ions which contain iron

You will need the following: solid iron(II) sulphate, '20 volume' hydrogen peroxide, sodium hydroxide solution, glass rod, 2 boiling-tubes.

What to do

YOU MUST WEAR YOUR SAFETY SPECTACLES THROUGHOUT THIS EXPERIMENT.

1   Take 2–3 spatula-measures of iron(II) sulphate and place them in the bottom of a boiling-tube. Add **distilled** water until the boiling-tube is about half-full, and then dissolve the iron(II) sulphate by stirring with a glass rod.

2   When all the iron(II) sulphate has dissolved, pour half of the solution into another boiling-tube, and put it to one side.

3   Take the solution left in the original boiling-tube to the fume-cupboard, where you will find some hydrogen peroxide solution. PUT ON THE RUBBER GLOVES WHICH YOU WILL FIND IN THE FUME-CUPBOARD, BEFORE YOU HANDLE THE BOTTLE OF HYDROGEN PEROXIDE. IF YOU LET ANY HYDROGEN PEROXIDE SOLUTION TOUCH YOUR SKIN, WASH IT OFF AT ONCE. Add several drops of the hydrogen peroxide solution to the solution in the boiling-tube, and take it back to your bench.

4   Carefully, boil the contents of the boiling-tube for about 1 minute.

5   Add sodium hydroxide solution to each of the two boiling-tubes which you have, remembering which is which.

6   **Discuss what you think you can decide from what you have seen. Write down what you have decided, and why you have decided it.**

What happened

You should have been able to see that the solution in the boiling-tube which you put to one side gave a green gelatinous precipitate when you added the sodium hydroxide solution. The solution which had been reacted with hydrogen peroxide solution gave a brown gelatinous precipitate.

What we can decide

The original solution contained Fe^{2+} ions, as you would expect. The solution which had been reacted with hydrogen peroxide contained Fe^{3+} ions.

A particular transition metal can be in many different ions. We can use a chemical reaction to change one ion into another ion.

Question

What type of a reaction took place between the solution of iron(II) sulphate and hydrogen peroxide solution? Write an equation which shows what happened to iron(II) ions during this reaction.

▶ EXPERIMENT 5.4

EXPERIMENT 5.4
Different ions which contain chromium

You will need the following: solid sodium dichromate, ethanol, ethanal (acetaldehyde), '20 volume' hydrogen peroxide, access to 2 fume-cupboards, 2 boiling-tubes, glass rod. Fume-cupboard 1 should be used to contain the ethanal (acetaldehyde) and the hydrogen peroxide. Fume-cupboard 2 should contain a large water-bath for heating solutions containing ethanal (see below).

Because of possible harmful interactions between ethanol and ethanal, it is suggested that in this case ethanol be kept on the demonstration bench, and the stopper replaced each time after use.

What to do

BE CAREFUL NOT TO GET ETHANOL AND ETHANAL MIXED UP. REMEMBER THAT THEY ARE BOTH FLAMMABLE. YOU MUST WEAR YOUR SAFETY SPECTACLES THROUGHOUT THIS EXPERIMENT.

1 Put 1 spatula-measure of sodium dichromate in a boiling-tube, and add distilled water until the tube is about quarter full. Add about $1 \, cm^3$ of dilute sulphuric acid and 1 drop of ethanol. Shake the mixture, and warm it gently until you see a colour change.

2 **Discuss what you have seen, and what you think it means. Write down what you have decided and why you have decided it.**

3 When the colour change is complete, pour half of the solution into another boiling-tube and put it to one side for the moment (tube 'B').

4 Take the solution left in the original tube (tube 'A') and add to it an equal volume of **distilled** water, and a few drops of dilute sulphuric acid. Now take the tube to the fume-cupboard which contains ethanal (acetaldehyde). PUT ON THE RUBBER GLOVES WHICH YOU WILL FIND IN THE FUME-CUPBOARD, BEFORE YOU HANDLE THE BOTTLE OF ETHANAL. IF ANY ETHANAL TOUCHES YOUR SKIN, WASH IT OFF AT ONCE. Add more ethanal than there was solution in the boiling-tube. Now take the boiling-tube and place it in the large water-bath in another fume-cupboard. (If you want you can place a label on your boiling-tube to make it easier to identify later.) Leave the boiling-tube in the water-bath until you see a colour change.

Discuss what you have seen, and what you think it means. Write down what you have decided and why you have decided it.

5 Now go back to tube 'B'. Add sodium hydroxide solution, a little at a time, until a murky green precipitate appears. Carry on adding sodium hydroxide solution until the precipitate dissolves. (If this does not happen easily, warm the boiling-tube, and then let it cool.) Take the boiling-tube to the fume-cupboard which contains hydrogen peroxide solution. PUT ON THE RUBBER GLOVES, BEFORE YOU HANDLE THE BOTTLE OF HYDROGEN PEROXIDE. IF YOU LET ANY HYDROGEN PEROXIDE SOLUTION TOUCH YOUR SKIN, WASH IT OFF AT ONCE. Add about 10 drops of the '20 volume' hydrogen peroxide solution. Take the boiling-tube back to your bench, and stir with a glass rod.

Discuss what you have seen, and what you think it means. Write down what you have decided and why you have decided it.

What happened

You should have been able to see the following changes:

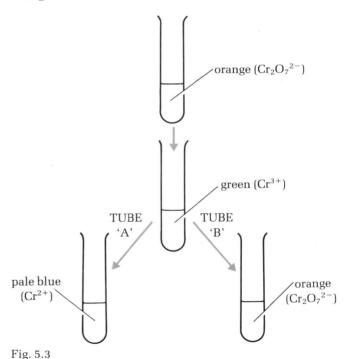

Fig. 5.3

What we can decide

Each time a new colour was produced, it was because the chemical reaction caused a different ion containing chromium to be formed. The different ions are shown in Fig. 5.3.

Fig. 5.4 *Iron is a transition metal, and it must be strong. This is the world's first bridge made of iron, built in 1779 and still standing. 'Ironbridge' is in Shropshire, in England*

So you have seen a number of examples in which a given transition metal can exist in more than one ion. Each different ion causes a different colour. It is generally true that all transition metals behave in this way. But what else can we say about transition metals?

As you were reminded above, you learned in Section 3 (Topic 3.3.3) that some molecules can act as ligands (you saw how water and ammonia do this with the Cu^{2+} ion). Transition metal ions are very good at acting as a centre for ligands. The ion which is formed when ligands attach themselves to an ion is called a COMPLEX ION. So transition metals form many complex ions.

If we represent a transition ion by the symbol M^{n+} (M is the symbol for the element, and n represents the number of positive charges which it has) and ligands by L, then we can write the following to express what happens when a complex ion forms:

$$M^{n+} + 6L \longrightarrow \begin{bmatrix} & & L & & \\ L & & & & L \\ & & M & & \\ L & & & & L \\ & & L & & \end{bmatrix}^{n+}$$

When we add ammonia to Cu^{2+}(aq) ions, the complex ion which forms is:

$$\begin{bmatrix} & OH_2 & \\ H_3N & & NH_3 \\ & Cu & \\ H_3N & & NH_3 \\ & H_2O & \end{bmatrix}^{2+}$$

the tetrammine copper (II) ion

This property of transition metal ions makes them vital to some of the chemical changes which happen in living things. For instance, the chemical in blood which carries oxygen from the lungs around the body is called HAEMOGLOBIN, and is blue in colour. In every haemoglobin molecule there is an atom of iron. This atom of iron 'picks up' an oxygen molecule (which behaves as a ligand), forming OXYHAEMOGLOBIN which is red:

BLUE

$$\underset{\text{haemoglobin molecule}}{\text{—Fe—}} + O_2 \longrightarrow \underset{}{\overset{O_2 \qquad \text{RED}}{\text{—Fe—}}}$$

haemoglobin   oxyhaemoglobin

When the oxyhaemoglobin reaches the part of the body which needs oxygen, the oxygen molecule can be given up easily.

As well as forming complex ions, transition metals have another important property. They can often act as CATALYSTS for chemical reactions. A catalyst is something which changes the speed of a chemical reaction. You will learn more about catalysts (and a more exact definition of them) in Section 6.

So we can make a list of the properties of transition metals (Table 5.3).

They are all similar to each other in that they:
are generally less reactive than other metals;
can form different ions which cause different colours;
can form complex ions with ligand molecules;
often act as catalysts for chemical reactions.

Table 5.3 *Properties of transition metals*

We should now ask ourselves why it is that transition metals behave in this way.

Some important transition metals – iron, copper and zinc

In Section 2 (Topic 2.2.2) you learned what the different steps were in obtaining chemicals from nature. You saw in outline how each of these steps (mining, separation, extraction, fabrication and assembly) is carried out for something made out of the metal zinc. You now need to learn in detail how we get from the ore to the pure metal for zinc and for two other transition metals – iron and copper.

You also learned in Topic 2.2.2 the origin of the ores of these three metals, where they are mined in the world, the uses to which each metal is put, the world reserves of each and the amount mined each year. You know roughly how long we expect our supplies of each metal to last. In Topic 2.4.3, you also saw those factors which have to be taken into account when we decide where to put an iron and steel plant.

You know that, of the three metals, copper is the least reactive. Because of this, it is sometimes found in nature as the element itself, although this is rare. It is much more usual to find copper as one of its compounds – and this is how we find iron and zinc.

When we take a compound of a metal and carry out a chemical reaction to get the metal, this reaction must be a **reduction of the metal compound to the metal**. So, to carry out this change we must have a suitable reducing agent.

In Experiment 4.21 in the last section, you learned that carbon (in the form of charcoal) will reduce lead(II) oxide to lead. So carbon must be more reactive than lead. Perhaps then, carbon is more reactive than all the metals in the reactivity series, and will reduce a compound of all of them to the metal.

▶ EXPERIMENT 5.5

EXPERIMENT 5.5

Is there a limit to the metals which we can get from their ores by reduction with carbon?

Your teacher will show you this experiment

The following will be needed: gas-jar filled with carbon dioxide, tongs, about 5 cm of cleaned magnesium ribbon.

What to do

DO NOT LOOK DIRECTLY AT BURNING MAGNESIUM.
WEAR EYE PROTECTION THROUGHOUT THIS EXPERIMENT.

1   Fill a gas-jar with carbon dioxide.

2   Clean a piece of magnesium ribbon which is about 5 cm long.

3   Hold one end of it with the tongs, and set it alight in a Bunsen burner flame. As quickly as you can, plunge the burning magnesium into the carbon dioxide.

4   When the magnesium stops burning, look at what is left in the gas-jar. What different colours can be seen in what remains?
    Discuss what you have seen, and try to decide what has happened. Write down what you have decided and why you have decided it.

What happened

You should have been able to see that the magnesium kept on burning in the carbon dioxide, and that there was carbon (black) and magnesium oxide (white) left in the gas-jar after the reaction.

What we can decide

Magnesium is more reactive than carbon, because it reduces carbon dioxide to carbon.

$$2Mg(s) + CO_2(g) \rightarrow 2MgO(s) + C(s)$$

So we can say that carbon would not be reactive enough to reduce magnesium oxide to magnesium.

In other words, we know that carbon is above lead but below magnesium in the reactivity series of metals. In fact, its true position is between aluminium and zinc.

Metal reactivity series
  sodium
  calcium
  magnesium
  aluminium
      ←——— carbon
  zinc
  iron
  lead
      ←——— hydrogen
  copper
  silver
  gold

So we can use carbon to get all those metals below aluminium from their ores, including iron, zinc and copper. For aluminium and the other reactive metals, we will have to find another method (as you will see shortly).

Iron (and steel)

Mining

The main ores of iron are:
  haematite, Fe_2O_3 (USA, Australia, USSR)
  magnetite, Fe_3O_4 (Sweden, Canada, USA)
  siderite, $FeCO_3$ (UK)

Separation

Crude separation is carried out at the point of mining, but this does not have to be complete since iron is separated from the impurities mined with it during the extraction stage.

Extraction

Whichever ore is being used, it is first roasted in air to give iron(III) oxide, Fe_2O_3. We then extract iron from the iron(III) oxide in a blast furnace.

There are really two processes which take place at the same time in the blast furnace – separation of iron(III) oxide from impurities, and extraction of iron from iron(III) oxide. We mix the iron(III) oxide with limestone (calcium carbonate), which is responsible for the separation and with coke (carbon) which is responsible for the extraction, and add the mixture to the top of the blast furnace. The other chemical involved is oxygen, which is pre-heated and then blown in to the bottom of the furnace as blasts (hence the name blast furnace) of air. The air inlets are called TUYERES.

The blast furnace is itself made of steel, lined on the inside with firebrick (because of the very high temperatures which are reached). It is usually about 30 m tall, and 8 m in diameter at the widest point.

Fig. 5.5 *These blast furnaces are at the British Steel Corporation's South Teesside works*

We must start to look at the chemical reactions which happen in the blast furnace by starting at the bottom of the furnace. It is here, where the temperature is highest, that oxygen from the air blown in via the air vents reacts with coke. The product of this exothermic reaction is carbon monoxide, which passes up through the furnace. The heat which is also produced helps to maintain the temperature of the furnace. Higher up, where the temperature is about 1000°C, the carbon monoxide meets iron(III) oxide and reduces it to iron. At this high temperature, iron is molten. So it runs down inside the furnace. Carbon dioxide passes up and out of the top of the furnace. (Equations 1 and 2).

At the same time that this is happening, the limestone (calcium carbonate) splits up because of the heat, making calcium oxide and carbon dioxide (which passes up and out of the furnace). The main impurity in the iron(III) oxide is silica (SiO_2). This reacts with calcium oxide, making the salt calcium silicate ($CaSiO_3$). Calcium oxide is a basic oxide and silica is an acidic oxide. (Find the element silicon, Si, in the Periodic Table. Why would you expect silica to

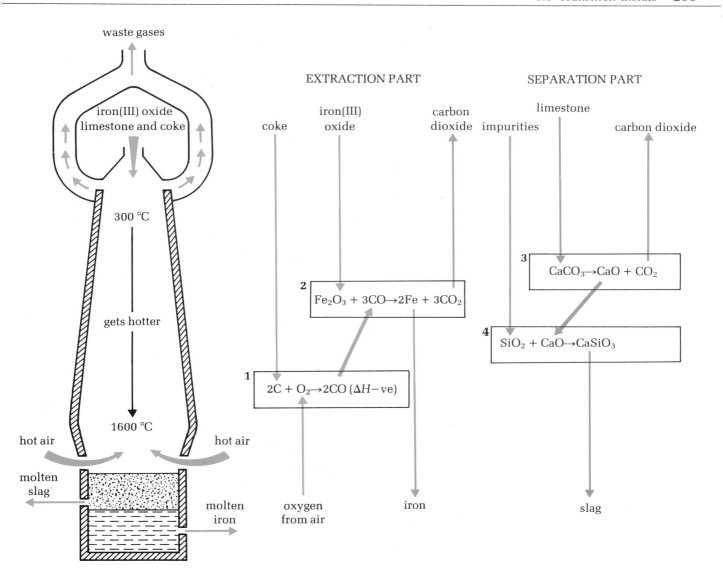

Fig. 5.6

be an acidic oxide?) Again because of the temperature, the calcium silicate (which we call SLAG) is also molten, and runs down inside the furnace. Molten slag is less dense than molten iron, and so it floats on the surface. This protects the molten iron from the oxygen in the air being blown into the furnace (what would happen if the two could meet together?).

Both the slag and the molten iron are run off from the bottom of the furnace. Slag is used for making roads. The iron is run into moulds about 1 metre long called PIGS. 'Pig iron' (which is sometimes called 'cast iron') is impure iron, containing about 4% of carbon and sulphur. 'Pig iron' is very brittle.

We can remove the carbon and sulphur impurities by reacting 'pig iron' with more iron(III) oxide. The oxygen in the oxide converts carbon to carbon dioxide, and sulphur to sulphur dioxide. Since both

are gases, they escape and the iron is purified. We call this pure form of iron WROUGHT IRON. It is tougher than 'pig iron' and can be hammered into shape and welded.

Steel

We start making steel by taking 'pig iron' from a blast furnace, and purifying it in much the same way as when we make wrought iron. Instead of adding iron(III) oxide, however, this is done by blowing a stream of air through molten 'pig iron' (in a Bessemer converter), or by using pure oxygen (in the Linz–Donawitz process). The advantage of using pure oxygen is that there is no nitrogen left in the iron – this can make it brittle.

Once the iron is pure, small amounts of impurities (usually between 0.5% and 1.0% carbon) are added in a precise, controlled way. This produces steel, which is harder and stronger than wrought iron. If we heat steel and suddenly cool it, we can make it even tougher. We call this process TEMPERING. Tempered steel is particularly good for making very sharp edges, like razor blades. If other impurities are added to steel, we can make specialist steels with particular properties. Some examples of impurities which are added are:

chromium – stainless steel
tungsten – very hard edges for drills and cutting
instruments

Rusting of iron

Although, like other transition metals, iron is fairly unreactive, one reaction which it does have is the process of RUSTING. Millions of pounds are lost each year because objects made of iron (bridges, cars, railway track for example) are attacked by rust. Rusting is a complicated chemical process, but it is possible to do experiments which show that for it to happen there must be
1. water,
2. oxygen,
3. carbon dioxide, or some other substance which forms ions when it dissolves in water (e.g. salt),
in contact with iron. The product, rust, has the chemical formula $Fe_2O_3 . xH_2O$ where x can vary. The simplest way to prevent rusting is to protect the surface of the iron. We often do this by GALVANISING or TIN-PLATING the iron.

Galvanising means coating with zinc. We do this by spraying, electrolysis or by dipping in molten zinc. Zinc develops a protective layer of zinc oxide when it is exposed to air, and this stops further attack.

Tin-plating is a similar process to galvanising. We pass the iron sheet through molten tin (which contains some zinc chloride to lower its melting point). Tin does not react with anything in the air, and so it protects the iron.

Other reactions of iron

If we take finely divided iron and heat it in air, we get the magnetic oxide of iron, called tri-iron tetroxide. The equation is:

$$3Fe(s) + 2O_2(g) \xrightarrow{\text{heat}} Fe_3O_4(s)$$
$$\text{tri-iron tetroxide}$$

You know that iron is above hydrogen in the reactivity series of metals, and you saw in Section 4, Topic 4.1.3, that it reacts with dilute acids to give the iron(II) salt and hydrogen (the reaction with dilute nitric acid is very complicated, however).

Question

Write balanced equations for the reaction between iron and

(a) dilute hydrochloric acid;
(b) dilute sulphuric acid.

So, iron is above hydrogen in the reactivity series. But is it reactive enough to liberate hydrogen from water?

▶ EXPERIMENT 5.6

Copper and zinc

You have already seen the different steps which we have to take to get zinc from zinc ore. The steps are almost similar for copper.

Zinc

The main ore of zinc is zinc sulphide, ZnS, which we call zinc blende. After it has been mined, we separate it from impurities by froth flotation. Then we roast it in air to obtain zinc oxide:

$$2ZnS(s) + 3O_2(g) \rightarrow 2ZnO(s) + 2SO_2(g)$$

We then heat the zinc oxide with coke (carbon) in a furnace to get impure zinc:

$$ZnO(s) + C(s) \rightarrow Zn(l) + CO(g)$$

We can make pure zinc by electrolysis.

Copper

The main ore of copper is copper pyrites, $CuFeS_2$. Like zinc blende, it is separated from impurities by froth flotation. Because of the iron which is present in the ore, the extraction of copper is more

Fig. 5.7 *This copper mine is in Australia*

EXPERIMENT 5.6
Will iron react with water?

> **Your teacher will show you this experiment**

The following will be needed: iron filings, mineral wool, hard-glass test-tube fitted with bung and delivery tube, small trough, 3 test-tubes and bungs.

What to do

PUPILS MUST WEAR THEIR SAFETY SPECTACLES.

1   Place some mineral wool loosely in the bottom of a hard-glass test-tubes, and soak this thoroughly with water.

2   Pass steam generated from the damp mineral wool over heated iron filings as shown. Do not heat the mineral wool directly.

3   Collect the gas produced over water, and seal in test-tubes with bungs.

4   Test each of three test-tubes for the presence of hydrogen.

What happened

You should have been able to see from the results of your teacher's experiment that red hot iron will decompose steam, giving hydrogen.

What we can decide

We can decide that iron is reactive enough to liberate hydrogen from water, but only under extreme conditions (the iron must be red hot, and the water must be in the form of steam).
The equation for this reaction is:

$$3Fe(s) + 4H_2O(g) \xrightarrow{\text{heat}} Fe_3O_4(s) + 4H_2(g)$$
$$\text{tri-iron tetroxide}$$

So, again, the product of the reaction is the magnetic oxide of iron, tri-iron tetroxide.

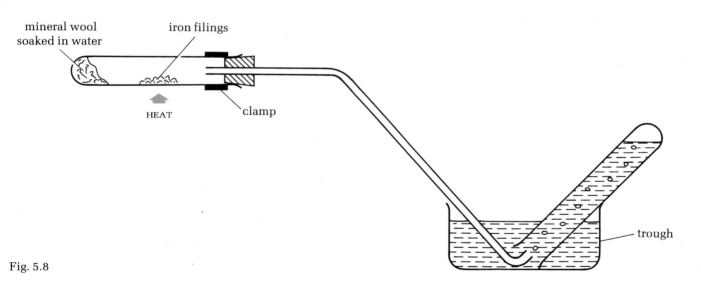

Fig. 5.8

complicated than for zinc. First, we roast the ore in air, to get copper(I) sulphide:

$$2CuFeS_2(s) + 4O_2(g) \rightarrow Cu_2S(s) + 3SO_2(g) + 2FeO(s)$$

We then add sand (silica) to convert the iron(II) oxide to a molten slag of iron(II) silicate, which we can pour away. Because copper is less reactive than zinc, we do not have to get the oxide and then reduce this with carbon. Instead, because copper will not react so

easily with oxygen, we can go straight from the sulphide to the metal:

$$Cu_2S(s) + O_2(g) \rightarrow 2Cu(l) + SO_2(g)$$

In order to get reasonably pure copper, all we have to do is to control the amount of oxygen which is present in the reaction – we use just enough to make the sulphur dioxide, without leaving any to react with the copper.

As with zinc, we can make the pure metal by using electrolysis. In the case of copper, we make the anode a lump of impure copper, the cathode pure copper, and the electrolyte a copper salt (see Fig. 4.54 on p. 242).

Fig. 5.9 *Copper is being purified in these electrolysis cells*

Question

Look back at Section 2 (Topic 2.4.3) where you learnt the different things which must be taken into account when we decide where to put a particular chemical plant. From what you have learned about how we get zinc and copper from their ores, make a list, for each metal separately, of the factors which you think are important in making this decision as far as their separation, extraction and purification are concerned. For each factor which you write down, say briefly why you think it is important.

You know that copper is not reactive enough to liberate hydrogen from dilute hydrochloric acid or dilute sulphuric acid. However it will react with hot concentrated sulphuric acid and with nitric acid. (These are **oxidising** agents. They oxidise copper atoms to copper(II) ions. You will see that, as no hydrogen is liberated in these reactions.)

With hot concentrated sulphuric acid, the products of the reaction are copper(II) sulphate, water, and sulphur dioxide:

$$\text{hot concentrated}$$
$$Cu(s) + 2H_2SO_4(aq) \rightarrow CuSO_4(aq) + 2H_2O(l) + SO_2(g)$$

If the nitric acid is dilute, we get a colourless gas, nitrogen oxide:

$$\text{dilute}$$
$$3Cu(s) + 8HNO_3(aq)$$

$$\text{colourless}$$
$$\longrightarrow 3Cu(NO_3)_2(aq) + 4H_2O(l) + 2NO(g)$$
$$\text{nitrogen oxide}$$

On the other hand, if we use concentrated nitric acid, we get a brown gas, nitrogen dioxide:

$$\text{brown}$$
$$Cu(s) + 4HNO_3(aq) \rightarrow Cu(NO_3)_2(aq) + 2H_2O(l) + 2NO_2(g)$$
$$\text{nitrogen dioxide}$$

UNIT 5.1
Summary and learning

1   You should remember the chemical behaviour and physical behaviour which is typical of all metals.

2   As well as having the properties of other metals, transition metals
(a) are generally less reactive;
(b) are generally stronger physically;
(c) can form more than one ion; different ions containing the same transition metal have different colours;
(d) can form complex ions with ligand molecules;
(e) often act as catalysts for chemical reactions.

3   You should be able to explain what we mean by a transition metal.

4   You should remember the details of how we get iron, copper and zinc from their ores, and how these metals react.

5   You should remember how wrought iron and steel are made, and how iron can be protected from rusting.

6   You have learnt the meaning of these words:

complex ion	pig iron
haemoglobin	wrought iron
oxyhaemoglobin	tempering
catalyst	rusting
tuyeres	galvanising
slag	tin-plating

UNIT 5.2 *Some important non-transition metals*

Transition metals are not the only metals which are important. In this unit you will study four metals which are not transition metals.

Three of these metals – sodium, magnesium and aluminium – are all more reactive than carbon. So we cannot get them from their ores by reduction with coke. Instead, we have to use electrolysis. The fourth metal is lead, which we can get from its ore in a similar way to the method which we use for zinc.

TOPIC 5.2.1

Sodium

You know that sodium is a very reactive metal. It is not found as the metal itself, but always as compounds of the element. Sodium compounds are very important, and so this is one of the reasons sodium metal is important. We can make sodium compounds from sodium metal. Another use for sodium is as a coolant in nuclear reactors (you learned this in Section 3, Topic 3.2.3) and the characteristic yellow colour which many street lights have is also due to sodium vapour. You know that lead is added to petrol. The compound of lead which we use is tetraethyl lead, and we make it using sodium metal. You learned in Section 2 that when we mix two or more metals together, we make something which we call an alloy. We can make an alloy of sodium and lead. If we react this with a compound called chloroethane, we make tetraethyl lead:

$$Pb(s) + 4Na(s) + 4C_2H_5Cl(g) \rightarrow 4NaCl(s) + Pb(C_2H_5)_4(l)$$

There are many different compounds of sodium which we can dig out of the ground, and we find them in many places on the surface of the Earth. The most common, however, is common salt, sodium chloride. We give the name ROCK SALT to sodium chloride when we find it as a mineral. There are a number of places where it is found, but one of the most important sources of rock salt is in Cheshire in England.

We get sodium metal from sodium chloride by melting it and then electrolysing it. The melting point of sodium chloride is about 800°C. So we have to use a lot of energy to reach this temperature, and this costs a lot of money. We can cut this down by finding a way to get sodium chloride to melt at a lower temperature. If we mix sodium chloride and calcium chloride together, the mixture melts at about 600°C. This cuts down the cost of the whole process (which is called the Downs Process, after the man who invented it).

The anode in the electrolysis cell is made of graphite (in the form of a cylinder). The cathode is a circle of steel around the anode. Sodium is produced at the cathode, and chlorine at the anode. At 600°C, these two would react together very violently (giving sodium chloride again) if they came into contact. So the Downs Cell contains a steel gauze around the anode which keeps them apart. If we cut a slice vertically through a Downs Cell, it would look something like Fig. 5.11.

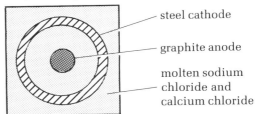

Fig. 5.10 *The Downs Cell (from above)*

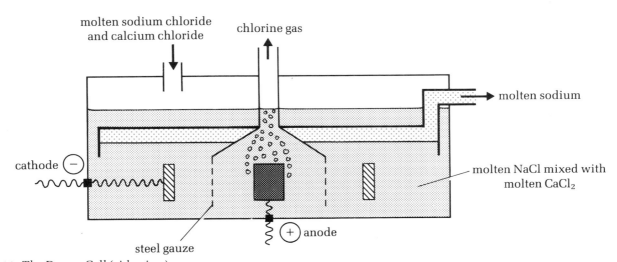

Fig. 5.11 *The Downs Cell (side view)*

	At the cathode	At the anode
Ions present:	$Na^+(l)$, $Ca^{2+}(l)$ $\underline{Na^+(l)\ preferred}$	$Cl^-(l)$
Electrode-equation:	$Na^+(l) + e^- \rightarrow Na(l)$	$2Cl^- \rightarrow Cl_2(g) + 2e^-$
Balanced electrode-equations:	$2Na^+(l) + 2e^- \rightarrow 2Na(l)$	$2Cl^- \rightarrow Cl_2(g) + 2e^-$

Sodium metal is produced at the cathode, and chlorine gas is produced at the anode.

You learned in Section 3 (Experiment 3.1) how sodium reacts with air, water and chlorine. You also saw in the same topic how the chemical behaviour of sodium is linked to the structure of the sodium atom.

PROJECT 5.1

(a) Make a list of all the things which you would have to take into account if you had to decide where to set up a plant to make sodium metal.

(b) From what you know about the structure of the sodium atom, and where sodium is found in the Periodic Table, explain each of the following in a few sentences:

    (i) why sodium forms the Na^+ cation when it reacts (and, therefore, why all its compounds are ionic);

    (ii) why sodium is so reactive.

(c) You know how to write balanced equations, starting from general word-equations. From what you have learnt about the reactions of sodium, write balanced equations (showing the sign of $\triangle H$), and draw a potential energy diagram for

    (i) the reaction of sodium with oxygen in the air
       (metal + oxygen → metal oxide)

    (ii) the reaction of sodium with water
       (metal + water → metal hydroxide
            + hydrogen)

    (iii) the reaction of sodium with chlorine
       (metal + non-metal → salt)

TOPIC 5.2.2

Magnesium

You have come across magnesium and its reactions in a number of places. It is important because we can make several different alloys between magnesium and aluminium. These alloys are extremely light, but very strong, and so they are used in making aeroplanes and spacecraft. Another use for magnesium is in the manufacture of flares and fireworks.

Fig. 5.12 *The brilliant light is caused by burning magnesium*

Our main source of magnesium is sea-water, which contains a high concentration of $Mg^{2+}(aq)$ ions. Since the main anion in sea-water is the $Cl^-(aq)$ ion, it is as if sea-water contains a lot of dissolved magnesium chloride. We can obtain magnesium from sea-water by precipitating out magnesium hydroxide:

$$Mg^{2+}(aq) + 2OH^-(aq) \rightarrow Mg(OH)_2(s)$$

So, after alkali has been added, we filter off the magnesium hydroxide and then heat it to 1600°C to obtain magnesium oxide:

$$Mg(OH)_2(s) \xrightarrow{1600°C} MgO(s) + H_2O(g)$$

If we heat magnesium oxide with coke in a stream of chlorine, we get magnesium chloride as one of the products:

$$MgO(s) + C(s) + Cl_2(g) \xrightarrow{heat} MgCl_2(l) + CO(g)$$

The other product of the reaction is the gas carbon monoxide, which escapes.

The melting point of pure magnesium chloride is even higher than that of pure sodium chloride. However, we can obtain a mixture which melts at a lower temperature (in this case, about 750°C) than either pure substance, by adding sodium chloride to the magnesium chloride. We can then get magnesium metal by electrolysis, using an arrangement which is similar to the Downs Cell (Fig. 5.13).

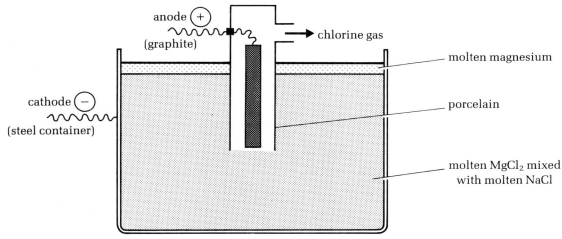

Fig. 5.13 *Electrolysis cell for magnesium*

	At the cathode	**At the anode**
Ions present:	$Mg^{2+}(l)$ $Mg^{2+}(l)$ preferred	$Cl^-(l)$
Electrode-equation:	$Mg^{2+}(l) + 2e^- \rightarrow Mg(l)$	$2Cl^-(l) \rightarrow Cl_2(g) + 2e^-$
Balanced electrode-equations:	$Mg^{2+}(l) + 2e^- \rightarrow Mg(l)$	$2Cl^-(l) \rightarrow Cl_2(g) + 2e^-$

Magnesium metal is produced at the cathode, and chlorine gas is produced at the anode.

The chlorine made at the anode is sold to reduce the cost of the process.

PROJECT 5.2

(a) In the same way that you did for sodium, make a list of the things which have to be considered when we decide where to set up a plant to make magnesium metal.

(b) Explain why magnesium forms the Mg^{2+} ion when it reacts, from what you know about the arrangement of electrons in a magnesium atom.

(c) From what you learned in Section 3, Topic 3.1.3 about the reactions of magnesium, write balanced equations for
  (i) the reaction of magnesium with oxygen in the air (given the sign of $\triangle H$);
  (ii) the reaction of magnesium with water (steam);
  (iii) the reaction of magnesium with dilute hydrochloric acid.

TOPIC 5.2.3

Aluminium

Aluminium is the most plentiful metal in the Earth's crust. Unfortunately, we cannot get at most of it because it is 'locked up' in materials such as clay, where it is combined with other elements. Nobody has yet come up with a way of getting aluminium metal from clay in an inexpensive way. If they did, then there would be many uses to which the aluminium could be put. You have already seen that we can make useful alloys between magnesium and aluminium, and aluminium on its own is used for making pots and pans for cooking, overhead electrical cables, aluminium paint, food packaging and for building. Aluminium is light, strong, does not corrode, and conducts heat and electricity well.

You learned about the places in the world where we mine aluminium ores, where these ores come from, the size of world reserves and the rate at which they are being used up, in Unit 2.2. We can obtain aluminium metal from a mineral called BAUXITE ($Al_2O_3 \cdot 2H_2O$). You should remember that most of the world's supplies of this mineral come from tropical regions.

Because bauxite deposits have come into being as a result of weathering (look back at p. 70 to remind yourself what 'weathering' means), they nearly always lie close to the surface, so we usually mine them by open-cast methods. When we dig up bauxite in this way, we also dig up impurities such as iron compounds. These have to be removed before we electrolyse the bauxite to obtain aluminium. Otherwise, iron would be deposited along with aluminium, making the product impure and useless for most purposes. You learned in Section 3 (Topic 3.1.3) that aluminium oxide is amphoteric. This means that it will dissolve in strong alkalki, whereas oxides of metals such as iron will not (because they are basic oxides). We use this fact to separate aluminium oxide (in the form of the soluble salt, sodium aluminate) from oxides of iron and other metals. These are left behind in an alkaline red slurry, which is a waste-product of the process and very difficult to get rid of. Often, it is simply pumped into the sea, which must be deep at the point where this happens, or else it is left to settle in huge lakes (so there must be cheap land available, because we need a large area to do this in).

We dissolve purified bauxite in molten cryolite (which is another compound containing aluminium), at about 100°C. If we then electrolyse this solution, the bauxite is used up, but the cryolite is not. So we simply add more purified bauxite from time to time. The electrolysis cell looks like Fig. 5.14.

Ions present:	**At the cathode**	**At the anode**
	$Al^{3+}(l)$, $Na^+(l)$	$O^{2-}(l)$, $AlF_6^{3-}(l)$
	$Al^{3+}(l)$ preferred	$O^{2-}(l)$ preferred
Electrode-equation:	$Al^{3+}(l) + 3e^-$ $\rightarrow Al(l)$	$2O^{2+}(l)$ $\rightarrow O_2(g) + 4e^-$
Balanced electrode-equations:	$4Al^{3+}(l) + 12e^-$ $\rightarrow 4Al(l)$	$6O^{2-}(l)$ $\rightarrow 3O_2(g) + 12e^-$

Aluminium metal is produced at the cathode, and oxygen gas is produced at the anode.

Molten sodium and magnesium are less dense than the electrolyte from which they were obtained. Aluminium is more dense, and so it sinks to the bottom of the cell, where it is run off. The other product of the electrolysis is oxygen. At 1000°C it reacts with the carbon anodes, forming carbon dioxide (which is another waste-product of the process). The anodes get worn away gradually and have to be replaced. So that the electrolysis does not have to be interrupted to do this, we use a row of separate carbon anodes which can be changed one at a time, as needed. This, of course, adds to the cost of the process.

However, by far the most expensive aspect of the extraction of aluminium from bauxite is the cost of the electricity needed. You learnt how to relate the amount of electricity used to the mass of a chemical deposited, at the end of Section 4. Since we need 3 moles of electrons to deposit 1 mole of aluminium, the amount of electricity used up in obtaining large amounts of aluminium is much more than for sodium, for example. The electrolysis cell runs at about 6 volts, and this means that it uses up about 16 000 kilowatt hours of electricity (enough to keep 16 000 single-bar electric fires running for an hour) to produce 1 tonne of aluminium. So it is important that the electrolysis stage of the extraction of aluminium takes place somewhere near a cheap source of electricity (for instance, from hydro-electric schemes). The needs of both the purification stage and electrolysis stage are difficult to meet in the same place, and so they are often carried out many thousands of miles apart. Of course, this also adds to the cost of the process, because of the cost of moving the purified ore.

▶ PROJECT 5.3

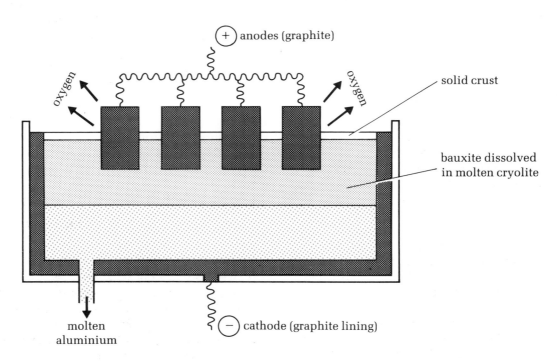

Fig. 5.14 *Electrolysis cell for aluminium*

PROJECT 5.3

(a) In the same way that you did for sodium and magnesium, make a list of the things which have to be considered when we decide where to set up a plant to make aluminium metal. Do this separately:

   (i) for the purification stage, and
   (ii) for the electrolysis stage.

(b) Explain why aluminium forms the Al^{3+} ion, from what you know about the arrangement of electrons in an aluminium atom. Explain why aluminium shows some properties which we would expect of a non-metal, alongside its metallic properties.

(c) From what you learned in Section 3, Topic 3.1.3 about the reactions of aluminium, write balanced equations for:

   (i) the reaction of aluminium with oxygen in the air;
   (ii) the reaction of aluminium with water (steam);
   (iii) the reaction of aluminium with dilute hydrochloric acid;
   (iv) the reaction of aluminium with dilute sodium hydroxide solution (the formula of sodium aluminate is $Na_3Al(OH)_6$. You will need water on the reactants side of the equation).

(d) Explain why the aluminium which we use in everyday life does not react with air or water (and therefore why it does not corrode away).

TOPIC 5.2.4

Lead

You learnt some of the uses of lead in Section 2 (Unit 2.2). Some others are in the production of solder (used for making electrical connections; solder is an alloy of lead and tin in the ratio 1 part of lead to 2 parts of tin), for making covers for underground cables, for making water pipes and gas pipes, and for making weather-proof seals on roofs and gutterings. The Romans knew about lead, and used it for making water-pipes (the Latin for lead is 'plumbum' – and this is where we get the symbol Pb and the word 'plumber'). You learned about the problem of lead pollution of the air in Section 2, Topic 2.3.1.

You also know from what you learnt in Unit 2.2 where we mine lead ores, where these ores come from, the size of world reserves and the rate at which they are being used up. The most important ore of lead is called GALENA and it is the compound lead sulphide, PbS.

We get lead from galena in much the same way as we get zinc from zinc blende. The first stage is to separate the mined ore from impurities, by froth flotation. The galena is then roasted with an excess of air, to give lead(II) oxide.

$$2PbS(s) + 3O_2(g) \rightarrow 2PbO(s) + 2SO_2(g)$$

We then use a small blast furnace to reduce lead(II) oxide to lead:

$$PbO(s) + C(s) \rightarrow Pb(s) + CO(g)$$

The molten lead is tapped off from the blast furnace in the same way as is used for iron.

You know that lead is not reactive enough to liberate hydrogen from dilute hydrochloric or sulphuric acids, or from water. However, like copper, it will react with oxidising acids. With hot concentrated sulphuric acid the reaction is:

$$\overset{\text{hot conc.}}{Pb(s) + 2H_2SO_4(aq)} \rightarrow PbSO_4(s) + 2H_2O(l) + SO_2(g)$$

Whether we use dilute or concentrated nitric acid, the product of the reaction with lead is always the colourless gas nitrogen oxide:

$$\overset{\text{dil./conc.}}{3Pb(s) + 8HNO_3(aq)}$$
$$\longrightarrow 3Pb(NO_3)_2(aq) + 4H_2O(l) + 2\overset{\text{colourless}}{\underset{\text{oxide}}{\underset{\text{nitrogen}}{NO(g)}}}$$

Again like copper, lead will react with the oxygen in the air if we heat it strongly. The product is a yellow solid called massicot (lead(II) oxide):

$$2Pb(s) + O_2(g) \overset{\text{heat}}{\longrightarrow} \overset{\text{yellow}}{\underset{\text{massicot}}{2PbO(s)}}$$

PROJECT 5.4

(a) Make a list of the things which have to be considered when we decide where to set up a plant to make lead from lead ore.

(b) Although lead is not a transition element, it is still fairly unreactive. Try to explain why this is, in terms of the position of lead in the Periodic Table (read through Topic 3.1.3 again before you do this). It may help to know that tin (symbol Sn) is also an unreactive metal.

UNIT 5.2
Summary and learning

1   For each of the metals studied (sodium, magnesium, aluminium and lead) you should remember:
(a) why it is important;
(b) where its ore occurs, and what that ore is;
(c) how we obtain the metal from its ore.

2   For each metal, you should be able to
(a) explain how it reacts in terms of its electronic structure;
(b) write balanced equations for its reaction with
   (i) the oxygen in the air (and with other non-metals);
   (ii) water;
   (iii) acids;
(c) list those things which have to be considered when we decide where to set up a plant to extract it from its core.

3   You have learnt the meaning of these words:

rock salt
bauxite
galena

UNIT 5.3   Compounds of metals

You have learned about important transition metals and non-transition metals. But it is not just metals which are important in providing us with the chemicals and products which we use in everyday life. There are two particularly important compounds of sodium, sodium carbonate and sodium hydroxide. We can also study the non-metal chlorine when we learn about sodium hydroxide, because we make both of them at the same time.

TOPIC 5.3.1

Sodium carbonate, sodium hydroxide (and chlorine)

Sodium carbonate

Sodium carbonate is important because we use it to make so many other things. It is used in huge quantities to make glass and glass fibre, and to make soap and other chemicals. Sodium carbonate is used to make textiles and dyes. It is used in the food and drink industry and in making a wide range of other chemical products. About 25 million tonnes of it are used each year in the world.

   The more expensive it is to get sodium carbonate, the more expensive will be all the things which we make from it. So we have to find the cheapest possible method. The best way of doing this is to start from chemicals which are cheap and plentiful. Sodium chloride (BRINE) and calcium carbonate (LIMESTONE) meet both of these criteria. But there is a simple obstacle to us reacting them together to make sodium carbonate – calcium carbonate is insoluble. If we put

Fig. 5.15 *Where most sodium carbonate ends up!*

the two chemicals together – nothing happens.
   It was not until 1864 that a man called Ernest Solvay (who lived in Belgium) came up with a way of using sodium chloride and calcium carbonate to make sodium carbonate. He did this by getting them to react together **indirectly**, using the gas ammonia.
   The overall reaction which happens during the Solvay Process is:

$$CaCO_3 + 2NaCl \rightarrow CaCl_2 + Na_2CO_3$$

However, calcium carbonate and sodium chloride never come into contact. The calcium carbonate is taken and heated, to make calcium oxide (QUICKLIME) and carbon dioxide:

$$CaCO_3(s) \rightarrow CaO(s) + CO_2(g) \qquad \text{STEP } 1$$

It is the carbon dioxide which is used to react with a SATURATED SOLUTION of ammonia in brine. (A saturated solution contains as much solute as will dissolve at a particular temperature. Since ammonia is very soluble, this is a lot of ammonia.) The carbon dioxide is forced up a tower (called a SOLVAY TOWER) down which the ammoniated brine is falling, passing over huge mushroom-shaped plates which give the solution a large surface area and make it take a long time to pass down the tower. This gives the carbon dioxide plenty of chance to react with the solution.

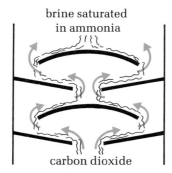

brine saturated in ammonia

carbon dioxide

Fig. 5.16 *Inside the Solvay tower*

The reaction which happens in the Solvay tower is:

$$NaCl(aq) + NH_3(aq) + H_2O(l) + CO_2(g)$$
$$\longrightarrow NaHCO_3(s) + NH_4Cl(aq) \qquad \text{STEP } 2$$

The lower part of the Solvay tower is cooled, and this makes the sodium hydrogencarbonate form as a precipitate. We filter off this precipitate and heat it. This gives us sodium carbonate:

$$2NaHCO_3(s) \rightarrow Na_2CO_3(s) + H_2O(g) + CO_2(g)$$
$$\text{STEP } 3$$

If you compare the equation for step 2 with that for step 3, you will see that 1 mole of carbon dioxide is used to make 1 mole of sodium hydrogencarbonate (step 2). So 2 moles of carbon dioxide are needed to make the 2 moles of sodium hydrogencarbonate which we use in step 3 to give us 1 mole of sodium carbonate and 1 mole of carbon dioxide. The carbon dioxide from step 3 is passed back into the Solvay tower, so we need 1 mole of carbon dioxide from another source (step 1) to make 1 mole of sodium carbonate. A simple way of putting this is that half the carbon dioxide passes round a **carbon dioxide cycle**, while the other half goes to making sodium carbonate.

So, we have got the product we were trying to make. But what about the other reactions which take place? We take the quicklime from step 1, and react it with an excess of water (we say that we SLAKE the lime):

$$CaO(s) + H_2O(l) \rightarrow Ca(OH)_2(aq) \qquad \text{STEP } 4$$

Then this calcium hydroxide is mixed with the ammonium chloride solution from step 2. This gives us all the ammonia we need for step 2.

$$2NH_4Cl(aq) + Ca(OH)_2(aq)$$
$$\xrightarrow{\text{heat}} CaCl_2(aq) + 2NH_3(g) + 2H_2O(l) \quad \text{STEP } 5$$

So, the ammonia gas also passes round a cycle, **the ammonia cycle**. Theoretically, none of it is used up, although small amounts escape and have to be replaced. The only by-product of the whole sequence of reactions is calcium chloride. We can represent the Solvay Process in a diagram (Fig. 5.17).

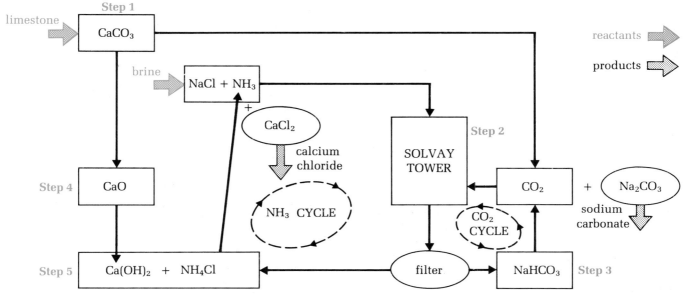

Fig. 5.17 *The Solvay Process*

If we take the five equations for steps 1–5, and 'add them up', we get the overall chemical change:

Step 1: $CaCO_3 \rightarrow CaO + CO_2$

Step 2: $2NH_3 + 2NaCl + 2H_2O + 2CO_2 \rightarrow$
$$\rightarrow 2NaHCO_3 + 2NH_4Cl$$

Step 3: $2NaHCO_3 \rightarrow Na_2CO_3 + H_2O + CO_2$

Step 4: $CaO + H_2O \rightarrow Ca(OH)_2$

Step 5: $2NH_4Cl + Ca(OH)_2 \rightarrow CaCl_2 + 2NH_3 + 2H_2O$

i.e. $CaCO_3 + 2NaCl \rightarrow Na_2CO_3 + CaCl_2$

The calcium chloride is sold to reduce the cost of making the sodium carbonate. We use calcium chloride in refrigerators, in concrete-making, and to help prevent erosion. Most of the sodium carbonate is transported in barges and tankers which can take up to 2000 tonnes at a time.

Like all industrial processes, the Solvay Process causes pollution. Pollution of the air comes from small amounts of ammonia gas which escape from the plant, and from sulphur dioxide gas which is made when we burn oil in the factory's power plant. There are two forms of water pollution – heat and chemicals. Water is used to cool the Solvay Tower, and we need about 50 m³ of water for every tonne of sodium carbonate which we make. We have to cool those large amounts of water down before they are returned to the river. The solutions which have passed through the chemical plant contain dissolved substances and tiny particles of solids in a SUSPENSION. If we let the suspension settle, we can take the solids out and return them to the mines where the original brine was obtained. This helps us to cut down the impact of the mining process. The main dissolved substance is calcium hydroxide, which we neutralise with dilute hydrochloric acid.

Plants which make sodium carbonate have to be sited close to sources of sodium chloride and calcium carbonate, and close to customers. This is particularly important because of the huge amounts of reactant and product chemicals which are involved, and which are very costly to transport. The plant should also be close to a navigable river (for transport of chemicals and for cooling water) and also where there are good canal, road and rail links.

Question

Figure 5.18 shows where one of ICI's plants which make sodium carbonate is situated (in Cheshire). Make a list of all the factors which you think were used to decide that the plant should be placed where it is.

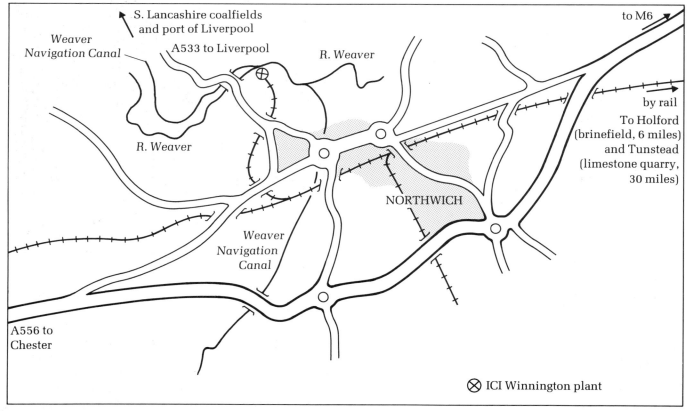

Fig. 5.18 *(courtesy ICI Mond Division)*

Sodium hydroxide

Sodium hydroxide, like sodium carbonate, is an important chemical because we can make a large number of other chemicals from it. If we react cold sodium hydroxide with chlorine, we get sodium hypochlorite, which is **bleach**:

$$2NaOH(aq) + Cl_2(g) \xrightarrow{\text{cold}} NaOCl(aq) + NaCl(aq) + H_2O(l)$$

If we warm the sodium hydroxide first, the product is sodium chlorate, which is a weedkiller:

$$6NaOH(aq) + 3Cl_2(g) \xrightarrow{\text{hot}} NaClO_3(aq) + 5NaCl(aq) + 3H_2O(l)$$

Obviously, both these chemicals are made in large amounts, starting from sodium hydroxide. We also use it to make RAYON (artificial silk), soaps and detergents, paper, in the purification of bauxite for making aluminium (see Topic 5.2.3) and for the many occasions in industry when we need to neutralise an acidic solution. About 30 million tonnes of sodium hydroxide are made each year in the world.

PROJECT 5.5

You know that, chemically, sodium hydroxide is an alkali. So its reactions are those of an alkali, which you have already met in a number of different places.

Use what you know to write balanced equations:

(a) in the full form, and
(b) in the form of ionic equations,
for the reactions of a solution of sodium hydroxide with each of the following.

1. dilute hydrochloric acid;
2. a solution of iron(II) sulphate;
3. a solution of iron(III) sulphate;
4. a solution of copper(II) sulphate;
5. aluminium metal (where have you seen this before?); the aluminate ion is $Al(OH)_6^{3-}$;
6. zinc metal: like aluminium, zinc forms amphoteric compounds; the formula of sodium zincate is $Na_2Zn(OH)_4$ and the zincate ion is $Zn(OH)_4^{2-}$;
7. chlorine (in the cold);
8. chlorine (hot solution).

Chlorine

Chlorine is an important element, because we can make a vast number of useful chemicals from it. We use it to make the chemical **vinyl chloride** (you will learn how we do this in Section 8), from which we make **polyvinyl chloride** (PVC, a plastic). We use PVC to make all kinds of plastic goods such as containers, electrical insulators, tubing, protective clothing, records and building materials.

Another chemical which we make using chlorine is called **propene oxide**. We use this to make a range of pharmaceutical chemicals (remember from Section 2 how important these are in the UK chemical industry), polyurethane plastics and car brake fluid.

We also use chlorine to make solvents (such as those used in paints and in dry-cleaning), 'chloroform' (trichloromethane), which was once used as an anaesthetic, 'carbon tetrachloride' (tetrachloromethane), chemicals used in refrigerators, gases used in aerosol cans, disinfectants and insecticides.

As with sodium hydroxide, about 30 million tonnes of chlorine are made in the world each year.

Fig. 5.19 *All these items are, or contain, chemicals which have been made using chlorine*

You know that chlorine is a non-metal, an oxidising agent and a member of the halogen group in the Periodic Table. You have come across it several times in earlier parts of this book. You know how to make it in the laboratory (Experiment 4.20, p. 226) and you know how it reacts with iron (p. 130), with hydrogen sulphide gas (p. 226) and with sodium hydroxide solution (see above). You can now see some more reactions of chlorine.

EXPERIMENT 5.7
More reactions of chlorine

> **Your teacher will show you a reaction of chlorine, and you will carry out others for yourself**

A   The following will be needed by your teacher: gas-jar full of chlorine, yellow (or white) phosphorus, deflagrating spoon.

B   You will need the following: chlorine generator, solution of sulphur dioxide in water, iron(II) chloride, barium chloride solution.

What to do

A   YOUR TEACHER WILL SHOW YOU THIS PART OF THE EXPERIMENT.
YOU MUST WEAR YOUR SAFETY SPECTACLES.

1   Take a gas-jar full of chlorine and place it in a prominent position in the fume-cupboard. Also in the fume-cupboard, cut a small pellet of white phosphorus from the body of the solid (under water, in a mortar). GREAT CARE IS ESSENTIAL, AS WHITE PHOSPHORUS GIVES OFF VERY POISONOUS FUMES, IS POISONOUS ITSELF, AND CAN EASILY BURST INTO FLAMES IN MOIST AIR.

2   Place the piece of phosphorus on a deflagrating spoon, and lower it into the gas-jar of chlorine.

B   YOU MAY CARRY OUT THIS PART OF THE EXPERIMENT FOR YOURSELF. TAKE GREAT CARE NOT TO BREATHE IN THE POISONOUS CHLORINE.

1   Make up a small amount of a solution of iron(II) chloride. To half of it, add a little sodium hydroxide solution. Take the other half to the fume-cupboard, and pass a stream of chlorine through it for a few seconds. Now add a little sodium hydroxide solution.

BARIUM CHLORIDE IS POISONOUS. TAKE CARE NOT TO TRANSFER ANY TO YOUR MOUTH. WASH YOUR HANDS AT THE END OF THE EXPERIMENT.

2   Take a little of the freshly prepared solution of sulphur dioxide in water which your teacher will have placed in a beaker in the fume-cupboard. Divide this into two parts, and then add a few drops of dilute hydrochloric acid and a few drops of barium chloride solution to the first half. Take the second half of the solution to the fume-cupboard, and pass a stream of chlorine through it for a few seconds. Now add a few drops of dilute hydrochloric acid, followed by a few drops of barium chloride solution.

3   **Discuss what you have seen, and what you think it means. Write down what you have decided, and why you have decided it.**

What happened

You should have been able to see the following.

1   The phosphorus burst into flames as soon as it met the chlorine. White smoke was produced.

2   When sodium hydroxide was added to a freshly prepared solution of iron(II) chloride, the product was a green gelatinous precipitate (iron(II) hydroxide). When this was repeated after chlorine had been passed through the solution, the product was a brown gelatinous precipitate.

3   When dilute hydrochloric acid and barium chloride solution were added to a freshly prepared solution of sulphur dioxide in water, no precipitate formed. When the same solutions were added to a solution of sulphur dioxide in water which had had chlorine passed through it, a white precipitate formed.

What we can decide

1   We can see that chlorine reacts with phosphorus exothermically. The product of the reaction is a mixture of the two gaseous chlorides of phosphorus – phosphorus trichloride (PCl_3) and phosphorus pentachloride (PCl_5).

2   You will remember from Section 1 the tests for Fe^{2+} ions and Fe^{3+} ions. Before chlorine was passed through the solution, Fe^{2+} ions were present. Afterwards, Fe^{3+} ions were present. So chlorine has oxidised Fe^{2+} ions to Fe^{3+} ions.

3   You will remember the test for sulphate ions. Before chlorine was passed through the solution of sulphurous acid (which contains sulphate ions, SO_3^{2-}), no sulphate ions were present. Afterwards, the solution contained sulphate ions, SO_4^{2-}. So chlorine has oxidised sulphite ions to sulphate ions.

PROJECT 5.6

Use what you know to write balanced equations

(a) in the full form, and
(b) in the form of ionic equations,
for the reactions of chlorine with the following.

1. Hydrogen sulphide (do not attempt to write an ionic equation).
2. Phosphorus. (Write two separate equa.ions. Would it be right to write an ionic equation? Remember what kind of elements are reacting, and what the nature of the compounds will be.)
3. Iron(II) chloride solution (in the ionic form, one of the products is the chloride ion, Cl^-).
4. A solution of sulphite ions (one of the products is hydrogen ions, H^+, and another is chloride ions, Cl^-).

The manufacture of sodium hydroxide and chlorine

We make sodium hydroxide and chlorine in the same process, starting from sodium chloride, by electrolysis. As you have seen, sodium hydroxide and chlorine react together. So we have to find a way of keeping the products of the electrolysis separate. A way of doing this was discovered as long ago as 1897, when the Castner–Kelner Company started making sodium hydroxide and chlorine at Runcorn, in Cheshire.

The modern process is very similar to that invented by Castner–Kelner. It involves using a flow of mercury as the cathode in the electrolysis. Sometimes we call the electrolysis cell a MERCURY-CATHODE cell.

The mercury-cathode cell is a long shallow trough. Along the bottom of the trough, there is a flow of mercury. Mercury is a liquid, but it is a metal and so it will allow electricity to pass easily. We connect it to the negative terminal of a power supply, and so it becomes a liquid cathode. Above the cathode is the electrolyte, a purified saturated solution of brine, which also flows continously through the cell. You

know that hydrogen would normally be discharged at the cathode when we electrolyse a solution of sodium chloride. However it is very difficult for hydrogen to form at a mercury surface, and so the sodium ions are discharged instead.

The anodes are a series of plates made out of titanium (a transition metal). These plates are fixed close to the mercury surface. Since the solution is a concentrated chloride, chloride ions are discharged at the anode, forming chlorine gas.

	At the cathode	**At the anode**
Ions present:	$Na^+(aq)$, $H^+(aq)$	$Cl^-(aq)$, $OH^-(aq)$
	$Na^+(aq)$ preferred at mercury surface	$Cl^-(aq)$ preferred, because conc.
Electrode-equation:	$Na^+(aq) + e^- \rightarrow Na(l)$	$2Cl^-(aq) \rightarrow Cl_2(g) + 2e^-$
Balanced electrode- equations:	$2Na^+(aq) + 2e^- \rightarrow 2Na(l)$	$2Cl^-(aq) \rightarrow Cl_2(g) + 2e^-$

Sodium is produced at the cathode (as an amalgam with mercury), and chlorine gas is produced at the anode.

Since sodium and chlorine are removed from the electrolyte, it becomes less concentrated as it passes through the cell. The reason for having a flow of brine is that its concentration is constantly renewed. As soon as the sodium forms at the cathode, it dissolves in the mercury, making an AMALGAM (a solution of another metal in mercury). Since the cathode also flows through the cell, pure mercury enters at one side and the amalgam leaves at the other. So in fact, no sodium hydroxide actually forms in the cell, and so there is no problem in keeping it separate from the chlorine gas produced at the anodes.

We react the sodium amalgam with water. It reacts as if it were itself sodium, and leaves behind mercury, which we use again:

$$2Na/Hg(l) + 2H_2O(l) \rightarrow 2NaOH(aq) + H_2(g) + 2Hg(l)$$

The amount of electricity which we need is very large. Each cell uses about 1800 kW (enough to keep 1800 single-bar electric fires burning) and a typical plant may have up to 100 cells, and uses the same amount of electricity as a large town.

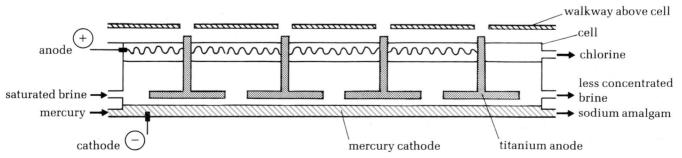

Fig. 5.20 *The mercury-cathode cell*

Fig. 5.21 *This room is full of mercury-cathode cells. The holes in the walkway are there so that the height of each titanium anode can be adjusted separately*

The hydrogen gas is compressed to form liquid hydrogen and sold to reduce the cost of running the plant. Chlorine is also compressed until it forms a liquid, to make transportation easier. For the same reason, the sodium hydroxide is concentrated before it is moved to the customer.

We place a plant which manufactures sodium hydroxide and chlorine:
(a) close to a source of brine (salt);
(b) close to an energy source (coal for converting into electricity, or hydro-electric power); and
(c) close to good transport facilities.

Question

How do you explain the presence of a sodium hydroxide/chlorine plant at Runcorn in Cheshire? Where do you think the energy supply is obtained?

TOPIC 5.3.2
How metal compounds behave chemically

It is important to be able to know, or to work out from what you know, how the different simple compounds of the metals in the reactivity series will behave.

In fact, you already know enough from the work you have done in earlier sections to be able to draw up a summary table of these properties.

1   In Section 1, you learnt that when a metal burns in air, the oxide produced is a base. If a base is soluble, it forms an alkali when it dissolves in water. You also learnt about the solubility of salts in Section 1.

2   In Section 3, you learnt some of the chemical

properties of the oxides, chlorides and hydrides of sodium, magnesium and aluminium.

3   In Section 4, you learnt that the salts of metals are harder to decompose by heat, the higher up in the reactivity series the metal is. You saw several examples of how the different salts of different metals behave when we heat them.

4   You know from the position of hydrogen (Section 4) and the position of carbon (Section 5) in the reactivity series which metal oxides are reduced by each of these elements. You also know which metals liberate hydrogen from dilute acids. In theory, lead will do this, but if we try this reaction we obtain no hydrogen gas. This is because it is difficult for hydrogen to form at a lead surface as well as at a mercury surface (see above).

Table 5.4 is a summary of what you know about the behaviour of metals and their simple compounds, in relation to the reactivity series of metals.

UNIT 5.3
Summary and learning

1   You should remember why sodium carbonate, sodium hydroxide and chlorine are important chemicals.

2   You should remember how we obtain each of these chemicals in industry, and you should know the factors which have to be taken into account in each case when we decide where to site the chemical plant.

3   You should remember how chlorine behaves
(a) as a member of the halogen group of elements (i.e. as a non-metal), and
(b) as an oxidising agent.

4   You should remember the way the simple compounds of metals behave chemically.

5   You have learnt the meaning of these words:

brine	slake
limestone	suspension
quicklime	rayon
saturated solution	mercury-cathode cell
Solvay tower	amalgam

	BEHAVIOUR OF METALS			BEHAVIOUR OF METAL COMPOUNDS			
Reaction with air	Reaction of oxide with water	Reaction of heated oxide	Reaction with dil. acids.	Nitrate	Sulphate	Carbonate	
Burn easily	Hydroxides soluble Oxides react with water to give solution of hydroxide (alkali)	REDUCED BY HYDROGEN ← REDUCED BY CARBON ←	React with dilute acids to give hydrogen	Soluble Heat decomposes to nitrate (+ oxygen)	Soluble Not affected by heat	Soluble Not affected by heat	Na
							Ca
	Hydroxides insoluble Oxides do not react with water			All soluble	All soluble except Ca and Pb	All insoluble	Mg
							Al
				Heat decomposes to oxide (+ nitrogen dioxide + oxygen)	Heat decomposes to oxide (+ sulphur dioxide + oxygen in most cases)	Heat decomposes to oxide (+ carbon dioxide)	Zn
							Fe
Form layer of oxide when heated strongly			Only react with dil. nitric acid (oxidising acid); no hydrogen				Pb
							Cu
NO REACTION	Hydroxides do not exist Oxides do not react with water		NO REACTION	Both soluble Heat decomposes to metal (+ nitrogen dioxide + oxygen)	Both soluble Heat decomposes to metal (+ sulphur trioxide + sulphur dioxide		Ag
							Au

Table 5.4

Chemical changes – 2

UNIT 6.1 *How can we alter the speed of a chemical change?*

In this section, we will look again at chemical changes. In this unit, you will learn more about the speed at which chemical reactions happen.

You know that some chemical changes happen more quickly than others. For instance, you learned in Section 1 (Topic 1.3.4) that, in general, the reactions of ionic compounds are more rapid than those of molecular compounds. But you also know many examples of fast and slow reactions. A good example of a rapid chemical change is an explosion. The chemicals react together so quickly (usually producing gases and heat), that the whole change is very destructive.

Fig. 6.1 *This explosion was caused by a very rapid chemical change*

Of course, we can harness the destructive power of rapid chemical reactions and put them to good use. You do this yourself every time you test for the gas hydrogen. If hydrogen is present in a test-tube which you hold to a flame, then it reacts very rapidly with oxygen in the air.

$$2H_2(g) + O_2(g) \xrightarrow{\text{rapidly}} 2H_2O(l)$$

The volume taken up by the chemicals suddenly drops (why?), and air rushes into the test-tube, making a 'pop' or 'squeak' which you can recognise.

Another example of how we can use controlled fast reactions is in the exploration of space. Space vehicles have to have a system of motors to power them and to allow them to manoeuvre. Since there is no oxygen in space, they cannot simply burn a fuel in the same way that, for instance, an aeroplane burns aviation-fuel in a jet engine. In space, we have to supply both of the reactants, which have to react together as soon as they meet. Liquid nitrogen dioxide is one of the chemicals which is used to power space vehicles.

THE FOLLOWING DEMONSTRATION SHOULD ONLY BE ATTEMPTED IF THE NECESSARY SAFETY EQUIPMENT IS AVAILABLE.

▶ DEMONSTRATION 6.1

By their very nature, chemical reactions which happen slowly are less dramatic, but they are equally important. Perhaps the best example is rusting, which you have already met.

Question

Write down three more chemical changes which happen quickly, and three more which happen slowly.

DEMONSTRATION 6.1
A rapid chemical reaction

Your teacher will demonstrate this reaction

The following will be needed: lead nitrate crystals, aniline, hard-glass test-tube fitted with bung and delivery tube to U-tube, salt/ice bath, long hard-glass 15 mm test-tube, Perspex safety screen and clamps, tall retort stand and clamps, teat-pipette.

What to do

1   Heat lead nitrate crystals and obtain liquid nitrogen dioxide using the apparatus shown in Fig. 6.2.

2   Continue heating, until 2–3 cm of liquid nitrogen dioxide has been collected.

3   Cool a long hard-glass 15 mm test-tube in the salt/ice bath, and then clamp it above the bench BEHIND A PERSPEX SAFETY SCREEN.

4   Immediately run the liquid nitrogen dioxide into the clamped tube. As quickly as possible, add 2–3 drops of aniline to the liquid nitrogen dioxide using a teat-pipette, and withdraw your arm. WEAR RUBBER GLOVES AND SAFETY SPECTACLES WHEN HANDLING ANILINE, AND AVOID BREATHING ITS VAPOUR.

5   **After the reaction is complete, ventilate the room thoroughly.**

What happens

You will see a long column of flame produced from the test-tube, showing that a rapid, exothermic reaction takes place.

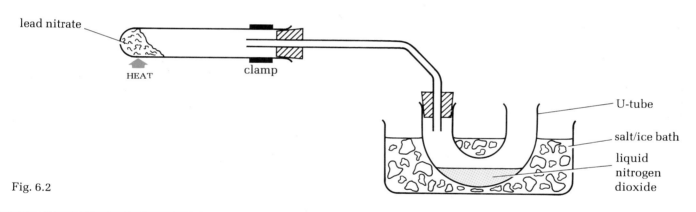

Fig. 6.2

So there are quick chemical reactions, and slow chemical reactions. But does a particular reaction have to have a particular speed? If so, then some chemical changes will be useless to us – because they will either be too slow for us to get reasonable amounts of the products in a reasonable amount of time, or because they will be too rapid for us to handle them safely.

Perhaps we ought to decide, before we go any further, just what we mean by 'the speed of reaction'. Since chemical reactions do not happen instantaneously (all at once), then while they happen the reactant chemicals are being used up, and the product chemicals are forming.

$$\boxed{\text{reactants}} \xrightarrow[\text{rate}]{\text{at a certain}} \boxed{\text{products}}$$

So we can measure the rate of a chemical reaction, by measuring the rate at which one of the reactant chemicals disappears, or by measuring the rate at which one of the product chemicals forms.

Think back to the experiment which you did in Section 4 (Experiment 4.13) which showed that chemicals react in fixed amounts. You added pieces of magnesium ribbon, 1 cm long, to a certain amount of dilute hydrochloric acid. You added one piece of magnesium ribbon at a time, and counted how many would react. Suppose you had **timed** the disappearance of each piece of magnesium. You would have been measuring the rate at which the reaction was happening ('1 cm of magnesium ribbon every *x* seconds'). As you went on adding pieces of magnesium ribbon, the time taken for each one to react got longer. So the reaction was getting slower. The rate of the reaction changed during the reaction. Why should this happen? The only thing that was changing as the reaction went on was the amount of hydrochloric acid which was left. The volume of the acid stayed the same, so it was actually the concentration of hydrochloric acid which got lower as time went on. So perhaps the reaction got slower because the concentration of the acid was getting less. If so, then perhaps the concentration of the reactant chemicals always has an effect on the rate of a chemical reaction.

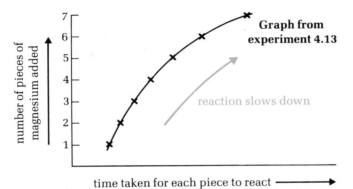

Fig. 6.3

In Experiment 4.13 you took a certain concentration of a chemical and you saw that the rate of the reaction got slower as it was used up and its concentration fell (if you had drawn a graph, it would have looked like Fig. 6.3). To test the idea that concentration might always affect the rate at which reactions happen, we ought to take the same chemical reaction and see how quickly it happens with different **starting** concentrations of one of the reactant chemicals.

TOPIC 6.1.1

The effect of the concentration of the reactant chemicals

The reaction which you can now investigate is one in which an element is produced by mixing two compounds in solution. The element is sulphur, and it is produced by mixing a solution of sodium thiosulphate with dilute hydrochloric acid. The reaction which takes place is:

sodium thiosulphate (aq) + dilute hydrochloric acid(aq)
$\longrightarrow$ sulphur(s) + sulphur dioxide(g)
+ sodium chloride(aq) + water(l)

$Na_2S_2O_3(aq) + 2HCl(aq)$
$\longrightarrow S(s) + SO_2(g) + 2NaCl(aq) + H_2O(l)$

EXPERIMENT 6.1
Could we make a 'chemical clock'?

You will need the following: boiling-tube, sodium thiosulphate solution, dilute hydrochloric acid.

What to do

1   Pour a solution of sodium thiosulphate into a boiling-tube until the depth of liquid is about 2 cm.

2   Add about 1 cm³ dilute hydrochloric acid.

3   Watch carefully what happens, until there is no further change.

4   From what you have seen, **discuss with the others in your group whether you think you could use this reaction to 'time' how quickly a reaction happens under different circumstances.** Would this be a fair test to compare the effect of different conditions on the speed of the reaction?

5   With your group, **design an experiment to test the effect of changing the concentration of the reactant chemicals on the rate of a reaction**.

What happened

You should have seen that the sulphur did not appear as soon as the two solutions were mixed together. It appears gradually, first as a milky coloration, and then as a yellow precipitate. It is obvious that the reaction is quite a slow one, because it takes some time to produce the sulphur. Since the solid sulphur is produced in a very finely divided state, it does not settle at the bottom of the test-tube but remains as a suspension in the solution. So the solution becomes harder and harder to see through as time goes on. Eventually, it becomes opaque (impossible to see through).

What we can decide

The amount of sulphur produced tells us how much reaction has taken place. The more reaction, the more sulphur. And the more sulphur, the more opaque the solution. If we carry out this reaction under different conditions, and time how long it takes for the solution to reach a certain degree of opaqueness, then we will be timing how long it takes for a certain amount of sulphur to be produced. So we have a way of investigating the effect of different conditions on the rate of the reaction. We have a kind of 'chemical clock'.

You can now carry out the experiment you have designed for yourself. Before you do, however, read through Experiment 6.2 to see whether you ought to make any alterations to your own experiment.

EXPERIMENT 6.2

The effect of the concentration of reactant chemicals on the speed of a reaction

You will need the following: stopclock (or watch that allows measurement in seconds), 100 cm³ beaker, 150 cm³ 0.2 M sodium thiosulphate solution, dilute hydrochloric acid, two 100 cm³ measuring cylinders.

What to do

1   Measure out 50 cm³ of the solution of sodium thiosulphate, using a measuring cylinder. Remember which measuring cylinder you have used, and be careful to use it only for measuring out sodium thiosulphate during the rest of the experiment.

2   Put the 50 cm³ of sodium thiosulphate solution in a 100 cm³ beaker, and place this on a piece of white paper on which you have drawn a thick black cross.

3   Use the other measuring cylinder to measure out 5 cm³ dilute hydrochloric acid. Have your stopclock or watch ready. At the same moment that you add the acid to the beaker which contains the 50 cm³ of sodium thiosulphate solution, start the stopclock or note the exact time on your watch.

4   Carefully swirl the contents of the beaker to make sure that they are mixed together. Watch the cross by looking down through the solution from above. When you can no longer see the cross, stop the clock or take the exact time from your watch. Write down the time taken for the cross to disappear.

5   Draw up a table like Table 6.1, and put in the time taken for the cross to disappear when you used 50 cm³ of sodium thiosulphate solution.

6   Wash out thoroughly the beaker you used in the first part of the experiment. Use the measuring cylinder which you have already used for sodium thiosulphate to measure out 40 cm³ of the solution and put it in the beaker. Now use the same measuring cylinder to add 10 cm³ of distilled water. You now have 50 cm³ of a solution of sodium thiosulphate as before, but this time it is less concentrated. Use the other measuring cylinder to add exactly 5 cm³ of dilute hydrochloric acid, and start timing straight away. Record in your table the time taken for the cross to disappear.

7   Repeat for the three other sodium thiosulphate solutions whose make-up is given in Table 6.1.

8   **Discuss your results with the others in your group.** Try to decide whether you can say anything about how the concentration of a reactant chemical alters the rate of a chemical reaction. **Write down what you have decided, and why you have decided it.**

What happened

You should have been able to see that the lower the concentration of the sodium thiosulphate solution, the slower the chemical reaction. It took longer each time for the same amount of product (sulphur) to be formed.

What we can decide

We can say that the speed of a chemical reaction is limited by the concentration of the reactant chemicals. The lower the concentration the slower the reaction. This means that the higher the concentration of the reactant chemicals, the faster the reaction will be. So one thing we can do to alter the speed of a chemical reaction is to alter the concentration of the chemicals.

Volume of sodium thiosulphate solution/cm³	Volume of distilled water/cm³	Concentration of reactant decreases	Time taken for cross to disappear/s
50	0		
40	10		
30	20		
20	30		
10	40		

Table 6.1

An increase in the concentration of reactant chemicals increases the speed of a chemical reaction.

A decrease in the concentration of reactant chemicals decreases the speed of a chemical reaction.

The effect of the temperature of the reactants

Think back to Experiment 4.13 again. When the reaction between dilute hydrochloric acid and magnesium became too slow, you speeded things up by heating the solution. So perhaps altering the temperature will always alter the speed of a chemical reaction. We can see whether or not this might be true by taking a closer look at the reaction between magnesium and dilute hydrochloric acid.

▶   EXPERIMENT 6.3

EXPERIMENT 6.3

The effect of the temperature of the reactant chemicals on the speed of a reaction

You will need the following: 250 cm³ beaker, 100 cm³ measuring cylinder, stirring thermometer, boiling-tube, stopclock (or watch that allows measurement in seconds), clean magnesium ribbon (cut into 1 cm lengths), dilute hydrochloric acid.

What to do

YOU MUST WEAR YOUR SAFETY SPECTACLES.

1   Use a measuring cylinder to measure out 20 cm³ of dilute hydrochloric acid, and put it in a boiling-tube. Measure the temperature of the acid using a thermometer, and record this in a table with these headings:

Temperature of acid/°C	Time taken for the 1 cm strip of magnesium ribbon to react/s

2   Have your stopclock or watch ready. At the same moment that you drop into the acid a strip of magnesium ribbon 1 cm long, start the stopclock or note the exact time on your watch. Measure the length of time that it takes for the magnesium to react completely, and add this to your table.

3   Empty the boiling-tube and clean it. Use the measuring cylinder to add 20 cm³ of fresh dilute hydrochloric acid, and put the boiling-tube in a 250 cm³ beaker which contains water. Put the beaker on a tripod and gauze.

4   Heat with the flame from a Bunsen burner, and stir the acid with the thermometer. When the temperature reaches about 30°C, stop heating. Carry on stirring for 1 minute, and then note down in the table the exact temperature of the acid. Start to time as you drop a

1 cm length of magnesium ribbon into the warm acid. Measure the length of time that it takes for the magnesium to react completely, and record this in your table.

5   Empty the boiling-tube and clean it. Start with another 20 cm³ of fresh dilute hydrochloric acid, and repeat the experiment, this time with the temperature of the acid about 45°C.

6   Carry out the whole procedure again, at a temperature of about 60°C.

7   **Discuss your results with the others in your group**. Try to decide whether you can say anything about how the temperature of a reactant chemical alters the rate of a chemical reaction. **Write down what you have decided, and why you have decided it.**

What happened

You should have been able to see that the higher the temperature, the more quickly the magnesium reacted. We know that the same amount of reaction took place each time, because the same quantities of magnesium and dilute hydrochloric acid were used. So it took less time for the same amount of reactant (magnesium) to be used up.

What we can decide

We can say that the speed of a chemical reaction is linked to the temperature of the reactant chemicals. The higher the temperature, the faster the reaction. This means that the lower the temperature, the slower the reaction will be. So we can also alter the speed of a chemical reaction by altering the temperature.

An increase in temperature of the reactants increases the speed of a chemical reaction.

A decrease in temperature of the reactants decreases the speed of a chemical reaction.

The effect of the size of the pieces of a solid reactant

When we react magnesium with dilute hydrochloric acid, a substance in solution has to react with a solid. Each time you have seen this reaction so far, the magnesium has been in the form of pieces of magnesium ribbon. But suppose we used a different form of magnesium, one in which the magnesium was in very tiny solid pieces. Would this have an effect on the speed of its reaction with dilute hydrochloric acid? You will have noticed that when magnesium ribbon reacts with dilute acid, bubbles of hydrogen form **on its surface**. If we chopped the same magnesium ribbon into smaller pieces, there would be more surface for the same mass of magnesium. So perhaps the reaction would be able to happen more quickly.

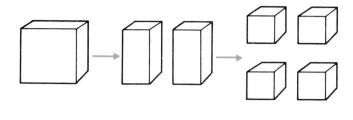

more surface area for the same amount of solid

Fig. 6.4 *More surface area for the same amount of solid*

▶ EXPERIMENT 6.4

EXPERIMENT 6.4

The effect of the size of the pieces of a solid reactant on the speed of a chemical reaction

You will need the following: access to a top-pan balance, glass rod, 100 cm³ beaker, clean magnesium ribbon (10 cm), magnesium powder, dilute hydrochloric acid, stopclock or watch with second hand.

What to do

YOU MUST WEAR YOUR SAFETY SPECTACLES.

1   Weigh a piece of clean magnesium ribbon about 10 cm long. Write down the mass of magnesium.

2   Put 50 cm³ of dilute hydrochloric acid into a 100 cm³ beaker. Drop the magnesium ribbon, coiled up, into the beaker. Time how long it takes for the magnesium to react completely, and write this down.

3   Weigh out on a piece of paper the same mass of magnesium powder as there was in the piece of ribbon you have just used. Do this as accurately as you can (it will be about 0.1 g).

4   Wash out the 100 cm³ beaker, and put 50 cm³ of dilute hydrochloric acid into it. Tip the magnesium powder into it, and stir with a glass rod. Time how long it takes for the magnesium powder to react completely, and write this down.

Discuss what you have seen, and try to draw any conclusions which you can. Write down what you have decided and why you have decided it.

What happened

You should have seen that it takes much less time for the magnesium powder to react than for the same mass of magnesium ribbon.

What we can decide

When we grind something into a powder, we give it a much larger surface area. The surface area of a powder is the surface area of all the specks added together. So the surface area of the magnesium powder which you used was much greater than that of the same mass of magnesium ribbon. The surface area of 0.1 g of magnesium powder is about the same as the area of a desk lid. So the reaction between the magnesium and the acid goes faster when the metal has a larger surface area. The same is true for any reaction which involves a solid – the more finely divided it is, the larger its surface area, and the faster it reacts. So if a reaction involves a solid, we can alter its rate by altering the size of the pieces of solid.

A decrease in the size of the pieces of solid reactant increases the speed of a chemical reaction in which it takes part.

An increase in the size of the pieces of a solid reactant decreases the speed of a chemical reaction in which it takes part.

The effect of the presence of a catalyst

You met the idea of a catalyst in the last section. A catalyst is a chemical which alters the rate of a chemical reaction, but which is itself left unchanged chemically at the end.

Note that the definition of a catalyst does not say that it increases the rate of a reaction. Some catalysts (we call them NEGATIVE CATALYSTS) slow reactions down. Negative catalysts are quite often useful, but the most common kind of catalyst is one that speeds a reaction up.

Catalysts are usually specific to a particular reaction. That is, a particular chemical acts as a catalyst to a particular reaction. While all chemicals are potentially catalysts, most have no reaction which they can catalyse. At the same time, most reactions have not had a catalyst found for them.

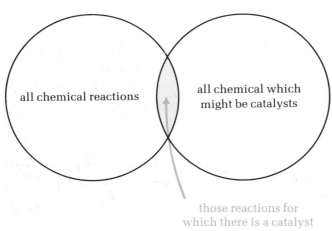

all chemical reactions   all chemical which might be catalysts

those reactions for which there is a catalyst

Fig. 6.5

Nevertheless, you know that transition metals often behave as catalysts for reactions. A dramatic example of this is the reaction between hydrogen and oxygen, which is catalysed by the transition metal platinum. If the lid is taken off a gas-jar full of hydrogen, it will simply mix with the oxygen in the air without reacting. But if a piece of platinum gauze or platinised ceramic fibre (which must be dry) is held in the mouth of the gas-jar, it will glow red, and there will be an explosion as the hydrogen and oxygen react.

(a) no catalyst   (b) with a catalyst

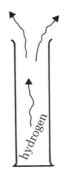 

hydrogen

Fig. 6.6

Even water can act as a catalyst, as the following demonstration shows.

DEMONSTRATION 6.2

Water as a catalyst

Your teacher will show you this reaction

The following will be needed: iodine crystals, aluminium powder, mortar and pestle, tin lid.

What to do

THIS REACTION MUST BE CARRIED OUT IN A FUME-CUPBOARD.

1   Grind 4–5 spatula-measures of dry iodine crystals to a fine powder in the mortar and pestle, in dry conditions.

2   Mix the ground iodine with 4–5 spatula-measures of powdered aluminium, and place the mixture on a tin lid in a fume-cupboard.

3   Add one drop of water.

What happened

You should have been able to see that a violent reaction took place, the heat causing clouds of vaporised iodine to form.

What we can decide

Water catalyses the reaction between aluminium and iodine by speeding it up.

You can now examine a different reaction for yourself.

EXPERIMENT 6.5
The effect of the presence of a catalyst on the speed of a chemical reaction

You will need the following: granulated zinc, copper turnings, dilute sulphuric acid, boiling-tube.

What to do

THIS REACTION MUST BE CARRIED OUT IN A FUME-CUPBOARD.

1   Take a few zinc granules and place them in the bottom of a boiling-tube.

2   Add dilute sulphuric acid, to a depth of 3–4 cm.

3   Observe the reaction for a short time, so that you get a clear idea of how quickly it is taking place.

4   Now add a few copper turnings, and make sure that they are **touching** the pieces of zinc.

5   Observe the reaction again, and decide whether the rate at which hydrogen is being produced has changed. Does the copper seem to have changed or be used up?

6   **Discuss what you have seen with the others in your group**. Can you decide how the copper is behaving? **Write down what you have decided, and why you have decided it**.

7   Write an equation for the reaction.

What happened

You should have been able to see that the reaction speeded up when the copper was added, and that the copper was not changed or used up.

What we can decide

Copper acts as a catalyst for the reaction between zinc and sulphuric acid by speeding it up.

A catalyst can speed up or slow down a chemical reaction without itself being changed chemically at the end. Not all chemical reactions are affected by a catalyst.

Many industrial chemical reactions use a catalyst. You will learn about two particular processes in Section 9. These are the manufacture of sulphuric acid (the catalyst for this reaction is vanadium pentoxide) and the manufacture of ammonia (the catalyst for this reaction is iron). Catalysts for industrial reactions are very often solids, and they come in all shapes and sizes.

It is not just people who have discovered catalysts. Nature found out about them many million of years ago! Many of the chemical reactions which happen in living organisms (like our own bodies) are catalysed by chemicals called ENZYMES. Enzymes are natural catalysts.

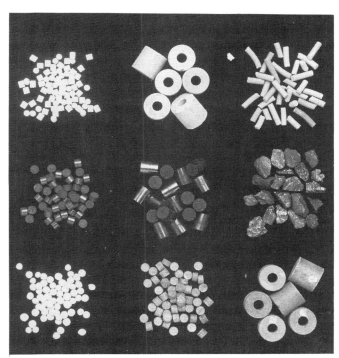

Fig. 6.7 *These pellets and granules of different chemicals are all catalysts*

The effect of light

In the same way that only a proportion of all chemical reactions are affected by a catalyst, so only a very small number are affected by light. But those that are affected, are affected dramatically!

EXPERIMENT 6.6

How light affects silver bromide

You will need the following: potassium bromide solution, silver nitrate solution, filter-funnel and filter-papers, magnesium ribbon (5 cm), tongs, glass rod, spatula.

What to do

1   You know that silver bromide is insoluble. So we can make it by mixing together a solution of potassium bromide and a solution of silver nitrate. Fill about one-third of a test-tube with potassium bromide solution, and add to it several drops of silver nitrate solution. DO NOT LET THE SILVER NITRATE SOLUTION TOUCH YOUR SKIN. IF IT DOES, WASH IT OFF IMMEDIATELY.

2   A precipitate of silver bromide will form in the test-tube. Stir the mixture with the glass rod to make sure it is properly mixed. Now place two folded filter-papers (your teacher will show you how to fold a filter-paper if you are not sure) on top of each other in the filter-funnel. Filter the chemicals in the test-tube through the twin filter-papers.

3   Have ready a flat, solid object, which can be any shape. A coin or an irregularly shaped piece of cardboard would be good examples.

4   Open out the filter-paper onto a flat surface, and use a spatula to spread out the silver bromide precipitate into a thin layer.

5   Put the flat object on the layer of silver bromide so that it covers part of it (Fig. 6.8).

6   YOU MUST WEAR YOUR SAFETY SPECTACLES FOR THIS PART OF THE EXPERIMENT.

Take the piece of magnesium ribbon in a pair of tongs, and burn it a few inches above the surface of the silver bromide. When the magnesium has finished burning, lift up the solid object and compare the area beneath it with the rest of the silver bromide.

7   **Discuss what you have seen, and try to decide what has happened. Write down what you have decided and why you have decided it.**

What happened

You should have been able to see that the silver bromide which received the light from the burning magnesium turned from pale yellow to a much darker shade. There should be a clear outline of the shape of the object which you placed on top of the silver bromide.

What we can decide

The dark colour is caused by metallic silver. This is produced when silver bromide decomposes. The rate at which this happens depends on the amount of light which falls on it.

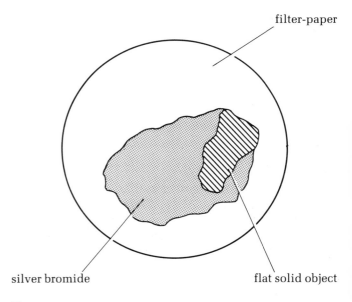

filter-paper

silver bromide

flat solid object

Fig. 6.8

The rate at which some chemical reactions happen depends on the amount of light which falls on the reactant chemicals.

The image that you made in Experiment 6.6 was a 'negative' of the flat object which you used. This process is the basis of black-and-white photography. The photographic film in the camera is coated with a silver salt, which reacts to the light which falls on it, at a rate which depends on the intensity of the light. So the 'lighter' parts of the image which falls on the photographic film end up darker, and vice versa. So we get a complete negative of the object which we are photographing. If we then 'take a photograph of the negative', we get a true image of the object which we photographed.

Fig. 6.9A. *The object*

Fig. 6.9B. *The negative*

Fig. 6.9C. *The photograph*

TOPIC 6.1.6

Why can we alter the rate of a chemical reaction?

We have seen that we can do the following things to increase the speed at which chemical reactions happen:

for all reactions
- increase the concentration of one or both reactants
- increase the temperature of the reactants
- decrease the size of the pieces of a solid reactant

for some reactions
- add a catalyst to the reactants
- increase the intensity of the light falling on the reactants

Why do these changes work? Catalysts work by providing a different route for the chemical reaction – one which has a lower activation energy.

We can look at the effect of all the above changes in the same way. For any reaction, there is an activation energy. (You should now go back and read pages 180–181.) This means that before a reaction will happen, **the particles of the reactant chemicals must come together and have a certain amount of energy**.

If the reactant particles do not meet – there is no reaction. If, when they meet, they have less energy than the activation energy – there is still no reaction.

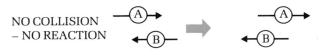

NO COLLISION – NO REACTION

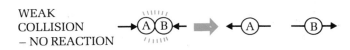

WEAK COLLISION – NO REACTION

ENERGETIC COLLISION – REACTION

Fig. 6.10

For a particular reaction, the rate at which it happens depends upon the rate at which reactant particles come together with more energy than the activation energy.

Imagine the following situation. Suppose we had a class of 30 children, each with a box of tennis balls, and faced with a high wall. If we told them all to try to throw their tennis balls over the wall together for five minutes, only some tennis balls would have arrived on the other side at the end. These would be the tennis balls which were thrown with enough energy to get over the wall.

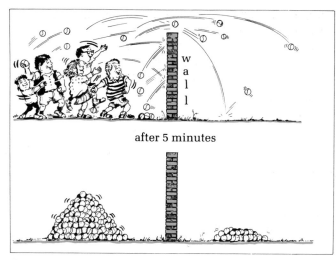

after 5 minutes

Fig. 6.11

The energy with which each individual tennis ball is thrown represents the activation energy of one collision between reactant particles. The height of the wall represents the activation energy of the reaction. The number of tennis balls getting to the other side in five minutes represents the speed of the chemical reaction. So the more tennis balls there are which are thrown with enough energy to get over the wall in five minutes, the greater the speed of the reaction.

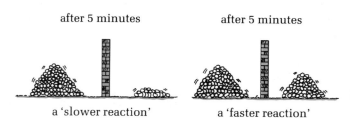

after 5 minutes   after 5 minutes

a 'slower reaction'   a 'faster reaction'

Fig. 6.12

To increase the speed of a reaction we must increase the 'number of tennis balls which get over the wall in five minutes'. There are two ways we can do this – by increasing the 'energy with which the tennis balls are thrown', or by decreasing the 'height of the wall'.

(YOU SHOULD STOP READING AT THIS POINT AND START AGAIN AT THE BEGINNING OF THE TOPIC.)

Temperature

To 'increase the energy with which the tennis balls are thrown', we must increase the energy with which the reactant particles collide. The amount of energy which the particles have depends on the speed at which they move. The faster they move, the more energy they have. The more slowly they move, the less energy they have. At a certain temperature, the average speed of the particles is fixed – as is the number of particles which are moving more quickly than the average, and the number which are moving more slowly than the average. Most particles have a speed close to the average, and a small number are moving very quickly and a small number very slowly.

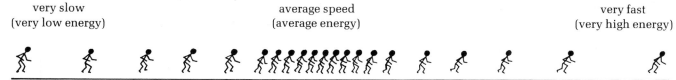

Fig. 6.13

Particles are like people. Most have average (or near average) energy and can run at an average (or near average) speed. Only a few have high energy and can run very fast, only a few have low energy and can only run very slowly.

So, at a certain temperature, only a few particles will be moving quickly enough to have more energy than the activation energy. But at a higher temperature, the average speed of the particles will be greater, and more will be moving quickly enough to have more energy than the activation energy.

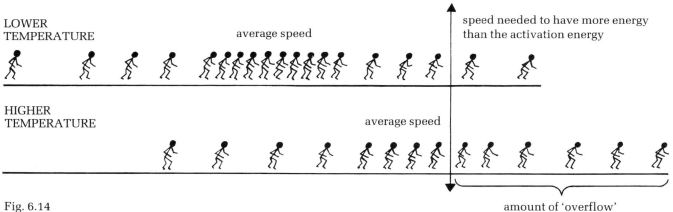

Fig. 6.14

This is the equivalent of adding a little bit of energy to all the tennis balls thrown by our class of children. The average energy is higher, and so more will have enough energy to get over the wall. So, without changing the height of the wall, we have increased the number of tennis balls which would get to the other side in five minutes.

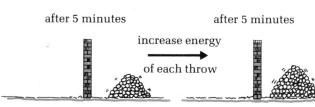

Fig. 6.15

Increasing the temperature of a chemical reaction increases the number of collisions with more energy than the activation energy. So increasing the temperature always increases the speed of a chemical reaction.

When we increase the temperature, we increase the energy with which particles collide, because we increase the speed at which they move. We also increase the number of collisions which happen each second. Imagine 50 pupils running around in random directions in your school gymnasium. There would be many collisions each second! But if the pupils were running at twice the speed, there would be many more. It is like this with the particles of reactant chemicals. The faster they move, the more often there are collisions. This also increases the number of tennis balls with enough energy to get over the wall in a given length of time. It is as if the class of children were throwing their tennis balls more frequently as well as with more energy.

Concentration

But there is another way in which we can increase the number of collisions each second, without increasing the temperature. Suppose instead of having 50 pupils running around in the school gymnasium, there were 100, running at the same speed. Because the space was more crowded, there would be many more collisions each second. We can make chemicals more crowded, by increasing their concentration.

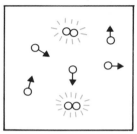
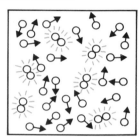

less concentrated –
fewer collisions

more concentrated –
more collisions

Fig. 6.16

The more concentrated the chemicals are, the more collisions there are each second. So, each second, there are more collisions which have more energy than the activation energy of the reaction. So, increasing the concentration of the reactant chemicals also increases 'the number of tennis balls with enough energy to get over the wall' in a given time. It is as if the children were throwing tennis balls more frequently during the five minutes. Increasing the concentration always increases the speed of a chemical reaction. For chemicals in solution, the concentration is the number of moles of solute per dm^3 of solution. For a reactant chemical which is a gas, the concentration means the pressure of the gas. So increasing the pressure of reactant chemicals which are gases increases the rate at which they react.

The size of the pieces of a solid

But what does the concentration of a solid reactant mean? We have seen that the important factor is the number of collisions between particles of the reactant chemicals (and how much energy those collisions have). Suppose we react a solid with another chemical which is a liquid or a solution. The particles can only collide **at the surface** of the solid. So the more surface there is (the bigger the 'surface area'), the more collisions there will be. So the more collisions there will be each second which have more energy than the activation energy, and the faster the reaction

will happen (because the 'number of tennis balls getting over the wall' in a given length of time is greater).

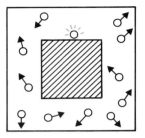
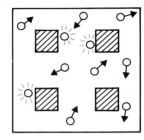

larger particles of solid –
fewer collisions

smaller particles of solid –
more collisions

Fig. 6.17

You saw earlier that the smaller the pieces of the solid are, the larger the total surface area. So a decrease in the size of the pieces of a solid reactant always increases the speed of a chemical reaction.

Catalysts

So far, we have seen ways in which we can increase the number of collisions each second which have more energy than the activation energy. But if we can simply make the activation energy for the reaction lower, then we can decrease the 'height of the wall'. So with the same 'average energy of tennis balls', the 'number getting over the wall' in a given time will be greater, and so the reaction will happen more quickly.

after 5 minutes   after 5 minutes

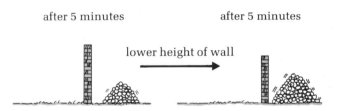

lower height of wall

Fig. 6.18

A catalyst works by making possible a different route for the chemical reaction, which has a lower activation energy. This is the same as 'lowering the wall' in our diagram. (Of course, a negative catalyst would **increase** the height of the wall.)

So a catalyst always speeds up a chemical reaction, if it lowers the activation energy.

Light

Light is a form of energy, and it has a particular range of wavelengths (see p. 297). For some chemical reactions, the reactant chemicals are able to absorb the amount of energy in light, and then they use this for the activation energy for the reaction. Most chemicals cannot do this, and so the presence or absence of light energy does not affect the speed at which they react.

So we can think of light as artificially 'increasing the average energy of the tennis balls', by giving reactant chemicals more energy than they would otherwise have.

UNIT 6.1
Summary and learning

1   You should remember the examples which you have seen of fast chemical reactions and of slow chemical reactions.

2   We can measure the rate of a chemical reaction by measuring the rate at which one of the reactant chemicals disappears, or by measuring the rate at which one of the product chemicals forms.

3   We can increase the speed of all chemical reactions by:

(a) increasing the concentration of one or both reactants;
(b) increasing the temperature;
(c) decreasing the size of the pieces of a solid reactant.

4   We can increase the speed of some chemical reactions by:
(a) adding a catalyst;
(b) increasing the light intensity.

5   You should be able to remember the details of experiments which you have done which show each of the five ways in which we can alter the rate of chemical reactions.

6   You should be able to explain why each of those five ways alters the rate of a chemical reaction.

7   You have learnt the meaning of these words:

negative catalyst
enzyme

UNIT 6.2   *How completely do chemicals react?*

This might seem a strange question at first. A chemical change, surely, is a chemical change. We go from the reactant chemicals to the product chemicals.

You have already reacted magnesium metal with dilute hydrochloric acid many times. When you do this (as long as there is enough acid left) all the magnesium reacts, and none is left over. The reaction is a good example when we want to think of chemical reactions in a simple way – the reactants react, and we get the products. In other words, it seems as though the reaction goes to COMPLETION.

You can probably think of many other examples of reactions which seem to go to completion. Here are a few:

Reactions which 'go to completion'

$CaCO_3(s) + 2HCl(aq) \rightarrow CaCl_2(aq) + H_2O(l) + CO_2(g)$
$2Na(s) + 2H_2O(l) \rightarrow 2NaOH(aq) + H_2(g)$
$Ba(NO_3)_2(aq) + Na_2SO_4(aq) \rightarrow BaSO_4(s) + 2NaNO_3(aq)$
$Pb(NO_3)_2(aq) + 2KI(aq) \rightarrow PbI_2(s) + 2KNO_3(aq)$

Questions

1   Write down the balanced equations for as many reactions as you can think of which 'go to completion'. (You should see whether your teacher agrees with all those you have written down.)

2   As we shall shortly see, all reactions which seem to go to completion have something in common. From the list above and from what you have written down, can you see what it might be?

So in many reactions, the reactant chemicals go on reacting until one or both of them is completely used up. You also know that many other chemical reactions which might happen, do not. An example would be:

$Cu(s) + HCl(aq) \rightarrow$ NO REACTION (under 'normal conditions')

Question

Write down as many starting chemicals as you can which we might expect to react together (they make up one of the general reaction types on p. 199), but which in fact do not.

We can explain the fact that some reactions do not happen, of course, in terms of the reactivity of the chemicals which are involved. So we seem to have reactions which happen completely, and reactions which do not happen at all. Are these the only categories for chemical reactions? Or is the true picture more complicated than this?

TOPIC 6.2.1

Are chemical reactions one-way changes?

In Section 4 (Topic 4.2.1) you met an example of a chemical change which can 'go both ways'. This was the change:

hydrated copper(II) sulphate

$\xrightarrow{\text{heat}}$ anhydrous copper(II) sulphate + water

You should remember that we said there that 'heat drove the chemicals up the reactivity hill', and that hydrated copper(II) sulphate was the unreactive

chemical. Because the water was driven off in the form of steam, anhydrous copper(II) sulphate and water 'couldn't get at each other to react'.

Now you have just seen (in Topic 6.1.1) that the rate of a chemical reaction depends upon the concentration of the reactant chemicals. In the case of the reaction between anhydrous copper(II) sulphate and water, if the water is not able to contact the other reactant (because it is in the form of steam), then its effective concentration is zero. So the **backward reaction cannot happen at all**. In other words, it seems as though for some reactions, the conditions decide 'which way' the reaction goes.

Before we look at this a little more deeply, we can see some further examples of reactions which can 'go both ways'.

▶ EXPERIMENT 6.7

EXPERIMENT 6.7

What happens when we heat ammonium chloride?

You will need the following: ammonium chloride crystals, long 15 mm hard-glass test-tube, retort stand and clamp.

What to do

YOU MUST WEAR YOUR SAFETY SPECTACLES.

1   Place a spatula-full of ammonium chloride crystals in a long hard-glass test-tube. Clamp the test-tube above the bench at an angle of 45°.

2   Heat the crystals gently and observe what happens.

3   Discuss what you have seen, and what you think it might mean. **Write down what you have decided, and why you have decided it**.

What happened

You should have been able to see that the amount of ammonium chloride solid got less, and that solid formed at the upper (cooler) part of the tube.

What we can decide

When ammonium chloride is heated, it splits up into ammonia and hydrogen chloride gases:

$$NH_4Cl(s) \xrightarrow{\text{heat}} NH_3(g) + HCl(g)$$

When these gases together meet a cold surface, they form ammonium chloride solid again:

$$NH_3(g) + HCl(g) \xrightarrow{\text{cool}} NH_4Cl(s)$$

So this reaction can 'go both ways'. The direction in which it moves depends on the temperature.

So the ammonium chloride 'system' is very like the hydrated copper(II) sulphate 'system'. The direction in which it moves depends on the temperature. But perhaps for other chemical changes, the direction depends on other things.

▶ EXPERIMENT 6.8

EXPERIMENT 6.8

The reaction between bromine and water

You will need the following: bromine water, dilute hydrochloric acid, sodium hydroxide solution, boiling-tube, white tile.

What to do

YOU MUST WEAR YOUR SAFETY SPECTACLES.

1   Take some bromine water (about 10 cm³) and place it in a boiling-tube.

2   Hold the boiling-tube above a white tile, and add sodium hydroxide solution to it until you see a change.

3   Now add dilute hydrochloric acid to the mixture of chemicals in the boiling-tube until you see no change.

4   Carry on adding alkali and acid alternately, several times.

5   Discuss what you have seen, and what you think it might mean. **Write down what you have decided, and why you have decided it**.

What happened

You should have been able to see that when alkali was added to the bromine water, the red colour of bromine disappeared. When you added acid, bromine was formed again.

What we can decide

You know that bromine dissolves in water to form an acid (Section 3, Topic 3.1.3). So bromine is used up in making an acid, but unless we do something to the reaction, not **all** the bromine is used up (the solution stays red in colour). But we can make bromine react more completely if we add alkali.

Adding alkali in this case is a bit like what happens when we heat hydrated copper(II) sulphate when water in the form of steam is one of the products. We take away one of the product chemicals so that it cannot react again to make the reactant chemicals. In this case, we take away the acid by adding alkali. Acid and alkali react, making water.

When we add acid again, the reverse reaction (which makes bromine) starts once more. We can go round this cycle as many times as we like.

The forward reaction is:

$$Br_2(aq) + H_2O(l) \rightarrow \underbrace{H^+(aq) + Br^-(aq)}_{\text{hydrobromic acid}} + \underset{\text{acid}}{\underset{\text{hydrobromous}}{HOBr(aq)}}$$

The only chemical which has a colour is bromine. So we can see when it reacts (when we add alkali), and when it is formed (when we add acid).

The reverse reaction is:

$$H^+(aq) + Br^-(aq) + HOBr(aq) \rightarrow Br_2(aq) + H_2O(l)$$

So in the case of the 'bromine/water system', the direction in which the reaction moves depends upon the concentration of acid or alkali which is present in the solution.

We can now look again at the reactions which you wrote down earlier as being those which 'go to completion'. In very many cases, one of the product chemicals is a gas or is insoluble. In either case, the chemical concerned cannot actually take part in the reverse reaction. This is because its effective concentration is zero (it is not 'available to react'). So, were it not for this fact, these reactions (which we are used to thinking of as being the most common, or typical, chemical reactions) would also be reactions which could go in both directions.

So it seems that many, if not all, chemical reactions are not in reality one-way processes, but are capable of going in either direction, depending on the conditions (such as temperature and the concentration of the chemicals). What is the exact nature of these chemical changes?

TOPIC 6.2.2

What is the true nature of chemical reactions that do not 'go to completion'?

Most chemical changes can happen in either direction, depending on the conditions. So almost always, neither the forward reaction nor the backward reaction happens on its own. This means that, to some extent, we always have at least some of each of the chemicals involved in the reaction (all those on the reactants side, and all those on the products side) present in the test-tube or beaker. We say that we have a REACTION MIXTURE.

How do we get a 'reaction mixture' and what is it like?

EXPERIMENT 6.9
Getting a 'reaction mixture'

You will need the following: iodine crystals, potassium iodide solution (approximately 1M), 1,1,1-trichloroethane, test-tubes and bungs.

What to do

1 Take a **small** iodine crystal, and place it in a test-tube. Add potassium iodide solution, so that there is a depth of about 2 cm. Put a bung in the tube, and shake until the iodine crystal has dissolved. Write down the colour of iodine dissolved in potassium iodide, and keep the contents of the tube.

2 Repeat step 1, but use 1,1,1-trichloroethane ('trike') instead of potassium iodide solution. Write down the colour of iodine dissolved in 'trike', and keep the contents of the tube.

3 Add an equal volume of 'trike' to the test-tube from step 1. Add an equal volume of potassium iodide solution to the test-tube from step 2. Potassium iodide floats on top of 'trike'. Figure 6.19 shows what will happen.

4 Check that your two test-tubes look like those in the diagram. Now put the bung back into each test-tube and shake gently for a short time.

5 At this point you should discuss with the others in your group what you have seen, and what you think it means. **Write down what you have decided, and why you have decided it**.

6 Now shake each tube rapidly, for several seconds. Discuss with the others in your group whether what you have seen means that you have to change your mind about what you think is happening in the two test-tubes.

What happened

You should have been able to see that when the fresh solvents (potassium iodide solution and 'trike') were added, each may have become darker but only slightly. When you shook gently each of the fresh solvents became darker, and showed the colour of iodine when dissolved in it. So in each test-tube, iodine was moving from one solvent to the other. In one test-tube the iodine moved in one direction and in the other it moved in the opposite direction.

When you shook the two tubes rapidly, you should have seen that they both looked the same at the end. No matter how much you shook each tube, it would look the same and not change any more.

What we can decide

What you have seen in this experiment is a picture of what happens in a chemical reaction which does not go to completion. We can think of one solvent (say potassium iodide) as representing the reactants side of a reaction and the other ('trike') as representing the products side.

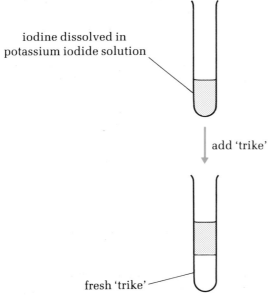

iodine dissolved in potassium iodide solution

add 'trike'

fresh 'trike'

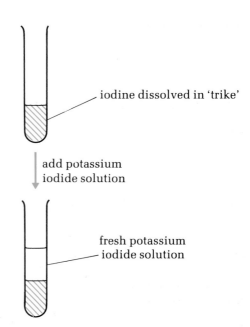

iodine dissolved in 'trike'

add potassium iodide solution

fresh potassium iodide solution

Fig. 6.19

In one test-tube we started with all the iodine in the potassium iodide solution (so it is as if we had only the reactants for the chemical reaction present). In the other test-tube we started with all the iodine in the 'trike' (so it is as if we had only the products of the chemical reaction present). When you shook the first test-tube, some iodine moved into the 'trike' layer (some reactants reacted, and made some product chemicals). When you shook the second test-tube, some iodine moved into the potassium iodide layer (some products reacted, and made some reactant chemicals).

We have seen that the iodine will always move across the boundary between the two solvents in both directions (this is the same as saying that the chemical reaction will move in both directions). So in the first test-tube iodine will have started to move back into the potassium iodide solution straight away (product chemicals will react to form reactant chemicals again straight away). (You can write down for yourself what happens in the other test-tube.) But when you 'stopped the reaction', by stopping shaking, there was more iodine in the 'trike' and less in the potassium iodide than at the start (more product

chemicals and less reactant chemicals than at the start). So although the change was happening in both directions at the same time, the **rate** was faster in the forward direction than in the backward direction. (This should make sense, because we have a much higher concentration of 'reactant chemicals', than 'product chemicals'.) In the other test-tube, the rate at which the change was happening was faster in the reverse direction than in the forward direction.

When you 'started the reaction' again (by shaking), the reaction continued in each tube until the concentration of the reactants (the amount of iodine in potassium iodide) and the concentration of the products (the amount of iodine in the 'trike') stayed the same. But we know that the iodine was still moving from one solvent to the other (the reaction was still going on in both directions). When the final position was reached, the iodine was moving **in both directions at the same rate** (the forward and reverse chemical reactions were happening at the same rate). We call this a position of EQUILIBRIUM ('balance') and we say that a chemical reaction in which the forward reaction and the reverse reaction are happening at the same rate has reached CHEMICAL EQUILIBRIUM.

We can imagine how the reaction mixture for a chemical reaction reaches chemical equilibrium, starting either from the reactants or from the products: (The lengths of the arrows stand for the rate of the forward and the reverse reactions.)

Starting from the reactants:

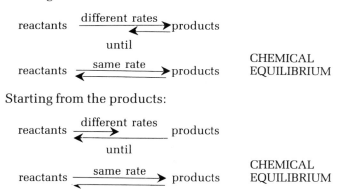

Starting from the products:

If a chemical reaction 'goes to completion', we do not get a chemical equilibrium. But such reactions are in the minority. For most reactions, after a certain time we end up with a mixture of reactant chemicals and product chemicals 'in chemical equilibrium' with each other. That means that the forward reaction and the reverse reaction are happening at the same rate.

For two different chemical reactions which have got to a position of equilibrium, the mixture of reactant

chemicals and product chemicals can be very different. In one reaction, the 'equilibrium mixture' might be made up mostly of product chemicals. In the other, it might be mostly reactant chemicals. In fact, all chemical reactions have a different make-up to their equilibrium mixture.

We can think of a simple situation to help us with the idea of chemical equilibrium. Suppose we had two rooms which are connected to each other by a revolving door:

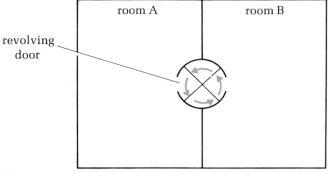

Fig. 6.20

Suppose now that room A contains people, all wandering around on their own. To go through into room B, through the revolving door, they have to join together into groups of three people, all holding hands. When they get into room B, they have to stay holding hands in their threes. They can come back through the door, but if they do they have to split up again into people on their own.

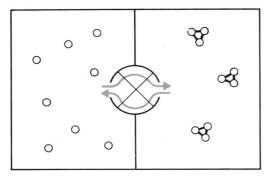

Fig. 6.21

This moving of people and groups of people between the two rooms could go on all the time, and in both directions at the same time. Imagine a situation where the number of people going through the door from room A to room B in a certain time is the same as the number of people coming out of the revolving door from room B into room A in the same time. The total number of people in room A would stay the same all the time. What would be happening to the number of groups of three people in room B? Well, every time a group of three people came through into room B from room A, a group of three people would leave room B and go into room A. If two groups of three people came into room B, two groups of three people would have to leave it. So if the total number of people in room A stays the same all the time, then the number of groups of three people in room B must stay the same all the time. There is a position of *equilibrium* (Fig. 6.22).

EQUILIBRIUM

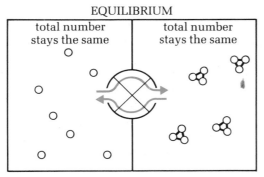

Fig. 6.22

Now we can use our model of the rooms and the revolving door to think of any chemical reaction which does not go to completion. Room A represents the reactants side of the reaction, and the number of people in it represents the amount of reactant chemicals. Room B represents the products side of the reaction, and the number of groups in it represents the amount of product chemicals. For different chemical

reactions which form an equilibrium mixture, the relationship between the number of people in room A and the number of groups of people in room B (at equilibrium) can be different in each case (Fig. 6.23).

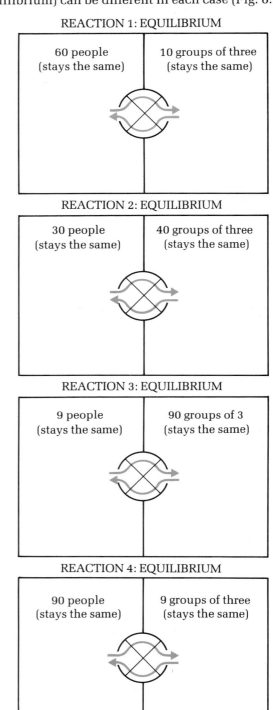

Fig. 6.23

So different chemical reactions can have different amounts of reactant and product chemicals mixed together when they are in their equilibrium positions. We saw earlier that we seemed to be able to move more to the reactants side or more to the products side of a reversible reaction, simply by altering the conditions. How can this be, if each reaction has its own position of balance (its own position of equilibrium)?

Using chemical equilibrium – Le Chatelier's Principle

A chemical reaction is in equilibrium when the rate of the forward reaction is the same as the rate of the reverse reaction. You know that the rate of a chemical reaction always depends on the concentration of the reactant chemicals. So, in a reaction which can go both ways, the rate of the forward reaction depends on the concentrations of the different reactant chemicals, and the rate of the reverse reaction depends on the concentrations of the different product chemicals.

Suppose that we take a particular chemical reaction which has already reached a position of chemical equilibrium, and suppose we alter some of the conditions. Can we work out what will happen to the position of the equilibrium (the balance between the amount of reactant chemicals and the amount of product chemicals) when we make different sorts of change in the conditions? For most of the changes which can happen, we need only think about the concentrations of the different chemicals to find out what will happen, as we shall see. This will lead us to a simple rule (called Le Chatelier's Principle) which we can use to work out the effect of any change on the make-up of the equilibrium mixture of chemicals.

Changes in concentration

Look back at the work you did in Experiment 6.8 when you examined the reaction between bromine and water. The more alkali you added, the less bromine there was in the equilibrium mixture. The more acid you added, the more bromine there was in the equilibrium mixture. You know the equations for the forward and reverse reactions, so we can write an equation to show the chemical equilibrium. To do this, we use a special sign ($\rightleftharpoons$) which means 'equilibrium'.

$$Br_2(aq) + H_2O(l) \rightleftharpoons H^+(aq) + Br^-(aq) + HOBr(aq)$$

At equilibrium, there is a certain concentration of bromine in the equilibrium mixture. The balance between the total amounts of reactant chemicals and product chemicals is the one for this particular reaction.

Adding acid

If we add some acid, we increase the concentration of one of the products of the reaction (the H^+ ions). So this makes the rate of the reverse reaction increase. So bromine and water are made more quickly than before the acid was added, and the concentrations of both of them start to rise. This make the forward reaction go faster – and it will go on getting faster until it balances the rate of the reverse reaction again. We have got back to equilibrium. But the new position of equilibrium is not the same as the old position. We have more reactant chemicals than before (and so the concentration of bromine is greater), we have more product chemicals than before, and the rate of the forward reaction and the rate of the reverse reaction are both greater than before. (No matter has been created. Remember that we added some acid)

Think again of the 'revolving door' picture of equilibrium. In the new position of equilibrium, it is as if we had more people in room A, more groups of people in room B, and more people and groups of people passing through the door in the same amount of time, compared with the old position.

Because there is more bromine in the new equilibrium mixture than in the old one, we sometimes say 'The position of the equilibrium has moved to the left'. But this is only a kind of shorthand. We have more bromine than before, but we also have more acid than before.

Adding alkali

When you added alkali to the equilibrium mixture, the result was a lower concentration of bromine in the new equilibrium mixture. When we add alkali, the reaction

$$H^+(aq) + OH^-(aq) \rightarrow H_2O(l)$$

happens, and so some $H^+(aq)$ from the reaction mixture is used up. This lowers its concentration and slows down the reverse reaction. So bromine and water are made more slowly than before the alkali was added, and the concentration of both of them begins to fall. This makes the forward reaction go slower – and it will go on getting slower until it again balances with the rate of the reverse reaction. We have reached equilibrium, but it is a different position of equilibrium.

In the new position, the concentration of bromine is less than it was in the old position. There are fewer reactant chemicals as well as fewer product chemicals than before we added the alkali. (Some acid was 'taken away' by the alkali.) The rates of the forward and reverse reactions are both slower than before.

Think of the 'revolving door' picture of equilibrium. In the new position, it is as if we had fewer people in room A, fewer groups of people in room B, and fewer people and groups of people passing through the door in the same amount of time, compared with the old position.

Because there is less bromine in the new equilibrium mixture, we sometimes say 'the equilibrium has moved to the right'.

We can make a summary of the effects of adding acid and alkali to the equilibrium mixture (Table 6.3).

Change	Effect on rate of reverse reaction	How rate of forward reaction must change to regain equilibrium	Change in concentration of bromine at equilibrium, compared with original
Add acid	faster	faster	increase
Add alkali	slower	slower	decrease

Table 6.3

You can now look at another chemical equilibrium for yourself.

EXPERIMENT 6.10

The reaction between bismuth(III) chloride and water

You will need the following: bismuth(III) chloride, concentrated hydrochloric acid, 5 test-tubes and test-tube rack, glass rod, two teat-pipettes.

What to do

YOU MUST WEAR YOUR SAFETY SPECTACLES.

1   Place the five test-tubes in the test-tube rack. Put a spatula-measure of bismuth(III) chloride into the first tube, and dissolve it in about 2 cm³ of concentrated hydrochloric acid. YOU SHOULD WEAR RUBBER GLOVES WHEN YOU USE THE CONCENTRATED HYDROCHLORIC ACID.

2   Fill all the other test-tubes about two-thirds full of distilled water. Use a teat-pipette to add 5 drops of concentrated hydrochloric acid to the first tube containing water, 10 drops to the second, 15 to the third and 20 to the fourth.

3   Take a fresh teat-pipette, and use it to add 5 drops of the bismuth(III) chloride solution to each of the four test-tubes.

4   Use a glass rod to stir each tube, but wash it carefully with distilled water between each tube.

5   Compare the amount of white precipitate which forms in each tube.

What happened, and what we can decide

The equation for the chemical equilibrium is:

$$BiCl_3(aq) + H_2O(l) \rightleftharpoons \underset{\substack{\text{bismuth} \\ \text{oxychloride}}}{\overset{\text{white}}{BiOCl(s)}} + 2HCl(aq)$$

Explain the results of your experiment using the equation above, and what you have learned about chemical equilibrium. It will help if you imagine a particular equilibrium (in which there is a certain equilibrium concentration of bismuth oxychloride), to which more and more hydrochloric acid is added in stages.

So, you should now be able to work out, for any equilibrium, the effect on the equilibrium concentrations of the different chemicals of a change in the amount of any reactant or product chemical.

Question

Suppose we had a chemical reaction, which comes to equilibrium as represented by:

$$A + B \rightleftharpoons C + D$$

Copy out the following tables, and complete them:

Change	Effect on rate of forward reaction	How rate of reverse reaction must change to regain equilibrium	Change in concentration of products (C + D) compared with original
Increase concentration of A or of B			
Decrease concentration of A or of B			

Change	Effect on rate of forward reaction	How rate of reverse reaction must change to regain equilibrium	Change in concentration of products (C + D) compared with original
Increase concentration of C or of D			
Decrease concentration of C or of D			

Changes in pressure (reactions which involve gases)

There are many chemical reactions which involve gases and which come to a chemical equilibrium. In Section 4 (Topic 4.4.3) you learned that the number of moles of a gas, and the volume which it occupies (at constant pressure and temperature) are directly related.

We need only consider here the effect of changing the pressure (or the volume) of the whole system.

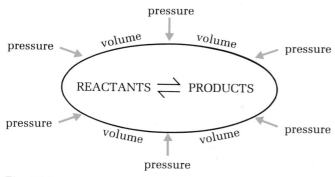

Fig. 6.24

Suppose we take the reaction between sulphur dioxide and oxygen, making sulphur trioxide. The equation for the equilibrium is:

$$2SO_2(g) + O_2(g) \rightleftharpoons 2SO_3(g)$$

By Avogadro's Hypothesis: 3 moles / 3 volumes → 2 moles / 2 volumes

Imagine that the equilibrium was set up inside a container whose volume can be altered, by alterations to the total pressure from the outside. If we increase the pressure from the outside, the volume of the container will decrease. If we decrease the pressure from the outside, the volume of the container will increase.

Suppose the total pressure increases, making the volume of the container smaller. The total number of moles of reactants is greater than the total number of moles of products. So making the container smaller crowds the reactant molecules closer together to a greater extent than the product molecules are crowded together (because there are more reactant molecules in the same space). In other words, the effective concentration of the reactants (taken together) is increased more than the effective concentration of the product chemical is increased. So the forward reaction will speed up to a greater extent than the reverse reaction. The concentration of the product chemical will increase, until the rate of the reverse reaction becomes equal to the rate of the forward reaction. In the new position of equilibrium, the concentration of sulphur trioxide is greater than before, and the concentrations of both sulphur dioxide and oxygen are less than before. So we really can say that the position of equilibrium has 'moved to the right':

$$\underrightarrow{\text{pressure increase}} \text{(volume decrease)}$$
$$2SO_2(g) + O_2(g) \rightleftharpoons 2SO_3(g)$$

If we take the same equilibrium, and decrease the total pressure from the outside, we make the container larger. By reversing the argument above, we can see that we 'un-crowd' the reactant molecules to a greater extent than the product molecules. So the effective concentration of the reactants (taken together) is decreased more than the effective concentration of the product chemical is decreased. The forward reaction will slow down more than the reverse reaction. The concentration of the product chemicals will fall until the rate of the reverse reaction becomes equal to the rate of the forward reaction. In the new position of equilibrium, the concentration of sulphur trioxide is less than before, and the concentrations of sulphur dioxide and oxygen are greater than before. So we can say that the position of equilibrium has 'moved to the left'.

pressure decrease (volume increase)

$$2SO_2(g) + O_2(g) \rightleftharpoons 2SO_3(g)$$

Suppose now that we take an example where the number of moles on the products side is **greater** than the number on the reactants side, such as the dissociation of ozone into oxygen:

	$2O_3(g)$	$\rightleftharpoons 3O_2(g)$
	2 moles	3 moles
By Avogadro's	2 volumes	3 volumes
Hypothesis		

The argument used above still applies, but in reverse. So than an increase in pressure (decrease in volume) will result in a new equilibrium position to the left (more ozone and less oxygen). A decrease in pressure (increase in volume) will result in a new position of equilibrium to the right (less ozone and more oxygen):

pressure increase (volume decrease)

pressure decrease (volume increase)

$$2O_3(g) \rightleftharpoons 3O_2(g)$$

If the number of moles of reactants which are gases is the same as the number of moles of products which are gases, then the position of equilibrium will not be changed by changes in the total pressure (or volume). An example would be the reaction between hydrogen and iodine, making hydrogen iodide:

$$H_2(g) + I_2(g) \rightleftharpoons 2HI(g)$$

	2 moles	2 moles
By Avogadro's	2 volumes	2 volumes
Hypothesis		

Position of equilibrium unchanged by changes in external pressure or total volume

Le Chatelier's Principle

The surest way to decide what will happen to the equilibrium mixture of chemicals when we change the conditions is to think in terms of the concentrations of the chemicals, and the effect on the rates of the forward and reverse reactions. However, if we look at what we have learned so far by doing this, we will see that there is a simple rule which summarises all the possibilities. We can then use this rule to decide what will happen to chemical reactions which are in equilibrium when we alter something which does not alter the concentration of the chemicals – such as the temperature.

We have seen that when we add one of the reactants of a reaction, the equilibrium will take some of that added reactant away. If we add one of the products, the equilibrium will take some of the added product away. If we ourselves take away some of one of the reactant chemicals, the equilibrium will replace some of the reactant we have taken away. If we take some of one of the products chemicals, the equilibrium will replace some of the product we have taken away. (Think back to an equilibrium like

$$Br_2(aq) + H_2O(l) \rightleftharpoons H^+(aq) + Br^- + HOBr(aq),$$

and work through each of these four possible changes for yourself.)

So, by restoring the chemical equilibrium, the system will always offset to some extent the change which was made. We can see that this also describes what happens with reactions which involve gases. If we increase the pressure from the outside, the position of the equilibrium moves in the direction which leaves it with a lower number of molecules of the different chemicals, and therefore a slightly lower pressure than there would otherwise have been. If we decrease the pressure from the outside, the position of the equilibrium moves in the direction which leaves it with a greater number of molecules of the different chemicals, and therefore a slightly greater pressure than there would otherwise have been.

We can therefore devise the following rule.

If a chemical system is in equilibrium and one of the conditions which is involved in the reaction is changed, then the equilibrium will find a new position in which the extent of the change has been offset.

We call this rule **Le Chatelier's Principle**.

Questions

1   The following equation represents a chemical equilibrium:

$$Ag^+(aq) + Fe^{2+}(aq) \rightleftharpoons Ag(s) + Fe^{3+}(aq)$$

Use Le Chatelier's Principle to decide **all** the changes which would be caused by:
(a) adding silver nitrate solution to the equilibrium mixture;

(b) adding iron(III) nitrate solution to the equilibrium mixture;

(c) adding dilute hydrochloric acid to the equilibrium mixture (silver chloride is insoluble).

2   The reaction between iron and water sets up the following equilibrium:

$$3Fe(s) + 4H_2O(g) \rightleftharpoons Fe_3O_4(s) + 4H_2(g)$$

Use Le Chatelier's Principle to decide all the changes which would be caused by:

(a) doubling the total pressure;

(b) adding more iron metal to the equilibrium mixture;

(c) heating iron in a constant stream of steam instead of in a closed space.

Changes in temperature (exothermic and endothermic reactions)

In the equilibrium which is set up between sulphur dioxide and oxygen, the forward reaction is exothermic:

$$2SO_2(g) + O_2(g) \rightleftharpoons 2SO_3(g)$$
$\triangle H$ negative as we move from left to right

The reverse reaction will, therefore be endothermic by the same amount.

Suppose we have such a system in equilibrium, and that we increase the temperature of the surroundings. Le Chatelier's Principle tells us that the new position of equilibrium will have offset the change to some extent. The only way the reaction can do this is to take in some heat from the surroundings – in other words the position of the equilibrium will move to the left, making more sulphur dioxide and oxygen. Consequently, we can say that the proportion of sulphur trioxide in the equilibrium mixture gets less the higher the temperature of the surroundings.

For a chemical equilibrium which is endothermic in the forward direction, Le Chatelier's Principle tells us that the proportion of product chemical in the reaction mixture will be greater the higher the temperature. If a chemical reaction is neither exothermic nor endothermic, the position of any equilibrium is not affected by the temperature of the surroundings.

You will see the importance of Le Chatelier's Principle to some industrial processes in which the chemical reactions are equilibria, in Section 9.

UNIT 6.2
Summary and learning

1   Most chemical reactions are capable of going in either direction, depending on the conditions. Reactions which 'go to completion' almost always involve a product which is a gas or one which is insoluble.

2   Reactions which do not 'go to completion' form a chemical equilibrium in which the rate of the forward reaction is equal to the rate of the reverse reaction.

3   The make-up of the 'equilibrium mixture' varies from one reaction to another. For some reactions it has a high proportion of product chemicals, while for others it has a low proportion of product chemicals.

4   We can summarise the effect of changing the conditions on the position of a chemical equilibrium in Le Chatelier's Principle.

If a chemical system is in equilibrium and one of the conditions which is involved in the reaction is changed, then the equilibrium will find a new position in which the extent of the change has been offset.

5   You should be able to describe the effect of changes in:
(a) the concentration of reactants and products;
(b) the total outside pressure (reactions which involve gases);
(c) the temperature (exothermic and endothermic reactions);
for chemical systems in equilibrium.

6   You have learnt the meaning of these words:

to completion
reaction mixture
equilibrium
chemical equilibrium

The structure of substances

UNIT 7.1 *The nature of solids*

You learned in Section 1 (Topic 1.2.2) that a solid is one of the three main states in which substances exist. The other two are the liquid state and the gaseous state.

You have also seen that we can understand which of the three states a particular substance will be in at room temperature, if we know how strong the forces are which act between its particles. The strength of these forces depends to a large extent on the chemical nature of the substance, and the type of chemical bonds which it contains. So you know that most metals are solids, that many non-metals are gases, that ionic compounds are usually solids, and that molecular compounds are often gases or liquids. **The important factor is the strength of the force between the particles of the substance**.

You also know a little of what solids, liquids and gases are like, and what happens when a solid melts or when a liquid boils. We use **the kinetic theory** to explain what the three states of matter are like and how they behave. We can summarise these properties in the following table.

	Fixed shape?	Fixed volume?
solids	yes	yes
liquids	no	yes
gases	no	no

Table 7.1

You have already met metals and ionic compounds as examples of solids. You know that many solids form crystals, and the reason for them having such a regular shape. You know that we call the arrangement of particles in a solid a 'lattice'. We can now go on to look at metals and ionic compounds in more detail, and to see that there are two more important types of solid – those formed by some ordinary molecular substances, and the types of solid we get when 'giant' molecules form. Before we do this, however, it is important to know how we can find out what the structure of a solid is.

Finding the structure of solids

By 'structure' we mean the pattern in which the particles of the solid are arranged. How can we find out what this is, when the particles themselves are much too small to see?

For a long time, scientists could not find an answer to this question. So they had to rely on studying very carefully the external shapes of crystals using microscopes, in the hope that this would reveal something about the nature of solids. Unfortunately, in spite of very many hours of painstaking labour, it did not!

Then, in 1912, von Laue suggested something new. He had heard about X-rays (which had been discovered a few years earlier in 1895), and he knew that they were like visible light, but with a much shorter wavelength (shorter even than ultraviolet rays, see Fig. 7.1). He worked out that the distance between the different layers of atoms or ions in a lattice would be about the same as the wavelength of X-rays. From this he calculated that a beam of X-rays would probably be DIFFRACTED when it passed through a solid. This would split the single beam of X-rays into a pattern of beams, which would be different for every solid. By recording the pattern (on photographic film) and studying it, the exact position of the different types of atoms or ions in the solid could be found. So von Laue's idea was tried – and it worked (Fig. 7.2).

Nowadays, X-RAY DIFFRACTION is a very precise technique indeed, and we can use it to find the exact structure of any crystalline solid. You can get some idea of how X-ray diffraction works for yourself, in the following experiment.

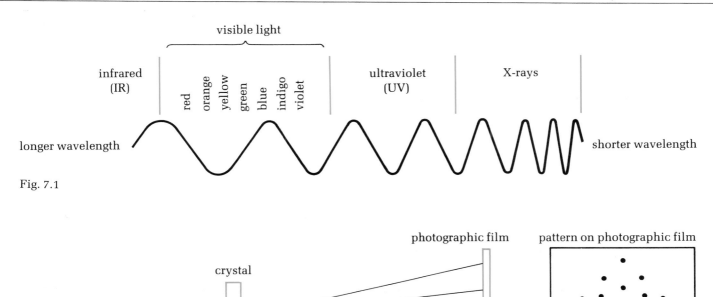

Fig. 7.1

Fig. 7.2

EXPERIMENT 7.1
Mimicking X-ray diffraction

You will need the following: several pieces of material (e.g. handkerchief, nylon, terylene), 6-volt bulb and holder, battery, card with pin-hole, hand-lens.

What to do

THE ROOM SHOULD BE DARKENED.

1 Set up the battery, bulb and piece of card so that the light shines brightly through the pin-hole.

2 Take one of the pieces of material, and hold it up to the pin-point of light. Try tilting it, rotating it and stretching it.

3 Repeat with all the other pieces of material which are available.

4 Look at each piece of cloth with the hand-lens, and try to decide whether the light patterns which you have seen are the same as the patterns of holes in them. If they are not **the same**, are they related in any way? Discuss what you have seen and whether you can decide anything as a result. **Write down what you have decided, and why you have decided it.**

What happened

You should have been able to see a different pattern of spots of light for each material. When the material was turned, the pattern turned as well. When the cloth was tilted or stretched, the pattern changed.

What we can decide

The light pattern is not the same as the pattern of holes, but it is related to it. The closer the holes are together, the wider the light pattern is spread out.

In your experiment, the pin-point of light represented a beam of X-rays, and the holes in the pieces of material represented rows of atoms or ions in a solid. So the results of an X-ray diffraction experiment are similar to the results of your experiment. The pattern which we get from a particular solid is **related to** the position of atoms or ions in it, but not identical to it. Fortunately, we have found ways of using the patterns which we get to give us an exact picture of how the particles in solids are arranged.

Fig. 7.3 *This pattern was produced when X-rays passed through a crystal of synthetic sapphire*

TOPIC 7.1.2

Metals

Metals exist as crystals. This might seem an odd thought at first, because we are not used to thinking of crystals as having the same sorts of properties as metals. Most of the substances which are crystalline and which you have come across before are very weak physically, and will easily shatter. As we shall shortly find out, it is the size of the individual crystals in a metal which can make it strong – or weak!

▶ EXPERIMENT 7.2

You learned in Section 3 that the atoms of metals are so close to each other that they actually touch. When we pack atoms together so that the maximum number are squashed together without any space being wasted, we say that they are CLOSE-PACKED. Again, it might seem strange, but there are two different patterns which are possible with the atoms close-packed in both cases.

▶ DEMONSTRATION 7.1

EXPERIMENT 7.2
Growing metal crystals

You will need the following: petri-dishes, copper wire, silver nitrate solution, zinc foil, lead ethanoate solution, hand-lens.

What to do

1   Just cover the bottom of a petri-dish with silver nitrate solution. Take a piece of clean copper wire, and drop it into the silver nitrate solution. Observe what happens, and examine any crystals with the hand-lens.

2   Half-fill a test-tube with lead ethanoate solution. Take a piece of zinc foil and lower it into the solution. Loop the top of the zinc over the rim of the test-tube and leave it there. Observe what happens (after a few hours), and examine any crystals with the hand-lens.

What happened, and what we can decide

You should have been able to see crystals of silver forming in the petri-dish, and crystals of lead forming on the surface of the zinc. This shows us that metals form crystals.

Fig. 7.4 *You can see crystals in this photograph of a piece of antimony*

DEMONSTRATION 7.1
Two ways of close-packing atoms

The following will be needed: overhead projector, about 40 polystyrene spheres, suitable triangular frame (this can be made using suitably sized books if necessary).

What to do

1   Place the triangular frame on the projector.

2   Add a single layer of spheres, which students will be able to see clearly on the screen.

3   A second layer blocks out more light, showing that the spheres are not directly above those in the first layer.

4   Now show that there are two ways of adding the third layer – completely blocking out the remaining light (and showing that the third row is not directly above either of the first two), or in such a way that the projection on the screen remains unchanged (and showing that the third row **is** directly above one of the other layers, and this must of course be the first layer not the second).

The two types of close-packing are called CUBIC CLOSE-PACKING and HEXAGONAL CLOSE-PACKING. When the three layers are not directly above each other (when all the light was blotted out in your teacher's demonstration), we say the arrangement of the layers is 'a, b, c' (to show that the three layers are different). This is the cubic arrangement. When the third layer is directly above the first layer, we call the arrangement of the layers 'a, b, a'. This is the hexagonal arrangement.

Arrangement of layers	Name	Example of a metal which has this arrangement
a, b, c	cubic close-packing	copper
a, b, a	hexagonal close-packing	zinc

Table 7.2

Some other metals take up an arrangement in which the atoms are not close-packed. We can show what the whole lattice looks like by drawing the smallest part of it which can be repeated to give the whole. We call this 'building block' of the lattice the UNIT CELL. The unit cell for the third type of arrangement in metals is called the BODY-CENTRED CUBIC lattice (Fig. 7.5). You will learn more about unit cells shortly.

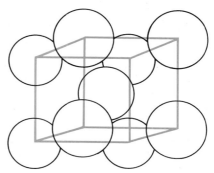

Fig. 7.5 *A body-centred cubic lattice*

The different arrangements of the atoms in different metals gives their crystals different shapes. As a result, the physical properties of the metals are different. But there is one important thing which we can do ourselves to alter the physical properties of a metal.

You saw in Section 3 that metals do not normally 'snap' easily, but they can be drawn into wires, with the rows of atoms 'slipping' over each other. This means that metals will also bend, because bending involves the metal's atoms 'slipping' in the same way. So to make a metal harder, we must simply make it more difficult for the rows of atoms to do this.

If we have pure metal, containing only one type of atom, and if the crystals of that metal are large, then the rows of atoms have nothing to stop them moving.

But suppose that in the layers of atoms there were some other atoms, bigger than the rest. Those bigger atoms would not slip past each other easily. This would make it more difficult to bend the metal – it would be harder (Fig. 7.6(b)).

(a)

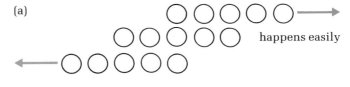

happens easily

(b)

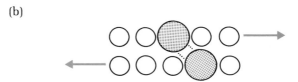

bigger atoms will not slip past each other

Fig. 7.6

This is what happens when we make an **alloy** by adding a small amount of another metal to the main one. Alloys are nearly always harder than either of the metals which make them up.

You know that steel is an alloy, and that there is another way in which we can make it tougher. You saw in Section 5 that we often temper steel in order to make a sharp cutting edge (like a razor blade). If we take something which is molten and cool it very quickly, the atoms do not have much time to line up and form a large, regular lattice. They are 'frozen' in a more irregular pattern. In other words, the more quickly we cool a molten metal, the smaller are the crystals which form. The smaller the crystals, the tougher the metal. The reason is the same as before – if the crystals are small, the rows of atoms cannot slip over each other easily. This is the case, because if we have many small crystals, they are all lined up in different directions. So there simply are no long rows of atoms, and when we apply a force the metal is not distorted.

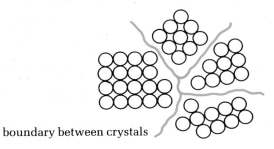

boundary between crystals

Fig. 7.7

So a metal edge which has been sharpened will stay the same shape more easily if the crystals in the metal are small. A tempered metal will allow us to make a sharp edge, which will stay sharp.

So whenever we want to use a metal for some engineering or industrial purpose, we have to make the right alloy, and also treat it in such a way that we get the size of crystals that we need.

TOPIC 7.1.3
Ionic compounds

You have seen that the particles in a metal (atoms) usually arrange themselves so that they are close-packed. It is easy for them to do this because:
(a) the particles are all the same size, and
(b) the particles do not carry positive or negative charges.
(The atoms can get very close together, because there are no strong repulsions between ions which have the same type of charge. Once they are close together, a very regular arrangement can form, because all the particles are identical.)

Ionic compounds do not have either of these advantages. They are made up of cations which have a positive charge, and anions which have a negative charge. Also, most cations are much smaller than

Fig. 7.8   *This Samurai sword has been made from tempered steel*

most anions. So it is not possible for the particles in ionic solids to form a close-packed arrangement.

Suppose we imagine what happens when an ionic solid forms. You know that the forces which hold the particles in an ionic solid together are the attractions between the oppositely charged ions. You also know that charges with the same sign repel each other. So what happens?

At first, when the lattice is beginning to form it is the attractive forces between the cations and anions which are important. So the ions get pulled closer together.

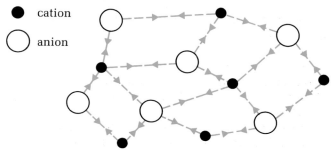

● cation
○ anion

Fig. 7.9

As the ions draw closer together, the repulsive forces between the ions with the same charge become more important. Eventually these repulsions become so strong that they stop the ions moving any closer together. A balance point between the attractive forces and the repulsive forces has been reached – and the lattice has formed.

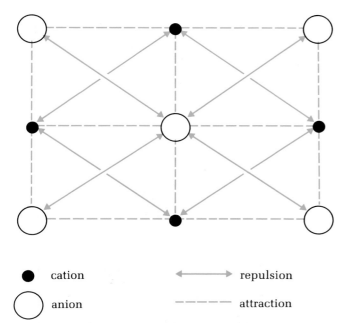

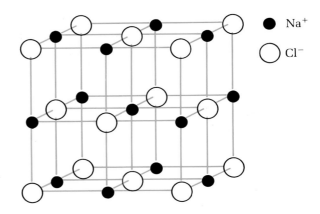

Fig. 7.11 *The sodium chloride lattice*

Fig. 7.10 *The balance of forces in an ionic lattice*

Figure 7.10 shows the sort of situation which arises when the lattice has formed. In fact, the oppositely charged ions get as close as possible to each other as their different sizes will let them, but without ever becoming close-packed. This means that the actual arrangement in space of the cations and anions depends to a large extent on their size, relative to each other.

So each ionic compound has a particular unit cell, because the ratio of the size of the cation to the size of the anion is always the same for that compound. Another ionic compound will always form its own unit cell.

So, are there as many different unit cells as there are ionic compounds? The answer to this question is 'no'. We can prove that there is only a limited number of truly different unit cells – seven in all. If we try to make any more, then the shape will always be a multiple of one of the original seven.

Each ionic compound forms one of the seven possible unit cells – depending on the ratio of the size of the cation to the size of the anion. Different compounds in which this ratio is similar will tend to form the same unit cell.

One of the most common unit cells is that formed by sodium chloride. We call this unit cell a FACED-CENTRED CUBIC lattice.

Look at Fig. 7.11 and concentrate on the chloride ions (the open circles). You will see that they form a cube, but with an extra chloride ion in the centre of each face of the cube. This is where the word 'face-centred' comes from. Now look at the sodium ions (the black dots). They too form a face-centred cube, although we would have to put in another row in one direction or another to see the whole cube. So it is as if we have two interlocking lattices – one of chloride ions arranged into face-centred cubes, and another of sodium ions also arranged into face-centred cubes. Magnesium oxide is another common ionic compound which has exactly the same structure as sodium chloride.

TOPIC 7.1.4
Molecular compounds

You know that the particles in a molecular compound are molecules. The atoms in a molecule are held together strongly by the covalent bonds between them, and molecules have a definite shape depending on the direction of these bonds (see Section 3, Topic 3.3.2). Compared with the forces between the ions of an ionic compound, the forces **between** individual molecules are very weak (see Section 1, Topic 1.3.4). However these forces, which we call VAN DER WAALS' FORCES, do exist. So, while it is generally true that molecular compounds have much lower melting points and boiling points than ionic compounds (and therefore usually exist as gases or liquids at room temperature), nevertheless there are a few that are solids at room temperature.

We have seen that a solid will form as crystals, if the arrangement of its particles is regular. We know that this nearly always happens with solids which are ionic. But does it happen with those which are molecular. Will molecular compounds form crystals?

▶ EXPERIMENT 7.3 (p. 302)

EXPERIMENT 7.3
Will molecular compounds form crystals?

You will need the following: crude naphthalene, ethanol, test-tube to fit centrifuge, 100 cm³ beakers, glass rod, access to centrifuge, access to Buchner funnel, stirring thermometer (−10°C to 110°C), test-tube, hand-lens.

What to do

YOU MUST WEAR YOUR SAFETY SPECTACLES. REMEMBER THAT ETHANOL IS FLAMMABLE.

1   Fill a 100 cm³ beaker about two-thirds full with water. Heat it on a tripod and gauze. Use a stirring thermometer to record the temperature. Stop heating when the temperature reaches about 75°C. Put the beaker on a mat, on the bench.
DO NOT GO ON TO THE NEXT STEP UNTIL ALL THE BUNSEN BURNERS IN THE ROOM HAVE BEEN TURNED OUT.

2   Obtain one of the special test-tubes which can be used in a centrifuge. Put crude naphthalene in this tube, to a depth of about 2 cm. Now add ethanol until the tube is about half-full.

3   Stir the tube with a glass rod, until all the naphthalene has dissolved. Take the tube at once to the centrifuge. **If you have not used a centrifuge before, or if you are uncertain how to, ask your teacher**. Make sure the centrifuge is properly balanced, and centrifuge for about 30 seconds. Have another (ordinary) test-tube ready.

4   As soon as you take the tube out of the centrifuge, pour the liquid part of what it contains into another test-tube. You can leave the solid in the original tube.

5   Take the tube containing the liquid to a tap, and cool it with running water. Keep doing this until solid appears in the tube.

6   Your teacher will have set up some special filter pumps in the laboratory. Go to one of these with your test-tube and one of the filter-papers for using in the funnel attached to the pump. Put the filter-paper in the funnel, and pour the contents of the tube through it, so that it is filtered.

7   Take your filter-paper back to your bench and dry any solid **very carefully** by pressing gently with another (dry) piece of filter-paper. Use a hand-lens to examine what you have made.

What happened and what we can decide

You should have been able to see that the white (or slightly yellow) solid was made up of crystals. Try to describe the shape of these crystals, and draw a picture of them.

What you have just done is to take some crude naphthalene, and to purify it. Naphthalene is a molecular compound which contains the elements carbon and hydrogen.

So at least in some cases, molecular compounds can be crystalline solids.

If molecular **compounds** can form crystals, then so can molecular **elements**. You know that iodine, for instance, is a non-metallic element whose molecules have the formula I_2. You also know that iodine exists as black/purple crystals. We know from the results of X-ray diffraction experiments that the molecules of iodine in its crystals are arranged in a kind of zig-zag pattern. Instead of all the molecules in the pattern being in the same layer, every other molecule is in the next layer above. So it takes two layers of molecules to make up the complete zig-zag ('herring-bone') pattern.

Another molecular element which you have come across is sulphur. You will learn more about sulphur and its reaction in Section 9. But for the moment we are interested in the structure of the element itself. Sulphur forms two different types of crystal, each of which we can make in the laboratory.

▶ PREPARATION 7.1

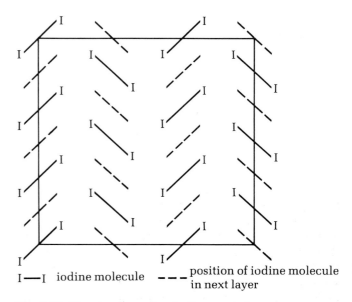

I—I   iodine molecule   - - - position of iodine molecule in next layer

Fig. 7.12 *The structure of an iodine crystal*

PREPARATION 7.1
Making different crystals of sulphur

You will need the following: powdered sulphur, methylbenzene, filter-funnel and filter-paper, boiling-tube, large crucible or evaporating basin, spatula, hand-lens.

What to do

YOU MUST WEAR YOUR SAFETY SPECTACLES. METHYLBENZENE IS HIGHLY FLAMMABLE AND ITS VAPOUR IS HARMFUL. THE ROOM MUST BE WELL VENTILATED.

A Making 'diamond-shaped' sulphur crystals

1   Put 4–5 spatula-measures of powdered sulphur in a test-tube.

2   Now add methylbenzene until the test-tube is one-third full. Heat the test-tube VERY GENTLY in a water-bath (see Experiment 7.3) until all the sulphur dissolves.

3   Filter the solution into a clean test-tube and let it cool. You will see crystals of sulphur beginning to appear. When no more crystals form, take some out using a spatula, and put them on a piece of filter-paper.

4   Use a hand-lens to examine the crystals. Try to draw a diagram of their shape.

BEFORE YOU START THE NEXT PART OF THE PREPARATION, MAKE SURE THAT EVERYONE IN THE ROOM HAS FINISHED WITH METHYLBENZENE AND THAT IT HAS ALL BEEN PUT AWAY.

MAKE SURE THAT YOU KNOW WHERE YOUR TEACHER HAS PLACED THE NEAREST DAMP CLOTH, IN CASE YOU NEED TO USE IT.

B Making 'needle-shaped' sulphur crystals

1   Put about 10 spatula-measures of powdered sulphur in a large crucible or evaporating basin. Heat the basin with a low Bunsen flame and when the sulphur starts to melt, add some more. Carry on until the container is about half-full of molten sulphur. IF THE SULPHUR STARTS TO BURN, TAKE AWAY THE BUNSEN BURNER, FETCH A DAMP CLOTH AND COVER THE CRUCIBLE WITH IT. TELL YOUR TEACHER WHAT HAS HAPPENED.

2   Now put the basin on one side to cool. A crust of solid sulphur will form on the surface.

3   When the crust has fully formed, make two holes in it with a spatula, at either side of the basin. Pour out the liquid sulphur.

4   Now use the spatula to break open the crust all the way round the basin, and lift it out onto a filter-paper.

5   You will see that needle-shaped crystals of sulphur have formed under the crust. Use a hand-lens to examine them. Try to draw a diagram of their shape.

We know that sulphur forms molecules which contain eight sulphur atoms (S_8). These molecules have the shape of a crown.

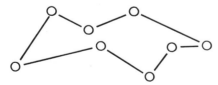

Fig. 7.13 *A sulphur molecule (S_8)*

You have already learnt that crystals are regular on the outside because of the regular arrangement of the particles which make them up. If the same particles arrange themselves in different ways, we can get more than one type of crystal. When sulphur crystallises at a temperature which is below 96°C, the S_8 molecules arrange themselves in such a way that the crystal looks like a diamond, with the top and bottom cut off. We call this form of sulphur RHOMBIC SULPHUR.

If we let sulphur crystallise at a temperature above 96°C however, the S_8 molecules take up different positions, with the result that the crystals which form are needle-shaped. We call this form of sulphur MONOCLINIC SULPHUR.

(a) rhombic sulphur   (b) monoclinic sulphur

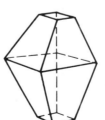
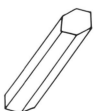

Fig. 7.14

We call the different forms of sulphur its ALLOTROPES, and we say that sulphur is capable of ALLOTROPY. Allotropes are different crystalline forms of the same elements. Any element which has more than one crystalline form is capable of allotropy. Another element which has more than one allotrope is carbon.

Giant molecules

You have met carbon before, and you know that it always forms covalent bonds. As you will see in Section 8, carbon atoms are particularly good at forming covalent bonds **with other carbon atoms**. This means, in the first place, that we can make an almost limitless number of different compounds of carbon. It also means that the element carbon itself can have a very special structure.

Diamond

You learned in Section 3 that a carbon atom (for instance in the compound methane) can form four covalent bonds pointing to the four corners of a tetrahedron. If we start with a single carbon atom, and put four others at the corners of the tetrahedron, each of them can form three more covalent bonds to other carbon atoms. We can go on like this as long as we wish, until we have a molecule which contains literally millions of atoms of carbon.

Because a tetrahedron is a regular shape, the arrangement of carbon atoms in this giant molecule is also regular – and so we get a crystal. The name of the crystal is – a diamond!

Fig. 7.15 *A tiny part of the giant molecule 'diamond'*

You can see in Fig. 7.15 that the carbon atoms in diamond form rings containing six atoms. You should also be able to see the beginnings of a shape that actually looks like a diamond! The arrangement of carbon atoms in diamond is regular, and open. This makes diamonds shiny and transparent. You can also see that it would be very difficult to shatter or bend diamond, because each atom is held firmly in place by its four bonds. To split a piece off a diamond would mean breaking millions of covalent bonds. As a result, diamond is one of the hardest substances which exist, and diamonds are (almost) indestructible. You have probably heard the phrase 'diamonds are forever'!

Diamonds are so tough that we use them as the cutting edge in drills for cutting through rock.

Fig. 7.16 *The cutting edge of the tool used to engrave this silver bangle is a row of man-made diamonds*

Graphite

But diamond is only one allotrope of carbon. As well as forming a tetrahedral shape, carbon atoms are able to form a triangular shape and a linear shape (as in carbon dioxide, see p. 158). If many carbon atoms join together using the triangular shape, then flat sheets of atoms (in rings of six) will be formed. This is what happens when the allotrope of carbon called 'graphite' forms. The sheets of atoms are held together weakly by van der Waals' forces.

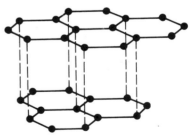

Fig. 7.17 *Part of the parallel sheets of carbon atoms in 'graphite'*

In graphite, the sheets of carbon atoms easily slip over each other. So graphite is not a strong solid. Instead, because of its 'slippery' nature, we sometimes add it to oil used in car engines to make the oil more effective. The layers can also be separated from each other – if you rub graphite on a piece of paper it leaves a mark (several layers of atoms have stayed behind on the paper).

You know that carbon is a non-metal, but that graphite allows electricity to pass through itself (like a metal). Turn back to Section 3 (p. 162) and read again the explanation of how metals allow electricity to pass.

You should be able to remember that a carbon atom has four electrons in its outermost shell. If it forms four covalent bonds (as in diamond), each of these electrons is paired with one from another atom. So each of the four electrons is being 'used'. In graphite, each carbon atom uses only three of its outermost electrons to form covalent bonds, and so each has one electron 'left over'. As with a metal, then, each carbon atom has one electron from its outermost shell which goes with all the others to make a 'sea' of electrons over the whole structure. So, as with a metal, if we put another electron in at one end of a piece of graphite, another electron is pushed out at the other end. Graphite allows electricity to pass.

Because its atoms are arranged in a regular way, graphite is crystalline. However, the crystals are very fine. Other forms of carbon that you know about, such as soot, are also made of the same sort of crystal, although these are extremely small. As we have seen, graphite is a very soft solid. However, there is one way in which it can add strength to other substances. If we heat it to a very high temperature, about 1500°C, we can make it form long strands called FIBRES. When these fibres are built into a plastic, the reinforced material is light and strong. Such substances are particularly good for making sports equipment.

Fig. 7.18 *These rackets have been reinforced with graphite fibres*

We have seen that because the carbon atoms are arranged differently in diamond and graphite, the two allotropes have different properties. Another difference between them is that the carbon atoms are, on average, closer together in diamond than in graphite. So diamond is the denser form. The differences between diamond and graphite are summarised in Table 7.3.

	Diamond	Graphite
Appearance	colourless, clear and shiny	black and opaque, with small crystal grains visible
Hardness	very hard	soft
Allow electricity to pass	no	yes
Density	$3.5\,\mathrm{g\,cm^{-3}}$	$2.2\,\mathrm{g\,cm^{-3}}$

Table 7.3

UNIT 7.1
Summary and learning

1   Solids are one of the three main states of matter. They have a fixed shape and a fixed volume. If the particles which make up the solid are arranged in a regular way, the solid has a regular shape (it forms crystals).

2   We can find the arrangement of the particles in a crystalline solid, using X-ray diffraction.

3   Metals are crystalline solids. Normally, their atoms are 'close-packed', and there are two different ways of producing this arrangement. We can make metals stronger by adding a few atoms of another element (forming an alloy). We can also make them stronger by making the size of the metal crystals smaller.

4   When an ionic crystal forms, the ions come together until the forces of attraction between oppositely charged ions are balanced by the forces of repulsion between ions having the same sign of charge. All ionic crystals fit into one of seven basic 'unit cells'. You should be able to describe the arrangement of the ions in a unit cell of sodium chloride.

5   Some molecular substances are solids at room temperature. If the molecules are arranged in a regular way, these solids are crystalline. You should be able to describe the arrangement of the molecules in an iodine crystal.

6   If there is more than one regular way to arrange the molecules in a molecular element, it forms different allotropes. You should remember how to make the two allotropes of sulphur, and you should be able to describe their shape.

7   If a molecular substance forms giant molecules in which the atoms are arranged in a regular pattern, the molecule itself forms a crystal. Diamond, which is one of the allotropes of the element carbon, forms such a molecular crystal. The other allotrope of carbon is graphite. You should remember the arrangement of

carbon atoms in diamond and graphite, and you should be able to explain their different properties.

8   You have learnt the meaning of these words:

diffracted
X-ray diffraction
close-packed
cubic close-packing
hexagonal close-packing
unit cell
body-centred cubic
   (lattice)
face-centred cubic
   (lattice)

van der Waals' forces
rhombic sulphur
monoclinic sulphur
allotropes
allotropy
fibres

UNIT 7.2   *The nature of liquids, solutions and gases*

You learned in Section 1 (Topic 1.2.2) that liquids and gases have no definite structure. That is why neither of these stages of matter has a fixed shape (see Table 7.1).

In liquids, the particles move about constantly, forming clusters which break up and form again somewhere else. The constant movement of the particles in a liquid in a random manner leads to the Brownian motion of any small particle of a solid which finds itself on the surface of a liquid (see Section 1, p. 22).

In gases, the particles move about independently of each other, at tremendous speeds. As a result, a gas will always take up any space into which it can escape.

You also saw in Section 1, that it is the strength of the forces between the particles of a substance which decide whether it will be a solid, a liquid or a gas at room temperature. You also know that these forces are strongest in ionic compounds and weakest in substances which are molecular. So, in general, ionic compounds are solids at room temperature. Other substances which exist normally as solids will also have strong forces between the particles, as is the case with most metals, and some non-metals like iodine, sulphur and carbon. Other molecular substances will be liquids or gases.

The theory which explains the nature of substances as solids, liquids or gases in terms of the movement of particles and the forces between them is called **the**

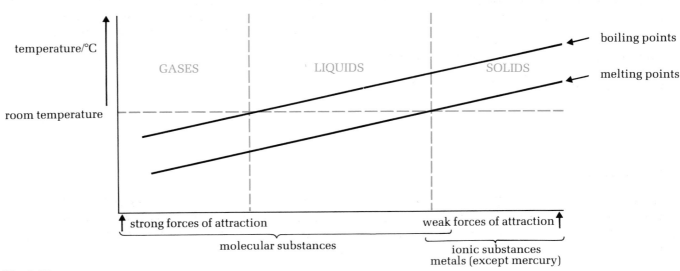

Fig. 7.19

kinetic theory. This theory tells us that energy is needed to change a solid into a liquid, or a liquid into a gas. Enthalpy of fusion and enthalpy of vaporisation were also defined in Section 1.

We can now go on to look more closely at these changes of state, at liquids (particularly water) and at gases.

TOPIC 7.2.1

Pure liquids – changes of state

EXPERIMENT 7.4

What happens when a liquid freezes?

You will need the following: solid to be melted (suitable solids are hexadecan-1-ol, octadecan-1-ol, hexadecanoic acid and octadecanoic acid: naphthalene should not be used), long stirring thermometer, boiling-tube, apparatus to set up water-bath, graph paper, stopclock or watch with second hand.

What to do

THE ROOM MUST BE WELL VENTILATED.

1   Set up a water-bath using a beaker big enough to hold a boiling-tube.

2   Fill a boiling-tube about half-full of pieces of the solid which you have been given, and place it in the water-bath.

3   Heat the water-bath until the solid just melts, and place the stirring thermometer in the boiling-tube.

4   Take the boiling-tube out of the water-bath, stir and record the temperature of the liquid

5   Keep stirring, and record the temperature every minute. Carry on recording the temperature of the liquid at one-minute intervals, even after it solidifies, until a temperature of about 65 °C is reached.

6   **Discuss your results with the others in your group, and try to decide what has happened. Write down what you have decided, and why you have decided it.**

7   Draw a graph, using the results of your experiment, with temperature on the vertical axis and time along the horizontal axis.

What happened

You should have been able to see that the temperature of the liquid stayed almost constant as it solidified. When all the liquid had frozen, the temperature started to fall again.

What we can decide

We know that when we melt a solid, we have to supply energy. Melting is endothermic. The reverse change, freezing, must be exothermic. The temperature of the naphthalene stayed constant all the time it was freezing, because the heat given out was enough to keep it at its freezing temperature (melting point).

PROJECT 7.1

Design an experiment like Experiment 7.4, but which will answer the question, 'What happens when a liquid boils?' You should use water as the liquid.

When you have shown your experimental design to your teacher, carry out the experiment. Record your results in the form of a graph.

When a liquid boils, we have to supply energy in the form of heat. The heat is used to convert the particles of the substance from the liquid to the gaseous state. So, while the liquid boils, the temperature does not rise. We could combine the results of Experiment 7.4 and of your own experiment to show what happens to the temperature as we heat a solid, melt it, heat the liquid, continue heating as the liquid boils, and then heat the gas. A graph of temperature v. time would look like Fig. 7.20.

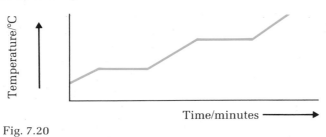

Fig. 7.20

Questions

1　Copy out Fig. 7.20. Mark the following on the graph.
(a) The melting point of the solid.
(b) The boiling point of the liquid.
(c) The period during which the solid was being heated.
(d) The period during which the solid was melting.
(e) The period during which the liquid was being heated.
(f) The period during which the liquid was boiling.
(g) The period during which the gas was being heated.

2　Use the kinetic theory to explain
(a) why melting is endothermic and freezing is exothermic;
(b) why boiling is endothermic and condensing is exothermic.

▶　EXPERIMENT 7.5

EXPERIMENT 7.5

How are the pressure of the surrounding gas and the boiling point of a liquid linked?

> **Your teacher will show you this experiment**

The following will be needed: round-bottomed flask (500 cm³), bung with two holes (one fitted with short delivery tube, rubber tubing and clip), thermometer ($-10°C$ to $110°C$), anti-bumping granules, cloth, distilled water, Perspex screen.

What to do

A SCREEN SHOULD BE PLACED BETWEEN THE APPARATUS AND THE CLASS, AND THE TEACHER SHOULD BE SIMILARLY PROTECTED.

1　Put the thermometer through the bung, and position it just at the entrance to the neck of the flask.

2　Remove the bung, add anti-bumping granules, and fill the flask about one-third full of distilled water.

3　Boil the water and replace the bung with the rubber tubing unclipped. Allow the water to continue boiling for about half a minute to drive out any remaining air. During this time, take the temperature being recorded on the thermometer.

4　Now take the heat away, and immediately clip the rubber tubing firmly. Clamp the flask upside-down. The thermometer bulb should not be in the water.

5　Soak a cloth in cold water, and place it on the flask. The water will start to boil, and its temperature can be recorded.

6　Carry on cooling the flask using the damp cloth, until no further lowering of the boiling point of the water can be achieved.

What happened

When the flask was cooled, some of the steam which it contained condensed. This caused the pressure above the water to be lowered. The more steam that was condensed, the lower the pressure became. At the same time, the water continued to boil, at lower and lower temperatures.

What we can decide

A liquid boils when the vapour pressure above its surface caused by evaporation is equal to the pressure of the surrounding gases. When the pressure of the surrounding gases is lowered, the vapour pressure which has to be reached before the liquid boils is also lowered. So the temperature which is needed to achieve this vapour pressure is lowered. The lower the pressure of the surrounding gases, the lower the boiling point of a liquid.

We can use the results of Experiment 7.5 to tell us something about all liquids. The lower the pressure of the surrounding gases, the lower the boiling point of any liquid will be. It is therefore also the case that the higher the pressure of the surrounding gases, the higher the boiling point of any liquid will be.

Question

Use the kinetic theory to explain

(a) why lowering the pressure of the surrounding gases lowers the boiling point of a liquid; and
(b) why increasing the pressure of the surrounding gases increases the boiling point of a liquid.

Since the boiling point of a liquid depends on the pressure of the surrounding gas, we should always be careful to mention along with the boiling point of a liquid the pressure at which the boiling point was measured. For instance, the boiling point of pure water is 100°C, at 1 atmosphere pressure. We normally give boiling points measured at a pressure of 1 atmosphere.

As well as depending on the pressure, we know that the boiling point of a liquid depends on the strength of the forces of attraction between the particles. That is why the boiling points of different liquids (measured at the same pressure) are different.

When a given liquid is boiling, we have to supply the energy needed to pull the particles away from each other. This energy is called the enthalpy of vaporisation. You learned the definition of enthalpy of vaporisation in Section 1. In order to compare the enthalpy of vaporisation for one substance with that for another, we have to take a certain amount of each. We could take 1 g or 1000 g, or any particular mass. It would be fairer, though, to take the same number of particles. So we normally measure enthalpies of vaporisation in kilojoules **per mole** (kJ mol^{-1}).

We can measure the enthalpies of vaporisation of different liquids in the laboratory. All we have to do is to measure the amount of energy given out per second by a Bunsen burner, or some other source of heat like an electrical heater, and then use it to boil a liquid. If we measure for how long the liquid boils, and how much of it boils away during this time (by weighing the container before and after we start timing) we can work out how much energy we need to boil a certain amount of it.

Suppose we have an electrical heater which gives out 50 joules per second, and suppose we put it into 100 g of the liquid benzene already at the boiling point. If we heat for 5 minutes, the mass of benzene will go down to 64 g. The heater gives out 50 joules per second. So in 5 minutes it gives out

$$5 \times 60 \times 50 = 15\,000 \text{ joules} = 15 \text{ kJ}$$

The mass of benzene converted to vapour by 15 kJ is $100 - 64$ g $= 36$ g. 1 mole of benzene has a mass of 72 g. So 36 g is $36/72 = \frac{1}{2}$ mole.

So, if it takes 15 kJ to convert $\frac{1}{2}$ mole of benzene from the liquid to vapour at the boiling point, it will take 30 kJ to convert 1 mole. So we can say that the **enthalpy of vaporisation of benzene is 30 kJ mol^{-1}**.

Once we have measured the enthalpy of vaporisation for different liquids, we can use it to find out more about liquids. For instance, we have seen that enthalpies of vaporisation depend on the strength of the forces between the particles of a liquid. It is this same factor which influences the boiling point of the liquid. So, the stronger the forces of attraction, the higher the boiling point and the higher the enthalpy of vaporisation. If we compare different liquids, do boiling point and enthalpy of vaporisation march hand-in-hand? Is there always a relationship between these two quantities for a liquid? If so, how strong is this relationship?

PROJECT 7.2
The relationship between boiling point and enthalpy of vaporisation

Here is some information about some typical chemicals:

Name	Boiling point/°C	Enthalpy of vaporisation/kJ mol^{-1}
hydrogen chloride	−85.1	16.1
hydrogen bromide	−66.7	17.6
hydrogen sulphide	−61.8	18.6
dimethyl ether	−24.8	21.5
ethoxyethane	35.0	26.0
carbon disulphide	46.3	27.2
trichloromethane	61.2	29.4
hexane	69.0	29.5
tetrachloromethane	76.8	30.4
benzene	80.1	30.9
tin(IV) chloride	114.1	34.7
tin(IV) bromide	205	41.0

Table 7.4

Draw a graph of boiling point against enthalpy of vaporisation for these twelve compounds. Put enthalpy of vaporisation on the vertical axis and boiling point on the horizontal axis.

You will see from the graph which you have drawn in Project 7.2 that there is the same relationship between boiling point and enthalpy of vaporisation for most chemical substances. One substance for which this relationship does not hold is water – but water is a very special compound, as we shall shortly see. Before then we should look at the properties of liquids which contain dissolved substances.

TOPIC 7.2.2

Liquids which contain dissolved substances

You already know that water is good at dissolving other chemicals – solids, liquids and gases. We say that water is a good **solvent**. It will dissolve most ionic compounds and many molecular compounds. But are there other types of solvent? And what types of chemical will they dissolve?

▶   EXPERIMENT 7.6

EXPERIMENT 7.6
Solvents other than water

You will need the following: naphthalene (or the solid used in Experiment 7.4), salt, ethanol, 1,1,1-trichloroethane.

What to do

ETHANOL IS HIGHLY INFLAMMABLE. AVOID BREATHING THE FUMES OF ETHANOL AND THOSE OF 1,1,1-TRICHLOROETHANE. THE ROOM SHOULD BE WELL VENTILATED.

1   You have two solutes – naphthalene (or a similar solid) and salt, and three solvents – water, ethanol and 1,1,1-trichloroethane. Try dissolving a small amount of each of the solids in each solvent in turn. (Try about 2 spatula-measures in a third of a test-tube full of solvent.) DO NOT ATTEMPT TO WARM – if a solid will not dissolve in one of the solvents, try stirring and shaking.

2   Try dissolving a little of each of the other two solvents in water in a test-tube.

3   **Discuss what you have seen and what you think you can decide. Write down what you have decided and why you have decided it.**

What happened

You should have been able to see that salt dissolves in water, but not in the other two solvents, and that the reverse was true for naphthalene (or the other solid you were given). Ethanol dissolves in water, but 1,1,1-trichloroethane does not.

What we can decide

Naphthalene (or the solid you were given which is like naphthalene) is a typical molecular compound, and salt is a typical ionic compound. Ethanol and 1,1,1-trichloroethane are molecular compounds.

Molecular compounds which will not dissolve in water will often dissolve in other molecular compounds which are liquids. We call these molecular solvents ORGANIC SOLVENTS, because they contain the element carbon (see Section 8: most of the compounds which contain carbon are called ORGANIC COMPOUNDS). Organic solvents are usually very poor at dissolving ionic compounds such as sodium chloride.

Most organic solvents are insoluble in water. We say they are IMMISCIBLE with water (they do not mix with water). A few organic compounds do dissolve in water. We say they are MISCIBLE with water. Ethanol is miscible with water – you will see the reason for this shortly.

So, most molecular compounds will only dissolve in liquids which are molecular (organic solvents) and will not dissolve in water. Most ionic compounds will only dissolve in water and will not dissolve in organic solvents. A few molecular compounds such as ethanol and sugar will dissolve in organic solvents and in water. We can represent this state of affairs in a Venn diagram (Fig. 7.21).

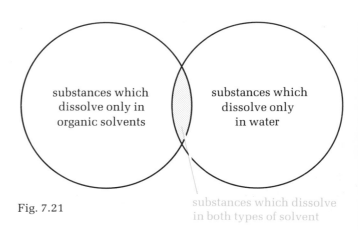

Fig. 7.21

substances which dissolve only in organic solvents

substances which dissolve only in water

substances which dissolve in both types of solvent

We shall look more closely at the process of dissolving shortly. But first, we should ask ourselves a simple question about solutions. Are they the same in their properties as pure solvents, or are they different? If they are different, in what way?

In Section 1, you learnt that the melting point and boiling point of a substance can be used to decide whether or not it is pure. So, if we think of a solution as a pure substance (the solvent) which contains a small amount of impurity (the solute), we might expect its freezing point to be slightly different from that of the pure solvent. We should also expect the boiling point of a solution to be slightly different from that of the pure solvent. We can get an idea of what happens by looking at a simple, and common, system – ice and salt.

EXPERIMENT 7.7

How does salt alter the freezing point of water?

You will need the following: filter-funnel, 250 cm³ beaker, thermometer (−10°C to 110°C), crushed ice, salt.

What to do

1 Gently clamp a filter-funnel above the bench, over a 250 cm³ beaker.

2 Fill the funnel with crushed ice, and place the thermometer in the middle of the ice, with its bulb below the surface.

crushed ice

Fig. 7.22

3 After a few minutes, the reading on the thermometer will stop falling. Write down the temperature of the ice.

4 Now add several spatula-measures of salt to the ice.

5 Notice and record all the changes which happen. **Discuss what you have seen and try to decide what is happening. Write down what you have decided, and why you have decided it**.

What happens

You should have been able to see that the ice started to melt when salt was added to it. At the same time, the reading on the thermometer fell.

What we can decide

Salt is very soluble in water. So when it is added to ice, a little dissolves. The freezing point of a solution of salt in water is lower than the freezing point of pure water. So the ice begins to melt, because in the presence of salt it is now above its freezing point. You know that when we warm a pure solid and it melts, the temperature remains constant because the enthalpy of fusion is being taken in (Fig. 7.20). In this case, however, we are not warming the ice, and energy is also needed to pull the sodium chloride lattice apart. So heat has to be taken from somewhere in the solution of salt in water. As a result, the solution which forms is cooled down as the salt makes more ice melt, and the reading on the thermometer falls to below 0°C.

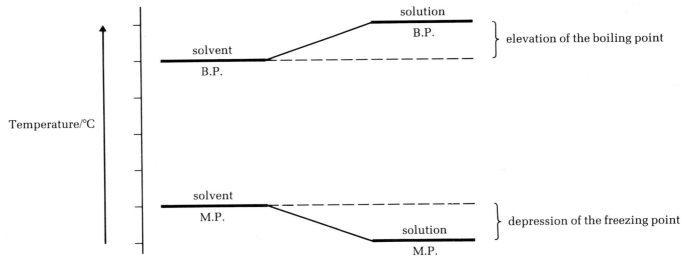

Fig. 7.23

We can put the above simply by saying that salt lowers the freezing point of water. Any solute dissolved in any solvent DEPRESSES the freezing point of that solvent. So solutions freeze at lower temperatures than pure solvents. In a similar way, any solute dissolved in any solvent increases the boiling point of that solvent. We say that the boiling point of the solvent is ELEVATED (Fig. 7.23).

Question

Why does spreading salt on icy roads in winter make them safer?

We have seen the changes which are brought about at the freezing point and boiling point by dissolving a substance in a liquid. But what about the normal process of dissolving? What energy changes take place when a substance dissolves? We must answer this question in two parts – what energy change is involved in just dissolving a solute, and what is involved in making a more dilute solution? The reason for this is that when we 'dissolve' a solid in a liquid, we do two things – we first of all dissolve it, then we make a more dilute solution.

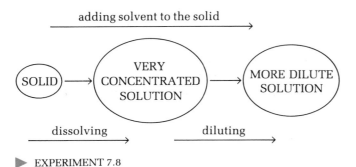

▶ EXPERIMENT 7.8

We should be able to understand why dissolving is endothermic and why diluting is exothermic, because we know from Section 4 (Topic 4.2.2) what causes the energy change during a reaction. A chemical change is endothermic if the forces of attraction (or bonds) which are broken are stronger than those which form. When we dissolve an ionic solid, we have to overcome the very strong forces of attraction between the oppositely charged ions in the lattice. This needs more energy than is given out by the forces of attraction between the ions and the solvent molecules. So dissolving is endothermic.

Diluting, on the other hand, must involve stronger bonds being formed, since it is exothermic. In a very concentrated solution each ion may be attached to only one solvent molecule. If more solvent molecules are suddenly available, many more become attached to each ion – sometimes in several layers. New bonds are forming all the time, and so energy is given out.

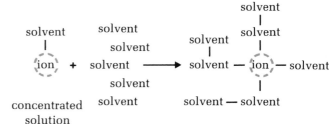

Fig. 7.24 *Dilution*

We call the energy given out by this process the SOLVATION ENERGY, because the process itself is called SOLVATION. The energy which has to be supplied during **dissolving** is the energy needed to break down the lattice – or the LATTICE ENERGY. For a particular solid, the overall process of dissolving the solid and making a dilute solution may be exothermic or

EXPERIMENT 7.8
What energy changes take place during dissolving and diluting?

You will need the following: stirring thermometer graduated in 0.1°C, 250 cm³ beaker, finely divided crystals of sodium nitrate and ammonium nitrate, copper(II) sulphate crystals.

What to do

DO NOT GRIND AMMONIUM NITRATE IN A MORTAR AND PESTLE.

A   Dissolving

1   Half fill a 250 cm³ beaker with water. Record its temperature. Place several spatula-measures of finely divided sodium nitrate crystals on a piece of paper. Tip all the solid into the beaker in one go, and stir with the thermometer. Record what happens to the temperature as the solid dissolves.

2   Repeat, using ammonium nitrate instead of sodium nitrate

B   Diluting

1   Make a concentrated solution of copper(II) sulphate in the bottom of a beaker by dissolving 4−5

spatula-measures of copper(II) sulphate crystals in the smallest possible amount of water.

2   Let the beaker stand for several minutes, until it returns to room temperature.

3   Place the thermometer in the concentrated solution, and record its temperature.

4   Add a very small amount of water (about 5 cm³), and stir with the thermometer. Record what happens to the temperature. Keep adding water, 5 cm³ at a time, and recording any temperature change, until nothing further happens

What happened

You should have been able to see that when sodium nitrate and ammonium nitrate dissolved, the temperature fell. When a solution of copper(II) sulphate was made more dilute, the temperature rose.

What we can decide

Dissolving is an endothermic process. Dilution is an exothermic process.

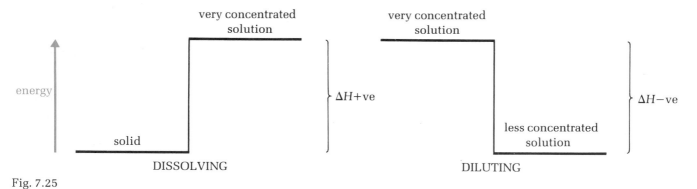

Fig. 7.25

endothermic. If the lattice energy is greater than the solvation energy, overall the change will be endothermic. If the solvation energy is larger, overall the change will be exothermic.

When we dissolve most ionic solids, and make a dilute solution, energy is given out. This is because the solvation energy is normally larger than the lattice energy. But it is important that you remember that this change takes place in two parts – and that **dissolving is itself an endothermic process**.

You know that most ionic compounds are soluble in water. But how soluble? We could not, for instance,

go on adding solute to a solution for ever. At some point, the solvent would not be able to dissolve any more solid, and the solution would be 'saturated'. You first met saturated solutions in Section 1.

A saturated solution of a certain solute in a certain solvent is one which contains as much solute as will dissolve at that temperature, and must have some undissolved solute present.

Suppose we took a saturated solution and warmed it. Some more solid might dissolve. So the solubility of substances may change with the temperature.

Before we can go on to find out more about this possibility, we must have a clear idea of what we mean by the solubility of a solid. Obviously, the amount of a solid which will dissolve depends on the amount of solvent present, and on the temperature. So we must always compare solubilities using the same amount of solvent, and we must record the temperature at which we measure the solubility.

The solubility of a certain solute in a certain solvent is the number of grams of the solute which are needed to saturate 100 g of the solvent, at that particular temperature.

▶ EXPERIMENT 7.9

You saw in Section 1 (Topic 1.1.2) that we can use the fact that the solubility of different salts changes with temperature to a different extent, in order to separate them by fractional crystallisation. You should turn to Experiment 1.3 (p. 9) and read through the explanation of what happened when you separated potassium nitrate from copper(II) sulphate using this method.

Questions

Answer these questions using the information in Fig. 7.26.

1   For which salt does solubility increase most rapidly as the temperature increases?

2   For which salt does solubility increase least rapidly as the temperature increases?

3   At what temperature are the solubilities of potassium chloride and potassium chlorate equal?

EXPERIMENT 7.9
How do solubilities change with temperature?

You will need the following: stirring thermometer, access to top-pan balance, boiling-tube, measuring cylinder, either of the following solids – sodium chloride, potassium chloride.

What to do

1   Carry out the experiment on one of the salts listed above. Weigh out the following amounts,depending on which solid you are using:
    sodium chloride   3.8 g
    potassium chloride   5.0 g

2   Put the solid you have weighed out into the boiling-tube. Add 10 cm³ of water using a measuring cylinder. Warm the boiling-tube until all the solid dissolves.

3   Let the solution cool, and stir with the thermometer. As soon as crystals appear, note the temperature. The solution is saturated, and the temperature you have noted is the temperature at which the solubility is 38 g per 100 g of water for sodium chloride and 50 g per 100 g of water for potassium chloride.

4   Add another 10 cm³ of water, and repeat the above. When crystals form again, note the temperature and work out the number of grams of solute dissolved per 100 g of water.

5   Carry on until you have added 60 g of water.

6   Record your results on a graph of solubility against temperature.

What happened, and what we can decide

You should have been able to see that the solubility of the salt which you investigated decreased as the temperature decreased. The change is more dramatic for some salts than for others. Figure 7.26 shows the 'solubility curves' for some common salts.

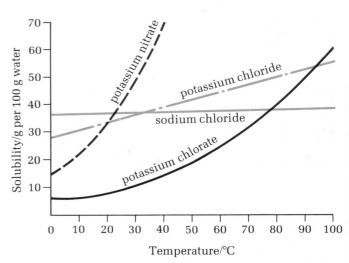

Fig. 7.26

4 Suppose you had a solution which contained the same number of grams of potassium chloride and potassium chlorate, at a temperature of 90°C. If you cooled the solution, which salt would crystallise first?

5 Suppose that in question 4 you had 100 g of water containing 40 g of each salt. What mass of the first salt to crystallise could you obtain on its own before any of the second salt started to crystallise?

PROJECT 7.3

For both the salts which you investigated in Experiment 7.9, solubility of the substance increased as the temperature increased.

We can think of a saturated solution as being a system in equilibrium. The solution is obviously very concentrated, so if any more solute were to dissolve, the process would be dissolving (endothermic), not diluting (exothermic). Would you expect from Le Chatelier's Principle that solubility would increase with increasing temperature, or not? Explain your answer.

TOPIC 7.2.3

Water – a very special liquid

Fig. 7.27 *The blue planet*

As far as we know, the Earth is the only planet which has seas of the chemical which we call water. It is certainly the only planet in the inner part of our own solar system which has this. We saw in Section 2 (Topic 2.1.3) that 70% of the surface of the Earth is covered with water and that only 30% is dry land.

Many scientists believe that it is possible for life to exist only where there are large amounts of water. Water is a good solvent for different types of chemical, and so it allows them to come into contact with each other, starting the chemical reactions which almost certainly lead to the evolution of life. Water vapour in the atmosphere also cuts out harmful ultraviolet radiations from space which would otherwise damage all living things. Water does one more important thing – it provides an environment in which the temperature does not vary too much. It takes a lot of heat to increase the temperature of water, and a lot of cooling to lower its temperature. So the Earth's water acts as a kind of 'buffer' to large temperature changes. Compare the maximum and minimum temperature figures for the surface of the sea on the Earth and the surface of Mars (where there is very little water).

	Earth	Mars
Minimum temperature recorded	−2°C	−85°C
Maximum temperature recorded	35.6°C	−30°C
Temperature range	37.6 Celsius degrees	55 Celsius degrees

Table 7.5

So water is a very important chemical, but it is also a very special one because of the special properties which it has. Why does water behave the way it does?

At the start of any investigation of water, we should consider its composition and formula. We can show both simply, by passing an electric current through it in an apparatus called a voltameter.

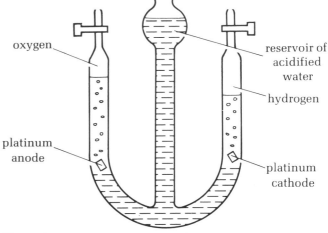

Fig. 7.28

You know from the rules of electrolysis (Section 4) that passing an electric current through acidified water using platinum electrodes causes hydrogen to be discharged at the cathode and oxygen to be discharged at the anode. In effect, water is split into the elements which make it up.

We can use the apparatus shown in Fig. 7.28 to measure the volumes of the gases produced at the two electrodes. When the current is switched off, we can use the reservoir of acidified water to push out of the apparatus the gas which has collected in each limb in turn, by opening the relevant tap. We can connect an apparatus which lets us measure the volume of gas which is pushed out. If we do this, we discover that the volume of hydrogen is always exactly twice the volume of oxygen. By Avogadro's Hypothesis, there are twice as many molecules of hydrogen. Since both elements are diatomic, the water molecule must contain twice as many hydrogen atoms as oxygen atoms. In other words, the empirical formula for water is H_2O. We know that the relative molecular mass of water is 18, and so its molecular formula is H_2O.

You learned about the bonding in the water molecule, and about its shape in Section 3 (Topic 3.3.2). But we need some more information before we can start to explain exactly why water behaves as it does. We can find a clue to the reasons for its properties if we look at the values for the enthalpy of vaporisation and the boiling points of water and of ethanol, and compare these with the graph produced in Project 7.2.

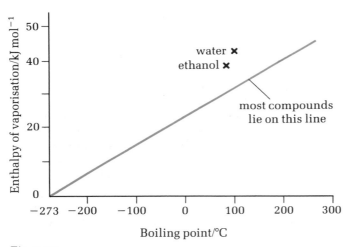

Fig. 7.29

For both water and ethanol, the enthalpy of vaporisation is higher than 'expected' if they were to lie on the same line as other compounds. This means that there must be an extra force of attraction between the molecules in these compounds. This extra attraction results in its needing more energy to separate their molecules than would otherwise be the case.

You learned in Section 3 (Topic 3.3.3) that water takes part in hydrogen bonding, because it contains a hydrogen atom covalently bonded to a non-metal atom (oxygen).

The formula for ethanol is C_2H_5OH, and it too has hydrogen bonds.

If water and ethanol can form hydrogen bonds with themselves, they can do so with each other, and this explains the ability of water to dissolve ethanol and other molecular compounds which contain the –O–H grouping (such as sugars). The existence of hydrogen bonds in water also explains its ability to absorb heat without too great a rise in temperature. Because there is a stronger than usual force of attraction between the molecules in water, it takes more energy to get them moving at a particular speed than for other compounds. It is as if the hydrogen bonds in water 'glue' the molecules together, or make them 'sticky'.

The hydrogen bonds in water also give it another strange property. Water is one of only a handful of chemical substances for which the solid form is less dense than the liquid. When water freezes, the hydrogen bonds hold the molecules in an open arrangement in which the average distance between them is actually greater than the average distance between the molecules when water is in the liquid form.

There is one important property of water which we have not yet explained – its ability to dissolve ionic compounds. Water is a molecular compound so we might expect it to dissolve only other molecular compounds. But it is in fact better at dissolving ionic compounds than molecular compounds. How can this be?

If we take a rod (made of plastic or some other suitable material) which has been charged with static electricity, and hold it close to a stream of water coming from a tap, the stream of water is bent towards the rod! This happens because, in the first place, a molecule of water is slightly charged, even though it is a molecule. The electrons in a water molecule are attracted more towards the two hydrogen atoms. We say that water is a POLAR molecule.

So if a water molecule comes close to a strong positive charge, say, the negative end of it is attracted, and the positive end is repelled.

In the stream of water passing the charged rod, **all** the water molecules are attracted in this way. Their negative ends will be attracted if the rod has a positive charge, and their positive ends are attracted if it has a negative charge. What happens then is that each water molecule becomes **more polar**. The electrons in the bonds in a water molecule are able, to some extent, to move – closer to the oxygen atom, or closer to the hydrogen atoms. Electrons have a negative charge, so they are attracted towards a positive charge, or away from a negative charge. Whether the rod is positively charged or negatively charged, then, the effect is the same – to make the water molecules more charged.

We say that water molecules, as well as being **polar**, are POLARISABLE. Because each molecule is more strongly charged as a result, it is strongly attracted to the charged rod (whether this is itself positive or negative). The overall effect on a stream of water is

strong enough to make it move physically.

When we put an ionic compound in water, the cations and anions polarise the surrounding water molecules, which then attach themselves strongly. A polarised water molecule can polarise the next water molecule, and so on. In the end, each cation and each anion has many water molecules attached to it. For instance, sodium chloride dissolved in water $(Na^+(aq) + Cl^-(aq))$ looks like this:

This explains two things:
1. the ability of water to dissolve ionic compounds;
2. the fact that solvation energies are large and exothermic (because so many 'bonds' are formed).

So water is able to dissolve ionic compounds and many molecular compounds. We saw in Section 2 (Topic 2.3.2) that this means that water easily becomes polluted – with industrial waste, sewage, fertilisers as well as in other ways (such as by heat). But of course water was a very good solvent long before there was man-made pollution. What substances dissolve in water in nature, and what effect do they have?

Natural pollution of water

Water that falls as rain is the purest form of water in nature. But even this contains dissolved gases – nitrogen, oxygen and carbon dioxide. As soon as it falls and passes through soil and rocks, it starts to dissolve any soluble chemicals which it meets. These chemicals, unless they are removed, will still be present when the water is used. They may affect the way the water behaves.

Take the everyday process of washing with soap. In

parts of the country where the water is 'hard', it is difficult to form a lather with soap and instead a 'scum' forms on the surface of the water. In a 'soft' water area, these problems do not occur.

So we know what hard water is – it is water that does not easily form a lather with soap (so it is much less easy to wash in). But what dissolved chemicals does hard water contain that soft water does not? We can test samples of water in which different chemicals have been dissolved to see if we can find the cause of 'hardness'.

▶ EXPERIMENT 7.10

If calcium ions cause water to be 'hard', how do they get into water? One obvious way in which calcium ions get into water is by a soluble salt of calcium in the ground dissolving as water passes over it. The most common soluble calcium salt in the ground is calcium sulphate.

Water which contains dissolved calcium sulphate is called 'permanently' hard. This is to distinguish it from water which contains a different calcium salt, and in which the hardness is 'temporary'.

The most common calcium compound in rocks and the soil is calcium carbonate. Limestone, chalk and marble are all different forms of calcium carbonate.

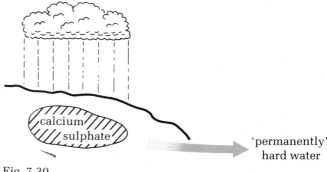

Fig. 7.30

But calcium carbonate is insoluble, and so if pure rainwater falls on it, it will not dissolve. However, if the water which runs over the calcium carbonate contains enough carbon dioxide, it will dissolve. Your teacher may show you this by passing a stream of carbon dioxide through a suspension of calcium carbonate in water. The cloudiness clears – showing that a solution has formed. The soluble calcium compound is calcium hydrogencarbonate.

$$CaCO_3(s) + H_2O(l) + CO_2(g) \rightarrow Ca(HCO_3)_2(aq)$$

When rainwater which contains dissolved carbon dioxide falls on an area in which the rocks are made of

---

EXPERIMENT 7.10
Which chemicals cause 'hardness' in water?

You will need the following; test-tubes and test-tube rack, teat-pipette, soap solution, samples of water containing the following dissolved chemicals (about $10 \, g \, dm^{-3}$): sodium sulphate, sodium chloride, potassium nitrate, calcium chloride, calcium sulphate, potassium chloride.

What to do

1   Take a depth of 1 cm of distilled water in a test-tube, and add 5 drops of soap solution to it with a teat-pipette. Shake it for several seconds, and then put it in the test-tube rack. This shows the lather that will form in water which contains no dissolved chemicals.

2   Repeat, using each of the solutions in turn. Observe whether a lather forms easily or not, in each case.

3   You know the cation and the anion which are present in each of the solutions which you have tested. Discuss the results which you have seen with the others in your group, and try to decide what has happened. **Write down what you have decided, and why you have decided it**.

What happened

You should have been able to see that only the solutions of calcium chloride and calcium sulphate behaved like 'hard' water.

What we can decide

Calcium chloride causes hardness, but sodium chloride and potassium chloride do not. All three contain chloride anions, but different cations. Clearly, chloride ions cannot be the cause of hardness. By the same token, sulphate ions (in sodium sulphate) and nitrate ions (in potassium nitrate) do not cause hardness. Neither do sodium or potassium ions.

The only source of hardness with which we are left is **calcium ions**.

Fig. 7.31 *The Avon gorge at Bristol: the rocks have dissolved, forming 'temporarily' hard water*

limestone, the rocks dissolve. Where a river flows through a limestone area, a GORGE forms. One of the most famous examples in England is the Avon Gorge.

Calcium ions in water make it difficult for soap to form a lather. Why is this? Soap is the chemical SODIUM STEARATE. Like all sodium salts, it is soluble. Soap is the sodium salt of STEARIC ACID. Since you know that sodium salts in general do not behave like soap, it must be the stearate anion which causes soap to act as it does. Water washes things, but water which contains soap washes them better. Dirt (for instance on clothes) often clings to tiny droplets of grease. Grease does not mix with water, so the dirt does not dissolve in water, and is not washed away by it. If we could make grease dissolve in water, we could wash away more dirt.

The stearate anion has two parts – a long chain of carbon atoms which prefers to dissolve in an 'organic' liquid like grease, and a charged part which prefers to dissolve in a 'polar' liquid like water.

When we put stearate ions (soap) into water, they immediately break down any droplets of grease. The carbon chain parts of the ion dissolve in the grease, and the charged parts are left in the water. So from the outside the grease droplet appears to be made up of particles which prefer water – and the droplet becomes soluble.

So, as long as the stearate anions are present, a solution of soap will work normally. Unfortunately, there is one major drawback with soap – its calcium salt is insoluble. Therefore, when soap is added to water which contains calcium ions, a precipitate of calcium stearate ('SCUM') forms:

$$Ca^{2+}(aq) \quad + \quad 2St^-(aq) \quad \rightarrow \quad CaSt_2(s)$$
$$\text{from hard water} \quad \text{from soap} \quad \text{scum}$$

This removes all the stearate ions from solution, and the soap will not work (it will not form a lather). We say the water is 'hard'.

Since it is calcium ions in solution which cause hardness, all we have to do is to remove them. If the dissolved salt is calcium hydrogencarbonate, this is easy.

▶ EXPERIMENT 7.11 (p. 320)

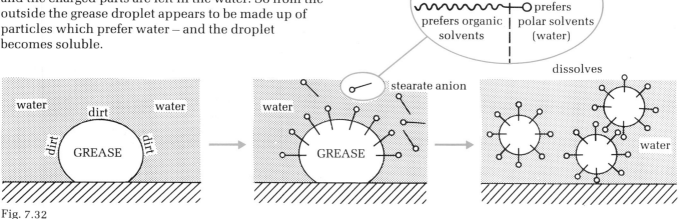

Fig. 7.32

EXPERIMENT 7.11

How are permanent and temporary hardness different?

You will need the following: test-tubes and test-tube rack, teat-pipette, soap solution, samples of water containing calcium sulphate and water containing calcium hydrogencarbonate, two 250 cm³ beakers.

What to do

1   Test each solution as described in Experiment 7.10 to see how easily a lather forms with soap solution.

2   Now take a sample of each, enough to fill a 250 cm³ beaker about one-third full, and boil for about 5 minutes. Notice any changes which have taken place.

3   Allow each boiled solution to cool, and test a sample to see how easily it will lather.

4   Discuss what you have seen and try to decide what has happened. **Write down what you have decided and why you have decided it**.

What happened

You should have been able to see that, after it was boiled, the water containing dissolved calcium hydrogencarbonate lathered much more easily. It had been 'softened' by boiling. When it was boiled, a white precipitate formed. The water containing dissolved calcium sulphate stayed hard even after boiling.

What we can decide

The white precipitate which formed when the solution of calcium hydrogencarbonate was boiled was calcium carbonate. Calcium hydrogencarbonate undergoes thermal decomposition:

$$Ca(HCO_3)_2(aq) \xrightarrow{heat} CaCO_3(s) + CO_2(g) + H_2O(l)$$

The calcium ions are removed from the solution, in the solid calcium carbonate. As a result, the water is no longer hard.

When we boil a solution which contains calcium sulphate, no chemical changes happen, and the calcium ions stay in solution. The water stays hard.

Temporary hardness is hardness which can be removed by boiling.
Permanent hardness is hardness which cannot be removed by boiling.

If the hardness of water in a particular area is temporary hardness, every time water is boiled, a precipitate of calcium carbonate forms. So the insides of kettles and boilers and pipes in industry become coated with a 'fur' of calcium carbonate. Pipes become blocked, and boilers become useless as a result. Over many years, the cost of replacements is enormous. This is another reason for wanting to be able to remove the hardness from water.

To remove the hardness from water, we have to remove the calcium ions. One obvious way of doing this is to add a chemical which will cause the calcium ions to be removed as part of a solid precipitate. Calcium carbonate is insoluble, and sodium carbonate is soluble. So if we add sodium carbonate to hard water, it will soften it.

$$Ca^{2+}(aq) + CO_3^{2+}(aq) \rightarrow CaCO_3(s)$$

    ↑   ↑
from hard water   from sodium
                 carbonate

You learnt about the many uses of sodium carbonate in Section 5, where you also saw how we can make

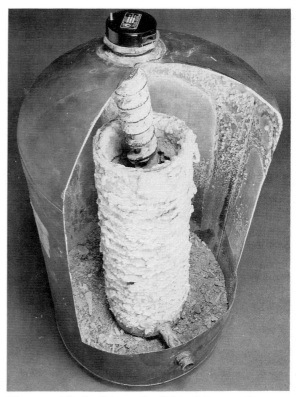

Fig. 7.33 *The build-up of solid in this water heater is caused by temporary hard water*

large quantities of it. Another use for sodium carbonate is as a water-softener. Because of this the old name for sodium carbonate is 'washing soda'.

A modern way of removing hardness is to pass water through an ION EXCHANGE COLUMN. This is a long column, the inside of which is packed with tiny spheres of a substance called a RESIN. The surface of the resin is coated with cations which do not cause hardness, such as sodium. When hard water passes through the column, the calcium ions which it contains change places with the sodium ions. The result is water which contains sodium ions (soft water) and an ion exchange column which contains a resin coated with calcium ions.

hard water

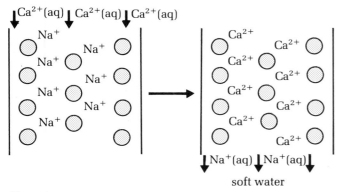
soft water

Fig. 7.34

Instead of removing the hardness from water, there is one other thing which we can do – we can get round its harmful effects. Hard water blocks the action of soap, because calcium stearate is insoluble. Suppose we made something which behaved like soap, but whose calcium salt was soluble. It would not be affected by the hardness in water. Such a chemical can be made with chemicals which we can get from crude oil, and it is called a DETERGENT. A detergent is the sodium salt of a SULPHONIC ACID, and is man-made. (The chemicals which we use to make soap come from animal fats.) The sulphonate anion looks very much like the stearate anion, since it has a long chain of carbon atoms which prefer to dissolve in an 'organic' liquid and a charged part which prefers to dissolve in water.

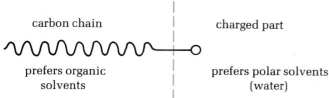
carbon chain   charged part

prefers organic   prefers polar solvents
solvents   (water)

Fig. 7.35

A detergent breaks up grease in exactly the same way as soap.

TOPIC 7.2.4

Gases – ideal behaviour

You already know a great deal about how gases behave. You saw in Section 4 (Topic 4.4.3) how we can describe this behaviour using Gay Lussac's Law, Avogadro's Hypothesis, Boyle's Law and Charles' Law. Read through Topic 4.4.3 again, before going any further.

Standard temperature and pressure (s.t.p.) and the Ideal Gas Equation were also introduced in Topic 4.4.3, although the use of the word 'ideal' was not explained. You saw in Section 1 how the behaviour of gases (for instance diffusion) could be explained using the kinetic theory. When we use the kinetic theory, we assume certain things about gases. Each of these assumptions is true only approximately for real gases, such as hydrogen and nitrogen. So most real gases are only approximately 'ideal'.

An 'ideal' gas would be one for which we could assume the following.

1. The molecules of the gas move about randomly, travelling in straight lines. They change direction only because they collide with each other, or with the walls of the container. No energy is lost in these collisions.
2. The molecules in the gas do not attract or repel each other.
3. The volume taken up by the molecules themselves can be ignored.

In such a gas, the Ideal Gas Equation

$$\frac{P_1V_1}{T_1} = \frac{P_2V_2}{T_2}$$

would be obeyed perfectly. Real gases obey the Ideal Gas Equation only approximately, but accurately enough for us to use it to carry out the kinds of calculation you saw in Section 4.

Dalton's Law of Partial Pressures

There is one further law which gases obey, and which we can explain using the idea of an 'ideal' gas. This law is called Dalton's Law of Partial Pressures, and is to do with **mixtures** of gases. The law says that in a mixture of gases, each gas behaves as if it were alone in the container, and that the total pressure of the mixture is equal to the sum of the **partial pressures** of the gases in the mixture.

So, if we have a mixture of nitrogen and oxygen in a container, the total pressure of the mixture is equal to the sum of the partial pressure of oxygen added to the partial pressure of nitrogen. Each partial pressure is the pressure which the gas would exert if it were in the container on its own.

$P_t = P_n + P_o$ (P_t = total pressure
P_n = partial pressure of nitrogen
P_o = partial pressure of oxygen)

We can explain Dalton's Law of Partial Pressures by considering an ideal gas. Since the molecules of a single gas do not attract or repel each other, the molecules in a mixture of gases do not attract or repel each other. They move in straight lines, hitting each other and the walls of the container. In a mixture of gases, each gas causes a pressure by this means (its partial pressure) and the total pressure of the mixture is caused by all the collisions of the molecules of the different gases with the container added together. This is the same as all the partial pressures added together.

Finding out whether a gas is 'heavier' or 'lighter' than air

We know from Avogadro's Hypothesis that 1 mole of any gas occupies the same volume, at the same temperature and pressure. So 2 g of H_2 occupies the same volume as 32 g of oxygen, for example.

It is clear that hydrogen is much less dense than oxygen, since the mass of it which takes up a certain volume is much less than the mass of oxygen which would take up the same volume. So to compare the density of different gases, we need only compare their relative molecular masses. Very often in chemistry we need to know whether a gas is less dense ('lighter')

than air, or more dense ('heavier') than air. A 'lighter' gas will rise up in air, and a 'heavier' gas will move towards the ground.

We know the relative molecular masses of different gases, but what is the 'relative molecular mass' of air? Very roughly, we can think of the air as being made up of 4/5 N_2 and 1/5 O_2. If we assume that the gases behave ideally, and do not interfere with each other, we can work out an 'average relative molecular mass' for air, as follows.

Air is 4/5 N_2 and 1/5 O_2. So in 5 parts of air, we have 4 parts of N_2 and 1 part of O_2 mixed together. To find the 'average relative molecular mass' of air, we have to find the average mass of the molecules in this mixture (the mass of molecules in 1 part of air mixture).
Rel. mol. mass of $N_2 = 2 \times 14 = 28$
Rel. mol. mass of $O_2 = 2 \times 16 = 32$
In 5 parts of air mixture, mass of N_2 $= 4 \times 28$
$= 112$
In 5 parts of air mixture, mass of O_2 $= 1 \times 32$
$= 32$

Total mass of molecules in 5 parts of air mixture $= 144$
Mass of molecules in 1 part of air mixture $= \frac{144}{5} = 28.8$

So the 'average relative molecular mass of air' is about 28.8. A gas which has a lower molecular mass than 28.8 will be less dense than air, and one which has a higher relative molecular mass than 28.8 will be more dense than air (Fig. 7.36).

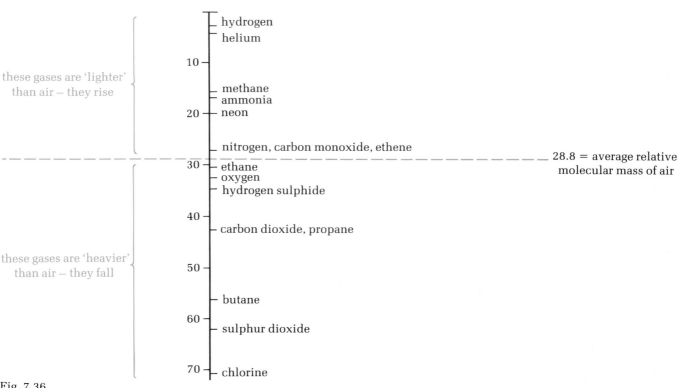

Fig. 7.36

UNIT 7.2
Summary and learning

1   You should be able to explain why some substances are solids, some are liquids and others are gases at room temperature, in terms of the strength of the forces between their particles.

2   You should be able to use the kinetic theory to explain why melting is endothermic and freezing exothermic, and why boiling is endothermic and condensing exothermic.

3   You should be able to explain the effect of changing the pressure of the surrounding gases on the boiling point of a liquid, using the kinetic theory.

4   You should remember how we can measure the enthalpy of vaporisation of different liquids in the laboratory. You should remember the relationship which holds between enthalpy of vaporisation and boiling point for most substances.

5   Molecular substances tend to be more soluble in organic solvents than in polar solvents such as water. The reverse is true for ionic compounds.

6   You should remember that a dissolved substance elevates the boiling point and depresses the freezing point of a pure liquid.

7   You should be able to explain why dissolving is an endothermic process, and why diluting is an exothermic process.

8   You should remember the definitions of
(a) a saturated solution, and
(b) the solubility of a solute.

9   You should remember how we can investigate how the solubilities of different solutes change with temperature.

10   You should be able to make lists of
(a) the ways water helps life to exist on Earth, and
(b) the special properties of water.

11   You should be able to explain water's properties, using the ideas of
(a) hydrogen bonding, and
(b) polarity and polarisability of the water molecule.

12   You should remember the different forms of hardness in water, how they occur, how they are harmful, and how they can be removed.

13   You should be able to explain how a soap or a detergent breaks down grease, and why detergents are more useful than soaps in hard water.

14   You should be able to explain the properties of gases using the idea of an 'ideal' gas, and you should remember Dalton's Law of Partial Pressures.

15   You should remember how to decide whether a gas is 'lighter' or 'heavier' than air.

16   You have learnt the meaning of these words:

organic solvent
organic compound
immiscible
miscible
depress (freezing point)
elevate (boiling point)
solvation
solvation energy
lattice energy
polar

polarisable
gorge
sodium stearate
stearic acid
scum
ion exchange column
resin
detergent
sulphonic acid

SECTION 8
The chemical world – carbon

UNIT 8.1 Carbon and systematic organic chemistry

Fig. 8.1 '. . . like a diamond in the sky'

The Universe contains plenty of carbon. Section 2 (Topic 2.1.1) contains a description of how the element is formed in supernova explosions, and how (under the right conditions) a star like our own sun will eventually become a slowly fading ember – made of carbon. Many of the stars in the photograph will become – may have already become – 'diamonds in the sky'. We also know that the clouds which exist in inter-stellar ('between star') space contains compounds of carbon.

Table 2.2 on p. 67 shows that carbon is the fourth most abundant element in our own solar system. This carbon came originally from a supernova explosion which happened long before our sun was born. Topic 2.2.1 also described how carbon is found in the form of carbon dioxide in the atmospheres of Venus and Mars, and in the form of the simple carbon compound 'methane' in the very make-up of planets like Uranus and Neptune. On the Earth, there is very little carbon in the form of carbon dioxide left in the atmosphere (see Fig. 2.15 on p. 67). Over millions of years, the carbon has become 'trapped' as carbonates in the shells of dead marine animals (which become chalky rocks), or as the remains of dead fish and plants on the sea-bed. The Earth has about 70 thousand million tonnes of carbon, of which 99.94% is 'trapped' in this way. The remainder is carbon in carbon dioxide in the air, carbon dioxide dissolved in the sea, or carbon **in living plants and animals**.

We call this latter the BIOSPHERE. We can think of the carbon in the biosphere as passing round a cycle (Fig. 8.2).

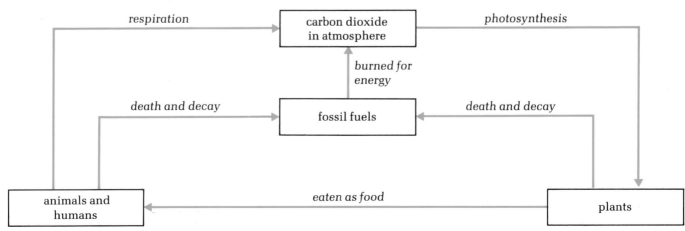

Fig 8.2 The 'carbon cycle'

But how does carbon become part of these living systems?

The element carbon and its place in the biosphere

Chemists in the seventeenth and eighteenth centuries knew that the chemicals which can be obtained from plants and animals – sugar, fats, oils and alcohol for instance – are different from the chemicals which we obtain from rocks. They tend to be insoluble in water, but soluble in organic solvents (see Section 7, Topic 7.2.2), and they are much more sensitive to heat. Most melt or decompose below 300°C – and typical 'mineral' substances like sodium chloride are completely unaffected by such temperatures.

So for a long time, chemists believed that only living systems were able to make 'organic' chemicals. They imagined that there was a special VITAL FORCE which was contained in living things and in the chemicals which make them up. So you could only make an 'organic' chemical if you started from other 'organic' chemicals – substances which possessed 'vital force'.

Ideas had to change very quickly, however, when a German chemist called Wohler made a typical 'organic' chemical, urea, from a typical 'inorganic' chemical, ammonium cyanate. This was in 1828 (see the Chart of Scientific History on p. 74). Soon after, many more organic chemicals were made without the presence of 'vital force', and it became clear that the chemicals in living things and the chemicals in the non-living world are all part of the same system. However, we still use the word 'organic chemistry', because it is a convenient label for the branch of chemistry in which we study the 1 million – or so – compounds of the element carbon. (A few carbon compounds – such as carbonates, hydrogen-carbonates, carbon dioxide and carbon monoxide – are classed as 'inorganic' along with all other chemicals: see Unit 8.3).

We shall shortly go on to look at exactly how carbon manages to form so many compounds, and also to begin studying some of them. But first we should ask ourselves just how widely carbon compounds are found in nature.

▶ EXPERIMENT 8.1 (p. 326)

In fact, all living things contain carbon, and there are more compounds of this one element than of all the others put together (apart from hydrogen which is also in most organic compounds). Why can carbon form so many compounds, and what are they like?

Look at the position of carbon in the Periodic Table:

Group	1	2	3	4	5	6	7	8
Electrons in outer shell	1	2	3	4	5	6	7	8

Li	Be	B	C	N	O	F	Ne

Carbon has four electrons in its outermost shell, and so it forms four covalent bonds to other atoms. It can form one, two or even three bonds **with other carbon atoms**. This means that

chains of carbon atoms

$$-\overset{|}{\underset{|}{C}} - \overset{|}{\underset{|}{C}} - \overset{|}{\underset{|}{C}} - \overset{|}{\underset{|}{C}} - \overset{|}{\underset{|}{C}} - \overset{|}{\underset{|}{C}}$$

rings of carbon atoms

and chains linked to rings

are possible.

As a result, the possibilities for variety are enormous. The same 'skeleton' of carbon atoms can result in very many different compounds just by changing one of the atoms which is bonded to the chain, or by keeping the same atom and moving its position. For instance

$$\text{H} - \overset{\overset{\text{H}}{|}}{\underset{\underset{\text{H}}{|}}{\text{C}}} - \overset{\overset{\text{Cl}}{|}}{\underset{\underset{\text{H}}{|}}{\text{C}}} - \overset{\overset{\text{H}}{|}}{\underset{\underset{\text{H}}{|}}{\text{C}}} - \text{H}$$

is a different chemical from

$$\text{H} - \overset{\overset{\text{Cl}}{|}}{\underset{\underset{\text{H}}{|}}{\text{C}}} - \overset{\overset{\text{H}}{|}}{\underset{\underset{\text{H}}{|}}{\text{C}}} - \overset{\overset{\text{H}}{|}}{\underset{\underset{\text{H}}{|}}{\text{C}}} - \text{H}$$

and

$$\text{H} - \overset{\overset{\text{H}}{|}}{\underset{\underset{\text{H}}{|}}{\text{C}}} - \overset{\overset{\text{Cl}}{|}}{\underset{\underset{\text{H}}{|}}{\text{C}}} - \overset{\overset{\text{H}}{|}}{\underset{\underset{\text{H}}{|}}{\text{C}}} - \text{H}$$

is a different chemical from

$$\text{H} - \overset{\overset{\text{H}}{|}}{\underset{\underset{\text{H}}{|}}{\text{C}}} - \overset{\overset{\text{Br}}{|}}{\underset{\underset{\text{H}}{|}}{\text{C}}} - \overset{\overset{\text{H}}{|}}{\underset{\underset{\text{H}}{|}}{\text{C}}} - \text{H}$$

151, 166

EXPERIMENT 8.1
In which 'natural' substances can we find carbon?

You will need the following: test-tube fitted with bung and delivery tube, copper(II) oxide, lime-water, naturally occurring substances (e.g. sugar, starch, custard powder, rice, butter).

What to do

YOU MUST WEAR YOUR SAFETY SPECTACLES.

1   Mix a little of the substance being tested with copper(II) oxide and heat strongly.

2   Pass the gases which are produced through a little lime-water, and observe any changes. Be careful not to let any lime-water suck back into the hot test-tube.

What happened

In each case, you should have been able to see that the lime-water turned 'milky'.

What we can decide

You know that when lime-water turns 'milky', it shows that carbon dioxide is present. You also know that carbon is a more reactive element than copper (see Section 5, Topic 5.1.2). So if any carbon is present in the substance which is heated with copper(II) oxide, it will reduce the copper(II) oxide to copper, and form carbon dioxide.

carbon + copper(II) oxide → copper + carbon dioxide
(in 'natural'
substance)

We can decide that carbon is found in all the 'natural' substances which were tested.

So where do we begin in studying the 'organic' compounds of carbon? You will remember that we are able to simplify our study of the chemical elements because they fall into groups of similar elements. In the same way, the compounds of carbon fall into series of similar compounds. We call these series HOMOLOGOUS SERIES.

Carbon is in the 'middle' of the Periodic Table – halfway between the metals and the non-metals. You know that hydrogen is also 'halfway' between a metal and a non-metal in its properties – because it can behave sometimes as a metal and sometimes as a non-metal. The 'polar' nature of a water molecule was mentioned in Section 7. The covalent bond between carbon and hydrogen, because both are halfway between the metals and the non-metals, is completely non-polar.

So, if we take a compound based on a carbon chain, and add one more carbon atom whose other bonds are to two hydrogen atoms, for instance

$$\begin{array}{ccc} Cl & H \\ | & | \\ H-C-C-H \\ | & | \\ H & H \end{array} \longrightarrow \begin{array}{cccc} Cl & H & H \\ | & | & | \\ H-C+C+C-H \\ | & | & | \\ H & H & H \end{array}$$

then the unit we have added (–CH$_2$–) has not really changed the chemical nature of the substance. All we have done is added something which is almost completely unreactive itself – but we have increased the length of the chain, and made a new chemical.

So, carbon compounds whose formulae differ from each other only by the unit (–CH$_2$–) are bound to be similar to each other chemically. They are part of the same 'homologous series'.

A simple chain of carbon atoms made up of (–CH$_2$–) units is very unreactive chemically. The chemical nature of an organic compound is therefore almost completely dependent on other atoms, or groups of atoms, which are attached to the unreactive skeleton. We call these 'active' parts of the molecule FUNCTIONAL GROUPS.

So a particular homologous series is a group of chemicals, which have the same 'functional group', but whose molecular formulae differ by a (–CH$_2$–) unit each time.

$$\begin{array}{c} ⊗ \quad \text{functional} \\ | \quad\;\; \text{group} \\ H-C-H \\ | \\ H \end{array}$$
first member of
homologous series

$$\begin{array}{cc} ⊗ & H \\ | & | \\ H-C-C-H \\ | & | \\ H & H \end{array}$$
second member of
homologous series

$$\begin{array}{ccc} ⊗ & H & H \\ | & | & | \\ H-C-C-C-H \\ | & | & | \\ H & H & H \end{array}$$
third member of
homologous series

We can now look at some of the simpler homologous

series of organic compounds. A good place to start is with compounds which contain only carbon and hydrogen. Such compounds are called HYDROCARBONS (you first met these in Section 4), and we shall consider two different homologous series of hydrocarbons – the ALKANES and the ALKENES.

TOPIC 8.1.2
The alkanes

We can think of the alkanes as being compounds whose molecules are the 'unreactive skeletons' mentioned above. They have no 'functional groups', and so they are much less reactive than other organic compounds. (The old name for the alkanes – 'the paraffins' – was given because of this low reactivity. The word paraffin comes from the Latin for 'little reactivity'.)

In the alkanes, each carbon atom can form four **single** covalent bonds to other atoms (hydrogen atoms or other carbon atoms). Each carbon atom is therefore at the centre of a regular tetrahedron (see Section 3, Topic 3.3.2).

In the smallest alkane, one carbon atom is joined to four hydrogen atoms. The compound is methane, CH_4. We draw the molecule on paper as a 'flattened out' shape, although it is really three-dimensional:

$$
\begin{array}{c}
H \\
| \\
H - C - H \quad \text{methane} \\
| \\
H
\end{array}
$$

The next member of the alkanes has another (–CH_2–) unit. So its formula is C_2H_6 and it is called **ethane**. We draw it as:

$$
\begin{array}{c}
H \quad H \\
| \quad | \\
H - C - C - H \quad \text{ethane} \\
| \quad | \\
H \quad H
\end{array}
$$

If we add another (–CH_2–) unit, we get the next alkane, **propane**, C_3H_8:

$$
\begin{array}{c}
H \quad H \quad H \\
| \quad | \quad | \\
H - C - C - C - H \quad \text{propane} \\
| \quad | \quad | \\
H \quad H \quad H
\end{array}
$$

The next member has a formula C_4H_{10}, and it is called **butane**:

$$
\begin{array}{c}
H \quad H \quad H \quad H \\
| \quad | \quad | \quad | \\
H - C - C - C - C - H \quad \text{butane} \\
| \quad | \quad | \quad | \\
H \quad H \quad H \quad H
\end{array}
$$

There are in fact two different alkane molecules which we can draw which have the formula C_4H_{10}. Suppose that instead of adding a (–CH_2–) unit to propane by adding to the length of the chain, we had done this by starting a side-chain. The molecule would have looked like:

$$
\begin{array}{c}
H \\
| \\
H - C - H \\
H \quad | \quad H \\
| \quad | \quad | \\
H - C - C - C - H \quad \text{methylpropane} \\
| \quad | \quad | \\
H \quad H \quad H
\end{array}
$$

So butane and methyl propane are different compounds which have the same formula but a different arrangement of atoms. We say that they are ISOMERS of each other. But why is one called 'butane', and the other 'methyl propane'?

Giving names to organic compounds

1   The end of the name tells us which homologous series the compound belongs to. Alkanes always end in -ane.

2   The beginning of the name tells us **the number of carbon atoms in the longest straight chain**.

carbon atoms:	1	2	3	4	5	6
	meth-	eth-	prop-	but-	pent-	hex-

3   A side-chain is called an 'alkyl' group, and we give it a name based on the number of carbon atoms it contains.

carbon atoms:	1	2	3	4	5	6
	methyl	ethyl	propyl	butyl	pentyl	hexyl

4   If we need to, we show the position of the side-chain, by giving the number of the carbon atom in the main chain to which it is attached.

Examples

$$
\begin{array}{c}
H \\
| \\
H - C - H \\
H \quad | \quad H \\
| \quad | \quad | \\
H - C - C - C - H \\
| \quad | \quad | \\
H \quad | \quad H \\
H - C - H \\
| \\
H
\end{array}
$$

2,2–dimethylpropane

$$
\begin{array}{c}
H \\
| \\
H - C - H \\
H \quad | \quad H \quad H \\
| \quad | \quad | \quad | \\
H - C - C - C - C - H \\
| \quad | \quad | \quad | \\
H \quad H \quad H \quad H
\end{array}
$$

methylbutane

2,3–dimethylbutane

2–ethyl–4–methylhexane

The smallest alkanes are gases, but as the molecules get larger further along the series, we get liquids, and eventually solids (Table 8.1).

Alkane	State at room temperature
methane, CH_4	gas
ethane, C_2H_6	gas
propane, C_3H_8	gas
butane, C_4H_{10}	gas
pentane, C_5H_{12}	liquid
hexane, C_6H_{14}	liquids
↓	↓
heptadecane, $C_{17}H_{36}$	solids
↓	↓

Table 8.1

A general formula for alkanes

If you asked your teacher to give you the formula for the alkane which has 10 carbon atoms, he/she would say '$C_{10}H_{22}$' straight away! Or if the number of carbons was 12, the answer would be '$C_{12}H_{26}$'. You can do this as many times as you like:

$C_{19} \longrightarrow$ '$C_{19}H_{40}$'
$C_{100} \longrightarrow$ '$C_{100}H_{202}$'
and so on

How does your teacher always know the formula straight away? The answer is simple. We could write methane as H-(-CH_2-)-H, and ethane as H-(-CH_2-)-(-CH_2-)-H or H-(-CH_2-)$_2$-H. Each new member of the series is made by adding a (-CH_2-) unit.

If n stands for any whole number, then the general formula, H-(-CH_2-)$_n$-H stands for any alkane. All we have to do is supply 'n', and we get the answer.

n	formula
10	H-(-CH_2-)$_{10}$-H = $C_{10}H_{22}$
30	H-(-CH_2-)$_{30}$-H = $C_{30}H_{62}$
40	H-(-CH_2-)$_{40}$-H = $C_{40}H_{82}$

Perhaps you can see from these examples that there is an even simpler way of writing the general formula of an alkane. Each time we work out the number of hydrogen atoms, we take the number of carbons, double it, and then add on the two hydrogens at each end of the chain. So we could say that the general formula of the alkanes is:

C_nH_{2n+2} where n is any whole number

Reactions of alkanes

We have seen that alkanes are generally unreactive. However, one important property which they all have is that they will burn in air. These reactions are very exothermic, and so alkanes are used as fuels. Methane is 'natural gas', and pentane is one of the main chemicals in petrol.

methane $CH_4(g) + 2O_2(g) \rightarrow CO_2(g) + 2H_2O(g)$
$\triangle H$ −890 kJ

pentane $C_5H_{12}(g) + 8O_2(g) \rightarrow 5CO_2(g) + 6H_2O(g)$
$\triangle H$ −3509 kJ

If there is plenty of oxygen present, the products are carbon dioxide and water (in the form of steam, because of the temperature). If there is only a limited amount of oxygen, carbon monoxide is formed instead of carbon dioxide (see Unit 8.3).

A more reactive group of hydrocarbons is the **alkenes**.

TOPIC 8.1.3
The alkenes

An alkene is a hydrocarbon which contains at least one carbon–carbon double bond. The double bond is the functional group in the molecule, since almost all the reactions of alkenes involve it in some way.

The smallest alkene, in which there are just two carbon atoms, is called **ethene**. (The names of alkenes always end in -ene). Its formula is C_2H_4, since the remaining two bonds of each carbon atom are taken up by hydrogen atoms.

ethene (a gas)

The next member of the alkenes has another (-CH_2-) unit, and so its formula is C_3H_6:

propene (a gas)

The next alkene would be butene, and its formula would be C_4H_8. So it is easy to see that the general formula for the alkenes is:

C_nH_{2n} where n is any whole number

Reactions of alkenes

Because the alkenes have a double bond and the alkanes do not, they are much more reactive.

EXPERIMENT 8.2
How do alkenes react differently from alkanes?

> **Your teacher will show you the first part of this experiment**

A The following will be needed: test-tubes containing methane and ethene, acidified potassium permanganate solution, bromine water.

B You will need the following: cyclohexane, cyclohexene, acidified potassium permanganate solution, bromine water.

What to do

ALKANES AND ALKENES ARE HIGHLY INFLAMMABLE. AVOID BREATHING THE FUMES. YOU MUST WEAR YOUR SAFETY SPECTACLES.

A
1 Your teacher will shake
   (a) some acidified potassium permanganate, and
   (b) some bromine water
   with methane in a test-tube.
2 The above will be repeated, using ethene instead of methane.
3 Observe what happens, in each case.

B
1 You can now repeat your teacher's experiment, but using a liquid alkane and alkene. The alkane is cyclohexane, and the alkene is cyclohexene.
2 Take 2–3 cm³ of the liquid which you are testing and shake with a few drops of
   (a) acidified potassium permanganate, and
   (b) bromine water
   in separate test-tubes.
3 Observe what happens in each case.
4 Discuss what you have seen and try to decide what has happened.
   Write down what you have decided, and why you have decided it.

What happened and what we can decide

You should have been able to see that, both in your teacher's experiment and in your own, the colour of acidified potassium permanganate and of bromine water was removed by the alkene but not by the alkane. We can use these reactions to test a hydrocarbon to see whether it is an alkane or an alkene. Alkenes always 'decolorise' these chemicals, but alkanes never do.

The reaction of bromine with ethene is a model for many of the reactions of all alkenes with other chemicals. The bromine molecule is simply added to the ethene molecule.

$$\begin{array}{c} H \\ H \end{array}\!\!\diagup\!\!\!C=C\!\!\!\diagup\!\!\begin{array}{c} H \\ H \end{array} \xrightarrow{\text{addition}} \begin{array}{c} H \quad H \\ | \quad | \\ H-C-C-H \\ | \quad | \\ Br \quad Br \end{array}$$

Br — Br
red/orange

1,2–dibromoethane
colourless

Reactions where a whole molecule is added across a double bond are called ADDITION reactions. Almost all the reactions of alkenes are addition reactions. We say that alkenes are UNSATURATED (can be added to), but that alkanes are SATURATED (cannot be added to).

If we add a hydrogen molecule to an alkene, we convert it into an alkane.

$$\begin{array}{c}\text{alkene}\\ \diagup\!\!\!C=C\!\!\!\diagdown \\ H-H \end{array} \xrightarrow[\text{high temperature}]{\text{addition}\atop\text{catalyst}} \begin{array}{c}\text{alkane}\\ |\quad| \\ -C-C- \\ |\quad| \end{array}$$

This reaction is used to convert vegetable oils (which contain one double bond per molecule) into vegetable fats (margarine).

Like alkanes, the alkenes burn to give carbon dioxide and water. In the case of alkenes the flame tends to be smoky due to unburned carbon (there is a higher proportion of carbon in alkenes than in alkanes).

Another important reaction of alkenes is their ability to join together to make large molecules (see Unit 8.2).

The alcohols

We can think of an alcohol as being an alkane in which one of the hydrogen atoms has been replaced by an oxygen atom and hydrogen atom bonded together (–O–H).

The simplest alcohol has one carbon atom and is called **methanol**. (The names of alcohols always end in -ol). Its formula is CH₃OH.

methanol (a liquid)

Methanol is a deadly poison. Even small amounts cause blindness and even death.

The most important alcohol by far is the next member of the series, which has another (–CH₂–) unit. Its formula is C_2H_5OH, and its name is **ethanol**.

ethanol (a liquid)

It is often said that making ethanol is the oldest chemical reaction known to man, because ethanol is the 'alcohol' in drinks like wine, beer and whisky.

Ethanol can be made from chemicals made by plants. Topic 4.2.3 explained how green plants make sugars and then store them in the form of starch. A starch molecule is many sugar molecules joined together. Starch is the raw material from which ethanol can be made, and we can get large quantities of it from, for instance, potatoes.

If we take the starch from potatoes and treat it with malt, an enzyme in malt (you met enzymes in Section 6 – they are natural catalysts) catalyses the breakdown of the large starch molecules. The enzyme is called **diastase**, and it breaks starch down into 2-sugar units, called **maltose**.

Each time the starch molecule is split up, water is added.

Because water is added, we call this change HYDROLYSIS. Before we can get to ethanol, the maltose molecules have to be split up further by another reaction, into single sugar molecules called **glucose**. We can do this by adding yeast. Yeast contains an enzyme called **maltase** which catalyses the hydrolysis of maltose to glucose.

There is another enzyme in yeast, called **zymase**. This catalyses the breakdown of glucose molecules to ethanol and carbon dioxide.

$$C_6H_{12}O_6 \xrightarrow{\text{zymase}} 2C_2H_5OH + 2CO_2$$
glucose ethanol carbon dioxide

So, we can summarise the brewing process as follows.

If we start with glucose, it is easy to carry out the brewing process in the laboratory. The chemical change involved is called FERMENTATION.

▶ PREPARATION 8.1

PREPARATION 8.1
Making ethanol by fermentation

You will need the following: 250 cm³ conical flask fitted with bung and bent delivery tube, test-tube, 50 cm³ of solution of glucose (about 10%), lime-water, yeast. For the teacher: large fractional distillation apparatus.

What to do

1 Put about 50 cm³ of the glucose solution in the conical flask, and add 1 spatula-measure of yeast.

2 Fit the bung and delivery tube, so that any gas coming out of the flask passes through a little lime-water in a test-tube.

3 Leave the apparatus to stand for about 1 week, in a warm place.

4 At the end of this time, a precipitate will have formed in the test-tube, showing that carbon dioxide has been produced during fermentation.

5 If your teacher pools the filtered contents of all the flasks, and carries out a large-scale fractional distillation, enough ethanol can be collected to burn.

Ethanol is a drug

Beer contains about 5% of ethanol, and wine about 10%. Whisky and other spirits are more concentrated still – a single 'measure' of whisky contains as much ethanol as half a pint of beer. Ethanol and water mix together completely (see Section 7, Topic 7.2.2), and so we can dilute ethanol in order to make it drinkable. Pure ethanol is extremely poisonous!

Fig. 8.3 *Some forms of dilute ethanol solution!*

In more dilute form, however, ethanol is a very popular drink. In fact, ethanol must be sold in more different forms than any other liquid, a tribute to human ingenuity. But why is ethanol so popular? (It is important to remember that it is not popular with everybody, of course. Many people make a decision never to drink ethanol, and some religions ban it.)

Ethanol is a drug. In fact it is a DEPRESSANT drug. This may seem strange – surely people would not drink something that would depress them! But this is exactly what ethanol does. Drinking a small amount of ethanol gives people a feeling of well-being, because a small amount depresses their worries and makes them feel more sociable. At the same time, even a small amount of ethanol can make people less physically skilful and slower to react to new situations – and is therefore the cause of many road accidents when drivers have been drinking.

Large amounts of ethanol can cause genuine depression, and it is not unusual for people who have had too much to drink to feel suicidal. Large amounts of ethanol taken over a long period cause brain damage and destruction of the liver – sometimes resulting in death. With this in mind, it should be remembered that ethanol is not only a drug – it is also an addictive drug. People can become dependent upon it to 'feel all right'. Most doctors would say that drinking more than the equivalent of about two pints of beer a day on a regular basis is harmful, and may lead to ethanol addiction.

Reactions of ethanol

Most of the reactions of alcohols, and therefore of ethanol, involve directly or indirectly the –O–H functional group.

▶ EXPERIMENT 8.3 (p. 332)

EXPERIMENT 8.3
What happens if we pass ethanol over a very hot surface?

You will need the following: test-tube fitted with bung and delivery tube, broken porous pot, mineral wool, industrial methylated spirits (ethanol), bromine water, 250 cm³ beaker.

What to do

YOU MUST WEAR YOUR SAFETY SPECTACLES.

1   Put a little mineral wool into the bottom of a test-tube, and soak it with about 2 cm³ of industrial methylated spirits (ethanol). Fill the rest of the test-tube with pieces of broken porous pot, and set up the apparatus as in Fig. 8.4.

2   Have three test-tubes filled with water ready to collect the gas which is produced by the reaction. Heat the porous pot strongly – there is no need to heat the ethanol directly. Allow the air in the apparatus to be driven out, and then collect two test-tubes of gas, while heating the porous pot strongly all the time. BE CAREFUL NOT TO LET ANY WATER SUCK BACK INTO THE HOT TEST-TUBE.

3   Use the two test-tubes of gas to carry out the following tests.
(a) Bring a lighted splint up to one of the test-tubes of gas to see if it will burn.
(b) Add a little bromine water to the other test-tube of gas, and shake.

What happened

You should have been able to see that the gas produced when ethanol is passed over a very hot surface behaves as follows.
  (a) It burns with a smoky flame.
  (b) It 'decolorises' bromine water.

What we can decide

The gas produced has the properties of an alkene. The only alkene which could be produced from ethanol is ethene. So we can write the equation:

$$C_2H_5OH(g) \xrightarrow[\text{porous pot}]{\text{heated}} C_2H_4(g) + H_2O(g)$$
$$\text{ethanol} \qquad\qquad \text{ethene} \quad \text{water}$$

If we look at the structure of ethanol and ethene:

ethanol ethene

We can see that the double bond in ethene has been formed by a hydrogen atom being taken away from one carbon atom in ethanol, and by the –O–H group being taken away from the carbon atom next to it. Altogether, the elements which make up water have been taken away, and so we say that this is a DEHYDRATION reaction.

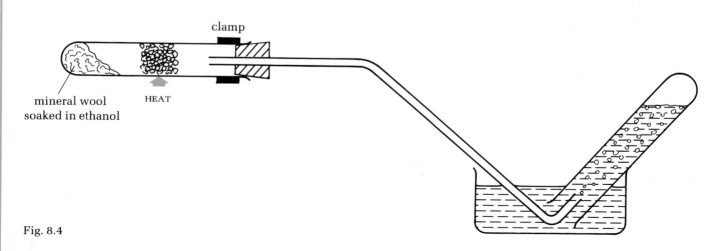

mineral wool
soaked in ethanol   HEAT

clamp

Fig. 8.4

2/2

EXPERIMENT 8.4
What happens if we react ethanol with an oxidising agent?

You will need the following: acidified sodium dichromate solution, ethanol, boiling-tube, teat-pipette.

What to do

1   Put about 5 cm³ of the acidified sodium dichromate solution into the boiling-tube.

2   Use a teat-pipette to add a few drops of ethanol. Keep the mixture cool by holding the boiling-tube under a running tap. Smell the product of the reaction by putting the palm of your hand over the mouth of the tube, and then smelling your hand. (This method lets you smell a small amount of the gas – a large amount might be harmful.) Is it a sweet or a sour smell?

3   Now warm the tube very gently, and use the same method to smell it again. Has the smell stayed the same, or is it different. Is the smell sweet or sour?

What happened, and what we can decide

You should have been able to notice a sweet smell at first, but this changed when the tube was warmed to give a sour acidic smell. The final product of the

reaction is in fact an acid, ethanoic acid (once called acetic acid). The sweet smell was caused by a chemical which is made on the way from an alcohol to an acid. These compounds are called ALKANALS.

The names of alkanals end in -al. So the alkanal made by oxidising ethanol is ethanal.

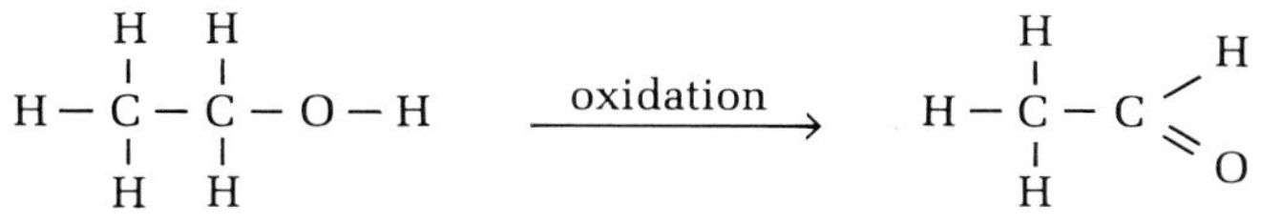

ethanol   ethanal

If we oxidise an alkanal, we get an ALKANOIC ACID. The names of alkanoic acids end in -oic acid. So the alkanoic acid made by oxidising ethanal is ethanoic acid:

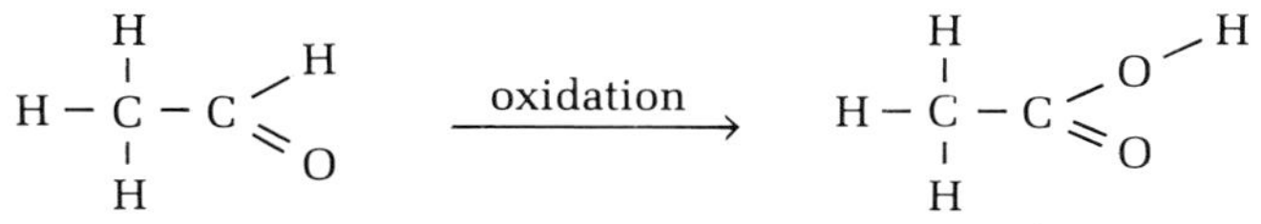

ethanal   ethanoic acid

Another name for ethanoic acid is acetic acid. Vinegar is mostly acetic acid. If wine is left in contact with the air for a long time, the ethanol in it is oxidised to ethanal and then to ethanoic acid.

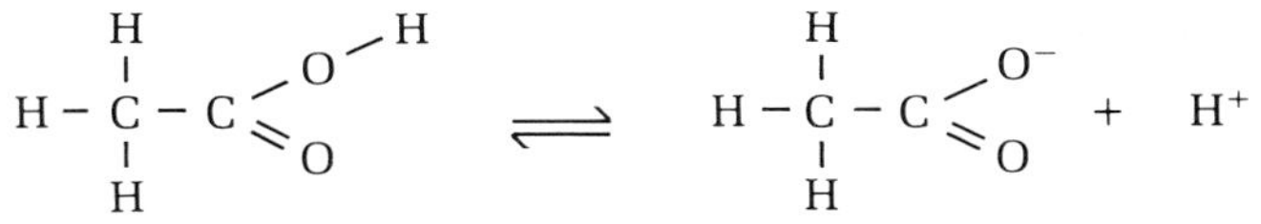

ethanoic acid   ethanoate anion

Question

Look back to Section 4 (Topic 4.5.1) and the different definitions of oxidation and reduction. In what way can
(a) the conversion of ethanol to ethanal, and
(b) the conversion of ethanal to ethanoic acid
be defined as oxidation reactions?

EXPERIMENT 8.5 (p. 334)

Alkanoic acids are weak acids (not completely split up to give H⁺ ions – see Section 1, Topic 1.3.3). The acidic hydrogen is the one attached to oxygen, and the functional group in alkanoic acids is the

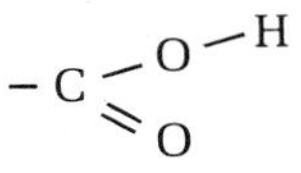

group. So in solution ethanoic acid splits up.

EXPERIMENT 8.5
What happens if we react ethanol with ethanoic acid?

You will need the following: glacial ethanoic acid, ethanol, concentrated sulphuric acid, boiling-tube.

What to do

ETHANOL IS FLAMMABLE.

GLACIAL ETHANOIC ACID AND CONCENTRATED SULPHURIC ACID SHOULD BE KEPT IN THE FUME-CUPBOARD. GLACIAL ETHANOIC ACID IS FLAMMABLE, WILL BURN YOUR SKIN ON CONTACT, AND GIVES OFF VERY UNPLEASANT FUMES. CONCENTRATED SULPHURIC ACID WILL ALSO BURN YOUR SKIN. IF YOU SPILL ANY, TELL YOUR TEACHER. IF ANY OF EITHER LIQUID TOUCHES YOUR SKIN, WASH IT OFF WITH PLENTY OF WATER AND TELL YOUR TEACHER.

YOU SHOULD WEAR YOUR SAFETY SPECTACLES.

1   Mix $1 \, cm^3$ of ethanol, 5 drops of glacial ethanoic acid and 2 drops of concentrated sulphuric acid in a test-tube. DO THIS IN A FUME-CUPBOARD and then carry the tube very carefully back to your bench.

2   Warm the mixture CAREFULLY for about 10 minutes in a water-bath and then pour the contents of the tube into a boiling-tube which is half-full of water.

3   Note what happens, and smell the product of the reaction using the same method as in the last experiment (using the palm of your hand).

What happened and what we can decide

You should have been able to see that the product of the reaction between ethanol and ethanoic acid did not mix with water. It formed a separate layer, floating on top of the water.

The product also had a familiar, sweet smell, which is like pear-drops. A new class of compounds has been formed, called ESTERS. The name of this particular ester is ethylethanoate. We name esters as if they were the alkyl salt of the alkanoic acid.

We will come across esters again shortly.

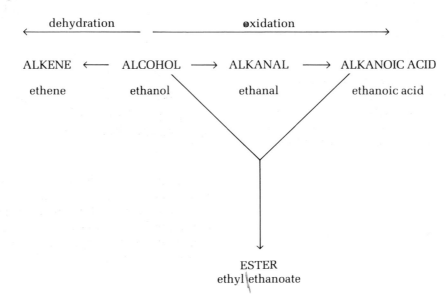

In summary, we have seen the following reactions of alcohols, by looking at the reactions of ethanol:

So far, we have looked at compounds based on a **chain** of carbon atoms. But we saw earlier that carbon atoms can link together to make **rings**, as well as chains. There are a number of different types of ring which are possible, depending on the nature of the atoms in the ring and how they are linked together. The most important compounds which contain rings are called AROMATIC compounds.

TOPIC 8.1.5

Aromatic compounds

Aromatic compounds got their name originally because so many of them have a strong 'aroma' (smell). They all contain a ring of six carbon atoms linked together in a special way. The simplest aromatic compound is benzene. Benzene is a colourless liquid, and its molecular formula is C_6H_6. We can think of the structure of a benzene molecule as being a six-sided flat ring made up of three single bonds and three double bonds.

simplified to

This representation of the benzene molecule is often called the Kekulé structure after the German chemist who first suggested it. However, we know that it is not a perfect picture of the benzene molecule, since
(a) all the six C–C bonds in benzene are exactly the same, and
(b) none of the bonds in benzene behaves like the double bonds in an alkene.

We saw earlier that molecules can be added to a double bond in an alkene – part to one side and part to the other. This happens only rarely with benzene. Instead, it is more typical of benzene that one of its hydrogen atoms is SUBSTITUTED by another atom, or group of atoms. This leaves the structure of the carbon ring intact.

Alkene: ADDITION

$$\text{>C}=\text{C<} + \text{AB} \longrightarrow \begin{array}{c} \text{A} \quad \text{B} \\ | \quad | \\ -\text{C}-\text{C}- \\ | \quad | \end{array}$$

Benzene: SUBSTITUTION

$$ + \text{AB} \longrightarrow + \text{HB}$$

Benzene is the 'parent' molecule for all aromatic compounds. They may be larger molecules containing only carbon and hydrogen, or molecules made by carrying out a substitution on benzene. Some examples are:

naphthalene   methylbenzene   phenylethene (styrene)

phenol   phenylamine (aniline)

All these aromatic compounds behave in a similar way to benzene. We can understand the behaviour of aromatic compounds by thinking of them somewhat as we thought of metals (Section 3, Topic 3.3.3) and of graphite (Section 7, Topic 7.1.5). It is as if the electrons of the double bonds are spread out around. the ring of carbon atoms, making a 'cloud' of electrons above the ring, and a similar cloud below.

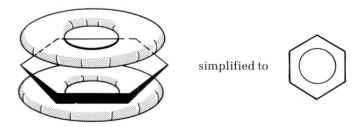

simplified to

We can now see that all the bonds in the ring are the same, and are not actual double bonds as in ethene. We can also see that the 'benzene ring' in aromatic compounds tends to survive their chemical reactions intact, the only change being in the atoms or groups of atoms which are attached to it.

UNIT 8.1
Summary and learning

1   Most of the carbon on Earth is 'trapped' in carbonate rocks, or in the remains of dead fish and plants on the sea-bed. The remainder is part of the 'carbon cycle' which includes living things.

2   The compounds of carbon (other than carbonates, hydrogencarbonates, carbon dioxide and carbon monoxide) are called 'organic compounds'. Everything living, or that once lived, contains organic compounds. There are more compounds of carbon than of all the other elements put together (apart from hydrogen).

3   There are so many carbon compounds because carbon atoms can link together forming chains and rings, and this allows for an enormous amount of variety. Chains made up of carbon and hydrogen atoms only are fairly unreactive, but most organic compounds have a 'functional group' of other atoms or groups of atoms attached to this skeleton. Carbon compounds whose formulae differ from each other by the unit ($-CH_2-$) are part of the same 'homologous series'.

4   Organic compounds which contain only carbon and hydrogen are called 'hydrocarbons'. The alkanes have a general formula C_nH_{2n+2}, where n is any whole number. They are much less reactive than the alkenes, whose general formula is C_nH_{2n}. Alkanes are 'saturated' hydrocarbons, but alkenes are 'unsaturated', and can have whole molecules added to them, across a double bond. You should remember how to name simple organic compounds, and how to test to see whether a hydrocarbon is an alkane or an alkene.

5   The alcohols contain the functional group $-O-H$. The most important alcohol is ethanol. You should remember how we can make ethanol from chemicals made by plants, and how it behaves as a drug. You should remember the reactions of ethanol.

6   Aromatic compounds contain a ring of six carbon atoms held together in the same way as in benzene. You should remember how benzene and other aromatic compounds are different chemically from alkenes.

7   You have learnt the meaning of these words:

biosphere	saturated
vital force	hydrolysis
homologous series	fermentation
functional groups	depressant (drug)
hydrocarbons	dehydration
alkanes	alkanals
alkenes	alkanoic acids
isomers	esters
addition reactions	aromatic (compounds)
unsaturated	substituted

UNIT 8.2   *Making new materials with carbon compounds*

We have seen how nature can build up giant molecules out of smaller molecules (such as starch, from glucose). Scientists have found ways of copying nature, to make new materials which we can use in everyday life. These materials, called POLYMERS, are a very important part of the way in which the chemical industry helps us to improve our standard of living (see Section 2, Unit 2.2).

When we make a polymer chemical, we take small organic molecules, and link them together to form a long chain. The small molecules are called MONOMERS ('mono' = one), and the long chain is called the polymer ('poly' = many). The process is called POLYMERISATION. Because these man-made giant molecules are themselves organic chemicals (containing long chains of carbon atoms linked together), they have the same properties as other organic chemicals – e.g. they are unaffected by water. So man-made polymers are particularly useful where something waterproof has to be made.

POLYMER

many × │ MONOMER │ ──*polymerisation*──→   · · · – MONOMER – MONOMER – MONOMER – · · ·

Polymer molecules can be very long indeed. Some have molecular weights of up to 1 000 000!! As a result, they are solids at room temperature, but liquids at higher temperatures. This means we can mould them into almost any shape we want.

So polymers are waterproof and can be shaped easily. Some of them are also very tough.

Two types of polymer

If we make polymer molecules which are simply long chains, we make a polymer which is called a THERMOPLASTIC. We can make a thermoplastic 'runny' by heating it up, then make it 'set' by letting it cool, as many times as we want. Almost all the objects we think of as being made of 'plastic' are in fact made of thermoplastic materials.

However, if we make a polymer in such a way that there are cross-links between the long chains, we make a polymer which can only be set once. We call such a polymer a THERMOSETTING POLYMER.

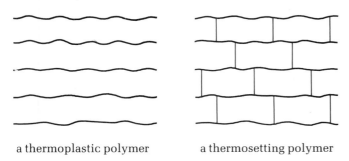

a thermoplastic polymer   a thermosetting polymer

Fig. 8.5

We use thermosetting polymers in situations where we want something which is strong and permanent – such as in glues, in paints and in certain types of construction (e.g. boat-building).

Fig. 8.6 *The Royal Navy's 'Hunt' class mine countermeasures vessels all have hull, decks and superstructure moulded in fibreglass composites (made from a thermosetting polymer called an unsaturated polyester).*

Thermoplastic polymers find an even wider range of uses – from plastic baths to nylon carpets, from non-stick frying pans to pipes for domestic plumbing. We must divide them into two groups – depending on how we make the polymer from the monomer.

TOPIC 8.2.1

Addition polymers

An ADDITION POLYMER is one where the monomer molecules simply join up with each other to make the polymer molecule. No atoms or groups of atoms are lost when this happens (so the polymer molecule has the same **empirical** formula as the monomer).

We can think of all addition polymers as being based on the monomer ethene. If we make a polymer from ethene itself, we make polyethene, or 'polythene'.

Polythene

...and so on...   ethene   ethene   ...and so on...

polyethene

Ethene molecules will polymerise if they are brought together under high pressure (this was discovered by scientists working for ICI in England in 1933). It is as if the second bond between the two carbon atoms 'jumps' to form a link to the next molecule. This 'jumping' of bonds then repeats itself down the chain, until a single huge molecule of polythene forms. We use polythene for making a vast range of items.

Fig. 8.7 *These goods are all made of polythene*

Polyvinyl chloride (PVC)

chloroethene
(vinyl chloride)

polychloroethene
(polyvinyl chloride, PVC)

If we start from chloroethene (vinyl chloride) instead of ethene, the polymer we make is polychloroethene (polyvinyl chloride). Polychloroethene has become known by the initials of its older name – PVC.

PVC is slightly stronger and harder than polythene, so it is particularly good for making pipes for plumbing.

Fig. 8.8 *These pipes are made from PVC*

Polystyrene

phenylethene
(styrene)

polyphenylethene
(polystyrene)

Polystyrene is a poor conductor of heat. It also is light and cheap, so as well as being used as a heat insulator, it is used for making packaging and containers. Polystyrene is obviously ideal where we need to do both these things: for instance, where we have to make a container for something which also has to be kept hot – or cold.

Polytetrafluoroethene (PTFE)

tetrafluoroethene

polytetrafluoroethene (PTFE)

Polytetrafluoroethene (PTFE) has some unusual properties. It will stand up to very high temperatures, it is a very good electrical insulator and it forms a very slippery surface. PTFE makes an ideal 'non-stick' coating for frying pans.

Polymethyl 2-methylpropenoate (Perspex)

methyl 2–methylpropenoate

Perspex

Propenoic acid (acrylic acid) is $CH_2=CH.COOH$, an alkanoic acid made from ethene. 2-methyl propenoic acid is $CH_2=C(CH_3).COOH$, and its methyl ester is methyl 2-methylpropenoate $CH_2=C(CH_3).COOCH_3$. If we polymerise this substance, we make Perspex.

▶ PREPARATION 8.2

Perspex is as transparent as glass, but does not break so easily. It is therefore used to make laboratory safety screens, plastic lenses for spectacles and plastic contact lenses, cases for museum displays, aeroplane windows and cashiers' screens in Banks and Building Societies for example. In a slightly different form it is used to mould plastic baths and to make false teeth.

TOPIC 8.2.2

Condensation polymers

When starch is split down into glucose molecules, water is added each time a 'link in the chain' is broken. So we call the process hydrolysis. In the reverse process, in which starch is built up from glucose molecules, a water molecule is **lost** each time a new link in the chain forms. This process is called CONDENSATION POLYMERISATION.

Man-made condensation polymers copy the process in nature by which starch is built up. Molecules are used as monomers which can link up to their neighbours at either end, with a molecule of water being lost each time. Nature manages to do this with a

PREPARATION 8.2
Breaking down and re-making Perspex

You will need the following: chips of Perspex, lauroyl peroxide, hard-glass test-tube fitted with bung and delivery tube, 250 cm³ beaker, thermometer.

What to do

THE LABORATORY MUST BE WELL VENTILATED. DO NOT BREATHE THE VAPOUR PRODUCED BY HEATING PERSPEX, AND REMEMBER THAT THE VAPOUR IS VERY FLAMMABLE. YOU MUST WEAR YOUR SAFETY SPECTACLES.

1   Put a few Perspex chips into a test-tube which is fitted with a bung and delivery tube. Heat the Perspex with a medium flame, and condense the gas produced in a test-tube which is standing in a beaker of water.

2   The liquid which collects in the tube is the monomer. Warm the water in the beaker until the temperature is about 50°C, and then add a tiny amount of lauroyl peroxide (dip the end of a spatula into the powder, and stir the few grains collected into the liquid). This catalyses the polymerisation, and clear Perspex solid forms in about 1–2 hours.

---

single molecule (glucose) but man-made condensation polymers usually need two different monomer molecules – one with -H at either end, and one with -OH at either end.

$$H-\boxed{A}H \quad HO-\boxed{B}OH \quad H-\boxed{A}H \quad HO-\boxed{B}OH$$

$$\rightarrow \quad \ldots A-B-A-B \ldots \quad + nH_2O$$

A good example of a condensation polymer is nylon.

Nylon

$$H-HN(CH_2)_6NH-H \quad HO-CO(CH_2)_4CO-OH$$
1,6-diaminohexane   hexane-1,6-dioic acid

$$\longrightarrow \ldots NH(CH_2)_6NH-CO(CH_2)_4CO-NH(CH_2)_6NH-\ldots$$
nylon

We condense an AMINE (-NH_2) with alkanoic acid, to make an AMIDE (-NH–$\overset{\overset{\textstyle O}{\|}}{C}$ -). The result of doing this with a molecule which has two amine groups and one which has two alkanoic acid groups, is a chain held together by amide links. So nylon is a POLYAMIDE.

Nylon is made on a large scale in industry. It forms as a solid, which is melted and forced through small holes. This makes long filaments of solid nylon again, which are stretched and dried. What results is a yarn which can be woven into a fabric (to make socks, shirts, ties, handkerchiefs, scarves, underclothes, waterproof coats and so on) or turned into ropes, nets and racket strings. Such clothes and articles are very strong and hard-wearing.

In bulk, nylon is a thermoplastic, and so it can be moulded to make objects of different shapes and sizes. Because nylon has a very smooth surface and is so hard-wearing, we often use it for the moving parts in machinery, such as wheel-bearings in cars.

PREPARATION 8.3
Making nylon

You will need the following: 5% solution of hexane-1,6-dioylchloride in 1,1,1-trichloroethane, 5% solution of 1,6-diaminohexane in water, tweezers, glass rod, 100 cm³ beaker.

What to do

YOU MUST WEAR YOUR SAFETY SPECTACLES.

1   Place a few cm³ of the solution of hexane-1,6-dioylchloride in the beaker. (You will notice that you are not using quite the same monomer as mentioned in the text. This is simply to make the reaction easier – the product will be exactly the same.)

2   Now carefully add the other solution, so that a separate layer forms above the first.

3   You will see a 'cloudiness' where the layers meet. This is solid nylon. Use a pair of tweezers to draw out a thread from the skin of nylon which has formed, and wind it round a glass rod which is being held horizontally.

4   You can make a lump of solid nylon by using the glass rod to mix the two solutions together.

YOU MUST NOT TOUCH THE NYLON WITH YOUR BARE FINGERS.

If we were to carry out a condensation reaction between other monomer molecules, we would obtain different polymers which had different properties. We saw earlier that ethanol and ethanoic acid react together to make the ester, ethyl ethanoate. This reaction is a condensation reaction, but it cannot cause a chain to form, because both ethanol and ethanoic acid have only one functional group. However, if we had an alcohol which had an –O–H group at each end of the molecule, and an acid which had a –COOH group at each end, then a chain POLYESTER would be possible. Terylene is a typical polyester.

Terylene

$$HO - (CH_2)_2 - OH \qquad HOOC - \underset{}{\bigcirc} - COOH \longrightarrow$$

ethane–1,2–diol $\qquad$ benzene–1,4–dicarboxylic acid

$$\longrightarrow \;...O(CH_2)_2O - CO - \underset{}{\bigcirc} - CO - O(CH_2)_2O...$$

Terylene

Terylene, like nylon, can be turned into a yarn which can be woven. Many polyesters are now used together with natural materials like cotton and wool to give a 'mixed cloth' which has the benefit of being hard-wearing (like a polyester), but still with the appearance and feel of the natural fibre.

Sources of raw materials for making polymers

The source of organic molecules which can be used to make polymers must be 'organic' itself. For a long time, chemicals derived from coal were the only ones available. But since the expansion of the oil chemistry in the 1950s and 1960s, crude oil has become the main source, and still is today. However, you learnt about the length of time that coal supplies will last, in Section 2. It is highly probable that attention will soon have to switch to this old source of organic monomers. Fortunately, both coal and oil can supply most of our needs.

Chemicals from coal

If we take coal and heat it in a place where there is no air, one of the products is a very thick liquid called 'coal tar'. If we take coal tar and distil it, we obtain various chemicals which can be used to make some of the monomers we need. Most of the rest can be obtained from one of the other products of heating coal away from the air – coke.

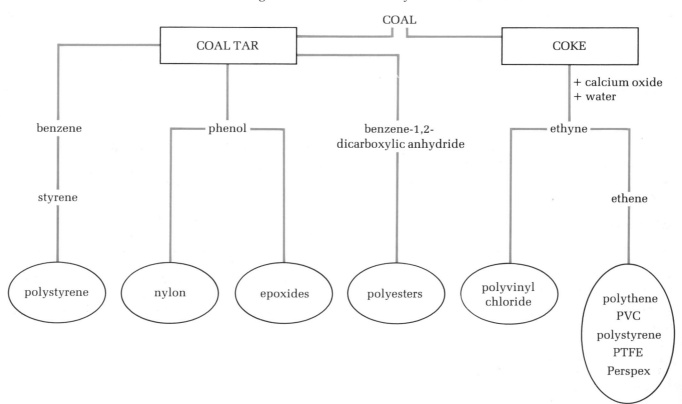

Fig. 8.9

Chemicals from oil

The different chemicals which we get from distilling crude oil can be used to obtain suitable monomers. Most of the monomers which we need are relatively small and, as Fig. 8.18 shows, are obtained from relatively small molecules such as methane, ethene and propene. On the other hand, many of the higher-boiling point chemicals which we get from crude oil by distilling it have much bigger molecules than these. So we could increase the amount of useful chemicals from a given amount of oil if we could break the bigger molecules down into smaller ones.

▶ EXPERIMENT 8.6

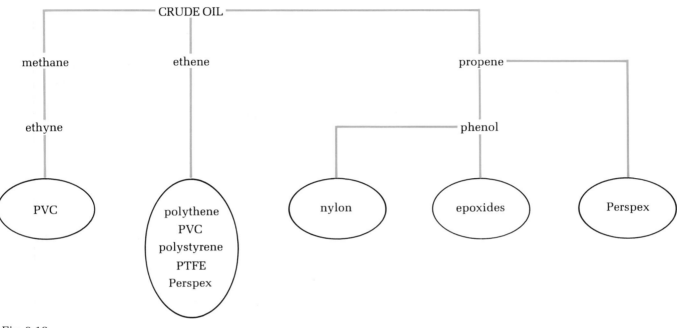

Fig. 8.10

EXPERIMENT 8.6

Can we 'crack' the bigger molecules which we get from oil?

You will need the following: medicinal paraffin, dilute bromine water, mineral wool, test-tube fitted with bung and delivery tube, pieces of broken porous pot, 250 cm³ beaker.

What to do

YOU MUST WEAR YOUR SAFETY SPECTACLES.

1 Follow the instructions of Experiment 8.3 (p. 332), but use medicinal paraffin instead of ethanol.

2 Use the gas you collect to carry out the following tests.
(a) Bring a lighted splint up to one of the test-tubes of gas to see if it will burn.
(b) Add a little dilute bromine water to another test-tube of gas, and shake.

What happened and what we can decide

You should have been able to see that the gas produced when medicinal paraffin is passed over a very hot surface
(a) burns with a yellow flame, and
(b) 'decolorises' dilute bromine water.
Medicinal paraffin contains alkanes which have a relatively high molecular weight. The gas produced in the experiment contained a mixture of alkenes, all of which are relatively small molecules. So 'cracking' appears to work, and give molecules suitable for use as monomers.

In industry, cracking is carried out in large columns, which often contain a catalyst. The mixture of gases which is produced is fractionally distilled in order to obtain pure chemicals.

UNIT 8.2
Summary and learning

1 We can copy nature and make new materials by building up large molecules from small ones. Thermoplastic polymers are solids which can be heated and re-set as many times as we like. Thermosetting polymers can only be set once.

2 Addition polymers are based on the monomer ethene, or chemicals which are made from it. You should remember the names of the different addition polymers, the monomers from which they are made, and the uses to which they are put.

3 Condensation polymers are ones in which water (or another molecule) is lost each time a new link in the polymer chain forms. You should remember how we make nylon and Terylene, and the uses to which they are put.

4 You should remember the outline of how we obtain the monomer chemicals which we need from coal and from oil.

5 You have learnt the meaning of these words:

polymers	condensation polymer
monomers	amine
polymerisation	amide
thermoplastic polymer	polyamide
thermosetting polymer	polyester
addition polymer	

UNIT 8.3   *Inorganic carbon compounds*

It was mentioned at the start of this section that most of the carbon on Earth is not part of the 'biosphere'. A large proportion of it is carbon which is trapped in carbonate rocks. So we usually think of carbonates, the related hydrogencarbonates and carbon dioxide, and carbon monoxide as being 'inorganic' chemicals. Certainly, they do not fit anywhere into systematic organic chemistry.

Almost all the reactions of these inorganic carbon compounds which can be carried out easily in the laboratory have already been mentioned in earlier sections. So what follows is mostly a drawing-together of facts and ideas of which you should already be aware.

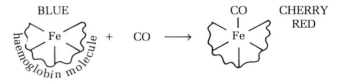

haemoglobin   carboxyhaemoglobin

When this happens, the result can be death through lack of oxygen.

The gases which come out of car exhausts and cigarette smoke both contain carbon monoxide. Air which contains even very low concentrations of carbon monoxide (as low as 0.1%) can be harmful.

▶ PREPARATION 8.4

TOPIC 8.3.1
Carbon monoxide

Carbon monoxide is a colourless gas, which has no special smell. It is about as dense as air (see Fig. 7.36 on p. 322). It is almost insoluble in water.

Carbon monoxide is extremely poisonous, since it combines with the haemoglobin in blood more easily than does oxygen (see Section 5, p. 252). When carbon monoxide is present in the air which someone breathes, oxyhaemoglobin cannot form, because carboxyhaemoglobin forms instead.

Reactions of carbon monoxide

Carbon monoxide burns in air with a blue flame, forming carbon dioxide.

$$2CO(g) + O_2(g) \rightarrow 2CO_2(g)$$

Carbon monoxide is a reducing agent (see Section 4, Topic 4.5.1). It reduces the oxides of lead, copper and iron to the metals.

$$PbO(s) + CO(g) \rightarrow Pb(s) + CO_2(g)$$
$$CuO(s) + CO(g) \rightarrow Cu(s) + CO_2(g)$$
$$Fe_2O_3 + 3CO(g) \rightarrow 2Fe(s) + 3CO_2(g)$$

PREPARATION 8.4
Making carbon monoxide in the laboratory

> **Your teacher will show you this preparation**

The following will be needed: apparatus as shown below, crystals of ethanedioic acid, concentrated sulphuric acid, concentrated potassium hydroxide solution.

What to do

THE PREPARATION MUST BE CARRIED OUT IN A FUME-CUPBOARD.

1 Use a tap-funnel to add concentrated sulphuric acid to some ethanedioic acid crystals in a round-bottomed flask, connected to the apparatus as shown.

Warm gently, and the following reaction takes place (the sulphuric acid 'removes' water from the ethanedioic acid, leaving carbon monoxide and carbon dioxide).

$$H_2C_2O_4(s) \rightarrow CO(g) + CO_2(g) + H_2O(l)$$

2 The mixture of carbon monoxide and carbon dioxide which is produced passes through concentrated potassium hydroxide solution. This removes the carbon dioxide.

$$CO_2(g) + 2KOH(aq) \rightarrow K_2CO_3(aq) + H_2O(l)$$

3 The carbon monoxide passes on, and, since it does not dissolve in water, is collected in gas-jars in a trough of water.

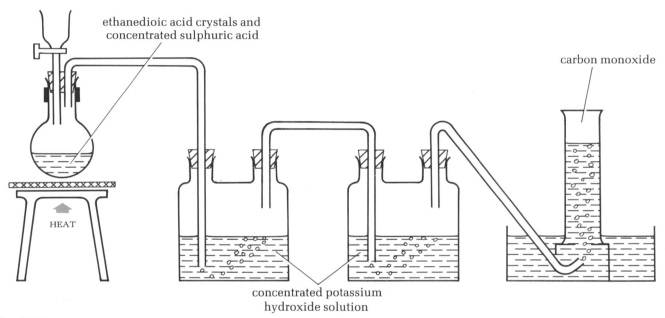

ethanedioic acid crystals and concentrated sulphuric acid

carbon monoxide

HEAT

concentrated potassium hydroxide solution

Fig. 8.11

TOPIC 8.3.2
Carbon dioxide

Like carbon monoxide, carbon dioxide is a colourless gas which has no special smell. It is much denser than air (see Fig. 7.36 on p. 322), and will form a layer around objects, pushing air out of the way. For this reason, carbon dioxide is a useful fire-extinguisher and is used in many modern fire-fighting devices. (Unlike carbon monoxide, carbon dioxide does not burn!)

Carbon dioxide will dissolve very readily in water, particularly if it is forced to do so by being at a high pressure. When the pressure is released, bubbles of gas form in the water, making a 'fizzy' drink.

The effect of carbon dioxide pollution in the atmosphere was mentioned in Section 2 (Topic 2.3.1). The structure and shape of the carbon dioxide molecule were explained in Section 3 (Topic 3.3.2).

▶ PREPARATIONS 8.5 (p. 344)

PREPARATION 8.5
Making carbon dioxide in the laboratory

Your teacher will show this preparation

The following will be needed: apparatus as shown below, marble chips, dilute hydrochloric acid.

What to do

1   Use a thistle-funnel to add dilute hydrochloric acid to some marble chips in a flat-bottomed flask,

connected to the apparatus as shown. Marble is a form of calcium carbonate, and the following reaction takes place:

$$CaCO_3(s) + 2HCl(aq) \rightarrow CaCl_2(aq) + H_2O(l) + CO_2(g)$$
marble

2   Carbon dioxide can be collected by pushing the water out of gas jars in a trough of water. Some carbon dioxide dissolves and is lost, but not enough to make any other method preferable.

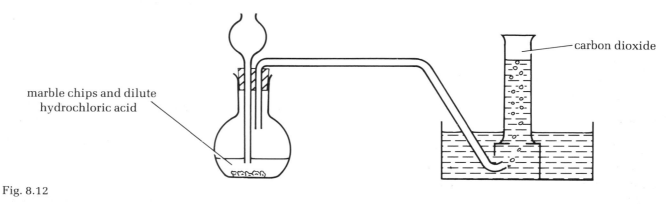

marble chips and dilute hydrochloric acid

carbon dioxide

Fig. 8.12

Reactions of carbon dioxide

Carbon dioxide puts out a lighted splint which is plunged into it.

It reacts with a solution of calcium hydroxide, making a precipitate of calcium carbonate. This is the basis of the chemical test for carbon dioxide, in which lime-water turns 'milky' if carbon dioxide is present. If we keep passing carbon dioxide through it, the liquid goes clear again (see below, Topic 8.3.3). The equation for the formation of the white precipitate of calcium carbonate is:

$$Ca(OH)_2(aq) + CO_2(g) \rightarrow CaCO_3(s) + H_2O(l)$$
lime-water

When carbon dioxide dissolves in water, it also reacts. The product of this reaction is a weak acid, carbonic acid.

$$\overset{\text{slightly}}{H_2O(l) + CO_2(g) \rightleftharpoons H_2CO_3(aq) \rightleftharpoons 2H^+(aq) + CO_3^{2-}(aq)}$$

If a burning piece of magnesium is plunged into a gas-jar of carbon dioxide, a redox reaction takes place. The products are carbon (black solid) and magnesium oxide (white solid).

$$2Mg(s) + CO_2(g) \rightarrow 2MgO(s) + C(s)$$

TOPIC 8.3.3
Hydrogencarbonates

You saw in Section 7 (Topic 7.2.3) that carbon dioxide dissolved in rainwater will react with rocks which are made of calcium carbonate, forming a solution of calcium hydrogencarbonate:

$$CaCO_3(s) + H_2O(l) + CO_2(g) \rightarrow Ca(HCO_3)_2(aq)$$

We can copy this reaction in the laboratory by passing carbon dioxide into lime-water until it becomes milky. If more carbon dioxide is passed through the suspension which has formed, it eventually clears because calcium hydrogencarbonate has formed.

The hydrogencarbonate anion has the formula HCO_3^-, and we might expect that it would form many salts with metal cations. However, the only important hydrogencarbonates which are stable are calcium hydrogencarbonate and sodium hydrogencarbonate.

We can make sodium hydrogencarbonate in the same way that we make calcium hydrogencarbonate. Sodium carbonate is soluble, so all we have to do is pass carbon dioxide through a solution of it in water.

$$Na_2CO_3(aq) + CO_2(g) + H_2O(l) \rightarrow 2NaHCO_3(s)$$

Sodium hydrogencarbonate forms as a white solid.

You saw that sodium hydrogencarbonate is formed in one of the earlier steps in the Solvay Process in Section 5 (Topic 5.3.1). However, we manufacture it from the final product of the Solvay Process, sodium carbonate, by saturating a slurry of it in water with carbon dioxide. Sodium hydrogencarbonate is called 'baking soda', and we use it in making baking powders. Why is this?

EXPERIMENT 8.7

Why is sodium hydrogencarbonate used in baking powders?

You will need the following: sodium hydrogencarbonate, lime-water.

What to do

YOU MUST WEAR YOUR SAFETY SPECTACLES.

1   Put several spatula-measures of sodium hydrogencarbonate in a test-tube and heat strongly.

2   Test for carbon dioxide gas in the usual way, and notice any other changes which happen.

What happened and what we can decide

You should have been able to see that when sodium hydrogencarbonate is heated, it decomposes giving carbon dioxide. Water is also produced, and forms droplets on the cooler parts of the test-tube.

$$2NaHCO_3(s) \rightarrow Na_2CO_3 + H_2O(l) + CO_2(g)$$

When sodium hydrogencarbonate is used in baking powders, the carbon dioxide produced during baking helps cakes to 'rise' and form something light, by making spaces between the solid pieces of cake.

TOPIC 8.3.4

Carbonates

You learned about the solubility of carbonates in Section 1 (Topic 1.4.2), about the effect of heat on carbonates in Section 5 (Topic 5.3.2), and how to identify carbonates in Section 1 (Topic 1.4.3). In summary, these properties are:

Na	soluble	not affected by heat
Ca Mg Al Zn Fe Pb Cu	insoluble	heat decomposes to oxide and carbon dioxide

give carbon dioxide with any acid

Question

If you were given two white powders and were told that one of them is sodium carbonate, and the other is sodium hydrogencarbonate, how could you test to see which was which?

The most important carbonate in industry is sodium carbonate, and you learned about it Section 5 (Topic 5.3.1).

As we have seen, the most important carbonate in nature is calcium carbonate. Limestone, marble and chalk are all forms of calcium carbonate. All derive originally from the 'bony' parts of the bodies of dead organisms which once lived in the sea. In the form of bone, calcium carbonate is quite strong. It provides support and protection in the bodies of all animals, including our own.

UNIT 8.3
Summary and learning

1   You should remember the properties of carbon monoxide and how to prepare it in the laboratory.

2   You should remember the properties of carbon dioxide and how to prepare it in the laboratory. Remember how it can be useful to us, and why.

3   You should remember how to make sodium hydrogencarbonate, and why it is useful as 'baking soda'.

4   You should remember the properties of carbonates, and particularly how sodium carbonate is different from most other carbonates. Remember also how to tell the difference between sodium carbonate and sodium hydrogencarbonate.

The chemical world – nitrogen and sulphur

UNIT 9.1 *Nitrogen, and some of its compounds*

We have seen that the Earth's atmosphere is about 4/5 nitrogen. It also exists as the element in the atmospheres of Venus and Mars, and in compounds of nitrogen (mostly ammonia) in the atmospheres of Jupiter and Saturn and in the actual make-up of the planets Uranus and Neptune. So there is plenty of nitrogen in the Universe – in fact, it is the fifth most plentiful element.

The Earth is a 'nitrogen world', because of the large amount of it in the atmosphere. We shall see shortly how important nitrogen is to the existence of life. Nitrogen is present in many of the most essential chemical substances in living things. This might lead us to wonder whether there are any other 'nitrogen worlds' in the Universe, and if so, whether life exists there.

In fact, we have already found one other 'nitrogen world' within the solar system. One of the moons of Saturn, called Titan, had been known for a long time to have some sort of atmosphere. Until very recently, it was thought that this was made up mainly of methane. However, when the Voyager space probes reached Titan in 1980 and 1981, they found that it was completely covered in dense clouds about 200 km thick, and that the atmosphere was 85% nitrogen! The pressure of the atmosphere on Titan is about half as great again as Earth's atmospheric pressure, and Titan itself is between the Earth and the Moon in size (Fig. 9.2).

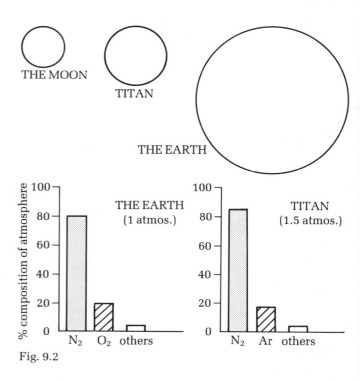

Fig. 9.2

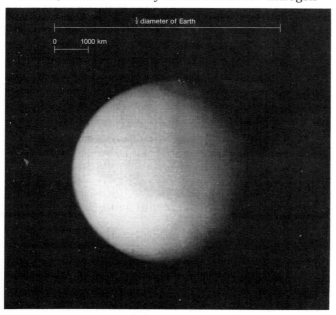

Fig. 9.1 *Titan, which circles round Saturn, is the largest moon in the solar system. Like the Earth, it is a 'nitrogen world'*

You know that the oxygen in the Earth's atmosphere has come from photosynthesis in plants over millions of years. Originally, the atmosphere contained no oxygen. It was probably made up of carbon dioxide, nitrogen, carbon monoxide, water vapour and a little hydrogen. This is important, because (it might seem strange, but it's true!) life would almost certainly not begin where the atmosphere contains much oxygen. In an OXIDISING ATMOSPHERE, instead of chains and rings of carbon atoms forming (see Section 8), all that would be produced would be carbon dioxide. So the 'backbone' of organic chemicals, with all the variety involved, could not come about.

The present atmosphere of the Earth is an oxidising atmosphere, and we need to breathe oxygen to live. But the Earth's early atmosphere was a mild REDUCING ATMOSPHERE, like the present atmosphere of Titan. Scientists have passed a spark repeatedly through a mixture of gases like that in the Earth's early atmosphere. When they have investigated the mixture of chemicals which is produced, they have found many organic molecules, including those which go together to make DNA. DNA is the 'messenger molecule' which organises chemicals into a living system (see photograph on p. 18).

So, is life being created at this moment on Titan? We think it is not, because the temperature is too low (Titan is much further from the sun than the Earth is). However, people may go to Titan one day, and carry out huge-scale experiments by heating up a few square miles of its surface at a time, and see what happens!

It seems, then, that nitrogen (like carbon) is an element which is essential to living things. Is this so; and if so, why?

TOPIC 9.1.1

The place of nitrogen in the biosphere

If we find carbon in all living things (see Section 8), can we say that we also find nitrogen there too? This is the first question which we must ask ourselves – where do we find nitrogen in the living world?

If we heat something which contains the element nitrogen with a strong alkali, we get ammonia gas. We can spot ammonia easily, because of its smell and because it is the only common alkaline gas.

▶ EXPERIMENT 9.1

The ammonia is proof of the presence of nitrogen in the substance – and when there was no ammonia, the substance contained no nitrogen. So we can decide that

(a) nitrogen is present in very many living things, but

(b) nitrogen is not present in all the chemicals which come from living things.

Another way of saying this is that nitrogen is needed for some of the chemicals in living things, but not all of them. What are those substances which contain nitrogen?

Proteins

We saw in Section 8 (Topic 8.2.2) that we can make the polymer 'nylon' by condensing a molecule with two amine groups with one with two carboxylic acid

---

EXPERIMENT 9.1

Where do we find nitrogen in the living world?

You will need the following: soda lime (a mixture of sodium hydroxide and calcium hydroxide), glucose, starch, as many of the following as possible: gelatin, dried peas, wool, milk powder, hair, meat, fingernail cuttings.

What to do

YOU MUST WEAR YOUR SAFETY SPECTACLES.

1 Take the substance which you are testing, and break it down into small pieces. Put it in a test-tube.

2 Add about twice the volume of soda lime to the substance, and mix the two together with a spatula.

3 Heat the mixture strongly, and test the gas given off with damp universal indicator paper.

4 Do this with glucose and starch, and with as many of the other substances as you can.

What happened, and what we can decide

You should have seen that an alkaline gas (ammonia) was given off in each case, except for glucose and starch.

groups. The result was a substance which can be used for making things (either as a fibre or as a plastic).

The substances which nature uses to 'make things' are called PROTEINS. Proteins are in many ways similar to nylon. To start with, we can call them 'polyamides', because proteins are polymers in which the monomers are held together by amide links. What makes a protein different, however, is that the amine group and alkanoic acid group are at opposite ends of **the same molecule**.

We call a chemical which contains both an amine group and a alkanoic acid group an AMINO ACID.

H — NH —☐— COOH

an amino acid

Two amino acids can condense together to form an amide:

H — NH —☐— COOH   H — NH —☐— COOH

amino acid   amino acid

→ H — NH —☐— CO — NH —☐— COOH

amide

This leaves an amine group free at one end of the molecule (which will condense with the alkanoic acid group of another amino acid molecule), and an amino acid group free at the other end of the molecule (which will condense with the amino acid group of a fourth amino acid). This process can go on many hundreds of times, building a polymer molecule.

Depending on the different amino acids which go together to make the protein, we get slightly different types. There are only 24 different amino acids which exist in the living substances on Earth, but out of these are built all the different forms of animal and vegetable protein which exist. A substance like a sugar or starch is not part of the 'building material' of living things – only an energy store. So they are not proteins, and contain no nitrogen.

When we eat some plant material or some meat, we are taking in proteins. These are not in exactly the right form for the needs of our own body, because it needs human protein to carry out repairs and to grow. So we break down the protein we eat into amino acids – and then put these back together again in such a way that we make human protein. So humans, like other animals, get the nitrogen which they need by eating. But where do plants get their nitrogen in the first place?

The element nitrogen, and the nitrogen cycle

We can think of the nitrogen which exists in living things as having come originally from the nitrogen in the air. To understand how living things get hold of nitrogen, we must look first at the element itself.

Look at the position of nitrogen in the Periodic Table:

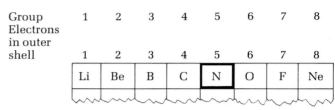

Group	1	2	3	4	5	6	7	8
Electrons in outer shell	1	2	3	4	5	6	7	8
	Li	Be	B	C	N	O	F	Ne

Nitrogen has five electrons in its outermost shell, and needs three more to obtain a filled shell. So it forms three covalent bonds, and the element itself is diatomic (see Section 3, Topic 3.3.2.).

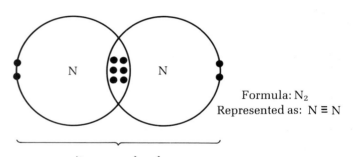

Formula: N_2
Represented as: $N \equiv N$

nitrogen molecule

Fig. 9.3

So the nitrogen in the air is in the form of diatomic molecules, held together very strongly by those covalent bonds. In fact, the bonding between the two nitrogen atoms in a nitrogen molecule is so strong that it can hardly be broken by the amounts of energy available in chemical reactions. This means that **nitrogen is a very unreactive element**.

However, nitrogen and oxygen will combine together to make oxides of nitrogen (gases) if a spark is passed through the mixture. This happens in the cylinders of a car engine (see Section 2, Topic 2.3.1), and occasionally in nature as a result of lightning. The oxides of nitrogen end up as soluble nitrates in the soil, which plants can obtain through their roots.

There is one other method by which some plants (the legume family: peas and beans) can get nitrogen from the air. Their roots contain special bacteria in little growths called ROOT NODULES. Those bacteria have become able to take atmospheric nitrogen and turn it into nitrogen compounds such as ammonia, without using a spark, or a high pressure, or high temperature. We call this process NITROGEN FIXATION. We do not understand how this happens, although it is probable that the nitrogen molecule is forced to act as a ligand in a complex with a transition metal (almost certainly molybdenum) (see Section 5, Topic 5.1.1). Once the nitrogen molecule has been held in this way, other systems then set about reducing it to ammonia. Some artificial systems have been made which copy the nitrogen-fixing behaviour of these bacteria, although only feebly. A full understanding of the chemistry of nitrogen fixation is one of the biggest unsolved scientific problems of our age. As we shall see shortly, the possible consequences of such knowledge for our ability to feed the world's population are enormous.

We need to eat plenty of protein every day, because our bodies continually break down old 'worn out' protein, and replace it with new. The nitrogen from the old protein passes out of our bodies in the chemical urea, which breaks down in the soil to ammonium compounds. When plants die and decay, the nitrogen in them also ends up in the form of ammonium compounds.

Ammonium compounds in the soil are oxidised by bacteria to nitrates – which are then picked up again by plant roots. So we can think of there being a cycle around which the nitrogen in living things passes (Fig. 9.4).

Fertilisers

In nature, there is a balance between the amount of essential chemicals in the soil, and the number of plants that will grow. When we farm land to obtain a particular crop, however, we may soon exhaust the chemicals which are in the soil 'naturally'.

So we have to add fertilisers – chemicals which supply the essential elements for plants to grow. You saw in Section 2 that naturally occurring sodium nitrate can be used to add nitrogen (N) to soils, and that we also need to add the elements phosphorus (P) and potassium (K). If we add all three elements together, we have what we call an 'NPK' fertiliser. An example would be a mixture of ammonium nitrate, ammonium phosphate and potassium chloride.

We have to use fertilisers in very large quantities. Part of the cost involved is the cost of transporting heavy solids over large distances. So we want to get the most nitrogen (for instance) per gram of fertiliser that we can. We can easily work out the percentage of the mass of a particular solid which is nitrogen or phosphorus or potassium (Table 9.1).

Compound	Formula	Mass of 1 mole/g	Percentages N	P	K
Sodium nitrate	$NaNO_3$	85	16	–	–
Calcium phosphate	$Ca_3(PO_4)_2$	310	–	20	–
Ammonium phosphate	$(NH_4)_3PO_4$	149	28	21	–
Ammonium nitrate	NH_4NO_3	80	35	–	–
Potassium phosphate	K_3PO_4	212	–	15	18
Potassium chloride	KCl	74.5	–	–	52
Potassium nitrate	KNO_3	101	14	–	39

Table 9.1

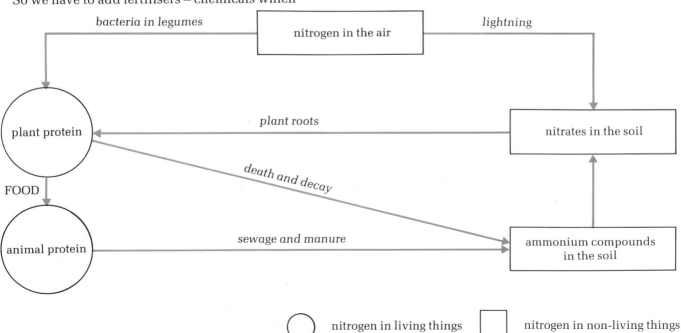

Fig. 9.4 *The nitrogen cycle*

Question

Which of the chemicals in Table 9.1 has:

(a) the highest proportion by weight of nitrogen;
(b) the highest proportion by weight of phosphorus;
(c) the highest proportion by weight of potassium;
(d) the best combination of nitrogen and phosphorus;
(e) the best combination of nitrogen and potassium;
(f) the best combination of phosphorus and potassium?

For a particular fertiliser, the 'NPK value' will depend on the chemicals which it contains, and the proportion in which they are mixed together.

Fig. 9.5 *NPK values are quoted on fertiliser bags*

You will see from Table 9.1 that ammonium compounds have a much higher proportion of nitrogen than do nitrates. So in spite of the existence of natural deposits of nitrates, we make ammonium compounds in order to use them as nitrogen fertilisers. We do this by making ammonia.

TOPIC 9.1.2

Ammonia

We have already seen that ammonia is a common substance in our solar system – especially amongst the outer planets (Jupiter, Saturn, Uranus and Neptune). It is one of the main gases in the atmospheres of Jupiter and Saturn, and it is part of the actual make-up of Uranus and Neptune (see Section 2, Topic 2.1.2).

Fig. 9.6 *These huge swirling clouds on Jupiter are made partly of ammonia*

You already know that the formula of ammonia is NH_3, that it is a gas which is 'lighter' than air, and that when it dissolves in water an alkali forms. But how can we make it in the laboratory, and what other properties does it have?

▶ EXPERIMENT 9.2

So, you have seen how to make ammonia in the laboratory, and how it behaves. We can easily make ammonium salts from ammonia, and so if we can make ammonia cheaply, we can have a plentiful supply of nitrogen fertilisers. How can we make ammonia on a large scale?

Making ammonia in industry – the Haber Process

About 80% of the ammonia which we make in industry goes for the manufacture of fertilisers – ammonium compounds. So the first thing we can say is that it would not make sense to make ammonia in industry the same way that we make it in the laboratory – by reacting an ammonium compound. We would just be going round a cycle – making ammonia from ammonium compounds and then remaking the ammonium compounds. So we have to

⟶ p. 352

EXPERIMENT 9.2

How can we make ammonia, and how does it behave?

You will need the following: test-tube and bung fitted with bent delivery tube, ammonium chloride, calcium hydroxide, concentrated hydrochloric acid, universal indicator paper.

What to do

YOU MUST CARRY OUT THIS WORK IN A FUME-CUPBOARD.

1   Put a few spatula-measures of ammonium chloride in a test-tube. Add the same amount of calcium hydroxide, and mix the two solids together. Set up the apparatus as shown in Fig. 9.7, and heat to obtain ammonia.

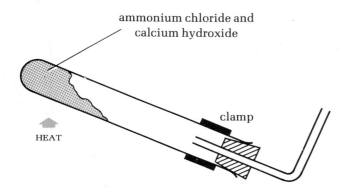

Fig. 9.7

Make sure that the mouth of the test-tube is the lower end. If you do not do this, the water which is formed will run back and crack the test-tube.

2   Place a test-tube over the end of the delivery tube so that ammonia gas is delivered upwards into it. Take a piece of damp universal indicator paper, and hold it just below the mouth of the test-tube which is collecting the gas. When the indicator paper turns blue, you will know that the test-tube is full of ammonia.

3   Take the test-tube full of ammonia and, keeping it upside-down so that the ammonia does not escape, place its mouth below the surface of some water in a beaker. If no change happens, shake the test-tube gently. Observe what happens, and then drop a piece of universal indicator paper into the beaker. **Discuss what you have seen, and try to decide what has happened to the ammonia.**

4   Take the stopper out of a bottle of concentrated hydrochloric acid, and hold it close to the delivery tube opening, while heating the mixture again to make more ammonia. What do you see?

5   Now collect another test-tube full of ammonia, keeping it upside-down. Take a lighted splint and hold it just above the mouth of the test-tube as you turn it the 'right way' up. The ammonia will rise past the flame as it mixes with the air. Does ammonia burn in air?

What happened and what we can decide

You should have been able to see the following.
1   We can make ammonia by heating ammonium chloride and calcium hydroxide mixed together:

$2NH_4Cl(s) + Ca(OH)_2(s)$
$$\xrightarrow{\text{heat}} CaCl_2(s) + 2H_2O(g) + 2NH_3(g)$$

2   Ammonia turns damp universal indicator paper blue. So it dissolves in water to form an alkali (ammonium hydroxide):

$NH_3(g) + H_2O(l) \rightarrow NH_4OH(aq)$

3   Ammonia is extremely soluble in water. It is so soluble that if ammonia and water are together in an enclosed space, a vacuum forms as the ammonia dissolves.

4   When ammonia meets hydrogen chloride gas (which is given off from tiny amounts of concentrated hydrochloric acid), a white 'smoke' forms. This is made up of tiny particles of the salt, ammonium chloride:

$NH_3(g) + HCl(g) \rightarrow NH_4Cl(s)$

5   Ammonia does not burn in air.

find a way to break into this cycle, by making 'new' ammonia.

The only way that we can do this is to 'put together' ammonia molecules from the elements in them – nitrogen and hydrogen. In other words, we have to find a way to 'fix' nitrogen from the air by reacting it with hydrogen.

Fortunately, a German scientist called Haber discovered (in 1911) that nitrogen and hydrogen will react together to make ammonia, if there is a catalyst of iron present. The reaction does not 'go to completion', but forms an equilibrium mixture (see Section 6, Topic 6.2.2).

$$N_2(g) + 3H_2(g) \underset{\text{catalyst}}{\overset{\text{iron}}{\rightleftharpoons}} 2NH_3(g) \qquad \triangle H \text{ negative in the forward direction}$$

We can use Le Chatelier's Principle to work out the conditions which would give us the highest equilibrium concentration of ammonia.

(a) The reaction is exothermic in the forward direction, so the lower the temperature, the greater the concentration of ammonia in the equilibrium mixture. But a very low temperature would mean that both the forward and reverse reactions would happen only very slowly, meaning that it would take a very long time before equilibrium was reached. This would increase the cost of making a given amount of ammonia in a given time.

(b) All the chemicals in the equilibrium are gases, and the total number of moles of reactant is greater than the total number of moles of product. So the reaction mixture takes up a smaller volume the higher the proportion of ammonia at equilibrium. So the 'yield' of ammonia is higher the higher the pressure, as is the speed at which equilibrium is obtained. But the higher the pressure, the higher the cost of supplying the energy which is needed to pressurise the gases, and the higher the cost of the

equipment – which has to be made stronger to withstand the pressure.

So, for both the temperature and pressure at which the reaction takes place, we have to find a compromise between yield of ammonia and cost. We have to make a reasonable amount of ammonia reasonably quickly – but at a reasonable cost (Table 9.2).

Change	Effect on equilibrium conc. of NH_3	Effect on rate of reaction	Effect on cost per tonne per day
Increase temperature	lower	faster	If too high – too little NH_3 and too costly. If too low – too slow
Increase pressure	higher	faster	If too high – too costly. If too low – too little NH_3 and too slow

Table 9.2

The compromise which Haber worked out was a temperature of 500°C and a pressure of 200 atmospheres, in the presence of an iron catalyst (which makes the reaction come to equilibrium more quickly).

We obtain a mixture of nitrogen and hydrogen (in the ratio of 1 volume to 3 volumes) by reacting methane (from natural gas) first with steam and then with air. The gases are compressed, heated and passed over the iron catalyst. The result is an equilibrium mixture of which 15% is ammonia. We then cool the mixture until the ammonia liquifies and it is then run off into pressurised tanks where it remains in liquid form. The nitrogen and hydrogen which have not reacted have more of the mixture added, and are passed over the catalyst again. So the process is a continuous flow process (see Section 2, Topic 2.4.2).

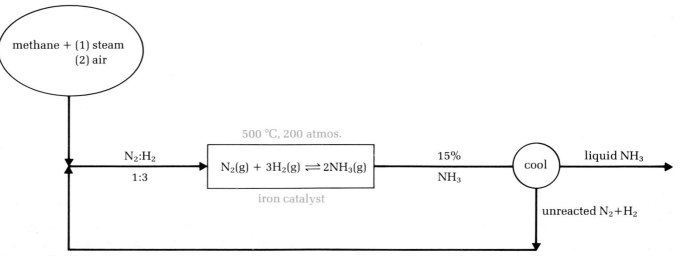

Fig. 9.8 *The Haber Process*

Fig. 9.9 *An ammonia plant, at Billingham on the River Tees*

A typical ammonia plant will make about 1000 tonnes of ammonia per day. An ammonia plant needs the following things:

1. a supply of methane (natural gas);
2. a supply of energy (to make steam from water, and to create a high temperature and pressure);
3. a supply of water;
4. good transport facilities.

Billingham in Teesside is the main site in Britain for the manufacture of ammonia. It is close to the North Sea and its natural gas and oil, and also to large coalfields. Water comes from the River Tees, and road, rail, river and sea transport are available. In overseas countries, ammonia plants are often sited close to oilfields, where methane and energy are available in abundance.

Of the 20% of ammonia which is not used for making ammonium fertilisers, most is converted into nitric acid, and from nitric acid, nitrates. We shall look at how this is done shortly. But first, how can we make nitric acid (and nitrates) in the laboratory, and how do they behave?

TOPIC 9.1.3
Nitric acid and nitrates

Today, we would not normally make nitric acid in the laboratory, since it is much easier to buy it from a supplier. However, there is a simple method for making it, using potassium nitrate and concentrated sulphuric acid. If we heat these two chemicals together in a piece of apparatus called a RETORT, nitric acid is given off as a vapour. We can then collect liquid nitric acid by passing the vapour into a cool vessel, where it condenses. (Fig. 9.10).

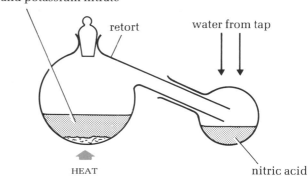

Fig. 9.10

$$KNO_3(s) + H_2SO_4(aq) \xrightarrow{\text{conc.}} KHSO_4(aq) + HNO_3(g)$$
potassium hydrogensulphate

You have seen all the important reactions of nitric acid before. It is both an acid, and an oxidising agent (see Section 4).

Nitric acid behaves as an acid

Like all acids, it will neutralise bases, forming nitrates. It will also react with carbonates to give carbon dioxide, and with metals above hydrogen in the reactivity series to give hydrogen. The following equations are for typical reactions of nitric acid when it is behaving as an acid.

$$CuO(s) + 2HNO_3(aq) \rightarrow Cu(NO_3)_2(aq) + H_2O(l)$$
$$NaOH(aq) + HNO_3(aq) \rightarrow NaNO_3(aq) + H_2O(l)$$
$$CaCO_3(s) + 2HNO_3(aq)$$
$$\longrightarrow Ca(NO_3)_2(aq) + H_2O(l) + CO_2(g)$$
$$Zn(s) + 2HNO_3(aq) \rightarrow Zn(NO_3)_2(aq) + H_2(g)$$

Nitric acid behaves as an oxidising agent

Dilute nitric acid and concentrated nitric acid are both oxidising agents. So both react with metals **below** hydrogen in the reactivity series, but not by giving hydrogen. You saw in Topic 5.1.2 how dilute and concentrated nitric acid react with copper.

dilute
$$3Cu(s) + 8HNO_3(aq)$$
colourless
$$\longrightarrow 3Cu(NO_3)_2(aq) + 4H_2O(l) + 2NO(g)$$
nitrogen oxide

conc.
$$Cu(s) + 4HNO_3(aq)$$
brown
$$\longrightarrow Cu(NO_3)_2(aq) + 2H_2O(l) + 2NO_2(g)$$
nitrogen dioxide

Concentrated nitric acid will also oxidise acidified iron(II) salts (green) to iron(III) salts (brown/yellow).

dil. H_2SO_4 conc. HNO_3
$$3Fe^{2+}(aq) + 4H^+(aq) + NO_3^-(aq)$$
green
$$\longrightarrow 3Fe^{3+}(aq) + 2H_2O(l) + NO(g)$$
brown/yellow

Nitrates

It is obviously easy to make nitrates from nitric acid. You learnt that all nitrates are soluble and how to test for a nitrate in Section 1. You saw in Sections 4 and 5 how the effect of heat on solid nitrates depends on the position in the reactivity series of the metal concerned (see Table 5.4, p. 271). You also saw the importance of nitrates (and their solubility) in the nitrogen cycle earlier in this section.

PROJECT 9.1

Use the sources given above to write down briefly, in your own words, the important properties of nitrates.

Making nitric acid in industry

As was the case with ammonia, we would not make nitric acid in industry by the same method that is used in the laboratory. The reason is the same – we use nitric acid in order to make nitrates (amongst other things) so it does not make sense to make nitric acid from a nitrate.

Instead, we make nitric acid from ammonia, which has itself been made from nitrogen in the air. You saw earlier that ammonia does not burn in air. However, if we increase the amount of oxygen in the air, ammonia will burn with a yellow flame. When this happens, the nitrogen is released from ammonia as the element itself.

$$4NH_3(g) + 3O_2(g) \rightarrow 2N_2(g) + 6H_2O(g)$$

As a means of getting nitric acid from ammonia, this reaction is not very promising – in fact we have achieved the opposite of what we want, because we have 'unfixed' the nitrogen.

Fortunately, however, if we use a catalyst of a red-hot gauze made of platinum (90%) and rhodium (10%) (note: both are transition metals) the product of the reaction is not nitrogen, but nitrogen oxide. The reaction is exothermic, so once it has started we do not have to supply any more heat to keep the gauze at the right temperature.

$$4NH_3(g) + 5O_2(g) \xrightarrow{\text{Pt/Rh}} 4NO(g) + 6H_2O(l)$$
catalyst
(red-hot) $\triangle H$ negative

Nitrogen oxide reacts very easily with oxygen in the air to form the brown gas nitrogen dioxide, which will itself react with more air and water to form nitric acid. So we pass nitrogen oxide, air and water into a tower, where the following reactions happen:

$$2NO(g) + O_2 \rightarrow 2NO_2(g)$$
$$4NO_2(g) + 2H_2O(l) + O_2(g) \rightarrow 4HNO_3(aq)$$

So we can now see how the fixation of nitrogen from the air in the Haber Process is used to form different sorts of nitrogen-containing fertilisers

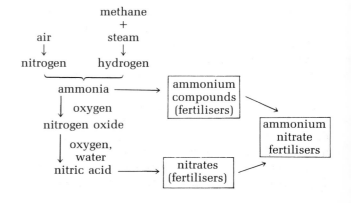

UNIT 9.1
Summary and learning

1   Nitrogen is one of the most plentiful elements in the Universe. It makes up (either as the element, or as ammonia) large parts of the atmospheres of many planets in the solar system, and is part of the make-up of planets like Uranus and Neptune.

2   Nitrogen is essential to life. It is part of the make-up of the DNA molecule and of proteins. All living things contain nitrogen. When life evolved on Earth, the atmosphere was probably very similar to that which exists today on Titan, one of the moons of Saturn, which is a 'nitrogen world'.

3   The element nitrogen is unreactive, since it exists as diatomic molecules in which each atom is held by three covalent bonds. You should remember how nitrogen from the air is made available to plants, and through plants to animals (the nitrogen cycle).

4   The most useful fertilisers are those which provide nitrogen (N), phosphorus (P) and potassium (K) for growing crops, and are called NPK fertilisers. You should remember what is meant by 'NPK value' for a particular chemical. Ammonium compounds generally contain more nitrogen per gram than do nitrates, and so they are popular fertilisers.

5   You should remember how we can make ammonia in the laboratory, and how it behaves. You should also remember the details of the Haber Process in which ammonia is manufactured on a large scale, and in particular you should be able to explain the reasons for the choice of the temperature and pressure at which the reaction is carried out. You should remember the factors which are important in deciding where to put an ammonia plant.

6   You should remember how we can make nitric acid in the laboratory, and how it behaves. You should also remember how nitric acid is manufactured in industry, and the uses to which it is put.

7   You have learnt the meaning of these words:

oxidising atmosphere	root nodules
reducing atmosphere	nitrogen fixation
protein	retort
amino acids	

UNIT 9.2   *Sulphur, and some of its compounds*

Sulphur is not so plentiful an element as nitrogen. It is, however, the tenth most abundant element in the Universe. So we should expect to find sulphur turning up in many places in the solar system. The importance of sulphur for us on Earth is its link with sulphuric acid, from which we make many useful chemicals, as we shall see.

We saw in Section 2 (Topic 2.1.2) that there are clouds of sulphuric acid on Venus. In fact, it is quite possible that solid sulphur exists on the surface of Venus and that this burns because of the high temperature. The sulphur dioxide which is produced is converted in the atmosphere to sulphuric acid – which falls as rain. So there may be a 'sulphur cycle' on Venus which is like our nitrogen cycle on Earth.

Most of the sulphur on Earth is trapped inside the core and so is not available to us. However, volcanoes bring some sulphur to the surface, or near to it, and so we do have a supply (see below). But the most dramatic appearance of sulphur is on Jupiter and one of its moons, Io. On Jupiter (which, remember, is the largest object in the Solar System – see Fig. 2.19 on p. 68) there exists what has become called the Great Red Spot. In fact, the Great Red Spot (which was first seen by Robert Hooke in 1664) is a cloud formation 39 000 kilometres long (the diameter of the Earth is about 13 000 km!). We are not certain what gives the spot its colour, but it is possible that it is molecular sulphur (Fig. 9.12).

In the same way that we have found a 'nitrogen world' in Titan, one of the moons of Saturn, so we have found a 'sulphur world' in Io, one of the moons of Jupiter. Io is about the same size as our own Moon. Its surface colour is a mixture of brown, orange and yellow – probably sulphur or mixtures containing sulphur. There are also white patches, which we believe are solid sulphur dioxide – sulphur dioxide 'snow'). The crust of Io is probably solid sulphur and sulphur dioxide mixed together, floating on layers of molten sulphur. Io is a 'sulphur world' because of the tremendous amount of volcanic activity there: there are at least eight active volcanoes on its surface all the time). Sulphur is constantly brought up to the surface by these volcanoes, and in fact we believe that the whole of the material which makes up Io has been 're-cycled' several times during its existence.

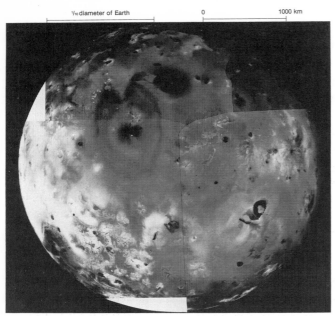

Fig. 9.11 *Io's surface is made up of volcanoes and sulphur deposits. This picture is a mosaic made up of four separate photographs*

So sulphur provides us with some of the most spectacular sights in the solar system. But what is it like chemically, where do we find it on Earth, and how can we use it?

TOPIC 9.2.1

The element sulphur and how it behaves

You have already seen some of the properties of sulphur (for instance in Section 1). You know that it exists as a yellow powder or yellow lumps. In the following experiment, you can investigate more fully how it behaves.

▶ EXPERIMENT 9.3

We can now look at the behaviour of sulphur in terms of its position in the Periodic Table.

Group	1	2	3	4	5	6	7	8
Electrons in outer shell	1	2	3	4	5	6	7	8

Li	Be	B	C	N	O	F	Ne
Na	Mg	Al	Si	P	S	Cl	Ar

Each sulphur atom has six electrons in its outermost shell, and so it needs two more to obtain a filled shell.

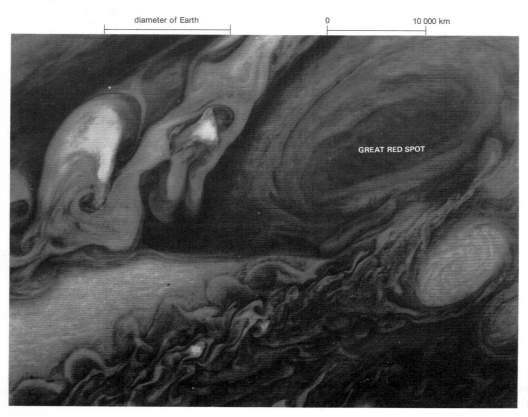

GREAT RED SPOT

Fig. 9.12 *The Earth would fit two and a half times across the Great Red Spot on Jupiter*

EXPERIMENT 9.3

How does sulphur behave when we heat it (a) without air, (b) with air and (c) with a metal?

You will need the following: powdered roll sulphur, iron filings, deflagrating spoon, gas-jar, test-tube, paper soaked in acidified potassium dichromate solution, universal indicator paper.

What to do

THE LABORATORY MUST BE WELL VENTILATED. YOU MUST WEAR YOUR SAFETY SPECTACLES.

WARNING: YOU ARE GOING TO HEAT SULPHUR — IF IT CATCHES FIRE, TAKE IT AWAY FROM THE HEAT AT ONCE. IF THE FLAME DOES NOT GO OUT, WALK CAREFULLY TO THE FUME-CUPBOARD WITH THE TUBE AND HOLD IT THERE. SOMEONE MUST THEN TELL YOUR TEACHER WHAT HAS HAPPENED.

1 Put several spatula-measures of powdered roll sulphur in a test-tube. Warm it gently, moving the tube about in the flame. Continue to heat, noting all the changes in the colour and 'runniness' of the sulphur which take place. When no further change happens, let the sulphur cool and see if the same changes happen in reverse order.

2 Place some powdered roll sulphur in a deflagrating spoon. Heat it until it burns, and then plunge it into a gas-jar which contains air. Note what happens.
  When the reaction has finished, test the gas in the gas-jar with
    (a) damp universal indicator paper, and
    (b) paper soaked in acidified potassium dichromate solution.

3 Put 3—4 spatula-measures of iron filings on a piece of paper and then add an equal volume of powdered roll sulphur. Mix the two together thoroughly, and then put them in a test-tube and heat strongly. When the reaction has finished scrape the contents of the test-tube onto a piece of paper, and examine what is there. Does a new substance seem to have been formed?

What happened, and what we can decide

1 If we heat a large amount of sulphur in a narrow test-tube, air cannot get at most of it, and so it is as if we were heating the sulphur without air. When we do this, the sulphur melts (at about 115°C) and turns into an orange-yellow runny liquid. As the temperature gets higher, the sulphur becomes darker in colour and at 160°C it becomes much less runny (more VISCOUS). At higher temperatures still, it becomes runny again and red-brown in colour. It eventually boils at 444°C.

2 A small amount of burning sulphur in a gas-jar has plenty of oxygen with which to react. It burns with a blue flame. The gas which is produced turns universal indicator red (showing that it is an acidic oxide) and turns paper which has been soaked in acidified potassium dichromate solution from orange to green (showing that it is a reducing agent (see Section 4, Topic 4.5.1). Sulphur dioxide is the only common gas which will do both these things so we know that this is the gas which forms when sulphur burns in air.

$$S(s) + O_2(g) \rightarrow SO_2(g)$$

3 Sulphur will combine directly with many metals, forming metal sulphides. When we heat iron and sulphur together, iron(II) sulphide (which is black in colour) forms.

$$Fe(s) + S(s) \rightarrow FeS(s)$$

So it forms two covalent bonds. In the element itself, each atom forms one covalent bond to each of two others. Sulphur is in the same group as oxygen, and so as with covalently bonded oxygen in water, we have two lone pairs and two bonded pairs in the outer shell (see Section 3, Topic 3.3.2). The result is an angle between the covalent bonds of about 107° – similar to that in water. (Fig. 9.13).

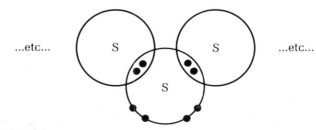

Fig. 9.13

Because of this angle between the bonds, sulphur atoms can join together to form rings containing eight atoms, shaped like a crown. You saw in Section 7 (Topic 7.1.4) how these S_8 molecules can arrange themselves in different ways to form the different allotropes of sulphur.

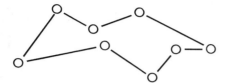

Fig. 9.14

We can also see from its position in the Periodic Table that sulphur is a non-metal. So we would expect it to burn in air to form an oxide which dissolves in water to give an acid. We would also expect it not to pass electricity (see Section 1, Topic 1.3.2) and to form an acid with hydrogen.

The compound between hydrogen and sulphur is hydrogen sulphide, a gas whose formula is H_2S. You saw in Section 4 that hydrogen sulphide is a reducing agent. We can also think of it as being the parent acid of sulphide salts, although it is a very weak acid indeed. Sulphides will also form by direct combination between metals and sulphur, as seen above with iron. It will also form sulphides with non-metals such as carbon (carbon disulphide, CS_2, is a useful solvent, although it is very toxic and flammable).

Uses and sources of sulphur

The world economy uses about 30 million tonnes of sulphur each year. As we have already seen, the main use for the element is to convert it to sulphuric acid (see below). Other uses are:

1. For making natural rubber (which is soft and pliable) much harder (such as in car tyres): this process is called VULCANISATION (because of the association of sulphur with **volcanoes**);
2. For preventing the growth of harmful fungi on vines (sulphur powder is dusted directly onto the vines);
3. for making other sulphur compounds (such as carbon disulphide) and for making dyes and fireworks.

Sulphur occurs on the Earth in the following ways:

(a) as the element itself (deposits in USA, Mexico and Poland);
(b) as H_2S in natural gas (at Lacq in France and Alberta in Canada);
(c) as metal sulphides (metal ores);
(d) as sulphates (such as gypsum).

Only the first two provide us with easy ways of obtaining the sulphur. The deposits of sulphur in America are about 150 metres under the ground, and were discovered about 100 years ago by people who were looking for oil. They could not be mined in the usual way because they were covered by difficult ground, much of it quicksand. The answer was found by Frasch, who realised that the sulphur could be

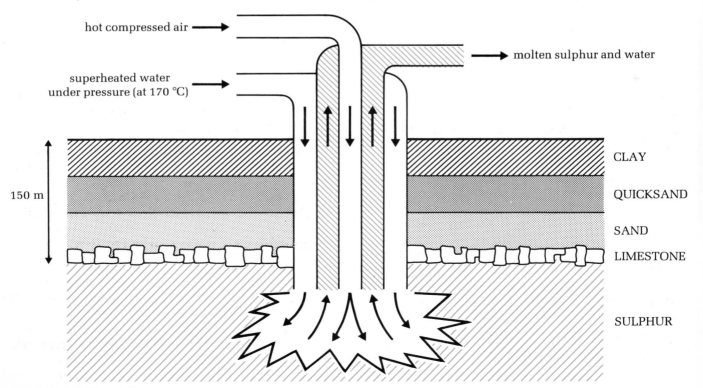

Fig. 9.15 *The Frasch Process*

melted under the ground, and forced to the surface by compressed air.

In the Frasch Process, water heated to 170°C and under 10 atmospheres pressure to stop it from boiling (SUPERHEATED water) is used to melt the sulphur. Liquid sulphur and water are forced to the surface by compressed air at about 15 atmospheres. The sulphur and water separate in large tanks.

The amount of hydrogen sulphide in natural gas varies considerably from one place to another on the Earth's surface. Gas from the North Sea contains hardly any, whilst that found at Lacq in France is about 15% H_2S, and that at Alberta in Canada about 30% H_2S. The sulphur is obtained by reacting hydrogen sulphide with sulphur dioxide (obtained by burning sulphur).

$$2H_2S(g) + SO_2(g) \rightarrow 3S(s) + 2H_2O(l)$$

Once sulphur has been obtained, most of it is converted into sulphur dioxide (and eventually to sulphuric acid).

<hr>

TOPIC 9.2.2

Sulphur dioxide

You already know a little about sulphur dioxide from the Experiment 9.3. But to investigate it properly you need to know how to make it in the laboratory, and to carry out several reactions with it.

We can use the apparatus shown in Fig. 9.16 to make sulphur dioxide (but nowadays we normally obtain a supply of the gas from a cannister).

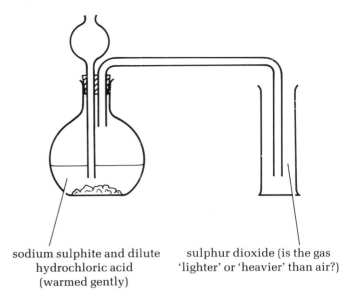

sodium sulphite and dilute hydrochloric acid (warmed gently)

sulphur dioxide (is the gas 'lighter' or 'heavier' than air?)

Fig. 9.16

The reaction is:

$$Na_2SO_3(aq) + 2HCl(aq) \rightarrow 2NaCl(aq) + H_2O(l) + SO_2(g)$$

Use your source of sulphur dioxide to carry out the reactions in Experiment 9.4.

<hr>

EXPERIMENT 9.4

How does sulphur dioxide behave?

You will need the following: test-tube and bung, gas-jar containing hydrogen sulphide, concentrated nitric acid, barium chloride solution, iron(III) sulphate solution, boiling-tubes.

What to do

YOU MUST CARRY OUT THIS WORK IN A FUME-CUPBOARD.

1   Fill a test-tube with sulphur dioxide and put a bung in the opening. Place the mouth of the tube below the surface of some water in a beaker, and take the bung out. Observe what happens, and then drop a piece of Universal Indicator paper into the beaker. **Discuss what you have seen, and try to decide what has happened to the sulphur dioxide.**

2   Fill a gas-jar with sulphur dioxide, and add a little water to it. Take a gas-jar full of hydrogen sulphide, and put the sulphur dioxide jar on top of it, and let the gases mix. **Write down what you see, and try to decide what has happened**.

3   Put some concentrated nitric acid in a boiling-tube, and pass a stream of sulphur dioxide through it. Write down what you see, and then after several minutes pour some of the liquid in the boiling-tube into a test-tube, and add a little water. Now add dilute hydrochloric acid and barium chloride solution. **Write down what you see, and try to decide what has happened**.

4   Put a few crystals of iron(III) sulphate into a boiling-tube, and then add 2–3 cm depth of water. Stir until the solid dissolves. Now pass a stream of sulphur dioxide through the solution. **Write down what you see, and try to decide what has happened**.

Continued overleaf

What happened, and what we can decide

You should have been able to see the following.

1   Sulphur dioxide is extremely soluble in water (but not as soluble as ammonia). It reacts with water as it dissolves to form an acid, sulphurous acid:

$$SO_2(g) + H_2O(l) \rightarrow H_2SO_3(aq)$$
$$\text{sulphurous acid}$$

2   Sulphur dioxide reacts with hydrogen sulphide, and one of the products is sulphur. The full equation is:

oxidation

$$SO_2(g) + 2H_2S(g) \rightarrow 3S(s) + 2H_2O(l)$$

reduction

This is a redox reaction in which sulphur dioxide acts as an oxidising agent. However, sulphur dioxide reacts much more often as a reducing agent, as the following reactions show.

3   When we pass sulphur dioxide into concentrated nitric acid, brown fumes (of nitrogen dioxide gas) are given off, and the solution gets hot. When the solution is tested with barium chloride solution, a white precipitate forms, proving that sulphate ions are now present. In fact, the sulphate which has formed is sulphuric acid.

oxidation

$$SO_2(g) + 2HNO_3(aq) \rightarrow H_2SO_4(aq) + 2NO_2(g)$$

reduction

4   Sulphur dioxide reduces $Fe^{3+}(aq)$ ions (brown) to $Fe^{2+}(aq)$ ions (light green):

oxidation

$$2Fe^{3+}(aq) + SO_2(g) + 2H_2O(l) \rightarrow 2Fe^{2+}(aq) + H_2SO_4(aq) + 2H^+(aq)$$

reduction

You also know that sulphur dioxide turns an acidified solution of potassium dichromate from orange to green:

oxidation

$$\begin{array}{c}\text{orange} \hspace{4cm} \text{green} \\ 3SO_2(g) + Cr_2O_7^{2-}(aq) + 2H^+(aq) \rightarrow 3SO_4^{2-}(aq) + 2Cr^{3+}(aq) + H_2O(l) \\ \text{dichromate} \hspace{4cm} \text{chromium(III)}\end{array}$$

reduction

The effects of sulphur dioxide and how we use it

Sulphur dioxide is an acidic oxide, and a reducing agent (except when it reacts with hydrogen sulphide).

You saw in Section 2 (Topic 2.3.1) how sulphur dioxide gets into the air, the effects which it has, and how it can be removed. The harmful effects of sulphur dioxide pollution come from the acidic side of its nature, and are not limited to Germany and Scandinavia. Many stone buildings in this country have been attacked by the sulphurous acid which forms when sulphur dioxide in the air dissolves in rain.

Fig. 9.17 *This statue has been eroded by acid rain caused by sulphur dioxide in the air*

When sulphur dioxide dissolves in water, an equilibrium is set up:

$$H_2O(l) + SO_2(g)$$

$$\Updownarrow$$

$$H_2SO_3(aq) \quad \text{sulphurous acid}$$

$$\Updownarrow$$

$$H^+(aq) + HSO_3{}^-(aq) \quad \text{hydrogensulphite ion}$$

$$\Updownarrow$$

$$2H^+(aq) + SO_3{}^{2-}(aq) \quad \text{sulphite ion}$$

So when we have a solution of sulphur dioxide in water, we will always have some sulphurous acid and some water and sulphur dioxide molecules present as well. **So a solution of sulphurous acid smells of sulphur dioxide, and has all its chemical properties**.

Sulphurous acid itself is a fairly strong acid (fairly completely split up to give $H^+(aq)$ ions), but it is not so strong as sulphuric acid. Like sulphuric acid, sulphurous acid is dibasic, and so forms two sodium salts when we react it with sodium hydroxide – sodium hydrogensulphite and sodium sulphite.

$$H_2SO_3(aq) + NaOH(aq) \rightarrow NaHSO_3(aq) + H_2O(l)$$
$$H_2SO_3(aq) + 2NaOH(aq) \rightarrow Na_2SO_3(aq) + 2H_2O(l)$$

If we add an acid to a solution of sodium hydrogensulphite or a solution of sodium sulphite, we soon get a strong smell of sulphur dioxide (see the equilibrium above). This gives us an easy way of making sulphur dioxide in the laboratory, and also of making solutions which have its properties. We use this in home brewing, when we make a 'sterilizing solution' by dissolving 'sodium metabisulphite' (sodium hydrogensulphite) and adding a few crystals of citric acid. We use similar chemicals to make a sterilizing solution for a baby's feeding utensils. Sulphur dioxide kills germs because it can behave as an oxidising/reducing agent. We also use it as a bleach and (in low concentrations) as a food preservative. But the main use for sulphur dioxide is in making sulphuric acid.

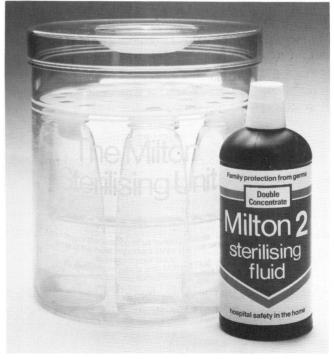

Fig. 9.18 *The sulphur dioxide released in this solution sterilises the things it comes into contact with*

Sulphuric acid and sulphates

As with nitric acid, we would not normally make sulphuric acid in the laboratory. It is made in such huge amounts in industry (see below) that it is easily available and cheap.

Sulphuric acid behaves as an acid

You already know all the important reactions of dilute sulphuric acid. It is a strong, dibasic acid. The following equations are for typical reactions of dilute sulphuric acid.

$$Mg(s) + H_2SO_4(aq) \rightarrow MgSO_4(aq) + H_2(g)$$
$$CuO(s) + H_2SO_4(aq) \rightarrow CuSO_4(aq) + H_2O(l)$$
$$NaOH(aq) + H_2SO_4(aq) \rightarrow NaHSO_4(aq) + H_2O(l)$$
$$2NaOH(aq) + H_2SO_4(aq) \rightarrow Na_2SO_4(aq) + 2H_2O(l)$$
$$CaCO_3(s) + H_2SO_4(aq) \rightarrow CaSO_4(aq) + H_2O(l) + CO_2(g)$$

Like sulphurous acid, sulphuric acid forms two sodium salts – sodium hydrogensulphate and sodium sulphate (see the third and fourth equations above).

As well as being an acid, concentrated sulphuric acid behaves as a DEHYDRATING AGENT (something that removes water from other chemicals) and as an oxidising agent. So, in addition to the reactions given above for dilute sulphuric acid, concentrated sulphuric acid will also have the following properties.

Concentrated sulphuric acid behaves as a dehydrating agent

If we leave an open beaker of concentrated sulphuric acid in a safe place for several days, we find that the level of the liquid rises. This is because sulphuric acid 'captures' water vapour from the air and so becomes more dilute. In fact, this process is very exothermic, and **so dangerous that we must never add water to concentrated sulphuric acid**. If we do, the heat given out causes boiling, and hot, very concentrated sulphuric acid can splash out of the container. We can, however, add sulphuric acid to water. (The way to remember the safe method is this. If we add water to acid there is a lot of acid and a little water when they meet (dangerous). If we add acid to water there is a little acid and a lot of water when they meet (safe).) (Fig. 9.19)

Concentrated sulphuric acid has such a strong attraction for water that it will take away ligand water molecules from hydrated copper(II) sulphate.

$$CuSO_4.5H_2O \xrightarrow{\text{conc. } H_2SO_4} CuSO_4 \; [+5H_2O]$$
$$\text{blue} \qquad\qquad\qquad \text{white}$$

If will even demolish a molecule to get at the water which it contains (Fig. 9.20).

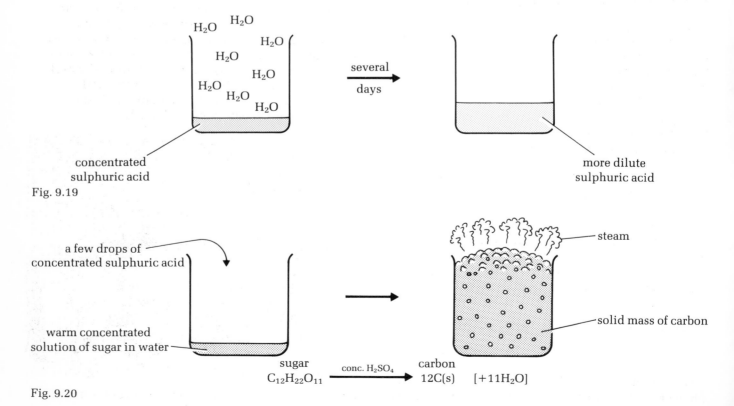

Fig. 9.19

Fig. 9.20

Concentrated sulphuric acid behaves as an oxidising agent

Concentrated sulphuric acid will react with metals which are **below** hydrogen in the reactivity series (unlike dilute sulphuric acid, which will not). For instance, it will react with copper, giving sulphur dioxide:

$$Cu(s) + 2H_2SO_4(aq) \xrightarrow{\text{heat}} CuSO_4(s) + 2H_2O(l) + SO_2(g)$$

(conc.) (anhydrous)

Note that in this reaction we obtain anhydrous copper(II) sulphate, rather than an aqueous solution of hydrated copper(II) sulphate. This is because concentrated sulphuric acid is still a dehydrating agent. So we get a white/grey sludge rather than a blue solution. If we add water to this sludge, it will of course turn blue.

Sulphates

As with nitrates, sulphates are easy to make. You learnt which sulphates are insoluble and how to make one of them (barium sulphate), and how to make two soluble sulphates, in Section 1. You also saw there how to test for a sulphate. The effect of heat on solid sulphates was investigated in Sections 4 and 5 (see Table 5.4 on p. 271).

Making sulphuric acid in industry – the Contact Process

Section 2 (Topic 2.2.1) explained how important the chemical industry of the world is to our standard of living. The chemical industry creates wealth by turning natural chemical resources into something which we can use.

Well, as the chemical industry is to the wealth of the world, so sulphuric acid is to the chemical industry. That is to say, sulphuric acid is the single most important chemical, taken overall, in the world economy.

Why should this be? If just so happens that sulphuric acid is needed to make almost all the world's important chemicals – fertilisers, medicines, plastics, paints, detergents and soaps, man-made fibres, and so on. For instance, we make phosphate fertilisers (see p. 349) by reacting calcium phosphate (which we dig out of the ground) with sulphuric acid. This makes a more soluble product, called 'superphosphate'.

$$Ca_3(PO_4)_2(s) + 2H_2SO_4(aq) \rightarrow Ca(H_2PO_4)_2(s) + 2CaSO_4(s)$$

superphosphate fertiliser

So important is sulphuric acid, that we can tell how prosperous a country (or indeed the whole world) is,

by how much sulphuric acid it uses. The world as a whole uses about 100 million tonnes of sulphuric acid each year. The UK is responsible for about 3% of this total – just over 3.4 million tonnes per year.

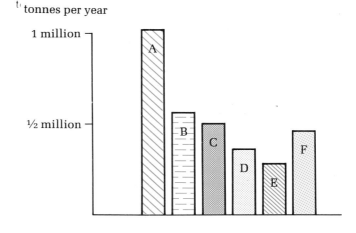

tonnes per year

A fertilisers
B making chemicals
C paints
D detergents/soaps
E fibres
F all others

Fig. 9.21 *Use of sulphuric acid in the UK*

About one-third of the sulphuric acid used in the UK (about 1 million tonnes each year) goes for making phosphate fertilisers. The various chemicals made using sulphuric acid come next in importance (these are medicines, plastics and explosives, and account for about 16% of the sulphuric acid) followed closely by paints and pigments (about 15% of the total). 'Brilliant White' paint contains titanium dioxide, which is purified using sulphuric acid.

Fig. 9.22 *These objects were all made using sulphuric acid*

So sulphuric acid is important – but how do we make it? We have seen that if we react sulphur dioxide with water, we get sulphurous acid (H_2SO_3). To get sulphuric acid (H_2SO_4) we need to react sulphur trioxide with water. We know that we can get hold of supplies of sulphur and we know how to use them to make sulphur dioxide. If we could find an easy way of getting from this sulphur dioxide to sulphur trioxide – then we would be able to make sulphuric acid fairly easily.

We can convert sulphur dioxide to sulphur trioxide by reacting it with the oxygen in the air, if there is a catalyst of vanadium pentoxide present. Like the reaction in the Haber Process for ammonia, this reaction does not 'go to completion', but forms an equilibrium mixture (see Section 6, Topic 6.2.2).

$$2SO_2(g) + O_2(g) \overset{V_2O_5}{\rightleftharpoons} 2SO_3(g) \quad \triangle H \text{ negative}$$
$$\text{in the forward direction}$$

This reaction forms the basis of the Contact Process for making sulphuric acid (so called because of the need to have **contact** with a catalyst).

We can use Le Chatelier's Principle to work out the conditions which would give us the highest equilibrium concentration of sulphur trioxide.

(a) Because the reaction gives out heat in the forward direction, the proportion of sulphur trioxide in the equilibrium mixture will be greater the lower the temperature. But too low a temperature would mean that it would take a long time to reach equilibrium and this would increase the cost.

(b) All the chemicals in the equilibrium are gases, and the total number of moles of reactant is greater than the total number of moles of product. So the reaction mixture takes up a smaller volume the higher the concentration of sulphur trioxide at equilibrium. So the 'yield' of sulphur trioxide is higher the higher the pressure. The apparatus needed for a high pressure process is expensive, however.

(c) If we were able to take the product of the reaction (sulphur trioxide) out of the reaction mixture, this would cause more sulphur dioxide and oxygen to react together to give a new equilibrium. This would mean that more sulphur dioxide would be converted to sulphur trioxide, and the overall yield of sulphur trioxide would be improved.

We can summarise these effects in Table 9.3 (below).

Because the vanadium pentoxide catalyst makes the reaction come to equilibrium more quickly, a relatively low temperature (450°C) and a relatively low pressure (about 1 atmosphere) can be used. Under these conditions, after being recycled over the catalyst for a second time, about 90% of the sulphur dioxide has been converted to sulphur trioxide. However, this is not good enough. The unreacted sulphur dioxide has to be allowed to escape into the air – causing pollution which results in acid rain (see p. 93). In the UK the law demands that 99.5% at least of the sulphur dioxide is converted to sulphur trioxide. This cannot be achieved by simply passing the equilibrium mixture over the catalyst if we use 450°C and 1 atmosphere of pressure. So at this point (90% conversion), the equilibrium mixture is passed into 98% sulphuric acid. The sulphur trioxide dissolves, forming a compound called 'oleum', $H_2S_2O_7$. This can be diluted later to give sulphuric acid again.

$$\overset{98\%}{H_2SO_4(aq)} + SO_3(g) \rightarrow \overset{oleum}{H_2S_2O_7(aq)}$$

$$H_2S_2O_7(aq) + H_2O(l) \rightarrow \overset{98\%}{2H_2SO_4(aq)}$$

The sulphur dioxide and oxygen from the reaction mixture do not react with the sulphuric acid, so they pass on. We now have these two gases on their own, with no sulphur trioxide present. They are passed over the catalyst again, making more sulphur trioxide. This results in 99.5% of the **original** sulphur dioxide having been converted, and the rest can be allowed to escape. The new sulphur trioxide reacts with 98% sulphuric acid as before, with water being added to keep the acid at the right concentration.

The sulphur dioxide for the reaction comes from one of two sources.

Change	Effect on equilibrium concentration of SO_3	Effect on rate of reaction	Effect on cost per tonne per day
Increase temperature	lower	faster	If too high – too little SO_3 and too costly
			If too low – too slow
Increase pressure	higher	faster	If too high – too costly
			If too low – too little SO_3 and too slow
Remove SO_3	higher	faster	Saves having to remove unreacted SO_2 and therefore gives more SO_3 at no net extra cost

Table 9.3

1. Roasting metal sulphide ores in air as part of the process of extracting them (e.g. copper, zinc, lead, iron).

   e.g. $2ZnS(s) + 3O_2(g) \rightarrow 2ZnO(s) + 2SO_2(g)$

2. From sulphur itself (obtained by the Frasch process, or from H_2S contained in natural gas).

The second of these two sources is by far the most important in the UK and so almost all the sulphur for conversion into sulphuric acid has to be imported (since our own North Sea gas contains almost no H_2S). To produce sulphur dioxide for the Contact Process, liquid sulphur is sprayed into a furnace where it burns in a flame at 1000°C.

We can now summarise the whole of the Contact Process in a diagram (Fig. 9.23).

A typical sulphuric acid plant will make about 750 tonnes per day. A sulphuric acid plant needs the following:

1. good transport facilities, close to a port (for importing sulphur);
2. a supply of water;
3. customers close by;
4. location and prevailing wind direction to take waste SO_2 away from inhabited areas.

Overall, the Contact Process gives out energy. This is used to make steam, which is sold to somebody who needs it for another chemical process (such as the Haber process). The income from selling steam covers all the running costs of the Contact Process, except for the cost of the sulphur. This means that sulphuric acid can be sold for a low price (about £30 per tonne in 1980), which in turn means that all the things which we make from it are much cheaper than they would otherwise be. A good thing, since so much of our material wealth depends upon sulphuric acid and the things we can make from it.

UNIT 9.2
Summary and learning

1 Sulphur is the tenth most abundant element in the Universe. It makes up (as the element, or as sulphur dioxide or sulphuric acid) part of a number of planets, including the Earth. Io, one of the moons of Jupiter is a 'sulphur world'.

2 You should remember how sulphur behaves chemically, and be able to explain this in terms of its position in the Periodic Table.

3 You should remember how we can use sulphur, and the ways in which we can obtain it.

4 You should remember how we can make sulphur dioxide in the laboratory, how it behaves, how we can use it, and its harmful effects when it pollutes the air.

5 You should be able to explain in detail how we make sulphuric acid, how it behaves (both dilute and concentrated), and the uses to which it can be put. You should be able to explain why sulphuric acid is such an important chemical.

6 You have learnt the meaning of these words:

viscous
vulcanisation
superheated
dehydrating agent

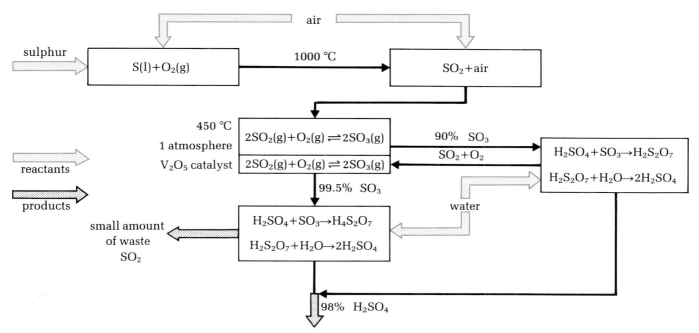

Fig. 9.23 *The Contact Process*

GCSE chemistry – now what?

Chemistry is worth studying for itself. In this book you have seen what chemistry is, and how it helps us to understand the world.

You have seen how chemistry fits into the Universe, and how scientists believe the Universe came about in the first place. Of course, chemistry is only part of how we go about trying to understand the Universe in which we live, but it is an important part.

You may be thinking of going on to study chemistry in greater depth, or you may be leaving it at this point. You may be studying other subjects in the future, or you may be ending your school career. Whatever is the case for you, what you have seen during your GCSE chemistry course should have left you with a clearer picture of the world – from one particular point of view.

Chemistry is about some of the basic things which affect our lives. So what you have learned should help you throughout your life. It should help you to make up your mind about issues such as whether lead should be banned from petrol, whether we should use nuclear fuels as we do, whether the cost we pay in terms of pollution and the using up of our natural resources is worth the increase in our standard of living which we get, and many others.

Scientific ideas are certain to become more and more important to the everyday world of the future – your world. So you need to carry with you an understanding of how science and scientists work. Your GCSE chemistry course should have given you some feeling for the way scientific ideas come about, and how they change.

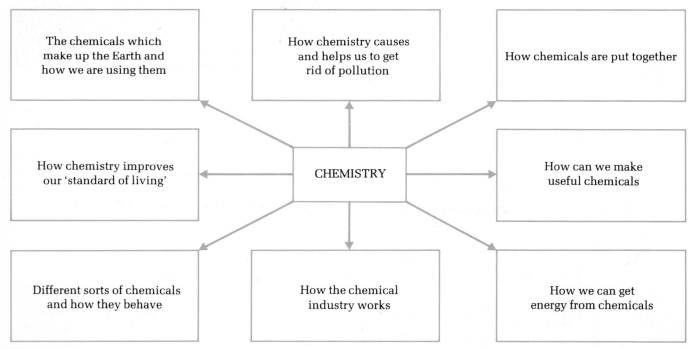

The chemicals which make up the Earth and how we are using them

How chemistry causes and helps us to get rid of pollution

How chemicals are put together

How chemistry improves our 'standard of living'

CHEMISTRY

How can we make useful chemicals

Different sorts of chemicals and how they behave

How the chemical industry works

How we can get energy from chemicals

Fig. 10.1

But chemistry is itself a useful skill. It is the most central of the sciences, and you need to understand chemistry to study geology, medicine and whole ares of technology such as materials science, fuel technology and metallurgy. Chemistry comes into manufacturing industry and into agriculture. It is essential in chemical engineering and in the nuclear power industry.

So knowing chemistry, as well as helping you in the world, should also be useful when it comes to finding a job. Below is a list of just some of the jobs that having studied chemistry will help you to get.

conservationist	oil engineer
archaeologist	agricultural engineer
nurse	doctor
photographer	biochemical engineer
horticulturalist	geologist
forensic scientist	veterinary surgeon
brewer	chemical engineer
animal nurse	hairdresser
mining engineer	pharmacist

Your careers teacher or local careers officer is the best person to find out more from. But here is a brief description of some of the above jobs.

Animal nurse

Animal nurses work for veterinary surgeons, and for organisations like the RSPCA (The Royal Society for the Prevention of Cruelty to Animals) and the PDSA (The People's Dispensary for Sick Animals). Animal nurses help diagnose and treat diseases and injuries.

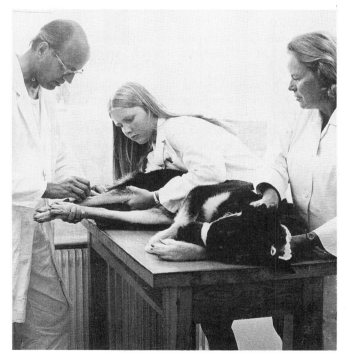

Fig. 10.2

Animal nursing is hard and sometimes unpleasant work. You need to care for animals, to be tough and fit, and to be able to cope with dirty and dangerous work – including evenings and weekends – before you think of becoming an animal nurse.

You can become an animal treatment assistant by joining the PDSA as a trainee. You must be over 18 years old, and have a good standard of GCSEs. If you have a slightly higher level of qualifications, you can train to be an animal nursing auxiliary with the Royal College of Veterinary Surgeons.

Photographer

Photographers take photographs and process photographic film. They can work in science and industry (for instance, using microscope cameras), in forensic science (for instance, recording the scene of a crime), in medicine (for instance, recording surgical techniques by photographing operations), in advertising, fashion and journalism.

Fig. 10.3

Photographers need to be able to communicate their ideas to other people, and they need to be painstaking and patient, and have a good visual imagination.

It is possible to enter photography at a variety of levels and with a range of qualifications. Courses take place at colleges at different levels, from CGLI courses to degree courses. In all of these, GCSE chemistry is useful.

Pharmacist

Pharmacists work in 'chemists' shops, in hospitals and in industry. They make up and dispense medicines, order them, store them and check on their quality. They advise doctors and nurses on the correct use of new drugs, or they may be involved in the development of the new drugs themselves.

Fig. 10.4

To become a pharmacist, you need to be able to study scientific subjects to at least degree level. You need to be responsible, with a logical mind and the ability to organise your own work and that of other people.

Pharmacists need to have obtained a degree in pharmacy from a university or a polytechnic, and to enter these it is normally necessary to have a good grade in GCSE chemistry, 'A' level chemistry, together with other 'A' levels.

Engineer

The word 'engineer' covers a wide variety of jobs, and there are a wide variety of entry requirements.

Engineers are people who use their knowledge to solve problems. This is true for a motor vehicle mechanic just as much as it is true for a TV maintenance electrician, or a professional engineer with a degree. Larger and larger numbers of women are making their living by becoming engineers – a field which used to be dominated by men.

Fig. 10.5

Fig. 10.6

Engineers work in offices and factories, on oil-rigs and construction sites – and all over the world. All engineers need to be able to work as part of a team, to plan ahead and see the consequences of what they are doing, and to be accurate, responsible and imaginative.

Engineers can be aircraft and engine designers, farm machinery or soil erosion experts, chemical plant designers, builders of bridges, dams and big buildings, they can be radar, TV and computer engineers, boat designers, mining engineers, factory planners and managers – the list is endless. You can go into engineering as a professional engineer with a degree, as a skilled craft worker, or as the technician engineer who provides the link – and often the detailed knowledge – between the two.

You can train as a mechanic, an electrician or machine operator with some or maybe even no GCSE subjects. To become a craft (skilled) machinist you will need moderate or good GCSE grades, and good grades if you want to become a technician engineer. To become a professional engineer, you will need to have 'A' levels, and to go on to get a degree.

Whatever you think the future holds for you, it might be worth taking the trouble to find out now how your GCSE chemistry qualification can help you. Remember, the above are just some of the many possibilities.

Index

Numbers in **bold** type show pages where the word or phrase is explained.